AF657578

JAYAPRAKASH NARAYAN

SELECTED WORKS

Volume Five (1948-1950)

Jayaprakash Narayan

SELECTED WORKS

Volume Five (1948-1950)

Edited by

B I M A L   P R A S A D

Issued under the auspices of
Nehru Memorial Museum & Library

MANOHAR
2005

First published 2005

ISBN 81-7304-353-1 (Series)
ISBN 81-7304-596-8

Published by
Ajay Kumar Jain for
Manohar Publishers & Distributors
4753/23 Ansari Road, Daryaganj
New Delhi 110002

Typeset by
A J Software Publishing Co. Pvt. Ltd.
New Delhi 110005

Printed at
Lordson Publishers Pvt. Ltd.
Delhi 110007

CONTENTS

Appendices

ILLUSTRATIONS

FOREWORD

It is pleasure to place before the reading public Volume 5 edited by Prof. Bimal Prasad of the *Selected Works of Jayaprakash Narayan.* It covers the period between the end of the Nasik Conference of the Socialist Party (March 1948), where the Party decided to leave the Congress and function as a completely independent political party, and the Madras Conference of the party (July 1950), where J.P. lucidly explained the main contents of the ideal of Democratic Socialism as also the ways of achieving it. The volume contains the texts of J.P.'s speeches, writings and letters not only on the theories and practices of socialism, but also on a myriad of other topics such as the problems of industrial labour, the state of civil liberties in the country, the way of ensuring free and fair elections and some issues related of India's economic and foreign policies. It is hoped that this volume will add to our knowledge of the history of the socialist and trade union movements in India during the period covered, and illustrate the role played by J.P. in them and the ideas propounded by him.

14 September 2004 K. JAYAKUMAR

ACKNOWLEDGEMENTS

I shall be failing in my duty if I do not thank all those who have helped me in preparing this volume. First and foremost, my thanks are due to Srimati Sonia Gandhi for her kind permission to consult and use the Nehru Papers after September 1946, as also the Nehru–J.P. correspondence preserved in a separate folio marked 'Files at Home'. I must also thank Dr. O.P. Kejriwal, who retired as Director of the Nehru Memorial Museum & Library on 29 February 2004 and Sri K. Jayakumar, who took over as Director on 1 March 2004. Both took keen interest in the J.P. Project and gladly helped me whenever required.

The members of the research team attached to the J.P. Project, namely Sri J.L. Gera, Dr. Maya Gupta and Ms. Sangita Malik (Research Officers) and Sri S.A. Abidi, Dr. Kapileshwar Labh and Sri Vas Dev Lakhanpal (Assistant Research Officers), helped me in collecting and arranging the materials that appear in this volume as also in seeing them through the press. I am thankful to all of them.

My thanks are also due to Dr. N. Balakrishnan, Head of the Research and Publications Division of NMML, for his willing cooperation whenever required. The same applies to Sri Deshraj, Administrative Officer of the institution. Ms. Deepa Sharma and Ms. Neha Bhardwaj attended to all the typing work. I am thankful to all of them.

BIMAL PRASAD

ACKNOWLEDGEMENTS

[illegible]

INTRODUCTION

This volume covers the period between the Nasik Conference of the Socialist Party (March 1948) and the Madras Conference (July 1950). The main preoccupation of J.P. as the General Secretary of the Socialist Party during 1948-50, was with the building up of the Party as an independent political entity, functioning in opposition to the Congress, which was the ruling party, and developing its ideology and strengthening its legitimacy in the eyes of the masses in the country. The Party had since 1947, without renouncing Marxism, adopted Democratic Socialism as its creed. However its organizational structure, based on a select group of members preparing for a revolution, continued to be the same as settled at the time of its foundation in 1934. After Nasik J.P., along with his leading colleagues in the National Executive of the Socialist Party like Narendra Deva, Yusuf Meharally, Achyut Patwardhan, Rammanohar Lohia and Asoka Mehta, felt that the old structure would not serve the need of the Party in the new situation where it had adopted Democratic Socialism as its ideology and was trying to develop itself as an opposition party in a democratic dispensation. The need of the hour, he felt, was a party with a mass and open membership.

The best exposition of J.P.'s thinking on this topic is to be found in his article entitled 'The structure of the Socialist Party' published in 1948 and included in this volume. Here J.P. strongly commends open membership of the party instead of the closed one on which it had been based till then. Rejecting the argument that the unchecked influx of the masses would dilute the ideological purity of the Party, he asserted that there was nothing in Marxist theory, which ordained that a socialist party must restrict its membership to a chosen few. In Czarist days there was no democracy in Russia and hence there was every justification for the Bolshevik Party to organize itself on the basis of a restricted membership. But India of 1948 was different from Russia of 1917. Here a democratic constitution was on the anvil and adult franchise as well as civil liberty were going to be provided for. In such a situation democratic functioning would be quite feasible and there would be no necessity of building up a party on the basis of restricted membership. Such a membership might suit the requirements of a communist party seeking to establish its own dictatorship but not of a socialist party working for the establishment of a democratic socialist society. At the same time, J.P. warned against having only individuals as members. Such individuals, he asserted, would have no control over the leaders and that would open the door to dictatorship and betrayal. The solution lay in following the organizational pattern of the British Labour Party and providing for admission to the Party of class organizations of peasants and workers, having the power to control the functioning of the Party and prevent it from being manipulated by leaders for their own selfish ends. All the members of the Socialist Party were not in agreement with J.P.'s ideas and there was quite a serious debate on them at the Patna Conference of the Socialist Party (March 1949), but J.P. finally had his way and the new constitution, based on his ideas, was adopted by consensus. It could not, however, be fully implemented. Membership was indeed thrown open to all individuals interested in the objectives of the Socialist Party, but the affiliation of organizations of peasants and workers to it remained merely a dream.

J.P. attached even greater importance to fostering ideological clarity among the member of the Socialist Party. He gave this task high priority and seldom missed an opportunity to inculcate faith in the ideals of Democratic Socialism. This vision of a democratic socialist society found a very powerful expression in his political report presented to Madras Conference of the Socialist Party in July 1950, which was also published as a pamphlet under the title *Democratic Socialism: the Ideal and the Method*. Here he pointed out that the values of socialism were more important than its theories and in case of a clash between the two it was the former, which must prevail. Socialism, for instance, could not be equated with mere nationalization of industry and collectivization of agriculture. It must also lead to the end of exploitation, injustice, oppression and insecurity; equality of opportunity; and an equitable distribution of the good things of life. All these might not necessarily be attained by merely nationalizing industry and collectivizing agriculture. 'If under such an economy,' wrote J.P. 'all political and economic power is concentrated in the hands of a party oligarchy, irreplaceable and self-perpetuating, there can be no Socialism but its suppression, no revolution but reaction.' He, therefore emphasized that it was necessary to define the goals or values of socialism clearly so that the social revolution, if and when it materialized, was not betrayed by self-seeking and power-hungry leaders entrenched in the government. Attempting such a definition himself, he observed in his report to the Madras Conference of the Party (1950):

> The aims of the socialist movement which needed to be emphasized were not mere overthrow of the capitalist order and establishment of a party dictatorship, but the creation of a society of free and equal peoples, a society based on certain values of human and social life, values which could never be sacrificed in the name of theory or the Party line or expedience of any sort.

J.P. felt called upon to dilate at length on the ideals and methods of Democratic Socialism not because he had something entirely new to say. Democratic Socialism had already been accepted as the creed of the Socialist Party at its Kanpur Conference (1947) and J.P. had again and again been explaining its rationale as also its implications. However, while going round the country and addressing public meetings he also came in to close contact with his party's cadres and found that the new creed had not been fully accepted by them from their hearts. The main reason for this was that the party, ever since its birth in 1934, had been organized with Marxism as its creed and many of its members thought that the party was going back on its ideals by adopting Democratic Socialism as its creed. An idea of how worried J.P. was on this account can be had by going through the text of his Madras address included in this volume. That address also represents one of the best expositions of the ideals of Democratic Socialism by anyone in India.

While expounding the ideology and explaining the methods of Democratic Socialism, J.P. as General Secretary of the Socialist Party, also had to arrange for funds for meeting the expenses not only of the central office of the party, but also of several of its allied organizations and branches in the various states. Then there were certain institutions like the Khoj Parishad, which had been set up by him with the cooperation of several of his leading colleagues in the Party, with a view to carrying on research on some of the urgent socio-economic problems of the country. The responsibility for their funding fell largely on J.P.'s shoulders. Some of his letters included here throw light on the way he carried on this financial burden. As will be found by a perusal of these letters J.P's incessant tours constituted the main source of fund for the party and other allied activities. He collected funds at almost all places, which he visited in course of his incessant tours. Often the party workers utilized his visits to collect money from sympathizers, which was presented to him as a purse at the meetings that he addressed. However, J.P. also had to himself solicit funds from well-to-do sympathizers, particularly during his visits to big cities like Bombay, Calcutta, Madras and Delhi, and remind them of unfulfilled promises through letters whenever found necessary. Many of the letters included in this volume throw light on this aspect of J.P.'s work. Several other letters similarly throw light on J.P.'s ideas on and his role in the organization of students, peasants and industrial workers. While working on behalf of his Party, it was his endeavour to develop the latter's organizations on independent lines as far as practicable and to ensure that they did not become pawns in the hands of political parties, including his own. For instance, while not opposed to different political parties working among students, he initiated the move to organize the National Students Union of India, which was expected to function on national lines, without being affiliated to or controlled by any political party. Similarly, while taking the lead in organizing the Hind Kisan Panchayat and the Hind Mazdur Panchayat which would both be affiliated to the Socialist Party, he advised its leaders and organizers to develop these organizations as independent class organizations of peasants and industrial workers and not exploit them for party ends. The leaders of other political parties, however, were not so broad-minded. J.P. had to face great difficulty in this regard, particularly because of the partisan attitude of the Congress Governments, both at the centre and in the states, which took keen interest in organizing labour unions under the aegis of the Indian National Trade Union Congress (I.N.T.U.C), which was founded by the Congress, and showed no scruples in using State power in this regard. J.P.'s correspondence with the Congress leaders, both at the centre and state levels, included in this volume, relating to the organization of labour at Jamshedpur and Dalmianagar in Bihar, should be found useful in understanding J.P.'s predicament and in providing us an insight into the working of Indian democracy in the labour field.

J.P. headed the two largest organizations of Government of India's employees—the All India Railwaymen's Federation (A.I.R.F.) and the All India Postmen and Lower Grade Staff Union. They were neither affiliated to the Socialist Party nor did they function under its control, but had elected J.P. as their president. J.P. scrupulously refrained from bringing them within the sphere of influence of his party and led them as completely independent labour organizations. This, however, did not save him from difficulties at the hands of Government of India. For the I.N.T.U.C was trying to form its own rival organization parallel to the A.I.R.F. Such efforts had the full backing of certain ministers in the Government of India, who tried to help the I.N.T.U.C by sitting pretty over some of the key demands of the organization headed by J.P. Undeterred by the partisan attitude of the Government, J.P. continued to lead the A.I.R.F. in a purely non-partisan manner and sought to ensure that whatever it did, it kept the nation's interests in view. This led him, in the context of the then deteriorating India-Pakistan relations, which seemed likely to lead to war, to advise the A.I.R.F. in early 1949 not to go ahead with the strike-ballot, earlier decided upon under his own leadership, in the interest of national security. For this he was fiercely denounced by the Communist Party of India and its associates in the labour field who accused him of working in league with the Government of India and betraying the cause of labour, but this had no impact on J.P. or on his leadership of A.I.R.F where he continued to enjoy overwhelming support. On the other hand, when the threat of outbreak of war with Pakistan evaporated and J.P. found that the Government continued to be insensitive to the demands of railwaymen as also the postal workers, he supported the taking of strike-ballot by them and the decision again not to go ahead with strike was taken only after the Government showed an accommodating attitude and conceded some of the vital demands of the railwaymen. The same applied to the postal workers' demands. In the latter a piquant situation arose after the Government went back on its assurance—conveyed by the Minister of Communications, Rafi Ahmed Kidwai, to J.P. in course of their conversation about the problems of postal employees—to find a solution, helpful to the latter, on the question of the payment of their salaries during the pendency of a strike in some form or the other. J.P's repeated knockings at the doors of the Government failed to secure the fulfilment of Kidwai's assurance. His correspondence with Gopalaswamy Ayyangar, Minister for Railways, Rafi Ahmed Kidwai as well as with Nehru, included in the present volume, will be useful in understanding the role of J.P. in leading the two major organizations of Government employees as also on the methods and practices of the Government in dealing with them.

During these two years (1948-50) J.P. was increasingly worried by the worsening state of civil liberties in the country, exemplified by the fact that even Rammanohar Lohia, one of the towering figures of the Socialist Party, had to face arrest in 1949 and again in 1950. Achyut Patwardhan, another towering figure of the Party, met the same fate. J.P. did his best to protest against this state of affairs and to make the general public conscious of the value of civil liberties by organizing or addressing conferences on them. The texts of some of his statements, addresses and letters on this issue will be found in this volume.

This state of civil liberties made J.P. seriously concerned with the prospect of free and fair elections, which was being expected soon, in the country. He had a foretaste of the shape of things to come during the by-elections to the U.P. Assembly caused by the resignation of its socialist members in 1948. The behaviour of the officers and policemen under the guidance of the Congress ministry made J.P. so worried and angry that he publicly warned about the possibility of the emergence of a Fascist State in India if the Indian people remained indifferent to what was happening in the field of politics. Indeed, he spent a good deal of his time in trying to make the Indian people conscious of the importance of free and fair elections in determining the future of the country as also their own living conditions. It was his initiative which led to the holding of the first All-India Conference on Free and Fair Elections in July 1950, attended not merely by leaders of the various opposition parties, but also by some eminent public men not associated with any political party and some experts. J.P.'s purpose in convening this conference was not to create a platform for attacking the Congress or the governments controlled by it, but to formulate concrete proposals for ensuring free and fair elections in the country. The conference was quite a success from this point of view. Some of the documents included in this volume bear ample testimony to this.

J.P. was interested not merely in the political and economic developments in India, but also in the world at large. Several of his statements and letters included in this volume will show that he was keen to see India playing an important role in world affairs, with a view to promoting the cause of peace and freedom all over the world. He was among an extremely limited number of Indians during the early years after the achievement of independence to see in some of the actions of the Soviet Union signs of its expansionism. On the Korean issue, his sympathies were clearly on the southern side. This was, however, not caused by any bias in favour of the United States. This is clearly borne by his statement on 14 February 1950 strongly denouncing American policy towards China, both with regard to issue of Formosa and the Chinese seat in the U.N. Security Council. Nearer home he showed keen interest in the struggle for democracy in Nepal being carried on under the leadership of B.P. Koirala. Some of J.P.'s statements and letters included in the volume illustrate the sincerity and depth of his interest.

J.P. had been a strong opponent of the Muslim League's demand for Pakistan and denounced it on several occasions on various grounds. He had also opposed the preparedness of the Congress leaders to accept Partition as a necessary price for the achievement of independence. However, once Pakistan was created, he began to emphasize in course of his speeches the extreme desirability of having friendly relations with that country. Again and again, he strongly denounced those communal elements among Hindus whose activities he thought were not merely spreading ill-will among the Hindus and Muslims in India, but also between India and Pakistan. Yet when in the beginning of 1950, Hindus in East Pakistan were facing violent attacks from the Muslims and being forced to think of migrating to India, J.P. took the matter seriously and urged the Government of India to treat the matter as most urgent and work for the restoration of normalcy in East Pakistan. As the situation continued to worsen he openly expressed the view in early March 1950 that if all efforts of the Government failed, it should consider the despatch of the Army to East Pakistan, not with a view to conquering it, but for ensuring the safety of the minorities there. However, the situation changed within a matter of weeks and an agreement was signed by Nehru and Liaquat Ali Khan, Prime Minister of Pakistan, in Delhi in the middle of April 1950, providing due safeguards for the protection of minorities in both India and Pakistan. This became famous as the Delhi Agreement or the Nehru-Liaquat Pact. J.P. now changed his line and withdrew his suggestion regarding the despatch of Indian troops to East Pakistan. Several of his statements on that issue included in this volume should be found useful by the reader in understanding J.P.'s point of view.

This short Introduction does not deal with all the facets of J.P.'s personality or his activities as revealed by his speeches, statements, articles and letters included in this volume, but only with a few selected ones. Those who want to have a fuller view must go through the whole volume. They can be safely assured that they will find such an exercise most rewarding and it will give them an insight into J.P.'s thinking and all the myriad activities and programmes with which he was deeply involved between 1948 and 1950.

1. To the Provincial Secretaries of the Socialist Party, 25 March 1948[1]

Circular No. 5

To

The Secretaries,
All Provincial Branches

Resignation of Party Members from the Congress

Dear Friend,

I am enclosing herewith a model letter of resignation for Party Members to withdraw from the Congress in view of the decision of the Nasik Convention. You should note that Party members are to resign their primary membership (as well as that) of all elected Congress Committees, and nominated or elected sub-committees.

The national Executive decided that Party members while resigning from the Congress should also relinquish the seats they might be holding as Congressmen on local bodies and legislatures, including the Constituent Assembly. The Executive decided further that all resignations should be submitted by the 15th of April.

Members of the Party who might have been nominated on committees in connection with the Mahatma Gandhi Memorial fund need not resign their seats. Members are also not to resign from committees appointed by Provincial and Central Governments.

In connection with these resignations, I should like to suggest that the members resigning should not issue any press statements nor give any other publicity to their resignation. You (i.e. the Provincial Secretary) should announce, after collecting the accurate figures, the number of resignations and their nature, i.e. the number of resignations from primary and other Congress Committees, and from local bodies and legislatures.

In connection further with these resignations, I should like to suggest that there should be no demonstrations, such as public meetings, with a view to announce and publicize them.

I hope you will give effect to this circular within the time prescribed.

Sincerely yours,
Jayaprakash Narayan,
General Secretary

[1] *J.P. Papers*, Nehru Memorial Museum & Library (herein after referred to as NMML).

Model Letter of resignation that Party members are to write in view of the decisions of the Nasik Convention and of the National Executive Committee.

To

The Secretary,
Provincial Congress Committee,

Dear Friend,

In pursuance of the decision of the Sixth Convention of the Socialist Party held at Nasik, I hereby resign from the primary membership of the Congress and from all elective positions I hold in the Congress organization.

I remain,

Sincerely yours,

Note: (1) If the Party member holds a Congress seat in any Local body, Provincial Legislative Assembly or the Constituent Assembly, he should add the following paragraph to the letter above:

"I resign further my seat on the …."

(2) Party members who are members of local bodies and legislatures should, in addition to the letter to the Provincial Congress Secretary, also write a separate letter of resignation, on the lines of the model letter above, to the appropriate authority, such as Chairman of the local body or leader of the legislative party.

2. To Jawaharlal Nehru, 27 March 1948[1]

My dear Bhai,

Aruna[2] gave me your letter[3] at Nasik. I need hardly say what a personal wrench it has been to most of us to separate from old friends. What it means personally for me I can hardly express. But I have no doubt that politically there was no alternative; and I hope that in the act of separation we have done nothing that would embitter our relations. I, together with many other senior members of the Socialist Party, do fervently hope that we will continue to receive inspiration and guidance from you and that the personal bonds and loyalties will endure.

[1] *Brahmanand Papers* (NMML).

[2] Aruna Asaf Ali (1909-96); freedom fighter; born and educated at Lahore, married Asaf Ali, a prominent Congress leader in Delhi; joined Civil Disobedience Movement, 1930; imprisoned for a year in Lahore; played an important role in the Quit India Movement and remained underground till 1946; joined the Socialist Party, but left it after sometime; elected President of Delhi Pradesh Congress Committee, 1947; first Mayor of Delhi 1958; recipient of Nehru Award for International Understanding in 1992.

[3] Not available either in *J.N. Papers* or in *J.P. Papers*.

I am sending you under separate cover a copy of the policy report.'[4] I made to the Conference.[5] I shall be happy if you can find time to go through it.

There are a few matters I should like to write to you about. The first of these is the Digwadih[6] Colliery strike about which you had sent me two telegrams a few days before our Conference. I had written you a longish letter[7] then, and I am glad to say that the surmise I had made has subsequently turned out to be correct. After receiving your telegrams I had sent a friend from here to Jharia to inquire into the whole matter. He came back at the time of the Conference and has submitted a written report. I wrote to you at that time that I was extremely doubtful that any pumps had been damaged or put out of action. That surmise has been confirmed. In your second wire to me you wrote: "Strike of safety men has resulted in serious damage to the pump which cannot be replaced for two years." The fact is that no damage whatever was done to any of the pumps. The Tatas completely misled you in this matter and tried by creating panic to influence you.

In both your telegrams you had referred to Tripathi's[8] "irresponsibility". Tripathi is the best worker we have in Jharia and he has a tremendous hold over the colliery workers. He is undoubtedly hot-tempered as many of us are, but he is incorruptible, hard-working and a fine speaker. He led the thirty days' general strike in the Tata Collieries with great ability and distinction. During all these thirty days there was not one case of violence or of violent speech by any one. You may verify this from the local authorities. In view of the magnificent way in which the Tata general Strike was conducted, all the colliery owners have made common cause against Tripathi so as to force Government to take action against him. They are afraid of him and they do not want him in Jharia. They have succeeded as Tripathi is in jail now.

Reverting to the Digwadih strike, Tripathi was not at all responsible for it nor was the strike called by the socialist union. Winding machine *khalasis* (12 of them in number) decided suddenly on a Sunday not to work because they were told that only half of them would be able to work on Sundays. The winding machines having stopped, nobody could go down the pit. Thus 150 of the safety men who had collected for work at the pithead could not go down. Work however started from the next Monday morning. On the next Sunday again the *khalasis* refused to work and again the 150 safety men could not go down the pit. On the next Monday morning, when work

[4] For Policy Report see item no. 160 in Vol. IV.

[5] Refers to Socialist Party's Sixth Annual Convention, Nasik, 19-21 March 1948.

[6] A place in Jharia District of Bihar.

[7] See item no. 157 in Vol. IV

[8] An active member of the Congress Socialist Party and Trade Union leader in Jharia.

was to be resumed, the 150 safety men refused to go down not because the Union or Tripathi had instigated them but because they demanded payment for the forced idleness on the previous Sunday which they were refused. That same night, at about 9 p.m., a settlement was brought about at the intervention of the S.D.O.; and the Union representatives including Tripathi and the representatives of the Management including Mr. Ghosh, the superintendent of all the Tata mines, agreed that the Digwadih dispute be referred to the Conciliation Officer whose award would be accepted by both the Management and the Union. After the settlement was reached, at 10 p.m. a meeting was held—this was on the 1st of March, two days before you sent me your first wire—at which the S.D.O. and Tripathi spoke and explained the settlement, and the workers resumed work. Two days later, when the Union referred this dispute to the Conciliation Officer, the latter was informed by the Superintendent of the Tatas that the Management was not bound to accept his award. This was a breach of the agreement. The following remarks of the S.D.O., made in writing on the Union's letter, referring the dispute to him, leave no doubt that the Tata Management had agreed to accept the award of the Conciliation Officer:

Forwarded to the Conciliation Officer, Camp: Jamdoba.[9] The workers were assured by me last evening that their grievances and demands would be looked into by the Conciliation Officer.

The leaders as well as Mr. Ghosh on behalf of the Management assured me that *they would abide by the decision of the Conciliation Officer*. The C.O. is, therefore, requested to look into the grievances and do the needful.

Now the Management has gone back on their word. This is the manner in which the Tatas, who take advantage of their position to approach Ministers directly, carry on. I could send you a lot of material to show how Tata Managements always constantly try to disrupt labour and put one union against the other; to corrupt union leaders and to misrepresent the workers to the Government. It is a common fact that in the face of high Tata officials the local authorities find themselves helpless. Magistrates and Deputy Commissioners are always afraid of the Tata bosses, because the latter have direct access to Delhi, Patna or Calcutta. This has a demoralizing effect on the local administration. I believe the S.D.O, Dhanbad, who was responsible for settling the Digwadih Strike has been transferred from his post. I take very strong objection to the manner in which in this Digwadih affair attempt was made to misguide you and I hope that future attempts of this nature will not be taken seriously by you.

The other matter of which I wish to write is the I.N.A.[10] affair. Gen.

[9] A place in Jharia.

[10] For note on I.N.A. see item no. 2 in Vol. IV.

Bhonsle[11] met me the other day and discussed this matter with me. I had understood from you that the British officers, particularly Auchinleck,[12] stood in the way of the I.N.A. being absorbed into the army. Now that Auchinleck is gone, I had hoped that it would be possible to do something for these unfortunate people. I dare say there are difficulties but the country owes to the I.N.A. a great debt which it should try to repay. I have no doubt that had Subhas Babu[13] been alive no Government in the country would have been able to refuse to the I.N.A. its due. The I.N.A. men may not be the kind of heroes we depicted them to be, but history will always hold that they played a great part in securing the country's freedom. This single undeniable fact should be sufficient to remove all difficulties and to secure justice for the I.N.A. I hope therefore that justice will be done to them.

The third matter concerns the talks I had with you about Sri Aurobindo[14] and Ramana Maharshi.[15] Further talks I had with friends here, including Maurice Friedman[16] and Rao Patwardhan,[17] have compelled me to drop the idea, though personally I still think that something should have been done in this matter. But I do not find it possible to go ahead with the idea alone.

I am leaving for Madras in an hour.

As ever,
J.P.

[11] Jagannath Rao Bhonsle (1906-); selected for training at the Prince of Wales College, Dehradun, 1926; joined British Indian Army, 1928, and served till 1942; joined Azad Hind Fauj as Quarter Master General and later became its Commander-in-Chief. At the end of War in 1945 he was captured by British forces and imprisoned at Bangkok and faced trial at Red Fort, Delhi.

[12] Field-Marshal Sir Claude John Eyre Auchinleck (1884-1981); joined 62 Punjabis 1904; served Egypt, 1914-15, Mesopotamia, 1916-19; G.O.C.-in-C Southern Command 1940, General to king 1941-6; Governor of Wellington College, 1946-59; Field Marshal, 1946; Supreme Commander India and Pakistan, 1947.

[13] For biographical note on Subhas Chandra Bose see *JPSW*, Vol. I, p. 114.

[14] For biographical note on Sri Aurobindo see item no. 161 in Vol. IV.

[15] For biographical note on Ramana Maharishi see item no. 161 in Vol. IV.

[16] A friend of Jayaprakash Narayan, a Polish engineer who became a Hindu and was known as Swami Bharatananda.

[17] P.H. alias Raosaheb Patwardhan (1903-69); formed Nachiketa Mandal along with Harindranath Chattopadhyay to encourage student participation in cultural activities, participated in Freedom Movement and imprisoned in 1930-2, 1940-2, and detained 1942-5; Member Maharashtra P.C.C. and A.I.C.C., edited *Sadhna*, a Marathi weekly founded by Sane Guruji 1950-6; after 1952 devoted himself to Bhoodan and Gramdan Movements, edited *Bhoodan*, an English weekly; founder editor *Sanghashakti*, a Marathi weekly; Member Indian delegation to U.N.E.S.C.O. and Board of Trustees, Rashtra Seva Dal.

3. Presidential Address at the Open Session of the First Tamil Nadu Socialist Party Convention, Madura, 28 March 1948[1]

The Congress has become a political party representing certain vested interests who having been all along miles away from it have infiltrated into it and have taken control of it to a certain extent. While the Congress talks of Socialism, it is not prepared to put it into practice. I took upon the Congress as the Kuomintang in China, which while being wedded to the democratic and socialist principles of Dr. Sun Yat Sen had not put them into practice. The fact is that the Kuomintang, the ruling party in China today, has become corrupt and inefficient. Though the Congress today has not become what Kuomintang has become in China, I am afraid it is fast moving in that direction.

The Congress has turned to be a political party working in the name of the people but largely with the purpose of maintaining the *status quo*. Having found it impossible to convert the Congress into a Socialist Party, the Socialists have come to the conclusion that if they really want to establish in the country a Socialist Government and create a Socialist Society the only way to do it is to go outside the Congress and build up a Socialist Party, based on the working classes and the peasantry. Another object in severing connections from the Congress is to provide a healthy opposition to the party in power. There is hardly any non-communal party in the country, whose patriotism is above suspicion, to play the role of opposition which is essential in a secular democratic State. As things stand today it is possible for the Congress to go ahead and rule the country on the basis of one party Government, thus leading towards totalitarianism. Further, the present Congress Governments are showing scant regard for the civil liberties of the people.

As an opposition party, Socialists would not act irresponsibly without any regard for the interests of the country. We would not subvert the State which we have established by our joint efforts. We would work within the four corners of the law and with loyalty to the country. Our separation from the Congress does not mean that we have lost sight of problems facing the country. We are eager to defend the freedom of the country. As the party in opposition, the Socialist Party will always be ready to join hands with the Congress to fight the common foes, both external and internal. Communalism and provincialism are our eternal enemies and these must be rooted out. If we do not do that, nothing will be left of our hard won freedom.

[1] Adapted from *Bombay Chronicle*, 30 March 1948.

[2] For biographical note on Dr. Sun Yat Sen see *JPSW*, Vol. II, p.129.

After our historic decision to separate from the Congress Party we should expand ourselves gradually and become representative not merely of a few devoted revolutionaries but of the mass of the people. I would like our organization to be developed on the lines of the British Labour Party. I want Trade Unions and Peasant Unions organized in every part of the country and affiliated to the Socialist Party. When we have succeeded in building a Party of that kind, we can succeed in establishing Socialism in the country.

Our objective is to create a workers' society in which there will be no vested interests and in which the workers can enjoy freely the fruits of their labour. We know this kind of society can not be created in a day. It will take time. We must steadily and steadfastly move in that direction, undaunted by any obstacle in our path. The basic transformation of society can not obviously be brought about without certain disturbances in our present society. The Congress also talks of certain Socialist programmes. But on one ground or another it has decided to go slow. It may be that those people who will be hit by Socialist measures will sabotage the efforts of a Socialist Government and that they will have to be suppressed. This may happen in the beginning. People who have no vision and faith may be frightened and may say that instead of going forward we are going backward, ruining instead of augmenting the prosperity of the country. All these criticisms have to be faced boldly. Those who have faith in socialism and have the courage to work for brining about a fundamental social revolution must go forward, disregarding difficulties in the way. I appeal to the Socialists in Tamil Nad to launch on this new, big task with faith and courage.

4. To Jawaharlal Nehru, 2 April 1948[1]

My Dear Bhai,

I hope Aruna gave you my letter.[2] There were two other points about which I was to write to you but forgot to do so owing to the rush in which I wrote.

The Nasik convention of the Socialist party passed the following resolution:

"This convention of the Socialist party appeals to the Government of India to declare the 1st of May a public holiday. The Convention further appeals to the working people of India to observe the May Day as a great festival of international working class solidarity."

I need not try to tell you what the May Day means to the socialists and labour movements all over the world. I think it will be proper and graceful for the Government of India to declare 1st May a public holiday.

[1] *J.P. Papers* (NMML)
[2] Item no. 2 in this volume.

The other point about which I was asked by the National Executive of the party to write to you was the ban on the R.S.D.[3] in Madras and also perhaps in C.P. You know better than I do what kind of organization the Rashtra Seva Dal has been and what service it has done to the cause of freedom and nationalism. It seems a great pity that the provincial governments should ban an organization such as this. I request you earnestly to look into this matter.

I have read with disappointment the announcement of policy regarding I.N.A. It is sad to reflect that you should have seen fit to issue such a statement. However, there seems little that one can do to influence Government's policy.

With regards and love,

Yours sincerely,
J.P.

[3] Rashtra Seva Dal was a voluntary organization founded in 1941 to help the downtrodden people. Raosaheb P.H. Patwardhan and S.M. Joshi were founding members and leaders of this organization.

5. Appeal to Railwaymen to avoid Strike, Trichy, 8 April 1948[1]

You should not be narrow in your outlook but view your problems from the larger interests of the country as a whole.

I advise you not to become victims of the propaganda of any political party and resort to strike but to remain patient and await the final outcome of the present negotiations between the All-India Railwaymen's Federation and the Railway Board. I sympathize with your lot but would like to remind you of your duties and responsibilities in free India. I am sure that all your legitimate grievances would soon be redressed.

In any collective bargaining there can not be hundred per cent success. In the negotiations which the All-India Railwaymen's Federation is now carrying on with the Railway Board it is quite likely you will win on some points and lose in regard to others. You should adopt a policy of give and take.

The very existence of free India today depends on transport. The country is experiencing food shortage and large supplies of food have to be transported to deficit areas. Moreover, a war is going on in Kashmir. In view of these factors, railwaymen should look at their problems in the context of the larger interests of the country. If, unfortunately, in the midst

[1] Adapted from *Bombay Chronicle*, 10 April 1948.

of the negotiations to which you yourselves are a party you resort to strike, you would not only be ruining yourselves but also the country.

I feel certain that if you discharge your duties to the entire satisfaction of the people at large, your legitimate grievances will soon be redressed.

I regret the delay in the implementation of the Pay Commission's recommendations. This is due to causes beyond any one's control such as the partition of the country and the mass killings that followed.

6. Address to French India Socialist Party, Pondicherry, 11 April 1948[1]

France can save herself from being placed under American or Russian domination, only if she sheds her colonial possessions wherever they may be, whether in Africa, Viet Nam or French India.

The French India problem is very simple. The primary and fundamental issue is freedom. Nobody likes alien rule. Every French Indian should carry the "Quit India" slogan. The next issue after complete freedom from foreign domination is self-determination for merging in the Indian Union or remaining an independent unit. I know almost the whole population desires merger with the Indian Union, the French Indians also being Indians. The Government of India has confused the French India issue by suggesting a plebiscite. According to Mr. Nehru's declaration in the Dominion Parliament, the Indian Republic might enter into an agreement with any nation, France, Russia, America or Britain for the creation of a world state which should be built up with free peoples and not with slaves. Some people belonging to cultural institutions in French India entertain doubts regarding the Indian Government. I am certain that the Indian Union will preserve French India's traditions—cultural, political and economic.

I am surprised at the attitude of the French India Socialist Party in confusing French India's issues. They do no service either to the country, people or Socialism itself. The French India Socialist Party should have a patriotic attitude and amalgamate with the National Congress. The Communist Party, wherever it exists, owes allegiance only to the Soviet Government and French Indian Communists are no exception. I wish French Indians all success. Your future lies absolutely in your hands whatever be the trend of the Delhi Negotiations.

[1] Adapted from *Hindu*, 12 April 1948.

7. Speech at Public Meeting, Triplicane, Madras, 14 April 1948[1]

For the past many days I have been touring in Tamil Nad and it has helped me to correct my impression of the people here. I had been told earlier by some friends that the people of Tamil Nad were cold and calculating as compared with the people in the other parts of the country. I find, on the other hand, that the people in Tamil Nad are as warm-hearted and emotional and as enthusiastic as people in other parts of the country. This has warmed up my heart, because I know that for the changes that we like to make in the social and economic system of the country, we need not only calculation, but also a great deal of enthusiasm. I am sure from what I have seen that Tamil Nad would not lag behind in the revolution that would have to be brought about in the society.

Thanks to the magnificent leadership of Mahatma Gandhi we have been able to achieve freedom. This freedom has brought its own problems and unless we face these problems with wisdom and courage, our freedom would lose its meaning and merit. The secret of our success in achieving freedom was the unity we were able to forge in the midst of various disagreements. If the country had to be divided ultimately that was not the fault of the Muslim League or Mr. Jinnah, it was the fault of all of us as we were not able to forge unity in the country. However, we should not forget that a very large part of the country is with us to-day and if we act with wisdom there is no doubt that India will make such progress politically, economically and culturally that it will become the pride of Asia. I also believe that if Socialist States are set up in both India and Pakistan, there can be hope that the two Indias would again be united. I do not see any other way of achieving that object. Communal politics has no chance of bringing this about, but there is, on the other hand, every chance of the India of to-day being further cut up into many parts. It is our duty today to preserve our hard-won freedom.

We notice to-day fissiparous tendencies threatening this freedom. I refer to the talk of Hindu Raj, Sikh Raj and Dravidasthan. It is true that there are various cultural and linguistic groups in the country. India is not the only country where various nationalities have been blended together into one great nationality. No one wants the different cultural identities to be destroyed, because each culture has its own beauty and contribution to make to the national culture. At the same time, however it should not be forgotten that we have to build up a powerful spirit of Indian nationhood. Till every Indian begins to feel that he is an Indian first and anything else after that, there can be no future for the country.

[1] Adapted from *Hindu*, 15 April 1948.

During my tour in Tamil Nad I have noticed the emergence of certain divisive issues such as linguistic provinces, Dravidian separatism, Brahmin-Non-Brahmin antagonism, hostility to the north, the question of national language, etc. I urge that we should bring to bear on these questions reason and a national outlook. Otherwise, disintegration would set in and the freedom and unity of the country would be in danger. Redistribution of provinces will have to be made scientifically, so that the cultural and economic life of the units can be carried on with ease and efficiency and to the benefit of the people. There should be not only linguistic and cultural homogeneity, they should also have economic solvency. Besides, there should be some kind of geographical unity.

I want that the caste system should go. I wonder if the Brahmins would be prepared to drink water from the hands of Harijans. I also deprecate the agitation against Aryans. The theory that the Aryans came from Central Asia is no longer accepted. On the contrary, the theory that they lived and grew in India itself has been acquiring credibility. Whatever that may be, we are aware of the history of Nazism in Germany and Fascism in Italy and the havoc wrought by them through their emphasis on the racial issue. As far as India is concerned, we should remember that there is only one race—the Indian race; and there is only one nation—the Indian nation.

On the economic question, the most important issue before the country is how to eradicate poverty. This problem of poverty has two aspects, viz., distribution and production. There is a tendency in the country to emphasize one aspect and neglect the other. I recall Dr. Shyama Prasad Mookherjee's recent remark in Parliament that equitable distribution of the present production would mean distribution of poverty and a similar note was struck by the Prime Minister. The Congress had pledged to supply food for all. Now, when we have won freedom, we are told by our leaders that the main question to-day is production. There would be the urge for greater production on the part of workers only if they are assured that the additional income would benefit them also instead of merely increasing the profit of capitalists. They must be convinced that attempts are being made to create a new system of distribution of wealth in which justice would be done to the producers. The Government has been so much impressed by the wisdom, policy and expert knowledge of capitalists that they have come to believe that unless they secure the co-operation of those capitalists on their own terms and conditions, production would not go on in this country. They point out to the lack of technical personnel. On the other hand there are very few working capitalists and in most cases the capitalists are depending on managers. If the Government takes over the industries, the some managers would be there to carry on the work. Moreover, the Government will have more facilities for training technical personnel and getting the necessary equipment. The Congress should solve the problems of distribution and production, so that poverty is abolished in the country. When workers demand higher wages, they are asked to produce more in the first instance, whereas the capitalists would not be content with lesser profit. This is queer logic and one does not know how at this rate they can solve the industrial crisis facing the country. I assure you that, so far as the Socialist Party is concerned we have offered our fullest co-operation to the Central and Provincial Governments in the cause of industrial truce. The country is facing an economic crisis and there is the danger of inflation if more goods are not produced. But certain elementary principles must be fulfilled if there is to be an industrial truce.

The Congress Governments have not yet been able to evolve a sound labour policy or sound industrial policy. The industrial policy that the Central Government has announced will have to be revised and reformed in many ways before it becomes a sound instrument for the industrialization of the country. Some months ago, the Labour and Industry Departments of the Government of India jointly called an industrial conference[2] and passed a resolution. But so far nothing has been done to implement any item of the resolution. At the same time, our leaders are going on sermonizing to labour that there should be no strike. That is not a wise way of handling a difficult situation. Therefore the Socialist Party advocates a policy of redistribution of wealth, here and now. I suggest that the minimum income of an individual should be Rs.100 per month and the maximum should be restricted to Rs.1,000 per month. I also suggest that the Constituent Assembly[3] should revise the salary of Ministers.

The Congress ceased to be a national organization the moment its object of achieving the freedom of the country was fulfilled. Thereafter it has become the ruling party in the country. Many persons like Acharya Narendra Deva[4], who have been members of the Congress for a long time have come out of it now. On the other hand, several persons, who were once even afraid of the name of Congress, have now got into it, perhaps, because it is now profitable to do so. The Socialist Party has realized that it will not be possible for them to push through their programme by remaining inside the Congress. There are many good and well-meaning people in the Congress, as for instance, Pandit Jawaharlal Nehru. There is the least doubt that Pandit Nehru wants to go in the same direction as the Socialists. However, all the good people in the Congress are caught up in a machine which is stronger than themselves. In order to make democracy function effectively in the country, an opposition party is essential and the socialist Party wants to act

[2] For note on Industrial Conference see *JPSW*, Vol. IV, p. 209.

[3] For note on Constituent Assembly see *JPSW*, Vol. IV, p. 41.

[4] For biographical note on Acharya Narendra Deva, see *JPSW*, Vol. I, p. 61.

as such. But it does not mean that the Socialist Party is opposed to cooperation with the Congress under all circumstances. The country is facing a crisis today. The Socialist Party is prepared to work hand in hand with the Congress and the Government for meeting the crisis and overcoming it. Whenever it is a question of relations with Pakistan, or solving the problem of Hyderabad, or the communal trouble or the economic crisis, the socialist Party's co-operation is always there. The Socialist Party has its own programme and would try to rally the people under their flag. The defence of the nation is the Party's first aim and it will not do anything to weaken the Government.

The aims and programme of the Socialists and the Communists are poles apart. While the Socialists derive their strength from the people of the country, the Communist Party owes its allegiance to Moscow. While the Socialist Party wants to bring about a classless and casteless Society and form a truly democratic Government, the Communists want an authoritarian Government. The role played by the Communists in India during the 1942 crisis was most deplorable.

Hyderbad is not a question that is very difficult to solve. It is not like Kashmir. It is a question which can be easily solved. The solution lies with Delhi, in the hands of the Government of India. The day the Government of India make up their mind, the Hyderabad issue can be solved immediately. The only solution I can think of is to merge the different areas of the State of Hyderabad in the respective provinces like the Maharatta area into Maharashtra; Kannada into Karnataka; and Andhra into Andhradesa. I am sure that the Central Government must have reasons for moving cautiously. I have not the least doubt that Hyderabad will become part of India and part of Indian democracy.

I appeal to the people to rally round the Socialist Party. It is easy to set up a Socialist society if only the people make up their mind. Adult franchise would be enforced in the next election and the choice of the form of Government will be in the hands of the people themselves.

8. To N.G. Goray, 20 April 1948[1]

My Dear N.G.,[2]

I had your letter and also Suresh's[3] during my tour of the South. I gave K.B.[4] the letter that you had given me and he promised to send you all the required information. Meanwhile I should like to say that the tour was a

[1] *Brahmanad Papers* (NMML).

[2] For biographical note on N.G. Goray see *JPSW*, Vol. IV, p. 153.

[3] For biographical note on Suresh Desai see *JPSW*, Vol. IV, p. 225.

[4] For biographical note on K.B. Menon see *JPSW*, Vol. IV, p. 52.

great success as far as crowds and propaganda went, but it was a failure as far as collections were concerned. I believe that they did not collect more than Rs. 20,000/- and in Madras City I doubt if there were any collections at all. I feel therefore that the strenuous back-breaking tour was rather wasted. The Provincial Tamilnad Conference was a success as far as the demonstration part went but organizationally it did not result in a step forward. Due to group intrigues K.B. and other friends decided that there should be no elections held at the Conference which was rather deplorable. It was decided that an Electrol College of five representatives from each district would meet in Madras to elect the Provincial Executive and the office bearers. This was done in my presence at Madras but here too things went rather wrong and I am afraid I upset K.B. a great deal. S.R. Subramanium[5] was unanimously elected Provincial Secretary. They did not decide where the Provincial office would be located, but you may send all circulars to Subramanium at Coimbatore and separately to K.B. in his capacity as regional secretary. I found great enthusiasm for the Party in Tamilnad, but I doubt if there are the proper kind of workers or the proper kind of leadership to make use of this enthusiasm and build up a strong socialist movement there.

I was rather surprised to find from you letter[6] that the Foreign Affairs Committee of the Party decided not to send any delegation to the Milan-Paris Conference. The last sentence of the decision which you had quoted in your letter I found rather annoying. It was not I alone who had agreed that we should participate in that Conference but the National Executive itself had decided to do so and as late as Nasik the Executive felt that there was no need to change that decision. However, though it is rather queer for the Foreign Affairs Committee to upset the decision of the Executive, I do not have more to say in this matter. I wish the Secretary of the Foreign Affairs Committee would write to all those concerned particularly Dantwala[7] informing them of the change.

Neither you nor Suresh has said anything about the progress made in the preparation and publication of the Nasik Conference report.[8] I am anxious that the report should be published as soon as possible. Will you please write to me at my Patna address and let me know what progress has been made?

[5] S.R. Subramaniam (1915 -); began his career as a journalist; joined freedom movement in 1938; participated in the Quit India Movement in 1942, arrested and sentenced in 1943; became active in the socialist movement: later, joined the Sarvodaya movement.

[6] See Appendix 1 for N.G. Goray's letter dated 6 April 1948.

[7] For biographical note on M.L. Dantwala see *JPSW*, Vol. III, p. 51.

[8] For note on Nasik Conference Report see *JPSW*, Vol. IV, p. 225.

I should also like to know if all the decisions made by the Executive at Nasik have been implemented, i.e. as far as the Office is concerned have steps been taken towards their implementation? There was a decision, for instance, about the student movement. During my tour of the South I was often asked about our policy regarding the students and I replied in terms of our Nasik decision. Have steps been taken to see that these decisions are implemented? Similarly with other decisions. Regarding Keshav Gore's[9] department, has he made any progress, i.e. has he prepared any schemes, curriculums etc. for the training of Party cadres? I should like him to send me at Patna whatever material he might have got ready by now.

During my tour of the South I was often asked about the Party's policy regarding controls. I think it would be advisable if we asked Dr. Lohia to prepare a small pamphlet explaining and defending the Party's policy in this regard. Similarly a pamphlet fully explaining the Party's foreign policy is necessary. We should plan other pamphlets also and allot them to various persons to write.

You probably know that I was scheduled to tour Sourashtra from the 29th of May for 10 days. I shall be extremely thankful if this tour could be cancelled. The Madras tour was more strenuous than you can imagine and the Bihar tour in this hot summer is going to be more than I can stand. Therefore will you please write to Chhotubhai[10] and request him to cancel the tour? There is enough time yet for this change to be made without any adverse affect. If, the tour of Sourashtra is absolutely necessary, somebody else might be sent there.

I hope you have settled in Bombay now and that the office is humming with work.

Yours affectionately
J.P.

[9] Keshave Gore (1920-58); youth leader, C.S.P.; Secretary Municipal Kamgar Sangh, Poona, 1939; worked underground during Quit India Movement 1942; in prison, 1943-6; became active in the Socialist Party in Bombay and was elected its Secretary in 1955; became Chairman, Maharashtra Socialist Party 1956.

[10] Ishwarlal Chhotubhai Desai (1907-66); participated in the Civil Disobedience Movement 1930; imprisoned 1930, 1932-4, joined C.S.P. in 1934; Member A.I.C.C. 1937; active in Quit India Movement; Member National Executive P.S.P. 1953-4; took part in Bhoodan Movement 1954, Goa Liberation Movement 1955-6; Member Gujarat Legislative Assembly 1962-5.

9. Jawaharlal Nehru, 21 April 1948[1]

Dear Bhai,

According to the talk I had with you about the Draft Constitution, I am sending herewith two documents: one in which we have tried to point out the more glaring defects of the Constitution and to suggest ways of removing them;[2] the other in which we have summarized the recommendations made by the Socialist Party in its own Draft Constitution, a copy of which is being sent separately.[3] I am also sending these papers to sir B.N. Rau.[4]

I hope you will find time to go through these papers and that some, at least, of our suggestions will be acceptable to you.

With the highest regards,

Yours affectionately
J.P.

[1] *J.P. Papers* (NMML).

[2] See next item in this volume.

[3] See Appendix 18 in *JPSW*, Vol. IV.

[4] Senegal Narsing Rau (1887 -): Entered I.C.S. in 1910; District and Session Judge Murshidabad 1919-20; Sylhat and Cachar 1920-5; Secretary to the Government of Assam 1925-33; Joint Secretary, Government of India, Legislative Department 1934-5; Judge, High Court Calcutta 1939; Chairman, Hindu Law Committee 1941, Indus Commission 1941-2; Constitutional Advisor, Constituent Assembly of India and Member of International Law Commission of the United Nations, India's Permanent Representative with United Nations, 1940.

10. Some Thoughts on Our Constitution, 21 April 1948[1]

The Constituent Assembly, as it is at present constituted, does not represent 85% of the people. Even the remaining 15% have not directly participated in its election. The Provincial legislative Assemblies of today are based on the Government of India Act of 1935 which permitted only 15% of the people to exercise their franchise and it was these assemblies which nominated (free election being out of the question) the members of the present Constituent Assembly. According to the May 16 Plan of the British Cabinet Mission which the Congress accepted some sort of "constitution-making body" had to be created to serve the emergency caused by the British decision to hand over power to Indians. It was in that hot haste that the Consembly was formed. At that time, certain inhibitions restricting the scope and sovereignty of the body were also there. Especially the Grouping Clause

[1] Sent as an annexure to item no. 9.

of the Plan was the bone of contention between the Congress and the Muslim League and ultimately proved to be its own wreck.

The serious discrepancy between the interpretations laid on the grouping clause by the Congress and the League, necessitated an award from the British Premier, which award, as expected, went in favour of Mr. Jinnah. Even he unequivocal Congress acquiescence in the interpretation did not improve matters and what followed is recent history.

Between June 1946, when the Cabinet Plan was accepted by both the parties, and June 1947, when the Mountbatten Formula was announced, the Constituent Assembly underwent a lot of changes in its scope and status. Nevertheless its representative capacity remained unchanged. What was intended to be a mere "constitution-making body" with no powers whatsoever to execute its own draft, and bound down to the dictates of the foreigner, emerged as a Sovereign Constituent Assembly, destined to draft and enforce the constitution of free India. No doubt, it was a happy change, but without the necessary metamorphosis in its set up, it was hollow.

It is worse still in the case of the States. Either the nominees of the rulers or the favourites of the States Peoples Conference have been hand-picked and solemnized as States' representatives in the Consembly. Thus by no stretch of imagination can the present Constituent Assembly be described as a representative body of Indians. A handful of people dominate the whole show while the voice of the millions is left in the wilderness. Democratic principle concedes the right of a free people to frame their own constitution. Such a right is being negatived by the present Constituent Assembly in practice. So I say, dissolve the Assembly and form another on adult franchise. Then and then only can the people be said to have ratified the constitution which will govern them for generations.

After 15 August 1947, there has been a tendency among certain people to deprecate the existence of parties other than the Party in power. A lot of confusion has set in, underrating the difference between Democratic Socialism and National Socialism. It is a grave danger. What happened in Russia in 1917 is too well known. People had no liberty to vote or to organize themselves, absolute power was in the hands of the capitalists and the landlords. Under the tyranny of the Czar there was no scope for a democratic atmosphere. Hitler did the same thing in Germany and similarly in Spain today. Though there was no foreign domination in all these cases, freedom remained to be achieved by the people. In such conditions no party except the Party in power, is allowed to function. Civil liberties of the peoples are curtailed.

In Russia, the Communist Party is the only Party and through its unquestioned dominance, Russia has become a totalitarian State. It is better than a capitalist state, in the sense that it has a planned economy, a classless society and absence of exploitation machinery. But as far as political democracy is concerned, no other party except the Communist Party is allowed to exist. It is not true that a single class will have a single political party. In America, both the Republican Party and the Democratic Party voice the views of a single privileged class. Similarly the working class of Russia will like to have different parties and different leaders, if only they are allowed to. This denial of liberty to join and form a Party of one's own choice, so long as one's loyalty to the State is assured, is the ugliest feature of totalitarianism.

Unfortunately, such trends are today seen in our country also. "Crushing" democratic opposition seems to be looked upon as an achievement by some. The irony of it is, that even he limited individual liberty available under the British is now snatched away under the plea of emergancy. When the Rowlatt Acts were promulgated, the people under the head [leadership?] of the Congress protested and agitated against them. At present under the Congress raj itself, more severe legislation is being carried out and a word against them is considered as disloyalty to the State itself.

The people also are mostly indifferent to these things. Their attention is rivetted on food and cloth. It is but natural that scarcity and want should thus narrow down their outlook. Nevertheless, they must widen their vision and look beyond their homes. Political rights are as important as economic wants. In the long run, they make or unmake the nation. If these conditions continue and the people's mentality remains unchanged, an autocratic rule will soon devolve on their heads.

The Press is also muzzled. It is in constant fear of the Government, for through the emergency legislation and ordinance rule, it can build up or destroy the whole machinery as it is for or against the Party in power. As in the case of civil liberties, so also in the case of the Press, its freedom and privileges should be zealously guarded and upheld by every democratic Government, unless the essential loyalty to the State was absent. Undoubtedly there is no such emergency in the country today as to necessitate the existing restrictions on the Press and individual freedom, yet the grip of the Public Security Acts is being tightened day by day. No democratic country would keep its press under the supervision of the Police as the Congress Governments in India are doing at present.

Such being the first taste of freedom, it is natural that we should demand adequate safeguards in the constitution. There are too many loopholes in it, enabling the people in power to take back with the left hand what is given with the right. Extraordinary powers have been vested in the President and the Governors under the heading "emergency". Emergencies can be very easily created and maintained, as in the case of the Weimer Republic of Germany which ultimately led to the dictatorship of Hitler. There are many such dangerous omissions and anomalies, all of which deserve to be brought before the public and rectified according to people's wishes.

According to our Draft Constitution, 21 years is the minimum age for enfranchisement. In many other countries, adult franchise means every one above eighteen years of age will have the power to vote. I don't see any reason for enhancing it to 21 in our country where the average life of man is far less than that in other countries.

The Congress leaders often brush aside these objections as unfounded. Will the very same leaders who led the people to freedom, betray them thus, they ask? Then there is no need for a constitution at all, because our leaders will know how to govern us. Some of our leaders may not have such dictatorial ambitions, they may not wish anything but the good of India. But there may be some others, or some ambitious power politicians may come up in course of time and take advantage of these defects in the constitution. India is going to be governed by this constitution at least for the coming fifty years. That point should not be lost sight of when framing or discussing the constitution. The present limitations of our people will not be there after a few years, percentage of literacy is bound to swell, civic and political consciousness is bound to increase, economic standards will not remain at the present tardy levels. All these will create new conditions in the country, which demand new adjustments.

11. To All Railwaymen, 23 April 1948[1]

Comrades,

I have learnt with grave concern that another union is being organized on the E.I.R. by certain Congressmen under the leadership of Dr. P.C. Ghosh.[2]

As you know, there are already two unions on the E.I.R., namely, the E.I. Railwaymen's Union and the E.I.R. Employees' Association. The existence of these two unions has been a source of weakness to railway workers; and both the organizations have come to realize that the interests of the workers demand that they merge into a single union. You may be aware that plans for such a merger are complete, and we are awaiting only certain technical requirements to be fulfilled for the merger to become a fact.

In view of this growing unity among you, it is sad that certain Congressmen should seek to disrupt your ranks. They cannot but do incalculable harm to you by these disruptionist methods.

[1] *J.P. Papers* (NMML).

[2] For biographical note on P.C. Ghosh see *JPSW*, Vol. III, p. 187.

There would have been justification for the formation of a new union if the present organizations were not patriotic or conscious of their obligations to the State, and if they were not zealous in the service of the workers. As it is, no one can doubt the patriotism of either the Union or the Association or accuse them of irresponsibility to the State. At the same time, both organizations have faithfully served the cause of the workers, and I am not aware of any dissatisfaction with them. I therefore find it difficult to understand why another organization is necessary, except to serve political ends and to bring the workers under the whip-hand of the Government. I have always believed in the independence of working class organizations, and I hope railwaymen will not sell their independence upon any inducement whatever.

It is likely that some of you may be persuaded to join the new union on the plea that a Congress sponsored union would be able to secure for you greater benefits. I should like you to remember that your strength lies not in official patronage, but in your unity and solidarity. A Congress sponsored union, which in the present circumstances is the same as a Government-sponsored organization, cannot but act as a fetter on your independence, and cannot but endeavour to make you subservient to Government policy in the matter of wages and conditions of work and in all other labour political matters.

If you need an example of how a Congress sponsored union functions, you may consider the B.B. & C.I. Rly. Employees' Association[3] of which the Hon'ble Sardar Vallabhbhai Patel is still the president. No one can claim that the B.B. & C.I. Employees' Association has any outstanding record of achievements or service.

Before I close, I should like to warn you further that the present move to form a new union on the E.I.R. is only the thin end of the wedge. The ultimate step in this conspiracy is to set up a rival Federation of Railwaymen. That would be an evil day for Indian railwaymen when a new Federation should come into being, for then that remarkable unity achieved under the flag of the A.I.R.F. would cease to be and railwaymen would fight among themselves while the Railway board would look on happily, playing its own little part in instigating the fight, much as the Railway Administrations do today when they try to play one rival union against the other.

I, therefore, appeal to you all, if you value your unity and independence of action, to keep away from the new move and press forward to an immediate merger of the two existing unions, which would bring together under one flag the hundred and fifty thousand of the E.I. Railwaymen.

[3] B.B. & C.I. Rly. Association—Refers to Bombay, Baroda and Central India Railway Association.

Yours would then be an irresistible force, and justice would no longer be denied to you.

I remain,
Yours fraternally,
Jayaprakash Narayan

12. Role of Trade Unions in Free India, 1 May 1948[1]

Our country having crossed the threshold of freedom, the Indian working class must be prepared to play its role in the creation of a free and prosperous India. This cannot be done unless we have a new type of trade union worker created.

The industrial prospects are gloomy today. Workers everywhere in our country are restless and worried. The dawn of freedom has on the one hand created hopes of a new life, free from want and exploitation, and improved economic conditions and, on the other, created a feeling of despair and despondency. This is a very dangerous situation.

Irresponsible elements such as the Communists who hope to gain their objective by fishing in troubled waters are interested in creating conditions of anarchy in this country. In this transitional period in which our newly won freedom is fraught on all sides with danger, such anarchy will lead to untold suffering and complete political and economic collapse of the country.

The trade union worker must know that there is a great responsibility to-day resting on his shoulders. He has, on the one hand, the task of organizing the worker and educating him, of protecting his interests and fighting for them and at the same time he has the task of making the worker aware of his larger responsibilities to the State and to society as a whole. It is my firm conviction that if the workers in India are to reach their economic and political goal, they must conduct their movement in an organized, disciplined and peaceful manner.

It is the worker's universal demand today that his wages must rise and his conditions of work and living must improve. I have not the least doubt that this must be so. The primary need of our worker, that is, the need for a living wage and for adequate shelter must be fulfilled. The industry that fails to give its workers living wage has no justification to exist. At the same time, it is for the worker to realize that his wages cannot rise in reality unless he produces more. If his wages rise and production remains at standstill or comes down, the result would be the rise in prices which will cancel out the rise in wages. If there are not more commodities produced, the worker cannot have more commodities to consume.

[1] Adapted from *Janata*, 1 May 1948.

It is the duty of the trade union movement to tell the workers that in their own interest they must produce more. At the same time, I should like to draw the attention of the Government and those responsible for economic policies in this country that unless there is a psychological revolution, the worker is likely to remain listless and disinterested. Unless the worker is assured that he is getting a new deal now, that he has acquired now a stake in industry and the economic and political life of the country, that he has become a partner both in the ownership and management of the State and the economic resources and institutions his attitude towards his work is not likely to change. If labour is to be fully productive, it must be provided with adequate incentives. And where material incentive may be wanting real psychological incentives must be created by a change in the social order.

Living wage and shelter are, however, not the ultimate objectives of labour. Labour in India as elsewhere must eventually come into its own and become the Government of the country. A Worker's Democracy, including in the term 'Worker' all those who live by their labour, whether they work in fields, factories or offices, is the ultimate objective of a labour movement. In the conditions of India such an objective is not difficult of fulfilment, but it is necessary for this that the labour movement should now enter the political field and the field of constructive work.

A Worker's Democracy will be a lie, unless the workers are developed morally, intellectually and politically. The Labour movement in this country must create an extensive workers' educational movement which, through visual and oral instructions, must bring about a mental change in the worker and raise him to a higher level of understanding and culture. I further believe that the labour movement must develop such other constructive activities as workers' co-operatives, prohibition, etc.

The new type of trade union worker must be trained in all these activities and he must also belong to a political party. I am looking to the day in the near future when the Indian workers in their millions will gather under the flag of the Socialist Party. That will be a great day for Indian labour and the beginning of a new political life in this country.

13. To Sardar Daljit Singh, 1 May 1948[1]

My dear Sardar Daljit Singhji,[2]

I am very sorry for the delay in replying to your letter. When I was in Delhi last, I tried to get into touch with you but failed. I thank you warmly for the

[1] *J.P. Papers* (NMML).

[2] A Delhi-based businessman interested in the Socialist Party.

cheque of Rs. 5000/- that you sent with your letter. The installment for April is due now and also the installment for May if that is possible. In any case please send me the April installment here at my Patna address.

I was very happy to find from the papers that you have already decided to leave the Congress and join the Socialist Party. I always thought that was the only right course for you or any young man who is inspired with ideals of social and economic justice. I wish you success in your new career and I am sure you will make a valuable contribution to the growth of the socialist movement in Delhi and the East Punjab.

I hope you will keep in mind my request for premises in your new building that is being built near the Regal theatre. When is that building likely to be ready?

Please remember me to your father and give him my regards,

With best wishes,

Sincerely yours,
Jayaprakash Narayan

14. To Purshottam Trikamdas, 1 May 1948[1]

My dear P.T.,[2]

Suresh[3] spoke to me about your impressions of Jharia. You should not take the word of the Indian colliery owners seriously. With rare exceptions they are a roguish lot. While our workers in Jharia are not at all perfect, they are on the average good people. One or two use intemperate language—though nothing like what the owners allege; and at least one I know is corrupt. But work in the collieries is difficult and workers don't stick there. It has been our plan slowly to withdraw the bad types after workers of the right type have been found and trained to do the work.

Suresh said that you would be prepared to go to Jharia for a week before the National Executive to study the situation on the spot. Nothing could be better; and I would greatly appreciate it if you could do that. I would be in Jharia on the 14th. If you could reach there before or on the same day, I could discuss the matter with you and give you certain old papers and background material. 14th would be a week before the Executive and ought to fit in with your programme. Do send me a wire at Patna if you are coming.

[1] *J.P. Papers* (NMML).
[2] For biographical note on Purshottam Trikamdas see *JPSW*, Vol. I, p. 88.
[3] Suresh Desai.

I shall be touring Bihar till the 15th and be leaving Patna on the 16th night for Bombay.

As ever,
Jayaprakash Narayan

15. Interview to the Associated Press of India, Patna, 15 May 1948[1]

Question: What are the reasons of the failure of the Socialist Party in District Board Elections in the United Provinces?

Jayaprakash Narayan: I guess that the failure of the Socialist Party was due to want of sufficient time for propaganda. I understand also that the Congress Party made improper use of the machinery of administration to coerce the voters. For instance, the Muslims are alleged to have been warned by officials that unless they voted Congress, their loyalty to the Union would be in question. Whatever may have been the reason for our failure in U.P. I do not take a gloomy view of it.

Question: What is your view regarding the accession of Hyderabad with Indian Union?

J.P: The issue in Hyderabad is whether 11 per cent or 89 per cent of the people should prevail. The issue is not communal but one of freedom and democracy—whether Hyderabad is to accede to India or otherwise. It is a question that the people of the state must decide. Before they do so, their sovereignty must be established and full democratic government instituted. The issue of accession could then be settled by the people in a free plebiscite.

Question: What should be the role of the Indian people in alleviating sufferings of the people of Hyderabad?

J.P.: The people of India must help the people of Hyderabad to win their independence. India had sent volunteers to Spain to fight against fascist tyranny; there is no less tyranny in Hyderabad today. It is the duty of every lover of freedom, not only in India but also elsewhere, to give every possible support to the suffering people of Hyderabad.

Question: Do you think that the Socialist Parties of Pakistan and India should have common policies?

J.P: The Socialist Party of Pakistan is now independent of the Indian Socialist Party; nevertheless the two parties should try to evolve common policies.

Question: Do you think that the Socialist Party of Pakistan is justified in lending its support to the Azad Kashmir Government?

[1] Adapted from *National Herald*, 16 May 1948.

J.P: It is not true that the Pakistan Socialist Party lent its support to the Azad Kashmir Government. It is, however, true that the party has advised the people of Kashmir to vote for Pakistan in the plebiscite. I believe that as loyal citizens of Pakistan, members of the party were justified in this stand.

16. To Sardar Daljit Singh, 29 May 1948[1]

My dear Sardar Daljit Singh,

I am sorry for the delay in replying to your very nice letter. I am happy to find you so enthusiastic about the Party and about your own work. As a friend and a sort of an elder brother, may I advise you not to think of positions as of the service that you may render to the cause? Position will come to you if you are patient and do not hanker after it. I have not the least doubt that a person of your standing would have great influence over the Sikh community in the East Punjab and I should like you very much to take up active work there. I also don't want you to remain merely a donor to the Party. Rather I would like you to become one of its foremost workers which would then entitle you to any position that you may desire. I have spoken to my friend, Prem Bhasin, about you and he is very keen that you should take up work in the East Punjab and help him in his arduous task there.

I am sorry to keep on reminding you every time of the promises that we want in your brother's new building near the Regal. I hope our claim would get first priority. We have decided now to shift the Head Office to Delhi as soon as possible. We will also require building space for our various other activities. Therefore I hope that we will be able to get a whole floor of your new building at whatever rent your brother may consider reasonable.

I have not yet received the cheques which you promised to send after your father returns to Delhi.

With best wishes,

Sincerely yours,
J.P.

[1]*J.P. Papers* (NMML).

17. To the President, Constituent Assembly of India, New Delhi, 30 May 1948[1]

To
The Hon'ble President,[2]
Constituent Assembly of India,
1, Queen Victoria Road,
New Delhi.

Dear Sir,

I have the honour to forward to you herewith three resolutions passed by the National Executive of the Socialist Party. These resolutions are of vital importance, and I hope they will receive due consideration.[3]

The resolutions deal with the following questions:

(1) Dissolution of the present Constituent Assembly (as distinct from the Central Assembly) and convening of a new Constituent Assembly elected on the basis of adult franchise;
(2) Indo-British relations and the status of the Indian State;
(3) Language and the delimitation of provinces.

Regarding the first, it need hardly be argued that the present Constituent Assembly has become wholly unrepresentative. Elected before the partition of the country and the transfer of power and by Provincial Assemblies which were elected still earlier and on a very restricted franchise; and containing as it does nominees of the Rulers, the present assembly is not only out of date but also unrepresentative of the people. Had this Assembly been functioning for normal legislative business, its present character might not have been found to be so objectionable, though even for that purpose a freshly elected body would be more desirable. But when the organic law of a newly born nation has to be written, justice requires that the law-making body is as up to date and representative as possible. Any other course would mean the betrayal of the principles of democracy and of the rights of the people.

I therefore trust that the suggestions made in our resolution would be accepted both by the Constituent Assembly and the Government of India.

[1] *J.P. Papers* (NMML).

[2] Rajendra Prasad. For biographical note see *JPSW*, Vol. I, p. 112.

[3] See Appendix 2 for Rajendra Prasad's reply dated 13 June 1948.

As for the other two resolutions their texts are clear enough and I need not write any further to elucidate them.

With kind regards,

Sincerely yours,
Jayaprakash Narayan

18. To Siddique Lodhi, 4 June 1948[1]

My dear Lodhi Saheb,[2]

Your letter of 19th May. I have thought over your letter carefully and have come to the conclusion that it would be more desirable for you to stay in Pakistan and develop the Socialist Party there. If all our old comrades come away then who will build up the Party there? Already there is so much misunderstanding between India and Pakistan which is harmful to both these countries. If this growing misunderstanding has to be removed it can only be done by independent Socialist Parties developing in both these countries. I should therefore like to advise you not to leave Pakistan but try to serve the cause of the common people of that country to the best of your ability. I hope you will accept this advice.

With best wishes,

Yours sincerely,
Jayaprakash Narayan

[1] *J.P. Papers* (NMML).

[2] Siddique Lodhi; Stockists and Suppliers of Iron, Paints and Hardware, Rawalpindi, Pakistan.

19. To Reyasat Karim, 9 June 1948[1]

My dear Reyasat Saheb,[2]

You will recall that some months ago I had sent Comrade Mahesh Desai[3] to bring the report on the situation in Jharia. At that time it was my intention to send Mahesh to Jameshedpur because the Bombay Party had found it

[1] *J.P. Papers* (NMML).

[2] For biographical note on Reyasat Karim see *JPSW*, Vol. IV, p. 222

[3] Mahesh Desai (1925-); General Secretary Hind Mazdoor Sabha, 1967-78; Convener, Central Steel and Engineering Committee since 1974.

difficult to spare Bagaram Tulpule.[4] Now the Bombay Party has agreed to let Tulpule go to Jamshedpur. This means that Mahesh Desai would be available for coal fields. I discussed the matter with him a couple of days ago and I was happy to find hat he was agreeable to go to Jharia. I hope you and all the other comrades in Jharia will welcome Comrade Mahesh Desai and fully cooperate with him. He will be going to Jharia by the end of this month. I expect to be in Patna in the first week of July and I hope it will be possible for us to meet then.

With best wishes,

Yours sincerely,
Jayaprakash Narayan

[4] Bagaram Tulpule (1922-); worked underground in Quit India Movement 1942, arrested in 1943, released in 1945, organized steel workers in Jamshedpur 1948, Secretary, Bombay Socialist Party in 1951, General Secretary, Mill Mazdoor Sabha 1956-63 and its President in 1971, President, Mazagon Dock Workers Union 1977-80.

20. Statement on Hyderabad Affairs, Madras, 12 June 1948[1]

The primary object of my tour is to find out what can be done by the people inside and outside Hyderabad State and to extend to the people of the State the full sympathy and co-operation of my party in their struggle for freedom. So far I have toured the Chanda border areas adjoining the Central Provinces and my impression is that the people inside the State should be encouraged to intensify their struggle. I propose to stay in Bezwada for three days to study the conditions in the border areas there. From Bezwada I will proceed to Kurnool and Bombay side and reach Delhi on June 18.

In my opinion the stage is now reached when the Government of India have no alternative except to march their forces into Hyderabad. What I expect out of the recent negotiations between India and Hyderabad Governments is some definite action when the parleys break down. The only action that can be taken by the Government of India is to chase out the Razakars. This power, the Government has already got under the present constitutional position. They should have done this long before. The delay on their part has made the Razakars stronger and aggressive. So far, the Government of India, in my view, has failed to utilize the time to strengthen its position on the border areas with a view to removing the feeling of helplessness prevailing among the people inside the State. I shall try to find out in what way the resources of my Party can be harnessed to solve the present impasse and to give sufficient encouragement to the people to organize and carry on their struggle for freedom.

[1] Adapted from *Hindu*, 12 June 1948.

21. Statement on By-elections to the U.P. Legislative Assembly, Bombay, 14 June 1948[1]

The by-elections to the U.P. Legislative Assembly are drawing near. At times of election it is usual for contesting parties to put temporarily away all considerations for truth, decorum and propriety. I should like earnestly to appeal to all members and friends of the Socialist Party to avoid this usual failing. Abuse and slander have never won any votes. Moreover, it amounts to a betrayal of the people to indulge in such practice. An election campaign should educate the electorate and not confuse and befuddle it.

Therefore, while we must criticize the party in power, and even criticize it strongly, we must avoid personal attack, lie, abuse and slander. That the Congress party may not have similar scruples should be no justification for misconduct on our part. If we too do what the opposite party is doing, we should forfeit our claim to be preferred to our opponents.

[1] *National Herald*, 15 June 1948.

22. Speech at Public Meeting, Kurnool, 16 June 1948[1]

The affairs inside Hyderabad tend to the establishment of a totalitarian state, which cannot be tolerated by the Indian Union. The cry of Hyderabad's, independence was the result of Anglo-American collaboration to keep Asia under their grip. Dr. Grady's[2] reference at ECAFE, to Hyderabad, bracketing it with Indonesia, has proved it.

I call upon the Nizam to transfer power to the people as has been done in Kashmir. Though the Nizam has accepted plebiscite, conditions prevailing in the state are not propitious and no plebiscite will be fair, before the restoration of a free atmosphere. The state atmosphere is now surcharged with anarchy. The Indian Union should not fight shy of a plebiscite either in Kashmir or Hyderabad.

An isolated, independent Hyderabad is a source of danger to Indian freedom and hence can not be tolerated. If Hyderabad persists, the Indian Union will be compelled to force Hyderabad to accede to it.

[1] Adapted from *National Herald*, 17 June 1948.

[2] For biographical note on Dr. Grady see *JPSW*, Vol. III, p. 140.

23. To John Matthai, 17 June 1948[1]

My dear Dr. Matthai,[2]

May I draw you attention to the following points:

The Pay Commission Report

1. The long drawn-out negotiations between us on the question of implementation of the Pay Commission Report have now reached the final stage. The Workshop Staff Classification Tribunal has already submitted its report, and the various Railway administrations too should have by now submitted their final report on their discussions with their respective unions. It is time now that final decisions are made.

The men as you know have been extremely restive at the long delay that has already occurred and the unions are pressing me to convene the General Council of the Federation without further delay. I have accordingly fixed the middle of July for this meeting. It is necessary before then (a) that the Railway Board should complete its review of the reports on the discussions between the Railway and the Unions and (b) that representatives of the Board and the Federation should meet and finalise the result of their negotiations on this whole vaxed question of the Pay Commission. I hope it would be possible to hold this meeting by the first week of July at the latest. This meeting would clearly take some days to conclude, and provision should be made accordingly.

Demands Unconnected with the Pay Commission

2. Our recent negotiation have been concerned mainly with the Pay Commission. But if you refer to the resolution of the Gorakhpur Convention of the Federation[3] (copy enclosed) you will find that there were several other demands, unconnected with the Commission's report, that too were placed before the Board. I am enclosing herewith an explanatory note on

[1] *Janata*, 25 July 1948.

[2] John Matthai (1886-1959) B.A., B.L. (Madras) D.Sc. (London) Professor of Economies Presidency College, Madras 1920-5, Member Madras Legislative Council 1922-5, Indian Tariff Board, 1925-31, President Tariff Board 1931-4, Director-General of Commercial Intelligence & Statistics, 1935-40, joined Tata Sons 1940. Minister for Industries, 1946-7, Minister of Finance Govt. of India 1948-50.

[3] Gorakhpur Convention: All India Railwaymen's Federation met at Gorakhpur on 5 June 1947 to discuss the Pay Commission's recommendations and railwaymen's demands. It also fixed 27 June 1947 as a special day for demonstrating the unity and solidarity of the railwaymen.

the Gorakhpur resolution that the Negotiating Committee of the Federation had submitted to the Board soon after the Convention.

A resolution (copy enclosed) of the General Council of the Federation, adopted on 4 August 1947, at New Delhi, allowed twelve months for negotiations on these demands to be completed. The resolution said inter alia: ". . . the General Council while reiterating with all the emphasis at its command the just and reasonable demands of railwaymen as presented to the Railway Board by the Negotiating Committee appointed by the Gorakhpur Convention expresses its willingness purely as a gesture of its sincere co-operation in the tasks lying ahead to stay further action on all the demands of the Federation for a period of time not exceeding twelve months provided the Railway Board pass orders for immediate and full implementation of the favourable recommendations of the Pay Commission as a whole. . . ."

Many months have elapsed since the meeting of the General Council, and it will be a year in less than two months. I do not know what the Railway Board has done with respect to these demands. But in order that no further time is lost and the grievances of railwaymen do not pile up, leading to discontent and lowering of efficiency, I should like to suggest that this matter be taken up as one of the highest priority and a high level officer be immediately put on the job, so that as soon as the Pay Commission business is out of the way, these questions may be taken up and decisions arrived at expeditiously.

The Adjudicator's Award

3. The long awaited Rajadhyaksha award has been out for some time now, and it was hoped that the Government would take immediate action on it. There should be no further delay in putting the award into force. The Federation should like to discuss any difficulties that might arise in carrying out the award.

Press Note on Tribunal's Award

4. I fear I must protest against certain parts of your department's press note on the findings of the Workshop Tribunal. The tribunal, it seems to me—and in this I agree with Mr. Khedgikar[4]—has gone beyond its powers in deciding matters which were not subject to dispute between the Federation and the Railway Board. I shall in this connection draw your attention to the following excerpt from a letter of the Board to the Federation (E48CPC/20 dated 26.2.48; para 7):

[4] For biographical note on Khadgikar see *JPSW*, Vol. I, p. 93.

As regards the classification of a trade as skilled or semi-skilled the procedure would be to accept a trade as skilled or semi-skilled in regard to which the practice on Railways is uniform. As regards trades in which the practice was not uniform, there would be in the first instance, a discussion between the Railway Board and the Federation. If an agreement was reached, the classification would be according to such agreement. If, however, there was no agreement, the matter would be referred to a Tribunal consisting of a representative of the Railway Board and a neutral Chairman. Government would issue orders without any avoidable delay in regard to the classification of trades where the practice on all Railways was uniform.

This letter makes it clear beyond argument that categories that had already been accepted by the Board as skilled would not be subject to re-examination by the Tribunal and they naturally cannot be affected by its decisions. It is a clear breach of agreement, therefore, for the Board to have decided, according to the press note, that in those cases where, under previous orders, any categories have already been classified as skilled and paid as such but the Award of the tribunal would only entitle them to a lower classification, the individual already admitted to the skilled rate of pay should be permitted to draw as personal to himself pay in the scale of Rs. 55-3-85-4, 94, i.e. up to the efficiency bar.

I request that orders be immediately issued to rectify this breach.

Running Staff

5. The unhappy strike of the S.I.R. running staff has spotlighted the grievances of railwaymen in this category. There is grave discontent among this staff, not only on the S.I.R. but everywhere. This discontent, as you must be aware is seriously affecting the running of trains, and should not be allowed to become chronic. The case of the running staff deserves careful and sympathetic consideration.

Passes

6. It is amazing how the Railway Board sometimes goes out of its way to create dissatisfaction among the men. The recent pass rules are an instance in point. I do not see where was the need in times that are already so full of trouble to further exacerbate feelings. Speaking for myself, I do not see why should there be such elaborate class distinctions even in the matter of passes to railway employees. Be that as it may, it is clear to me that it was unwisdom to have upset existing privileges. These privileges were certainly not undue; and to have reduced them further was unjust.

I therefore strongly urge that the new pass rules be immediately withdrawn. Here I should like to draw your attention to point no. 20 of the note of the Negotiating Committee already referred to. This point says: Existing pass and P.T.O. facilities should continue subject to a uniform minimum of three sets for all categories so far as privilege passes are concerned. In view of this old demand of the Federation, made months back, it was not right for the Board to have framed new pass rules without reference to the Federation.

Grainshop Enquiry Committee

7. There are reports current that the Board intend taking action on the interim recommendations of the Grainshop Enquiry Committee. I trust that no decisions will be taken in this respect until the Federation has been given an opportunity to express its opinion.

I hope these points will receive your urgent attention.

With kindest regards,

Sincerely yours,
Jayaprakash Narayan

24. Statement on the Rampur Elections, Lucknow, 21 June 1948[1]

The people of Rampur were ill-advised to accept the official assurance of non-interference in elections and not to press for the immediate formation of a popular interim government when the January declaration of reforms with certain agreed amendments, was accepted in March last.

The authorities and officials of the state were anyhow expected to be absolutely neutral in elections to the legislature. They, however, did not choose to remain neutral. They actively and almost openly interfered in the interests of their henchmen and other reactionaries with a view to perpetuating their autocratic rule. To stifle the voice of democracy even the use of microphone and loudspeakers were prohibited during the period of elections.

Under such circumstances the National Conference was perfectly justified in boycotting the elections and demanding the formation of a popular interim government prior to the elections to the legislature. I am glad to know that the call of the National Conference was readily responded to by the bulk of

[1] *National Herald*, 22 June 1948.

the voters and that at one polling both only three out of six thousand votes were cast.

A legislature so elected cannot claim to represent the people and lay the foundation of democracy in the state. These elections must be set aside and popular interim government should immediately be formed. The state authorities must remember that autocracy cannot be allowed to be perpetuated and buttressed by election manipulations and packed legislature. Willing transference of power to progressive forces is the only peaceful solution of the political problem of the state.

I hope all the progressive forces of the state will rally round the National Conference and thus strengthen it to compel despotism, bureaucracy, and communalism to yield to democratic progress. The establishment of full responsible government and foundation of secular democratic public life on the basis of common and equal citizenship are the primary tasks of the people of the Rampur State and they must be attended to first.

25. *Janata*: Organ of the Socialist Party, 28 June 1948[1]

I have great news for members and friends of the Party:

The lack of a full-fledged central organ of the Party has been keenly felt for many months. On this account, not only has the Party lacked an authoritative interpreter, but it has also been extremely difficult to coordinate the work of the provincial branches and the various departments of Party activity. The first twelve months, if not more, after our separation from the Congress are going to be the formative period for the Party. This formative work has been suffering greatly in the absence of a regular Party organ.

Accordingly, I am sure all members and friends of the Party will hail the news with pleasure that *Janata*, from its issue of July 4 this year will become an official organ of the Party. From that day the Party takes full responsibility for the management and editorial policy of the paper. Comrade Narayanan,[2] who has been editing the paper with such distinction and devotion, will continue to be the editor.

When *Janata* is about to launch upon a new career, it would be profitable to review its past.

During their underground days Aruna Asaf Ali[3] and Achyut Patwardhan,[4] with whom was closely associated Edatata Narayanan, keenly felt the need of a printed medium through which they could reach the minds of the youth

[1] *Janata*, 28 June 1948.

[2] For biographical note on E. Narayanan see *JPSW*, Vol. IV, p. 222.

[3] For biographical note on Aruna Asaf Ali see *JPSW*, Vol. III, p. 278.

[4] For biographical note on Achyut Patwardhan see *JPSW*, Vol. IV, p. 162.

and fight the prevailing mood of defeatism. Thus the idea of starting *Janata* as such a medium was born during the summer of 1945. It was not however, till January '46 that the idea could take practical shape. The first issue of *Janata* appeared on Independence Day: 26 January 1946. E. Narayanan became its editor and Aruna and Achyut its guiding spirits, who wrote regularly under assumed names.

From the very first number, *Janata* leaped into popularity and became a ray of light and hope in the enveloping atmosphere of darkness and groping. Thousands of fighters for freedom throughout the country took courage and guidance from *Janata*; and the common citizen who read it saw hope rising on the dim political horizon.

Those were days when there was no formal organization of the Party functioning. The Party, so to say, was in cold storage, though all its members, who were not in prison, were active in the underground movement. *Janata* was then the open voice of the underground. When, after Rammanohar Lohia and I were released from the Agra jail, it was decided to reorganize the Party. *Janata* became its unofficial organ. The Party, however, was in a more or less disorganized condition for many months and therefore it was not possible to forge those links with *Janata* that should exist between a party and even, its unofficial mouthpiece. Nevertheless, *Janata* made a considerable contribution to the reorganization of the Party and propagation of its views. In recent months, however, the Party and *Janata* had somehow drifted apart but even during this period *Janata* continued broadly to support the Party. It should be a matter of great satisfaction to all concerned, as it is to me, that this long association is being turned now into complete identification and *Janata* becomes an official organ of the Party.

While I have no doubt that this news will be received with enthusiasm by all the members of the Party, every member must realize that he too must bear his share of responsibility for running *Janata*. Every member and friend of the Party must give his best to *Janata* in whatever manner possible.

The first thing for every member to do is obviously to enroll enough subscribers of *Janata* to make it financially as secure as possible. Quotas have been allotted to every province which must be fulfilled by the 31st of August this year. It is the duty of every member to see that this provincial quota is fulfilled within the prescribed period.

The next important thing to do in order to make *Janata* a successful Party organ is for every provincial Party to send to the editor regularly-every week, at least—a full report on Party activities, political developments in the province, events of interest, etc. Further, members of the Party who are in a position to do so should make it a first priority job to send to *Janata* regularly, articles, notes or other material for publication.

Last but not the least, every member of the Party who reads English must make it a point regularly to read *Janata*, and, if he desires, send to it comments, suggestions or criticism.

Apart from this appeal to Party members, may I also make an appeal to the general reader and all those who may be interested in the cause which *Janata* and the Socialist Party endeavour to serve? I appeal to all such friends to help us in any manner they can, whether by contributing articles, notes, letters, comments or otherwise.

Lastly let me wish *Janata* all success in its new career. The future of India is with socialism. Let *Janata* lead the people to their destiny.

26. Statement Condemning Assault on a Party Worker, Faizabad, 28 June 1948[1]

I have seen and heard of many strange and unbelievable things during this bye-election campaign in the U.P. When I have a little more time, I shall tell of these strange happenings because the people should know of them. But the story of Nawabganj in the district of Gonda I must tell immediately because delay would mean encouragement to the dark forces of evil that are abroad.

After my meeting at Nawabganj, I was taken to the house of Gaya Prasad Azad, an old Congress and Socialist worker, who was lying in bed with unnumbered bruises and severe injuries. The doctor who was attending on him said it was a miracle that Gaya Prasad did not die.

Gaya Prasad is a selfless and fearless servant of the people who love and respect him. On the night of June 21 as he was returning home after the day's propaganda tour for the Socialist Party, he was set upon by a dozen or more Congress hirelings and beaten up mercilessly.

The next day there was a spontaneous hartal in the township and hundreds of people streamed to the doors of Gaya Prasad to inquire after his health and give him their sympathy.

It is not many months that Mahatma Gandhi left us. Congressmen do not hesitate to trade in his name and yet they have already so forgotten him in Gonda at least as to sink even to goondaism.

[1] Adapted from *National Herald*, 29 June 1948.

27. 'Towards Fascism', *Janata*, 4 July 1948[1]

For the first time in my life I went out electioneering. From the 19th June to the 28th, I toured the United Provinces from Aligarh to Ghazipur.

[1] *Janata*, 4 July 1948.

This is the first of July and the results would not be out before another couple of days or more. What the results will be, I cannot tell; although, if our candidates are defeated, it should cause no surprise. The Party is only a few months old and a great deal of work will have to be put in both organizationally and in the field of constructive work and service of the people and educative propaganda, before we may reasonably be sure of success. These by-elections have given us valuable lessons and experience which could not have been gained otherwise. As such they have been of incalculable value to us.

The results of the U.P. elections in terms of a party's defeat or success have little immediate bearing, however, on the country's future. What is of far greater significance is the manner in which the elections were conducted by the U.P. Government and the Provincial Congress. In the past months there has been a growing disregard shown by the provincial governments for the liberties of the people. This was serious enough. But the utter disregard shown by the U.P. Government for the methods of democracy and the attitude of mind exhibited by Congress leaders of the Province can lead not only to an early strangulation of Indian democracy and enthronement of fascism but also to the complete divorce of public life from decency and honesty.

In an election it is customary for public tastes to be lowered, though from a country so dear to Mahatma Gandhi, better standards could be expected. While it is possible, that on the socialist side in the U.P. elections some speeches in low or vulgar taste were made, none can accuse any of the prominent socialist leaders of the Province, or those who had gone from outside, of any cheapness or vulgarity. The speeches of Narendra Deva, Rammanohar Lohia, Aruna Asaf Ali, Achyut Patwardhan maintained a high level of political propaganda. On the other hand, Pandit Govind Vallabh Pant, the Prime Minister of the Province, from his very inaugural speech at Lucknow descended to personalities, cheapness and vulgarity. Here are some gems cast about by Pandit Pant:

1. There is no need of an opposition;
2. We shall crush any opposition as we crushed the Muslim league, the Hindu Mahasabha, the RSS, the Communists, etc.;
3. The socialists are self-seekers and they left the Congress for self-aggrandisement;
4. The socialists are snakes;
5. To vote for the socialists is to vote for the Razakars and the Frontier tribesmen raiding Kashmir;
6. To vote for Congress is to give peace to Gandhiji's soul;
7. The U.P. Government have made Hindi the official language, the socialists will replace it with Hindustani;

8. The socialists do not believe in religion and if they come to power, temples would cease to be;
9. Choose between Nehru and Patel on one side and Jayaprakash and Lohia on the other;
10. To vote against the Congress is to weaken the country; and similar other gems.

It can be imagined what the lesser Congress luminaries must have said when Pt. Pant himself set the tone in such fashion. Almost alone among Congressmen in the U.P. was Babu Purushottamdas Tandon, who neither forgot his manners nor the decencies of life.

But let us leave aside the low taste of Pandit Pant and his supporters. I whish here to draw attention to two vitally important aspects of the matter.

Pandit Pant declared repeatedly, and in this he was supported by Tandonji, which added great weight to his declarations, that there was no need of an opposition whatever and that opposition after all was a western political device unsuited to our country. It is remarkable that after the Congress had copied the entire western system of government, a Congress leader of the standing of Pt. Pant should strike at the concept of democratic opposition on the ground of its being western. But the ground is immaterial: it was trotted out merely to pander to the cheap anti-western sentiment of the obscurantists in our society whose number is not small. It is the frank denial of the need of an opposition and the impatience and annoyance shown over it, that are of far greater significance. Only a fascist mind can function in this manner.

This attitude of mind becomes infinitely more serious when we take into consideration its translation into practice.

Everywhere that I went, people told me that an atmosphere of fear had been deliberately created in which the people were afraid to exercise the franchise freely. Congress leaders, ministers, parliamentary secretaries, members of the Services, the Provincial Home Guards, all cooperated in creating this fear psychology. The people were told that the Socialists were against the Government and therefore any one who voted for them would be considered as an enemy of the government and dealt with as such. With the background of the recent suppression of the RSS and other organizations, this powerful intimidation had a disastrous effect on the voters who, suppressing their discontent with Congress rule, stayed away at home or voted against their hearts' wish out of fear.

When such methods are used, it is immaterial who wins because, in any case, the country loses. If a sound democracy is our goal, these methods, as I have said, can only result in strangling democracy and all the freedoms of the people. If Pandit Pant and Congressmen of his kind are not checked they will soon make of India a slave nation. The freedom that the people won from the British, they would soon lose to a fascist junta.

The second aspect of Pandit Pant's election campaign to which I wish to draw attention is his pandering to the communal sentiments of the people. His description of the socialists as anti-religious, his constant playing up of the Hindi-Hindustani issue are examples. In one breath he said, to vote for the Congress was to give peace to Gandhiji's soul; and in the next, disregarding all that Gandhiji stood for, he asked for votes on the ground that his government had made Hindi the official language, whereas if the socialists came to power they would replace it with Hindustani.

I had thought that there were certain things that were common ground between us and the Congress, such as: defence of freedom and democracy; a clean and decent public life; opposition to communalism and racialism. In a democracy, unless opposite parties have some common basis of this sort, democracy cannot function. If the Congress begins to pander to communalism just to catch votes, what will happen to India?

I wonder if there is enough vitality in the people to prevent these trends at the very beginning of free political life. I wonder too if there is any one in the Congress now since the death of Gandhiji interested enough in the future of Indian democracy and with detachment enough from partisanship and the path of power, to raise his voice against these fatal trends. Pandit Nehru? Perhaps. But will he act?

The people may still continue to vote for the Congress out of habit or fear, but I know that today if they have any faith in the Congress left, it is almost solely because Pandit Nehru is still there. Will Panditji therefore vindicate the people's faith in him by fighting for their liberties, if need be, even against his own party? Much may depend on the answer, but unless the people realize that the only guarantee against enslavement is their own eternal vigilance, no one and nothing can save them.

28. To Madhu Limaye, 9 July 1948[1]

My dear Madhu,[2]

In the *Janata* of 4th July, there was a note on foreign affairs which was not bad as far as it went. But I was surprised that in the reference made to the Paris Conference there was no mention of the Party's representative. I think it was a serious omission.

[1] *Brahmanand Papers* (NMML).

[2] Madhu Limaye (1922-95); took part in national movement, imprisoned 1940-1, 1943-5, Joint Secretary Socialist Party, 1951-2 and P.S.P. 1953-5, Chairman Socialist Party, 1958, M.P. Lok Sabha 1964-7, 1967-70, 1973-6 and 1977-9.

I have cabled to Phulan Babu[3] to send me a report on the Conference before the General Council. If I get it in time, I shall send a copy to the *Janata*. I hope you will approve of that.

Another suggestion I have to make after reading your note in the 4th July issue, is about the change in Russia's policy regarding popular front tactics. The note said that the Cominform has ordered that communist-socialist unity should be broken up and that the many Socialists have been left high and dry. I think this is a matter of the greatest importance and you should collect all the necessary material immediately and write a full length independent article on this in your own name. In your article you should make a reference to the unity moves made by the communists in India and whatever their present position may be.

Your foreign notes should be more factual rather than commentative. If you wish to comment on important international events, you should do so in signed articles. Opinions expressed in unsigned notes are not of much value. The reader wants to know whose opinions he is reading. Your opinions on foreign events will be of far more value for the reader and certainly for the Party member than opinions anonymously expressed.

I hope you are keeping fit.

Yours sincerely,
Jayaprakash Narayan

[3] Phulan Prasad Verma, for biographical note see *JPSW*, Vol. I, p. 62.

29. Lessons from the U.P. Elections, *Janata*, 11 July 1948[1]

We have taken an awful beating in the U.P. bye-elections. The defeat of Narendra Deva[2] must have come to many of you as a shock, as it has to hundreds of thousands of others. His defeat was, aptly enough, a victory for the Congress; but it was a defeat of all that is good and noble in our public life.

What are the lessons we draw from this unmitigated defeat in U.P.? It would be fatal to brush aside the results of the election on the plea of restricted franchise, or the plea that democracy is a mere farce under Congress fascism. Undoubtedly, if the franchise had been wider, the results would have been different. Again, if the Congress party had not used the administrative machine to intimidate and coerce the electorate and create a fear psychology, the results would have been different.

[1] *Janata*, 11 July 1948.

[2] For biographical note on Acharya Narendra Deva see *JPSW*, Vol. I, p. 61.

But, it would be suicidal for us to draw facile satisfaction from such reasoning and pat oursalves on the back for the "good fight" we put up, and then drop into inactivity.

During the course of the election campaign, I often asked myself this question: if I were a U.P. villager, should I vote for the Socialist Party. My answer invariably was, no. Why? Because, I argued, I did not know anything about this party; its workers had never come to me before the election campaign, nor had they ever done any thing for me.

Why, then, were so many thousands of votes cast for Socialist candidates? Mainly, because of the candidates' personal influence and reputation, and, secondarily, due to the prevailing discontent with the Congress. In the rural areas, at least, there was very little knowledge of the Socialist Party. Even in the towns, while there was a livelier understanding of the ideological contest, there was practically no Party organization existent.

Take Meerut, for instance. We had there a candidate, Raghukul Tilak,[3] who by virtue of his personal merit, should have won hands down. He withdrew from the contest, as you know, on account of Congress interference with the polling. But had he not, his defeat was yet certain. Why? Because prior to the election there were only three members of the Party in Meerut town and no organization worth the name! On the other side, the Congress had an old-established organization, which till the other day Tilakji and other socialists had themselves been so ably assisting to run. In every ward the Congress had its committees and large number of workers. As compared with the Congress organization—apart from the resources of money and other things—ours was a most primitive affair. At election time, no doubt, a number of new workers had come forward, but they were all raw and inexperienced; and in any case, a quickly improvised election machine cannot take the place of a well-established political organization.

In these circumstances, the lesson to be drawn from Meerut—which was typical of all the constituencies—was obvious enough. The lesson was, to use only two words: organization and work.

But surprisingly enough this was not the lesson that many of our comrades who had gone to Meerut drew. Their moral was something to this effect. It is moonshine to talk of democracy in India; the party in power is bent upon remaining in power, even if need be, at the cost of democracy. So let us stop talking of democracy and democratic methods and prepare for revolution. I was told that some comrades in Delhi were even discussing how they would break up Pant's meetings now—perhaps to inaugurate the revolution!

All this is the utterest infantilism. For anyone who understands socialism,

[3] For biographical note on Raghukul Tilak see *JPSW*, Vol. I, p. 62.

the problem is not of choosing from two equally available methods, the democratic and the revolutionary. A good socialist knows that in a given situation there is only one path that will lead to success and he follows that path unswervingly. But whatever is the method followed, there can be no success without organization and without the support of the masses. The revolutionary method is not equivalent to a conspiratorial act. A revolution, particularly a social revolution, is a voluntary and even fanatical participation of the masses in a rising against the established order. Partly social forces drive the masses into such participation and partly it is the result of the activities of a revolutionary party. In fact, without such active political work, a mass rising is bound to dissipate its energies in aimless disorders.

So, whatever the method used, the primary essential is Party organization and active work to organize and educate the masses and to bring them under the Party's political leadership. The U.P. elections show that we are far, far behind the fulfilment of these primary essentials.

Therefore, the reaction of a true socialist to the debacle in U.P. should be not that he should break up Pant's meetings now, but that he should work harder to build up the Party and extend its activities to every village and town, school and office, mine and factory. Let a missionary zeal inspire every worker of the Party so that he knows no rest till he has taken the message of the Party to the home of every Indian workingman—whether he works by hand or by brain. Let us not find escape from work in wordy debates about the futility of democratic methods.

Some may argue that our preparatory work will be different, depending on the different methods that will eventually be used. To an extent this argument is valid, but only to an extent. A socialist party does not prepare for a social revolution by manufacturing bombs. It takes the fullest advantage of all the existing liberties to organize the masses and to inspire them with the message of socialism. It makes the fullest use of parliamentary institutions. Lenin sent his comrades even to the reactionary and powerless Duma. In India today who can deny that any party that secures a majority in the National Parliament could change the face of the country. The elections to the Parliament are going to be held on the basis of adult franchise. It would be foolish for the Socialist Party to refuse to make use of this wide franchise. The Party in power might try to reduce elections to a farce, but let us not forget that defence of democracy is not the concern of only those who are in power. The people too and the parties in opposition have a vital role to play. If we lost our elementary liberties it would be as much due to the people's apathy and our own inaction as to any designs of the party in power. If the voter is frightened into voting against his wish it is as much due to our negligence as official intimidation. If we had worked among the voters and educated them, they would surely know their rights better and have the courage to exercise them. Therefore, to give in to fascist methods without fighting to protect the liberties of the people is to betray not only freedom but also socialism. The fight for socialism in India includes the fight against the gathering forces of fascism. The fight for socialism requires that we do not play into the hands of the fascist party. The fascists in the Congress are waiting at this moment for one false step from us. The moment we give them a chance, they would jump at the opportunity, and one fine morning you may read that the Socialist Party has become an outlaw. That would make the task of Indian socialism doubly difficult. It would be criminal folly deliberately to multiply our difficulties. At this moment we need desperately all the civil liberties that there may be in order to build up the socialist movement. It has been unfortunately the practice of a certain type of socialists first to do all in their power to put fascism on the throne and then start an anti-fascist campaign! Let us not repeat that mistake. The way to fight the nascent fascism in India is to fight doggedly for the preservation of the people's democratic liberties.

The lesson of the U.P. elections, therefore, I repeat is none other than organization and work: harder work and better and better organization.

30. Dissolve the Constituent Assembly, *Janata*, 18 July 1948[1]

One of the most depressing things in our country is the apathy of the people to the problems of their freedom. There was enthusiasm enough when we were fighting the British. But having won freedom from the foreigner, the people seem to have lost all further interest in it. To most of them perhaps freedom is equivalent to national freedom: they fondly believe that having got rid of the foreigner, they are now as a matter of fact a free people, and that there is nothing further to be done about it. Not having been used to a free way of life, it does not occur to them that the freedom they have won from the foreigner they might lose to a handful of their own countrymen. They have yet to learn that there are other forms of slavery different from foreign slavery.

Unfortunately, those who have come to power in this country too are not interested, in spite of the fine traditions of the independence movement, in the problems of freedom. Their main interest is power. All this nonsense about democratic liberties when we are passing through a crisis is fashionable talk in the ruling circles of the country. In these circles they glibly talk of this or that danger: Hyderabad is in danger, Kashmir is in danger, and so on. But they do not see that the thing that is most in danger

[1] *Janata*, 18 July 1948.

is freedom itself. If the people lose their freedom what good is Hyderabad or Kashmir to them?

The attitude of the rulers should not have mattered much, had the people been keen about their freedom and vigilant in its protection. The indifference of the people and the cynicism of the rulers combine to create a situation in which the people's freedoms are in serious jeopardy and the road to dictatorship is fairly easy.

Perhaps the apathy of the people is not better exemplified than in their attitude towards the work of the Constituent Assembly. For a country about to begin life as a free nation, there is nothing so important as its constitution. It is the constitution that determines the structure of political organization, the quality of freedom, the outlines of social and economic life. Yet, the people of India have hitherto shown singular indifference to the business of constitution-making. Indeed their indifference is so great that if the rulers of the country desired to deprive the people even of their franchise and replace the proposed adult franchise with something for more restricted, they would most likely get away with it. The people might be assuaged with slogans such as: Why need you vote at all when Nehru and Patel are looking after you?

Taking advantage of the people's indifference, the rulers of the country have got a draft constitution prepared that is a most unsatisfactory document. It would be a tragedy for India if this document becomes the foundation of our national life. This draft constitution would neither guarantee the freedoms of the people nor make social change possible.

The constitution in its present form would be a bulwark of conservatism and a powerful hindrance to full democracy. The fundamental rights of the people have been so hedged in as to nearly nullify them; the Executive has been armed with such sweeping special powers as to encourage dictatorship; bicameralism even in the provinces assures conservatism; the guarantees regarding compensation for property acquired makes progressive economic policy too burdensome to be undertaken; there is no assurance that one-third of the country comprised by the States will possess the same democratic institutions as the rest of the country; finally, the provisions for amending the constitution are so difficult as to make this monstrous document well-nigh unalterable.

The draft constitution must be radically changed if India is to march towards full freedom and democracy. There is little chance, however, that the Constituent Assembly, as it is constituted today, will make any drastic change in the draft constitution.

Only a new Constituent Assembly freshly and directly elected by the whole people, including the people of the States, can do so. Only then perhaps would the people begin to take genuine interest in constitution-making.

The present draft constitution seeks to speak in the name of the Indian people. "WE THE PEOPLE OF INDIA having solemnly resolved etc." are the opening words of the draft constitution. But who can honestly claim that the present Constituent Assembly has any right to speak in the name of the Indian people? It was surely not elected by the people.

The Constituent Assembly, as is well known, is made up of representatives of the provinces and the States. The representatives of the provinces were elected not directly by the adult population but indirectly by the Provincial Assemblies, which in turn were elected under the Act of 1935 by no more than 15 per cent of the people. This means that 85 per cent of the people in the provinces have no representation whatever in the Constituent Assembly.

The unrepresentative character of the provincial representatives in the Constituent Assembly is further exposed when it is recalled that the members of the Provincial Assemblies had no mandate whatever to send their representatives to any such body as the Constituent Assembly.

When we turn to the representatives from the States their unrepresentative character becomes still more apparent. Out of a total of 69 members from the States, 28 are the nominees of the Rulers and 41 "elected". Clearly the nominees of the Rulers have no right to speak in the name of the people and use the phrase, "WE THE PEOPLE OF INDIA etc." Of the 41 elected, it can be imagined how unrepresentative they must be in the absence of true representative institutions in the States. None of the 41 was directly elected by the people concerned; and most of them were merely nominees of the Congress bosses who dominate the All India States' People's Conference.

The present Constituent Assembly thus is an utterly unrepresentative body; and in the name of all that is just and fair, it must go.

A new assembly elected on adult franchise by the entire people—of the provinces as well as the States—must be called to pass the final draft of India's constitution. Who that is a democrat and anxious to see the birth of a sound democracy in this country can refuse to support this demand? No mental laziness should stand in the way of what is right, nor petty questions of party politics.

Who shall dissolve the Constituent Assembly? The Constituent Assembly itself, which has sovereign powers.

31. The First Meeting of the Socialist Party's General Council after Nasik, *Janata*, 1 August 1948[1]

It was the first meeting of the General Council of the Party after the Nasik Conference. Bikaner is far away from most parts of the country but once you get there you are surprised to find a city of palaces flourishing like an exotic plant in a desert land. And yet if there were water enough this desert land would be a paradise: this one state, they told me, could feed one-fourth of the country: Out of 23,000 sq. miles only 1,000 is irrigated, the Ganganagar area, but this one-twentythird of the State grows enough to feed all its people.

I believe most members of the General Council kept away because of lack of knowledge of the routes to Bikaner. After all, it is little more than a night's travel from Delhi to Bikaner and from Ahmedabad it takes only 24 hours. Out of 94 elected members of the Council only 21 attended. Of the 24 members for the National Executive who are in India, 14 attended; Bombay and U.P. and Gujarat completely non-cooperated, though there were provinces which were not too far away. The non-cooperation of Bombay was complete: even members of the Executive from there kept away. Executive members from far away Assam, Orissa and Bengal came, but none came from Bombay and only Rammanohar Lohia from the United Provinces. I have a feeling that certain provinces deliberately non-cooperated because I did not agree to their suggestion to change the venue. Perhaps it is forgotten that I had no hand in fixing Bikaner as the venue nor any authority to change it. It was at the Nasik Conference that an assurance was given to the Rajputana Party that one meeting of the General Council would be held in Rajputana. In pursuance of this assurance the National Executive at Belgaum decided to hold the General Council in that province. The Provincial Party naturally had the authority to choose any venue within its province. At Belgaum it was hoped that Jaipur would be selected as the venue, but when the Rajputana Party chose Bikaner there was nothing that I could do about it. Nor do I find such a great deal of difference between Jaipur and Bikaner particularly when the Ambica Airways has a service now from Bombay and Ahmedabad to Bikaner. Any how, I cannot but express my concern over the attitude of even responsible members of the Party towards Party functions in case their convenience is not guaranteed. Bikaner may be for away, but it is a part of India and as a frontier area it is of vital importance. It is well for Party members to know something of this part of the country and of the people who live there.

Because of the small attendance, the General Council may not be considered to be a great success, but the fact that the General Council was

[1] *Janata*, 1 August 1948.

held in this isolated part of the country has gone far towards bringing the message of socialism to this vital frontier people. Here during the General Council session daily public meetings were held and each one of them was a tremendous success. The most important thing about the Bikaner General Council was the new and revolutionary departure made in conducting the business of the Council. It was felt at the Nagpur meeting of the Council and again at the Nasik Conference that when the National Executive places prepared resolutions before the meeting for discussion, the delegates feel that the decision has already been taken and that, in spite of the amendments they might move or the speeches they might make, the resolutions as they come from the Executive would be passed. This feeling gave to the house a sense of unreality and frustration. Therefore, the National Executive at Bikaner decided to make a new departure. When the Council met and after the Secretary's report was made and discussed, the House was divided into groups to discuss the questions before it. Members of the Council were asked, according to their choice, to join any group they pleased. In this manner the Council divided itself into four groups which discussed in two sittings the Kisan, the Labour, the States and the Hyderabad problems. Because of the small attendance it was not possible in the time available to form other groups to discuss other problems. The experiment with these groups was an unqualified success. Delegates felt that they were really shaping the policies of the Council and the discussion in the groups was conducted responsibly and with keen interest. It could be said without hesitation that successful conduct of the business of the Council in this collective manner was the main feature of the Bikaner meeting.

It was hoped that important organizational decisions would be taken at the Bikaner meeting, particularly in view of the debacle in U.P. But on account of the thin attendance this was not possible. I hope that the National Executive would be able to consider these organizational problems at its next meeting and give a new start to the party.

32. Interview to Press, Jaipur, 2 August 1948[1]

The question of Kashmir would not be solved by Kashmir Commission[2] or any compromise, but the armed forces will solve it on the battlefield and it is the only way. The policies of the U.N.O. are not guided by morality or

[1] Adapted from *Tribune*, 4 August 1948.

[2] Kashmir Commission: The U.N. Commission on India & Pakistan (UNCIP) was constituted in pursuance of the Security Council's resolution of 20 January 1948 to look into the Kashmir question. The Commission consisted of three members and its strength was raised to five later on Joseph Korbel was its chairman.

truth. The interests of the big powers dominate it and, therefore, there is no hope that the Kashmir Commission will solve the question. I apprehend the possibility of partition of the Kashmir State in two or three divisions, giving one each to India and Pakistan and third a semi-independent region.

I support India's foreign policy and the Government of India's policy of keeping aloof from power blocks, but I warn against the danger of such a policy leading to a passive and ineffective role. There is need of a positive and active foreign policy based on international morality and merit.

I suggest that India should come forward and form a third group with those countries whose policies are similar to its own, keeping aloof from power politics. I am of the opinion that the capitalism of America and expansionism of Russia are fundamentally the same in effect.

The Hyderabad question has not been handled properly from the beginning and the Government of India has committed a blunder by entering into a standstill agreement for one year with the Nizam. Steps like economic blockade, which the India Government has taken today, ought to have been taken in the very beginning and no time should have been given to the Nizam to consolidate his position by increasing his army, organizing the Razakars, opening new ordnance factories and importing weapons and war materials.

33. Address to All-India Railway Running Staff Conference, Jhansi, 2 August 1948[1]

The Congress has been creating dissensions in the ranks of the working class and breaking its solidarity to reduce it to a mere pawn in a political game.

The Congress is engaged in creating a rival labour organization in almost all the Railways and a plan to form a parallel railwaymen's federation is in the offing. This is nothing but fascism. The Congress wants to capture labour with a view to reducing it to a pawn in its political game. The Congress wants to regiment all labour activities in the country. The protestation of the Congress that its new found love for labour is the product of its desire to help the working class is sheer hypocrisy.

Congress leaders, when they are ruling at the centre and in the provinces, can help labour and improve its lot, then why create rival labour bodies and stage mock fights against the Government?

Congressmen are today the rulers of the country and if they also add to themselves the new status of being the representatives of the working class, the latter loses all its independence and initiative. Its interests are seriously endangered because Congressmen in government and in labour

[1] Adapted from *National Herald*, 5 August 1948.

organizations will make a common cause to exploit labour for their own political ends.

The Congress is developing a fascist mentality and the champions of freedom of yesterday are out to crush and regiment all political activities. There is ordinance raj in every province. Political workers whom Congress thinks to be rivals are rotting in prisons. During the British regime ordinances were promulgated on rare occasions, but today ordinance raj has become the order of the day. And now the Congress intends to organize labour which will only promote its fascist mentality.

The Indian labour must fight on two fronts, economic and political. While its immediate problem is the betterment of its economic standards, it can not limit its activities to the solution of the problems of bread and butter alone. Labour can rest only when a kisan-mazdoor raj is established in India. Such a raj can not be brought about through the forum of the All-India Trade Union Congress. Labour must have a political organization of its own which would carry on its fight for the establishment of a truly socialist state.

The time has definitely come when labour must take active and constructive part in politics. Those who advise you otherwise, take it from me, are pillars of capitalism and want to establish capitalist rule and control.

One of the salient features of the new constitution of India is adult franchise, though I am doubtful if the Government in their present temper intend to retain it. If labour is kept off politics how would it understand and grasp the currents and cross-currents in Indian politics and again, at the time of elections, how would it be able to discriminate between its exploiters and friends? The result would be its continued political and economic slavery. We require a politically conscious labour which must know what it stands for.

The immediate demand of the railway working class should be real and complete nationalization. The railways have been nationalized after the end of the British rule, yet it has led labour nowhere. The working class is still being exploited as ever before, is ill-clothed, ill-fed and ill-paid. The exploiters are still there. We, therefore, demand participation of labour in the railway administration. Efficient persons belonging to the working class must be given big jobs. In short, we want a share for the working class in the railway administration. Members of the working class and officers are engaged in common endeavours and, therefore, they deserve equal status. The workers do not want to appear before the Railway Board as supplicants.

I condemn the anti-national activities of the Communists. They are today promising to create a heaven on earth for the working class. They are instigating the workers to go on strikes. But I appeal to the workers to stand by the nation in this hour of crisis. The workers undoubtedly have genuine complaints against the railway administration and the Indian Government, but they can not have any complaint against the nation. There is a world of difference between the nation and the Government.

A great responsibility rests on the shoulders of the railway workers. Their role in the present conditions is more important than that of the Indian armed forces. It they are led astray, the nation is doomed and with it are doomed millions of workers and peasants. If the workers feel offended by the railway administration, they can agitate and get matters right. They can even strike if all other efforts fail, but to invite workers to strike on petty pretences is to invite a national disaster.

Workers should raise their moral stature. Today their credit is so low that they are accused of corruption. If they want people to co-operate with them in pushing their demands, they must work with honesty, sincerity and a sense of duty.

34. Message to *Blitz*, 10 August 1948[1]

Eternal vigilance, in the famous words of John Currant, is the price of liberty. If Indian liberty has to be preserved, the closest vigilance is necessary, for all manner of power-grabbers are trying in devious ways to steal the people's birth-right. The *Blitz*, in the past year, has been a watch-dog of freedom. I trust in the coming years too the *Blitz* will guard zealously the priceless freedoms of the people. I wish god speed to the *Blitz* in the noble task.

Jayaprakash Narayan

Bombay, 10 August 1948

[1] *J.P. Papers* (NMML).

35. To Uma Shanker Bajpai, 14 August 1948[1]

Dear Mr. Bajpai,[2]

I thank you for your letter[3] of 28th July (D.O. No. D. 2645-CA/48). I suggest that the articles, with one exception, that have so kindly been traced be

[1] *J.P. Papers* (NMML).

[2] Uma Shankar Bajpai (1921-); Member Indian Foreign Service, Under Secretary, Ministry of External Affairs, Govt. of India 1948-52, First Secretary Indian Embassy in Rome 1952-5; First Secretary Indian Embassy in Kathmandu, 1957-9, Paris 1959-61, Minister in Indian High Commission, London 1965-6, Deputy High Commissoner in Karachi, 1966-9.

[3] See Appendix 3 for U.S. Bajpai's letter to Jayaprakash Narayan, 28 July 1948.

dumped into the Jumna or into any convenient pit in or near New Delhi. The one exception that I should like to make is in the case of the two "Gandhi Rupees". If the Government of India have any plans for a National Museum I would suggest that the coins be kept there. If not, I should be obliged if the rupees are returned to me at Kadam Kuan, Patna.

I am very thankful to the Government of India for the painstaking search they have made for my seized articles.[4] I shall however be a hundredfold more thankful if the books that were seized are traced. If necessary, I shall send you a list of the books that the Nepal Government had taken possession of. To save your Department further trouble, let me say that I am not in the least interested in any articles, other than the books, that may be traced hereafter: you may do exactly as you please with them.

Thanking you kindly,

Sincerely yours,
Jayaprakash Narayan

[4] The reference here is to those articles, which were seized by the Nepalese Government from the place where J.P. was staying in the Terai area of Nepal in 1944 after his escape from the Hazaribagh Central Prison in India.

36. Stock-Taking, *Janata*, 15 August 1948[1]

The first year of freedom finds the people unenthusiastic. In small things as well as in big, the Government does not take the people into confidence. Corruption has increased and civil liberties are at the mercy of the Government.

An American the other day asked me, "How do you find your independence?" What I told him was my private opinion, but if the same question were put to the Indian people, I wonder if they would not reply: 'tasteless'. Except for the few "carpet-baggers" independence has turned into dust in the mouth of the people.

On this day a year ago there were mad celebrations throughout the land. The people approached the day with suspicion but when officialdom whipped up enthusiasm, they were convinced and entered with zest those unprecedented moments of joy-making.

The miseries and the muddles, the ascendant corruption and self-seeking, the runaway prices and the profiteering, the killings and the war, and, above all, the supreme blunder which cost us the life of the Nation's father have made of that independence festival a historic mockery.

[1] *Janata*, 15 August 1948.

There are many a great things wrong with us. But the thing that is most wrong is that there is no life in us today, no enthusiasm; the country looks dead. The great emotional flood that broke through the gates of Indian freedom on August 15 last was not harnessed to any national endeavour. And the hearts that were uplifted with faith and joy on that historic day sank before the grim reality of freedom.

It is not that the people expected a miracle on the morrow of Independence Day. Centuries of suffering have made them patient, and they would have waited with undimmed hope and faith for the day of deliverance—from want, exploitation, disease and ignorance—had they proof that the old order was changing. What they saw, however, was the same old system of rule continuing and the very same social order of which they had so long been the underdogs. The people were, as they are, steeped in poverty. They would have borne their hardships without despair or despondency, had they evidence that those who assumed power with their support were partaking of their poverty. In terms of money the salaries of ministers and their ways of living are of no importance. But as psychological factors their significance is overwhelming. It alienates the people and disillusions them to find that those who till yesterday preached the virtues of sacrifice and voluntary poverty have moved into the palaces vacated by the British and have surrounded themselves with all the pomp and panoply of power and, from the pockets of the poor, are drawing emoluments that are hundreds of times larger than the incomes of those who foot the bill.

A little sacrifice in high quarters, a sharing in the poverty of the people, would have evoked a generous response from the latter and cleared the capitals of India of the atmosphere of greed and selfishness that pervades them today.

But, in small things as in big, the people see no evidence of any real change since the days of slavery. So, they lose faith and sink into despondency.

Now, to construct a new India many things are needed but what is needed most is faith and enthusiasm. There must take place a psychological revolution in our country so that the people might be inspired to action. Today—for us—even a major war is being conducted without evoking any popular zeal. The loans that the Government asks for are treated by people and Government alike as peace time measures, and though there is such a grave emergency, the loans are not subscribed. Who will believe we are at war! The Indian soldier who fought as a mercenary in the British Army received little presents and tokens of love and appreciation from make-believe citizens' organizations at home. Has the soldier fighting so bravely—perhaps the soldier alone today is loyal to his country—in Kashmir, received any such cheering tokens of love?

No, in small things again as in big, our popular Government fails to make a popular approach. The hand that rules is still the old wooden hand of bureaucracy and the heart that never beats, or at least, that never beats in unison with the heart of the people.

Here then are two fundamental failings of the present Government, to which history has entrusted the task of giving flesh and blood to independence. The Government has failed to create popular enthusiasm, without which that national effort is impossible that alone can build a nation. The Government has failed in this, because it has shown no imagination, has kept intact what it inherited from the British, and taken no bold step to shatter the old rotten social system and mould it nearer to the people's desire.

The other failing is an extension of the first. It is the distrust of the people and the reluctance to get any thing done through popular initiative. Whether it is adult literacy, or recruitment for the army, raising loans or fighting the Nizam or anything else, it is the wooden machinery of bureaucracy through which the Government works. The result in every case is the same; the people are left cold and distrustful.

Wherever you go in India from Cabinet ministers to gossip-makers, every one will tell you how inefficient is the present system of administration, how lacking in initiative, how dilatory, how corrupt. The movement of files through labyrinthine channels, the laborious notings, the checks and counter-checks, the shifting of responsibility, the lack of imagination and the habits of inertia all these are common topics of conversation. That the present system of administration was fashioned by the British for the limited purpose of maintaining law and order and collecting revenues and that it cannot therefore fulfil the task of nation-building are propositions universally admitted. The pervading and mounting corruption is a source of the utmost national anxiety.

Yet, no steps have been taken to transform the administrative machinery nor to root out corruption. Responsible ministers whose duty is it to cast out corruption, have the brass to use it as an argument against progressive policies.

"Look at the Railways", they say, "what use is all this talk of nationalization in view of the mess we find on the Railways? There is no use taking industry from the hands of corrupt businessmen only to pass it on to equally corrupt bureaucrats."

Not only was no serious attempt made to check corruption in the Services, but actually there has been a widening of its sector. Corruption has invaded the ranks of the party in power, and a sort of link has been forged between corrupt officialdom, corrupt Congressmen and the profiteers and black-marketeers. Nothing has added more to the disillusionment of the people than this unholy alliance.

A secular democracy is the declared objective of the people. Yet, communalism has thrived and where strong, as among the Sikhs and Hindus of East Punjab, has received the imprimatur of nationalism. Everywhere the Congress has bowed before the politics of caste denomination and race. Even such long accepted national planks as that of Hindustanee have been sacrificed to assuage the communal monster.

Democracy should have been the most cherished ideal of free India. But the liberties of the people are today far more at the mercy of the Government than even under British rule. The citizen is less indepedent, thanks to the Public safety Acts, after a year of independence than he was in the days of slavery. Even the right of habeas corpus has been nullified. Those in power are impatient of criticism and intolerant of opposition. Totalitarianism is gathering force. The picture of democracy that the Constituent Assembly has drawn up is disheartening in the extreme.

It is not my intention here to make an inventory of the failures of the Government. The list would be too long and the task too boring. The muddles on the economic front with their attendant miseries are alone a story too long to be told here. I have drawn attention only to certain basic faults, which if not corrected will turn independence either into fascism or to a sorry mess similar to that in Kuomintang China.

37. To the President, Indonesian Independence Day Meeting, 17 August 1948[1]

Dear friend,

I regret very much that being held up on some urgent business, I am unable to come over to the meeting this evening to celebrate the Indonesian Independence Day. I hope you and the friends present at the meeting and also the Indonesian Independence Day Celebrations Committee will forgive me for this. I do send my warmest good wishes for the success of the Indonesian people in their fight for independence. I feel sure every Indian is in fullest sympathy with the Indonesian struggle. The Socialist Party would be ever ready to do whatever lies in its power to help the people of Indonesia in their struggle.

Thanking you all,

Fraternally yours,
J.P.

[1] *J.P. Papers* (NMML).

38. To the General Secretary, Bolshevik Leninist Party of India, 20 August 1948[1]

Dear Comrade,

I have great pleasure in informing you that the National Executive of the Socialist Party cordially welcomes the desire of the BLPI to merge into the Socialist Party.

Our Party believes that the only way to unite the genuine democratic socialist forces in the country is to forge a *single party* of socialism. The BLPI has shown unique loyalty and devotion to the cause of socialism by expressing its desire to merge with the Socialist Party in order to fulfil this crying need of unity.

The following terms for the proposed merger were agreed upon between representatives of the BLPI and the S.P.:

1. The BLPI would be dissolved and all its members and candidates would be admitted into the S.P. There may be an objection raised in the case of an individual or so on grounds of undesirability. But such cases are bound to be very rare and nothing will be decided before giving full satisfaction to the BLPI.
2. The BLPI will sever its connection with the 4th International and the Lanka branch of the Party.
3. Representatives of the BLPI should immediately after the merger become full members of the S.P. We accept this demand as reasonable in view of a merger. But on account of the Party's constitution, the National Executive is powerless in the matter. Therefore, let me assure you that though after the merger the members of the BLPI would be technically treated as probationers, they would for all practical purposes act as members, and at the expiry of three months they would all acquire the constitutional rights of membership. The candidates of the BLPI would in like manner be treated as probationers and be confirmed at the expiry of three months.

With fraternal greetings,

Sincerely yours,
Jayaprakash Narayan

[1] *J.P. Papers* (NMML).

39. Speech at the Convention of Economists, Calcutta, 27 August 1948[1]

The problem of inflation is undoubtedly the most serious problem before the country today. There are many reasons for it—monetary, financial and those concerning production and distribution—but the most important among them perhaps is the situation concerning production. The economic and industrial policy of the Government of India, which has resulted in this crisis in production, is responsible for the economic crisis through which India is passing today.

The main contributory reason for this crisis in production is the inability to obtain capital goods. It is true that the world today is suffering from a shortage of capital goods, but if the Government of India followed a sound policy and bestowed proper attention on this problem, the position of the country as regards capital goods would have been better. The foreign trade has so long been in the hands of private traders and there has been an absolute absence of any policy, so far as the Government is concerned, in the matter of foreign trade.

Coupled with this, the prevalence of countrywide corruption has contributed to a great extent to the failure on the part of the Government to secure capital goods which the country so badly needs for its industrial development. The Government of India also failed to take the fullest advantage of certain types of exports in which India had a privileged position. If the Government had mobilized the resources of the country, prepared in time some sort of an inventory of goods which India has to import and gone ahead with a determined policy and programme, the position would have been much better. It is now time for the Government to take over the entire foreign trade in their hands. But while taking over the foreign trade the Government should create an agency independent of their departments, with full power and authority to deal with it.

Another important thing connected with the production crisis is the refusal of the business community to be satisfied with a smaller margin of profit. Big business in the Country has been non-cooperating with the Government in respect of investing money in new enterprises with a view to securing better terms from the Government for itself. If big business had played its game well, the production situation in the country would not have been so bad. Unless all elements in the country come to an understanding as to the limits that should be placed on profits and prices, the economic problems in the country will not be solved peacefully—rather there will be every danger of upheavals, riots and revolutions.

[1] Adapted from *Janata*, 5 September 1948. The Convention had been convened by the Khoj Parishad (Calcutta) founded in Calcutta in April 1948.

The Government of India today are busy with huge projects which will take a long time to be implemented. It is unwise on the part of the Government to undertake such huge projects in imitation of the developed countries of the West, when the secondary and small industries need development and succour.

Those who are at the helm of affairs in the country today unfortunately have little faith in the policy and programme of decentralization of industries so strongly advocated by Gandhiji. In the present context of the economy of India, decentralisation of industries is the best way to solve the economic crisis. It is regrettable that except for paying lip-sympathy no attempt is being made by the Government in this direction. I would recommend to the Government to make a serious study of the secondary and small industries; their requirements of raw material and technical know-how; and their markets; and prepare a scheme within a few months in order to make a planned beginning in the field of these industries.

With regard to the development of agriculture, the mainstay of our people, though there have been huge schemes, no substantial work has been turned out by the Government since their assumption of power. The Government could have put into practice short-range schemes which might have yielded better results. If some minor projects had been undertaken by the Government at a lesser cost, but with a view to rendering benefit to the largest number of people, thousands of acres of land could have produced food for the people and it would not have been necessary to spend 67 crores of rupees on the Grow More Food campaign.

The problem of corruption is no less formidable. Unless there is a drastic reform made in the whole system of administration, unless a real attempt is made to check and root out corruption, nothing that the Government will undertake is going to succeed. If the Government have it in their mind to tackle this huge problem, they should organize an Economic Civil Service, formed of those who have knowledge, ability and practical experience and who are inspired by different ideals from those of law and order which are the sole inspiration of the existing civil service.

Indeed the rooting out of corruption should become the first national priority. For this the Government should enact new legislation providing for the award of exemplary punishment for corruption in the administration. The Government should appoint a secret commission drawn from the High Court and the Supreme Court judges and empower them with the fullest authority to enquire into all cases that might be brought before them and give a decision which should be final. Attached to the Home Ministry there should be a new secret service which should be appointed solely for the purpose of ferreting out corruption from the labyrinthine chambers of the Government Secretariat.

All employees of the Government should be asked to make a declaration of their properties, movable and immovable, at the end of every year or two. The Government also should have the right to enquire into any acquisition of property for which there is no basis. Neither controls nor any measure to fight inflation can succeed unless corruption is removed from the administration. It is suggested in some quarters that in fighting inflation labour should play its part. But labour in this country is greatly discontented because its primary living wage and housing have not been conceded.

Last, but not the least, is the need for austerity. Luxury and expenditure on unnecessary things must be curtailed. Compulsory savings and various forms of economies must be undertaken and payments may be deferred to a future date, whether they are payments of profit, bonus or interests of other kinds.

Unless every one in this country realizes that he or she will have to sacrifice and sacrifice in equal measure, we are not going either to pull out of this crisis or to make anything of the freedom that has been achieved at a great cost. Not only the people of India but the people of the whole of Asia are looking towards Delhi to see what will be done by the Government to solve the problems before them and usher in an era of prosperity and happiness for this vast continent.

40. Views on Linguistic Provinces, Bombay, 28 August 1948[1]

The Socialist Party considers Bombay city to be a part of Maharashtra, and believes that, if and when linguistic provinces are carved out, Bombay should go to the province of Samyukta Maharashtra.

The party's views on the whole question are clear and unequivocal. In view of the complexity of the subject and the emotional sentiments evoked by it, the whole question of linguistic provinces should be put aside for ten years as suggested by the Prime Minister, Pandit Jawaharlal Nehru. The Socialist Party has accepted the principle of linguistic provinces subject to two important conditions. First, the national language, namely, Hindustani must, within a reasonable period of time, replace English. Secondly, the linguistic provinces must satisfy the conditions of geographic integrity and economic solvency.

While, thus, the policy of the party in this matter is unequivocal, there is another overriding aspect of it, to which I must draw attention. The Indian political climate is in many ways abnormal and irrational today. Issues which

[1] Adapted from *Pioneer*, 30 August 1948.

should be decided objectively and with calm deliberation are complicated and vitiated by the introduction of a great deal of unnecessary emotion and animus.

The issue of linguistic provinces is an issue which should be decided in an atmosphere of calm and unity. Accordingly, the party supports the plea of the Prime Minister, Pandit Nehru, that the whole question of linguistic provinces be put aside for a period of 10 years. If all parties, including Congress, agree to accept the Prime Minister's suggestion, in the meantime, our energies can be applied to the more urgent tasks of construction. If, however, the issue is forced now, the party's views on the matter are clear and unequivocal.

41. Address at the Annual Convention of the All-India Railwaymen's Federation, Lillooah (near Calcutta), 30 August 1948[1]

We are meeting today not only in the shadow of all these past tragedies and misfortunes, but in the midst of a grave national crisis. The undeclared and treacherous war that Pakistan is waging against us in Kashmir, threat of disintegration in Hyderabad, the rising cost of living and inflation present a somber picture and must fill every Indian patriot with deep anxiety. It is in the context of this national crisis that we must view our problems and formulate our decisions. And I am confident that when we speak of "our problems", we include in the term not only the question of our demands and grievances, but also the question of providing an efficient and honest transport service to the nation. The well-being of railwaymen cannot be independent of the well-being of the Railways, and the one is as much our concern as the other.

While our achievements, as a result of our negotiations with the Railway Board and the Ministry of Railways, are not inconsiderable, let me frankly admit that large sections of railwaymen find themselves in deep dissatisfaction, and some even in despair. The Railway authorities at Delhi were no doubt overwhelmed with extra ordinary problems and difficulties, yet I cannot get away from the feeling that they failed to give the time and attention to the problems of railwaymen that they deserved. I have no doubt in my mind that the Hon'ble Dr. John Matthai has always had the good of the men at his heart, but I am sure he could have, if he so desired, given more personal attention to the problems of labour.

I find it necessary here to say a few words about the manner in which the Railway Board conducts negotiations with us. The manner is most

[1] Adapted from *Janata*, 12 September 1948.

perfunctory, dilatory and unsatisfactory. I should like in all earnestness to make the following two suggestions to the Ministry of Railways. The first is that a new department should be set up in the Railway Board to deal with labour problems and particularly with problems raised by the Federation. It would be necessary not to confuse this department with that of Personnel. This new department should be placed in the charge of a Member of the Board with an understanding of trade union and labour movements. My second suggestion, and a more important one, is that a permanent joint machinery representing both the Federation and the Board should be set up to deal with and dispose of issues as they arise from day to day.

II

I should also like to add a word about anomalies that have arisen as a result of the implementation of the CPC Report. While the grave anomalies that have resulted must be removed in the nature of things, it is impossible to remove each and every anomaly that may have been created. Any standardization of scales in the conditions that obtain on the Indian Railways would lead to anomalies and it is necessary to adjust ourselves to this fact.

It is a matter of gratification that the Government has accepted the Rajadhyaksha award and decided to give effect to it. It is not known in what manner this is going to be done, but the period of three years considered necessary for the implementation of certain of the recommendations does appear to be too long. I do not wish to comment at any length on the award itself except to say this that the recommendations made in respect of the running staff appear to me to be ill-considered. I hope the Board will rectify the situation.

Though about eighty per cent of the workers have received satisfaction in one form or another, there is real dissatisfaction among many classes of employees. I cannot say what steps you are going to take to remove this dissatisfaction. For my part, I do firmly believe that the same methods of organization, peaceful agitation and negotiation which we have used so far will stand us in good stead in the future too. There is after all no finality in the labour movement, till perhaps labour comes into its own and becomes the master of its own destiny by taking possession of the State. In any case, whatever be the nature of your decisions, I hope you will not overlook the grave situation in the country and the place of the Railways in the national effort that must be made to master the problems that face us. The future of the country is very much in your hands, and I am sure you will not let the country down. Voices of general strike might be raised, but let me frankly and unequivocally advise you against lending your ear to them. A general strike, except perhaps a token one, would be disastrous for the country, and, let me add, equally disastrous for your organized might and solidarity. For I am sure such a step would breach your ranks and while the engines of repression might be turned upon the AIRF, the rival Federation might be pushed forward. I also cannot conceive of any gain that you might secure in the existing conditions from the National Government by declaring an open offensive against it, such as a general strike would be. With these words on this question I turn to the consideration of other matters.

III

As a part of the unfulfilled tasks I might mention the problem of the Indian "State" Railways. The Federation has always visualized a unitary transport system for this country under one authority. The Government of India Act, 1935, also had made provision for a Federal Railway Authority to administer the railway systems in India. I have no doubt that such an Authority should soon be created by the National Parliament. This would give us an integrated countrywide railway system with uniform standards and rates and be a source of large revenues.

Considered from the point of view of railwaymen, the position is far from happy. While the State Railways are always quick to take advantage of any increase in rates and fares by the Government of India, they refuse to give their employees the terms of pay and service which the Central Government offers to its railwaymen. As a result, there have been many struggles of the employees of the State Railways in the past year. Jodhpur, Jaipur, Baroda and Mysore are cases in point. In the interest of the country as a whole, as well as of the railwaymen of the States, I once again give expression to your demand that the Government of India should take immediate steps to integrate all the railway systems in the country under one central authority. Pending that step, the Government should see that the same standards of pay, etc., are applied to the State Railway employees as the Government has accepted for its own.

IV

When I took over, we had a rather rudimentary constitution and many points used o be settled according to convention or the interpretation of the office-bearers. We have now a proper constitution. But a constitution is hardly anything more than the plan of a structure. We have yet only the skeleton of our organization. If the Federation is to serve the railwaymen well it will have among other things an efficient office with trained, specialized staff and experts, who will collect facts and figures and study problems; a journal to educate the men and ventilate their grievances and conduct their struggle and guide the Unions. The Federation should have a number of officers to travel on the lines and check up on organization and help the affiliated unions to function more efficiently. The Federation should help them further to develop constructive activities in such fields as co-operation, insurance, education and the like. Let us hope that the Federation would take up some of these functions in the coming year and widen and develop its organization and scope of work.

The Federation should also be in a position to check up on transport, finances and the policies of the Transport Ministry and suggest ways and means to improve the strength to fight corruption in the Railways and to ensure efficiency, honesty and devotion to work.

I should like to make a few tentative remarks about the organizational structure of the Federation and the Unions. Our organization today is of the pure industrial type. The problems of many classes of workers are either neglected or fail to be adequately emphasized. In the result we have many sectional or craft organizations developing, each independent of the other. This is not a very healthy state of affairs. I, therefore, suggest that you might consider a combination of the craft and industrial forms of organization so that all classes of workers, at any rate all important classes, may be organized in their sections, comprising together the unions. If the principle is accepted, it should not be difficult to work out the details.

While I view the future of the Federation with complete optimism, I consider it my duty to point out two potent dangers: one from within and the other from without.

The Federation embraces within its fold men of different political views. All these elements can work together only if the common interests of railwaymen and of the Federation as a whole are placed over partisan ends. I regret to say that there is at least one political element namely the communists, that has tried in the past few months, i.e. since the policies of the Communist Party have undergone a volte-face, to drag railwaymen into actions that had little to do with their organized struggle and much with the furtherance of a political line; the line being disorganization of the country's economic and political life and weakening of the free Indian State. I should like to warn railwaymen that no matter what be the character of the Indian Government and their differences with it, they have nothing to gain if there is chaos and anarchy in the land and the foundations of the Indian State are undermined.

Another danger to which I must draw attention comes from outside the Federation. You all know how the working class movement is split up in this country. But in the midst of this disunity, or Federation stands as a unique example of working class solidarity. This solidarity however is threatened today from a not unexpected quarter. Some Congressmen have tried to set up a rival organization in what is styled as the Indian National Railway Workers' Federation.

In view of our declared policy, there can be no justification whatever for a rival Federation to exist. So I am afraid the real reasons behind the establishment of the I.N.R.W.F. are different; and I consider it my duty to warn railwaymen of them. It appears to me that the fact that the A.I.R.F. is an independent labour organization not subservient to any party or government, is unpalatable to those in power; and so the attempt is being made to set up this new Federation in order that, through it, the Government might be able to control the railway workers. In the case of railwaymen, the Government itself is the employer and when the employer becomes the trade union boss too, there is no freedom. If railway workers value their solidarity and their independence, I would earnestly appeal to them to keep away from the new Federation and let it die a natural death.

42. To Suresh Desai, 8 September 1948[1]

My dear Suresh,

I wish you or Goray keep me in touch with developments at the Central Office and the progress made since I left Bombay.

We all expected you at the Khoj Parishad Economic Convention[2] which, as you might have seen from the papers, was a great success. Papers read at the Convention have already been sent to you and others that were to be printed might have been sent now.

I am going to Calcutta again on the 27th of this month and will be staying there for at least two days entirely for organizational matters. Could you also come to Calcutta about that time?

I sent a draft of Rs. 6000/- to Purushottam with Peter.[3] I also gave Rs. 1500/- to Bagaram Tulpule for expenses for the months of September

[1] *Brahmanand Papers* (NMML).

[2] Khoj Parishad was established at Calcutta in April 1948 with the object of promoting, organizing and conducting surveys and research on economic, political and social problems of the country. The management of the Parishad was vested in a Council of Governors and its research work was conducted under the guidance of a Research Advisory Council composed of distinguished economists and social thinkers like Prof. Khagendranath Sen, Satendranath Bose and Dwarkanath Ghosh. J.P., Lohia, Surendranath Dwivedy, etc., were members of Council of Governors.

[3] Peter Alvares (1908-75), freedom fighter, was imprisoned twice, associated with the Congress Socialist Party, member Bombay Legislative Assembly 1948-52, participated in Goa Freedom Movement from 1952 to 1961, President National Congress Goa, 1953-61; member Lok Sabha 1963-7, Secretary Joint Council of Action of Central Government Employees strikes in 1960 and 1968, President All India Railwaymen's Federation 1974.

and October. It seems you have also sent a cheque to Jamshedpur. I am asking Bagaram to keep that also with him which means that no money need be sent to Jamshedpur till the end of November. I have paid out other sums of money, details of which I will give you when I come to Bombay.

What progress has been made about the hill station meeting? You should write to the members of Executive definitely about the dates and how they are to reach the place and what are they supposed to bring with them in the matter of clothes, blankets, etc. I am preparing the agenda for the camp which I shall circularize from here and also send you a copy.

With best wishes,

Yours affectionately,
J.P.

43. To All Provincial Secretaries of the Socialist Party, 12 September 1948[1]

Dear Comrade,

You will recall the resolution of the National Executive on Left Unity passed at Belgaum some months ago. I am glad to inform you that after that resolution certain parties responded to the call for unity. Among them the Socialist Party of India of which Com. Rajdeo Singh[2] of Jaunpore, U.P. was the leader, has already merged into the Party. Another of the Socialist Parties, namely, the Bolshevik Leninist Party of India too opened negotiations with us for a merger. The BLPI is a branch of the Fourth International and wields considerable influence in Tamilnad and to some extent in Bengal and has important members in Bombay and publishes a fortnightly, the *New Spark*. The negotiations came to a successful end some time ago and in pursuance of the decision of the Bikaner meeting of the National Executive, we decided to accept the offer of merger made by the BLPI. I am enclosing herewith a copy of the letter I wrote to the General Secretary of the BLPI. The letter speaks for itself.

The BLPI is meeting in a conference in a few weeks to ratify the decision of merger.

I hope all provincial branches and every member of the Party will do everything possible to make this merger a success. Our Tamilnad comrades, I should add, did not feel very happy over this step, but I have no doubt that once the decision has been taken they too will fully co-operate to make it a success. It will perhaps take another couple of months for the formal merger

[1] *J.P. Papers* (NMML).

[2] Rajdeo Singh, an active socialist leader of Jaunpore, U.P.

to take place and if during this period we begin to work jointly with BLPI comrades the course of the merger would be smooth and easy.

With best wishes,

Sincerely yours,
J.P.

44. Address at Sriniketan, 13 September 1948[1]

It is a matter of lasting regret for me that it had not been possible for me to come to Santiniketan during the Poet's life time. I am glad to be at Sriniketan and to see the place of which I have heard so much. I have come here to know and learn and appreciate the work you have been doing. When we were struggling for independence, each one of us was busy in his or her particular sphere of activity, but the immediate objective was the same for all of us. After the achievement of our political freedom, however, the perspective has changed. We have now fallen apart. The problem of national reconstruction has therefore become more difficult than ever. And it is this crucial problem which you, the workers of Sriniketan, have devoted yourselves to solving.

India is a land of villages, of very poor and helpless villages. But we had never cared to give a single thought to the villages and villagers till Gandhiji came and taught us by his own example to view the problems of village life seriously. But even in this field, Gurudeva was the pioneer. He saw that national reconstruction must depend on the reconstruction of village life which should, before everything else, be extricated from the shackles of a foreign domination which had forced an artificial economy on the rural society and thus destroyed the old balance and equilibrium. The first step therefore was to go to villages, live among the villagers and study the problems of their life with sympathy and vision. This perhaps was the aim that led Gurudeva to establish Sriniketan.

The present system of village administration and the policy of the Government of India regarding the Panchyat system are not at all well-conceived. What is wanted is a system in which villages will become autonomous units, directing the State through their Panchayats.

India has now to face two sets of problems, one consequent upon the division of India which, in my opinion, amounted to a division of freedom, and the other due to the anomalous and still undecided position of India in the sphere of international politics. More complacency on our part might indeed be fatal for the future security and status of this new-born State.

[1] Adapted from *Visva-Bharatī News*, October-November 1948.

The independence we have won means nothing more than freedom from foreign domination and real political and economic freedom of the people has still to be achieved. This can only be done through Socialism—not necessarily of the Soviet type—rather a kind of socialism suited to the genius of India and based on its best traditions of love and brotherhood.

The new social order and human values, envisaged by a socialist like myself, has much in common with Gurudeva's vision. Many of the desirable conditions of a full and rich life that the rest of India would have to struggle long to secure are already existing at Santiniketan. We are following in your footsteps. The ideals of universal brotherhood and international amity which you have set before yourselves are also most dear to a socialist's heart. Santiniketan should continue to teach the people the meaning of life and demonstrate to them the value and significance of a social life based on human fellowship.

45. To Jawaharlal Nehru, 16 September 1948[1]

My dear Bhai,

Your letter[2] regarding Achyut. I have written to him today to accept your offer.

I shall write at length later.

With kind regards,

Affectionately yours,
Jayaprakash

[1] *Nehru Papers*—Files at home (NMML).
[2] See Appendix 4 for Nehru's letter to Achyut Patwardhan.

46. To the Provincial Secretaries, Socialist Party, 18 September 1948[1]

Dear Friend,

Kisan Day

As you must have learnt from the circular letter of Comrade Ramnandan Misra,[2] November 14th has been fixed as the Kisan Day in order to emphasize and popularise the basic kisan demands formulated by the Party

[1] *J.P. Papers* (NMML).
[2] For biographical note on Ramnandan Mishra see *JPSW*, Vol. II, p. 186.

and the Kisan Committee. I hope you will do everything possible to see that the programme is a fitting success. The details of the programme are given in Comrade Ramnandan Misra's letter.

Janvani (*Hindi Monthly*)

The U.P. Party, with the cooperation of the Bihar Party, is publishing a first-class Hindi monthly, *Janvani*. It is edited by Comrade Baijnath Singh 'Vinod',[3] who is a great Hindi scholar, and Acharya Narendra Deva and Shri Rambriksh Benipuri, along with the editor constitute the Editorial Board. *Janvani* is recognised on all hands as one of the best Hindi magazines.

It is a matter of great pity that Provincial Parties have not so far given the attention to *Janvani* that it deserves. Of the Hindi-speaking provinces, Bihar and U.P. have some subscribers, but C.P. (Mahakoshal) has very few. In the East Punjab, Delhi, Rajputana, Madhya Bharat, Vindhya Pradesh, there are hardly any subscribers. In the other provinces too and in Calcutta and Bombay cities there are large numbers of Hindi readers, but practically no subscribers for the *Janvani*.

May I therefore draw the attention of all the Provincial branches to the *Janvani*? Securing subscribers for the *Janvani* should be put on the list of Party activities and a drive should be made in that behalf.

The annual subscription is Rs. 8/- and semi-annual Rs. 4/8/-. Subscriptions should be sent to the Manager, *Janvani*, Kashi Vidyapith, Banaras Cantt.

Party members should also write for the *Janvani*.

Sincerely yours,
J.P.
General Secretary

[3] Baijnath Singh Vinod (1910-), author. Publications: *Mahabir*, *Gautam Buddha*, *Samrat Ashok*, *Dhara*, *Hindustan Fascism Ki Ore*, ed. *Dvivedi Patrika* (Letters), translated many books on Gandhi and Sarvodaya.

47. Foreword to the booklet entitled *The Party and Hyderabad*, 19 September 1948[1]

Events follow their inexorable course. One may prevaricate, one may vacillate, but a time comes when the force of events impels one forward or pushes one out of the way. Events in Hyderabad have been coming to a head all these past months, and a situation has now arisen in which even

[1] *Janata*, 19 September 1948.

the indecisive Government of India must act or lose the game. At a moment when a decision seems at last to have been taken and when the responsibilities arising out of that decision have to be shouldered unitedly by the nation, it seems futile to lament past inactivity or ineptitude. Yet when a review is being presented in the following pages of the fight that has been waged, it is only fair to the brave fighters to point out the mistakes and blunders that have been responsible for the ill-fortune that has attended their heroic efforts and the sacrifices of the suffering people of Hyderabad.

It has been our misfortune to differ on many matters of policy with the Government of India. But perhaps our difference with them was never so sharp as in the case of the policy pursued in Hyderabad. As it appears to me, two basic mistakes have been made in respect to Hyderabad. The first of these was acceptance of the Stand-still Agreement, which included the withdrawal of our forces from Secunderabad. By that agreement India not only accepted the fact that the Nizam stood on a footing different from that of the other Indian Rulers, but also surrendered the only means we had of preventing misrule, disorder and treachery.

The other mistake of no less proportion was our failure to help the people of the State adequately in their fight for freedom. For many months the people fought almost bare-handed against brutal, organized tyranny. The fighters for freedom in Hyderabad looked for help to the people and the Government of India, but the Government disowned them and the people gave them little else than sympathy. The Government of India is in the hands of men today who had themselves led a people's struggle for freedom. But having come into power these men have suddenly lost all faith in the people whether of Hyderabad or of India. From the very beginning the Government took up an attitude of contempt towards the people's struggle in Hyderabad. Occupying the seats of power, it seemed to them that whatever had to be done in Hyderabad was for them to do and the rabble need not presume to write on the pages of history. They said times without number that they were negotiating with the Nizam, and there was hardly any need for any one else to do anything. As a matter of fact, the Government was so sure of its prowess and position that from the beginning it underestimated the strength of the opposite party and followed accordingly such a complacent policy that the little boil that could have lanced and healed easily has grown so big as to require now a major operation. All the sacrifices that India may be called upon to make in order that a regime of law and justice may be established in Hyderabad would have been unnecessary had the Government of India been less sure of itself and shown greater confidence in the people. I am definite that six months ago a comparatively small aid to the fighters in Hyderabad would have yielded the same results as far greater efforts may do now. And the risk in aiding the people's struggle was much less than that involved in trying to re-station our forces in Secunderabad.

Some critics of this view bring up the issue of the Kashmir raiders, and the *Statesman* the other day flung into my face a quotation from a Nasik speech of Achyut Patwardhan. The analogy of the raiders hardly holds good in this case, and those who bring it up are not trying to think straight. The fighters in Hyderabad are not raiders by any stretch of imagination but are the people of the soil who are fighting to protect their hearths and homes and their liberties and to achieve the freedom to which every civilized man is entitled. Swami Ramanand Tirth was and is the leader of the people of Hyderabad and it was under his command and the command of the State Congress, of which the socialists are an integral part, that the Hyderabad struggle has been waged. To have refused to run to the aid of Swami Ramanand and the State Congress and the people who were fighting as it were with their bare hands, was to betray the cause of freedom and democracy. Men of goodwill all over the world had hastened to Republican Spain to save it from the jaws of international fascism. Millions of people of Hyderabad are in the grip of no lesser a fascist tyranny and I cannot imagine any one, European or Indian, who is a lover of freedom and who refuses to give all possible aid to the victims of *Asafia* fascism.

These then were the two basic mistakes—history will call them Himalayan blunders—that the Government made, and the people of India now have to pay a heavy penalty for them. However, let us hope that now at any rate there will be no prevarication and brave words will no longer be allowed to take the place of decisive deeds.

There is no room for any ruler in democratic India but I am sure the one ruler who has forfeited his right to his gadi is the Nizam of Hyderabad. The Nizam must go and his dominions merged into the respective linguistic areas.

48. Address to Tata Steel Workers, Jamshedpur, 29 September 1948[1]

The present problem before the socialist movement in India is no longer merely the destruction of capitalism. That is inevitable in the near future. Social dynamics has condemned capitalism all over the world, even in its ideal breeding ground, America. The problem is the positive one of erecting the structure of a socialist society. Nationalization of the means of production, abolition of vested interests, distribution of the national produce, the evolution of political democracy—these are some of the problems that

[1] Adapted from *Janata*, 10 October 1948.

the socialist movement is faced with to-day. It is up to the intelligentsia to give the correct theoretical and technical answers to these problems while the organized proletariat completed its task of the abolition of capitalism.

It is a fact that at present almost every political party claims as its objective the establishment of Socialism, of kisan mazdoor raj. Such claims are necessary to get the support of the people who are mostly kisans and mazdoors. Even the Conservative Party of England claims to exit for the good of the masses. But the truth of such claims has to be checked against the actual deeds and policies of each party.

The Congress, for instance, claims to work for the establishment of kisan mazdoor raj. But its policies and actions as the party in power does not bear out this claim. Even granting that the establishment of full Socialism would take a long time, at least a beginning can be made. The British Labour Party[2] laid the foundations of Socialism at a time of severe crisis. The Indian Government has however done nothing of the sort.

The foundations of socialism must consist of measures enforced by legislation which would firstly establish people's ownership of the means of production, fair and equitable distribution of the national produce, levelling of incomes and full political freedom. The present Government is doing no such thing. Its claim to be a people's government cannot be sustained. The Socialist Party stands for these measures even in the present crisis. A people's government must not allow the existence of the present structure of society based on exploitation to continue any longer. The Governor-General cannot claim a salary of over a lakh of rupees per month in a people's government. The existence of a crisis cannot be an excuse to delay laying the foundation for Socialism.

It is wrong to say that the existence of an opposition party weakens the nation. On the contrary, by criticizing the Government it helps to keep the Government from moving too far away from the people. In England even before the war was fully over; the two parties had pitted themselves in opposition to each other and the result had been to the benefit of England. Democratically expressed opposition concerns itself mainly with internal policies. On all occasions when the existence or progress of the nation is threatened, opposition parties join hands to fight common dangers.

The unification of left parties is possible only with people and parties who conform to certain common fundamentals of policy and ideology. With the Communists, for instance, no unity is possible as they owe loyalty to a foreign power, have no regard for the integrity and strength of the nation and have a long record of betrayal of the nationalist movement in India and elsewhere.

[2] For note on British Labour Party see *JPSW*, Vol. IV, p. 54.

The parties which decide to work together must merge into a single party and not exist as separate units often in rivalry to each other. The Socialist Party is moving along this line. The Bolshevik-Leninist Party of India has already merged with it.

The problem of increased production can be solved only when the worker is satisfied that increased production would go to make his life more comfortable and not to swell the bank balances of a few individuals. The production of steel is declining due to reasons which are beyond the powers of the workers. I would bring the matter to the notice of the Prime Minister and ask him to hold an investigation into the reasons for lower production.

49. Interview to the United Press of India, Bombay, 8 October 1948[1]

Even after taking into consideration the circumstances as they are to day, the authorities and the capital have not done for the workers what the latter were entitled to expect. It is not true that labour has not co-operated with the Government. I might rather say that the labour has been badly let down.

The working classes have been singularly patient and forbearing. You will realize this only when you take into consideration their conditions of life. Admittedly, Government have had to face tremendous problems and difficulties during the months that India has been free, yet, in spite of them, they could have achieved quite a lot in reorganizing the whole system of wages and bringing to the labouring classes a sense of security in the midst of the haunting specter of rising spiral of prices.

The Government have failed, because they have not yet implemented their own resolution on industrial truce in respect of the determination of fair wages and fair profits, bearing in mind the needs of each industry and the conditions of each area. It is true that they have set up a machinery for the settlement of industrial disputes. This machinery has not functioned satisfactorily, either because it has not had enough power or because it has been unduly influenced in favour of the captains of industry.

The first thing the Government ought to do is to check the rising prices. In my opinion, the anti-inflation programme announced by the Government of India does not take into consideration basic issues. It would not materially affect the prices of essential commodities unless the system of controls devised by Government is worked successfully. And unless prices are brought down to a reasonable level, the country would continue to suffer from economic instability.

[1] Adapted from *Tribune*, 10 October 1948.

50. Speech at the Twenty-Second Annual Conference of the All-India Postmen and Lower Grade Staff Union, Bombay, 9 October 1948[1]

I warn the postmen that unless they unite with the railwaymen and act together in fighting with the Government of India, they would not be able to win their case.

Belonging to such an important public service and performing duties of such utility with such devotion and honesty, the postmen deserve the utmost consideration from the society and State.

The meaning of freedom that has been achieved by the efforts of the common men has always seemed to me to be that in the new India the under dog should rise to his fullest stature. This, unfortunately, was the reverse in the British days.

The present Government of India have often made socialist professions, but if they have any living faith in their professions, they must at least in their administration give proof of it.

India has, on the one hand, a Governor-General who receives a salary of Rs. 10,000/- per month and on the other the postmen are even denied an adequate dearness allowance in the face of the ever-rising cost of living.

I whole heartedly endorse the demand that the recommendations of the Pay Commission be implemented by the Government of India. Though there is the grave problem of inflation facing the country, it is unjust to ask the labour alone to bear the cost of inflation.

While the Government of India has made large concessions to capitalists, I am at a loss to know why they have paid absolutely no regard to the cost of living of labour which is daily rising. And still they tirelessly sermonize the labour to produce more.

I feel sure that labour would give its fullest co-operation to the Government in any such scheme of disinflation, but it cannot allow itself to be sacrificed at the altar of disinflation for the benefit of the capitalist class.

Whatever the view of the Government's policy regarding nationalization of other industries, those services which were already nationalized such as railways, posts and telegraphs should be run jointly by the administration and the workers. The traditional employer-employee relationship and the mentality arising out of it should go for ever and the spirit of a joint undertaking to serve a common purpose should be fostered.

I am glad that the Communication Minister[2] is setting up a permanent machinery for joint consultation between his department and the postmen's union.

[1] Adapted from *National Herald*, 10 October 1948.

[2] Refers to Rafi Ahmed Kidwai. For biographical note see *JPSW*, Vol. IV, p. 229.

One of the main demands of the postmen is that they should be given the same pay as skilled workers as they have a certain standard of literacy and, therefore, are entitled to a higher scale.

51. To Indra Sen, 12 October 1948[1]

My Dear Comrade Indra Sen,[2]

It is not possible for me to say any thing definite about the list of members that you gave me. I must send the list to the Provinces and get a report from them. That, however, need not delay the merger. If, later on, there is any thing found objectionable against any member, the matter could be dealt with in consultation with you. At present there is only one name about which I remember objection was raised at Madras, the name of Comrade Selvraj.[3] I made independent enquiries also about him and I gather that he adopts rather unscrupulous methods and is not truthful. We may take up his case at the time of admission. Apart from his name, there is no other member of the B.L.P.I. about whom any definite objection can be raised by us. But, as I have said above, this matter need not delay the merger. I am sure there cannot but in the rarest of cases in which objection might be raised.

Wishing success to your conference,

Fraternally,
Jayaprakash Narayan

[1] *J.P. Papers* (NMML).

[2] Indra Sen (1903-); General Secretary, Bolshevik and Leninist Party of India, which had decided to merge with the Socialist Party.

[3] Selvraj, an active member of the Bolshevik and Leninist Party of India.

52. Address to All-India Railwaymen's Federation, Bombay, 14 October 1948[1]

The Railwaymen should be prepared for a showdown with the Government of India in the event of the Government's failure to concede the Railwaymen's demands by the end of this month. We stayed our hands so far, because the nation was passing through a crisis, following Partition, and in view of the various problems which arose out of it. But after the successful police action in Hyderabad the internal situation has distinctly improved. There is no internal danger to peace. We have to that extent become strong as a nation and can now consolidate our freedom without

[1] Adapted from *Hindustan Times*, 15 October 1948.

any difficulty. The Government cannot, therefore, advance any more their usual excuse, to delay consideration of labour's demands for a better deal, that the nation is confronted with difficulties.

We have decided to wait for the Government's final reply to our demands up to the end of this month. Our General Council will meet on November 25 and 26 to consider the reply we receive from the Government.

I cannot foretell what our ultimate decision will be, because it is difficult to forecast what the Government's reply will be. But if past experience is any indication, I am afraid Government's reply will not be in favour of labour, as is evident from their attitude of indifference towards labour in general and Railwaymen in particular. They will suppress labour with all their might, if labour goes on strike, but will try to woo the capitalists, even when they (the capitalists) go on strike, as admitted by Pandit Nehru himself, instead of punishing them.

All the same I hope and trust that the Government will change their attitude and will concede the just demands of the Railwaymen, and thus avoid a strike. We are not spoiling for a strike for the sake of a strike, but wish to avoid it, if possible. But no option will be left for us but to go on a strike, in the event of the Government's reply being unacceptable to the labour.

53. To Prominent Trade Unionists, 4 November 1948[1]

Dear friend,

The growing disparity between prices and earnings is causing serious discontent among the working people. There is an unprecedented urgency about the need to meet the developing situation.

2. The measures announced by the Government of India to combat inflation lack the strength to master the soaring prices and bring down the cost of living. The indifference shown by the Government to the suggestions towards disinflation made by the representatives of organized labour to the cabinet threatens to aggravate an already difficult situation. The Government's ineffective oscillations between control and de-control, rationing and de-rationing fail to inspire confidence. The working class, at this critical juncture, must therefore speak out its mind with the greatest possible unanimity and emphasis. An exchange of opinion among leading trade unionists is therefore generally desired.

3. The failure of the Government to implement the recommendations of the Central Pay Commission about linking dearness allowance with cost

[1] *Brahmanand Papers* (NMML).

of living has resulted in great loss and severe misery to workers, and Government employees in particular. So acute is the discontent on this score that not a few sections of Government employees are contemplating strike action. Here again there is a widespread desire to co-ordinate agitation and action. An irresistible mass mobilisation behind the demand for adequate dearness allowance, fluctuating with the cost of living, is today desirable and possible as never before.

4. The Government's legislation and machinery to solve industrial disputes are progressively robbing the workers of their basic rights. The workers are in the danger of being reduced to the position of slave labour. Here again united action is long overdue.

5. I feel that an informal conference of leading trade unionists to discuss these vital issues and chalk out a common policy is urgently called for. When I and Asoka Mehta[2] discussed the idea with Mr. N.M. Joshi,[3] Mr. Dinkarrao Desai,[4] Mr. Khedgikar,[5] Mr. Phadke,[6] Mr. Karnik,[7] Miss Maniben Kara[8] and Mr. Shibnath Banerji,[9] I found that my suggestion merely echoed the feelings of all others.

6. In consultation with friends mentioned above I propose to convene an informal conference of leading trade unionists in Bombay on 27th and 28th November 1948.

7. The agenda for the conference will be: To consider:

(i) Government's economic policy with special reference to the

[2] For biographical note on Asoka Mehta see *JPSW*, Vol. I, p. 122.

[3] For biographical note on N.M. Joshi see *JPSW*, Vol. III, p. 81.

[4] Dinkarrao Desai (1890-); began to take part in social and political work 1917, President of Bombay Municipality for 5 years. Member of Provincial Assembly 1937, went to jail several times, Minister of Law and Civil Supplies, Govt. of Bombay 1951.

[5] For biographical note on R.A. Khedgikar see *JPSW*, Vol. I, p. 93.

[6] Phadke: Not traceable.

[7] Vasant Bhagvat Karnik (1903-85); participated in the Non-Cooperation Movement 1921; Managing Editor, *Independent India* which later changed its name to *Radical Humanist*; Editor, *Freedom First*; First General Secretary of Radical Democratic Party and Indian Federation of Labour; publications include: *M.N. Roy—Political Biography*, *N.M. Joshi—Servant of India*, *Trade Unions in India—A Survey*, *Strikes in India*, *Trade Unions and Politics*, *Indian Labour: Problems and Prospects*.

[8] Maniben Kara (1905-79); veteran trade union leader from Bombay, social worker and freedom fighter; by turn President of the Hind Mazdoor Sabha, All India Railwaymen's Federation and member of the executive of the International Confederation of Free Trade Unions; was influenced by the ideology of M.N. Roy and became a radical Humanist.

[9] Sibnath Banerjee (1897-1982); member of Bengal P.C.C. 1932-4 and later A.I.C.C., convicted in Meerut Conspiracy Case in 1933; one of the founder member of C.S.P.; elected to Bengal Legislative Council in 1937; held the Howrah Labour Reserved constituency till 1952; by turn President, A.I.T.U.C. and Hind Mazdoor Sabha; joined J.P. Movement in 1975 and imprisoned for 3 months; after this retired from active politics.

measures recently announced to combat inflation.

(ii) The failure of the Government to implement the recommendations of the C.P.C. about linking dearness allowance with the cost of living.

(iii) Government's legislation and machinery for the solution of Industrial disputes that abridge the basic rights of workers Mr. N.M. Joshi has kindly agreed to preside over the conference and guide its deliberations.

8. In view of the importance of the Conference may I request you to accept this invitation and in spite of the short notice make it convenient to attend it? Without your active cooperation the results of the Conference will be incomplete.

9. Will you kindly wire your acceptance of this invitation to the care CONSOC Bombay, or to Mr. Asoka Mehta care SAMAJWADI, Bombay?

Yours sincerely,
J.P.

54. To Jagjivan Ram, 6 November 1948[1]

My dear Jagjivan Babu,

You may recall that some time ago when I had met you in Delhi I had spoken to you about the Bombay Textile Technicians Association. Subsequently they had sent you a memorandum which you were kind enough to consider for they have received a reply from your department which removes one of their main difficulties, viz., their being excluded from the purview of the Industrial Disputes Act. There were, however, other important questions that they had raised to which it appears sufficient attention has not been given, for instance, the need to appoint an enquiry committee and the desirability of their being nominated on the various committees appointed by Government. The technicians and supervisory staff are the key men in industry and, to my mind, the utmost attention should be given to them. I therefore request you to give a little time to one of the office-bearers of the Technicians Association, Mr. R. Krishnamachari, Vice-President, who is going over to Delhi on my suggestion to interview you. I request that you give him some time on the 13th November when I will also be present in Delhi and if you have no objection may bring him

[1] *Brahmanand Papers* (NMML).

with me. I will be reaching Delhi on the 12th morning and shall get into touch with you immediately.

Trusting you are well and with regards,

Very sincerely yours,
J.P.

55. The Party and the Student Movement, *Janata*, 7 November 1948[1]

There has been a great deal of confusion lately in the student movement, but in the midst of all the discordant voices there has been one remarkable unanimity. Everyone seems to agree that all the different student organizations that have sprung up should go and the student community as a whole should be united in one organization, viz., the National Union of Students. It is also agreed that this body should be a non-political body and should be concerned mainly with educational, cultural, recreational and social service activities. The Socialist Party has for some time been whole heartedly supporting this idea of a National Union.

Just at the time when there was such a general agreement, there was an unfortunate split at Bangalore in the All India Students Congress. It has been particularly painful to me that in this split some of those too who generally look up to the Socialist Party for political guidance are involved. However, it gives me pleasure to state that the attempt to repair the damage done at Bangalore has at last succeeded. It has been agreed that the Students Congress of which Shri Narendra Goyal was elected president at Bangalore would be dissolved and an organizing committee made up of an agreed list of members will be formed to organize the National Union. This committee will have powers to co-opt. I hope the organizing committee will succeed in re-building the student movement on a national and broad basis. I wish it all success.

While the National Union is conceived as an organization of the student community as a whole, a need will be felt by political parties to do their party political work among the students. The only way to do this without disrupting the unity of the student community is to organize groups outside the National Union to spread the influence of one's party among the student world. The Socialist Party has decided to set up socialist clubs or societies in the colleges and universities. These clubs will not interfere in any manner with the working of the National Union and will only be centres of socialist study and discussion. All the members of the clubs need not be members of

[1] *Janata*, 7 November 1948.

the Socialist Party, but the clubs will be built up around a core of Party members. The clubs would have a decentralised organization and there will be no district, provincial or national body or committee of them. At the most, the college clubs in the same city may be brought together into one organization. These college or university clubs will function under the guidance of the local branch or unit of the Socialist Party. These clubs, further, should not be confused with the Young Socialist League and should be kept apart from it.

The socialist movement must also have a youth movement allied to it. To this end the organization of the Young Socialist League had been suggested by the Executive. But at Mahabaleshwar the Executive re-examined the question and appointed a committee to go into the matter fully and report to the next meeting at Lucknow. This need not mean that YSL work should be stopped till then. The work may continue with the understanding that it will have to be reorganized in the light of later decisions.

56. The Next Annual Conference of the Party, *Janata*, 7 November 1948[1]

The next Annual Conference of the Party will meet at Patna in Bihar from February 20 to 24 [1949] inclusive.

It has been a convention that the National Executive selects the Chairman some time before the Conference meets. The election at the Conference is merely a formal affair. Members and sympathizers will be happy to learn that the Executive has selected Yusuf Meherally as the chairman of the next Conference. Meherally is one of the founders of the Party and his services to the cause of national freedom are second to none in the country. From his student days, he has been the idol of youth, and in his city, Bombay, his popularity is unrivalled. During his last imprisonment in the course of the August Revolution, Yusuf developed a serious heart illness that nearly cost him his life. After his release, when the Interim Government was installed, Yusuf, his health not improving, yielded, much against his will, to the pressure of friends to go to the United States for treatment. He has been away for a year and a half now and is coming back this month. The country, I am sure, will warmly welcome back its great son to its bosom. For us, his colleagues and followers, what could be a better form of welcome than to honour him with the gift of this highest office? I hope he will accept this offering and will guide and lead us to a brighter future.

The following is the procedure laid down by the Executive for the Conference:

[1] *Janata*, 7 November 1948.

All sub-committees of the National Executive, all provincial branches and individual party members are invited to send draft resolutions for the Conference, so as to reach the Central office not later than the 23rd December. These resolutions will be considered by the National Executive and on their basis resolutions will be drafted by it. These draft resolutions will be published for the information of delegates in the Party press, at least one month before the Conference.

The report of the General Secretary will be ready and printed and circulated at least one month before the Conference.

The procedure of business at the Conference will be as follows: after the Chairman's address and discussion on the General Secretary's report, the Conference will divide itself into groups according to subjects for discussion, such as labour, peasant, political, foreign policy, etc. These groups will discuss the draft resolutions selected by them and other items on the agenda and report to the Conference. The Conference will then consider the group reports and resolutions and take final decisions.

Each delegate will pay a delegate fee of Rs. 2 to the Central Office and Rs. 15 to the Reception Committee for board and lodging for five days, from February 20 to 24.

In no case will refund of any of these charges be made.

Other details of the Conference Programme will be published in due time.

57. Report of the Socialists Camp at Mahabaleshwar, Bombay, 7 November 1948[1]

It was Mrs. [Aruna] Asaf Ali who some time ago had suggested the idea of a camp where members of the National Executive and other prominent members of the party could get together and discuss, in conditions of comparative quiet and rest and at adequate length, the many problems that are before the Party and the country. The Bikaner Executive had readily accepted the suggestion and Comrade Achyut Patwardhan kindly undertook to make the necessary arrangements. Thus came about the Mahabaleshwar Camp.[2]

The camp was such an outstanding success and so much earnest and serious discussion and work were got through that it was decided to make this camp an annual feature. Every year about this season the Executive

[1] *Janata*, 7 November 1948.

[2] Mahabaleshwar Camp—The National Executive of the Socialist Party of India held a fortnight's camp at Mahabaleshwar (Bombay), starting from 25 October 1948, to formulate a plan for work in rural and urban areas of the country.

will hold a fortnight's camp to take stock of the year's work and plan for the future. The camp will meet at different places and an attempt will be made to find a quiet and cool place so as to provide rest and recreation along with work.

In some quarters, I am told there has been some criticism of the camp having been held at a place like Mahabaleshwar. I do not find any weight in this criticism. Mahabaleshwar was no more costly than, let us say, Bombay. Moreover, the men and women who gathered there were entitled, to my mind, to a fortnight's rest.

The camp was well attended. The only members of the Executive who could not attend were: Kamaladevi,[3] Ganga Sharan Sinha[4] and Maganlal Bagdi,[5] each one whom was unavoidably kept away either by some urgent work or illness. Among those specially invited, the following came to the Camp: S.M. Joshi,[6] Prof. [M.L.] Dantwala,[7] Prof. Mukut Bihari,[8] E. Narayanan,[9] Basawan Sinha,[10] Tilak Raj Chaddha,[11] Raghukal Tilak,[12] B.P. Sinha,[13] K.G. Sivaswamy,[14] Peter Alvares[15] and Pratap Shah.[16]

At the first sitting of the Executive, various sub-committees were formed to deal with the different questions on the agenda and report to the Executive. The following were the sub-committees formed: Constructive Work; Programme of the Party; Foreign Policy; Pakistan; The Party and the Government; Congress and other Parties; Labour Policy; Kisan Policy; Indian Constitution; States; Casteless Society; Backward Castes and Tribes;

[3] For biographical note on Kamaladevi Chattopadhyaya see *JPSW*, Vol. I, p. 47.

[4] For biographical note on Ganga Sharan Sinha see *JPSW*, Vol. II, p. 98.

[5] Maganlal Bagdi (1912-88); sentenced to five years rigorous imprisonment in connection with the 1st Nagpur conspiracy case 1932; arrested in 1939 for participating in Kisan Satyagraha; joined the Socialist Party in 1942; sentenced for life in 1943 for waging war against the king; released in 1946; member National Executive of the Socialist Party, 1948-52 and First Lok Sabha, 1952-7; subsequently joined the Congress.

[6] For biographical note on S.M. Joshi see *JPSW*, Vol. IV, p. 186.

[7] For biographical note on M.L. Dantwala see *JPSW*, Vol. III, p. 51.

[8] Mukut Behari Lal (1901-81); taught at Banares Hindu University (Department of Political Science) 1929-56; General Secretary All India Swadeshi Sangh 1933-5, Secretary Harijan Sewak Sangh 1933; founder member National Conference, Rampur State, 1946; member Central Council of all India States' People's Conference 1947; Provincial Executive U.P. Socialist Party 1948-9, U.P. Legislative Council 1952-4, National Executive Socialist Party 1956; Chairman U.P. P.S.P. 1957-8; Member of Parliament (Rajya Sabha), 1960-6.

[9] For biographical note on E. Narayanan see *JPSW*, Vol. IV, p. 222.

[10] For biographical note on Basawan Sinha see *JPSW*, Vol. III, p. 18.

[11] For biographical note on Tilakraj Chaddha see *JPSW*, Vol. III, pp. 82-3.

[12] For biographical note on Raghukul Tilak see *JPSW*, Vol. I, p. 62.

[13] For biographical note on B.P. Sinha see *JPSW*, Vol. I, p. 61.

[14] K.G. Sivaswamy (1922-); joined Quit Indian Movement in 1942; suffered imprisonment and was kept in Coimbatore Jail.

[15] For biographical note on Peter Alvares see item dated 8 September 1948 of the volume.

[16] Pratap Shah, Joint Secretary, Praja Socialist Party.

General Elections; Publicity and Party Journals; Research and Literature; Finance.

The sub-committees worked very diligently and produced able reports, which were then considered by the National Executive as a whole. For the structure of the Party, there was no sub-committee formed as I had a report ready for the Executive. The final reports, as adopted by the Executive, will soon be published in *Janata* and also as separate pamphlets.

Before the reports of the sub-committees were taken up, the Executive reviewed the progress made since the Nasik Conference. To enable the committee to do this, I had presented a written review. A most interesting discussion took place during which many fine suggestions were made. A point made by almost every one present was that there must be more literature produced and attention paid to the training of Party workers. To this end the Executive appointed a Research and Literature Committee with Narendra Deva as chairman. This Committee met at Mahabaleshwar and has planned a number of pamphlets and some basic literature. It would take about a year for the whole programme to be carried through.

As for the training of Party workers, it was decided that a permanent School of Politics be founded at Bombay. It was hoped that Yusuf Meherally, whom we will soon have the good fartune to have in our midst, may agree to act as Director of the School. There can be none more suited for the job. In Bombay there is also, fortunately, a group of socialist intellectuals and workers of adequate experience who could easily run an institution of this nature. Some of these friends are already running the Labour College with outstanding success.

Another striking point made by Rammanohar Lohia and commonly accepted was regarding the lack of a philosophy behind the socialist movement. This lack is largely responsible for that weakness of faith so often noticed in our movement. The creation of a philosophical basis is not a matter that can be entrusted to a committee, but it was good that so pointed an attention was drawn to this question. I have no doubt that just as our movement is trying to find deeper roots in the Indian soil and draw sustenance from the history of this country and of Asia, so, in course of time a philosophy would be developed that would be vital and indigenous enough to touch the core of our people's lives and move millions to action.

The Mahabaleshwar Camp was not convened merely to pass resolutions. In fact there were hardly any resolutions adopted. Many organizational decisions were taken, basic policies were determined and a plan of work was chalked out. The reports that will appear from week to week in *Janata* and that will be published as pamphlets will give some idea of the decisions made, and the rest will be conveyed to Party branches through circulars to which I draw the attention of every Party member.

The National Executive will meet again at Lucknow on December 29 and 30.

58. Address at Press Conference, Bombay, 7 November 1948[1]

A considerable time has elapsed since the Government of India announced their measures to fight inflation. These measures have so far failed to make any impression on the country's price structure. Government spokesmen have admitted this in their recent statements. I am sure the present policy gives no promise of future success.

The country is thus in the throes of a grave economic crisis out of which there appears to be no way in sight. All classes of people are affected by this crisis, but the class that is hardest hit is the class of the wage-earners and salaried employees in the lower and middle income groups. With the ever rising cost of living, their real wage is continuously falling and they are in the jaws of real hardship and misery. In certain sectors of our economy, such as in the textile industry in Bombay, the workers have fought for and won a system of dearness allowance that has some relation with the price index. But in most other sectors the workers and the fixed-income groups have no protection against rising prices. It is well known that for Central Government employees, the Central Pay Commission recommended a sliding scale of dearness allowance with a five-rupee equivalent for every twenty points of rise or fall in the index number. This was accepted by Government; but on one plea or another, it is not being implemented. This is causing widespread misery and disappointment and is seriously affecting the employees' output of work. A government that fails to protect the salaries and standard of living of its own employees fails in its primary task and demonstrates the utter bankruptcy of its economic policy.

It has been decided to call a consultative conference of labour representatives in Bombay on November 27 and 28 to consider the situation and devise ways and means to persuade the Government to change their present economic policy and adopt measures that would bring down prices or in the alternative, to consider how wage and fixed income-earners can fight to maintain their standard of living.

[1] *Tribune*, 8 November 1948.

59. Address at the Labour Forum, New Delhi, 13 November 1948[1]

There should be some sort of industrial truce for a certain period in the larger interest of the country especially at a time when there are bigger

[1] Adapted from *Hindustan Times*, 14 November 1948.

problems to be tackled. As a Socialist I think that there should be industrial truce particularly when priority has to be given to the nation-building programme. It means that labour should be prepared to keep in abeyance certain demands in national interest. To some it might sound as a sacrilege while others might call it a betrayal.

During the last 50 years, there had been occasions in the life of the labour movements when it was advantageous to restrain sectional and class interests in the larger interest of the country. In order to have industrial truce, it is obvious that both sides must accept certain compromises. There should be some limitations on profits of industrialists as well as wages of workers.

The reason for labour conditions in India steadily deteriorating is the absence of a proper relationship between the dearness allowance and cost of living. There is no intention on the part of labour to embarrass the Government, but the determination of a fair wage on the one hand and a fair profit on the other, must also be attended to.

Labour is patriotic and national, but it does not like to lose its fundamental rights. The right to strike is equivalent to the right to live. Industrial peace can be possible for a certain period, but it cannot be coercive. No civilized Government can think for a moment to take away the rights of labour.

60. Statement on Labour Unions' Strike, New Delhi, 15 November 1948[1]

The token strike called by labour unions in Delhi on November 13 has only been a partial success. This does not mean that the Delhi workers are not behind their unions and the Socialist Party that leads them, but only that labour has not as yet learned how to fight under conditions of fascism. We function in this country on the assumption that we are doing so under a democracy and are, therefore, surprised and confounded when we are baulked by methods of fascism.

The average man in the country is not conscious of the paradox that the achievement of national freedom has coincided with the eclipse of individual and civic freedom. The result is the deadening of the social conscience. It is a tragedy that in free India when a leader and patriot of the standing of Achyut Patwardhan is arrested, the people treat it as a common affair. Our present rulers no doubt justify everything on the ground that law and order must be maintained; but they should remember, if power has not dulled their memory that there is such a thing as a lawless law. A law which a person like Achyut Patwardhan felt compelled to defy, is a law of this kind

[1] *National Herald*, 16 November 1948.

and has no justification to be. The present indifference of the public to such vital matters provides a fertile soil for the growth of a nascent Indian fascism over which strangely enough a democrat like Pandit Nehru presides.

The Prime Minister, during his recent European tour, gave expression to high idealism, but right under his eyes, in his own capital things have happened apparently with his full approval that are an eloquent repudiation of all his idealistic talk. Here was a one-day token strike based on purely trade union demands and here were the authorities of free India who met the strike as if it were a call to revolution. Military was called out, indiscriminate arrests were made, trade union offices were raided at dead of night, and almost the entire executive of the local Socialist Party, Hind Mazdoor Panchayat and the Kisan Panchayat was put under arrest. Socialist workers who had no concern with labour work and had confined themselves to the peasantry alone were also rounded up. Congressmen worked not only as strike-breakers but also as police agents.

Fascism has not succeeded elsewhere and it cannot succeed here. But it will cause untold suffering to the people in the course of its attempt to rule their destiny. I wonder if there are enough people in this country who can unite to save the people from this suffering.

61. To Indra Sen, 16 November 1948[1]

Dear Comrade Sen,

I am very sorry that I was not able to write earlier. I hope your Central Committee is still in session and this letter will not be too late. Even if it is, the talk that I had with you should have been enough for the Central Committee to take a decision.

Regarding the probationary period, as I had told you before, the National Executive has absolutely no power to amend the constitution in any respect, but as I also told you there would be no difficulty whatever in confirmation of members of the BLPI[2] after the required period of three months is over. I therefore urge your Central Committee not to attach any importance to this matter.

As I told you in Bombay, if the applications of BLPI comrades are sent immediately they would be able to participate in the next annual conference; by then the probationary period of three months would be over. The applications could be made collectively as I explained to you, i.e. you could send in a list with a letter saying that all the persons listed seek admission into the Socialist Party.

[1] *J.P. Papers* (NMML).

[2] Bolshevik Leninist Party of India.

Regarding the last point, i.e. objection to individuals, I am not in a position yet to send you any further names, but as I told you before I do not apprehend that there will be any objection except in very rare cases. As far as Comrade Selvraj is concerned, I have asked the Madras Party to send me the details.

With greetings,

Sincerely yours.
J.P.

62. To Ravindra Varma, 16 November 1948[1]

My dear Ravindra Varma,

I am extremely sorry for not replying earlier. It was good of your working committee to have agreed to the proposal for joint secretaryship. Ramkrishna in his letter to me had suggested that a distinction should be made between you and the other joint secretary: that is to say, you should be styled secretary, while the other person should be designed joint secretary. This was not what I understood you to say in your letter: nor these fine distinctions are to help us in our work. So I take it that it has been agreed that there shall be two joint secretaries, one among them being you and the other some one representing the so-called socialist group.

Now, regarding the selection of the other joint secretary, we would have been glad to have Ramchandra Shukla as suggested by you. But the difficulty is that the Goyal group are anxious to have some one who is more intimately connected with them. It appears Shukla is not even a member of Goyal's working committee. Therefore after consulting with them and taking your own wishes into consideration, it has been decided that Sugata Das Gupta should be the joint secretary along with you. He would be accepted readily, it seems, by other groups too such as the Bengal R.S.P. group. Das Gupta being already on the organizing committee (of ten), the procedure would be further simplified.

I hope now this arrangement will be accepted by you. If you experience any difficulty in working it out, do let me know. I shall do my best to smoothen the way, as I am anxious that the National Union [of students] should soon come into being.

With best wishes,

Sincerely yours,
J.P.

[1] *J.P. Papers* (NMML).

[2] Narendra Goyal, President of one of the two groups into which the students Congress had split.

63. Views on the Draft Constitution, 17 November 1948[1]

The overwhelming defeat of the amendment that Seth Damodar Swarup[2] moved asking for a new Constituent Assembly to be elected on adult franchise will cause no surprise. Since the achievement of freedom all our values seem to have undergone a sea change. What was vice in the white ruler has become virtue in the brown. What was black then is white now, including the Governor-General's salary, the pomp and show and the corruption and the suppression of liberties. Even the blind can see that the present Constituent Assembly does not represent 85 per cent of the people of the Provinces and even a higher percentage of the people of the States. Yet, Damodar Swarup's simple home-truth was derided and run down and buried under a mechanical majority vote, a vote that is exercised not according to the merits of a question but in obedience to a so-called "high command".

It is sad to reflect that India is going to be saddled with such a cumbrous and defective constitution that will ever stand as a solid barrier against progress and social change.

The Socialist Party has repeatedly drawn attention to the glaring defects in the Draft Constitution. But unfortunately the people, more engrossed with the problems of bread and shelter, have remained indifferent to what the makers of their destiny were doing at Delhi. Encouraged by the people's indifference, the conservatives and reactionaries had easy going; and there seems to be nothing to stop them. The voice of one solitary socialist could hardly avail against the yellings of the band-boys.

Here in these columns once again the Socialist Party publishes its main criticism of the Draft Constitution in the hope that some at least may be made more aware of the dismal destiny to which the self-satisfied law-makers are driving the country.

[1] *Janata*, 17 November 1948.

[2] For biographical note on Seth Damodar Swarup see *JPSW*, Vol. I, p. 85.

64. Address at the Annual Conference of East Indian Railway Employees' Union, Moghalsarai, 18 November 1948[1]

Up-till now I used to advise the labour all over India not to resort to strike but now I find a vast change in the attitude of the Government of India towards labour and hence I cannot now give the same advice.

I am aware that our Government is busy in the Kashmir war. If the

[1] Adapted from *Searchlight*, 20 November 1948.

Government is busy in war against another country that does not mean that Labour should not fight for its legitimate demands by resorting to strikes. This can not be found in the history of labour movement of any country.

Prior to the Government's Police Action in Hyderabad the situation in India was no doubt delicate, but after successfully solving the Hyderabad problem, the national spirit has stabilised and the deep wound in the country's chest has completely healed up. Now it is the time for labour in the country to show that no power can suppress them any more. Up-till now they had a firm belief that the Government of India would not resort to any action which might prove detrimental to the working class. But their difficulties are increasing every day due to ever mounting inflation.

In order to solve the inflation problem the Nehru Government convened many conferences of Ministers, Officials, Professors, Economists and Capitalists without whom the Government cannot take a single step. But the anti-inflation policy announced by the Government after much delay has made it clear that labour all over the country should get ready for self-protection.

The Government had surrendered to the capitalists who wanted many facilities including relief from certain taxes without which they said it was not possible to increase all-round production, but the Government did nothing to bring relief to labour. Without any ambiguity I want to warn our Government that their new anti-inflation policy would prove quite ineffective. We cannot now tie down labour by advising them not to launch any movement for improving their condition.

The Nehru Government has said that it has no money to improve the lot of working classes in the country, but at the same time it allows the Governor-General and high officers to draw fat salaries which run into thousands. The Government claims that in order to maintain the country's dignity and prestige it is necessary for the Governor-General to maintain the old standards. How the Government can have dignity if the working classes in the country remain half-starved and hard-pressed under such conditions. There is no sense in clinging to old notions of dignity and prestige.

Labour has full right to fight for their bread. How this fight is to be conducted should be decided by labour itself. They themselves should think over their problems with a calm and quiet mind. For this I do not want to instigate them. Strikes are a form of non-violence so dear to Mahatma Gandhi; a very long time ago in the list of Fundamental Rights adopted by the Karachi Congress (1931) the Congress had recognized them. They are also recognized all over the world in democratic countries, including even a capitalist country like the United States of America.

But now the Congress Government is enacting laws which aim at depriving the labour of its birth-right. For this I cite the action of the Bombay Government and the recent action of the Delhi Administration, which went so far as to declare the Textile Industry as an essential and public utility service.

In order to suppress the Labour Movement the Nehru Government is adopting fascist methods of the bygone British era by declaring strikes illegal, effecting countrywide arrests of labour leaders and the show of military and police force. I, therefore, warn labour that if they remain submissive at this stage they would remain in slavery and bondage for ever.

65. Inaugural Address at the Conference of the Anti-Communal Students' Front, Benaras Hindu University, 19 November 1948[1]

Communalism is a great obstacle to the progress of the country and if this disease is allowed to continue it will eat up the body politic. Had this evil not existed in our land we would have reached our goal earlier and would not have seen independent India divided. If we want to fulfil our dream of one united India we have to improve the lot of the common man in the country.

All communal organizations like R.S.S., Hindu Mahasabha, Muslim League and others must go. As far as my information goes none of the members of R.S.S, or Hindu Mahasabha courted arrest in connection with the fight for independence for or motherland.

The unity of two States [India and Pakistan] by means of force cannot be permanent unless the inhabitants of these States like it. The only means of bringing about the reunion of Pakistan with India is a change of heart. To attract our Pakistani brothers to join us we have to create the necessary conditions in our country. The lot of the common man has to be improved and we have to establish a fully secular state. Communal organizations should be immediately banned. If we allow them to grow they will create greater harm than what they did during the British rule. Four crores of Muslims cannot be driven away from this land. If we follow the policy of discrimination and communal hatred there will be chaos in the country and we will be thrown away hundreds of years back and ultimately lose our independence for which we shed our blood.

I warn the audience against the disruptive forces in the country. Movements for the establishment of a Dravidian homeland under the auspices of the Dravidian Youth League, narrow provincialism and the disputes of Hindi, Urdu and Hindustani have made matters worse. Such problems always mar the progress of a country.

[1] Adapted from *National Herald*, 21 November 1948.

66. Address at Kashi Vidyapeeth, 20 November 1948[1]

Many of our Socialist friends so far believed that by bringing about an economic revolution in the country they would be able to create an ideal socialist state, but we have now come to the conclusion that to achieve our goal we have to improve the morals of individuals as well.

There was demoralization of the middle class during the British rule when the education imparted made the people forget their own culture, I appeal to young men to raise the moral standard of society to make the country powerful.

Gandhiji did not differ with the socialists as regards the establishment of a State in which there was no exploitation. He had repeatedly said that he aimed at an equal distribution of wealth in society, the only difference from the socialists being that he believed in trusteeship of the capitalists while the socialists did not. In the later period of his life, however, Gandhiji began to realize that the exploiting classes could not be reformed beyond a certain stage, Acharya Vinoba Bhave,[2] a great disciple of Gandhiji, and also an original thinker, has come to the conclusion that the textile industry should be nationalized.

Two classes of thinkers are found in our country today, one emphasizing the necessity of improving the lot of the common man and the other favouring reformation of society on the moral plane. We have to harmonise both ways of thinking in order to establish true socialism in our land.

[1] Adapted from *National Herald*, 22 November 1948.

[2] Vinayak Narahari Bhave (1895-1994); popularly known as Vinoba Bhave, a very learned person and a devout disciple of Mahatma Gandhi, generally hailed as Gandhi's spiritual heir; leapt into fame in 1941 when Gandhi selected him as the first satyagrahi in the Individual Civil Disobedience Movement launched that year; started the Bhoodan Movement in 1951 and later the Gram-dan Movement in order to provide land to the landless and establish an exploitation free society in the village.

67. Appeal to the Party Members to boost Subscription for *Janata*, 21 November 1948[1]

I fail to understand the attitude of Party members to *Janata*. There is such a cry for Party literature. Yet, I wonder how many members, who read English, read *Janata*. I wonder too how many Party branches there are which subscribe for *Janata*. The other day I had gone to Udaipur in Rajputana. I was utterly surprised to find that the Udaipur district unit did not subscribe even for a single copy of *Janata*. In the whole district there

[1] *Janata*, 21 November 1948.

was not one copy of *Janata* sold. And yet Udaipur is one of the noted educational centres of Rajputana. I have no doubt that had the Udaipur comrades given even a day to it, they could have enrolled at least fifty subscribers for *Janata*.

Then there is that quota of 2000 subscribers yet to be fulfilled. This subscription drive—a small test for Party members—has been a painful revelation. Will the struggling provinces even now wake up? The whole of the south, i.e. the Southern Party branches, has behaved inexcusably. While elaborate schemes have been discussed, much valuable opportunity for propaganda has been missed and the English *Janata* has remained practically unknown in the vital south. Will the Regional Office and the southern branches do something concrete now in this matter?

To the East Punjab goes great credit, that in spite of the diseased communal climate in which it has to function, the Party there has exceeded its quota. Bombay too has come up. But other provinces have far to go, C.P. particularly and Bengal. The U.P. and Bihar too have not done so well. May I put it to comrades in these provinces that it does no credit to them that they should lag so far behind. Buck up comrades! If you do well in little things, you will not fail in the bigger trials. Let the middle of December see the fulfilment of your quotas.

68. The Structure of the Socialist Party: *Janata*, 21 and 28 November 1948[1]

The structure of the Party has not changed in any basic manner since its inception. The Party grew up as a group within the Congress, and even though it had an independent membership, its own constitution and rules, it never grew out of the role of being an ideological group within a great mass movement. The salient points of the Party's structure, as it took shape at the beginning and stands till today, are: (1) small, selected membership; (2) admission to membership depending upon fulfilment of certain work quota; (3) a probationary period for all members, scrutiny and confirmation or rejection of membership.

This structure served its purpose as long as the Party functioned mainly as an ideological group within the Congress. But can it fit the Party's new role? The Party is not only an independent political party now: it aspires to become a party of the toiling millions, and it aspires too, by its own political action, to destroy feudalism and capitalism in India and establish a socialist society. These are not objects that a handful of persons can achieve. Unless

[1] *Janata*, 21 and 28 November 1948. Article by J.P. in two installments.

the Party succeeds in rallying the workers, the peasants, the exploited middle classes, under its banner, unless it is able to organize them and inspire them to political action, the Party's objective shall remain unrealized. The Party must become the Party not only *for* the toilers but also *of* the toilers.

For many months past one of the slogans of the Party has been: '*Mazdooron ki parti*: Socialist Party'; '*Kisanon ki parti*: Socialist Party', etc. The question is, how can the Party become in fact, and not in theory alone, the party of the peasants and workers? If the Party is made up of a handful of socialist workers and the masses are barred from coming in, how can we be justified in claiming that we are the party of the masses? We constantly invite the masses to come into the Party; what value has this when we at the same time bar their way? It is obvious that the Party must expand and broaden out: it must become a mass party. It cannot do it all of a sudden, but the structural goal of the Party is fairly definite.

The thought of a mass party is disturbing to some friends. The influx of the masses is supposed to dilute the ideological purity of a party and blunt its revolutionary edge and make it too cumbrous and heavy for revolutionary action. According to such friends a revolutionary party must be a party of chosen workers. To them the structure of the communist party appears to be ideally suited to a revolutionary purpose.

In Marxist theory and common logic, there is no reason why a party that desires to serve the masses must restrict its membership to a chosen few. The more logical and natural course for it should be to include as large sections of the masses as possible. Restricted membership is no essential attribute of revolutionism. Rather, it is the resultant of special objective conditions.

In Czarist days, there were no civil liberties in Russia, and the Bolshevik[2] Party, or its parent, the Social Democratic Party, had to function in conditions of illegality, secrecy and underground life. Under those conditions, it was physically impossible to build up a mass party. Only tested members could be admitted and strict vigilance and discipline were necessary to prevent betrayal and to ensure devoted work in the face of suffering and danger.

It was not only in Russia that these organizational needs were felt and patterns found to meet them. In every country where Czarist conditions existed, revolutionary organizations followed a similar pattern. The revolutionary parties in India too did the same during British days. It was the genius of Mahatma Gandhi that in *satyagraha* he devised a revolutionary method that even under conditions of Czarism could be used openly.

[2] Bolshevik Party—the name assumed by members of the radical left wing (functioning under the leadership of V.I. Lenin) of Russian Social Democratic Labour Party in 1903 spearheaded the famous October Revolution of 1917, which became known as the Bolshevik Revolution.

Communist methods having been perfected to suit certain given conditions, it is unwise to attempt to apply them universally. Where the civil liberties of the people are guaranteed and all the avenues for open political propaganda, organization and action are available, the methods of secret societies cannot but lead to failure. In democratic countries, communist methods have yielded meagre results.

In Great Britain, America and France, communist parties were and are legal and have functioned within the framework of democracy. In Weimar Germany too, the Communist Party functioned as a legal party. Of these countries, only in Germany till the rise of Hitler[3] was the Communist Party of any great political significance; and the reasons for that were many. The course of the German Revolution and the consequent split in the German Social Democratic Party[4] and the formation of the Spartakus League under the leadership of such famous international figures as Rosa Luxemburg[5] and Karl Leibknecht[6] and the contemporary victory of the Russian Revolution, were directly responsible for the initial success of the Communist Party in Germany. The weaknesses of Social Democracy and the worsening economic situation contributed to its steady growth. But in France, America and England, communist methods hardly produced any results. The present strength of the French Communist Party is due to the political conditions in Europe and the disintegration of French democracy, rather than to any marked success of the methods of the French Communist Party. Furthermore, it should be remembered that even the rigid communist methods undergo a sea change under democratic conditions. The French and Italian communist parties, for instance, are no longer parties of chosen revolutionaries, but mass parties, with hundreds of thousands of members.

Communist methods thus do not flourish in a democratic climate nor in conditions of tolerable economic well-being. It is for this reason that a vital element in the communist method is a deliberate and planned attempt to bring about political instability and depressed economic conditions.

An undemocratic society develops internal strains and stresses that result eventually in a violent break-up. Communist methods having been perfected to be used under undemocratic conditions, they are ultimately based on the

[3] For biographical note on Adolf Hitler see *JPSW*, Vol. III, p. 2.

[4] German Social Democratic Party was founded in 1875; its leaders were devout Marxists but refused to accept dictatorship of the proletariat and functioned as a parliamentary party, aiming at the assumption of political power by constitutional electoral means.

[5] Rosa Luxemburg (1870-1919); one of the most famous women in the history of international socialism who played a notable part in shaping the Socialist Movement in Europe, particularly in Germany.

[6] Karl Liebknecht (1871-1919); a German left-wing socialist who went on to found the German Communist Party. He argued against bureaucratic leadership of Social Democratic Party and made himself known outside Germany by his defence of Russian revolutionaries.

possibility and desirability of a well-organized minority utilizing conditions of chaos to impose its rule over the rest of the community. During times of widespread social disorganization, social will is disintegrated and any minority that has a will of its own and the proper organizational set-up can force its will upon others. These methods require for their success periods of social unrest and disequilibrium. Wherever these conditions do not exist communists feel like fish out of water and they always attempt artificially to create the conditions in which their methods can succeed. Therefore they are everywhere the enemies of democracy and ordered change.

Under democratic conditions a party that believes in democratic socialism follows entirely different methods. A time might come when even a democratic party might find itself in the midst of anarchic conditions. Obviously in these conditions it must represent the largest possible crystallization of the social will and, as such, try to impose its will over society by means that cannot be democratic—because in those conditions the framework of democracy would have broken down—but are based on force. No doubt in these conditions too the democratic socialist party must try to rally round it as large a section of the toiling people as possible, but for the rest it must have to depend on force. To some this may not appear very different from communist methods, but will amount to saying that communist methods were evolved primarily to suit conditions of chaos. I am sure Lenin would have been forced by history to adopt other methods had democracy developed further in Russia and had not Russian society collapsed round him like a house of cards in 1917. And then Leninists would have sung to a different tune.

The important thing for us to consider is, when conditions are different from what they were in Russia under the Czar, shall we follow the same methods?

Some have the fear that while democratic conditions might exist today they may not be present tomorrow and if the Party is organized so as to function under today's conditions, it may not be able to function properly in the conditions of tomorrow. This fear is unfounded. If democratic methods are not divorced from a revolutionary outlook, the Socialist Party, if it has functioned properly as a democratic party under conditions of democracy, would have the organizational strength, the popularity, the necessary mass contact, the resilience and the revolutionary will to function equally effectively in conditions of social breakdown. The Congress functioned alternately for years as a legal organization, utilizing democratic freedoms that existed, and as a revolutionary party functioning illegally and carrying on a mass struggle. The resilience of the Congress was largely due to the revolutionary will of its great leader, but its success in struggle was due to its widespread organization and mass influence built up through democratic functioning.

What is a revolutionary will, I may be asked. It is (1) the will that allows no compromise with fundamentals or blurring of the final objectives: (2) it is the will that does not flinch before danger and suffering and deviate from the right path on their account. I believe the Socialist Party is possessed of such a will; and as long as it has that will, it cannot fail.

A word more about communist methods. Not only are these methods inapplicable to a democratic society, their use does not lead to the goal of democratic socialism. Since 1917 the Communist Party in Russia has been the ruling party. After the victory of the Revolution the main task before the Communist Party has been that of shaping and maintaining its dictatorship. Every organizational change that has taken place in the Russian Communist Party[7] has been influenced by this all-important consideration. Inside the party itself, the struggle for leadership and the ruthless faction-fight led to the perfection of a system of control and management from the top that left very little internal democracy. The party was thus moulded not only to maintain its grip over Russia but also to enable the *Vozd*, the Russian equivalent of the *Fuehrer*, to maintain his grip over the party itself. Those who denounce totalitarianism when practiced by others, but are eager to practise it themselves on others find the methods of the Russian Communist Party peculiarly acceptable. But those who believe in freedom and democratic socialism and have a living faith in it, must reject communist methods.

Let me turn to the conditions in our own country. It need hardly be pointed out that the India of today is not the Russia of Czarist days. There is no Czar in India. We have considerable freedom and there is going to be adult franchise. There is, no doubt, every danger of severe curtailment of the liberties of the people, yet there is ample opportunity for open political work, and there is every hope that, with the development of the socialist movement, the liberties of the people will be preserved. Indian feudalism and capitalism have not been the ruling class in this country, but understudies of the Imperial power. The loyalty of the armed and civil services has not been given to these classes. These classes, moreover, are on the defensive today and cannot hope to maintain their position except with the support of a popular mass organization, such as the Congress. The Congress is not yet a capitalist party, but largely an agrarian party passing slowly under capitalist control. Again, 1948 is not 1917. The frontiers of capitalism are receding, and those of socialism and communism are advancing. Capitalism is old and discredited. The chances of socialism are far brighter today than they were thirty years ago.

In view of this situation communist methods of organization are patently unsuited to India. We must devise our own pattern of organization, which

[7] Russian Communist Party: see note 2 above.

will suit the given conditions and further the objectives of democratic socialism. As I said at the outset, if our Party is to succeed in establishing socialism in India by the consent of the people, it must bring the majority of them under its influence and organization. It must become a mass party.

Should the Socialist Party, then, become a people's party? Is a mass socialist party the same as a people's party? Some friends have suggested that in order that the party might rapidly become an alternative to the Congress, it should convert itself from a socialist party into a people's party. The view of these friends is that the socialist party with a clear-cut socialist policy and programme has a restricted appeal; whereas a people's party with a 'non-sectarian' programme that offers the people good government and enough food, cloth, and shelter, may quickly grow to the proportions of the Congress: the two parties being something like the Republican and Democratic parties in the U.S.A.

I reject this suggestion because, firstly, such a people's party cannot establish a socialist society and I am more interested in that than in merely replacing the Congress government. Secondly, it seems fantastic to me to suppose that a socialist party should fail to win the allegiance of that section of the upper class which is not satisfied with Congress rule and wants an alternative party. It happens in bourgeois society everywhere that the bourgeois class itself is split into at least two rival political camps. In India too the suggestion about a people's party, as distinct from a socialist party, merely means that a section of the Indian bourgeoisie which is not satisfied with the Congress wants to create under its domination a rival organization to the Congress. When friends suggest that a people's party will grow rapidly, they are mainly thinking of the financial resources that such a party might be able to command. From financial resources to organization and propaganda appears to them, and not wrongly, to be only one long jump. But such a people's party would be another mass party functioning under bourgeois control and playing at parliamentary politics, as rival bourgeois parties do elsewhere, without ever desiring to effect any vital social transformation. This suggestion, therefore, of converting the party into a people's party must be rejected.

This, however, does not mean that a socialist party is not, or cannot be, a people's party. To be effective and to fulfil its purpose, a socialist party must in a real sense be a people's party. But it can be so only when it has succeeded by organization and propaganda in convincing the people that socialism is nothing more than the realization of their needs, desires and aspirations. A socialist party becomes a people's party when the people generally are converted to socialism.

We reach then the conclusion that the Party must function as a socialist party with a definite socialist ideology and programme and that it should grow into a mass party, rather than remain a party of the select. What shall be the mass party pattern into which the Party should grow? I find in the world two types of mass party patterns. One, a pattern similar to the Congress pattern of organization (as it was till recently): i.e. having a mass membership, of which every member is individually enrolled. The other, the British Labour Party[8] pattern, which combines individual mass membership with organizational membership. The Cooperative Commonwealth Federation of Canada[9] is the only other socialist party in the world which I have found to follow the British pattern.

I recommend for our Party the Labour Party pattern. It has many advantages. It links the political party with the class organizations of the masses and with their day-to-day struggles. In this manner, the political party in reality becomes the party of the masses. Secondly, it makes possible a rapid growth and development of the Party. Individual enrolment might take long to bring millions of workers and peasants into the Party, whereas through trade-union and kisan-panchayat membership, the period of time might be considerably reduced. Thirdly, the attachment of individual members to the Party, especially when enrolled in the mass, will not be so deep as when their unions or panchayats are affiliated to the Party. Fourthly, an individual toiler may be just a Hindu or Muslim, Harijan or Thakur, but as a member of a trade union or kisan panchayat he will be more often than not a loboursr or a peasant. That is, when he enters the Party through his class organization, he brings with him a consciousness of class: and that puts him in tune with socialism.

In following the British pattern there are obvious difficulties. That pattern was an organic growth and was made possible by the fact that British labour had one single trade union organization. The growth of our Party too has hitherto been organic, and this has been its strength. Its further growth too must not be artificial. But in adapting the British party structure to our purpose, I find no artificiality: much less artificiality, at any rate, than if we were to adopt the Russian pattern. It is true that trade unionism is divided in India, but whether trade unions are affiliated or not to the Socialist Party, the Party cannot hope to achieve success unless the preponderant part of Indian labour comes under its political leadership. In Britain too while there is one Trade Union Congress,[10] there are many unions that are not affiliated

[8] For note on British Labour Party see *JPSW*, Vol. IV, p. 54.

[9] The Cooperative Commonwealth Federation of Canada: The economic depression of 1930s gave rise to a number of parties in Canada, one of them being Cooperative Commonwealth Federation (C.C.F.), a farmer-labour party with a socialist intelligentsia in 1935.

[10] Trade Union Congress (Britain): It was founded in 1868 at annual conferences for the exposition of trade union principles. From 1871 it had permanent standing Committee, T.U.C. was composed mainly of unions of skilled workers until 1889 but later on it included

to the Labour Party and many union officials who are members of rival parties. Leaving the question of party structure aside, let it be remembered that the Socialist Party has no future unless it becomes the dominant party among Indian labour. If that be the definite goal of the Party, the adoption of the British pattern should rather pave the way than present obstacles.

To the mass enrolment of individuals an objection may be raised on the plea that these persons may have no knowledge of socialism. But if socialism is the concretization of the aspirations of the masses it is wrong to think that every toiler must first be converted to socialism before he can belong to the Socialist Party. Rather, the Socialist Party should be a party that expresses the feeling and aspirations of the toilers. I would, therefore, rather let the millions come into the Party and shape it than have the Party adopt a doctrinaire attitude. Every toiler, there can be little doubt, will happily subscribe to the ideal of a classless society. There is no doubt that socialist philosophy is much more than that, and that the Party does start with a definite set of well-defined principles, but it does so precisely because it feels that the principles ideate the interests of the masses. If they do not do so, they must change in the course of the movement. It is also true that the Party starts out to imbue the toilers with certain ideas. But these ideas too can be accepted by the masses only when they find them in actual practice to be in their interest. Thus, while socialist theory is an ideation of the miseries and needs and desires of the masses, the test of the theory lies in its acceptance by the masses. Therefore, I do not apprehend any danger in throwing open the doors of the Party to the actual toilers. I would qualify these remarks when applied to the middle-class. This class, economically and socially, is peculiarly situated. Its outlook oscillates between the outlooks of the upper and the toiling classes. Therefore, there may be a certain danger in mass enrolment of middle-class individuals; and so, a certain caution may be exercised in this regard. But, here too there is no need to insist on any work quota as a necessary condition for membership. Any individual who agrees with the principles, policy and programme of the Socialist Party may be admitted. I am conscious of the danger pointed out by some friends, of undesirable elements coming into the Party in this manner, but to my mind, even this danger can be fought only if the Party becomes a mass party.

I therefore propose that the Party should consist of the following elements: individual members; organizations that become members such as trade unions, artisans' associations; associations of professionals; kisan panchayats, kisan mazdoor panchayats; representatives of the Socialist Youth

---

unskilled unions also. It assumed its modern form after World war I. Its membership rose to 1,20,00,000 in 1979. It supports British Labour Party. It is affiliated with International Confederation of Free Trade Unions (I.C.F.T.U.).

Organizations; culture; associations and clubs. I should also have included in this list co-operative societies, but the Congress governments are so petty-minded that this may become an obstacle in the growth of co-operation in this country.

All representatives of member organizations must also have ward units, in urban areas, and in rural areas, local units. The units will be the only Party committees where all members will function in the capacity of individual members.

Above the unit will be higher bodies: Constituency Branches, District Branches, Provincial Branches. In these bodies representatives will come from the units, representing the individual membership, and from the member organizations, representing them.

An important point that must be cleared up is that collective membership of a trade union or Kisan Panchayat does not mean that the Hind Mazdoor Panchayat (H.M.P.) or Hind Kisan Panchayat (H.K.P.) as a whole is to be affiliated to the Party. These are both independent organizations and will live their own life, in accordance with their will. Only the primary unions and panchayats will be affiliated to the Party; and there may be even such primary bodies that are affiliated to the H.M.P. or the H.K.P. and yet are not allied to the Party. Nor would it be necessary for every member or official of a union or panchayat to be a member of the Party.

I should like here to digress a little and say a few words about politics and the trade union movement. There are still people in this country who would keep the workers away from politics. Nothing could be of greater disservice to the working class. The working class has a dual role to play: economic and political. A trade union cannot merely be satisfied with collective bargaining, it must also attempt to influence legislation and government. In the picture I have presented, a trade union performs the function of collective bargaining through the H.M.P. and the political function by sending its representatives to the Socialist Party. The trade union thus is the base on which two structures are built up, each autonomous, but each expressing the will of the organized working class, namely, the central trade union body (H.M.P.) and the political party (S.P.).

In recommending this Party structure I am also influenced by certain other considerations. First, such an organizational set-up might attract many trade unionists, kisan workers, social workers, individual socialists, even socialist groups, who keep away today on the ground that the Socialist Party is merely a caucus and not a party.

Second, it will remove the growth of authoritarianism and sectarianism in the Party. At present admission of new members is practically entirely in the hands of the Provincial executives, for the Scrutiny Board does little more than put its seal of approval on the recommendations received from them. This has resulted in some provinces in stagnation and shutting out of newcomers. Group politics and the will to leadership also get the chance for full play in these circumstances. Thc recommended structure, by allowing the democratic principle full scope, will help the growth of the Party.

Third, I have often been asked what guarantee there was that when in power socialists too would not go the way of Congressmen. Among other things, the Party structure I have suggested should be a powerful guarantee against this. Congressmen theoretically represent the masses. But the masses they represent are like amorphous sand, they have no organized will to exert over their representatives. It is merely individuals who choose the Congress representatives. In the Socialist Party under the new structure, on the other hand, the masses will come largely through their class organizations, i.e. through workers and peasants unions. The representatives of these unions would be under a conscious discipline and would be liable to be brought to book if they went wrong. In the British Labour Party, for instance, the trade union representatives cannot flout their unions and hope to remain in the Labour Party. Collective membership is thus a guarantee against opportunism and self-seeking.

69. Appeal to Railwaymen to Contribute Generously to their Emergency Fund, Nagpur, 22 November 1948[1]

Nearly a year ago I had appealed to you to give your best, in spite of your troubles and difficulties, to you country. I was grateful for your ready response. You passed through trying times and your patience was sorely tested, but you proved your loyalty to your country by your devoted service.

In these circumstances, it was your right to be treated with consideration. But it is a pity that after long months of negotiation and bargaining, there are still so many of your grievances outstanding. I have been aware for the past several months of your growing feeling of discontent. At the Lillooah Convention I had fresh evidence. And yet I counselled patience all along and you were patriotic enough to realize that the interests of the country demanded that you acted with self-restraint. Lillooah Convention, however, as all of you know, for the last time formulated your demands and grievances and set a time limit before which the Ministry of Railways should communicate to the Federation its reply. The demands and grievances were many, but mainly they concerned the rising cost of living and the implementation of the C.P.C. Report. In this connection I should like to draw your earnest attention to the following resolution raised by the Working Committee of your Federation recently at Bombay:

[1] *Janata*, 28 November 1948.

Whereas the Working Committee of the All-India Railwaymen's Federation is apprehensive that in view of the unsympathetic and dilatory attitude of the Government of India and of the unsatisfactory nature of their general economic policy, as exemplified in their anti-inflation measures, and further in view of the continuously rising cost of living, Railwaymen may soon have to face a grave emergency; and

Whereas it is essential that the Federation and the affiliated unions and railwaymen generally should prepare for ever possible contingency without loss of any further time, be it resolved that an emergency reserve fund be raised immediately.

I am sure railwaymen throughout the country will share this apprehension of the Working Committee. I for one fully do so. It has come to me as a great shock that while in the midst of serious economic crisis such as the ever rising cost of living, labour behaved with such singular sense of responsibility, in contradistinction to the treacherous strike of capital, it was not suffering labour that received any consideration in Government's disinflation policy, but capital. In view of Government's policy, I cannot but be apprehensive of the future.

Labour has so far sacrificed in the national interest. Now after the solution of the Hyderabad problem the nation is secure from the internal disorder and immediate national danger has passed. In view of this improved position labour would be completely justified in pressing its demands. The plea of crisis has too long been used as excuse for inaction. The plea no longer can hold water. In any case, there is no justice in asking labour alone to bear all the burdens of crisis. The time has come for labour to act.

Visualizing all this the Working Committee of your Federation decided that Railwaymen should be prepared for any emergency that might arise. As a first step towards this preparation, the Committee decided to raise a Railwaymen's Emergency Fund. The Fund will be raised by the affiliated unions under the direct supervision and control of the Federation. This fund will be used only for the purpose of meeting the emergency as and when it may arise and not for the day-to-day work of the unions or of the Federation. In case no emergency arises and there is an amicable settlement, for which all of us pray and hope, this Fund will be kept as a reserve for future emergencies or put to such use as the Federation may decide. Fifty per cent of the Fund will be left with the unions and the remaining will be deposited with the Federation. All contributions received towards this Fund must be put in a separate account with banks that are sanctioned by the Federation in consultation with the unions concerned.

I appeal to everyone of you to contribute as generously as you can to this Fund. No one should contribute less than a rupee.

During my contacts with you in every part of the country at meetings, conferences and private discussions I found among you a feeling of impatience at the Federation's cautious ways and I got the impression that you were all itching for action and that only a word was necessary to be given for all the nine lakhs of railwaymen to rally to the call of the Federation and to do or die. Here then is a test for you. This Emergency Fund will test your earnestness and seriousness.

I shall judge more by your contributions to this Fund, than by your slogans and shows of enthusiasm, your seriousness of purpose. If you do not contribute to this Fund I shall know that you are not serious about the struggle of which so many of you talked so bravely. I hope you will succeed in this preliminary test. Remember, if things do not go well you have far severer tests facing you. Let me warn you before I close against giving your contributions to false and fraudulent men. The coupon books for this Fund are being printed by the Federation and will bear the name of Mr. S. Guruswamy, the General Secretary of your Federation, and the stamp of your union. Do not give any money except for such authentic coupons. I hope by that time the General Council meets at Nagpur on the 25th of November this Emergency Fund will have been fully subscribed to and everyone of you will have paid his due.

Wishing you all success.

70. Address to the General Council of the All-India Railwaymen's Federation, Nagpur, 24 November 1948[1]

At Lilooah I had advised railwaymen to exercise restraint and desist from strike action in view of the grave situation in the country. Circumstances have changed since then and I am not prepared now to tender you the same advice. What action you should take is a matter which you alone should decide. I am not a railwayman and am not liable to suffer on account of any decision you might take. But I am no longer prepared to hold you back. I shall briefly explain how my position has altered in the past few months.

When I counselled restraint at Lilooah, I received universal praise for what was described as my sanity and good sense. I have not lost my sanity or my good sense nor have I begun to look at problems from any point of view other than that of national good and the good of the common people.

When we met at Lilooah, conditions in our country were grave and all of us were filled with anxiety. Hyderabad was like a knife thrust into the very heart of the country and the people and the Government were undecided as to how to meet that grave calamity. There were also fears of internal instability, howsoever remote, and of a war with Pakistan. The brilliant

[1] *Janata*, 5 December 1948.

success of the police action in Hyderabad and the demonstration of national solidarity during the course of those anxious days have removed all fear of internal danger and disintegration. Nor is there any longer any fear of a war with Pakistan. Those who even now talk of the nation as if it were a house of cards, ready to collapse at the mildest breath of misfortune, are merely trying to create fear complex in the people so that they might be made subservient to their dictatorial rule.

Under these improved conditions, it is no longer necessary for labour or any other section of the people to hold in abeyance its struggle for a better life. It is true that economic conditions in the country continue to be grave and a truce on the industrial front is still as desirable as before. I am sure that except for a small section, the working class in India is still prepared to play ball, but it is wrong to ask labour to play the game while the other side folds up its arms and refuses to field. As the Labour Minister, Mr. Jagjivan Ram, said the other day, labour has responded to the call of the nation and acted with a due sense of responsibility. It is the other side, namely, the employers and the State which have failed to do their duty. In the meanwhile, the condition of labour has deteriorated to such an extent that if concerted action is not taken by labour the whole economic life of the country will go to rack and ruin and there will be chaos and anarchy.

Therefore, paradoxical as it might appear, the time has come when labour must act deliberately and concertedly even if it means a break of the truce, to which in any case, no one except labour has adhered, so that the essential conditions for an industrial truce might be created in this country.

If labour did not do so now, I am afraid, it will not be able to act in a concerted manner in the future. Fetters are being fashioned to bind labour hand and foot and allow it no freedom of action. Had the Government taken steps in the economic sphere that had convinced labour that it was serious about checking the steady fall in working class standard of living. I should have continued to advocate a policy of restraint. But in spite of so many months of ceaseless agitation by all the labour organizations in this country, the Government, in spite of its pious professions, has failed to do anything concrete to lighten the burden of the working class. Prices have continuously been rising. The index number today, I am sure, is not less than 380 as compared with 260 on the basis of which the recommendations of the Central Pay Commission were made. In the face of this steady fall in the real wages of labour, the latter has hitherto acted with exemplary self-control and in the spirit of patriotism. But it is unfair to expect labour alone to bear the full brunt of inflation.

As I have said above, had the Government shown that it were serious in the matter and was taking adequate steps to reduce prices, labour would have held its patience some time longer. But the past months have shown that the Government have only been tinkering with the problem and are not serious. Their disinflation policy has failed hitherto to check prices and there is hardly any one except the Government who believes that it will produce any result in the future.

In its disinflation policy the Government made considerable concessions to capital but paid no heed to labour at all.

It is true that the Prime Minister said the other day that his Government was considering the problem of the rising cost of living. The Government had more than a year now in which to consider this question, but with no result. I am convinced, therefore, that unless there is a concerted action on the part of labour, the Government will not wake up to the reality of the situation. If the anti-inflation policy of the Government results only in a steady cut in the real wages of the working class, that policy should be described as an anti-labour policy rather than anti-inflation. I do say that the present economic policy of the Government is not anti-inflation so much as anti-labour.

As regards the Railway Ministry's reply to the resolutions of the Lilooah Conference, I shall not pre-judge the issue by expressing my opinion. It is for you to determine how far the Government has met the demands of the Railwaymen. I must however, draw your attention to the Railway Ministry's changed attitude towards the Federation. It seems clear to me that the Ministry is trying to bypass the Federation and ultimately destroy it.

The present Government and its supporters are ever ready to stigmatise everything that the independent labour organizations are doing today as partisan and actuated by political motives. But recent developments have shown that there can hardly be a Government more partisan and actuated by motives of Party gain than the present one. Since 1930, during even the darkest days of British rule, the all-India Railwaymen's Federation has been treated as the sole representative of Indian railwaymen. The Federation has never been the tool of any party though men of all political views have been its members. It has always been, as it is today, a non-political industrial organization of railwaymen. Yet, today the Railway Administrations, under instructions from above, are trying their best to disrupt the Federation, in the interest of the party in power, by bolstering up a rival Federation and assisting the Congress Railway unions. Just the other day the Railway Ministry administered another blow to the Federation by negotiating with a sectional organization outside the fold of the Federation. I, therefore, urge you to keep in view this serious danger to your great organization and refuse to play into the hands of the Government.

Thus, taking into consideration the improved political conditions in the country and the Government's anti-labour policy, I have come to the conclusion that it would be wrong to ask labour to hold itself back. In fact, I do definitely believe that the time has come for concerted action by the whole working class or at least by all the employees of the State. The Post and Telegraph employees have already decided to take a strike ballot, as you know, and they are anxious to act in concert with railwaymen. I am sure railwaymen are equally anxious to act in concert with them. There may be employees of other departments of the Government also eager to join such a move. We should welcome their co-operation and so determine our course of action that they may also be able to fall in line with us.

There is a personal aspect of the question which has been causing me some anxiety, and I wish to place it before you. I am not a railwayman as you know and belong to a party that is in opposition to the party in power. This is apt to create misunderstanding and injure your cause. Whatever advice I may give you or whatever action I might take, is likely to be interpreted by the Government and its subservient press, which, I am sorry to say, has consistently shown an anti-labour attitude in the past months, to have been actuated by partisan motives. Therefore, if you think that my being at the head of your organization will handicap you and will place your struggle in a partisan light, I shall be happy if you choose another person for this high office. In this matter as in every other I am completely at your disposal.

Lastly let me assure you that whatever decision you might take, I shall be with you through thick and thin till the end and do anything that lies in my power to help your cause.

71. To Jawaharlal Nehru, 30 November 1948[1]

My dear Bhai,

Mr. Dalvi[2] with another representative of the Postmen met you a few days ago. Yesterday representatives of the three largest unions of P & T workers, i.e., The All India Postmen & Lower Grade Staff Union, The Federation of Post and Telegraph Unions and the Union of Post and Telegraph Workers, met here and decided jointly to seek an interview with you. They have asked me to lead their delegation. I happen to be president of the first two organizations.

I shall be grateful if you could give us some time in the afternoon of the 10th December. It is not right for me to name the date and time, but I am in difficulty as on no other day about that time I am free to go to Delhi. So, I hope you will find it possible to grant us an interview on the 10th December at any time in the afternoon. I shall be grateful for a reply.

[1] *J.P. Papers* (NMML).

[2] V.G. Dalvi; Advocate, Bombay High Court and General Secretary of the All India Postmen and Lower Grade Staff Union.

I hope you will excuse me for writing a personal letter in a matter such as this.

With kindest regards,

Affectionately,
J.P.

72. Inaugural Address at Socialists Workers' Training Class, Ahmedabad, 1 December 1948[1]

There is no fundamental difference between Gandhism and Socialism. But the way in which the Government of the country is being conducted in the name of Gandhism since the attainment of freedom shows that the country is heading towards Fascism and not Socialism.

There can be no democracy without civil liberties, but in India with a Socialist Premier there is no civil liberty for a party in opposition as in Russia.

Men like Mr. Achyut Patwardhan are being arrested by a Mamlatdar, and treated like ordinary criminals. Sec.144 is being applied to suppress all labour movements except that of the Indian National Trade Union Congress.

There can be only armed rebellion where civil liberties are suppressed. The Socialist Party of India is still following the principle of non-violence, but non-violence is not possible for all. Even Mahatma Gandhi preferred violence to cowardice.

After seceding from the Congress the Socialist Party is trying to unite with all parties except the Communists, who are fifth columnists, so as to form a united socialist party pledged to establish a classless and casteless society on the lines of Mahatma Gandhi's thinking.

[1] Adapted from *Bombay Chronicle*, 2 December 1948.

73. Interview to the Press, Bombay, 3 December 1948[1]

Question: What are the minimum demands the satisfaction of which would induce labour to reconsider their attitude?

Jayaprakash Narayan: The minimum the workers would accept as the basis for negotiation would be the linking up of dearness allowance with the cost of living index. This would go a long way in satisfying the main grievance of labour. Absolute implementation of the Pay Commission's recom-

[1] Adapted from *Hindu*, 4 December 1948.

mendations in this respect is essential. The minimum dearness allowance of Rs. 55 for a wage of Rs. 30 per month should immediately be granted. It would then be possible to negotiate the satisfaction of certain sectional demands of the different groups of workers. It is unjustifiable on the part of the Government not to link the rising cost of living with proper wages and dearness allowance.

Q: What line of approach you would adopt when you meet Pandit Nehru?

J.P.: The recent consultative conference of non-Communist and non-Congress trade union workers has already expressed their clear opinion on the Central Government's economic and labour policy, describing it as more anti-labour than anti-inflation. The resolution had already been forwarded to Pandit Nehru. We shall wait for his reaction before deciding our future policy. In the meanwhile we shall do whatever we can to mobilize public opinion in favour of labour's point of view regarding their demands.

The next conference of labour representatives is to be held at Calcutta on December 24 and 25 to form a new labour organization on an all-India basis and the various trade unions in the country outside the Congress and Communist groups would be sending their delegates to this conference. The name and constitution of the new body would also be decided at that meeting.

Q: Is the Industrial Truce being implemented? Will it not be contrary to that understanding if labour organizes a coordinated strike now?

J.P.: When the Industrial Truce decision was arrived at eleven months ago, certain important conditions had been attached to it. From Labour's point of view, these conditions have not been fulfilled from the other side. The Central Advisory Committee of Labour, which sat at Lucknow to decide the question of fair wages and industrial relations, has done nothing to meet labour's demands. The Government have shown great hesitancy and in-decision in tackling the problems seriously and this has caused great anxiety in the ranks of labour. If the Government were serious, they could adopt the suggestion of Mr. N.M. Joshi to set up a statutory committee which should meet continuously at Delhi and consider the problems determinedly and not break up unless and until certain concrete decisions are made.

The government themselves, as an employer of labour should be a model to other employers and see that labour is not harassed from all sides.

Q: Is the labour justified in going on strike when a national crisis faced India and increased production is of utmost importance?

J.P.: In my opinion, the national crisis is now over and labour would be justified in taking action because nothing has been done even on such a clear issue as dearness allowance. Conditions today are more stable than a year ago and unless labour takes timely action, undesirable elements would infiltrate into the labour organizations and create chaos in their ranks. Organized action on the part of labour would obviate that danger and also compel the Government to look into their demands. If the people as a whole realized that something grave might happen, public opinion too would persuade the government to apply their minds to the question in a spirit of urgency.

As regards increased production and output, this can only be achieved if all the elements involved were satisfied. Production can not be increased by giving one-sided concessions to capitalists, for example, in the matter of taxation and import and supply facilities and expecting labour alone to be patriotic. Under such conditions, all efforts to fight the economic crisis would fail. Capital is refusing to make sacrifices. They are not contributing according to their capacity to Government loans or savings schemes. On the other hand, they indulge in anti-national activities such as operations in the blackmarket. The remedy for this situation is nationalization. But even now in the partial nationalization that has been carried out, old-time bureaucrats are still in control at the top and labour has no hand in management. True industrial democracy is only possible when labour is able to participate in the control and management of industries to an appreciable extent.

Q: Is there any justification for the charge that Socialists are playing a role that the Communists welcomed and whether the socialists would support the Government in the event of a Communist movement like that in Malaya and Burma developing?

J.P.: The Communists have never been successful in exploiting the ideals of the Socialists. The Socialists are much more anti-communist than the Congress and they are fighting the Communists with greater determination and a clearer understanding of issues than the Congress. It is the Congress people as a matter of fact, who are responsible for some trade unions going into the hands of Communists, as for example in Cawnpore and in Bengal.

74. To Jitendra Mehta, 4 December 1948[1]

My dear Jitubhai,[2]

I thank you for the Gujarati papers you have sent. My Indore tour has been cancelled and I am here [Bombay] till the 10th morning. I shall be very

[1] *J.P. Papers* (NMML).

[2] A prominent Socialist Leader of Ahmadabad.

grateful if you could send me at least 5000 rupees for the Khoj Parishad before I leave Bombay. Instead of sending the money by post you might come down to Bombay for a day or telephone to some firm or bank here to send me the cheque. In any case, please give me a ring at Purshottam's place on any night between 10 and 10.30 p.m.

Thanking you,

Very sincerely yours,
J.P.

75. To Pratap Shah, 4 December 1948[1]

My dear Pratap,

Thank you for your letter of the 1st December. I was very keen, as you know, to meet Indulalbhai[2] but due to the crowded programme I could not do so to my great regret. I am, however, enclosing a letter for him which I would like you to hand over to him.

Regarding Swamiji,[3] I had some talks with him. He has broken away from the Communists but he is now working with the Forward Bloc in Bihar. I do not know if it would be possible for the Bihar comrades to associate themselves with Swamiji's 60th birthday celebrations. I should like to leave the matter entirely in the hands of the Bihar friends. I am, however, working for an understanding with Swamiji and I am hopeful that it would be achieved. The consolidation arrived at the Labour Conference will help in bringing Swamiji closer to us.

I am writing to Jitu to send me at least 5000 rupees for the Khoj Parishad before I leave Bombay on the 10th morning. Please see that Jitu does not go slack in this matter.

Yours affectionately,
J.P.

[1] *J.P. Papers* (NMML).
[2] For biographical note on Indulal Yagnik see item 82 of this volume.
[3] For biographical note on Swami Sahajanand Saraswati, see *JPSW*, Vol. I, p. 147.

76. To Jawaharlal Nehru, 6 December 1948[1]

6 December 1948

To
The Prime Minister,
Government of India,
New Delhi,

Dear Sir,

I have the honour of forwarding a report on the conference of trade unionists which had been convened a few days ago at Bombay to consider:

1. Government's economic policy with special reference to the measures recently announced to combat inflation;
2. The failure of the Government to implement the recommendations of the Central Pay Commission about linking dearness allowance with the cost of living; and
3. Government's legislation and machinery for the solution of industrial disputes that abridge the basic rights of the workers.

The report contains a brief introduction, the resolutions of the Conference, my welcome speech and the address of the President, Mr. N.M. Joshi. I like particularly to draw your attention to the resolutions and the concrete proposals made by Mr. Joshi, and I hope they will receive your earnest consideration.

The trade unionists gathered at the Conference are meeting again at Calcutta at Christmas and I shall be obliged to have your reactions to the proposals of the Conference, so that we might determine our future course of action in their light.

With the highest regards,

Sincerely yours,
Jayaprakash Narayan

[1] *Brahmanand Papers* (NMML).

77. To Madhu Limaye, 7 December 1948[1]

Dear Madhu,

I should have written to you earlier about the meeting of the Executive. At Patna I had a talk with Ramnandan regarding the All India Kisan Conference.

[1] *J.P. Papers* (NMML).

You probably know that the C.P. Party was not in a position to hold the conference in December. So Ramnandan postponed the conference and told me that he was fixing the dates sometime in the third or fourth week of January, and he suggested that the Party Executive should also meet at about the same time and same place. Ramnandan told me later that the dates of the Kisan Conference have been fixed immediately after the National Executive dates, which should also meet at Raigarh. I do not think it would be possible for members of the Executive to travel to two different places at the same time, once for the Kisan Conference and then again for the Executive. Therefore, if the Kisan Conference is going to be held at about that time the Executive should meet a few days earlier and at the same place. You may send a wire to Ramnandan at Patna and find out from him where and when the Kisan Conference is meeting and you may fix the dates of the Executive accordingly.

Affectionately yours,
J.P.

P.S. I had telephoned to Rammanohar from Patna to enquire about his accident. He suggested to me then to call the National Executive to consider the international situation. I told him that it would be better if he called the Foreign Policy Committee. He agreed. I suggested the end of December and Bombay for the time and venue. To that also he agreed. I do not know if he has written to you. If not, please call a meeting of the Foreign Policy Committee on the 29th December at Bombay. Please write to Rammanohar also.

J.P.

78. To Jawaharlal Nehru, 10 December 1948[1]

My dear Bhai,

You may remember the letter you had written me some time ago—it was delivered by hand when I was in Delhi. I have been waiting for some time to reply to that letter but never had the necessary time to do it. Had not a recent incident occurred I would not have written this letter at all?

A few days ago I was at Nagpur in connection with the meeting of the Railwaymen's Federation. The local branch of the Socialist Party wanted to hold a public meeting for me, and they applied for permission—there being Section 144 in force in Nagpur. The Magistrate refused permission;

[1] *Brahmanand Papers* (NMML).

my friends went up to Pandit Misra:[2] he too said no. The plea was that since a communist meeting had been prohibited a few days before, it was not possible to permit a socialist meeting! Meetings of the Congress could of course be held.

You wrote in your letter of the growing bitterness among Congressmen and us. But can it be otherwise, if this is how the Congress behaves? I cannot tell you how I felt when I heard that my meeting was not permitted. There is nothing that I ask for from freedom—no dividends of any kind; but at least I expect to enjoy the ordinary freedom of a citizen in a free society. If there is danger of the peace being disturbed as a result of my speech, then all that I can say is that in that case the peace deserves to be disturbed.

The day I had seen you in Delhi last, I had read in the morning of Achyut's arrest. How that news had upset me I cannot describe. I had intended to speak to you about it, but your mind was naturally on your recent European visit and then Pandit Pant came in and I felt I had no right to intrude upon your time any longer. But there cannot be a more eloquent commentary on the freedom that the Congress has bestowed upon the country than the manner of Achyut's arrest and his treatment by the police and the prison authorities. Here is a man of the eminence of Achyut, whose services to the country are second to none and whose character and patriotism are unsurpassed, being hustled into prison by a petty Mamlatdar for no reason whatever. You probably do not know the story. Achyut was about to address a peaceful audience of about 3000 in a small town when about 30 Congress goondas tried by raising persistent slogans to prevent the meeting from proceeding. The crowd was patient and quietly stood its ground. The goondas, however, went on raising slogans upon which the Mamlatdar went up to Achyut and suggested that the meeting be disbanded. That was an extraordinary proposition, and it was amazing that the custodian of peace should make it. Achyut naturally protested upon which the official announced that he would promulgate Section 144 which he did. The crowd refused to disperse and Achyut announced that he would not leave the platform; on that he and his colleagues were arrested! I cannot imagine a grosser mis-application of law and commonsense. That goondas who deliberately attempt to prevent peaceful citizens from carrying on their legitimate activities, should be left untouched and men of position and character should be treated as goondas and punished is an example of misrule of which the British imperialists could well have been proud. Will you please imagine what would have happened if the roles at Achyut's meeting were reversed. Imagine the meeting to have been convened by the Congress

[2] For biographical note on D.P. Misra see *JPSW*, Vol. II, p. 173.

and that Mr. Shankerrao Deo[3] was to have addressed it, and that instead of the 30 goondas being Congressmen suppose they were socialists. Can you imagine the Mamlatdar arresting Mr. Shankerrao Deo? It were far more likely that there would have been a lathi charge, if not shooting, and instead of only the 30 goondas being arrested three hundred would have been jailed. After his arrest, Achyut was taken in an open truck to the police station and in the same manner to the Nasik Prison and lodged there together with ordinary criminal under-trials. During the British days I was arrested many times but not once was I taken to prison in an open truck, and they always treated men like you with great consideration and respect. Under your rule even an Achyut Patwardhan is no different from an ordinary criminal. I am enclosing herewith a story of the arrest and release as related by Achyut himself to the Free Press. If you have the time and the inclination you might glance through it. Such things are happening to lesser socialists in worse forms all over the country and our Congress carpet-baggers have hardly time left from their pursuit of happiness even to find out what is happening.

In these conditions I wonder what else can happen than bitterness. But yet, strange as it would appear, the bitterness is more marked on the other side rather than on ours. The Congress people are bitter because they are Almighty God and none may dare criticize or oppose them. They have developed a totalitarian attitude and they believe that none except them has any business to live in this country. Sardar Patel is reported to have said at Nagpur that "those who disagree with us are free to leave the country". Whether it is encouragement to charkha, organization of cooperatives, celebration of Independence Day or Gandhi Jayanti or anything else, big or small, the Congress is not prepared to work with any one else except its own hangers-on and yes men. The Congress is determined by hook or crook, by intimidation and coercion, by corruption, by falsehood and misrepresentation, by trading in the name of Mahatma Gandhi, to remain in the ruling party in the country. Democracy, socialism are mere words that the Congress bandies about with no faith in either and with the open cynicism of all those who would rape the masses. If the Congress has any regard for democracy, the first thing it ought to do now is to repeal all the Public Safety Acts. There is no emergency now to justify them in the least.

No one doubts, least of all I, that you are determined honestly to lead the country as you said in your letter in a particular direction. But a solitary leader, no matter how great, cannot by himself lead a whole nation to Socialism. I am not writing in disparagement. You are undoubtedly a great man, and there is no need for me to repeat it, but even you cannot lead millions of people and a vast country like India to the goal of Socialism

[3] For biographical note on Shankerrao Deo see *JPSW*, Vol. IV, p. 88.

without the active support of a widespread socialist movement reflected strongly in the highest councils of the nation. How many socialists are there in your Cabinet, how many in the Party you lead in the Constituent Assembly? How many provincial ministries are socialist? How many Provincial Congresses are socialist? Is it Socialism that is the driving force behind the Congress or is it, in the vast majority of cases, the hunger for personal gain and power? Since you came into Government what steps has it taken towards Socialism? What planning has been done for it? Everywhere and at every turn Socialism is being put on the shelf. Even where an opportunity offered itself to build up a sector of the national economy on a basis of Socialism, the opportunity was thrown away. In the East Punjab and elsewhere hundreds and thousands of refugees were settled on the land. No socialist government would have allowed such a golden opportunity to slip away. All the refugees would have been compulsorily settled in cooperative communities. But if you want to know how keen your Government has been to develop such colonies, you have only to enquire from Kamaladevi who has a heart-breaking story to tell. Even the halting agrarian legislations in the provinces are being put off on one excuse or the other. Nationalization has been shelved for 10 years. In the disinflation policy, corrupt, non-cooperative, unpatriotic, tax-evading capitalism has been given large concessions whereas labour, which has played the game, has been left in the cold on pretexts that even a school boy should think twice to advance. The only method your Government can think of to check inflation is to allow the real wages of the workers to fall steadily. There is no doubt that you will hold fast to the faith that you are leading the country to Socialism, but let me say without malice or rancour that in spite of your best intentions, the country is drifting in the opposite direction. You are trying to ride two horses which may be possible in circuses but not in a historical evolution. History can move only in one direction and not two at the same time. You want to go towards Socialism, but you want the Capitalists to help in that. You want to build Socialism with the help of Capitalism. You are bound to fail in that. If you want Capitalism to play its role in industrializing the country, it will demand its price and if you pay the price, you will give a go-by to Socialism. That is exactly what is happening today. Bold and drastic measures are necessary, in the place of which we get half-hearted diluted measures.

You are a believer in first things first, but I thought the very first thing you would do today was to reform the whole system of administration and the Services. You cannot make the present system yield results which it never was intended to do. But I do not see that any step has been taken in this direction. There was corruption under British rule against which all of us spoke strongly. There is more corruption under Congress rule and I see no instance of any serious attempt being made to root it out or even to check it. Nepotism and favouritism are prevalent in the highest quarters, and it is often the corrupt civil servant, who being conversant with the art of pleasing his masters whoever they may be, that prospers. You have tremendous personal popularity in the country and the Congress has still a vast capital of past services to draw upon, and therefore you may not realize what is happening or where are we drifting. Take the Constitution that is being drafted. Future generations will realize, even if we do not, how difficult any progressive social legislation would become on account of the safeguards which have been deliberately introduced. I am afraid I may annoy you by my bluntness, but I am confident, that had you been in my place you would have used far stronger language.

I shall be meeting you in the evening with representatives of post and telegraph workers. I have no authority from the Railwaymen's Federation to speak to you on their behalf but as one who is genuinely interested in helping the Indian State to go forward and one who loves and admires you, I should like to say that had not politics entered into the Transport Ministry, the Federation would not have been driven to the strike decision. Men like Khandubhai Desai[4] are going about exclaiming that it is the socialists who are trying to exploit labour for their own political ends. I assure you if there is anyone who wants to exploit labour more than anyone else, it is men like Khandubhai Desai. Every thing that these gentlemen are doing, as legislators or labour ministers or trade union leaders, has been actuated by a single motive, namely, how to control labour and deliver it to the Congress tied hand and foot. The INTUC is to my mind the greatest danger to free trade unionism in this country. No one would have minded if the INTUC used ordinary trade union methods to fight rivals in the field. But they are using legislation, going to the length of illegalising strikes, the Public Safety Act, the Government machinery and the employers to suppress independent trade unions. The chief role of the Congress unions today is that of strike-breaking. They talk of Gandhian methods, but they are no better than the communists in the matter of bogus membership, and they do not stop at hooliganism.

The dock-workers in Bombay are on strike again. The tiny-gods at Delhi must be feeling indignant and gnashing their teeth over the irresponsibility of labour leaders. Well, this is not a socialist union, but I have the fullest sympathy with the workers. According to the recent Conciliation Board decision, 1500 new hands have to be recruited. The Port Trust is recruiting these hands from amongst Sindhi refugees through the rival Congress union. The older Union, which undoubtedly holds sway today, peacefully

[4] Khandubhai Karsanji Desai (1898-1975); joined the Non-Cooperation Movement (1920) was Secretary of I.N.T.U.C., 1947-50 and later its President, 1950-3; a member of Bombay Legislative Assembly, 1937-9 and 1946-50, the Constituent Assembly of India 1946-50, Lok Sabha, 1952-7, and Rajya Sabha, 1959-68, Union Minister of Labour 1954-7.

demonstrated against this before the Port Trust. The Union's claim may be right or wrong and its demonstration unwarranted. But the demonstration was entirely peaceful. The Port Trust Authority did not complain to the Police or seek their help. Yet, seven of the leaders of the Union were hauled up after the demonstration and thrown into prison under the Public Security Act on the fictitious plea that breach of peace was apprehended! The workers have struck in protest and are demanding the release of their leaders. They are completely justified. But the Government says, go back to work first. The real motive behind all this is to smash the inconvenient union and bring forward the Congress union. The INTUC, the Police, the Government, the stevedores all against the helpless workers. The Pathan striking workers, I should add, have been warned privately by the Pathan Police—the Bombay Police have a Pathan Branch of the Force—that if they did not return to work, they would be repatriated to their home! Can you imagine a worse form of coercion?

To return to the Railwaymen. I am sure that had Dr. Matthai been in the Transport Ministry this break between the Ministry and the Federation would have been avoided. But I am afraid, Mr. Santhanam's[5] coming into the Ministry and his being made responsible for its labour policy, has introduced an overdose of politics. It is true that I am the President of the Railwaymen's Federation, but my being its president does not make the Federation a socialist body any more than your being the Prime Minister makes the Central Government socialist. I am sure that had I not been there, the strike would have come earlier. Today I am attacked and abused for exploiting railwaymen for political purposes, but till the Lilooah conference of the Federation, i.e. for nearly a year and a half it was I who ceaselessly tried to keep the men in check and dissuade them from taking extreme steps. Why did I not try to exploit the men before? Why must, I do it only now? I have it on good authority that the plan of Santhanam and Khandubhai Desai and people higher up is to force us into a fight and then let loose the weapons of repression and crush us and then bring forward the official, or company union, the rival Indian National Railwaymen's Federation. The total membership of the affiliated unions of our Federation is $4^1/_2$ lakhs whereas the membership of the rival federation is no more than 50,000. It was formed on the ground that certain unions were not allowed to affiliate with us. This is false because all those unions that are entitled to join the Federation are free to do so. I have no doubt that you can put us all in jail and crush the strike if it comes off, but repression is no solution either of a national or a labour problem. It will only lead to bitterness and perhaps more desperate forms of opposition. Also it must be realized that the workers cannot be

[5] For biographical note on K. Santhanam see *JPSW*, Vol. II, p. 262.

made to work by repression. You may break their strike and drive them back to work, but you cannot by force make them work. As Mr. [N.M.] Joshi reminded the Government the other day, you can take the horse to the water, but you cannot make him drink. Further, I must add that I too do have a certain self-respect and as long as I am the President of the Federation, I will not allow it to be crushed. I do not think that it is too late even now. The General Council of the Federation in its strike resolution has expressly said that the door to negotiations was not closed. I don't, however, think that Mr. Santhanam would be able to rise to the occasion. You alone can do something effective in the matter, but you must realize that mere words will not do. The railwaymen and other State employees have a strong case and substantial concessions must be made before they are expected to compromise.

I should like to draw your attention to another aspect of the question. As Socialists we all believe in nationalization, but if labour is going to have the same status in nationalized industries as railwaymen have in the Railway industry, then nationalization would have no meaning at all. Nationalization does't mean bureaucratisation and bureancratic rule. Nationalization is a step towards industrial democracy. What democracy is there in the Railways? They are being run today by a handful of bureaucrats, just as they were in the days of the British. These bureaucrats may be members of Parliament but the meaning of industrial democracy is not only that a few ministers responsible to Parliament will hold in their hands all the economic power in the country. That would be centralization of economic power worse than what we have in Capitalism. I am sure you are conscious of this problem. I mentioned it to you once before, but I do not see that anything is being done in this behalf. The Railwaymen's Federation has been and is the sole representative of the railwaymen. As such it should have been given a share in the running of the Railways equal to that of the bureaucrats. But since Mr. Santhanam's coming, even the position that the Federation had before has deteriorated. For instance, it was the practice that the Railway Board never came to any major decisions concerning conditions of service, etc., without first consulting the Federation. Recently the Railway Ministry has taken vital decisions without any reference to us. For instance, their decision regarding the Grain Shops. I am enclosing herewith a copy of my letter to Mr. Iyengar[6] which further puts our point of view. Therefore, if your mind has not already been made up, and if you have not decided to have it out once for all with the so-called trouble-makers like us, I suggest that you

[6] N. Gopalaswami Ayyangar (1882-1953); served in the Madras Civil Service, 1905-37, member, Indian Legislative Assembly, 1927, member, Council of States 1944-6, Dewan Jammu & Kashmir, 1937; joined Central Cabinet in 1947 as minister without portfolio, Minister of Railways, 1948-April 1952, Minister of Defence, 1952-3.

take the initiative and call the representatives of the Federation and try to find a way out. I have written all this because it is difficult for me to say these things when I meet you, and I also want you to have read this letter if possible before I meet you, so that you might be able to tell me something definite about the matter. The strike ballot on the railways does not begin before the 1st of January and therefore there is the whole of December in which negotiations may be held. I would be happy if matters concerning labour were left in the hands of Mr. Iyengar rather than in those of Mr. Santhanam because the latter is bound to take a partisan view on every issue, if for nothing else because of the reason that I happen to be the unfortunate president of the Railwaymen's Federation.

Yours,
J.P.

79. To Gopalaswami Ayyangar, 13 December 1948[1]

The Federation understands fully that the general basis of the recommendations of the Central Pay Commission cannot be altered. The Federation has not demanded such alteration. The Railway Board, however, must be aware that in several specific instances the recommendations of the C.P.C. have, in fact, been modified. For instance, the limit of Rs. 2,000 as the highest salary recommended by the C.P.C. was raised to Rs. 3,000. Again, on the representation of the Federation the minimum scale of skilled workshop staff was raised from Rs. 50 to Rs. 55 a month.

The creation of many unauthorized grades by the Railway Board is another instance in point. Many other instances can be adduced, but these are enough to establish that the recommendations of the C.P.C. have often been altered. Yet, our demand is not for alteration of the C.P.C. basis. Wherever the demand of the Federation, when superficially considered, appears to be a demand for alteration of the basis of the C.P.C. recommendations, closer examination would show that the demand seeks only the removal of a grave anomaly or an injustice that a literal application of the C.P.C. has led to.

Regarding the demand for dearness allowance to be linked to the price index, it is strange that it does not occur to the Government that it is they who are altering the basic recommendations of the C.P.C. The Federation, on the other hand, is demanding nothing more than that the recommendations of the C.P.C. should be put into force.

Regarding the disinflation measures adopted by the Government, the

[1] The letter was sent to Gopalaswami Ayyangar, then Minister of Railways and Transport, Government of India on 13 December 1948 and released to the press by J.P. on 26 December 1948, *Hindustan Times*, 28 December 1948.

Federation is in emphatic disagreement with the Railway Board. We are sure that these measures will never succeed in bringing down prices. Indeed, experience has shown that they have so far utterly failed. Therefore, the time-lag cannot be brushed aside on the plea that efforts are being made to shorten the period of the lag as far as possible. The 'regrets' of the Government cannot fill the stomachs of the workmen.

The reply of the Board to the demand regarding the States railway staff is wholly unsatisfactory. Even though the Constituent Assembly has not decided the relation of the States to the Centre, the latter has surely enough powers in the sphere of currency, communication and defence to interfere effectively in regard to them. We do to accept the plea that the Central Government are helpless in the matter, nor do we separate the Railway Board from the Central Government. If the Government, for instance, can impose Ministers and administrators of their own choice on the States, surely, they can interfere in the matter of working conditions and scales of pay on the State railways.

Before I close I should like to say a word about the charge that I am trying to exploit railwaymen for my own party ends. I have been President of the Federation for over a year and a half. Till recently I restrained railwaymen and appealed to them to give their best to the railway and to their country. I received praise from all concerned for my sobriety and good sense. Today I am being accused of exploiting labour. Why did I not try to exploit them before? And how am I exploiting them? It is not I who asked them to decide to take the strike ballot. It was entirely the decision of the affiliated unions. All I said was that I was not prepared to hold them back any more. The plea of national crisis no longer has the same force as before. There is still an economic crisis, it is true, but it is very largely the Government's own creation. I am sure that unless labour and the people generally compelled the Government to change their present economic policy, the economic crisis will not be mastered.

In the matter of the grain shops a grave injustice has been done to railwaymen and to the Federation. All the sins of that system have been laid at the door of labour, when it is quite clear that inefficient management and absence of a clear-cut policy and corruption among the higher officers are the chief causes of the enormous waste to and loss of revenue. The Federation itself had raised the question of efficient and honest working of the grain shops and the Railway Board had agreed to set up a joint committee to go into the matter. A resolution on this question was passed by the General Council of the Federation in October 1947 a copy of which has been sent to the Railway Board. Among other things the resolution appointed a committee of five representatives to discuss with the committee of the Railway Board ways and means of improving the working of the grain shops. The Railway Board never carried out this promise and this joint-committee never met. When the Grain Shop Inquiry Committee reported it was proper and just that the Federation should have been consulted before the recommendations were finally acted upon.

In this matter, as in many others, the Railway Board has not acted according to the undertaking that it had given to the Federation that no decision of importance affecting the railwaymen would be taken without consulting the Federation. The grain shops, as you know, were not established on a demand from the railway workers, but by the old Government of India because the British were anxious to get the full co-operation of the Indian Railways. Now when an existing privilage is being taken away at-a-time when life is as hard as it can be for the low-salaried employee, he cannot be expected to submit meekly. Even the grain shop concessions as they are today do not fully compensate for the rise in prices. In these circumstances, I fail to understand what justification there can be in closing down the grain shops. Because other Government employees do not get the same concession, that is no reason for taking it away from railwaymen. Rather, that is one more reason why the others too should not get at least the same concession. However, this question of grain shops is only a part of the larger question of an adequate dearness allowance. What the workers want is full compensation to make up for the rise in prices according to the formulas laid down by the C.P.C. itself. If full compensation is granted, the workers might not press for concessions in kind.

I think the grossest breach of agreement with the Federation has been in connection with the procedure agreed upon for reaching final conclusions on the implementation of the Pay Commission's recommendations.

It was definitely agreed between the Board and the Federation that after the railway administration had discussed with the Union concerned all questions connected with the implementation, the Board would formulate its decisions on every point which would then be discussed by the Federation, and only then would final decisions be taken.

Fourteen hundred references were made by the Board as deserving consideration. Even these were not all discussed with the Federation. There are still very serious anomalies and I am advised by competent railwaymen that unless they are removed the very functioning of the railways would be affected.

There are other such instances, but there is no need to lengthen this letter unduly. They can be discussed with the Railway Board if they are prepared to do so. The manner in which this whole question has been summarily dealt with by the Board created the impression that the Board did not care to secure the cooperation of the Federation and was indifferent to the cause of organized labour. A department which has to deal with nearly nine lakhs of employees cannot dispose of the labour issue so summarily and treat the largest industrial organization of Indian working men so cavalierly. In an industry of such dimensions, thousands of disputed questions are bound to arise and there must be a joint machinery at the highest level—for most questions are only for railway workers and the Railway Board to decide—to settle them. Those not settled should be sent to a tribunal or to an arbitrator.

The need for fixing of grades and of classification came up, but the Railway Board never showed any desire to win the confidence and co-operation of labour and treat it as an equal partner in a joint undertaking. The railways are a nationalized industry. What meaning has nationalization if company management is merely to be substituted with a bureaucratic management? Nationalization must lead to industrial democracy. Where is industrial democracy in railways?

Regarding the adjudication of the dispute regarding hours of work and leave rules, if one takes into account the uncondonable delays, one must appreciate the patience of the staff. The Adjudicator was appointed in April 1946. He gave his award in May 1947. The Government sat tight over it for a year and accepted only parts of it in May 1948. Even to-date the award has not been put into force. The award, as is well known, caused great discontentment among the running staff, and I had occasion to write about the matter to your predecessor in office, Dr. John Matthai. A special committee was then appointed by the Government, but so far no decisions have been announced.

Certain categories of workshop staff are sore on many wrong decisions of classification. In my last letter in June 1948, on which no appropriate action was ever taken, I had drawn the Railway Minister's attention to another grave breach of agreement with us. When the Workshop Tribunal was appointed, it was agreed that only those points would be referred to it as were in dispute between the Board and the Federation. In fact, even agreed points were referred to the Tribunal, which in the very nature of things was fantastic as only a dispute is sent to a tribunal and not an agreement. The Tribunal gave in many such cases decisions that were contrary to what was agreed upon between the Board and us. We protested and demanded a rectification of this wrong, but to no effect.

About several matters that fall out of the C.P.C. and the Adjudicator's award, the Board has replied that its reply is final. This is rather unfortunate, for these surely need further examination, and settlement in some other manner if mutual settlement is impossible. The Railway Board is in the position of an employer, and if in a dispute to which it is itself a party, it also becomes the final arbiter, it is surely assuming extraordinary powers to which no employer should be entitled.

You will excuse me for saying so, but a good deal of politics has recently entered into the Railway Ministry and those very gentlemen who accuse me of exploiting labour are themselves playing with the life of workers and turning them into pawns in their political game.

You know a rival railwaymen's federation has been brought into being, and the founders of this body are conspiring to destroy the A.I.R.F. by forcing it into a strike and then inducing the Government to crush it by repression. I am sure you are not a party to this conspiracy, but unless you take matters into your hand, unnecessary distress would be caused to hundreds of thousands of men and loss and inconvenience to the people and the Government.

The Federation is the sole representative of Indian railwaymen and it was treated as such even by the British, but the Railway Ministry is trying to disregard it and eventually destroy it. Hitherto, the Railway Department used to deal only with us. But now sectional organizations are being encouraged in the hope of dividing our ranks. Only recently the sectional running staff was called in for discussion. I protest against this action and consider it as a deliberate attempt to weaken the Federation.

Finally, I draw your attention to the Nagpur resolution which desires to inform the Government that the Federation is always prepared for an honourable settlement. I shall be glad to know what steps you suggest to that end.

80. To Jawaharlal Nehru, 13 December 1948[1]

My dear Bhai,

It was very kind of you to meet the Post and Telegraph Workers. I must confess, however, that they were rather disappointed. I too was not prepared to hear from you a rather common speech on the relation between inflation and wages. You will forgive me for saying that you did not seem to have applied your mind to the question. The disinflation policy of your Government came to labour as a great shock. Labour is not interested only in dearness allowance. Primarily it is interested in lowering of the price level. To that purpose it has made concrete suggestions, but they have gone unheeded. Proper disinflationary measures cannot be offset by rise in dearness allowance. In any case, what are workers to do when they are faced with continually falling wages? They do not hope to move the conservatives of the Finance Department and a somewhat complacent and slow-moving Government except by concerted action. I hope your

[1] *Brahmanand Papers* (NMML).

[2] See Appendix 4 for Nehru's reply to this letter.

Government will not use the cheap argument that they cannot yield to threats.

I should like to say a word about the Railwaymen. I have no authority from the Railwaymen's Federation to speak to you on their behalf but as one who is genuinely interested in helping the Indian State go forward, I should like to say that had not politics entered into the Transport Ministry, the Federation would not have been driven to the strike decision. Men like Khandubhai Desai are going about exclaiming that it is the socialists who are trying to exploit labour for their own political ends. I assure you if there is any group of persons who want, to exploit labour more than all others it is Khandubhai Desai and his friends. Every thing that these gentlemen are doing as legislators, Labour Ministers or trade union leaders—is actuated by a single motive, namely, how to control labour and deliver it to the Congress tied hand and foot. The INTUC is to my mind the greatest danger to free trade unionism in this country. No one would have minded if the INTUC used ordinary trade union methods to fight rivals in the field. But they are using legislation, going to the length of illegalising strikes, the Public Safety Act, the Administrative machinery and even the employers to suppress independent trade unionism. The chief role of the Congress Unions today is that of strike-breaking. They talk of Gandhian methods, but they are no better than the communists in the matter of bogus membership; and they do not stop at hooliganism.

The dock-workers were on strike in Bombay just a few days ago. The tin-gods at Delhi must have been indignant over the irresponsibility of labour leaders. Well, the union concerned is not a socialist union, but I had the fullest sympathy with the strikers. According to the recent Conciliation Board decision, many new hands had to be recruited. The Port Trust was recruiting these hands from amongst Sindhi refugees through the rival Congress union. The older union, which undoubtedly holds sway to-day, peacefully demonstrated against this before the Port Trust buildings. The Union's claim might have been right or wrong and its demonstration unwarranted. But the demonstration was entirely peaceful. The Port Trust Authority according to their won admission, did not complain to the police or seek their help. Yet, seven of the leaders of the union were hauled up after the demonstration and thrown into prison under the Public Security Act on the fictitious plea that breach of peace was apprehended. (Was Public Security Act meant for this purpose?). The workers struck in protest and demanded the release of their leaders. They were completely justified. But the Government said: go back to work first. The real motive behind all this was to smash the inconvenient union and bring forward the Congress Union. The INTUC, the Police, the Government, the stevedores were all in league against the helpless workers. The Pathans among the strikers, I should add, were warned privately by the Pathan Police—the Bombay Police Pathan branch of the Force—that if they did not return to work they would be repatriated to their home. Can you imagine a worse form of coercion? Well, the workers were coerced back to work, because otherwise their union would have been smashed and the Government union would have taken the front seat.

To return to the Railwaymen, I am sure that had Mr. Matthai been in the Transport Ministry this break between the Ministry and the Federation could not have occurred. But I am afraid, Mr. Santhanam's coming into the Ministry and his being made responsible for its labour policy, has introduced an overdose of politics. It is true that I am the President of the Railwaymen's Federation, but my being its President does not make the Federation a Socialist body any more than you being the Prime Minister makes the Central Government socialist. I am sure that had I not been there, the strike would have come earlier. Today I am attacked and abused for exploiting railwaymen to political ends, but till the Lilooah Conference of the Federation, i.e., for nearly a year and a half I ceaselessly tried o keep the men in check and dissuade them from taking extreme steps. Why did I not try to exploit the men before? Why must I do it only now? I have it on good authority that the plan of Santhanam and Khandubhai Desai and people higher up is to force us into a fight and then let lose the weapons of repression and crush us and bring forward the official, or company union, the rival Indian National Railwaymen's Federation. The total membership of the affiliated unions of our Federation is four and a half lakhs, whereas the membership of the rival Federation is no more than fifty thousand. It was formed on the ground that certain unions were not allowed to affiliate with us. This is false because all those unions that are entitled to join the Federation are free to do so.

I have no doubt that you can put us all in jail and may succeed even in crushing the strike if it comes off. But repression is no solution either of a national or a labour problem. It will only lead to bitterness and perhaps more desperate forms of opposition. Also it must be realized that the workers can not be made to work by repression. You may break their unity and drive them back to work, but you cannot by force make them work. As Mr. Joshi reminded the Government the other day, you can take the horse to the water, but you cannot make him drink. Further, I must add that I too do have a certain self respect and as long as I am the President of the Federation, I will not allow it to be crushed. I do not think that it is too late even now. The General Council of the Federation in its strike resolution has expressly said that the door to negotiations was not closed. I do not, however, think that Mr. Santhanam would be able to rise to the occasion. You alone can do something effective in the matter, but you must realize that more words will not do. The railwaymen and other State employees have a strong case and substantial concessions must be made before they are expected to compromise.

I should like to draw your attention to another aspect of the question. As

Socialists we all believe in nationalization, but if Labour is going to have the same status in nationalized industries as Railwaymen have in the Railway Industry, then nationalization would have no meaning at all. Nationalization is a step towards Industrial Democracy. What democracy is there in the Railways? They are being run to-day by a handful of bureaucrats, just as they were in the days of the British. These bureaucrats may be ministers of Parliament, but the meaning of Industrial Democracy is not that a few ministers responsible to Parliament will hold in their hands all the economic power in the country. That would be centralization of economic power worse than that we have in capitalism. I am sure you are conscious of this problem. I had mentioned it to you once before. But I do not see that any thing is being done in this behalf. The Railwaymen's Federation has been and is the sole representative of the railwaymen. As such it should have been given a share in the running of the Railways equal to that of the bureaucrats.

But since Mr. Santhanam's coming, even the position that the Federation had before has deteriorated. For instance, it was the practice that the Railway Board never came to any major decisions concerning conditions of service, etc., without first consulting the Federation. Recently the Railway Ministry has taken vital decisions without any reference to us. For instance, their decision regarding the Grain Shops. I am enclosing herewith a copy of my letter to Mr. Ayyangar which further puts our points of view. Therefore, if your mind has not already been made up, and if you have not decided to have it out once for all with the so-called trouble-makers like us, I suggest that you take the initiative and call the representatives of the Federation and try to find out a way. I have written all this because it is difficult for me to say these things when I meet you, and I also want you to have read this letter if possible before I meet you, so that you might be able to tell me something definite about the matter. The strike ballot on the railways does not begin before the 1st of January and therefore there is the whole of December in which negotiations may be held. I would be happy if matters concerning labour were left in the hands of Mr. Ayyangar rather than in those of Mr. Santhanam because the latter is bound to take a partisan view on every issue, if for nothing else because of the reason that I happen to be the unfortunate president of the Railwaymen's Federation.

Yours
J.P.

81. Address to the Students of the Lucknow University, 16 December 1948[1]

The Congress decision to stay in the Commonwealth, as also the pro-capitalist policy of the Government pursued at the cost of the common man, is to be condemned.

The country today is in a state of confusion since the leaders of its destiny are themselves divided over the goal to which they should steer the ship of the State. While Pandit Nehru talks of establishing Socialism, Sardar Patel pats the capitalists and asks them not to worry about the enemies of Capitalism. The Government are following a policy of mixed economy, staving off nationalization for the next 10 years, with disastrous results of high prices and inflation. The Government have succumbed to the blackmail of blackmarketeers, tax-evaders and unpatriotic capitalists and are now trying to deprive labour of its last weapon of strike to secure a living wage.

The ministers and Congress leaders are describing me as a traitor since I have asked labour to fight for its rights. These tendencies smell of fascism. Labour struck work in capitalist countries like America and Britain during the last war, but even Churchill did not call them traitors. But in India there are ministers like Mr. K. Santhanam who cannot think of a strike by labour under a government of the people. The intention of Mr. Santhanam is probably to reduce the trade union movement to something like Hitler's labour Front.

The Congress Working Committee's draft resolution about India's staying in the Commonwealth is a great shock to me because I cannot believe that the Lahore resolution of complete independence would be completely reversed. More strange, however, is the way the Constituent Assembly is enacting the constitution, where amendments after amendments are being withdrawn just on party-whips. I am surprised at the statement of Dr. Rajendra Prasad expressing himself against adult franchise.

The decision to stay in the Commonwealth would mean tying India's foreign policy to the apron-strings of the British Foreign Office and joining a fraternity of nations like South Africa and Australia which practise racial discrimination against Indians. Over and above this, India would become a perpetual enemy of the Soviet Union since she would be joining the American bloc.

I plead for an independent foreign policy aiming at a confederation of Asian and African countries pursuing progressive ideals with no designs of expansion. Arguments are being advanced that India's stay in the Commonwealth would enable her to carry out rapid industrialization and help her to organize her defence. But all these arguments are untenable

[1] Adapted from *Hindustan Times*, 30 December 1948.

because Britain would not be able to supply even ordinary capital goods for three years to come and because her defence system is entirely dependent on American aid.

Most of the princes in the states would have been popularly deposed but for the Government of India who have installed them as Rajpramukhs. Traitors like the Nizam, who had taken recourse to open resurrection against the Indian Government, are still princes of their domains and issue firmans.

I exhort the students to act as torchbearers and spread out in the country with the message of Socialism, and thus awaken the people to their tasks. The country, contrary to expectations that there would be a flush of new life after attainment of freedom, is dead today and it needs people to reawaken it and to shake off the belief which the mass of the people hold that they have now no responsibility except to depend on the Government for everything.

82. Statement to the Press, Lucknow, 29 December 1948[1]

The decision for a strike ballot is not mine nor of the Socialist Party, but of the railwaymen themselves. Actually, I have been telling them repeatedly that the country has been passing through delicate times, and that if they have any quarrel, it is with the Government and certainly not with the country. At the same time of course, I have told them plainly that if they thought a strike was necessary to press their demands, which I thought were reasonable, then I would be with them.

While Pandit Nehru told me on December 10 that the prices would gradually come down, the Finance Minister publicly stated that there was no intention to bring down prices but to stabilize them. I think that if prices obtaining now are to be stabilized, then the workers' allowance should also be stabilized on the basis of the existing prices. In spite of what Mr. Santhanam and others said, how can I dissociate myself from this just demand of the workers.

Half the responsibility for the present ills of the country belongs to those traitors who sustained the British Government and who are still enjoying the same power and position. Immediately after the British withdrawal they had begun to behave better, fearing that their old methods might put them in trouble. But they have again settled down to their old habits, thinking that their new masters are quite as good to them as the British. They are incapable of adjusting themselves to the changed conditions.

[1] Adapted from *National Herald*, 17 December 1948.

83. To Indulal Yagnik, 1 January 1949[1]

My dear Indulal bhai,[2]

Thanks for your letter of 8th December.

We have decided to convene a conference in the third week of February at Patna of Kisan workers in the country to form an all-India body. I will send you an invitation letter later.

The experience of the Labour Conference has not been very happy as far as little political groups and certain ambitious individuals are concerned. In calling this conference we shall be guided by the experience of the trade union movement. It is not possible in the context of political tasks to bring about unity on the mass front without even a working unity on the political front. Our party as an alternative to the Congress must be able to give to the masses a clear-cut political lead. This task is confused when the Party gets itself associated with a lot of little groups which are always quarrelling among themselves and which by themselves have no mass following. I hope this aspect of the peasant and labour movement will be kept in mind by you.

We shall be happy to have your co-operation and we hope to win Swamiji's[3] co-operation also, but if we aim at getting every little leftist group to join, the organization will lose all political significance. And what is a mass organization worth if it does not give a clear political lead to the people?

I have spoken to Chhotubhai already and I am sure our comrades in Gujarat will be very happy to have your co-operation. You may write at my Patna address.

With regards,

Sincerely yours,
Jayaprakash Narayan

[1] *J.P. Papers* (NMML).

[2] Indulal Yagnik (1892-1972). Lawyer and journalist; joined Servants of India Society and Home Rule Movement in Gujarat, 1917; participated in Kaira Satyagraha, 1918; Secretary, Gujarat, P.C.C., 1921; Secretary, Satyagraha Committee, Gujarat, 1923; imprisoned 1924-5; Assistant Editor, *Bombay Chronicle*, 1930; visited Germany, England and Ireland, 1932-3; returned and joined Kisan Sabha, 1936-9; imprisoned 1940-1; led Maha-Gujarat Movement, 1956; member, Lok Sabha, 1957-72.

[3] The reference here is to Swami Sahjanand Saraswati.

84. To Jawaharlal Nehru, 4 January 1949[1]

Dear Bhai,

I seem destined to trouble you every now and then about petty affairs. You will perhaps recall that towards the end of November last I had met you in Delhi with Rafi Saheb regarding certain demands of the All India Postmen & Lower Grade Staff Union, of which I happen to be the President. A serious situation has arisen now in connection with these demands.

Let me go back a little. The All India Postmen Union, like the All India Railwaymen's Federation, had decided at the beginning of last year to take a strike ballot which had resulted in an overwhelming vote in favour of a general strike. Negotiations in the meanwhile had been conducted between the Ministry and the representatives of the Union. In the middle of February last I submitted a report to the General Council of the Union at Delhi on the result of these negotiations. Upon my report and advice the strike was postponed *sine die*. Among the points that had been settled between the union and the Ministry were the following:

1. Rafi Saheb had given me an assurance that after three months he would do what was possible to settle the demand for payment for the period of the strike of 1946. He had further told me that he would have a formula worked out to make this payment not in the shape of payment for a strike period but as payment against leave due or special leave.
2. Last January, as result of pressure from the Railwaymen's Federation and the P. & T. Unions, the Government of India announced a flat increment of Rs.10/- per month as the minimum dearness allowance. As it happened, certain categories of postmen and lower grade staff in the P. & T. Department had been given an extra interim dearness allowance sometime earlier. In these cases the sum already sanctioned as interim allowance was deducted from the additional ten rupees that the Government granted in January. My Union protested vigorously against this cut and Rafi Saheb was good enough to assure us that there would be no deduction made from the additional dearness allowance of ten rupees granted by the January announcement.

It is ten months now that these assurances were given but they yet remain to be implemented. At no time during the last ten months Rafi Saheb disowned his word, as of course as an honourable man he could not do. It

[1] *J.P. Papers* (NMML).

seems however that the Ministry of Finance and the Cabinet have overruled him. This puts labour and its representatives in an awkward position, and it seems to me that the Government too cannot be in an enviable position when its assurances and pledges carry no weight. When I met you last with Rafi Saheb I tried to impress upon you that whatever the financial difficulties, the Government was honour bound to carry out the assurances given by one of its Ministers to labour. After a Minister of Cabinet rank has made definite promises to labour, on the basis of which labour makes a responsive gesture, it is meaningless for the Government or any other Ministry to go into the right or wrong of the question concerned. Internally the Cabinet may say what it likes to the Minister concerned but his promise must be carried out. As a matter of fact, I cannot see how Rafi Saheb can permit himself to continue in his present position when he is unable to carry out his word himself.

I might add here that the other demands which were the subject matter of negotiations between us and the Ministry of Communications have also not been satisfactorily disposed of. Some years ago the Government had appointed an Expert Committee to examine the working of the P. & T. Department in relation to the staff. The representatives of the P. & T. Unions were also associated with this Committee which made an unanimous report. This report was published by the Government after an inexcusable delay, after which again a great deal of time was taken to "examine" the recommendations of the Expert Committee. Officially our Union was informed that the Department was ready to discuss its final orders on the recommendations of the Committee. But when the representatives of the Union met the Hon'ble Minister and his colleagues they were told that there was no purpose in discussing the matter because no recommendation of the Expert Committee which involved the expenditure even of a single additional pie could be implemented. This has given to the employees a very rude shock indeed.

I am not in favour of using the method of fasting to solve industrial dispute but we are dealing here not with an industrial dispute but a moral issue. No less a person than a Cabinet Minister gave me certain assurances and I find that these assurances are not being carried out. It is wrong of any government to act in this manner, but it is much more so for a Congress government because the Congress had in the past years laid so much stress on truth. I therefore find that the only course open to me is to undertake a fast till your Government agrees to carry out the promises made by a member of your Cabinet. The other course open before us is to declare a general strike. As a matter of fact, at the last annual conference of the All India Postmen Union, it was practically decided to declare a strike if the assurances in question were not fulfilled and certain other of the major demands were not accepted. I however do not desire to put the public to serious inconvenience or to make the men suffer the privations and difficulties of a strike. So I propose to undertake a fast from the 5th of February next.

I am in Bombay till the 11th January, after which I shall be touring C.P.

I hope you are well.

With kind regards,

Affectionately yours,
Jayaprakash

85. Press Statement Refuting Charges of Exploitation of Labour, New Delhi, 7 January 1949[1]

The All India Railwaymen's Federation and the All India Postmen and Lower Grade Staff Union and the Union of Post and Telegraph Workers have decided to take strike ballot.[2] All the ballots would probably be taken at the same time, that is, during the first half of January. If the ballot is affirmative, nearly a million Government employees, in two of the most vital services, will be involved. The stoppage of the railways and the post and telegraph would cause considerable inconvenience to the public. So, the proposed action has come in for a good deal of criticism, and every thing is being done to alienate public sympathy from the workers.

As an humble servant of labour, and as one who has some responsibility in the matter, I consider it my duty to place before the country the case of the railway and the post and telegraph employees, if not of other state employees too.

I am attacked by men like Sardar Vallabhbhai Patel, Mr. K. Santhanam and Mr. Khandubhai Desai for exploiting labour for my own political ends. This is an easy charge to make, and when you have an obliging press and a gullible public, you may make it without fear of contradiction. But were it possible, by abusing me, to fill the stomachs of hungry workmen and to settle serious labour disputes, I should have rejoiced to be made the target of all the venom the Congress leaders are capable of. Unfortunately, however, socialist-baiting is not likely to ease the situation.

Let me place before the public the facts regarding this charge of political exploitation. It was a year and a half ago that I took over the presidentship of the All India Railwaymen's Federation. Since then, till about a couple of

[1] Published in *National Herald*, 7 January 1949, *Statesman*, 9 January 1949, and in several other papers on different dates.

[2] The decision to go ahead with strike ballot was taken at the Nagpur Conference on 24 November 1948.

months ago, I consistently advised the men against extreme steps and pleaded for the method of negotiation. Once, in 1947, when the general council of the federation had actually decided to take a strike ballot, I persuaded the council to rescind the resolution and adopt another offering a year's time to the Central Government for negotiations. At a time when efficiency and production were falling in the railways I issued an appeal to the men, parts of which were broadcast by All India Radio. I may be permitted here to quote from that appeal:

I do not know how many of you realize that the railways today are carrying a responsibility and a burden heavier than that borne by any other department of the Government. If the railways go under, there will be stark ruin and chaos in the country which will hit the entire nation, and hit the working class the hardest. Thus, you railwaymen carry today a burden heavier than what even the brave men of our army do. I want you to realize this.

I said further: you doubtless have your grievances; but on that account you must not allow the work to suffer. By not doing your duty you will hurt not any class of profiteers but your country, which includes yourselves.... You cannot be unaware of the very grave complaints that are being made about you by the public today. That you have grievances should be no reason for these complaints to arise.... It is the duty of organized labour movement not only to look after the immediate interests of the workers, but also to ensure honesty, discipline, a high standard of work and production, which are essential in the larger interests and which, naturally, embrace the interests of the workers themselves.

The then minister for Railways, Dr. John Matthai, was good enough to express his appreciation of my appeal and I was given to understand that the appeal had a salutary effect on production. At many railway centres, production conferences were held with my direct encouragement. One such in Bombay I had occasion to inaugurate. Throughout the past months, at every meeting of railwaymen that I addressed I pleaded, in spite of the outstanding grievances of the men for devotion to duty.

My Lillooah[3] speech, I believe, is still fresh in the minds of the public; and it may be recalled that it received general approbation. If I am not mistaken, the Prime Minister himself expressed his pleasure at the stand I had taken in this matter.

All these things, however, are forgotten today by the people who are expected to have longer memories and a keener sense of fairness. If all I am trying to do is to exploit the discontentment of railwaymen to political ends, why did I forbear till the other day?

It has been suggested that the unbroken series of defeats that the socialists

[3] For the text of Lillooah speech, 30 August 1948, see item 46 in this volume.

have sustained has made me desperate. These clever political analysts must have their heads buried in the sand. I at least have no such sense of defeat and have no reason to feel desperate. In fact, I have been surprised at the response we have received. I feel confident that if the Congress does not go completely fascist and turn the next general elections into a farce, the results would come as a shock to all our political ostriches.

It is suggested further that as long as I was a Congressman I counselled industrial truce; but as soon as I left the Congress, I started to incite labour in order to embarrass the Congress governments. Critics should have their facts right. I left the Congress in March last, and for months thereafter no one accused me of engineering strikes. In fact, till recently I was praised for my sobriety!

And even today what is it that I have done? Mr. Santhanam shows little regard for truth when he charges me with instigating the workers to strike. The fact is that it is Mr. Santhanam's policy, his arrogance, his threats, his attempts to break the solidarity of the workers, his lack of insight into the cause of the workers, that have driven them to take a strike ballot. For myself, all that I have done is to tell the men that while I was holding them back in the past I was not prepared to do so any longer, and that they were free to take any decision they considered best and that I would be with them in fair weather and foul. At the same time, I took the opportunity to point out that the decision must be their own. I was not a railway employee and did not stand to suffer the consequences of their decision.

At the general council of the federation at Nagpur,[4] one representative of the affiliated unions after another came on the rostrum and declared categorically that there was no other way left now except a general strike. There was only one exception. Most of the representatives were employees and there were only a few socialists or communists among them. It was the unmistaken voice of railwaymen.

I should say a word about the reasons that persuaded me not to hold back the men any more. The reasons were stated clearly in my address to the general council at Nagpur. Briefly, it was and is my view that after the settlement of the Hyderabad issue internal conditions had become far more stable than before and it was no longer unpatriotic or treasonous for labour to fight for its demands. Strikes are always upsetting, but nowhere in democratic countries are they treated as rebellion. The right to strike is a fundamental right guaranteed by law in all the democracies. In India, however, we find the dangerous practice of dealing with every strike as rebellions, a challenge to authority. Even during the last World War, there were strikes in Britain and the U.S.A. and not even the capitalist

[4] General Council of the Federation met at Nagpur on 24 November 1948.

administrations of those countries threatened to suppress them as rebellions, not even Churchill used the language that Santhanam used, for instance, at Calcutta.[5]

My other argument was that it was not right to ask labour to suffer patiently when the Government were deliberately pursuing an economic policy that resulted in a steady fall in working class standards and at the same time in substantial concessions to capital. The disinflation policy of the Government,[6] which had been announced some time ago, had come to me as a shock. Labour, which had played the game and had maintained the industrial peace, was given the go-bye and capital, that had been on strike according to the Prime Minister himself, was propitiated. I could not imagine a more iniquitous deal. Had any relief from rising prices been in sight, one would have felt justified, inspite of this inquity, in counselling patience. But I was convinced that the disinflation measures were not going to succeed. In that case, I was sure, there was no course left to labour but to exert the maximum pressure on the Government in order to compel them to change their policy and give to labour its due.

That my fears about the Government's disinflation measures were well-founded is borne out by the Finance Minister's recent admission that all he hoped to do was to stabilize prices and not to lower them. Then, if prices are to be stabilized at their present levels, labour is more than justified in demanding that its dearness allowances too be adjusted to these levels. As long as there was a hope for prices to go down, it was possible to ask Labour to hold its patience, but there can be no justification for it now. If the slow-moving and well-fed bureaucrats of New Delhi, who are the real rulers of free India today, cannot be moved by the sweet reasonableness of labour, the latter must use harsher methods to wake them up and make them face realities. These were the considerations that persuaded me not to instigate the workers to strike but merely to decline to hold them back any longer. If this is socialist exploitation of labour, I do not know what honest trade unionism is.

I might add here that anticipating the propaganda of Congressmen, I drew the attention of the general council at Nagpur to the danger of its case being misunderstood if I continued to be the President of the federation.

[5] K. Santhanam had delivered the speech referred to by J.P. at a public meeting in Calcutta on 14 December 1948.

[6] To contain inflation, the Economic Programme Committee of the Government of India had taken up certain decisions in December 1948. According to them, some type of statutory authority was to be set up at the Centre to review principal labour awards and to solve industrial disputes in a peaceful manner; to increase production by all means; to secure uniformity in wages and loans, and lastly, not to peg dearness allowance with the price index.

I pointed out that my being in that office would give a handle to the Government and their supporters to misrepresent the workers' economic struggle as a struggle between the Socialist Party and the Congress. I accordingly placed my resignation before the council, but they did not accept it. That was, of course, another instance of socialist exploitation of labour.

When so much has been said about political exploitation of labour, I may be permitted to add a word about the same type of exploitation by the Congress. Leaders of the Congress, from Sardar Patel downwards, are accusing all others of exploiting labour. But the experience of recent months has made it plain that if there is one party in the country that is exploiting labour politically, it is the Congress. The whole purpose of the INTUC is to bring labour by hook or by crook into the fold of the Congress. Congress leaders talk of Gandhian principles as applied to the labour movement, but if the methods of the INTUC are described as Gandhian, I cannot imagine a greater sacrilege. Starting with the common practice of inflating membership to goondaism and hooliganism, the INTUC stops at nothing. Had the INTUC unions functioned merely on a trade union level, no one would have cared a brass button for what they did. But the INTUC enters the field supported on the one hand by the employers and on the other by the Government. Legislation is enacted to help the labour unions of the Congress, and the Public Security Acts are invoked in their aid; arrestes are made; externment orders issued; meetings banned; strikes illegalised; employers forced to recognize them and give them every facility. Where the state is itself the employer, the officers either persuade or intimidate the employees to join the INTUC unions. The favourite method is to set up a Congress union in an industry, get the workers of the rival union arrested in one manner or another, and thus bolster up the official union. Every impartial observer can see that the Congress is in the labour movement not for the interest of the labour but for the interest of the Congress itself, which means for the party in power. Can there be a clearer example of political exploitation?

Before leaving this topic, let me point out that political exploitation of labour is not the same thing as the attempt to develop politics of the working class. No trade unionist in the modern world can be unconcerned with politics. As a socialist I naturally want labour to support the socialist Party. But first of all I am interested in developing a sound and independent trade union movement. The political aspect of the labour movement is not subsidiary to me; but I do not desire to impose a political party over the head of labour, as the Congress or the communists are trying to do. I want rather the political party to grow—in the manner of the British Labour Party—out of the labour movement. It is for this reason that I am advocating a change in the structure of the Socialist Party to allow the trade unions and peasant unions to control it rather than be controlled by it. I believe firmly that a sound trade union movement will automatically lead to sound Labour politics. Therefore, I have no need to exploit labour. I have only to serve it truly and leave the rest to the forces of history. If socialism is the historic goal of labour, I need not be impatient or adopt petty political manoeuvres.

All newspaper scribes deliver every now and then a homily on the unpatriotism of strikes only when higher authorities wake up to handle the issue. Under certain conditions a strike may be undesirable in the national interest. But I do not accept the proposition that only those who are in the seats of power understand patriotism. I wish this rather cheap method of public controversy should be given up. For my part, I wish to say in all humility that there is no one in this country, not even Pandit Nehru, from whom I am prepared to take a lesson in patriotism. Least of all I shall take it from Mr. Santhanam. At Calcutta he presumed to remind me of the national interest. We all have different conceptions of the national good. For instance, when in 1942 Mahatma Gandhi called "Quit India" and launched the greatest fight of his life, he was undoubtedly actuated by patriotic motives. Likewise, when in the same year Mr. Santhanam resigned from the Congress owing to his differences with Gandhiji, he too was acting in the national interest. Today he thinks he is serving his country by treating labour in the manner of the proverbial sun-dried bureaucrat. I disagree with him and think that he is, on the contrary, doing his country a great disservice. So, let us not preach patriotism to each other but consider each problem objectively and on its merits, without raising doubts about the bonafides of each other.

At Calcutta, Mr. Santhanam gave expression to some extremely dangerous views. The entire issue of democracy versus dictatorship hangs on the answer which the people of India will give to the poser which Mr. Santhanam placed before the country. He is reported to have said: "in the political field democracy could not co-exist with direct action" (*National Herald*, 15 December 1948). This is a dangerous proposition. That those who sat at the feet of Gandhiji should talk in such vein so soon after his death, is depressing in the extreme and fills one with anxiety and is surely not compatible with democracy. On the other hand, peaceful direct action is not only compatible with it but the essence of democracy is that it guarantees the right of the citizen to such action. A strike is not an attempt to overthrow established society by violence, rather it is a peaceful method of collective bargaining. Satyagraha too is a direct action. And democracy does not jeopardized by such action but is enriched, strengthened and purified by it. It is a dangerous symptom that the new rulers of the country are so intolerant of opposition even when the opposition is democratic and peaceful.

Mr. Santhanam further developed his dangerous thesis and is reported to have observed: "When the Government themselves owned an industry and were subject to parliamentary control and public opinion, I do not see how a strike could be a legitimate weapon. If there was a strike where was the impartial authority to judge between the employer (which was the state, with the backing of the people) and the workers?" (*National Herald*, 15 December 1948).

I am not sure if all those who read this report realized the mischief packed in these words. Every progressive citizen in this country today is looking forward to the end of the capitalist order and to an era of socialized economy. But if socialized industries are to be run in the manner of the railways, as at present, nationalization would become an instrument for the enslavement of labour. Nationalization, among other things, should lead to industrial democracy, the vital characteristic of which is participation of labour in the management and control of industry. There is no such participation of labour in the railways today—which are in effect a nationalized industry. On the other hand, we have a bureaucracy as sole authority in place of the private company's board of directors.

The Central Government inspite of the highfalutin resolutions and declarations of the Congress Party, have not yet shown that they are even conscious of this problem. Had steps been taken to introduce industrial democracy into the railways, and had the workers been given a new status and admitted into a joint and equal partnership in running the industry, the question of strike in those conditions could have been legitimately raised. Though, I for one would not be prepared to rule out strikes even under industrial democracy, I should think it would be a rare occurrence then. But under the present conditions, when the democratic state has not unfolded itself and is identical with the Council of Ministers, it is a complete denial of democracy to say that workers in state industries cannot claim the right to strike. Even the British never questioned that right. The fact that the place of the British has been taken by elected ministers does not vest the latter with unlimited powers. Where the state is the employer, it cannot, in a dispute with its employees constitute itself into the final authority. As a party to the dispute it cannot become the arbiter. The people must create other institutions which can arbitrate between the Government and the state employees.

Mr. Santhanam finds it difficult to imagine where an impartial authority can be found to deal with a dispute between the state and its employees. And yet, almost daily such impartial authorities are being set up in the shape of tribunals, arbitrators, adjudicators and so on. I have suggested several times before that not only a machinery should be set up whereby railwaymen are given an adequate share in the management and control of the railways, but also that a permanent tribunal of Supreme Court judges be formed to adjudicate on disputes referred to it either by the Government or the railwaymen's federation. In the absence of such institutions, we have the present rather sorry situation in which the Government are the employer and at the same time the final arbiter in a dispute. The result is bound to be no other than frequent clashes and conflicts. The surprise, in the present conditions, is not that there are conflicts but that there are so few.

Mr. Santhanam, in his Calcutta statement, went on to put me a question. Supposing his party was in power, he said, speaking of me, and somebody else threatened it with a strike, would he surrender to the threat or would he suppress it? If the Government surrendered, they would cease to be a Government.

I have no difficulty in answering Mr. Santhanam. First of all, I do not look upon a strike as a threat or a challenge to authority. It is a weapon of collective bargaining. As such, I am not faced only with Mr. Santhanam's two dire alternatives: surrender or suppression. There is a third and democratic course—settlement—which may mean surrender on both sides and suppression of none. Moreover, under a socialist government there will be industrial democracy and an adequate machinery for the settlement of disputes, and strikes will be among the rarest of events. So much for Mr. Santhanam's totalitarianism.

So far I have dealt with general and political aspects of the question. In my last letter to the Hon'ble Mr. Ayyangar which appeared recently in the press, I have shown how unsatisfactory have been the Government's attempts to meet the demands of the railwaymen.

I shall close this rather longish article with a few words about labour's universal problem i.e. dearness allowance. The public has been told that railway workers and other state employee are constantly putting up their demands. This is an unfair charge. The workers would be perfectly justified in demanding a revision of their basic scales of pay, but they are not doing so. They have, in fact, accepted the Pay Commission's scales. But since prices have been steadily rising, the workers have naturally been demanding that their dearness allowance should rise proportionately. This is not a demand for higher wages but merely for the protection of their present emoluments. The public is not generally aware that the Pay Commission itself recommended that dearness allowance should be linked to the price index, and laid down that for every rise of 20 points in the price index a minimum of five rupees should be added to the dearness allowance. The workers are demanding not a pie more than this. How can any one consider it to be unreasonable? The plea that such a course would lead to further inflation is untenable.

The public has been told that the railway worker enjoys more privileges than other state employees: as for example, witness the grain shops. It is true the railway workers have the benefit of cheap grain shops. But even with the grain shops concession the total dearness allowance in cash and kind that they received is not equivalent to what they are entitled according to the Central Pay Commission. The railwayman does not insist on the grain shop. It may be abolished, if the Government so desire, but he insists on adequate allowance to compensate fully for the rise in prices. The post and telegraph workers want the same. If the Government cannot give the latter what is their due, there is no justification for taking away from the former the little they were getting. And that is exactly what has been done. The Government have decided to curtail the grain shop concessions so drastically that there has actually been a cut in the workers' wages at a time when they were justly crying for more! What else can the unfortunate worker do but fight desperately to save himself?

86. Statement to the Press, New Delhi, 18 January 1949[1]

The Congress Party has decided to celebrate the 26th January as 'Remembrance Day'. I have been asked by members of the Socialist Party what should our attitude be. This day was observed in the past 20 years as a day when we renewed our pledge to complete independence. The Jaipur decision[2] of the Congress to preserve India's link with the British Commonwealth is a denial of that pledge. Therefore, the 26th of January, instead of being celebrated as a Day of Remembrance, should rather serve to remind the Indian people of the unfulfilled pledge and spur them on to its fulfilment, and to achievement of that full stature for their country which is the meaning of independence. Accordingly, it should be our duty to see that the people are not beguiled by official circuses and celebrations and that we utilize this day to remind the people of the task that remains undone.

I have also been asked to define the Party's attitude towards the observance of January 30. This day above all should be a Day of Remembrance, a day which millions of hearts in the country should, in humility and truth, call into devoted remembrance the Father of the Nation, his life and his teachings, his supreme sacrifice, his undying message. On this day India should dedicate herself anew to the memory of her master and to the service of truth, love and Daridranarayan.[3]

Mahatma Gandhi was not of a party, but of India and of the world. So it

[1] Adapted from *Bombay Chronicle*, 19 January 1949.

[2] The resolution adopted by the Congress at the Jaipur session on 8 December 1948, favoured the maintenance of India's association with the United Kingdom and the Commonwealth.

[3] Gandhi's favourite phrase equating the poor with God.

is wrong to confine the observance of a day dedicated to him within partisan bounds. In issuing its recent instructions regarding this matter the Congress Party again made the mistake of equating itself with the nation. The Working Committee of that Party went so far as to propose a message to be read on this day. There are millions in this country outside the fold of the Congress Party who too love and regard their Bapu.

But they should not like on this day to listen to the so-called message of merely one of the political parties in the country but only to the message of Bapu himself. Incidentally, the more the Congress Party deviates in action from the path of Gandhiji the more anxious it is to deliver high-sounding messages in his name.

Be that as it may, I should like to direct all branches of the Socialist Party to observe the 30th January as a day of dedication to the memory of Mahatma Gandhi and of service to the ideals of human equality and fellowship. Quiet and reverent processions should be taken out, with banners carrying Gandhiji's words and public meetings should be held where appropriate passages should be read from his writings. There should also be activities organized as a token of our preparedness to put into practice the ideals of the master.

87. To Asoka Mehta, 19 January 1949[1]

Dear Asoka,

I am afraid the Maharashtra Party has unnecessarily been brought in by certain elements in the Bombay Party to confuse the issue and to keep out someone they do not like. While we were in the Constitution Committee there was a telephone from Madhu Dandawate[2] to say that a telegram had just been received from Madhav Rao Gaekwad[3] suggesting N.G. Goray's name for the Railway seat. S.M. Joshi[4] and Madhu Limaye happened to be present and I asked them how things really stood. They were completely

[1] *J.P. Papers* (NMML).

[2] Madhu Ramchandra Dandawate, b. 1924; took part in Quit India Movement, 1942; Joint Secretary, P.S.P., 1954; participated in Goa Liberation Movement, 1955; member, Maharashtra Legislative Council, 1970-1, and Lok Sabha, 1971-7, 1977-9, 1980-4, 1985-90, and 1990-1; General Secretary, Socialist Party, 1972; imprisoned during emergency, 1975-7; Minister of Railways, 1977-9; and of Finance, 1989-90; Deputy Chairman, Planning Commission, 1996-8; publications include: *Gandhiji's Impact on Socialist Thinking; Three Decades of Indian Communism; Marx and Gandhi; Jayaprakash Narayan: The Man and His Ideas; Yusuf Meherally: Quest for New Horizons; Quest of Conscince, and Jayaprakash Narayan; Struggle with Values.*

[3] Madhav Rao Gaekwad, Socialist activist and one of the secretaries of Maharashtra Socialist Party.

[4] S.M. Joshi, for biographical note, see *JPSW*, Vol. IV, p. 186.

surprised and told me definitely that the matter was never discussed in the Maharashtra Executive and the idea that one of the two seats should go to Maharashtra never had even crossed their minds. They were sure that N.G. Goray himself had never thought of it. It appeared later that Gaekwad's telegram was in reply to a specific suggestion that the Maharashtra Party should recommend a prominent political (as different from labour) name.

So the question is really confined to the Bombay Party. I am afraid there are some people who are conspiring to keep Peter Alvares[5] out. Madhu Limaye confirmed this at the time I told him and S.M. of Dandawate's telephone. The whole thing is insufferably petty.

However, considering all aspects of the question, it is my definite view that Peter Alvares should be set up from the Railway seat and Purshottam from the E. & F. Ward constituency. I am sending you this opinion not because I want to interfere with the affairs of the Bombay party, but because you wanted me to express my definite view in the matter. And, with respect to the railway seat, I think I am entitled to have my say.[6]

I hope the Hyderabad trip did not ever strain you.

As ever,
Jayaprakash Narayan

[5] Peter Augusto Alvares (1909-75); a prominent socialist leader of Bombay; active on the Labour front; elected to the Bombay Assembly as a Socialist candidate, 1949; member of Parliament, 1962-7.

[6] Asoka Mehta in his letter dated 22 January had explained to J.P. about the situation in Maharashtra. See, Appendix 6.

88. To Phillip Gooneverdene, 23 January 1949[1]

My dear Phillip,[2]

Many thanks for your wire.[3] I discussed it with some of my colleagues and they generally liked the idea, but we thought that (a) our taking such a step might appear to be an imitation of the step taken by the Government of India and (b) it may be too late to do anything of such a kind. So we decided that instead of calling a conference forthwith we should get in touch with the various Asian Parties and sound them first. If we get a good response we might convene the conference at a time suitable to them all. Our Party

[1] *J.P. Papers* (NMML).

[2] Phillip Gooneverdene, founder-member of the Lanka Sama Samaja Party, 1935; President of the Youth League of the LSSP, 1949; formed the Viplavakari Lanka Sama Samaja Party, 1950; Cabinet Minister in Sri Lanka, 1956-8 and 1965-70; passed away in 1972.

[3] The proposed conference could not be held. See, J.P.'s telegram to Gooneverdene, 3 March 1949.

Conference is meeting in Patna from the 20th to 25th of February and we would like very much to hold this conference too at the same time and place. We have already sent telegrams to the Parties concerned and we are awaiting their reply.

I hope you are well and prospering.

With kindest regards,

Sincerely yours,
Jayaprakash Narayan

89. To Madhu Limaye, 23 January 1949[1]

My dear Madhu,

You remember Gooneverdene's telegram from Lanka. It was decided that we should sound the Asian Parties and then, if they agree with the suggestion, hold a conference at the time of our Party Conference. Have you sent out these telegrams? I hope you have got Lohia's programme so that you can inform him of the replies as you get them. I will be in Patna, so you can write to me there.[2]

Have you also sent out invitations to Asian, European and other parties for our Conference. You may also invite prominent individuals.

Hoping to see you in Patna soon,

Affectionately yours,
J.P.

[1] *J.P. Papers* (NMML).

[2] For Madhu Limaye's reply to J.P. dated 30 January 1949, see Appendix 7, dated 30 January 1949.

90. To N.G. Goray, 24 January 1949[1]

Dear N.G.,

I enclose a copy of a letter I have written to Dandawate. A railway seat seems to have fallen vacant due to the communist M.L.A. being underground: continued absence from the Assembly leading to his being unseated.

When I was in Bombay last, Asoka told me that as the question was a difficult one and he wanted me to decide it. After considering all aspects of the matter I decided that Peter should be set up for the seat. I received this morning a letter from Dandawate, of which I am enclosing a copy. This was like a sock in the eye. The whole thing is nauseating. There is so much

[1] *J.P. Papers* (NMML).

of petty intrigue behind all this. Your name too was also dragged in unnecessarily. Madhu Limaye will tell you.

However, I want you to take the matter in hand. The Bombay Party alone cannot decide it. The primary people to decide it are the railway workers, for after all it is they who are to send their representative. So, you will please ascertain the opinion of our unions in the B.B. & C.I. and G.I.P. Please also ascertain the opinion of the Maharashtra, Gujarat and Karnatak Branches of the Party. It may be difficult for the executives of all these bodies to meet. So, you should either get their opinion by circularization or secure the opinion of the office-bearers. If there is a clear majority for any name, he should be set up as our candidate. If, opinions are divided, the Central Parliamentary Committee or Asoka or Narendra Deva should decide.

As for my own view, I do hold strongly that Peter is the only candidate who should in fitness and propriety be set up by us. It is tiresome to argue a point that is obvious, so I shall not go into my reasons.

Hope Madhu Limaye is reaching Patna in the first week of February.

Affectionately,
Jayaprakash Narayan

91. To Asoka Mehta, 24 January 1949[1]

Dear Asoka,

This is a fine way to treat me. However, I have done with this sordid business, and do not want to be troubled about it any more.

Enclosed you will find copies of letters sent to Gore and Dandawate.

Hoping you are well,

Affectionately,
J.P.

P.S. I wrote the above last night. This morning when Madanlalji[2] came here he brought your letter of January 22.[3]

I have learned my lesson about the Bombay Party and shall be more careful in the future about it. It is very kind of you to be so considerate to the General Secretary—I did not miss the accent on the General Secretary rather than on poor Jayaprakash Narayan. However, as I have explained in

[1] *J.P. Papers* (NMML).

[2] Madanlal Sodhani, for biographical note see, *JPSW*, Vol. 4, p. 222.

[3] From Asoka Mehta to J.P., 22 January, see Appendix 6.

my letter to Dandawate, the General Secretary has no right to give a decision on a matter like this. I have given my own suggestion as President of the Federation. For the rest, I have suggested the procedure in the letter to Dandawate. If there is no time to go through the procedure, you, as Secretary of the Parliamentary Committee, or Narendra Deva, as President, could decide.

Regarding the railways, there is no empire that I have built up. Since I took over the Federation, I only know the strain it has been on me. And through it I have endeavoured to serve the Party. However, the only thing for me to do after what you have written is to resign my Presidentship. I shall be called a quitter if I did it in the present circumstances, for we are facing the biggest show-down with the communists. But I assure you the empire will be dissolved as soon as possible.

Yours,
J.P.

92. To M.R. Dandawate, 24 January 1949[1]

Dear Dandawate,

Your letter of January 20. I am rather surprised at the procedure the Bombay Party has adopted in this matter. I might have made a mistake, but I understood from Asoka that since the question was controversial he wanted me to decide it. I made my decision after hearing you all and communicated it to you. Now, you say you are awaiting my "final decision." If you had no intention to accept my decision, I do not see why I should thus have been humiliated by Asoka and the Bombay Executive.

However, since you gentlemen desire to follow strict constitutional procedure, let me state the position as I see it. I have no constitutional right to decide such questions. I gave my previous decision because Asoka asked me to do so. Where a railway constituency is concerned, the Railwaymen's Federation and the relevant railway unions must have the primary choice. If I wanted to play at politics as you gentlemen seem bent upon to do, I could have got a resolution passed by the Working Committee of the Federation which met here on the 21st, nominating the Federation's candidate. The G.I.P. and B.B. & C.I. unions too could, and still can, have their say. The Bombay Branch cannot speak for the Federation nor for either of these unions. If a provincial branch has any voice in the matter, at least the Gujarat and Maharashtra branches have as much voice as the Bombay branch. Even the Karnatak branch should have a voice in that case. In my last letter I wrote that the Maharashtra branch did not claim any voice in

[1] *J.P. Papers* (NMML).

the matter, but if the Bombay Branch wants to decide the issue by votes, the other branches too must be given the right to do the same. So, it should be noted that the decision does not rest with the Bombay Executive. I am writing to Gore about this matter, and am asking him to ascertain the views of our unions on the G.I.P. and B.B. & C.I. and of the Gujarat, Maharashtra and Karnatak branches. I am also writing to him that though the Federation has not considered the matter, I, as President, suggest the name of Peter Alvares, in anticipation of the sanction of the Federation's Working Committee.

Finally, I wish to place it on record for the information of the Bombay Executive, that Peter Alvares has been doing excellent work in the Federation. It is largely due to his organizational ability that the position of the Party in the Federation is so strong today. There is no other Party member who has been so helpful to me in my Federation work and I have found him to be ever loyal and devoted to the Party. I expected that the Bombay Executive would show appreciation of his hard and able work rather than slap him in the face. I expected also that the Bombay Executive would show great regard for my considered views. However, I have learned my lesson, and I know now where I stand with the Bombay Party.

So, let me sum up:

I have no authority to give final or other decisions in such matters.

In respect of a railway constituency such as the one in question, the Railwaymen's Federation, the railway unions and the provincial branches concerned have a say. If among the electoral colleges there are also representatives of dock or other labour, their unions too should have a say. In case there is no clear majority for any one name, the Central Parliamentary Committee should decide.

As President of the Federation I suggest the name of Peter Alvares for the seat.

Finally, I should like to make it clear that, though I have been deliberately humiliated, I have no intention to convert this issue into a personal one or fight to rehabilitate my *amour propre*. The Bombay Executive has elected to be constitutional and technical; so I have pointed out the other constitutional proprieties. For myself, I am content to make what, in my judgment, is the best suggestion and leave the rest to the processes of Party democracy.

You need not write to me any further in this matter (except if you wish to carry on an argument with me). Write to N.G. Goray for further advice and guidance.

Sincerely yours,
J.P.

93. To my Countrymen in Malaya, 27 January 1949[1]

Dear Friends,

It was a great pleasure to meet Sardar Budh Singh,[2] your leader and President of the Malayan Indian Congress.

You are facing difficult times, but times are changing. Asia is on the move and the remaining vestiges of European imperialism will soon entirely disappear. In the meanwhile, you must struggle and fight. Your cause is worthy as the cause of all oppressed peoples. India shall stand by you in your struggle and do all to help you.

Sardar Budh Singh has extended to me on your behalf an invitation to visit you. It shall give me the greatest pleasure to do so, but problems at home are so pressing that I cannot tell whether it will be possible for me to get away from home. However, I look forward to the day when I could be in your midst.

With fraternal greetings,

Sincerely yours,
J.P.

[1] *J.P. Papers* (NMML).

[2] Sardar Budh Singh, a member of Indian diaspora in Malaya; personally known to Nehru; leader of the Malayan Indian delegation to the Jaipur Session of the Indian National Congress, December 1948; visited India again in 1950.

94. To Peter Alvares, 30 January 1949[1]

My dear Peter,

I have your letters. As I have already written to the people concerned, I have withdrawn from this business. But the advice I gave you at Delhi still stands, and I hope fervently that you will accept it. It is in the interest of the Party that you withdraw from the contest—that is the only right course for you, just as it is the right course even now for me to suggest your name on behalf of the Federation. But I am absolutely clear, that if you are not thinking of yourself, but of the Party, you must withdraw from the contest.

Very sincerely yours,
Jayaprakash Narayan

[1] *J.P. Papers* (NMML).

95. Gandhi and Socialism, 30 January 1949[1]

Oh, he is a Gandhian Socialist: That, in certain quarters, is enough condemnation for a socialist. In certain other quarters, celebration of Gandhi Jayanti is regarded as apostasy punishable by excommunication. It is not Gandhism or Gandhiji who suffers on account of this blinkered vision, it is Socialism.

Gandhiji was a social phenomenon which Socialism must understand rather than explain away. The post-Gandhi world can never go on as if there never had been a Gandhi. At every turn, on every occasion, his great voice will echo forth.

Gandhiji was a seeker after truth. He sought for truth not away from life, not beyond it, but within life itself. He sought for truth in action. He sought it through service of the lowly and the dispossessed. Socialism too is a search for truth within life, in action and through service of the common man.

Gandhiji was a revolutionary, not a philosopher. He was not primarily interested in merely understanding life but in changing it. He changed history. In his very death he set the pace of social change so fast that men of sturdy hearts lost courage and dropped by the roadside. Socialism too is a revolutionary creed. By understanding society it endeavours to change it.

Gandhiji was a revolutionary because he had faith in the masses and believed in mass action. He was not a constitutionalist afraid to plunge society in turmoil. Socialism too believes in the masses and depends on mass action.

Gandhiji was a revolutionary because he had the courage of his convictions, took his logic to its end, and was not limited or inhibited by petty bourgeois prejudices. Socialism, too, has its inexorable logic and tears down the edifice of middle class Philistinism.

Gandhiji was not a dogmatist. He was pragmatic, experimental and dialectical. Likewise, Socialism.

Gandhiji emphasized the need to change man in order to change society. Socialism recognizes that social change is not secured without changing man.

Gandhiji was opposed to capitalism and feudalism. He wanted to reform them if possible by individual's reform. But, if necessary, he was prepared to abolish them by legislation. Socialism meets him halfway by trying to abolish capitalism and feudalism by legislation in a democracy, by revolution in the absence of democracy.

[1] *Janata*, 30 January 1949. This note was written by Jayaprakash Narayan, prior to Gandhi's first death anniversary.

Gandhiji was not opposed to large-scale industry but he wanted to nationalize them. Likewise Socialism.

Gandhiji stood for small-scale production in the spheres where simple techniques are possible. Socialism, in India at any rate, must plan a large-scale development of small-scale production to secure full employment and to utilize fully the country's productive capacity in view of the shortage of capital goods, savings, technical personnel, etc.

Gandhiji laid stress on decetralisation of political and economic power. Socialism too, if it is not to turn totalitarian, must do the same.

Gandhiji was opposed to violence. Socialism is not opposed to violence but it desires to destroy the social roots of violence.

Gandhiji was not a Marxist. He was himself. Marx too was no a Marxist. He was himself. Both were primarily men of action though both were profound in ideas.

World Socialism, more so Indian socialism, would hurt its own cause if it allowed dogmatism, masquerading as science or orthodoxy, to blind itself to the historic significance of Gandhi.

96. To Gyan Chand, 3 February 1949[1]

Dear Gyan Bhai,[2]

I have written to Narendra Deva if he could be in Calcutta on February 28 or March 1 or 2 for a meeting of the Khoj Parishad Governors. If he agrees, could you too find it possible to come over? A reorganization meeting would be very necessary. I am writing to M.L. Dantwala & Dhurjati Prasad[3] also to come.

Had I or Achyut left with you a monograph on coal nationalization prepared by one of the Khoj Parishad assistants? If you have the paper with

[1] *J.P. Papers* (NMML).

[2] Gyan Chand (1894-1983), an eminent economist; taught at Banares Hindu University 1920-6 and Patna University 1926-46; served in the International Monetary Fund as the Chief of its Far Eastern Financial Section, Washington, 1946-50; on return to India became Head of the Economic Section of the Cabinet Secretariate; contested Lok Sabha election from Patna as an independent candidate with socialist backing in 1952, but lost; works include, *Teeming Millions of India* (1939), *The New Economy of China* (1959) and *The Socialist Transformation of Indian Economy* (1965).

[3] Dhurjati Prasad Mukherjee (1894-1961), Lecturer Sociology later Reader of Economics, Lucknow University, 1922-34; worked (on leave) as Director of Information, U.P. Government, 1938-40; visited the Soviet Union, 1952; Visiting Professor in Social Science Institute, The Hague, 1953-4; Professor of Economics, Aligarh Muslim University, 1954-9; attended the Bandung Conference, 1955. Works include, *Basic Concepts of Sociology*, *On Indian History: Views and Controversies*, *Indian Music*; wrote several Bengali novels including *Antahshila*, *Abarta* and *Mohana*.

you, will you be able to find a little time to go through it and send it to me with your suggestions?

I shall be anxious to hear from you.

With kindest regards to you and Anu Bhabhi.

Affectionately yours,
Jayaprakash Narayan

97. To Khagendranath Sen, 3 February 1949[1]

My dear Khagen Babu,[2]

I have pleasure in inviting you to the meeting of the National Executive of the Socialist Party at Patna on March 4 and the following dates, and also to the Annual Conference of the Party on March 6 to 10. Please let me know the date and time of your arrival at Patna so that we could make the necessary arrangements.

I wanted to meet you at Calcutta when I was there last, but it could not be arranged. I was anxious to discuss with you the reorganization of the Khoj Parishad. A meeting had been arranged at Lucknow as you might know, but it had to be postponed due to the Science Congress.

Can we meet at Calcutta towards the end of the month? I have written to Narendradevji asking if he could go to Calcutta on February 28 or March 1 or 2. If he is able to do that, would it be convenient to friends in Calcutta? I shall try to get in touch with Lohia and find out if he too can come. I shall be anxious to hear from you.

Some time ago, we had decided that the Parishad should hold a conference on labour. I believe arrangements for that are in progress. But when I was in Delhi last some friends suggested that a conference on food was far more urgent. I rather liked the suggestion. Could you not think over it and let me have your suggestions?

A conference on food would be of far greater interest to the people and may prove to be of great practical value.

How about the monographs that I understood were ready—one on coal

[1] *J.P. Papers* (NMML).

[2] Khagendranath Sen (1903-82); Lecturer and later Professor, Calcutta University, Department of Economics, 1932-66; joined journalism as Assistant Editor, *Advance*, 1930; and *Hindustan Standard*, 1937; Editor-in-Chief, *The Nationalist*, 1944; attended Round Table Conference in London 1930-1; visited United States on Indo-American educational exchange programme, 1959; started a children's magazine, *Rangmahal*. Works include, *Economic Reconstruction of India*, *Education and the Nation*, *Indian Economics*, *Introduction to Social Science*, *New Constitution of Soviet Union*.

nationalization and another one? Dhurjati Babu had undertaken to go over the coal monograph. Have you heard from him?

With kindest regards,

Very sincerely yours,
J.P.

98. To Satyabrata Sen, 3 February 1949[1]

My dear Sattoo,[2]

I received your notice regarding the meeting of the Governing Body. I am sorry that I was not able to come. I feel however that a reorganization meeting of the Governors and friends interested in the Parishad is urgently necessary. The Lucknow meeting unfortunately had to be dropped on account of the clash of dates with the Science Congress. I am suggesting a meeting at Calcutta on any of the following dates: i.e. 28th February to March 2. I have already written to Khagen Babu and also to Narendra Deva, Lohia, Gyan Chand, Dhurjati Prasad and Dantwala. I hope that these dates will suit the Calcutta friends and as soon as I hear from the friends from outside I shall let you know.

I do not know how you have been running the Parishad with practically no financial support from us in the latter month. I am however, hoping to be able to give you some money after the Party Conference.

Hoping to hear from you soon and hoping you are well,

Sincerely yours,
J.P.

[1] *J.P. Papers* (NMML).

[2] Satyabrata Sen, Member of the Council of Governors, *Khoj Parishad*, Calcutta; economist and active member of the Socialist Party, Calcutta.

99. To B.P. Sinha, 3 February 1949[1]

Dear Comrade,[2]

I confirm the dates suggested by you, i.e. February 26 and 27, for my Jharia programme. Apart from other things, I hope it would be possible for you to take advantage of my visit to bring into existence a single union of mine workers. Please let me know what preliminary steps have already been taken in this regard.

With greetings,

Sincerely yours,
J.P.

[1] *J.P. Papers* (NMML).

[2] B.P. Sinha, head of the Socialist Labour Union in Jharia.

100. To Dhurjati Prasad Mukherji, 3 February 1949[1]

My dear Prof. Mukherji,

You remember it was arranged that a meeting of the Khoj Parishad should be held at Lucknow sometime in January, but due to the Science Congress the idea had to be dropped. A meeting however is urgently necessary to put through the reorganization plan. I have suggested that the Governors and friends interested in the Khoj Parishad should meet at Calcutta on any of the following dates: February 28 to March 2. I have written to Narendra Devji also to come, as also to Dr. Gyan Chand and Prof. Dantwala. I hope Rammanohar will also come. Could you find it convenient to attend this meeting? Please do let we know.

With regards,

Sincerely yours,
Jayaprakash Narayan

[1] *J.P. Papers* (NMML).

101. To M.L. Dantwala, 3 February 1949[1]

My dear Mohanlal,

I have the pleasure to invite you to the meeting of the National Executive at Patna on March 4 and also to the annual conference which will meet from March 6 to 10. I hope you will find it convenient to come.

I am trying to call a meeting at Calcutta of friends interested in the Khoj Parishad and of the Governors to discuss and finalize the reorganization plans. I should very much like to have you too at this meeting at Calcutta. We could then go together from there to Patna for the National Executive. The latest that we can have this meeting would be March 2. I must reach Patna a day before the National Executive meets. Do let me know which of these dates will suit you.

Have you completed that pamphlet on *kisan policy*. If so, please give the typescript to Suresh to send to the press. You and I have to do that constructive programme pamphlet also. I shall prepare a draft here and send it to you.

When I was in Delhi last, friends suggested that we should convene a conference on food. The Khoj Parishad has been planning to convene a conference on labour. I have written to the Director today if, instead of doing that, the Khoj Parishad could not convene this conference on food. It

[1] *J.P. Papers* (NMML).

is an urgent problem and I am sure it will evoke public response and the discussions might bring into light useful practical measures. I should like to have your opinions and suggestions regarding this matter. If you think that such a conference would be useful, I should like you to prepare a plan as to how the conference should be called, who should be invited, what papers should be asked to be prepared and so on. Give also the most suitable dates from your point of view.

Hoping you are well,

With love,

Affectionately yours,
J.P.

102. To Rammanohar Lohia, 3 February 1949[1]

My dear Rammanohar,

That Khoj Parishad meeting, as you know, which was arranged to be held at Lucknow did not come off. But a meeting is very essential as soon as possible to finalize the reorganization plans. Could you find it possible to be in Calcutta on any date between February 28 and March 2? I have asked Narendra Deva if he could also spare a day and come over to Calcutta. I have also written to Gyan Chand, Dantwala and Dhurjati Prasad. If you come to Calcutta, we could come to Patna together and stay on for the National Executive which is to meet on March 4. Please write soon.

Hoping you are well,

Affectionately yours,
J.P.

[1] *J.P. Papers* (NMML).

103. To Anugraha Narayan Sinha, 3 February 1949[1]

Dear Anugraha Babu,[2]

Pranam.

I am writing you this letter not as a politician but on account of personal intimacy.

[1] *J.P. Papers* (NMML). Original in Hindi

[2] Anugraha Narayan Sinha (1887-1957); actively participated in the Freedom Movement and imprisoned on several occasions; President of the Bihar Provincial Congress Committee, 1928-9; Minister of Finance, P.W.D., Labour, Commerce and Local self-Government, Bihar, 1937-9; Minister of Finance, Supply, Food and Labour, Bihar, 1946-57.

I have been extremely pained at whatever has happened with regard to the Dalmianagar strike.[3] A small dispute so adversely affected the province's main industry, caused so much loss to production, did so much harm to the interests of farmers and workers and so aggravated the hostility between two political parties. Even if we accept the plea, for argument's sake, that it was not proper to launch a strike on the issue of recognition, could the Government not have resolved the dispute in an impartial manner? When I had come here a month ago, I had accepted whatever might be the proper solution. When on the first day I met you at your residence, the proposal to submit the issue of recognition to the arbitration of Jeejeebhoy[4] was made from the Government side and I had said that if Basawan Babu[5] was sent for, I would reply after consulting him. When talks took place the next day in the Secretariat, I agreed to the arbitration, though Basawanji was hesitating. Pandit Hargobind Mishra[6] asked for 24 hours time, and you gave him time. I returned with the idea that if Mishraji did not agree to arbitration, you would devise some other way. Subsequently you put aside this matter by giving a label of violence to whatever had happened at Dolmianagar. If violence had indeed taken place, then punish those who committed violence. Why should all workers, thousand of farmers and the province's industry be ruined?

Let us take up the question of the mistake committed in the notice as per Raman Saheb's version.[7] If the mistake had in fact been committed, the Government itself should have rectified it. We had been assured that the mistake would be rectified, but that had not happened for a full month. You said that you had ordered the rectification of the mistake only after two-three days of the last meeting, but the notice was not issued because of laziness. Then the file was missing. So necessary work and such carelessness!

You are ruling today. You continue to rule, but your rule should have some objective; it should have some principles. If the people like the

[3] The strike began in Rohtas Industries, Dalmianagar on 4 December 1949. The main issue was recognition by the employers of a new union formed by the INTUC. The old union of which Basawan Sinha was the President felt that the recognition of the new union amounted to an attempt by the employers to break the existing one.

[4] Sir Jamsetjee Jeejeebhoy (1909-68); Member, Bombay Municipal Corporation, 1934-9; Honorary Presidency Megistrate 1935-58.

[5] For biographical note on Basawan Sinha, see *JPSW*, Vol. III, p. 18.

[6] President District Congress Committee, Shahbad (Bihar); belonged to INTUC.

[7] The Government notification of 2 December erroneously stated that the issue of the recognition of the new union would be referred to the Industrial Court by the new union itself when actually it had to be referred by the old union only. However, this mistake was rectified by the Government by a fresh notification on 31 January 1949. See item 103, dated 5 February.

Congress, the Congress must rule, no one can prevent it. But, is the interest of the Congress going to be served in any way by the manner in which the rule is being carried on today? The Government cannot last long with repression. The Congress cannot expect that its influence over workers will be established by either repression or under Government pressure or by winning over the owners. I do not know what information has been given to you, but if you conduct an impartial enquiry, you will find out that in recent times the influence of the Congress over the workers of Dalmianagar has not increased—perhaps it has decreased. In view of what happened during the strike, who will tell that Basawan Sinha has no strong influence there.

Now consider this issue of violence. You may perhaps remember which devices Bari Saheb[8] used against Homi[9] or other rivals in Jamshedpur. If we had resorted to similar extremely violent methods anywhere, we do not know what repression-cycle the Congress Government would have set in motion. After all, what violence took place in Dalmianagar? On the day I went there, some people got hurt. The people were angry over the demonstration staged against me. In view of that, whatever happened was not surprising. After that I did not hear that anyone's nose was broken. Yes, some workers had quarrelled among themselves, but when there is such tension, it is not impossible to get involved in such skirmishes. Over and above that the repression that was launched by the Government was a painful event. If you are not prepared to accept my point of view with regard to violence, I shall be happy if the Government institutes an impartial enquiry into violence—both workers' violence and its own—by a judge of the High Court or by any other person of the same position.

I was astounded to hear whatever you said today in the evening in connection with Jamshedpur. Does freedom of citizens has no value? Is there no difference between the British rule and the Congress rule? Do persons like Munshi Ahmed Din have no weight? The atmosphere at Jamshedpur was hostile, so those who went there from outside were arrested. What a surprise! Is this freedom? Munshi Ahmed Din is not a ruffian who should be put behind bars during disturbances. It is not only those who came from outside who have been arrested, but also several members of the Socialist Party who reside in Jamshedpur.

You have power in your hands, so you have a great responsibility. Democracy is the rule of the majority, but the rule of the majority and the tyranny of the majority are not the same. The fundamental rights of the people are embodied in the Constitution only in order to curb the tyranny

[8] For biographical note on Abdul Bari, see *JPSW*, Vol. IV, p. 42.

[9] Manick Homi; lawyer; worked in the Tata Iron and Steel Company; led TISCO strike in 1928, and became a full-fledged labour leader in Jamshedpur.

of the majority. Hope you will give heed to what I have written, and act with discretion and prudence. Power is not the be-all and end-all of life.

Regarding Dalmianagar I have already told you that after the rectification of errors in the notification, I wish to advise the workers to go to work. Out of 4500 permanent workers, more than 1200 workers are not going to work at present. After giving notice the Company has dismissed all workers who had gone on strike. Under these circumstances their returning to work has no meaning unless assurances are given that old workers would be reinstated. You should not parry this question by saying that the owner alone can respond to it. It would be enough for me if you give assurance from your side that you want that old workers be taken back.

Another matter in connection with Dalminagar is with regard to those who are in prison. Excepting those who are accused of assaulting some one, it will be proper to set free the rest. You should not set it aside by saying that it is a question of law and order. In this respect, only what you desire will happen.

Different kinds of versions are being given about the fire that broke out in the paper-mill.

I want to be excused for writing such a long letter. We are divided between mutually rival parties, still there are certain things that I cannot do. I shall not be able to issue any statements in newspapers against you or fight with you. But I do not understand what I should do in view of the attitude of the Bihar Government towards us. However, I have already told you what I had to say; you may now do what you think fit.

Yours affectionately,
Jayaprakash Narayan

104. To Anugraha Narayan Sinha, 5 February 1949[1]

Dear Anugraha Babu,
Pranam.

Phulan Babu told me what you said to him yesterday. I was very much disappointed. It is true that perhaps I do not realize your difficulties fully. But I do not understand what I should do. I have sent Basawanji for being arrested. He was very unhappy, and his living out (of the prison) was troubling him.

Under these circumstances I have decided that I should advise the workers' union to withdraw the strike. Perhaps they may also accept. Other problems will be solved subsequently. At first, let us see how many workers

[1] *J.P. Papers* (NMML).

are not reinstated by the owner. The workers' union will inform the Government that henceforth the union is prepared to cooperate with the Industrial Tribunal.

Today I am writing a letter to Shri Babu. Its copy is attached herewith. A meeting will be convened in order to withdraw the strike. Permission is needed for that. I am going to Calcutta today evening. If the permission becomes available prior to that, it will be good. The meeting will be held tomorrow or day after tomorrow.

Hope you are cheerful.

Yours affectionately,
Jayaprakash

105. To K. Rama Rao, 5 February 1949[1]

My dear Shri Rama Rao,[2]

I was very happy to hear that you have come over as editor of the *Searchlight*. Journalism in Bihar had touched rather low levels, but now I am sure that with you as editor of one of the premier papers here—even though it is owned by capitalist interests—there would be a toning up of our journalism and an improvement in the public life of the province. I have noticed visible effects in the *Searchlight* since it came under your stewardship. I am going out of Patna today but I hope that after I come back it will be possible for you to come over and have a cup of tea with me. I shall send you a message when I return.

I am enclosing herewith a short statement on the strike in Dalmianagar.[3] You may publish it as a note from me or as a letter to the editor or in any other way you see fit. I shall be thankful if you publish my statement not before Tuesday the 8th February.

Hoping you are well and with kind regards,

Sincerely yours,
J.P.

[1] *J.P. Papers* (NMML).

[2] K. Rama Rao (1896-1961); Editor, *Swarajya*, 1934-5; *National Herald*, 1938-46; *Searchlight*, 1948-50; and *Congress Sandesh*, 1951-2; member, Rajya Sabha, 1952-4.

[3] The statement appeared in *Searchlight* on 9 February, see next item (5 February 1949).

106. On the Strike in Dalmianagar, 5 February 1949[1]

A good deal has been written in the Bihar press about the strike in Dalmianagar. I do not desire to enter into a controversy with anyone but I should like to make clear a few points which, I am afraid, have not received public attention.

I believe it is well-known that the main issue involved in the strike was recognition by the employers of a new union formed by the INTUC. This point may not be considered to constitute a proper trade dispute, but the old union of which Shri Basawan Sinha is the President, and which has served labour in Dalmianagar with such distinction and success, felt that the recognition of the new union amounted to an attempt by the employers to break the existing one. No one can question the right of any section of workers in any industrial unit to form a union of their own whenever they like, but recognition of any mushroom union is always fraught with mischief and it should be regulated by law. Recent labour legislation tends towards making a distinction between unions and bestows special rights and privileges upon those unions which fulfill certain conditions, chief among which is some kind of a test of the representative character of the union concerned. The old union at Dalmianagar had contended that, while the INTUC union had every right to function, the employers should not recognize it unless it was shown that it controlled a certain percentage, let us say 20 per cent, of the total labour strength. This was, of course, not acceptable to the INTUC union and the strike began from the midnight of December 3.

I have felt from the beginning that it was rather unfortunate that a strike at such an important industrial centre of the province should be allowed to continue so long. I therefore tried, when I was in Patna on the 27th and 28th December last, to find a way to bring the strike to an end. During a discussion with the Hon'ble Minister for Labour and departmental chiefs and union representatives, a proposal was made that the issue of recognition of the new union should also be referred to the Industrial Court, and, if there was any legal bar to the Court considering such a point, it might be referred to Mr. Jeejeebhoy as an arbitrator by both the unions. I accepted this proposal on behalf of Shri Basawan Sinha and the old union. Unfortunately, the INTUC union found it impossible to accept this very reasonable proposal which would have set the wheels of industry running at Dalmianagar from the beginning of this year.

During the aforesaid discussion it was discovered that the Government's notification referring the dispute to the Industrial Court contained a clerical

[1] *J.P. Papers* (NMML).
The article was published in *Searchlight*, 9 February 1949.

mistake, i.e. instead of stating that the issue of recognition of the new union might also be taken up by the Industrial Court on reference by the old union, the Government notification had stated that it could be done on reference by the new union. It was said on behalf of the Labour Department that the clerical mistake would be corrected. I was very happy to find that on the 31st of January last, by a fresh notification, the Labour Department has made this correction. This offers the old union an opportunity to reconsider the strike decision and its earlier decision to keep away from the Industrial Court.

Taking everything into consideration and particularly the distress of the workers concerned and the loss to the industry and the province as also Government's fresh notification, I have decided, on my own responsibility, since Shri Basawan Sinha was arrested two days ago, to advise the Union authorities to call off the strike. I hope they will be good enough to accept my advice.

This however is not likely to be the last word on the subject because at least two outstanding questions will have to be solved. The first question is that of taking back into employment all the old staff who were discharged *en masse* by the Management sometime ago. I hope the Hon'ble Minister for Labour will exercise his great influence to see that there is no victimization and that all the old employees are taken back into service. The second question which will have to be settled concerns those who have been arrested and are imprisoned. I think it would be fair to set at liberty all such of them as were arrested on account of technical breach of the law, such as breach of Section 144 or participation in an illegal strike. In the case of those against whom there may be specific charges of violence the law might be allowed to take its course, though there too clemency would not be misplaced, particularly when the workers have suffered from a good deal of violence from the side of custodians of law and order. I hope public opinion in he province will support me in these views and help in the settlement of an issue which has unnecessarily been allowed to become so troublesome.

107. To Shri Krishna Sinha, 5 February 1949[1]

Dear Shri Babu,[2]
Pranam.

Some months ago when Ramanand Tewari[3] was on fast in prison, I had written you a letter. Subsequently I learnt from Phulan Babu that you had

[1] *J.P. Papers* (NMML). Original in Hindi.

[2] For biographical note on Shri Krishna Sinha, see *JPSW*, Vol. 2, pp. 221-2.

[3] Ramanand Tewari (1909-80); participated in the Quit India Movement, 1942; led the

been hurt by my letter. I am sorry that my letter hurt you, but I assure you that I had no idea in my mind, even in dream, that I should write anything against your dignity.

Last time when I wrote to you, I was very much aggrieved because I had no permission to meet one of my comrades in prison who had been on fast for 21 days. At the time of writing this letter also I am very sad at heart. Two days ago I heard the news of the arrest of my friend, Munshi Ahmed Din.[4] Munshiji had gone to Karachi in connection with his family work. After returning from there he came directly to me and left for Jamshedpur the same night. You are aware that Munshiji has been working for the Socialist Party at Jamshedpur for several months. During this period he has become extremely popular there among workers. When I had once gone to Jamshedpur, 50,000 workers in a meeting had, raising their hands, hailed him as their leader. Otherwise also Munshiji is an old nationalist and was one of the leaders of the Punjab Congress. At this time he is a member of the All-India Executive Committee of our party. Since he went to Jamshedpur he has worked very carefully and I believe the local authorities would have no complaints against him. John Saheb[5] will certainly have complaints, but that is because of party politics.

Under these circumstances, Munshiji's arrest without any reason is a gross injustice. In Jamshedpur some workers went on strike, so why should Munshiji and other Socialists be arrested? Are we like the *Doms* (persons belonging to the scavengers' castes) of the British period who were put behind bars if incidents of theft took place anywhere in the area? Is there no value of the freedom of citizens in free India? Is there no difference between the British regime and the Congress regime?

When the black legislation was introduced in the Legislative Assembly of Bihar,[6] Phulan Babu had expressed his apprehensions in the Select Committee that the law would be used not only in communal riots but also against Socialists. Then you had given an assurance that law would be used only in communal riots. Has Munshiji participated in communal riots? If he had been a communalist, he would have been a minister today in Pakistan, not in the prison of the Congress Government.

If you want to keep alive freedom and civil liberty, then I beseech you to

---

police strike 1947-8; member, Bihar Legislative Assembly, 1952-72; Home Minister Bihar Government, 1967-71; member, Lok Sabha, 1977-80.

[4] Munshi Ahmed Din. For biographical note see, *JPSW*, Vol. 2, p. 199.

[5] M. John, labour leader in Jamshedpur and a Congressman; President, Tata Steel and Wire Worker's Union.

[6] The Bihar Public Safety Act of March 1947 was extended in 1948 by a resolution of the Legislature. In March 1949, the Bihar Assembly passed a new amending Act, extending the previous Act for another year and including Chhotanagpur which was not there previously.

kindly release Munshiji and also other Socialists who have been imprisoned like the *Doms* of the British period. If you want to fight with the Socialist Party, then fight without using the power of the administration as two parties fight in a democracy.

I want to make a request to you with regard to Dalmianagar also. I want that the strike should be withdrawn in the wake of the Government's new notification. In this respect, I made two requests to Anugraha Babu: one, all old workers may be reinstated in their work; and second, those workers who have not been accused of being involved in violent activities may be released after the withdrawal of strike. I am repeating these two requests to you and I hope that you will accept them. Besides, there is a small request that I may be given permission to convene a meeting at Dalmianagar to withdraw the strike. I want to send one of my companions to speak at the meeting. We may call the meeting perhaps on 6 or 7. It will not be possible to withdraw the strike without calling a meeting. I shall leave for Calcutta at 5 P.M. today. So, I shall be obliged if I receive your reply prior to my departure.

I want to be excused for a long letter.

Yours,
Jayaprakash Narayan

108. To Shanti Prasad Jain, 6 February 1949[1]

Dear Shanti Prasadji,[2]

On that day I was surprised and pained that you talked to me with such impoliteness. I have also felt extremely sorry for the fire that broke out in the factory, but how did you accept the view that they were my "men" who set the fire. You know me and also Basawan Babu. Can you accept that we had ordered people to set fire? Up-till now there is no correct information as to how the fire broke out, but even if we accept that someone had wilfully set the fire, be rest assured that the union or the Socialist Party could never have had a hand in that.

You know that it has been my effort from the beginning that there should be a settlement of the strike. When I met Anugraha Babu on 28 December, I had accepted the proposal that the issue of recognition should be submitted to the arbitration of Jeejeebhoy. But those who had been loudly proclaiming their support for the method of arbitration, rejected it.

[1] *J.P. Papers* (NMML). Original in Hindi.

[2] Shanti Prasad Jain (1912-79); Chairman, Rohtas Industries Ltd., S.K.G. Sugar Ltd., Delhi-Rohtas Light Railway Ltd.; President, Bihar Industries Association, and Employers Association, Patna.

Subsequently the error in the Government notification was not rectified for a month. After my return to Patna and talking to Anugraha Babu, the error has been rectified and a new notification has been issued. In the circumstances, I am advising the labour union to withdraw the strike, and cooperate with the Industrial Tribunal. I hope the labour-union will accept the advice.

Now the question is one of the reinstatement of all the old workers in their jobs. I had wanted to talk to you on this question only, but you were so much distressed by the burning of the factory that you paid no attention to propriety in the talks. My suggestion to you is that you should deal with this question with tact and understanding. If you want that industrial peace should prevail in Dalmianagar in future, then do not dismiss any worker for his participation in the strike. Basawan Babu had assured workers at the time of his arrest that he would stake his life on this question. Then, what is the use of raising a new issue again? Here I am at Phulan Babu's residence [in Calcutta]. If you wish to talk, you may come here or send your Secretary. I am here till the 8th.

109. Appeal to the Workers of Dalmianagar (undated, but between 6 and 8 February 1949)[1]

Brother-workers of Dalmianagar,

I congratulate you on having conducted your strike with such bravery and firmness for so many days. You have proved by your sacrifice and patience what kind of faith you repose in your labour union and how you recognize your true interests and how much unwavering respect you have for your leader, Bhai Basawan Sinha.[2] You suffered lots of difficulties, but your suffering will not go in vain. Emerging from this fire of sacrifice, your organization has further become like shining gold on which there can never be any blot.

During the period of your strike a number of events have taken place and you have seen and heard so many things. The true image of that Congress union, over which your dispute arose, has come before you all. You have seen how far that union is of the workers and how far of the Government—the same Government that inflicted so much repression upon you. You have also seen how the owner and the Congress union have coalesced with each other like milk and water. Thus, even if no other benefit results from this strike, it will be enough, if it opens the workers' eyes and helps them to become aware of their friends and foes. Even if the Congress union continues to exist in Dalmianagar with the help of the police and military, it will

[1] *J.P. Papers* (NMML). Original in Hindi.

remain as the Company's union instead of the workers' union. And in this condition it cannot harm you in any way. If there is unity among workers, nobody can harm them.

Basawan Babu is in prison at present. In this situation you and I have to sit and think what should be done further. To prolong your pain further will be doing an injustice to you, and a new way also has been found of which you can take advantage. You would have known that I had accepted the proposal of the Government that the issue of recognition of the Congress union should be referred to Shri Jeejeebhoy's arbitration. But the Congress leaders, who have been beating the drum of the method of arbitration day and night, did not accept it. But now the Government itself has said by issuing a new notification that any party can refer the issue of recognition to the industrial court, that is, Shree Jeejeebhoy's arbitration. It cannot be said what the decision of the court will be on this issue; but at least you have got the right to refer this issue to the court. This is also a success for you.

Under the circumstances, my suggestion to the labour union and to all brother-workers is that you should now withdraw the strike, and the labour union should order you all to go to work.

My second suggestion is this that the labour union should inform both the Government and Shri Jeejeebhoy after the issue of the new notification, that it is prepared to cooperate with the industrial court.

I hope you will accept both of my suggestions.

All problems will not be resolved with the withdrawal of strike. It cannot be said with certainty as yet whether the company will take back all old workers or not, and whether those who are in prison will be released or not. But it is not proper to wait for decision on these matters. The labour union will continue to fight on these issues, and I shall extend you all possible help in this respect. Basawan Babu has told me before going (to prison) that he will stake his life on these issues. You know how Basawan Babu is true to his word. His life is not cheap and we shall not let it be endangered.

I would also like to tell that you should not regard those old brother-workers who went back to work during the strike, as your enemies. Perhaps they had to return because of their weakness or their difficulties, but I am confident that they too will not be prepared to join the Congress union. You should keep them also with you, and make them members of your union.

At the end, one thing more. I became very unhappy to hear that fire broke out in the paper-mill and heavy losses were suffered. Now it is not known how fire broke out, but if somebody set fire wilfully, than he greatly harmed both the workers and the country. It is treason to workers to damage a factory and machine in any way because the factory belongs not only to the capitalists but also to the workers, and is a means of their livelihood. I therefore hope that if someone had wilfully set fire, you will openly condemn him.

Your own,
Jayaprakash Narayan

110. To All Members of the National Executive, 9 February 1949[1]

Dear Friend,

I received on 6-2-49 the following telegram from Yusuf Meherally:[2]

"After fresh examinations doctors prohibit coming Patna or writing address therefore tendering resignation stop kindly elect new president deeply grieved giving all this trouble."

I have already replied to him saying that there is no question of his resigning or our accepting his resignation. The Executive has selected him for chairmanship of the Conference and his name has been announced, and I see no reason why we should change the Chairman only because Yusuf is ill. I therefore feel strongly that the Executive should not accept Yusuf's resignation. This view is strengthened when we consider the fact that we contemplate a change in the Party constitution according to which the Chairman of the Conference would also be the Party's Chairman for the year, i.e., he would also preside at meetings of the General Council, the National Executive and special Conferences. I hope you will agree with this view.

Even if you agree that Meherally should continue to be the Chairman-designate, we will have to have someone to deputise for him at the session in view of his illness and his inability even to write his address. Ordinarily, there need have been no hurry in selecting the deputy, but it would be advisable to give the person selected some time to prepare his address. As the Patna Conference has a rather exceptional importance, I personally thought that we should persuade Narendra Deva to act for Yusuf, because his address would receive wide publicity and attention. I cannot say, because I have not consulted him yet, if Narendra Deva would agree, but I see no reason why he should not.

Please consider this letter as urgent and reply as soon as you can, preferably by wire to me care *Janata*, New Delhi, up to the 14th and thereafter at Kadam Kuan, Patna.

Sincerely yours,
Jayaprakash Narayan

[1] *J.P. Papers* (NMML).

[2] Yusuf Meherally. For biographical note, see *JPSW*, Vol. 1, p. 156.

111. To Purshottam Trikamdas, 9 February 1949[1]

Patna
9 February 1949

Dear Purshottam,

I received your wire two days ago suggesting Sethji's[2] name in place of Yusuf for the chairmanship of the Conference. Just now there is a wire from Narendra Deva saying:

"WELCOME SETHJI'S PRESIDENTSHIP"

I find all this rather bewildering. I do not understand the terrific haste in which you people seem to be. It appears from Narendra Deva's wire that you must have wired to other members of the National Executive too. That was unnecessary. Yusuf's place is not vacant yet. It is true he has written to me relinquishing his chairmanship; but I have not accepted his resignation, nor has the Executive considered it, nor had I circularized yet the members for their opinion. It is my definite opinion, for what it is worth—and it is not worth much for the Bombay party—that we should not accept Yusuf's resignation. He need not attend nor need he send his written address, but yet he should be the Chairman-designate. Some one may deputise for him.

I have no objection to Sethji, but I was considering Narendra Deva. But that is not important, any one may deputise. What I felt and do so still, in spite of the weighty opinions of yourself, Asoka and Narendra Deva, is that Yusuf should remain the Chairman-designate.[3]

I am circularizing the members today. I shall act according to their wishes.

I hope Madam is better now.

Affectionately yours,
Jayaprakash

P.S. The names of Achyut and Asoka would naturally occur to you in this connection. They did to me too. But it is my wish that Achyut should be the Chairman next year and Asoka the year after that. It would not be good to have either of them as deputy. But Narendra Deva has been our Chairman before; in fact, he was our first Chairman. So it appears to me not inappropriate that he should deputise for Yusuf. It cannot be considered *infra dig* for any of us to be Yusuf's deputy.

[1] *J.P. Papers* (NMML).

[2] Damodarswarup Seth, see *JPSW*, Vol. I, p. 185.

[3] J.P.'s view finally prevailed and it was decided that Narendra Deva would be Chairman of the Conference with Yusuf Meherally remaining Chairman of the Party.

112. Address to the Railwaymen at Danapur, 16 February 1949[1]

Friends,

At Nagpur you decided that the unions should take a strike ballot. That decision was ratified by all the affiliated unions and the result of the ballot was overwhelmingly in favour of strike.

Meanwhile, I had certain talks with the Hon'ble Minister for Railways, and the Government's favourable decision regarding dearness allowance was published. The Working Committee that met at Delhi on January 21 according to your Nagpur decision, thought that these were new developments and required a fresh consideration of the step that had been contemplated. It is thus that we have met together again. I have no doubt that the General Council will decide the issue before it today, with the same wisdom as theretofore.

Before I place for your consideration the issue which faces you, I should like to say a few words by way of personal explanation. The communists have accused me of carrying on unauthorized negotiations and betraying the railwaymen. These are serious charges of which if found guilty I must be removed from the presidentship of the Federation. I should therefore like from you a clear verdict on these charges.

I shall briefly state my position. As President of the Federation it is my inherent right to correspond with or meet the Railway Minister if I considered that necessary from the point of view of the Federation. But it was not merely personal responsibility that led me to write to or meet Shri Gopalaswami Ayyangar. In acting thus I merely carried out your wishes. You will recall that the Nagpur resolution had directed "that active steps should be taken to enlighten the public and inform the Government that the Federation is always prepared for an honourable settlement".[2] It was in pursuance of this direction that I wrote to the Railway Minister early in December and the text of my letter has already appeared in the press and has been sent to the unions. In the course of that letter I had said after quoting the above direction:

"If the Government too are prepared for an honourable settlement I shall be glad to know what steps you suggest to that end." In reply to that letter Shri Ayyangar wired to me as follows:

> Your letter dated 13th from Meerut has just been delivered to me. I welcome your method of approach to the problem which confronts us both and the country as

[1] Adapted from *Janata*, 20 February 1949.

[2] The resolution was passed at the Nagpur Conference of the Federation on 24 November 1948.

well as your drawing attention to the preparedness for an honourable settlement on the part of the Federation. Government are equally desirous that their decisions should be regarded by the Federation as some thing which the workers can accept with honour. I would request you to make it convenient to meet me for the purpose of a frank talk on the whole matter. I shall be in Delhi till the 24th, in Madras from the 26th to 31st December, in Bombay from 2nd to 4th January and back in Delhi on the 6th January. I shall be delighted if you can meet me preferably in Madras on any one of the dates mentioned. If after this talk the Federation calls off the strike ballot, as I hope I shall be able to persuade you to advise it to do so, I assure you I am prepared to sit with you in January from day to day and discuss with you myself every issue specifically connected with the Railways which you have raised or may raise with a view to effect the honourable settlement which you have stressed.

When the Railway Minister had invited me so courteously to a personal talk it would have been churlish on my part, and I would have been injuring the interests of railwaymen, if I had refused to go or had said that I would see him only after the balloting was over. That would have caused unnecessary provocation and only multimplicd our difficulties.

I accordingly met Shri Ayyangar at Bombay on the 3rd and 4th January; and to help me at these talks I invited the General Secretary and the office-bearers of the Federation who reside in Bombay. Unfortunately, Shri Joglekar was out of town and was not able to accompany us.

After our two days' talks I felt that an understanding was possible on the issues discussed and a statement to that effect was made. In my own statement I had made it clear at the same time that the Nagpur resolution stood. Subsequently, we had further discussions with the Hon'ble Minister and his colleagues at Delhi, after which the working Committee met on the 21st of last month at Delhi.

I have been condemned for not calling the working Committee immediately after the talks in Bombay. This is a thoughtless accusation. As you know, a notice of ten days is necessary even for an emergent meeting and therefore the earliest that we could have called the working Committee after the 4th evening was the 15th of January. The Committee had already been scheduled to meet on the 21st to take action on the results of the strike ballot. Because the difference was only of six days I thought there was no need to call the Working Committee on the 15th and then again on the 21st, and so I carried on the talks with the Minister, assisted by such colleagues as I thought fit to invite. If you think I was wrong in doing what I did, please say so and I shall act accordingly.

As regards the charge of betrayal, our communist friends, being so well versed in that art, are always profuse in calling others names and accusing others for what they have been doing themselves. If you consider dispassionately all that the Communists have been doing in the railways for the past months you will agree with me that if there is any one who can be accused of betraying the workers, it is they. If they are allowed to carry on as at present, the result will be a complete disruption of our organization and the end of the Federation. I have come to the conclusion therefore that we have now reached a parting of the ways. But I shall revert to this question again.

I want you and all railwaymen to distinguish a friend from an enemy. You elected me President twice, and at Nagpur you gave me a unanimous vote of confidence. But these friends say now that I have turned a traitor. I have already explained to you what my role of treachery has been and it is for you now to decide. I have no private interests to serve and I am not seeking any favours or jobs of the Government. I am not in the running for ministry. If I were, there was no need for me to make secret pacts: I could have accepted an invitation to join months ago. So, where was the need for me to enter into any pact with Shri Ayyangar or Pandit Nehru? Further, I belong to a party that is in opposition to the party in power. So, I can gain no party advantage from any such pact. Nor has the Socialist Party, let this be well understood, any interest to serve, apart from the interest of the working men. Whatever is to the advantage of the worker is naturally of advantage to the Socialist Party. So, in all my actions, I only had the interests of the railwaymen in view, to the exclusion of all other considerations.

I never understood that it was the decision of the Federation that whatever happened there must be a strike. The General Council had said that we were always prepared for an honourable settlement. It is now for you to consider whether the results of my talks are sufficient for you to change your decision. There is no secret commitment that I have made. All I wish to do on my part is to tell you frankly and unequivocally my own personal view and leave it to you to make your decision.

II

Now let me first state briefly the result of my talks. The most important of our demands, as you know, was that for an adequate dearness allowance. In December last, by its grainshop decision, the Railway Ministry had effected a serious cut in the total emoluments which you were receiving.[3] This cut was made in the face of rising prices. As a result of your agitation the cut has been largely, if not wholly, restored. Though that cannot satisfy us, you must realize that it was a victory for your Federation, as for the Post and

[3] After the implementation of Pay Commission recommended salary to the railwaymen, the Railway Ministry had decided to cut the grain-shop facility (subsidized food shops), so long granted to the railway employees, and that had an adverse effect on their revised pay-packet which was not very high.

Telegraph unions who had forced the Central Government to make these fresh concessions. That even the present dearness allowance is not adequate and not in accordance with the C.P.C. recommendations is admitted by the Government. That too is a gain for us. The Government conceded in its communiqué that it had accepted the C.P.C. recommendations but its financial position did not allow it to implement those recommendations to the full. That strengthens our case for future negotiations. The Government conceded what the Pay Commission had pointed out, that dearness allowance of the employees should be revised every six months, in accordance with the price index. Therefore, it should be remembered that the last word has not been spoken on the subject and our efforts to win an adequate allowance need not be given up.

The question before you is not whether you accept the present dearness allowance as satisfactory but whether after this concession, you feel that a strike is necessary. The Government, you know, argues in the first place that it is trying its best to reduce prices; and that it is no solution of the problem of rising costs to let wages run after prices. That is a vicious circle and therefore the Government says it is trying and hoping to reduce prices in the near future. There has been no success achieved hitherto in this direction by the Government. But, as it has been the case of labour also that the main problem is reduction of prices and not of raising dearness allowances only it may be wise for us, in view of the concession made by the Government, to give the Government a chance for a few months. If the prices do not decline, we would be justified in pressing for a full dearness allowance.

I shall summarise below the other concessions made by the Government tentatively, their application depending upon the course of action we choose here:

Demand No. 1: On Pay Fixation Formulae

For the purpose of the fixation of the initial pay in the prescribed scale of a person who was on a pre-1931 scale of pay and who had elected for the prescribed scale of pay, the pay that on the date of his passing to the prescribed scale, he would have been entitled to on the post-31 scale of pay, should first be calculated on the assumption that he came on to the post-31 scale when he could have done so and his pay then was fixed under FR. 22. This applies only to posts for which the pre-1931 scale is inferior to the corresponding post-1931 scales. The Railway Board will have power to determine which post-1931 scale corresponds to which pre-1931 scale.

As regards other cases of pre-1931 entrants:

The Railway Board will examine the application of the rules for the fixation of the pay in the prescribed scales of pay in order to determine how and to what extent experience in the same category of service can be given due regard to fixing the initial pay in the prescribed scales.

Demand No. 2

The unauthorized scale 35-1-40 for unskilled supervisory staff will be abolished as demanded by the Federation and the scale 35-1-50 will be given in its place, not only for those who are correctly designated but also others whose work involved supervision in substance over unskilled workers.

Only persons who are responsible for the quality and outturn of work of a group of workers would be admitted to this group. Any unskilled employee whose post carries a measure of personal responsibility and who is not subject to direct supervision will be given Rs. 35-1-40 scale.

Any specific cases in which the scale of 35-1-40 had been allotted to any category and which the Federation considered, after an examination of the duties attached, to the post merited the scale of Rs. 35-1-40 will be examined.

As regards the splitting of 80-220 scale, the Railway Board held the view that this gave the matriculate clerks chances of promotion which they would not have got otherwise and as the initial recruitment for clerks is mostly in the lowest categories, and in the absence of any category of posts of clerks for which a university degree is insisted upon, the scale of 80-220 has not been adopted on the railways.

Demand No. 3

As regards the raising of the pay scales of different categories listed in the Federation's resolution, while the Government adhered to the view that the general structure of the C.P.C. scales cannot be disturbed, the Government were prepared to set up an Anomalies Committee for the following purpose: to examine anomalies arising out of the application of the C.P.C. recommendations to railway workers, and also to recommend how these might be corrected.

Any proposal which seeks to vary the Pay Commission recommendations must be justified on the score of serious injustice or hardship to any particular class of employees in the light of their previous condition of service.

Demand No. 4

As efficiency bars are recommended by the Central Pay Commission, this could not be abolished.

Demand No. 5

The scales of pay and allowances for Running Staff have been announced in the light of the recommendations of the Running Staff Committee and in some cases have been further improved.

Any post-1931 entrant drawing less emoluments under the new system to payment than he actually drew before 1.1.1949 for equivalent mileage performed will be protected in his emoluments.

Demand No. 6

With reference to the distribution of posts in the various grades in any category, if a comparison of the present ratios in any railway with similar ratios in the last three pre-war years shows that in the former there has been a considerable shift to the lower grades, the case will be re-examined.

In any other case if it is contended that there is serious injustice in the distribution of various grades in any particular category in a railway, it also will be examined.

Demand No. 7

This is covered by the reply to demands Nos. 3 and 5.

Demand No. 8

The Hon'ble Minister of State for Transport and Railways promised to take up personally with the Finance Ministry the question of enhanced local allowances on the basis of the latest population figures. The question was delayed due to differences of opinion on the tests to be evolved for verifying population claims.

Demand No. 9

The Government will be prepared to discuss with the federation the facilities required for running the railway grainshops on co-operative lines.

Demand No. 10

The Pay Commission scales and allowances will be applied to casual labour who will be treated a temporary labour as per the decision of the Railway Board that the limiting periods for casual employment not paid from contingencies should be six months.

Other temporary staff, Class III and IV, will be engaged at the prescribed scales of pay applicable to permanent railway servants and will, in accordance with rules, be eligible for dearness allowance, house rent and compensatory allowances sanctioned for the locality where the individual concerned is employed (Vide Railway Board's E. 48 CPC/150, dated 12-1-1949)

If the provincial scales of pay are lower, Railway school teachers will be entitled to minimum scales applicable to corresponding Railway subordinate staff recruited with matric or degree as minimum qualification. The question of granting Dearness Allowance as per Railway Rules for the Railway School Teachers will be reconsidered.

Demand No. 11

Protection of pay of non-permanent staff I the workshops on the same basis applicable to permanent staff is granted and other cases are under examination. Generally, excess payments due to bona fide mistakes will be waived recovery.

Demand No. 12

The decision of the Government on the Adjudicator's Award and the C.P.C. recommendations regarding the leave rules is expected before 1st March 1949.

Demand No. 13

The latest pass rules meet some of the objections raised against the previous rules. The question of retirement, passes for class IV staff, will be considered.

Demand No. 14

The basic minimum monthly pay should be deemed to be 48 working hours a week and that there will be no variations in emoluments from month to month provided the workman is present for normal working hours of the workshop even if the actual working hours in any month may exceed 208 hours or be lower.

A collective option to the staff in each workshop to decide whether they would accept the formula proposed by him or were prepared to be paid in accordance with the existing practice, after consultation with the Law Ministry.

Demand No. 15

C.P.C. recommendation regarding the temporary staff will be implemented.

The question of extension of the State Railway Educational Assistance Rules to railways, which did not apply them, will be considered.

Other C.P.C. recommendations will be implemented in the light of the decisions of the Government for other departments.

Demand No. 16

The Hon'ble Minister of State for Transport and Railways will look into the question of the conversion of temporary posts to permanent and the confirmation of temporary staff therein and the Federation will be informed of the position as soon as the necessary statistics are obtained about the action taken on the Railway Board's instructions.

Another chance for exercising option will be given if prescribed scale for any posts is altered.

These are not large concessions but you will agree with me that they are quite appreciable. And they would be available to us without going through the risk and trouble of a strike. The negotiations that would be continued, if you decide to follow the path of negotiation again and the Anomalies Committee would doubtless yield further results and further improvement of your lot.

Therefore, it is advisable for your to consider whether you should now take the risk of a strike and of earning public hostility and censure and of putting a vital sector of the nation's economy in turmoil.

III

In this reconsideration there are other factors which too you have to keep in view. You must have noticed that the press had generally been hostile to your case, and the public, to say the least, have been apathetic. Government spokesmen have done their best to create ill-feeling against you. In these circumstances, if you were to go on strike even after the concessions already made you will not receive any public support, I am afraid. On the other hand, the Government will not only justify suppressing our struggle but also receive solid public support in its action, in the absence of which our success would be extremely doubtful.

The history of recent strikes in the country has brought to light certain dangers which it would be foolish for us to overlook. First of all, there is an anti-strike sentiment created among the people on the plea of national crisis. Backed by this sentiment, the legislatures have enacted laws which lay down complicated procedures for the settlement of industrial disputes and vest extraordinary powers in the executive to deal with strikes as if they were acts of rebellion. To cap it all, there are the Public Safety Acts.[4] The conditions in their totality amount to semi-fascist circumstances and labour in this country must fully appreciate these difficulties and devise proper ways to wage its fight under them. There must be a far greater consolidation of labour organizations than at present and a higher political development

[4] To control widespread strike and agitations in the states, the Government enacted several laws to empower the state governments with the right to detain any person suspected of indulging in unlawful activities. The Public Safety Act and the Essential Services (Prevention of Strikes) Act were introduced in the Parliament in 1948. The Security Amendment Act and Armed Forces Act (Special Powers) were passed in West Bengal in September 1948. And in Madhya Pradesh, the Public Safety Bill was passed in the Assembly on 6 January 1949.

of the labour movement, before labour can hope to break the chain of fascism that holds it today. As recent experience has shown, premature action only leads to the strengthening of the fascist hold. Labour must attempt patiently to educate public opinion; there must be more independent labour representatives in the legislatures; labour must become a greater political force before it can give a major challenge to the forces of reaction. Therefore the strategy of the labour movement demands not foolhardy ventures but consolidation of present gains and existing organizations, propaganda and preparation for political action.

There is yet another aspect that you must bear in mind. It is true that there was an overwhelming vote in favour of strike. But it is my clear reading that notwithstanding the vote, a large section of our members and larger section of non-members while deeply dissatisfied, are unprepared to shoulder the risk of a strike. An index of this unpreparedness is the result of the drive for the Emergency Fund. The exact figures are not yet with me, but I doubt if the collections amount to more than 50,000 rupees, whereas at least four lakhs were expected from the members of the affiliated unions. It is true that many have not paid because they have not been approached, but even when approached, the response has been disappointing. There is no doubt there are many militants in the Federation whom nothing can cow down, but they alone cannot bring about a general strike. I should also tell you that my long experience of the national and labour struggles has shown me that there is no relation between brave words and brave deeds. I have found that many who came to the platform and spoke fiery words lost courage and fell by the roadside long before the goal was reached. So, I would urge you not to confuse words with action, and be carried away by the first to the detriment of the second.

I have often referred to the danger to our Federation from a rival body that has been formed.[5] I am sure that if we act wisely, this danger can be eliminated, for the realization is growing that it serves no purpose whatever to multiply organizations. But I am also sure that if we were to launch upon a strike in the present circumstances the rival body would be used to break our solidarity and destroy the unique position that our Federation holds.

I should like to take this opportunity to plead with the unions that have formed a rival federation that they should reconsider their step in the interest of the unity and solidarity of the railway workers. For our part, I should like to assure these unions that our doors are always open to them and that nothing could give us greater pleasure than to welcome them into the fold of the All-India Railwaymen's Federation.

Lastly, I should like to draw your attention to another serious danger, a

[5] Indian National Railway Workers Federation.

danger that comes from within. We have some unions which are controlled by our communist friends. The general policy of the communist parties in Asia today is that of creating chaos and confusion in all walks of national life. In India too, that is their present policy. It is a rather simple policy and does not take much effort to carry out. To create chaos and disorganization is easier than to construct and build. In pursuance of its policy, the Communist Party of India is trying its best to disorganize industry and government. They hope in this manner to prevent India from growing strong, and thereby they hope to serve the ends of Russian policy. Russia does not want any country in its neighbourhood to become powerful and remain outside its orbit of influence. Therefore, the communist ultimatum to every country is: walk into the Russian parlour or choose to remain weak and disunited. The communists in India are not fighting to build up a communist State, but, because India has refused to walk into the Russian parlour they aim to keep her in disorder. Communists are not trying to serve the interests of labour. Their aim, as I said, in all circumstances and at all costs is to create chaos, disorder and disruption. Reports of communist activities that have reached me go clearly to show that they have made preparations to take advantage of the strike to accomplish this basic task. They are advocating a strike even in the present changed circumstances not because they are convinced that a strike is advisable on the merits of the case but because they find it convenient to take advantage of your discontent in order to create disorder and chaos.

There may be some misguided friends who may argue that it is a revolutionary policy today to disorganize government and create anarchy. As a humble revolutionary myself, I should like to repeat the warning that I have given a hundred times before, against this infantile view. It is my definite opinion that if there is chaos in the country today it is not the forces of Socialism and progress that will win but the forces of reaction, i.e., the forces of feudalism, communalism and capitalism. Out of chaos in the present conditions of India, will arise a fascist dictatorship and not a socialist State. Nor can the communists' hope, on the strength of their own resources and unaided by agencies outside the country, to create a communist dictatorship out of chaos today. They are, as elsewhere, relying on support from outside—monetary, military and diplomatic. And remember, with foreign support no one can establish a workers' democracy, but only a slave State. And this is the most treacherous and pernicious part of world communism today.

India is a friend of Russia, but India will never allow Russia or America or any other power, great or small, to interfere with her internal affairs through their quislings and fifth columns. The sooner people in this country including railwaymen realize this, the better it would be for them.

IV

After taking into consideration all these aspects of the question I have come to the definite conclusion that you should not give notice of strike now but should stay your hands, carry on the negotiations that the Railway Minister has offered to hold with us, and consolidate our present gains and our organization. This is my unequivocal advice which, I do hope you will see the wisdom of accepting.

I may be asked why when most of the above considerations were present even at Nagpur I did not tender the same advice then. I did not, because the situation was very different then. We were faced then with the "final reply" of the Railway Board and there was no other course left to us but to decide on taking strike ballot. Subsequently, the Railway Minister in response to my letter offered to negotiate with us; some negotiations were actually held; certain concessions were promised; the Government of India published their decision to grant an extra dearness allowance over what we were getting since January 1st of this year; further negotiations, including an Anomalies Committee, were agreed upon. These are sufficient reasons for me to advise you now to change your Nagpur decision and desist from serving strike notice. I should add that I have been further persuaded to do so because I have been convinced of the sincere desire of Shri Gopalaswami Ayyangar to settle with us and do all that is possible for him in the present set-up of things.

Let me revert to the communists again. Reports of their activities prove that they are guilty of disloyalty to the Federation and have done their best to undermine its authority and to disrupt it from within. Disruption from within is more dangerous and culpable than the same thing attempted from without. I have therefore come to the conclusion that the communists have no place in the Federation any longer. To allow them to continue to use our organization and our platform is to allow them to complete their task of disruption. To build up a representative organization of nearly a million workers is a vast constructive task and it cannot be undertaken by people who have no sense of responsibility, who have no capacity to work with those who differ from them and who do not keep the interests of the workers in view but act according to extraneous influences and motives.

I had desisted hitherto from speaking even a word against the communists from the platform of the Federation, but the time has come now when it would be doing a great disservice to railwaymen if I do not now speak out. Do not for a moment think that I have been provoked to make these remarks because the communists have attacked me personally. Their attacks and abuses do not in the least affect me. I am used to them because they have been doing this sort of thing for years past. It was not many years ago that they called me a traitor to the country and a Japanese agent, just at the moment when I was fighting as a soldier of freedom. These people who are themselves guilty of the greatest betrayal of recent times accused Netaji, you will remember, of treachery. If you go through communist literature in this country you will find that they have in the past accused the Father of the Nation himself, not once but hundreds of times of being an agent of British imperialism and a lackey of Indian capitalism. You might have seen that they have recently been attacking Pandit Nehru, after having shouted for months "Nehru Zindabad", as a lackey of Anglo-American imperialism. Instead, therefore of being rattled by their invective I feel rather proud to find myself in the company of Mahatma Gandhi, Netaji Subhas Chandra Bose and the Prime Minister.

So it is not because the Communists have attacked me personally that I have denounced them, but because I have felt, as I said before, that the time had come to warn you of the dire danger from them. Railwaymen must realize that if the Federation is to be saved, the communists must go.

V

I have suggested above that our main task in the next few months should be that of consolidation. For that we require money and more workers. I hope railwaymen will give us the tools to carry out this business of reorganization and consolidation.

In this connection I should like to make a few suggestions. The trade union movement in this country, even though more than a quarter of a century old, is still in a primitive condition. There is practically no constructive activity that the unions undertake. There is very little educational work done; offices are inefficiently run, there is a dearth of experts. There is no research or study being carried on, and they have no journals. The Federation is almost a beggar when it comes to funds and we have no travelling organizers. This state of affairs must go. If railwaymen are really serious, the time has come now when they must put their shoulders to the wheel and create an efficient organization which would serve them efficiently in many ways. Among constructive activities I should lay stress particularly on the need of starting a co-operative movement among railwaymen, in which I hope Government and the Railway Administrations will give us all possible help. The problem of rising prices would have been less severe for railwaymen if they had their own co-operative stores, and in that case the loss to them from corruption and mismanagement would also have been much less.

It was at Lillooah that I had referred to the reorganization of the unions and the Federation. My further experience has proved to me that if we are to function effectively we must combine the principles of industrial unionism with those of craft unionism. While our unions must remain industrial orgnisations, as they are today, their internal structure should be such that each category of staff is adequately represented and whenever the interests of that staff are concerned its own representatives are in a position to participate in negotiations and settlement. At the Federation level also, such reorganization is essential. I hope the Working Committee will immediately turn its attention to this problem of reorgnisation.

I should like here to go further and suggest a revolutionary innovation. I think the time has come when the Federation type of organization should give place to the single union type. In other words, instead of having federation of autonomous unions, we should have a national, central union of railwaymen, with branches and locals. When there were different railway companies, there was justification for separate unions. But now we have only one employer (barring the case of the employees of the State Railways which too are bound sooner or later to be integrated with the national system). Most of the issues in dispute are to be taken either to the Railway Board or the Minister. In these circumstances, the Federation has to bear most of the burden of collective bargaining and yet because of the federal type of organization it has insufficient funds, insufficient control over the unions and is unable to build up a powerful, efficiently functioning organization. The change-over to the centralized union of organization would also solve the problem of rival unionism.

I was happy to find that such an experienced and able leader of the Federation as our General Secretary is in complete agreement with this view. Indeed he tells me that he has been trying exactly for this very thing for the last twenty years! Well, he was ahead of his time, I am afraid. But, time has caught up with him now, and I hope all of us will help him to realize his dream.

These are some of the important problems of consolidation and reorganization to which you must turn your attention in order to move forward and raise your organization and your struggle to a higher level.

VI

I should like now to address a few remarks to the Government. The newspapers are thick with rumours that the Government is contemplating an ordinance to deal with strikes of their employees. The Government has been in office for eighteen months now. Form its very birth it had to face discontented and clamorous employees and the eventuality of a strike threatened it from the very first day. Yet till to date the Government has not tried to make a new approach to the question. Pandit Nehru's Government has dealt with its labour problems much in the same manner as Wavell's Government, for instance, did. Our legislators and rulers should realize that outlawing of strikes is no solution of the labour problem. The Central Government is the biggest employer in the country and runs many commercial and industrial undertakings. It must set up a suitable and permanent machinery to dispose of labour disputes. For the Railways I have been advocating for some time the setting up of a Joint Standing Committee of the Railway Board and the Federation to deal with disputes and a Permanent Tribunal to decide questions which are not settled in the Joint Committee. The latter should not be a mere consultative body, but should have ample powers to call for relevant papers and facts and to take agreed decisions of a binding character; and its working should be regular and expeditious. In cases of difference, either party to the dispute may make a reference to the Permanent Tribunal, whose judgement should be binding on both with certain specified qualifications.

Together with this machinery there should be progressively greater association of labour with administration till, within a specified period of time, labour comes to acquire equal share in the administration of the Railways with the Railway Board and the Railway Administrations.

Experience has further shown that sometimes labour discontent grows not because the Railway Board is unreasonable, but because some other department of the Government stands in the way. More often than not it is the Finance Department that is the villain of the piece. I think that it is high time to realize that the Railways are an industry and a business and they must run on proper business lines and those responsible for running them must have freedom to carry on work according to their discretion. Questions of policy may be settled by Parliament or the Cabinet, but within the framework of that policy the Railway Ministry and Board must be made autonomous.

All this would require a drastic amendment of the Railway Act. I hope that such amendment would not be delayed much longer and that the Federation would be consulted before the new Act is prepared.

Friends, I have surveyed for you the whole position; and I hope you will take a comprehensive view and be guided by wisdom and farsight in making your decision. I thank you.

113. To Anugraha Narayan Sinha, 19 February 1949[1]

Dear Anugraha Babu,
Saprem Pranam.[2]

I am giving you trouble again regarding Dalmianagar. You had said with regard to old workers that the issue would be settled through Jeejeebhoy's arbitration. Now it is known that Jeejeebhoy cannot take up this issue unless the Government refers it to him. Meanwhile, the helpless workers are starving. In my opinion the Government does not lose anything if the question of future of these poor workers is sent to arbitration. I therefore hope you will order the needful in this respect.

Hope you are cheerful.

Yours affectionately,
Jayaprakash.

[1] *J.P. Papers* (NMML). Original in Hindi.
[2] Loving salutation.

114. Statement on Civil Liberties in Bihar, Patna, 21 February 1949[1]

There are a number of cases of suppression of civil liberties in the province, and I hope public opinion in Bihar would assert itself on the side of civil liberties in the absence of which freedom is a meaningless term.

I am not asking for freedom for the disturber of the peace, but am only insisting on the principle that no citizen should be deprived of his liberties unless found guilty of a proved charge. Under the law, emergency measures may be justified during war or large-scale rioting such as we had on the advent of freedom. But to take advantage of the emergency powers to crush political opponents or legitimate movements of the people is an injustice unworthy of an enlightened and democratic Government.

It will be recalled, that some weeks ago the well known Socialist leader, Munshi Ahmed Din, was arrested at Jamshedpur under the Security Act. He was released a few days ago and has returned to Jamshedpur. With Munshiji there were eleven other detenus in Purulia jail from Jamshedpur. They too have been released but they were all served at the jail with externment orders, externing some of them from Chhota Nagpur and others from the two districts of Singhbhum and Manbhum. The public perhaps do

[1] *Civil Liberties in India.* A collection of extracts from Socialist Party news letters, the *Hindu. Hitavada, Independent India* and the *Janata* weekly, published by K.G. Sivaswamy, Chairman of the Conference Committee, Madras, 1949.

not realize the enormity of such punishment. Among the persons externed there are many who were employed in the Tata Iron and Steel Company or some of the other companies there. They had worked there for years—one had a service of eighteen years, for instance. The externment order at one stroke deprives them of their employment. It is a very serious affair to deprive men of their livelihood. The Security Act does not require Government to give any reasons for their action and the men concerned have been rendered jobless and homeless for no offence that they know of.

115. To Achyut Patwardhan, 22 February 1949[1]

Dear Achyut,

Thanks for your letter.[2] Your note was fine. And, by the way, *Janata* is getting better week by week.

What happened to Asoka that day—I expected a ring from him. He did not write either, telling us about his talks with Jagjivan Ram regarding Jamshedpur.

Herewith the final draft of the Party Constitution. It should appear as a supplement in the next issue, and we would want 1000 reprints, O.K.?

I talked to Narendra Deva last night on the telephone. He has agreed to preside and write out his address. I am getting my report ready too. Both have to appear in the *Janata*, but how will you be able to manage it? The session is on March 6 when Narendra Deva will deliver his address. The address should appear in the daily press on the 7th morning, i.e., Monday morning. I should like my report to appear in the papers earlier, let us say on the 5th morning. This on the basis that the report would be submitted before the Executive on the 4th. In any case, the latest the report can appear is on the 5th morning. You will have the typescript latest by the 1st, i.e. Tuesday. I am asking Narendra Deva to send you his address too latest by then. Narendra Deva will have his address printed as a pamphlet at Lucknow and I shall have my report done at Calcutta, so you need not bother about reprints.

Regarding the money, I shall send you something in a couple of days and more later.

With love,

Yours,
Jayaprakash Narayan

[1] *J.P. Papers* (NMML).

[2] Appendix 8.

116. To Suresh Desai, 23 February 1949[1]

Dear Suresh,[2]

Thank you for your letter[3] which you sent through Madhu.[4] I have to make a few suggestions.

1. You should bring the office here latest on the 2nd, because it will take a day to settle down. The office should be in working order from the 3rd at the latest.
2. I do not know what you are doing about the resolutions. Whatever draft resolutions are ready should be printed in English and Hindi. Please have the translation made in Bombay and get it printed. If you do not get time to print the Hindi translation it can be done here provided you reach Patna on the 2nd.

Regarding money I shall send to P.T. [Purshottam Trikamdas] something on the 26th telegraphically. I am writing to him also.

More when we meet.

Affectionately yours,
Jayaprakash Narayan

[1] *J.P. Papers* (NMML).

[2] For biographical note see, *JPSW*, Vol. IV, p. 225.

[3] The letter from Suresh Desai dated 10 February suggested that the National Executive should meet on 4 and 5 March in accordance with the changed dates of Patna Conference from 6 to 10 March 1949.

[4] Madhu Limaye.

117. To Gopalaswami Ayyangar, 25 February 1949[1]

Dear Shri Ayyangar,

It is a great pity that the whole machinery of Government is so lacking in imagination and is so wooden. Our General Council decided on the 17th against strike and yet it was not possible for the Administration to advise the Police by the 19th afternoon that the list which they had supplied earlier must be radically altered. The result was that the very people who took a leading part at Danapore in deciding against a strike were hauled up unceremoniously. There can be absolutely no justification whatever for such a mad and senseless action. Inefficiency can be stretched to cover many sins but I cannot imagine inefficiency going to such extremes. In this connection I have a particular complaint to make against the divisional

[1] *J.P. Papers* (NMML).

Superintendent of Danapore who seems to have gone out of his way to victimize leading workers of our Union. The no-strike decision was taken right under his nose and he at least could not pretend that he did not know who was who and what was what. Office-bearers of Mohgalsarai, Gaya and Mokameh branches were arrested. It should have been the first duty of the Divisional Superintendent and, if I may say so, of Mr. Nilakantan, the General Manager, to issue fresh advices to the Police. I cannot tell you how much trouble, worry and annoyance all this has caused me. No doubt, you and the authorities concerned took prompt action, but the mistake should not have been made at all. Please remember that among those who were arrested there was hardly anyone about whom it could be said that he was a Communist.

This morning I was surprised to read Sardar Patel's attack on me at Madras. This old gentleman seems to have made up his mind never to understand our case. I am sending you a newspaper cutting giving my statement in question. You will see from it that I never asked for any leniency to be shown to the communist disruptors. What I had done was to warn the Government against police excesses and against treating all the members of the communist unions as communists. Sardar Patel's unjustified attack has greatly upset me. I am afraid he can understand nothing else than police action. But he will realize, after the country has paid heavily for his misconceptions, that communism cannot be beaten down by repression alone. Sardar Patel's clear and unequivocal declaration at Madras that there was going to be no attack on capitalism and that nationalisation was impractical is just the kind of food on which communism grows fat. People who are drunk with power always feel that iron chains and prison walls can choke up an idea, but all ideas with any vitality in them prosper under the very conditions of repression which are intended to destroy them.

To return to the railwaymen, Guruswami[2] might have sent you already copies of the resolutions passed at Danapore. I have been asked to nominate the Federation's three representatives on the Anomalies Committee. I shall do so by the end of this month. In the meanwhile, the Federation's Office is preparing a detailed memorandum in two parts, the first dealing with anomalies and the second with other matters arising out of the Pay Commission, the Adjudicator's Award and the Running Staff Committee's Report. As soon as this memorandum is ready it will be sent to you and to the Railway Board. After the Board has examined the questions raised we could meet together whenever convenient. The Anomalies Committee however could start functioning as soon as the Committee is constituted. I shall send you the names of our representatives early in March.

Pending the results of our further talks I should like once again to

[2] A Socialist leader, working in the railways.

emphasise the necessity of a change of outlook on the part of the Railway administrations and officers. I have received information to show that many officers are trying through their stooges, who are generally associated with the INTUC unions, to harass our workers. A glaring case is that of the Divisional Superintendent, Danapore. There is a man called A.P. Sharma at Moghalsarai who was a T.T. till lately. I cannot imagine a more unreliable and disloyal person. I am saying this not because he has left our Union to join the INTUC. While he was still with us he did everything to disrupt from within and did spying and informing for the D.S. and the Police. For that he was promoted from a T.T. to the post of Staff Warden. I do not mind his promotion nor do I want, by writing about him, to hurt his interests. I am merely giving you an example of how things are done. This man is a protege of the D.S., Danapore, and he has become such a terror at Moghalsarai that anyone who incurs his displeasure is liable to be transferred or punished in some other way at a moment's notice. The arrests at Moghalsarai were directly on the advice of this man.

If highly-placed officers are going to work through stooges and disloyal union busters I am afraid the labour policy of the Administration is going to go completely awry, landing both labour and the administration in unending misunderstandings and troubles. I believe this sort of thing is not rare. I do not care what happens to Sharma but I am absolutely clear that men like C.J. Singh, the D.S. at Danapore, have no business to hold posts of such high responsibility. If Singh is not removed from this division and not instructed to work impartially and according to well-defined standards there will be trouble on the E.I.R.

It has not been my practice to complain against any individual officer, and I am doing so now with the utmost reluctance and only after I have been convinced that the matter should be brought to your notice. The matter becomes deeply important in view of the fact that if C.J. Singhs are not common they are not exceptions either.

I will be in Patna from the 3rd of March to the 11th.

With kind regards,

Very sincerely yours,
Jayaprakash Narayan

118. To Jawaharlal Nehru (Telegram), 2 March 1949[1]

I strongly protest against new legislation to outlaw strikes in the essential services. The existing laws more than adequate to deal with all situations. Instead of repressive measures Government should try to apply remedy at

[1] *J.P. Papers* (NMML).

the root and remove discontent and provide speedy and impartial machinery for settlement of disputes. Satyanarayan Sinha's[2] bill[3] a blot on your administration and ugly example of growing Indian Fascism.

Jayaprakash Narayan

[2] Satya Naryayan Sinha (1900-83). Minister of State for Parliamentary Affairs, 1948-52; Minister of Parliamentary Affairs, 1952-67; Information and Broadcasting, 1963-4; Communications, 1964-7; Health, 1967-9; of Information, Broadcasting and Communications, 1969-71; Governor of Madhya Pradesh, 1971-7.

[3] The Essential Services Bill (Prevention of Strikes), presented by Sinha in October 1948, made strike illegal in all essential services and punishment by imprisonment obligatory for all participants, except when a court was of the opinion that it was not called for.

119. To Gooneverdene, Telegram, 3 March 1949[1]

Regret proposed Asian Socialist Conference on thirteen-fourteen March cannot be held. Proper contact not yet established with other Asian parties. Thanks for keen interest you have taken. Hope our common efforts will bear fruit and Asian Socialist co-operation will become a reality soon.

Jayaprakash

[1] *J.P. Papers* (NMML).

120. Statement to the Press opposing Repression, Calcutta, 3 March 1949[1]

It is one of the major puzzles of this age that the greatest democrat in Asia should preside over India's destiny and yet her Government should show such an insatiable appetite for ever larger punitive and coercive powers. The Indian Government was armed to the teeth already with the most sweeping powers and yet its hunger for more grows ever apace.

Every new situation of any gravity becomes only an excuse for assuming further extraordinary powers. At this rate, Pandit Nehru's semi-fascist Government will soon turn into a fully fascist regime, which can only give fresh impetus to the very forces of chaos and disaffection that are being sought to be suppressed. As a student of history, Pandit Nehru should know that repression and outlawry are poor remedies for mass discontent.

[1] Adapted from *Tribune*, 4 March 1949.

However, the adoption of security measures in Bengal and East Punjab, where conditions were anything but normal, is justified. One of the most dangerous forces of disorder in the country is the growing propensity towards goondaism and violence of certain trade unions.

I mention a specific case in which I was myself a victim during my recent visit to Asansol.[2] As soon as I arrived at a public meeting arranged at Burnpur by the Bardwan Socialist Party, loud slogans were raised, which, incidentally, showed that the disturbers were the supporters of a rival union there. As I got up on a table and began to speak into the microphone, slogans were added with more solid things. Brickbats, clods of earth and other missiles began to shower around me from all sides.

I spoke for twenty minutes and the attack continued for this entire period. My friends tried to protect my person, but nearly half a dozen missiles hit me on the back, the head and the hands. Some of my comrades were hit by missiles which caused wounds and drew blood.

The most curious thing was that though the police station was nearby, the custodians of law and order were conspicuous by their absence throughout the meeting. You can imagine what would have happened, had there been a Congress leader in my place. There would have been firing perhaps, and the newspaper headlines would have shrieked of Socialist goondaism the next morning. This was my first experience of its kind. Even during the British days I had never faced such hooliganism. Had the hooligans been communists or hired goondas of the employers, there would have been no cause for surprise. But the fact that people who claimed to organize and lead labour in accordance with the principles of Mahatma Gandhi, should have indulged in such behaviour was sad, to say the least.

I have been recently criticized for asking for leniency to be shown to the communists; Sardar Patel spoke about it in Madras. It is not the first time that the Sardar and the Press have misunderstood me. I never pleaded for leniency to those who are deliberately out to create chaos and anarchy. What I did was to sound a warning against police excesses. We have an extremely unimaginative and ignorant police and if in their excessive zeal they put innocent people into prison, it would be only adding fuel to the fire. I warn against treating all the railwaymen enrolled in the communist unions as communists. An imaginative and bold attempt should be made at this moment to win them over rather than throw them more definitely into the arms of the communists.

[2] J.P. visited Asansol (Bengal) on 27 February 1949.

121. General Secretary's Report submitted to the Socialist Party Conference, Patna, 6 March 1949[1]

Our practice has been that the General Secretary submits a written report. This time, I regret, I have deviated from this tradition. I apologize for the omission. It is true that we had decided at Nasik last year, that the General Secretary's report should be with the delegates for their consideration, at least 15 days before the Conference. But I could not prepare it this year because of pressure of work. During the last three months I was loaded with work. I have been preoccupied with difficult problems. There is for example the Railwaymen's question. It needed all the vigilance and hard work I could spare. Of course I agree that the preparation of the Report was also urgent. Yet somehow I could not do it. I admit my mistake. You have a right to censure me for this lapse. I am, however, submitting an oral report.

I wish to talk to you about our work, our organizational efforts and more particularly about matters of policy. We have now yet another year's experience behind us. What does it teach us? Where do we want to go? And how do we propose to proceed? We have to answer all these questions. Looking back I feel that last year was the most eventful year of our existence. We have been functioning and working as an independent party during this year. When we took that momentous decision at Nasik, we had hopes and apprehensions too. We had belonged to and were a part of the Congress organization till then. We had won a place for ourselves and people had heard us speak from the platform of the Congress. Our association with the Congress was, in a way, a source of strength. Naturally we had apprehensions about what would happen if we quit the Congress. Who would listen to us? Would we not get isolated and crushed? Yet we had hopes too because we felt, and rightly so, that if we broke the bonds which tied us to an organization which had come to stand for the preservation of the status quo, it would help us to take great strides and march forward to our goal. The close association with the national movement had strengthened us in the past. It had given us a mass base. But after the attainment of freedom this association became a cramping limitation, hindering the further growth of the Party. That is why we thought that if we tore ourselves asunder, we would be able to make progress. What has been our experience? It has proved that our apprehensions were largely groundless. For, despite Government's opposition and the indifference and even hostility of the Press we have managed to hold our own. The newspapers have lately passed under the capitalist-monopolist control. They have suppressed our news and maligned us in season and out of season. However, there are a few exceptions.

[1] *Report of the Seventh Annual Conference of the Socialist Party, Patna, 6-10 March 1949*. Jayaprakash Narayan was the General Secretary of the Socialist Party at that time.

National Herald, for instance, is one such paper. The *Herald* along with a few others, has treated us well. It has sought to place a new code of honour before the country. It has placed a high standard of journalism before India's Fourth Estate. I cannot but express my gratitude for its effort in the direction of bringing about a change in the climate of our public life.

As I have said, our work suffered because of the hostility of a large section of the Press, as we could not put across our policy to the people. We could not answer criticism; misrepresentations and distortions went uncorrected. Our propaganda has not been very efficient. We have not got any daily papers. And yet I must say that we have not become weak. We may not have progressed much but there is no setback. The hopes many of us had entertained at Nasik may not have been fulfilled completely, yet enough was achieved to sustain these hopes. Looking at the organizational report, I feel that we have not made any spectacular advance. The Party has no doubt grown in strength in some provinces and in some fields of activities. Yet much remains to be done. The East Punjab branch a year ago was very weak. They experienced the great communal massacres and uprooting of millions from their ancestral homes. There was complete disintegration of humanity. Our Punjab unit, which was once the pride of our party had gone to pieces. Is it not then surprising that our comrades not only managed to regroup their forces but also register a definite advance?

Similarly, the Bombay Party has made tremendous progress. Even before the World War the Bombay Party was an important unit of the Party. It has achieved phenomenal growth, particularly during the past two years. The elections to the Bombay Municipal Corporation and Assembly bye-elections are evidence of this new development.[2] Elections of course, are not the only barometer of progress. Yet it certainly proves to what extent the Party has rallied public opinion behind itself. Due to the tireless efforts of Asoka Mehta, Moinuddin Harris and Purshottam as well as young comrades like Nargolkar and Dandawate, the Party has been able to extend its influence to a large majority of workers and lower-middle classes. The protest general strike of 29th December last year, was an event of national significance. We are proud of the achievements of our Bombay comrades. This, however, cannot be said about other provinces.

The U.P. elections came as a great shock. As Acharyaji said, we suffered a great defeat. We felt it keenly because we had entertained great hopes. When we were in the Congress, the U.P. Party was considered to be very influential. It was the Province of our leaders Acharyaji and Dr. Lohia. Yet in the District Local Board elections we would not win more than 144

[2] Two Socialist Party members, Peter Alveres and Purshottam Trikamdas, had been elected to the Bombay Legislative Assembly. Some Socialists had also got elected to the Bombay Municipal Corporation.

seats. In the assembly bye-elections too we failed. The defeat of Acharyaji in particular was a great blow. Yet we should not lose perspective. If we take into consideration the voting percentage, we will realize that it is not a very depressing thing. We polled nearly 23% votes that is as much as we did in Bombay. The elections have enabled us to mobilize our strength. It has galvanized our ranks and has put new hope in the heart of our comrades. In Karnatak we have not made any progress. Assam is relatively a new Party unit. There we have made some progress. In south our progress has not been great. I went to the south. So did Achyut, Aruna and Asoka. I think the Party has a fund of goodwill there. Its prestige is very high. But organizationally we are weak.

Kerala is a better organized unit. I would say and since the BLPI comrades have joined our Party, our strength is likely to grow in Madras. The Hyderabad unit has passed through a great ordeal. The Party, as a result, has acquired some strength. It is not true that the Communists are very strong in Hyderabad. Even in Nalgonda and Warangal they are not as powerful as is claimed by them. The communists exploit the economic distress of the people and resort to terrorism and violent methods. Terror may induce people's submission, but it will not win their whole-hearted and sustained support. If our people succeed in organizing effective resistance to the communist terror, then the danger of disruption will rapidly disappear.

This then is the overall picture. It is not a very rosy picture. Yet it is not disheartening either.

There are two other things of vital importance which I must mention. There is an urgency about them and I am sure you will also feel it. The first and the foremost in my mind is the question of the structure of the Party. We have now assumed great responsibilities. We have to transform the Party into an effective instrument of social revolution. Will the present party structure meet our needs? Will it strengthen us and carry us forward? I am convinced that the present Party structure has outlived its utility. It needs revision. The Party must be reconstituted on a new basis. We must broadbase it if it is to fulfil the great task we have undertaken. A party of the select cannot achieve democratic socialism. We will have to mobilize the mass of people, bring them within the Party's fold. A change is, therefore, inevitable. Opinions may differ about the details but about the urgency of effecting structural changes there should be no two opinions. I will be pained if you think otherwise.

The other question relates to our propaganda work. Our means of propaganda are far from adequate. Our publicity organs have functioned inefficiently. We want to carry the message of democratic socialism to the remotest corner of our country. We want to educate the masses and place before them our alternative programme of reconstruction. How can we do all this without a chain of daily newspapers? We no doubt have Party Journals today, but they are weeklies. Essentially they cater for the needs of the Party workers. Party organs of this type cannot influence the broad mass of people. And it is the people, who under universal suffrage, are going to decide our political future. Unless we have daily newspapers, at least one in each provincial language, we will not be able to put across our policy and programme to the people. This, then, is our task in the next six months. There is also the urgent need for an English daily. Efforts are being made to start one and it is hoped that before the year is out, an English daily will appear either from Bombay or Delhi.

II

Now I turn to other problems. These are mainly ideological. At Nasik in the course of my report I spoke about the purity of means. Some people have ridiculed this. Yet I must say with all the emphasis at my command that our means must be good if we wish to attain noble ends. We talk about the decadence of the Congress. But let us not forget that the masses are observing us with watchful eyes. Every one is being tested, our Party included. We have yet to prove our faith and our integrity. We have got to convince them that we are clear about our objectives, that we know our own business and have the capacity to implement our programme. We must demonstrate that we are not merely critical and negative but are capable of shouldering national responsibilities and carrying out constructive tasks. Today the people feel that we are wearing the same cap and the same dress as Congressmen do. We talk about the same things and make the same promises which most Congressmen used to make in the pre-freedom days. Yet the people know that those who talked high and made big promises, have failed to live up to them. What guarantee is there, they ask, that we also will not go the same way? The Congress which was once a noble organization has fallen from its high pedestal today. It is easy enough to catalogue all the misdeeds of the Congress and its serious deviations from the revolutionary path. But mere criticism of the Congress will not lead us anywhere. Unless we identify ourselves with the aspirations, yearnings and miseries of the people, we won't be able to win their heart. I do not want to criticize anyone in particular. But it pains me to observe that we have not behaved as we ought to have, in the matter of trade union and Party accounts, etc. These may appear to be trivial things. Yet they are important. That is why I made a pointed reference to means and ends. This is not a thing to be laughed at. I do not believe in a doctrinaire philosophy. When I talk about the principles Gandhiji stood for, his teaching and practice and the lessons these have for the socialist movement, I am quite serious. It is a pity that you have nothing but ridicule for such a revaluation. I feel this has a direct bearing on our ideas. There is so much confusion in the socialist movement the world over. We are still moving in the old ruts and have refused to learn the lessons which experience has taught us. We must not forget the tragedy of European social democracy. Do we want to repeat the same tragedy in India?

Gandhiji tried to evolve a new method of social change. He preached a new set of values to lift up our public life from the morass into which it had fallen. We cannot poohpooh this by calling it surrender to Gandhism. If we remain dogmatic we will end up not by establishing socialism but a Party dictatorship. The Congress has fallen from the esteem of the people not so much because the masses have become disillusioned with its policy. As a matter of fact, they know mighty little about Government's industrial policy; their refusal to put through the nationalization programme, etc. They have another yardstick with which to judge the political parties. There is so much scramble for power, corruption and nepotism among Congressmen! Yet they are the same people who had once dedicated themselves to the service of the people. That is the reason why people are turning away from them. We must show the people that we are both intellectually and morally superior to Congressmen. If we do not measure up to their expectations, if we do not maintain our integrity, we will lose their confidence.

III

Then there is the question of democratic socialism. Some of you openly ridicule the word "democratic". Some say that the deep red of socialism has been rendered pink by the word democratic. But they are confusing democratic socialism with traditional social democracy. When we adopted the thesis of democratic socialism at Kanpur [1947], there was no great opposition to it. It had had a relatively smooth passage. I was wondering how it happened. Did the delegates not give serious thought to it? Did they support it out of real conviction or did they swallow it as a bitter pill, sugar-quoted though? I say with much regret, really it pains me profoundly to say so, that there is not enough strength within us; there is not that urge, that living faith in the creed of democratic socialism, which alone can sustain us and enable us to pay any price and make any sacrifice for attaining it. Does socialism merely mean solving the problem of bread and butter? Has it only an economic content? I refuse to accept this view. I am convinced that there can be no real socialism without the enlargement of our liberty and freedom, without complete democracy. I have read Marx. I have studied Lenin's writings. I was once a Communist. Marx and Lenin had both said that democracy and socialism are inseparable. Marx argued that under socialism alone will people get real freedom, freedom and equal opportunity to realize the best in themselves. But we know how their teaching has been distorted, how they have been caricatured. I have watched the Soviet experiment with anguish. In the name of Marx and Lenin awful things have been done. The revolution has led to a denial of freedom and liberty. I thought that the greater freedom, higher will be the level of socialism. The contradiction that obtains in Russia today, therefore, baffles me.

Democratic socialism must become our life's mission, the philosophy of our life. We must accept democracy and all that it stands for, then alone can we reach the goal of socialism. Democratic socialism involves acceptance of democratic means, peaceful methods and constructive approach, in the attainment of our goal. No Marxist can say that democracy and socialism are contradictory. Not even Stalin or Trotsky or Mao Tse-Tung. Even the communists shout about democracy.

It is often argued that democracy does not mean a thing to the exploited and starving millions. They have only one hunger, hunger for food, clothing and shelter. All the talk about democracy is so much nonsense. It does not feed empty stomachs. Neither does it clothe the naked bodies. It is utterly wrong to argue like this. This loose talk is dangerous. It is deliberately confusing the issues. I have no place among those who understand and explain socialism that way. We have before our eyes the example of the Soviet Union. It is more than 32 years now, since the Bolsheviks seized power in order to establish socialist society. Have they realized this ideal? I do not think so. There is ruthless dictatorship in Russia. No civil liberties exist. I do not know whether they have the problem of bread. Some even deny that. But I know one thing that without political liberty, socialism is incomplete. The Russian state is a product of a peculiar combination of circumstances and is essentially transitional in character. It is not an ideal thing that we can and must copy. If you want to establish a totalitarian State in the name of Socialism you can very well do so, but then I will not be a party to any such effort. The tragedy of contemporary socialist movement has only one lesson to teach. It is that we must have unassailable faith in the principles of democratic socialism. Why do you work night and day and brave all difficulties and dangers? To what end? What sustains you? What is your inspiration? Surely democratic socialism should be the source of your inspiration. It should permeate all your utterances and activities.

IV

I must now turn to other matters. The question of evolving an alternative trade union organization has been exercising our minds for the past few months. At Calcutta we succeeded in bringing together almost all non-communist, non-I.N.T.U.C. labour unions. We have launched the Hind Mazdoor Sabha.[3] Through this Central Organization we hope to build up a real democratic trade union movement, free from the domination of the Government as well as political parties. To my mind the question who should control the central labour organization is irrelevant and futile. It is improper to think in these terms. The trade union organization must be a workers' organization and they should control it. This does not men that it should remain aloof from politics. That is simply not possible. For why did we secede from the A.I.T.U.C.? Was it not because it failed to give correct lead to the workers in August 1942? Was it not because it failed to lead the class-battles of the working class against imperialist plunder and capitalist profiteering? On that historic occasion in the life of our nation, the A.I.T.U.C., under communist domination, closed its eyes and turned away from the great national struggle. We must, therefore, strive to keep the H.M.S. above Party politics, but not out of politics. It is unfortunate that some of the non-communist unions have not joined us. I still hope that light would dawn on them and they would realize their mistake and join in this common endeavour to create a mighty organization of the Indian working class.

Today there is so much talk about Left unity. It is an attractive slogan no doubt. In fact it is a worldwide phenomenon. This slogan has tragic associations. It has led to disunity more than to unity. We tried this experiment years ago. Why did we fail? In order to understand this we must inquire as to why various left parties came into existence. What is their basis? It will be seen then why this unity is impossible of realization. Some people say that we oppose Left unity and particularly unity with the communists because we have a vested interest to defend and that we fear that our leadership will be jeopardized! The Communists say that Jayaprakash is opposed to unity because he is unable to forget the past and bury the hatchet. This is a false propaganda. The Communists do not believe in truth. They have no honesty, no integrity. They are out Geobbelsing Geobbels. To them Left unity is merely a manoeuvre, a device of acquiring a mass base, by boring in from within other parties and organizations. They tried this technique in the past and not without success. Our organization, particularly in south India suffered greatly as a result of communist infiltration. We do not wish to repeat that experiment.

The communists talk about unity. Yet at the same time they are trying to discredit our Party. They have been carrying on slanderous propaganda

[3] The Hind Mazdoor Sabha was started at a Conference, of trade union representatives belonging to the Socialist Party held at Calcutta on 24 to 26 December 1948. By March 1949, the H.M.S. represented 427 unions with the membership of 6,05,172 workers from 15 provinces.

against me. They go to the extent of saying that I am an agent of the Railway Board, that I have betrayed the workers.

Under these circumstances how can we work with them? The question of unity with non-communist left parties is on a different footing. Our attitude is not sectarian. We have been sincerely trying to achieve the goal of a single United Party of socialism. At Belgaum we decided to throw open the doors of the Party to all such left groups and socialist parties as accept the fundamental principles of democratic socialism, and I am glad to say that some parties have responded magnificently. The Bolshevik-Leninist party has, for instance, merged with the Party. They are among us today. So also the socialist group of Rajdeo Singh[4] in the U.P. has joined us. A majority of the R.S.P. came in much earlier. I welcome all these comrades. I hope other parties would also emulate their example.

The bane of the Leftist parties has been their tendency to exaggerate minor differences. This outlook must change. We are prepared to do everything to bring all the left elements within a single Party.

At the Lucknow meeting of the National Executive we decided to convene an All-India Kisan Conference with a view to create a central organization of kisans. Invitations were issued to non-party people as well. Comrade Indulal Yagnik has accepted our invitation, but others have not. Shil Bhadra Yajee[5] of the Forward Block has rejected it. He talks about Left unity and yet he is not prepared to cooperate with us. He accuses us of having betrayed Socialism. He accuses us of fighting the Communists instead of cooperating with them in the interest of the working class. I fail to understand this attitude. What does he mean when he says that we fight the communists? We do criticize their policy and methods and will continue to do that. But we have not indulged in murders and stabbing of political opponents. Communists have. We can have no truck with them. Sometime back Shil Bhadra Yajee and others formed a united front of 18 left parties at Patna! What has happened to this grand edifice? It has collapsed like a pack of cards. The Belgaum way is the only way to Left unity. The creation of H.M.S. and H.K.P. is our contribution to Left unity. On the solid foundation of these class organizations will be erected, one day, the Indian socialist movement.

[4] Rajdeo Singh, a political activist, leading a group of socialists in the U.P.

[5] Shil Bhadra Yajee (1916-96), joined Bihar Socialist Party and got involved in Kisan Movement; imprisoned in 1930, 1932 and 1933; member Legislative Assembly Bihar, 1937-45; associated with Subhas Chandra Bose at the time of the formation of the Forward Bloc, 1939 and became its General Secretary; closely associated with INA Movement; arrested in 1940 and 1943; rejoined Congress, 1955; member Rajya Sabha, 1957 and 1964; Convener and Secretary General of All India United Left Front. Publications include *A Glimpse of Indian Labour Movement, Forward Bloc and its Stands; True Face of Manopolistic American Democracy.*

I have taken a lot of your time. I have poured out my heart. In the end I wish to make only one appeal. We may have differences. We may have criticism and discussion. But let there be no suspicion about each other, and let there be no lack of faith. If we have unassailable faith in our objective I have no doubt we will achieve our goal.

122. To Shri Krishna Sinha, 8 March 1949[1]

Dear Shri Babu,
Pranam.

I have received no reply yet to the letter which I had written regarding Jamshedpur. In the meanwhile, new difficulties arose. Munshiji had asked for permission to hold a meeting at Jamshedpur on 12 March. Shri Asoka Mehta and Shri Purshotam Trikamdas are to arrive at the meeting. Earlier I came to know that the D.C. has asked for the order of the Bihar Government. After telephoning to Shri L.P. Singh,[2] I came to know that both Munshiji and John Saheb[3] have not been given the permission to hold a meeting What sort of lawlessness is this? I do not understand what to do. Should I flee from Bihar? Has any report come to you until today from Jamshedpur that a breach of peace or a strike took place because of our holding a meeting there? The Chief Secretary mentioned the danger of railway strike. There was no limit to my surprise at this. Do you not know that these days my comrades are actively engaged all over the country only in ensuring that there is no railway strike? To this extent that those of my comrades who have been working in the railways have not even come for the Patna Conference (of the Socialist Party) and are sticking to their own places. If there is a threat of railway strike at Jamshedpur, that threat will lessen rather than increase, in case Bhai Asoka and Bhai Purushotam go there. If the Government does not understand such a simple matter, then only God may save us.

John Saheb also has not been given permission. By doing this an effort has been made to underline that the Government is impartial. The impartiality of the Government is world-famous, and daily we get its proof. If John Saheb had not received the strong support of the Government, and

[1] *J.P. Papers* (NMML). Original in Hindi.

[2] Lallan Prasad Singh (1912-98); Chief Secretary, Bihar, 1948-56; Member Secretary, Second Pay Commission, 1956-9; Addl. Secretary, Ministry of Home Affairs, 1960-4; Home Secretary, 1964-70; Ambassador to Nepal, 1971-3; Governor of Assam, Manipur, Meghalaya, Nagaland and Tripura, 1973-81.

[3] M. John, working in Tata Iron and Steel Company, Jamshedpur; Labour leader belonging to Congress; became President of the Tata Worker's Union in 1947 after the assassination of Abdul Bari.

his rivals had not been subjected to arbitrary repression, he would have been uprooted long ago. You would also be aware how peace-loving and follower of the Congress objectives he is. I myself have been a victim of the hooliganism of his companions at Burnpur the other day. There is no knowing what would have happened today if the socialists had done something similar.

Our comrades from outside cannot come to Bihar again and again. John Saheb will get the permission sometime again, if not, some minister himself will address his meeting after going there. You must be aware that Binoda Babu[4] has already gone there many times; no permission is required for his meeting, and John Saheb can speak at that meeting.

One thing more regarding Jamshedpur. According to the constitution of the Tata Workers Union, the election of the Union should be held every year. But the election has not taken place for two years. This has been the demand of Munshiji that there should be held open election. After months of campaignings when John Saheb was not prepared to accept the challenge of election, Munshiji declared that if the workers desired and thought it necessary, they could hold election of the Tata Workers Union at the meeting on 12 March. This is by all means a constitutional method (Bari Saheb's election also took place at a public meeting and how John Saheb was elected is, of course, not clear as yet).

If the authorities have told you that there would be disturbances in Jamshedur by our holding a meeting, then it is false. If John Saheb's hooligans do mischief, I cannot say, but there is no danger of breach of peace from any other direction. And John Saheb's hooligans are in his hands and he is in the Government's hands. Therefore, it is easy to prevent that hooliganism.

I hope you will reconsider this issue and grant us the permission to call a meeting. Munshiji will leave for Jamshedpur today evening by train. Therefore, if I get your message before the evening, I shall be obliged. I hope for justice from you.

Yours,
Jayaprakash Narayan

[4] Binodanand Jha (1900-71), Minister for Local Self Government and Public Health, Bihar, 1946; Chief Minister, Bihar, 1961-3.

123. Speech at the Socialist Party Conference moving the Motion for Consideration of the Draft Constitution of the Party, Patna, 8 March 1949[1]

In my report speech I had made a brief reference to the urgent need for a revision of the Party Constitution. Acharyajee has, in his presidential address, discussed this question at length. He has pointed out the defects from which the Party suffers. These need to be remedied.

For some time past this problem has been agitating my mind. I am convinced that our present constitution is not at all suitable to our needs. It needs immediate revision in view of the altered conditions. The structure of our Party has not changed in any basic manner since its inception, even though we effected two major changes at Kanpur [1947]. At Kanpur we dropped the prefix "Congress". The doors of the party were thrown open to those who were not members of the Congress.

Let us remember that the Party grew up as an ideological group within the Congress. The present constitution served its purpose as long as we were playing the role of an ideological group within a great mass movement. The political situation has materially changed since Kanpur. The changed conditions, the new objectives and policy of the Party, the ever widening sphere of our activities compel us to give serious consideration to the question of Party structure.... I felt that in the new context a revision of the Party Constitution was necessary. The Party has a new role to play. It is not only an independent political party now. It aspires to become a party of the masses. Therefore, I submitted a thesis to the National Executive when it met at Mahabaleshwar [1948]. That thesis was thoroughly discussed and a Drafting Sub-Committee was appointed. It has, since then, prepared a Draft Constitution.[2] The salient point of the proposed Party structure, according to me, is the affiliated membership clause. In this connection I would like to mention a few things which belong to the past. For they indicate how my mind has been working. At Lucknow, in 1936, the Congress appointed a Constitution Sub-Committee. I was a member of that Committee. The Committee met a number of times. In one of the meetings I moved that there should be a provision for collective affiliation. I had felt then that this could only be achieved if trade unions, Kisan organizations, etc., affiliated with the Congress as members. A questionnaire was issued. Answers were collected and carefully scrutinized. There was heated discussion. In the meeting held at the Sadaqat Ashram, [Patna], the Socialists pressed hard for the acceptance of collective affiliation. Jawaharlal also agreed

[1] Adapted from *Report of the Seventh Annual Conference of the Socialist Party, Patna, 6-10 March 1949.*

[2] For text see Appendix 10.

with us. But the majority was against introducing any material change.

The idea of collective affiliation has been in my mind since those days. This conviction has grown lately. Admission to membership [at present] depends upon fulfilment of a certain work quota, probationary period and scrutiny. Can we maintain this position? We approach people for contributions. We ask them to vote for us. We desire that they should support us in all possible ways. How can all this be achieved with the present party structure? These are not the objects which a handful of persons can achieve. If we alone constitute the Party, how can we say that the Socialist Party is a Party of the *Kisans* and *Mazdoors*? Our slogan has been 'Kisanon ki Party Socialist Party; Mazdooron ki Party Socialist Party'. And yet we prevent the masses from joining the Party. You can of course give a bookish answer, a theoretical explanation. But it will not satisfy the people.

Kisans and *Mazdoors* must be brought into the Party in large numbers. But how? Is it possible for us to approach every individual *Kisan* and *Mazdoor*, make him a socialist, and explain to him the conditions under which he can become a member of the Party? Individual approach is not possible and, therefore, we must have a provision for collective approach. We have a programme of building class organizations of *Kisans* and *Mazdoors*. We organize them. We strengthen their organizations by sustained organizational work and by increasing the class consciousness of *Kisans* and *Mazdoors*. If we leave this task at that, if we do not carry it to the logical conclusion and admit them to the membership of the Party, our strength will not increase. *Mazdoor Panchayats* should therefore, become members of the Party. *Kisan Panchayats* should become members of the Party. Then only they will feel that the Socialist Party is their party. Then the slogan 'Mazdooron ki Party-Kisano ki Party, Socialist Party' will be justified.

This then is the way to broadbase the Party. In that thesis I have discussed at length the advantages of collective affiliation and individual mass membership. I had before me the constitutions of the Socialist Parties of other countries. I studied them. The British Labour Party pattern appealed to me. Madhu Limaye says that the constitution of the Canadian Socialist Party (C.C.F.) provides for collective affiliation. Belgian Socialist Party was also formerly based on the same principle. My only mistake was that I made a mention of British Labour Party in my thesis and recommended that pattern. This mention has created misunderstanding. Some of you have resented it. But I am not a diplomat. I said what I honestly felt. I liked a certain constitution and I mentioned the name of the Party which had adopted it. Why are you afraid of the mention of the British Labour Party? There are many things which we can learn from that Party and other parties. However, you may leave it at that.

Looking ahead I feel that Socialist Party is the only party which can effectively influence the Trade Union Movement. A majority of organized *Mazdoors* and *Kisans* will one day come in to the Socialist Party. We must not forget that we have to work for the emancipation of Kisans and Mazdoors. We do not want to exploit them. Our problem can be solved by bringing in *Kisans* and *Mazdoors* in large numbers into the party.

The draft of the proposed constitution is with you. Collective affiliation is the soul of this proposed constitution. I do not suppose that there is any other alternative before us. The proposed constitution is elastic and not rigid like the present one. Being elastic it can be made to fit in the new set-up and changed conditions.

Then there is the proposal regarding individual membership. The draft suggests that individual membership should be open and not restrictive. The reasons are obvious. I want that millions should come into the Party—millions who subscribe to the aims and objects of the Party. You can adopt a doctrinaire attitude and oppose the proposals regarding individual membership. Please also consider one practical aspect. We move among the people, meet them, address public meetings. They hear us and our ideas spread. The people are attracted towards the Socialist Party. But the influence is short-lived. People gather and go away. It is, therefore, necessary that they should feel that they are an integral part of the party.

After Nasik we decided to enroll sympathizers. That only a few were enrolled is entirely our fault. We did not work hard enough. Misconception also spread amongst our members that sympathizers were being enrolled for monetary gains. It is unfortunate.

Some say that this is the age of Socialism. In the same breath people say that conditions are not yet ripe. Ours is a bourgeoisie society. Capitalist mentality has penetrated all the sections of society. How can both these things be possible?

It is true that middle class mentality prevails in this country. But the middle classes certainly do not want the rule of Tatas and Birlas. There is no sympathy for free enterprise. Then why keep on saying that there is bourgeoisie mentality and capitalist mentality? Let us understand the objective conditions. Why do you turn your face away from the realities and imagine things that do not exist. The masses do want socialism. There is no danger in admitting them to the Party.

Let us, therefore, throw our doors wide open to people who have sympathy for our cause, who are prepared to accept our objectives.

The only objection to the proposed individual membership is the danger of undesirable elements coming in to the Party. I am conscious of this danger. But then has the work-condition prevented infiltration of undesirable elements into the Party? Why should we be afraid of infiltration of undesirable elements into the Party? If there is vitality in the party, if there is life in the Party we can overcome this danger. I will not say anything more at this stage. The draft is before you. I am sure you will consider it dispassionately in the light of our needs and the stupendous tasks that lie ahead of us.

124. Reply to the Debate on the Draft Constitution, 9 March 1949[1]

I listened very carefully to your arguments.[2] Some of the speeches were able. I very much appreciate the way Ajit Roy, Nargolkar and Baburao Jagtap have spoken. Their criticism comes from a high theoretical level. Dandawate's speech in support of the Constitution was also very able. But nothing has been said which necessitates change in my approach. In fact the Opposition speakers replied to each other. No doubt, some of you gave expression to fears, doubts and apprehensions. I have no answer for these. A few of you even doubted my intention. This sort of attitude does not help.

The draft constitution has to be judged by one criterion: can it move the Party forward, bring the broad toiling masses into the Party and help it to achieve its goal? If it has that basic potentiality, minor errors in it can be eliminated by experience and trial. If, on the other hand, it proves to be a hurdle on the way of progress, it has to be rejected. Several kinds of activity—strikes, satyagraha, no-tax campaigns, constitutional activities—will have to be adopted to reach the goal of a democratic socialist society. The Party has no reason to fight shy of constitutional activity. The Bolshevik Party of Russia[3] is renowned for its revolutionary character but it did not desist from fighting on the constitutional front even though the Czarist Duma offered no opportunity for social change by constitutional means.

The example of the Bolshevik Party has often been quoted in favour of a party of the select. But it must be remembered that the Bolshevik Party did not create the revolution. If the war of 1914 had not taken place, if Czarism had not toppled down like a house of cards due to rampant corruption, inefficiency and unrelieved oppression, if the soldiers had not voted for the revolution with their feet, as Lenin put it, that is, with their arms, thus giving the revolution a ready-made army there would have been

[1] Adapted from *Report of the Seventh Annual Conference of the Socialist Party, Patna, 6-10 March 1949*.

[2] See Appendix 9 for the debate on the Draft Constitution of the Socialist Party.

[3] The Bolshevik Party was the radical group of the Russian Social Democratic Party and spearheaded the October Revolution in 1917.

no revolution in Russia inspite of Lenin and the Bolshevik Party. In France in 1789 and in Russia in 1917 conditions of unrelieved oppression obtained. A violent overthrow of the existing regime was inevitable under those conditions. Such conditions do not obtain in India. Where democracy and democratic conditions prevail, violent outbursts are uncommon and slow and organized change is the rule. The example of Britain is a case in point.

The British Labour Party is a working class party, but it did not come into power until it had attracted the general sympathy and support of the middle classes. Recent historical experience has proved that the support of the middle classes is necessary for all revolutionary parties. It was lack of this support which led the German Communist Party to its ruin. The fear that a mass party might not be able to take revolutionary decisions and actions is entirely unfounded. The Indian National Congress was a mass organization with millions of members on its rolls. But it remained a fighting organization as long as it was clear that mere constitutional means were incapable of realizing the object of national independence. Its constitution never prevented it from taking revolutionary decisions. The failure of the Social Democratic Party in Germany was not due to its constitution or mass character. It failed because when history demanded revolutionary action, when it had become clear that constitutional means alone would lead to failure, it faltered, hesitated and remained indecisive. The German Communist Party which at one time had polled five million votes, also failed, although it had a fool-proof, centralized constitution. It is clear, therefore, that constitutions do not make any party revolutionary. The success of the Russian revolution was not due to the centralized and so-called revolutionary constitution of the Bolshevik Party. Had the decision, made by Lenin and Trotsky, that the time was ripe for an insurrection not been accepted, the revolution might not have taken place. Stalin and others opposed the decision. In their opinion the material situation did not warrant an insurrection at that juncture. If Stalin's proposal had been accepted, there would have been no revolution. One wrong step would have destroyed the mighty Bolshevik Party. It is a lesson of history that parties are made or ruined by their leadership. Even the best constitution will not help a party if its leadership falters and fails to rise to the occasion or takes a hasty or wrong step.

It has been contended that the Socialist Party can be turned into a mass party by enrolling individual *Kisans* and *Mazdoors* on large scale, that a large number of trade unions and *Kisan Panchayats* are under the influence of the Party, and that collective affiliation is, therefore, unnecessary. But the Party must anchor itself to the collective organizations of kisans and workers and be influenced by them. No Marxist revolutionary can oppose the principle of collective affiliation for it helps to sharpen the class struggle and make peasants and workers class-conscious. The draft constitution will give a fillip to the party's organizational and educational activities and compel greater and more sustained effort from its members. Collective affiliation will strengthen the working class character of the Party, not weaken it.

Collective affiliation secures the mobilization of the affiliated bodies behind the Party. A party of the select, a party of actual workers, secures concentration alone. Without mobilization of the toiling masses, no social change is possible. The proposed structure of the party secures concentration as well as mobilization and will render the party a fit instrument of social change.

There will be a lot of difference between the individual membership of the Party and the individual membership of the Congress. The Congress individual members were enrolled in millions and left alone. The members of the Party will not be left alone—at least they should not be left alone. Anyone who comes into contact with the Party must be educated and trained systematically. If at present Party members are neither trained in Party work nor well versed in socialist ideology, it is due to a lack of enthusiasm among active workers of the Party, not to the unsuitability of individual membership.

Another issue has been raised which is based on the premise that civil liberties are being curtailed progressively and naked fascism will be established in due course. It is feared that under conditions of fascism the party will not have the stamina to exist and grow. This premise has to be rejected; its acceptance will be ruinous to the party and the socialist movement. It cannot be denied that civil liberties are being curtailed, but we still enjoy a large measure of democratic freedom. We can conduct peaceful strikes, organize agitations, distribute party literature and contest elections. The principle of adult franchise has been accepted and general elections are due to take place soon. Official pressure may be used, discrimination may take place and ballot boxes tampered with. But the British also tried all these tactics against the Congress and were unsuccessful. If the Congress after assuming power follows the British example, it will be possible to fight it with the support of the toiling masses. And if official interference and pressure seek to thwart the declared will of the masses, the masses are bound to rise in revolt and destroy the chains that bind them against their will, to an archaic and oppressive system. It must be our endeavour, therefore, to galvanize the masses and direct their energies into organizational channels.

Mere dictatorship is not fascism which is a socio-economic phenomenon, appearing at a certain stage in the evolution of capitalist society under certain conditions. Hitler was able to establish fascism in Germany on the basis of the feeling of mass resentment and humiliation against the victorious Powers.

He played upon the sentiments of national and racial pride of the people and exploited the aspirations of the middle and lower middle classes. His success was due to a great psychological factor. Such factors do not exist in India. But we should not underestimate the dangers of fascism or the importance of fighting it. The time to fight it is now, not when it has succeeded in planting itself firmly. Those who declare that fascism has already arrived, that it has already established itself firmly are unconsciously undermining the fight against fascism. This kind of fatalism is fatal to the Party and to the socialist movement in India.

It is impossible to fight fascism by internal resistance alone, once it has succeeded in establishing itself. After Hitler's rise to power, Communist Parties all over the world sponsored a movement for a *Front Populaire*. They organized an Anti-fascist Front, consisting of all parties maintaining that their fight at that moment lay not against capitalism, nor for socialism, but against fascism. It needed the greatest war in human history to defeat it. Fascism must, therefore, be fought before it gets established, not after it has come into being.

By giving up democratic methods and taking to disruptive and insurrectionary means we will only help in creating chaos and anarchy, giving fascism both a valid reason and a fertile ground for establishing its sway. We have to utilize all the democratic avenues open to us to organize the masses and with their organized might resist the advent of fascism. If fascism is successful in India it will be due more to our mistakes than to its inherent strength.

The constitution of the Party must be considered dispassionately. After all, constitutions do not make or mar a party. It is the workers who do it. Active, honest, diligent workers are always the life and backbone of a party. And whatever the constitution, if the workers devote themselves with energy and determination to the training and education of cadres, the party is bound to grow and acquire strength.

125. Statement Congratulating Railwaymen, Patna, 10 March 1949[1]

I congratulate Railwaymen on their magnificent demonstration of loyalty to All India Railwaymen's Federation, which is their sole representative body. When the communists were turned out of the Federation at Danapore, they threw out a challenge that the 9th of March would show whose lead Railwaymen were to follow. I had accepted their challenge. The utter failure of months of communist preparation and lieing propaganda has ended up in smoke and the 9th of March has proved to the hilt that Indian workers

[1] Adapted from *Searchlight*, 11 March 1949.

have totally repudiated communist policies and leadership. In certain parts of the country, such as in Calcutta, the communists had gone beyond their programme of Railway strike and given a call for a general strike. Life in Calcutta was running its normal course on the 9th March as on any other day of the year. I cannot imagine a more total repudiation of the Communist Party than this.

I should like to draw the attention of Railwaymen in this hour of relief and thankfulness to the tasks of organization and consolidation which are facing The All India Railwaymen's Federation and the affiliate unions, I hope all Railwaymen will address themselves to this task with devotion and loyalty.

As for as the negotiations with the Railway Ministry are concerned, I assure all Railway Workers that these shall be resumed as soon as possible. It will be recalled that one of the terms of the agreement arrived at with the Railway Ministry was the appointment of an Anomalies Committee[2] I am happy to announce that I have nominated Shri S. Guruswami, Shri Khedgi Kar and Shri Pratul Chatterjee to represent the Federation on the Anomdies Committee. The Committee will begin to function as soon as the preliminaries which are under way are completed.

[2] It was expected that the Anomalies Committee would look into the anomalies in the wage structure of railwaymen.

126. Address at the Foundation Conference of the Hind Kisan Panchayat, Patna, 10 March 1949[1]

The Kisan movement in our country has had a painful history, characterized by mutual discord, endless bickerings and party politics. This is true also of The Mazdoor movement. The original idea was to form an all party Kisan organization. But we have come to the conclusion that there are some groups in the country with whom it is impossible to work.

The Socialist Party has always believed that there is no good having merely a paper organization of Kisans, so the party has decided to form a Kisan organization from the primary units to the central organization, consisting of the chosen representatives of the primary units. Barring the Congress and the Communists, invitations were extended to all parties to join the socialists in forming a central organization.

These efforts, however, did not produce the desired result because some interested groups had formed blocs for opposing and frustrating the move of the Socialists. The Forward Bloc characterized the Socialists, move as

[1] Adapted from *Searchlight*, 12 March 1949. The office bearers of the new Kisan Organization were Ram Manohar Lohia, President, Indulal Yagnik, Vice-President, Ramanandan Misra, General Secretary, Swami Bhagwan and R.S. Rana, Joint Secretaries.

disruptive and directed against the Communists. The Party tried its best to bring all groups on a common platform, but failed in its efforts. In spite of what had happened in the past, the doors of the new organization that has been formed are still open for all groups in the country. But no condition would be accepted for their admittance into the organization. Compromise in such matters generally leads to obstruction of work; people tend to form groups and there is general disruption all round.

The Kisan organization therefore, will not be poorer in the absence of groups from certain organizations. I believe that this organization will become the most representative organization of the Kisans, leaving other organizations as paper ones or mere platforms of certain political parties. And I can assure the Conference that the Socialist Party will help it in every possible way.

127. To the Editor, *National Herald*, Lucknow, 10 March 1949[1]

Sir,[2]

My friend, Shri Ishwar Saran of Gonda, has told me an amazing story. It appears that on the death of Shrimati Sarojini Naidu, the local Socialist Party branch desired to take out a mourning procession and also hold a public meeting. Permission for the latter was given by the authorities, but the procession was disallowed. The Socialist Party quite rightly felt that this was an un warranted interference with citizens' elementary rights, and therefore decided to defy the ban. Consequently five processionist satyagrahis were arrested.

I have nothing to say about the arrests. Those who deliberately offer satyagraha must always be ready to suffer. But it does seem rather strange to me that District Officers should so abuse their powers. It is still more strange that instead of discountenancing such unjustified abridgment of civil liberties, the Police Minister, my esteemed friend, Shri Lal Bahadur Shastri,[3] should set the seal of his approval on it on the ground that the said procession was taken out merely to spite the District authority. How a procession taken out to mourn a national leader could be deemed to have been intended to spite authority, it is difficult for me to understand. But,

[1] *J.P. Papers* (NMML).

[2] M. Chalapathi Rau (1909-1983), Editor, *National Herald.*

[3] Lal Bhadur Shastri (1904-66); General Secretary, U.P.P.C.C., 1935-8; member, U.P. Legislative Assembly, 1937-52; Minister of Police and Transport, U.P. Government, 1947-51; member, Rajya Sabha, 1952-7; and Lok Sabha, 1957-66; Minister of Railways and Transport, 1952-6; Transport and Communication, 1957-8; Commerce and Industry, 1958-61; Home Affairs, 1961-3; and Minister without Portfolio, January to June 1964; Prime Minister and Minister of Atomic Energy, 1964-6.

granting that some people did want to spite authority, that should be no excuse for the latter to lose discretion and act in an irresponsible manner.

I hope the Police Minister will reconsider the position and take necessary action.

Sincerely yours,
Jayaprakash Narayan

128. Statement to the Press on Basawan Sinha's Fast, 14 March 1949[1]

On my way to Delhi from Calcutta I dropped this morning at Dalmianagar to see my friend, Shri Basawan Sinha, who is on an indefinite fast since the afternoon of the 8th March.[2] This is the seventh day of his fast, and though his general condition is satisfactory, his pulse and blood-pressure are low. He is taking only water with soda-bicarb and a few drops of sour lemon.

This self-invited suffering of this brave soldier of freedom and tireless servant of labour has so far passed unnoticed. This is in keeping with Basawan Sinha's character. He has always worked silently and never sought publicity or acclaim. However, it is our duty to see that such a valuable life is not put into jeopardy and his suffering is relieved as soon as possible.

The public are perhaps aware of the long drawn-out struggle at Dalmianagar.[3] The story of that struggle is a painful story of intrigue and injustice. But this is not the time to go into that. It is sufficient to remind that a few weeks ago, acting on my advice, the Union withdrew the strike which had been going on for over two months. But the Management refused to take back the strikers. I appealed personally to the Management and went down on my knees as it were before the Prime Minister and the Labour Minister of the Bihar Government to see that bare justice was done to the workers. But all that was of no avail. The workers and their families had suffered for long and were on the point of starvation. Basawan Babu, having tried every means open to him to have the workers reinstated found it impossible to witness quietly the suffering of those who had acted on his advice.

[1] *J.P. Papers* (NMML). The statement, written during the train journey from Delhi to Calcutta on 14 March 1949, was published in newspapers on 15 March 1949.

[2] To understand the background of Basawan Sinha's fast, see Appendix 11.

[3] In Dalmianagar there was only one representative union of the workers known as the Rohtas Industries Mazdoor Sangh. A parallel union was formed by the Indian National Trade Union Congress, funded and guided by the Congress. This did not have much following, but was being helped by the Congress to build up its base among the workers and to weaken the socialists. One of the most active socialist trade union workers, Bhagwat Tripathy, was externed by a Government order. But the workers refused to accept the INTUC leadership and the strike started on 4 December. See item no. 22 (J.P. to Anugraha Narayan Sinha, 3 February 1949).

While normally the weapon of fasting is unsuitable to the labour movement I am convinced that there was no alternative left open to Basawan Babu but to invite upon himself the same sufferings to which the workers had been exposed. It is common these days to take lightly fasting and hungerstrike. I should, however, like to warn the people that the fast undertaken by Shri Basawan Sinha should not be treated in such a manner. Those who know him will testify that he is incapable of doing any thing merely to produce an effect or for the purpose of propaganda. I, therefore, appeal to the good people of this province to exert their utmost to save this noble soul.

129. To Ramanandan Mishra; 14 March 1949[1]

Doon Express

Dear Ramanandan Babu,[2]

Just now I am coming after seeing Basawan Babu. It is the seventh day of fast. The health is all right so far, but there is weakness, and the pulse and blood pressure are low. No body from the province has enquired about him. You should come to see him and should think how to organize an agitation regarding him. Hue and cry should be raised through newspapers. The press correspondents from Patna should be sent to Dehri. Binay Babu[3] should also go. Interviews with Basawanji should be organized. Dalmianagar is under Section 144, but the meeting can be held in any neighbouring village. The striking and other workers, and the farmers of villages also should be asked to attend it through the distribution of leaflets. "Basawan-Day" should be observed throughout the province. Later on the members of the party can undertake a fast for a day; etc., etc. Various kinds of activities can be organized in this respect. Some one from among you should meet Shri Babu. I am writing him a letter,[4] its copy is attached herewith.

There is need to pay heed to this issue. You will show this letter to your colleagues. Send Reyasat[5] to Dalminagar for some days. I am also writing to Ganga Babu.[6] You all should consult collectively and take suitable action.

Yours,
Jayaprakash

[1] *J.P. Papers* (NMML).
[2] For biographical note on Ramanand Misra, see *JPSW*, Vol. II, p. 186.
[3] A Socialist Leader of Bihar.
[4] Letter to Sri Babu not found.
[5] For biographical note on Reyasat Karim, see *JPSW*, Vol. IV, p. 222.
[6] For biographical note on Gangasaran Sinha, see *JPSW*, Vol. II, p. 9.

130. To Basawan Sinha (Telegram), 26 March 1949[1]

My heart with you. You will win because your cause just. Even death is victory in such cause. Having launched on supreme sacrifice do not worry about settlement. Have wired Prime Minister and Dalmia.

Jayaprakash

[1] *J.P. Papers* (NMML).

131. To Shanti Prasad Jain (Telegram), 28 March 1949[1]

Bihar Prime Minister wires,[2] "it is entirely for management to decide whether or not they would reemploy the discharged men, and provincial government do not come into picture. A telegram has been sent to Shri Shanti Prasad Jain today stating this." Life of Basawanji entirely in hands of employers, hope you will do everything to save him, reaching Dalmianagar thirtieth night Bombay mail.

[1] *J.P. Papers* (NMML).
[2] Bihar Prime Minister to J.P., 28 March 1949.

132. Message for the Special Number of *Students Congress*, Patna, 30 March 1949[1]

I am happy to know that a special number of the "Students Congress" is soon to appear. I send my greetings on this occasion to "Students Congress" and all my good wishes.

Students in our country have not yet adjusted themselves to the new tasks and responsibilities that freedom has created for them. Meaningless strikes and demonstrations, disclosures of examination papers, absence of any constructive and creative activity, factionalism—all these are symptoms of the distemper of the student world. Students must pass quickly out of this destructive state and settle down to the tasks of construction, study and self-discipline.

One of the great constructive efforts being made today is the attempt to form the National Union of Students, which will rescue the student movement from destructive factionalism. I hope all students will cooperate in building up this national organization, so full of promise.

Jayaprakash Narayan

[1] *J.P. Papers* (NMML).

133. To Rafi Ahmed Kidwai, 30 March 1949[1]

My dear Rafi Saheb,

You may recall that I had spoken to you on the telephone from Patna at the time of the threatened strike about the arrest of Shri B.M. Dalvi,[2] postal employee and Assistant Secretary of the All India Postmen and Lower Grade (R.M.S.) Staff Union, of which I am the President. Dalvi apparently was arrested on suspicion of being a Communist. All my colleagues in the Union working in Bombay assure me that he is not a Communist, though at the meeting of the General Council he had spoken in favour of the strike. That, however, is no crime as every member of the Council was free to express his view. The continued detention of B.M. Dalvi is giving a handle to trouble-makers and is weakening our hands. I therefore urge that the Provincial Government be advised as soon as possible to set Dalvi at liberty.

A rather serious situation has developed of which I was informed at Bombay a couple of days ago. You will recall that when I had met you at Delhi with representatives of the All India Postmen and Lower Grade (R.M.S.) Staff Union, one of the questions discussed was whether the increment in dearness allowance of Rs.10/, then announced by the Central Government, would be available without any reduction to that category of staff also who were receiving an "interim allowance". It was argued on our side that the increment of Rs.10/- in the dearness allowance was sanctioned in view of the further rise in prices and that the prices had risen for all. The employees whose previous total emoluments were protected by the make-shift arrangement of the "interim allowance", should not be made to suffer by the absorption of the new increment in the interim allowance. If this were done, these poor men would have to suffer twice: once when the new rates were applied and their total emoluments were reduced (which were sought to be protected by the interim allowance); and again when the increment in dearness allowance due to rise in prices was virtually denied to them by the increment being absorbed in the interim allowance. Surely, prices have risen for these people as much, if not more, as for others. A concession made to employees in view of the rising cost of living should not be withdrawn in order to suit the clumsy formula of the Finance Department.

When we had pressed this point before you, it is my distinct recollection that we were assured that it would be conceded. At least, that was the

[1] *J.P. Papers* (NMML). The letter was written on the train to Dehri-on-Sone.

[2] B.M. Dalvi, a postal employee and Assistant Secretary of All India Postmen and Lower Grade Staff Employees (R.M.S.) Union.

impression that we had gathered. Mr. Jerath's[3] contrary reply, however, has created an ugly situation, and the men are angry with us for misleading them. I do very earnestly plead with you to look into this matter and have it rectified. If the question involves other Government employees too, that should be no reason why the Government should persist in a wrong. A dearness allowance—and an admittedly inadequate allowance—granted in order to give some relief to the employees from the demon of inflation should not be withdrawn in this manner, just because of certain rules which are in themselves not sound. I request an urgent decision on this matter.

I am enclosing a copy of Mr. Dalvi's letter and Mr. Jerath's reply.

Hoping you are well and with regards,

Very sincerely yours,
Jayaprakash Narayan

[3] Harbans Jerath (1899-); Dy. Director-General, Post and Telegraph, Government of India, 1947-9; represented India on the Executive & Liaison Commission of the Universal Postal Union in Montreaux (Switzerland), 1950.

134. To Jawaharlal Nehru (on the Train to Dehri-on-Sone), 30 March 1949[1]

Dear Bhai,

You probably know Pandit Baleshwar Dayal. He comes from the UP and has been working for the last 12 years among the Bhils of Central India and Rajputana. He has an ashram at Bamania (BB & CI) near Ratlam. From all accounts his work among the Bhils has been of an outstanding merit and he has won their universal love and admiration: he is known among them as Mamaji. A unique feature of his work has been that he has trained Bhils themselves to be his co-workers.

Since the advent of freedom, Pandit Baleshwar Dayal had been carrying on a campaign for the control and abolition of jagirdari. His campaign succeeded so far that after the Deputy Prime Minister of the Madhya Bharat Government had seen him, it was announced that in the whole of the Bhil area the Government would forthwith take over the functions of the jagirdars who would have nothing to do with the tenants, the latter dealing directly with the Government. Soon after, the Rajasthan Government too announced a similar policy. This was a great victory for Panditji, and this was not liked by the power-managers of the Congress in this part of the world.

[1] Enclosure of Nehru's letter to Patel, 6 April 1949, *Sardar Patel's Correspondence 1945-50,* edited by Durga Das, Ahmedabad, Navajiwan Publishing House, 1972, Vol. 8, pp. 507-9.

Baleshwar Dayal on his part went ahead with his work. Strangely enough his probation work has frowned upon by the authorities; and one of the strangest things I have seen happening in Free India is the drink campaign set afoot among the Bhils after the arrest of Panditji under official patronage and not a little of coercion!

Pandit Baleshwar Dayal was forced soon after the victory of his anti-jagirdari campaign to launch an agitation against certain newly imposed taxes on grass, firewood and timber. These taxes, I have been told, leave only two alternatives to the Bhils: either to take to thieving or to starve. This is probably an exaggeration. But I have no doubt that the effect of these taxes will be to break up Bhil economy—what little there exists of it—and expose a good part of their economic life to the depredations of outside contractors and open up great opportunities to petty forest officials to mulct the poor Bhils. It was at the height of this agitation that Baleshwar Dayal was invited by the Minister concerned to Udaipur for discussion. When he went there in response on February 3, he was put under arrest and sent to Tonk prison! For the first two days he was given no food in the prison.

Having gone into the matter carefully, I have no doubt that the Rajasthan Government has no cause whatever to put Panditji in prison. He has been shut up either because his strong criticism of the Government and his growing influence were too much for the little fellows who are in power; or because of a personal grudge that Manikyalal Varma bears him.

It is a great pity that when we have the opportunity now to put into practice all the fine things we used to say about tribal and depressed peoples, we are ourselves becoming the instruments of their exploitation by soulless money-grabbers.

The continued detention of Pandit Baleshwar Dayal is a crime against freedom and the simple Bhils. I do not know whom else to write but you in a matter like this. I hope you will take steps to have him set at liberty. The Madhya Bharat Government, I am told, has nothing against him. His ashram, by the way, is within the territory of Madhya Bharat. The District Officer of Banswara, in a recent letter to Baleshwar Dayal, praised his work among the Bhils and said there was great reformation visible of their life on account of his efforts.

Several Congress committees, notable among them the Ratlam Congress Committee, have passed resolutions condemning the arrest of this selfless man.

Yours affectionately,
Jayaprakash

135. To Sheikh Mohammad Abdullah, 8 April 1949[1]

My dear Sheikh Saheb,[2]

I need not introduce to you, Farid.[3] as you probably know he has not been well for the past whole year practically and the doctors have advised him to spend this summer also in a cool place. They have advised him to go to Kashmir and he is doing so. I shall be deeply obliged if you could make the necessary arrangements for him to stay there and for whatever help he may require. I regret that I am adding to your troubles but I am doing so in the hope that you will not mind it.

You might have read in the papers that I fractured my arm the other day, that the fracture has been well set and that I am progressing satisfactorily. So is my wife.[4]

With kindest regards,

Sincerely yours,
Jayaprakash Narayan

P.S. I am unable to write due to my fracture.

[1] *J.P. Papers* (NMML).

[2] For biographical note of Sheikh Mohammad Abdullah, see *JPSW*,-Vol. IV, p. 195.

[3] Faridul Haq Ansari (1895-1966); joined the Bar, 1925; member, A.I.C.C., 1927-48; Secretary, Delhi, P.C.C., 1929-30; and Delhi D.C.C., 1930-2; participated in Civil Disobedience Movement, 1930, 1932, and individual satyagraha, 1940; founder-member, C.S.P., 1934; in prison, 1942-5; member, P.S.P. 1952-8; Joint Secretary, P.S.P., 1954-8; member, Rajya Sabha, 1958-60 and 1960-6.

[4] While touring in Bihar, along with his wife Prabhavati Devi, Jayaprakash Naryayan met with a car accident near Daltonganj on 1 April and got his right arm fractured. Prabhavati escaped with minor injuries.

136. To Jawaharlal Nehru, 10 April 1949[1]

Dear Bhai,

I thank you for your letter of 6th April.[2]

I have a compound fracture in my right forearm which will immobilise me at least for two months. The bones have been set well and now it is only a question of time. Prabhavati is much better and her stitches have been removed and she is expected to move about in another week though because of her head injury she ought to take more rest than she is inclined to.

I thank you for the trouble you took in the matter of Pandit baleshwar Dayal. I was very happy to read a few days ago of his release.

[1] *Nehru Papers*—Files at home (NMML).

[2] See Appendix 12 for Nehru's reply to this letter.

There are two matters about which I am anxious to write to you before you leave for London. You remember I spoke to you about Bishweshwar Prasad Koirala. I am sending you a copy of another letter from him which he smuggled out to his friends in India. I hope it will be possible for you to do something in the matter. You know best what to do.

When I met you last you were good enough to explain to me your point of view regarding the Commonwealth link. Our talk however was not finished and I was not able to have a clear picture from you. Since it is expected, if one is to judge from newspaper reports, that this question is coming up at the Commonwealth Premiers' Conference, I should like to say that the point of view which you expressed to me the other day did not seem very convincing. As far as I was able to understand there were two important considerations in your mind: (1) that it was not good for India to be isolated; (2) that the Commonwealth link implied no commitments whatever on our side except our agreement to consult jointly on important and vital matters.

At the same time, your foreign policy in regard to the two power blocs continues to be that of complete neutrality. This seems to me to be rather inconsistent. But I should like to discuss this question separately from our foreign policy.

The British, throughout their rule here, made the Hindus and Muslims compete with each other for their support. They seem to be succeeding in the same policy even now and the competition of the two communities has now taken the form of competition between India and Pakistan. By seeking the support of Britain we are merely exposing our lack of self-confidence. National independence is a relative term in the present world, yet I believe India must learn to stand up on her own legs and give up the habit of leaning against Britain if she is to achieve real independence.

Your claim that association with the Commonwealth will mean no commitment whatever except that of mutual consultation is rather naive, if you will excuse me for saying so. To agree to consult mutually on every vital issue is a very deep commitment indeed. When India agrees to consult with A group of nations, that means she will not consult with B group of nations or others. That itself puts India on a different footing with different nations. Furthermore, it would be unreasonable to contend that the obligation to consult mutually leaves one completely free to take any line one chooses. When a group of nations habitually consult among themselves, all kinds of factors and considerations arise that bind them closer together. There would be no meaning in India consulting with the Commonwealth nations and following an independent line on vital matters of policy. That just cannot happen and, if it does happen, Great Britain and the other nations of the Commonwealth will lose all their interest in India and would be rather anxious for the day when the black sheep in the family would leave it.

Therefore, firstly the fear of isolation should be fought and India should be prepared psychologically to stand on her own legs. Secondly, the so-called non-commitment is indeed a far-reaching commitment.

Thirdly, if Iwere to come back to the neutrality question, I have no doubt that India's association with the Commonwealth will indubitably place her in one of the two power blocs.

I hope therefore that you will not commit the country to a cause against which we had set our face for so many years. All the old arguments are still valid and I have not heard of any new argument which in the least should affect our position.

With love and regards,

Affectionately yours,
Jayaprakash

137. To Asoka Mehta, 20 April 1949[1]

Dear Asoka,

It is very good of all of you to have made such affectionate enquiries about Prabhavati's and my condition. I am much better now but the bone-union will not take less than three months to be strong enough to allow me to resume my work. The doctors had told me in the beginning that it might be possible for me to move about in two months but now they have definitely told me that I would not be able to leave Patna before the first week of July. In these circumstances I think it will be unfair for me to continue during this period as General Secretary of the Party. I am therefore writing to you to request you earnestly to act in my place for the duration of my physical incapacity and I hope you will be good enough to accept my suggestion. Three of the Joint Secretaries are permanently in Bombay and therefore you will not find the new responsibility a great burden. I have spoken to Suresh about it when he was here. Please do not stand on ceremony and send me a negative reply because I shall not accept that.

I believe there is enough money with the Treasurer to carry us forward for a couple of months. After that you, Purshottam and Yusuf may put your heads together and raise a little money to tide the Central Office over for another month or so, or Purshottam may draw upon Rs. 25,000 which is with him to the credit of the Janata Publications Ltd.

I am sorry that I will not be in a position to literally hand over charge to you but that is not necessary. The office and the Secretaries being in Bombay,

[1] *J.P. Papers* (NMML).

you can take over charge from them. As soon as I hear from you I shall issue a press statement to this effect.

How is Purshottam's election going on? Please write to me whenever you have the time.

With love,

Affectionately yours,
Jayaprakash

138. To Asim Kumar Dutt, 22 April 1949[1]

My dear Asim Babu,[2]

A couple of days before my accident I had written to you in connection with the *Khoj Parishad*. Since the accident has incapacitated me for some months I have grown far more anxious about the finances of the *Khoj Parishad* than before and therefore I am giving you this trouble again. When I discussed the matter last with you I definitely got the impression that you would be able to arrange for a monthly contribution of 700 rupees. I learn from Satu[3] that he has so far received only your own personal contribution but not the rest of the monthly amount. Will you kindly see the friends concerned and fix up with them and make to Satu the remittances accordingly. The *Khoj Parishad* has great possibilities and in spite of serious difficulties it has done good work already and it needs all our support.

I am progressing fairly well. The first plaster will be removed in about a month's time and then a lighter plaster will be applied which I will have to keep for another month and a half. The doctors say that the bone-union will not take less than three months to be completely all right. This means I will have to be confined to Patna till the first week of July. I am otherwise fit. My wife is well now and has been discharged from the hospital.

Hoping all of you are well and with kind regards,

Affectionately yours,
Jayaprakash Narayan

[1] *J.P. Papers* (NMML).

[2] Asim Kumar Dutt, a socialist activist in West Bengal; one of the members of the Council of Governors, Khoj Parishad, Calcutta.

[3] Satyabrata Sen.

139. To Achyut Patwardhan, 22 April 1949[1]

Dear Achyut,

As you know, a friend in Delhi has promised a monthly contribution of Rs. 500 to the *Khoj Parishad*. Will you kindly arrange that the contribution is regularly remitted and if possible that cheques are made out in the name of the Treasurer, *Khoj Parishad*? Also, as soon as the dollar problem is solved, kindly arrange that the lump sum contribution promised, or such part of it as is possible, is also made at the earliest opportunity.

Please do not fail to have both these arrangements made.

Affectionately yours,
Jayaprakash

[1] *J.P. Papers* (NMML).

140. To Acharya Narendra Deva, 22 April 1949[1]

My dear Narendra Devji,

I do not know if you received the letter I wrote to you from the Bombay Mail just a couple of days before my accident. I had written to you about arranging to hold as soon as possible a meeting of the Research Council of the *Khoj Parishad*. You know, according to the reorganization plans, only if the Research Council meets and plans out the research work and allots it to various collaborators throughout the country, the work of the *Parishad* cannot progress very much. As most of the universities and colleges are going to have their vacations from the middle of May or so, I wish you would arrange a meeting during this period. But unless you get in touch with the members of the Research Council now it may not be possible to get all of them together because they might make their vacation programmes in the meanwhile. So I hope you will treat this matter as urgent and do the needful.

I discussed with Dantwala the question of opening a branch of the *Parishad* in Bombay and he said that as soon as the Research Council has met and the work is chalked out the branch will begin to function.

I tried to persuade the doctors to let me leave the hospital at the end of this month, but they would not listen to me. So I will have to be here till the first plaster is cut, which will be in the middle of May. Then they will apply a new plaster and only then will they let me go to my residence. After

[1] *J.P. Papers* (NMML).

returning to my residence, which maybe about the 18th or 19th of May, I should like to trouble you to come to Patna at your convenience in the later part of May or any time in June to stay here if possible for a week or so. I want you here so that we can move on with our literature production. I am sure if we spend some time together some of the pamphlets and booklets which we have planned might get a good start. I spoke to Lohia also about it and he also might come at the same time and of course Prof. Mukut Beharilal also. The dates will have to be suited to you all, and as far as I am concerned any time from the third week of May to the end of June will suit me. As you probably know, the National Executive also is to meet in Patna from the 8th to 10th June. But our meetings need not be at the same time. I hope you will consider my request and if your health permits will find time to come to Patna.

Prabhavati is well now and she has been discharged from the hospital. Hope you are keeping good health.

Affectionately yours,
Jayaprakash

141. Statement to the Press, Patna, 23 April 1949[1]

My friend, Prof. [M.L.] Dantwala of the School of Economics and Sociology, University of Bombay, informs me that he is standing as a candidate for the directorship of Oriental Life Assurance Co. Ltd. on behalf of the policy-holders, particularly the small policy-holders. Prof. Dantwala needs no introduction to the public or recommendation from any one. He is not only a distinguished economist but has also played an active part in the freedom movement. I first made his acquaintance in the Nasik Road Central Prison in 1933 where he was a civil disobedience prisoner. Since then he has participated in all the national struggles even though that meant frequent breaks in his academic career. Among other things he is at present a member of the Agrarian Policy Committee of the National Congress. I am sure that the interests of the policy-holders and of the public generally will be safe in the hands of Prof. Dantwala and I accordingly endorse his candidature wholeheartedly. I hope he will receive the unstinted support of the policy-holders.

[1] *J.P. Papers* (NMML).

142. Comment on the Government's Decision to Continue in the Commonwealth, 28 April 1949[1]

The Socialist Party would take the first opportunity, whenever it was in a position to do so, to undo this great blunder. This was the greatest mistake committed by the Congress Party after the Partition; the agreement was a triumph for British diplomacy and not for the Prime Minister of India.

India has been opposed to such a policy for the last 20 years and even today the people's verdict would be against it. I have no doubt that India's international position as an independent sovereign state, preserving its neutrality as between the two power blocs, had greatly suffered.

The Socialist Party would never agree to this kind of association with a group of nations with whom they had very little in common and with some of whom they had been in serious conflict, such as South Africa.

[1] *Janata*, 22 May 1949. Also published in *Statesman*. The decision to join Commonwealth was taken at the Prime Minister's Conference in London held between 21-27 April 1949. The communiqué issued on 27 April (London) noted that India intended to be a "Sovereign Independent Republic" under its new Constitution but that it desired to "continue her membership of the Commonwealth and accept the King as symbol of free association of its independent member nations" and as its head.

143. To Sir Biren Mukherjee, 28 April 1949[1]

My dear Sir Biren,[2]

The bearer of this letter is my friend Satyabrata Sen, General Secretary of the *Khoj Parishad*. You will perhaps recall that I had spoken to you about the *Khoj Parishad* at Mr. A.K. Basu's[3] place when I was in Calcutta last. I had requested you for a contribution that could set the *Parishad* on its feet and be appropriate to your own position. Before that, Asoka Mehta, I believe, had spoken to you about the same matter at Delhi. He had given me the impression that you were interested and would be prepared to help if I approached you personally. It was then that I took the liberty to speak to you about it at Calcutta.

The *Parishad*, I assure you, is an institute of social and economic research and is independent of party politics. It has already done useful work and I

[1] *J.P. Papers* (NMML).

[2] Sir Biren Mukherjee (1899-1982), engineer and industrialist; joined Martin Company in 1924; became partner of the company in 1931 and partner of Burns Company later on; Managing Director of Martin-Burns Company till 1946; founder of Indian Iron and Steel Company.

[3] Amiya Kanta Basu (b.1893), Government Counsel, Calcutta High Court, 1926-47; member, Lok Sabha, 1953-6.

am sure it has a very useful role to play in the future. We want to pattern it something after the Fabian Research in Great Britain.[4]

Some time after I had spoken to you I wrote to Mr. A.K. Basu to see you in the matter and finalize it. He probably did speak to you, but because he had to leave for Switzerland he was perhaps unable to conclude the talks. Due to my accident I am incapacitated from moving about and I am naturally much more anxious about the Parishad finances now than I was when I met you and I am therefore sending this SOS. Please do not disappoint us and for heaven's sake do not make this young friend run to you, as is the wont of rich men, a dozen times. I am sorry to give you this trouble and I hope you will excuse me for it.

With kindest greetings,

Very sincerely yours,
Jayaprakash Narayan

[4] Established in 1884 predominently by the middle-class intellectuals to spread and apply socialist ideas to Britain gradually through democratic means.

144. To Acharya Narendra Deva, 1 May 1949[1]

My dear Narendra Devji,

I am enclosing a copy of a letter [dated] 22 April[2] I wrote to you sometime ago and I should be obliged if you kindly send an early reply.

I had sent for Satyabrata Sen to discuss the financial position of the *Khoj Parishad*. Unfortunately the Delhi promise does not seem to work out well. I gave Satu a letter for a friend in Calcutta and he has contributed Rs. 5,000/-. This should remove Satu's immediate worry and set the *Parishad* going. The Research Council can now be called and work begun.

Hoping you are well,

Affectionately yours,
Jayaprakash Narayan

[1] *J.P. Papers* (NMML).
[2] See ante, item no. 56.

145. To Asoka Mehta, 7 May 1949[1]

Dear Asoka,

Thanks for both your letters of 2 May. I am very sorry and a little hurt that you did not find it possible to act for me during my illness. You say that you

[1] *J.P. Papers* (NMML).

will be out of Bombay for the whole of the month of May and therefore it was not possible for you to accept the responsibility. You know that I am out of Bombay for eleven months out of the twelve in a year, and yet the responsibility is thrust upon me year after year. After all, the job would not have taken much of your time. It would only have meant that you would have had to take decisions between meetings of the Executive which the other Joint Secretaries would probably have found a little difficult. It would also have meant some financial responsibility which, according to your previous letter, you and other Bombay friends have already undertaken till the end of August. However, there is no need to argue this point further since you are not prepared to accept my request.

Regarding your suggestion that Purshottam should act for me, I do not understand how it escaped your notice and that of Suresh, Madhu and Rohit that he was not a member of the National Executive. Not being a member, it is obvious that he cannot act as the General Secretary of the Party even for a short period. Nor is there a vacancy on the National Executive which he can fill in the meanwhile. As I do not want any further delay in the matter I have no alternative but to ask Prem Bhasin, who is the senior most Joint Secretary, to function for me during my illness. The National Executive, when it meets next, may decide further in regard to it. I am sending a copy of this letter to Purshottam and another to Suresh.

Regarding Hasmukh's letter[2] I am afraid I did agree to become a member of the Advisory Committee of the National Education & Information Films Ltd. I was not aware of the seriousness of the step I took till I read Hasmukh's letter. Now that he has drawn these matters to my notice I shall take steps to find something about this company and dissociate myself if I find it necessary. I should like Hasmukh to help me in finding out something about the concern. I cannot do all this till I come to Bombay which, I m afraid, will not be before the second week of July.

Regarding the P. & T. unions matter (ref. Jabbar's letter from Madras)[3] about which you wrote to me sometime ago, you probably do not know that when I was in Bombay last it had been arranged that the representatives of all the P. & T. unions should meet in Delhi on 15th of April, at which the problem of realignment and amalgamation would be considered. Due to my accident this meeting had to be cancelled. I am writing now to the persons concerned to find out if it would be possible for them to collect at

[2] Hasmukh Shah, businessman in Bombay.

[3] M.A. Jabbar in his letter dated 28 March had suggested that a formal meeting between the representatives of the P & T Unions and the Government officials would be useful in solving the then existing impasse by (1) obtaining release of P & T officials then in custody, and (2) seeking appointment of anomalies committee of standing conciliation machinery which had already been conceded by the Railway Board.

Patna in the first week of June. The Working Committee of the Railwaymen's Federation is meeting in the first week of June and the P. & T. people could also come at the same time. I shall let you know after I hear from the parties concerned.

Affectionately yours,
Jayaprakash Narayan

146. To Sir Biren Mukherjee, 7 May 1949[1]

Dear Sir Biren,

I thank you very warmly for your letter of 29th April and for what you did in the matter about which I had written to you.[2] By not making Shri Satyabrata Sen run to you many times, you gave another proof that you are different from others of your order.

I am progressing fairly well.

With greetings,

Very sincerely yours,
Jayaprakash Narayan

[1] *J.P. Papers* (NMML).

[2] The matter, discussed in the letter exchanged between J.P. and Sir Biren Mukherjee, was about raising funds for the Khoj Parishad.

147. To R.S. Ruikar, 9 May 1949[1]

Dear Com. Ruikar,[2]

Many thanks for your letter of 21st April.[3] I do not understand the remarks made by the Jharia comrade. As far as I remember when I went to Jharia no one on behalf of the Forward Bolc ever came to see me or ever sent me any message. Will you please find out from the comrade concerned what exactly he wants from me when and where he would meet me.

I have been worried by the recent trend in the Forward Bolc, at least on this side. There is very little to distinguish the policy and attitude of the Forward Bloc from that of the Communist Party. I do not know how long this confused state of affairs is going to continue. The Socialist Party gets nothing but the filthiest abuse from the Forward Bloc here and that naturally

[1] *J.P. Papers* (NMML).

[2] For biographical note see *JPSW*, Vol. 1, p. 64.

[3] Ruikar's letter is not available.

makes it impossible for members of the Socialist Party to work in any field with it. We, on our part, however, keep quiet and there is hardly ever anything that we say or write against them. The question of leftists working together is often raised but unless the leftists learn some self-restraint and refrain from attacking and abusing one another, such joint working is not possible. Dignified political criticism is one thing and hurling vulgar epithets at one another is different. Except for the Socialist Party, I am sorry to say, all other leftist groups seem to be doing little more than attacking and abusing one another. However, this is an international phenomenon and one must go ahead irrespective of it.

Hoping you are well and with kind regards,

Sincerely yours,
Jayaprakash Narayan

148. Statement to the Press in Support of the Democratic Struggle in Nepal, 10 May 1949[1]

For some days past there have been persistent rumours about the hunger strike of Shri Bishweshwar Prasad Koirala,[2] former President, Nepali National Congress, and his three colleagues in the prisons of the Nepal Government. Some days ago the Headquarters of the Nepali National Congress confirmed the news. Now confirmation has come afresh from the Nepal Government itself. In a communiqué,[3] briefly published in the daily papers, the Nepal Government admits that four prisoners are on hunger strike, presumably on account of the treatment they are receiving as prisoners. The communiqué describes the four hunger-strikers as revolutionaries, thus admitting in effect that they are political prisoners. In no civilized country in the world have revolutionaries been ever treated as common criminals. The people of India, who have the utmost friendship and goodwill for the people of Nepal and every sympathy with their struggle for freedom and democracy, cannot but condemn the action of the Nepal Government in treating inhumanly their political opponents. It is a great pity that the Ranas of Nepal are not able to take any warning from history. They should realize that no amount of tyranny and oppression is going to preserve their power and privilege and prevent the people of Nepal from establishing their democratic rule.

The people of India cannot be indifferent to the struggle of the Nepali

[1] *Janata*, 22 May 1949. This statement was published, in brief, in *Searchlight* on 12 May 1949.

[2] B.P. Koirala had gone on hunger strike from 1 May for better treatment to political prisoners in Nepal jail.

[3] The communiqué dated 7 May was published on 8 May.

people because recent history has proved that freedom and democracy are indivisible. Our hearts go out in sympathy to the people of Nepal as much as to those of Indonesia or other peoples fighting for freedom. Our sympathy is greater for the Nepali people not only because they are our neighbours, but also because they are our kith and kin and children, as ourselves, of Mother India and inheritors of the same culture and tradition. Moreover, the continued autocracy in Nepal constitutes a danger to our freedom too. The Ranas of Nepal had been, till the end of British Raj in India, the stooges and servitors of that Raj. If the people of Nepal are not able to establish their own democratic rule there is every danger of other foreign powers filling the vacuum created by the British. Therefore, it is our duty to take the liveliest possible interest in the struggle of the Nepali people. Let the hunger strike of Koirala and his colleagues create a wave of sympathy and interest that would shake the foundations of Rana autocracy. The Nepali National Congress, as it will be recalled, decided recently to launch a satyagraha movement against that autocracy and for the achievement of elementary civic rights and freedoms. I have no doubt the people of this country will do all that is possible to help their Nepali brethren in their impending struggle. Meanwhile, I appeal to the people generally and to the youth and the Socialist Party particularly to demonstrate peacefully throughout the country in sympathy with the Nepali hunger-strikers and for their immediate release.

149. Telephonic Message to the Maharaja (Prime Minister) of Nepal, undated but around 10 May 1949[1]

Deeply disturbed at barbarous ill treatment of Bishweshwar Prasad Koirala and his three colleagues and their consequent hunger strike. The charges preferred against them by your Government are of political nature and entitle them to treatment as political prisoners. To deny them that status is to deny humanity and to challenge all decent people in this country and beyond. I urge therefore immediate acceptance of demand of political prisoners. The Indian people cannot brook tyranny in Nepal or Indonesia or anywhere in the world. You will earn nothing but ill will and enmity of people of this country if you and your Government persist in your present policy of tyranny and oppression. You should take a lesson from the end of British tyranny in India.

Jayaprakash Narayan

[1] *J.P. Papers* (NMML). The message was sent through the Operator Telephone Exchange, Raxaul, a small town in Bihar close to the boarder with Nepal.

150. To Shri Krishna Sinha, 12 May 1949[1]

Dear Shri Babu,

Sadar Pranam.

Just now I received a letter from Phulan Babu, reading which I became puzzled. He has written that he talked to Rajendra Babu in Delhi regarding Dalmianagar. Rajendra Babu said that he was prepared to become an arbitrator, but the difficulty was that except Basawan Sinha no other contenders were prepared to accept him as the arbitrator. Shanti Prasad Jain has written to him that he wants him to decide whether or not Basawan Sinha's fast was proper. Hargovind Misra has written to him that he does not accept arbitration itself.

I have been very much pained after knowing these facts. You would remember that when you came to this hospital (to see me) Krishna Ballabh Babu[2] had told us that Shanti Prasad had told him on telephone that he had accepted Rajendra Babu's arbitration. After that I asked you if it should be accepted as a confirmed matter, then you replied that when Shanti Prasad said so to Krishna Ballabh Babu on telephone, that should be accepted as confirmed. Again, I asked what issues would be referred to arbitration. Then you yourself said that the same issues would be referred that have led Basawan Babu to undertake a fast.

After this talk I sent Ganga Babu[3] to Dalmianagar with the message that Basawan Babu should break his fast.

When I had talks with you, or prior to that with Anugraha Babu, there was no mention of Hargovind Misra as a party to this issue. I do not understand how he came into it now. I advised Basawan Babu to break his fast on assurance from you people. I see that we have been deceived. I cannot say as to who is responsible for it. Since I had talks with you, I would like to ask you as to what you want to do in this matter now. Reply promptly. I shall be obliged.

Yours,

Jayaprakash

[1] *J.P. Papers* (NMML). Original in Hindi.

[2] Krishna Ballabh Sahay, for biographical note, see *JPSW*, Vol. II, p. 254.

[3] Ganga Saran Sinha, for biographical note, see *JPSW*, Vol. II, p. 98.

151. To Jawaharlal Nehru, 12 May 1949[1]

Dear Bhai,

What we had feared for months past has finally come about. Now that we are faced with an accomplished fact I shall not trouble you by carrying forward the argument.[2] My only regret is that to the many existing controversial issues another grave issue—not an empty one as you have suggested—has been added, which will divide the nation into contending camps.

I hope you will excuse me for writing again about Bishweshwar Prasad Koirala. I am enclosing a press cutting which gives in brief a communique issued by the Nepal Government. We had private information that Koirala was on hunger-strike with three other political prisoners since the 1st of May. The Nepal Government's communique confirms this. The hunger strike is on the issue of better treatment of political prisoners. The Nepal Government, while describing the hunger-strikers as revolutionaries, refuses to class them as political prisoners or give them any preferential treatment. History is being repeated in Nepal. Throughout the world it has been the struggle of political prisoners which has improved the condition and lot of prisoners, political or otherwise. It is a pity however that in our immediate neighbourhood, nay on Indian soil itself as it were, such tyranny should flourish and that we should look on helplessly. The sympathies of the Indian people and of its present Government have been unbounded for the suffering peoples of Indonesia and elsewhere, but we have so far taken little interest in the plight of our brethern across the border.

This is the twelfth day of Bishweshwar's fasting, and because of his delicate health I fear greatly for his life. In a revolutionary struggle for the freedom of the people the life of one individual may not have a very large place. Yet those for whom the individual's life has value cannot remain indifferent. It is for this reason that I am giving you this trouble in the hope that you will be able to persuade the Ranas at least to treat their prisoners less barbarously if not humanely. In a few days Bishweshwar's elder brother, Matrika Prasad Koirala, who is now President of the Nepali National Congress, and Bishweshwar's wife will go to see you at Delhi. In the meanwhile, I am writing this letter because the matter is urgent.[3]

I hope you had a fine time in Europe and are the better for it. I read with

[1] *Nehru Papers*—Files at home (NMML).

[2] This refers to India's decision to continue to remain in the Commonwealth.

[3] See Appendix 13 for Nehru's reply to this letter.

great interest all the reports of your doings in England and on the Continent and could not help feeling proud at the great acclaim you received there.

Affectionately yours,
Jayaprakash

P.S. After writing the above I read your statement at the press conference. That you should have come down to such a level shows you have a weak case. However, history will show who is living in the past. For those of us who are certain that India's link with the Commonwealth is unnatural and cannot last long, there is no need to be impatient or to lose temper.

(J.P.)

152. To R.S. Ruikar, 13 May 1949[1]

Dear Com. Ruikar,

I wrote to you a couple of days ago. Now Asoka Mehta has sent me a copy of your letter of 3rd May to him regarding the non-cooperation of the Socialist trade union workers with you and with the H.M.S. in C.P.[2] I have been astounded to read your letter for I had no such information previously. I assure you that we will not allow this disruptive policy to continue. The H.M.S. is not a projection of any political party and all workers of the Socialist Party are expected to develop it on trade union lines and give it their fullest support.

As Asoka has written to you, we shall discuss this matter at the meeting of the National Executive in June. In the meanwhile, I am writing to the Secretary of the C.P. Provincial Socialist Party to send me an explanation of the conduct of the Nagpur comrades. I would like to repeat the counsel of patience that Asoka has given in his letter. I quite appreciate your annoyance, but you are too seasoned a political worker to be deflected from the correct path by difficulties and I shall write to you in the matter as soon as I hear from the C.P. Provincial Secretary.

Sincerely yours,
Jayaprakash Narayan

[1] *J.P. Papers* (NMML).

[2] Ruikar in his letter to Mehta dated 13 May, had expressed his anguish at the attitude of Nagpur party comrades, after his election as President of HMS. According to him the Socialist comrades even refused to cooperate and participate in the May Day celebrations held at Nagpur under the auspices of HMS and other affiliated trade unions. According to him their hostility was seriously affecting the work of HMS, not only at Nagpur but also at other centres like Burhanpur and Akola. He requested Mehta to forward a copy of his letter to J.P. Ibid.

153. To S. Pagare, 13 May 1949[1]

Dear Comrade Pagare,[2]

I am enclosing herewith a copy of a letter from Comrade Ruikar addressed to Comrade Asoka Mehta.[3] I should like to know from you what explanation the Nagpur comrades have to give for their non-cooperation with the H.M.S. of Nagpur. It also appears from Ruikar's letter that the non-cooperation with the H.M.S. is not confined to Nagpur alone but spreads to the whole province. This is a very sad state of affairs which I am completely at a loss to understand. Our party took such pains to build up the H.M.S. and I cannot understand our own Party comrades trying to disrupt it by non-cooperation and sectarian attitude.

I shall appreciate an immediate reply.

Sincerely yours,
Jayaprakash Narayan

[1] *J.P. Papers* (NMML).
[2] Sukumar Pagare, Provincial Secretary, Socialist Party, Nagpur (C.P.).
[3] See fn. 2 in the previous item (J.P.'s letter to Ruikar, 13 May 1949).

154. To Anugraha Narayan Sinha, 14 May 1949[1]

Dear Anugraha Babu,
Sadar Pranam.

After returning from Delhi Phulan Babu, who has written you a letter with regard to Dalmianagar, has also sent me its copy. I became perplexed after reading that letter. When you had placed a proposal before me that we should accept Rajendra Babu as an arbitrator in the affair relating to Dalmianagar, you would remember that I, on my own behalf and that of my comrades, had accepted that proposal immediately; but at the same time I had asked if Shanti Prasad would also accept that proposal. You replied that he could not have courage to refuse it. Later when Shri Babu and Krishna Ballabh Babu came to see me, Krishna Ballabh Babu said that Shanti Prasad had accepted Rajendra Babu's arbitration. Shri Babu had also told me that the terms of reference for the arbitration would be the issues that had led Basawan Babu to undertake a fast.

While these talks took place with you people, the question of Hargovind Misra had not arisen. Whatever that may be, it cannot be imagined in dream that Hargovind Misra will refuse Rajendra Babu's arbitration. I hear that

[1] *J.P. Papers* (NMML). Original in Hindi.

the I.N.T.U.C. has great trust in the method of arbitration. But Hargovind Misra has refused arbitration twice in the affairs of Dalmianagar alone. On both the occasions the proposal for arbitration came to me from you people. I accepted it both the times, but it is your followers who rejected it. It is such a riddle that is beyond my grasp.

Now tell me what should be done in this case. I had advised Basawan Babu to break his fast on assurances of you people. Now we realize that we were deceived. God alone knows who is responsible for this deception, but it is clear that I cannot sit quietly after this deception. Even then, before doing anything I would like to know what you want to do further in this matter. I shall be exceedingly obliged if you are kind enough to reply speedily.

Yours,
Jayaprakash

155. To Jawaharlal Nehru (Telegram), 15 May 1949[1]

News just received from Raxaul about Koirala's rumoured death, kindly enquire and confirm preferably telephonically Patna.[2]

Jayaprakash

[1] *J.P. Papers* (NMML).

[2] In his reply telegram dated 17 May, Nehru informed J.P. that Koirala was not dead but very weak. Nehru further mentioned that he had strongly represented to Nepal to allow Koirala's wife to fly to Kathmandu and visit him and further to release him immediately.

156. Statement to the Press on Rammanohar Lohia's Arrest, Patna, 26 May 1949[1]

The news of Dr. Lohia's arrest and injury from tear bomb shells[2] has come to me as a great shock. Free India is being slowly converted into a vast prison. Even citizens of standing are unable to carry on peaceful activities without let or hindrance. The Ranas of Nepal are bent upon murdering by slow death some of the noblest sons of Nepal, and citizens of India who have the deepest sympathy for the long suffering people of Nepal, are not even allowed to demonstrate peacefully before the representative of the Ranas in this country. The argument that a particular procession or a meeting

[1] Adapted from *Searchlight*, 28 May 1949.

[2] Rammanohar Lohia, and Prem Bhasin, along with nearly fifty other Socialists, had been arrested in New Delhi on 25 May for demonstrating in front of the Nepalese Embassy demanding release of B.P. Koirala and delivering speeches against the systematic curtailment of civil liberties in Nepal.

was unlawful begs the question. Citizens in a free country possess the fundamental right to assemble peacefully and the right can not be taken away by the simple device of declaring such assemblies as unlawful. During the British days the Congress was often declared to be an unlawful assembly, but no patriotic citizen ever accepted that and gave up his right. There are more restrictions on the liberties of the citizens in free India today under Congress rule than there ever were under the worst of British despots. This must cause deep anxiety to all freedom-lovers in this country and perhaps the day is not distant when they must all join together irrespective of Party creeds to save this country from fascism. Immediately I invite all branches of the Socialist Party and all peace loving organizations to organize demonstrations and meetings of protest against the arrest and ill-treatment of Dr. Lohia and comrade Prem Bhasin and fifty other members of Delhi Socialist Party.

157. To Shakti Bose, 26 May 1949[1]

My dear Shakti,

I am sorry for not replying to your letter earlier. You must have read the report in this morning's papers of the demonstration in New Delhi.[2] It is more necessary now to have a demonstration in Calcutta too. Matrika Babu[3] has gone on a tour of the U.P. side of the Nepal Terai and he will not be going to Calcutta for some time. He has given me the address of the representative of the Nepali National Congress in Calcutta, which is:

10-B, Rammohan Dutta Road,
Elgin Road Post.

You please meet this gentleman and arrange the demonstration in consultation with him. The two Nepali friends for whom you wanted letters from me you should contact through Asim Babu. Judging from the attitude of the Democratic Nepali Congress, I am doubtful whether they would be of much help to us. However, we should meet them in any case.

I have received the letter which Satu has sent me. Please let me know of further developments in the Tramway Mazdoor Panchayat affair.

Sincerely yours,
Jayaprakash Narayan

[1] *J.P. Papers* (NMML). Shakti Bose was a prominent Socialist leader of Bengal.

[2] This refers to the demonstration in front of the Nepalese Embassy in New Delhi on 25 May 1949, under Lohia's leadership, see fn. 2 of the previous item.

[3] Matrika Prasad Koirala (1912-97); founder-member of Nepali National Congress, 1946; President, Nepali Congress party, 1950; Prime Minister Nepal, 1951-2, and 1953-5; founded Rashtriya Praja Party, 1952; Ambassador to the United States and Permanent Representative at the United Nations, 1962-4.

158. Statement to the Press on B.P. Koirala's Fast, Patna, 28 May 1949[1]

It is a matter of deep regret that so much confusion has been created in the press about Mr. Bisheshwar Prasad Koirala, who is on hunger-strike in a Nepal prison since May1. Where a man's life is involved there should have been more care exercised in handing out information.

I am in a position to say categorically that Mr. Koirala had not given up his hunger-strike till yesterday. I received a telegram direct from Kathmandu which said that his hunger-strike was continuing. People have unnecessarily brought in Pandit Jawaharlal Nehru's name in this matter. In the nature of things he could not give any assurance to a prisoner in a foreign country. All he could do, and which I am sure he must have done, is to make a strong representation on grounds of humanity to the Nepal Government to treat political prisoners as human beings.

The news published in a section of the press to the effect that Mr. Koirala has given up his fast might lead to complacency and further endanger his life. Therefore I appeal to all concerned not to be misled by these false reports and to continue to make all possible efforts to save Mr. Koirala's life.

[1] *Searchlight*, 30 May 1949.

159. To the Maharaja of Nepal (Telegram), 29 May 1949[1]

Thank you for your decision to release Mr. Koirala although belated.[2] I hope Mr. Koirala's release means the beginning of a new era of democracy and liberal Government in Nepal.

[1] *Tribune*, 31 May 1949.

[2] B.P. Koirala had sent a telegram to J.P. on 28 May saying: "Myself released, broken-fast." He wanted to stay in Nepal for a fortnight convalescing and also having a talk with the Maharaja, there. See also Appendix 14.

160. To Faridul Huq Ansari, 2 June 1949[1]

My dear Farid,

I was very happy to have your letter of 22nd May and to know that Srinagar is agreeing with you and your health is steadily improving. I know of your

[1] *J.P. Papers* (NMML).

letters to Ganga Babu[2] and he told me that he had also written to you and he wondered, when he got your second letter, how his reply to your first letter had not reached you. I am sure he has written to you again. He has gone to Lucknow and is expected today. I will show him your letter when he comes back.

Prabhavati has completely recovered. I also have left the hospital and am back at my residence. But my recovery is rather slow. The bones have united but the union is not strong yet. Therefore, I still have the plaster on my arm which I will have to keep on till the end of June at least. Otherwise I am well. I will be in Bihar till the end of July, after which I will go over to Bombay for a month. I should have loved to go to Kashmir but it does not seem to be possible. My illness has taken so much time that as soon as I am able to work again I will have to take up my tours and my other activities.

Narendra Devji was here on his way to Assam and he did say that he was to go to Srinagar for a conference. I am sorry that the conference has been cancelled. I doubt whether he would be able to go now.

When Ganga Babu comes back I will discuss with him his future plans. It is just possible that he might be going over to Kashmir for a short time.

With best wishes for your health.

Affectionately yours,
Jayaprakash Narayan

[2] Ganga Saran Sinha.

161. To H.S. Addison, 2 June 1949[1]

Dear Mr. Addison,[2]

I am indeed very thankful to you for sending me an invitation to attend the World Assembly of the Moral Re-Armament Movement.[3] I should have liked very much to be present at this assembly, to take inspiration from it and be able to meet the leaders of this movement as well as of the socialist movement who, as you write, might also be present. I am however unable

[1] *J.P. Papers* (NMML).

[2] H.S. Addison: a British Missionary, London; one of the organizers of the Moral Rearmament Movement.

[3] The Moral Rearmament Movement, variously known as Buchmanism and also the 'Oxford Group' was a movement founded in 1938 by Frank N.D. Buchman (1878-1961), an American Evangelist. He got influential support at Oxford University and the movement came to be known as Oxford Group. The Group aimed at reconciling nations, races, management and labour. The movement stressed absolute honesty, purity, love and unselfishness. The work had spread to more than 50 countries. The first World Assembly of the movement was held in 1958.

for various reasons, among them a motor accident I had recently, to move about for some months yet. I shall no doubt be able to resume my work by August, but having been incapacitated for several months I would have so much to do here that I would hardly be in a position to leave the country for any length of time. I know the regret is all mine but I cannot do more than merely send my best wishes for the assembly.

With all good wishes.

Sincerely yours,
Jayaprakash Narayan

162. To Yusuf Meherally, 2 June 1949[1]

Dear Yusuf,

I am sorry for not having written to you earlier. I am also sorry for not returning the book yet. I have read a part of it only, but since you need it urgently I am sending it back today by registered post. I hope you will get it in time. I have liked what I have seen of the book. I am sure it is a good idea to have it published in India.

Irving Brown[2] did come over with Sokoloff.[3] They spent some hours with me and we had a very nice chat together. I rather liked Brown. He was so frank and outspoken.

How is your health now? I heard reports of your relapse again. I hope you are better now and are strictly following the doctor's advice, particularly in the matter of visitors and work.

Prabhavati is completely recovered. My own recovery is rather slow. I still have the plaster on and will have to keep it on for another month at least. Had it been only arm I would not have minded but during this period I have had several little troubles which have caused a good deal of deterioration in my general health. But I hope the worst is over now. I am moving about now and go out for a walk every evening. I shall be going out of Patna for three days to Darbhanga for the Provincial Party Conference, after which I will be back in Patna till the end of the month. Then I will go to a Provincial Party Camp for a fortnight in Monghyr District. I will probably be coming over to Bombay some time in August.

With love,

Affectionately yours,
Jayaprakash Narayan

[1] *J.P. Papers* (NMML).

[2] Irving Brown (b.1908), writer of text books on rhetoric and reading; Professor of Rhetoric, University of Minnesota, 1954; publications include *Efficient Reading* (1952), *Explorations in College Reading* (1959), *Visual Linguistic Reading Series* (six vols.), (1966-7).

[3] Henrif Sokoloff, a member East Asia House, New York.

163. Statement to the Press on likely Externment of B.P. Koirala, 4 June 1949[1]

After weeks of anxious waiting the news of Mr. B.P. Koirala's release came to us as a great relief and we felt justified in deducing that his release marked a change in the policy of the Nepal Government. But that Government's communiqué,[2] which said that Mr. Koirala would be sent back to India as soon as doctors advised, filled us with grave anxiety. Mr. Koirala is a citizen of Nepal and if he has been set at liberty he must be allowed complete freedom of movement in the State.

After he recovers he will naturally come to India to meet his friends and consult his doctors. It may be recalled that Mr. Koirala is a patient of cancer and when he was in India he had to visit the Tata Cancer Institute in Bombay every few months. But Mr. Koirala's coming to India must be in accordance with his own choice and not as a result of any externment order issued by the Nepal Government.

India is not Nepal's penal settlement and the Nepal Government has no right to deport such of its citizens to India as it does not like. The more straightforward course for the Nepal Government would be to send Koirala back to prison. I hope, however, that good sense will prevail in Kathmandu and the gesture of goodwill in releasing Mr. Koirala will not be set at naught by issuing any such orders as the Nepal Government communiqué hinted at.

[1] *Searchlight*, 6 June 1949.

[2] The Nepal Government's communiqué was released to press on 1 June 1949.

164. To Krishna Ballabh Sahay, 15 June 1949[1]

My dear Krishna Ballabh Babu,

I thank you for your letter of the 9th June. Your letter has greatly relieved me because recent developments had created serious misgivings in my mind. I am glad that you have confirmed that you had told me when you met me with Shri Babu in the hospital that Shri Shanti Prasad Jain had said to you on telephone that he was agreeable to the arbitration of Dr. Rajendra Prasad.

I am sorry that you do not remember my having raised the question of the terms of reference of the proposed arbitration. I hope, however, that Shri Babu might be able to recall the talk. In any case, is it not obvious that if Rajendra Babu's arbitration was considered in the context of Basawan Babu's fast, the issues which were the basis of that fast must certainly be

[1] *J.P. Papers* (NMML). Original in Hindi.

the main points to be referred to the arbitrator? It is possible that the other party might like to refer other points also to the arbitrator, but there can be no opposition to the issues directly related to the fast being the main points for arbitration.

You are quite right in saying that "there was no talk of Government forcing Mr. Shanti Prasad Jain to refer the dispute to the arbitration of Dr. Rajendra Prasad." Indeed, there could have been no point in anyone's talking about forcing Shri Jain to accept arbitration when he had already agreed, according to you, to the arbitration. If you refer to my letter to Shri Babu, you will find that I had not in any manner suggested that either you or Shri Babu had agreed or had undertaken to force Shri Jain to accept arbitration. It was earlier in a talk with Anugraha Babu, when he had asked me whether Rajendra Babu's arbitration would be acceptable to us and when I had enquired if Shri Jain would agree to his arbitration, that Anugraha Babu had replied that he dared not refuse to do so. At that time it was not known that there was any telephonic talk between you and him. Anugraha Babu in making this remark did not, of course, mean to say that he or the Government would force Shri Jain to accept arbitration. He merely expressed the view, and quite rightly, that it could not be possible for Shri Jain to decline such a reasonable proposal. While, therefore, I never for a moment thought that there was any commitment on the part of the Government to force Shri Jain to accept arbitration, I did naturally assume that, when he had told you on telephone that Rajendra Babu's arbitration was acceptable to him, he, as an honourable man, would keep his word; and, further, that if he did not, you would try to persuade him to carry out his pledge. Am I wrong in this assumption?

You write that you feel that the matter is between me and Shri Jain. I am rather surprised at this. It was not I who had talked to him on telephone and he had given me no promises. He told you something on telephone which you were good enough to communicate to me, and I acted on the basis of the information you gave me. Subsequently, it turned out that Shri Jain refused to honour his word. Don't you think that you have some moral responsibility in the matter? You are an important person in the public life of the province and a member of the Government. Would you allow yourself to be trifled with in this manner by any individual? Shri Babu told me that if someone made a promise and did not keep it, it was none of Government's business. It may not be so, though there may be two opinions about it. Government is an impersonal entity and it may afford to disregard moral issues, though I would still question its propriety in doing so. But individuals, whether in Government or outside, cannot but give the utmost consideration to the moral aspect of every question. Here is a man who tells you something which affects public issues and then goes back on his word. I should think it should be your concern to try at least to persuade this person to follow the right path. If persons of position are allowed in this manner to show utter disregard for their pledged word, the nation would face utter moral ruin. I am not suggesting that you have to use Government's powers of coercion to force Shri Jain to follow the path of righteousness. You have merely to tell him in a friendly manner that it was not right that he was refusing to act up to the undertaking he gave you, and I am sure that would be enough. If you were to tell me that you had tried this course but yet Shri Jain refused to honour his promise, I would be satisfied and would know what to do next.

Sincerely yours,
Jayaprakash

165. To Anugraha Narayan Sinha, 17 June 1949[1]

Dear Anugraha Babu,
Saprem Pranam.

When you returned from Delhi, I tried to meet you, but you had gone out somewhere. I am sending herewith a copy of Krishna Ballabh Babu's letter, together with my own reply also. That part of Krishna Ballabh Babu's letter which I have underlined will indicate that he has acknowledged that he told me in the hospital that Shanti Prasad Jain had accepted Rajendra Babu's arbitration. Regarding the rest of Krishna Ballabh Babu's letter, I have already said in reply to it what I had to say. Now some decision should be made speedily regarding this matter. If you are free today evening, I would like to meet you. I shall try to fix time after telephoning you.

Yours,
Jayaprakash

[1] *J.P. Papers* (NMML). Original in Hindi.

166. Speech at a Public Meeting on Lohia Day, Patna, 26 June 1949[1]

The conviction of Dr. Lohia and his colleagues must cause countrywide resentment and anger. It has made a profound impression on me and I am sure all those who are as sick of Congress rule as I am must have reacted equally strongly. For those who are dissatisfied with the present Government, there are two courses open. One, that is followed by the Communists,

[1] *Janata*, 3 July 1949. The speech was also published in *Searchlight*, on 28 June 1949. Lohia was convicted by the Delhi High Court for breaking the law on 23 June 1949.

namely, the path of chaos and anarchy; the other, the part of democratic opposition, including the method of satyagraha and other forms of peaceful resistance to evil.

In the interest of the country, the Socialist Party has chosen the second path. But the Congress Governments, with their present policy of suppression of liberties, are feeding the fires of anarchy, and it is clear that if they persist in these policies not all the ordinances and forces of coercion will be able to save the country from chaos.

Those in power today do not realize that the dissatisfaction with them is so all-sided and pervading that even a small band of desperadoes can create a situation which can easily get out of control. The present power-drunk and power-hungry rulers of India do not seem to realize that peace in society can never be maintained by force but by the consent and co-operation of the citizens.

The patience of the Indian citizen, harassed by high prices and scarcity of goods, is sorely tried, and he is in an ugly mood. Pandit Nehru is sitting on a huge powder-dump of discontent and disaffection, but he does not seem to know it. By treating men like Dr. Lohia and Prem Bhasin in this atrocious manner his Government has not exactly dampened that powder.

The apologists for Congress rule might reply that after all Dr. Lohia was guilty of defiance of the law and he had to be punished; the law is no respector of personalities. This is how little minds work. Dr. Lohia is no disturber of the peace. When a national leader of his stature feels compelled to defy the law, he obviously does it not as a common law-breaker, but in order to raise some fundamental issue and to defend a higher law of society.

After all, what did Dr. Lohia demand? Merely the right to march in a peaceful procession. There was no reason why this right should have been denied to him. Pandit Nehru talks lyrically about freedom and democracy, but there is under his rule today far greater denial of liberties than under British rule and with far lesser justification. When the law itself becomes lawless, disobedience becomes a duty.

Dr. Lohia and his colleagues have been punished for exercising a fundamental right of the citizen. At the same time the men who were guilty of the grave crime of lathi-charging and tear-gassing a peaceful and orderly procession have been left untouched because they were dressed with authority. This double standard applied to the enforcement of law is galling, and it saps the very foundations of society. When official lawlessness and excesses are condoned and decent citizens are punished, social peace is gravely endangered. It is doubtful whether those whom unchallenged power has corrupted so profoundly will take any warning from current history. But if they do not, not only will they go down themselves one day but will also take the country down with them.

167. To Yusuf Meherally, 27 June 1949[1]

Dear Yusuf,

I am sending herewith by registered post a copy of the prospectus of the Janata Publications Ltd., which has to be filed with the Registrar of Joint Stock Companies in Delhi. You and Achyut are two directors in the Company. Will you kindly put your signature on page 3, where Narendra Deva and I have signed, and also get Achyut to sign the document? I shall be much obliged if you do this as soon as possible and then send the document by registered post to

Shri S.Vaidyanath Aiyar,
C/o S. Vaidyanath Aiyar & Co.,
Registered Accountants,
Kashmere Gate, Delhi.

I was happy to hear from you and to learn you are better now. I am looking forward to seeing you early in August.

With love,

Affectionately yours,
Jayaprakash Narayan

[1] *J.P. Papers* (NMML).

168. To Ajit Roy, 27 June 1949[1]

My dear Ajit,[2]

I told you when you were here for the Executive meeting that I would be spending a week at Calcutta at the end of July and beginning of August and I asked you to study the situation in consultation with other comrades and prepare definite proposals as to what ought to be done in the present circumstances. In this connection I am making the following proposal. I would like you or someone else to get hold of all the recent literature published by the left parties in Bengal[3] and analyze them, particularly with

[1] *J.P. Papers* (NMML).

[2] Ajit Roy, a Communist, turned Socialist; close to J.P.; member of Khoj Parishad; author of a number of books, including *Indian Monopoly Capital: A brief outline* (1953); *Planning in India*; *Economics and Politics of "Garibi Hatao"*, *Euro-Communism: An Analytical Study*, *Political Power in India: Nature and Trends*, and *Aspects of World Politics* (1982).

a view to find out what their positive line of action is and what their criticism of our Party is. If this material is collected and an analysis is made on the lines I have suggested I would, when I am in Calcutta, like to prepare a detailed reply to all these parties, and that might become the starting point of our ideological offensive. Will you please have this done?

As at present arranged I expect to reach Calcutta on the 27th July, but it is possible that there might be a few days' delay. In any case I will give your prior notice.

Hoping you are well,
With greetings,

Sincerely yours,
J.P.

169. To Jawaharlal Nehru, 30 June 1949[1]

Dear Bhai,

I hope you will excuse me for troubling you about the Dalmianagar affair. You probably remember that one of our comrades, Shri Basawan Sinha, was on a 30 days' hunger-strike in this connection. You had made some reference to his hunger-strike in your Muzaffarpur speech.[2]

I do not wish to waste your time with the whole painful story of Dalmianagar. There was a strike which was called off on my advice. The Management, however, refused to take back the strikers—about 2500 in number when the strike ended. They had been discharged from service for participating in the strike, which was claimed to have been illegal. The workers and their families were faced with starvation. Basawan Sinha, who is the President of the Union, was in a difficult position. Dismissal of 2500 workers was a serious affair, and even if the strike was illegal, it was a severe punishment. Feeling helpless and faced with the combined malevolence of the employer (Shanti Prasad Jain), the new INTUC union and the Bihar Government, he saw no other course left open to him but to starve along with the workers and leave it to the conscience of the public to secure justice for them. It is easy to sermonize, as was done freely in this case, on the folly of introducing the method of fasts into the domain of industrial disputes. But I have no doubt that Basawan Sinha had no other alternative.

On the 29th or 30th day of the fast, two or three days after your Muzaffarpur Conference, Shri Anugraha Narayan Sinha, the Labour

[1] *J.P. Papers* (NMML).
[2] On 4 April 1949.

Minister, came to see me in the hospital. He asked me if we would agree to the matter being referred to Rajen Babu's arbitration. I readily agreed, but enquired if the other party, i.e., Shanti Prasad, would accept the proposal. He said he [Shanti Prasad] dared not refuse, upon which I told him [Sinha] that as soon as I was definitely informed that Shanti Prasad was agreeable to the arbitration, I would send a message to Basawan Sinha to give up his fast and accept Rajen Babu as arbitrator.

That same night Shri Krishna Sinha and Shri Krishna Ballabh Sahay came to see me. The latter informed me that Shanti Prasad Jain had told him on the telephone that he was prepared to accept Rajen Babu's arbitration. The next morning Basawan Sinha broke his fast on a message from me.

Days passed after that and nothing seemed to happen. Weeks afterwards my friend Shri Phulan Prasad Verma of Damodar Valley Corporation met Rajendra Babu at Delhi who told him that while he [Rajendra Prasad] was prepared to arbitrate, he could not do so in the absence of the parties agreeing to his arbitration. He further told Phulan Babu that only Basawan Sinha had written to him expressing his consent to his arbitration; but that Shanti Prasad Jain had merely asked him to decide the question whether Basawan Sinha's fast was in accordance with Gandhian principles, and Shri Hargovind Misra, President of the new INTUC Union at Dalmianagar, had plainly said that his Union was not agreeable to the arbitration at all.

You can imagine my consternation and annoyance when I learnt this. It was on the definite assurance given to me that Shanti Prasad had accepted arbitration that I advised Basawan to break his fast. And then I was faced with this *volte face*.

Further, when we first discussed that matter and an agreement was reached regarding Rajen Babu's arbitration, the INTUC Union was not in the picture at all. No one even mentioned Hargovind Misra's name or suggested that his agreement to the arbitration must also he secured. However, I do not object to the INTUC Union also placing its case before the arbitrator, but what I cannot understand is the refusal of any INTUC Union to accept a man like Rajen Babu as arbitrator. It is strange that we who are opposed to the Congress are prepared to put our trust in him but Congressmen themselves are declining to do so. And yet it is we who are abused all the time for introducing politics into the labour movement.

However, this is the position today as regards this Dalmianagar affair. You will appreciate my personal difficulty. One of my comrades had staked his life for the cause of 2500 dismissed and starving workers and he suffered for thirty days. He broke his fast on my advice and now he finds he had suffered in vain and I find that I had been cheated and made a fool of.

In the past weeks, since I learnt of the deception, I have done all that was possible. I went to see Shri Babu and Anugraha Babu, but with no result whatsoever. The Chief Minister was brutally frank and he said Government did not come into the picture at all and that if Shanti Prasad gave a promise once and broke it later, it was none of his Government business. After a few days Krishna Ballabh Sahay wrote me a letter of which I am enclosing a copy, as also of my reply. There the matter stands at present. Subsequently I met Anugraha Babu again, but he told me nothing definite.

I had long ago left all hope of ever receiving a fair deal at the hands of the Bihar Government, but I was not prepared for such downright roguery. Behind the entire Dalmianagar affair has been the Bihar Ministers' determination to break, no matter how, our hold over the workers there and smash up our Union. Basawan's fast undid all their efforts but at the same time they were not prepared to let him die. So, they manoeuvred to have his fast broken, and then, their purpose served, they have turned their back on us. All this talk of Shanti Prasad not being prepared to carry out his undertaking and of Hargovind Misra (President of the INTUC Union) not agreeing to the arbitration is just baloney. Shanti Prasad dare not go back on his word, particularly when he had given it to a malevolent person like Krishna Ballabh Sahay. I have no doubt that the latter himself has instigated Shanti Prasad to repudiate his pledge to him [Sahay]. As for Hargovind Misra, it is inconceivable that he would take such a serious step as declining Rajen Babu's arbitration unless instructed to do so by his superiors.

Be that as it may, I am faced with a serious moral problem, and I see no way out except, as Basawan Sinha, to undertake a fast. I do not want to do so, and my health is none too good and my arm is still under plaster. But as I have just said, there is no alternative before me. I had given an indication of this to the Bihar Ministers, but it seems to have left them unaffected.

The only issue involved in Basawan Sinha's fast was the reinstatement of the strikers. The only issue involved in my fast would be—if I were compelled to undertake it—that the question of reinstatement of the workers be referred to Dr. Rajendra Prasad for arbitration, as it was agreed upon by the parties concerned at the time Basawan Sinha was induced to give up his fast. In other words, all I am asking for is that the agreement arrived at with me be honoured.

I am sorry for having troubled you in this matter. But I know you are always impatient of hunger-strikes; so I wanted to place the matter before you in case I take any drastic step.

With the highest regards,

Affectionately yours,
Jayaprakash Narayan

170. To. K.G. Sivaswamy, 1 July 1949[1]

Dear Shri Sivaswamy,[2]

I had received your letter about your inability to attend the National Executive meeting at Patna. In the circumstances in which you were placed, I quite agree that it was not possible for you to attend the meeting. Unfortunately, many other members of the Executive did not turn up and the meeting was rather an unsuccessful one.

I am sorry I have not been able to write about the Civil Liberties Conference.[3] I am very happy to find that you have been able to secure the services of a prominent jurist like Shri P.R. Das[4] for the presidentship of the conference.

With every day that passes India sees a new shackle forged and I have no doubt that it is the supreme need today to organise effectively for the protection and maintenance of the people's liberties. So far the civil liberties movement, at least after the achievement of freedom, has proved ineffective and failed to arouse much public enthusiasm. This public indifference is a source of great danger because it encourages those in power to make further inroads into the liberties and rights of the citizen. The people are too much engrossed in the problems of food and clothing to take interest in what they consider to be abstract principles. It is our task to make the people understand that the question of civil liberties affects the very question of their bread and butter because unless they have these liberties, they will not be in a position to change the Government or to compel it to change its policies. In the absence of liberties the people will have no alternative to starvation. I hope the Civil Liberties Conference will be able to bring this realization home to the people of this country.

I send you my warmest good wishes for the success of the conference.

Very sincerely yours,
Jayaprakash Narayan

[1] *J.P. Papers* (NMML).

[2] K.G. Sivaswamy (b. 1916), took part in Quit India Movement in 1942, arrested and jailed for 6 months; started Civil Liberties Movement in Madras and played a key role in the organization of Civil Liberties Union in Madras, 1947.

[3] The Madras Civil Liberties Union had convened the Indian Civil Liberties Conference to be held in Madras, 16 and 17 July 1949.

[4] Prafulla Ranjan Das (1881-1963), Bar-at-Law; younger brother of Chittaranjan Das; practiced in Calcutta High Court, 1906-7; joined Patna High Court and became judge, 1920-9; joined Civil Liberties Movement and presided over Indian Civil Liberties Conference in Madras, 16 and 17 July 1949.

171. To Meherchand Ahuja, 1 July 1949[1]

My dear Meherchandji,[2]

I should have written to you earlier to send you my warm congratulations on the conspicuous success achieved by the East Punjab Party in the Hissar satyargraha.[3] I have always regarded the Punjab Party as one of the best in the country and the satyagraha victory has been another feather in your cap. I hope this victory will make your work smoother in the future.

The National Executive decided at its last meeting at Patna to hold the next October camp in the Simla Hills. You remember the Executive held a camp last year in October at Mahabaleshwar. The camp will last for 15 days. I remember Prem had spoken to me some months back when we happened to discuss this matter that this year's camp might be held in kullu or somewhere else in the Simla Hills. The Executive does not want to burden the East Punjab Party, but if you all feel you would be able to find the expenses and manage the camp, the Executive will be happy to meet in the Simla Hills. You have to make arrangements for not more than 35 persons.

Will you kindly let me know as soon as you can, whether you will be able to undertake this job?

With best wishes,

Sincerely yours,
Jayaprakash Narayan

[1]*J.P. Papers* (NMML).

[2]For biographical note on Meherchand Ahuja, see *JPSW*, Vol. IV, p. 226.

[3]In March 1949 the Kisan Panchayat took up the question of eviction of Kisans in the district of Hissar (Punjab). After having failed to get the Government's intervention the Panchayat decided to launch a Satyagraha which went on for several days and over 90 peasants were arrested. The satyagraha had such an impact on public opinion that the Congress ministry had to pass an ordinance stopping all ejectments in Hissar.

172. To Tilak Raj Chaddha, 1 July 1949[1]

My dear Tilak Rajji,

Your letter of 13th June along with a report of your talk with Giani Kartar Singh.[2] I do not know what to write to you in reply. I have heard that Giani

[1] J.P. Papers (NMML).

[2] Giani Kartar Singh (1905-74); elected to the Punjab Legislative Assembly, 1937, 1946, and 1957; General Secretary for many years and President of Akali Dal in 1947; after independence was frequently in and out of both the Punjab Cabinet and the Akali Dal.

Kartar Singh was the evil genius behind Master Tara Singh[3] and that he is a very shrewd person and not very dependable. I do not know if my impression is correct. However, I wonder if a mere declaration on the question of delimitation of Maha Purbi Punjab is going to bring the Sikh masses into the Party's fold. At this distance it is difficult for me to send you any definite reply. I should like to meet you and discuss the matter more fully before making up my mind. If the matter is not urgent, I suggest that you discuss this question in Madras when we meet for the General Council. If, however, you want an immediate reply, you must see me at Patna before the 27th July.

I hope Mrs. Chaddha and the Youngman are well and prospering.

With best wishes,

Affectionately yours,
Jayaprakash Narayan

[3]Master Tara Singh (1885-1967); prominent Sikh leader; joined Akali Movement and dominated Sikh politics for 40 years (1920-60); demanded 'Punjabi Suba', a separate State for the Sikhs.

173. To Basawan Sinha, 2 July 1949[1]

My dear Basawan ji,

I had hoped after I had written to you that you would be good enough to accept my suggestion to come to this camp [at Haveli Kharagpur Monghyr (Bihar)] even for a few days. I had no idea that you had fixed up a programme for the 6th and 7th at Gorakhpur.[2] I thought you knew that the Provincial Executive was to camp from the 28th June to the 12th July. However, even if you had to go to Gorakhpur you could have come here with us and left on the 4th or 5th.

It is because I was sure that you would be coming with us that I did not send you any money as you had asked for. I shall send you something after I return to Patna.

I am glad you are taking interest in the O.T. Railway. You probably are aware of the decision of Bholanath Chowdhury's Union. As usual, this decision too was taken without any regard to constitutional proprieties. However, if we make a concerted effort many of the branches and prominent workers of that Union will come over to your new organization.

[1]*J.P. Papers* (NMML).

[2]Basawan Sinha had explained that he had to go to Gorakhpur in order to attend a joint meeting of the different railway organizations and also a mass meeting proposed to be held on 8 July which would make it possible to form a strong union there.

I do not know what your plans are in this regard. You might contact at Gorakhpur, Com. B.N. Banerji, who is a member of the Working Committee of the AIRF. I am informed that he has not seen eye to eye with Bholanath in this matter. I have received other letters also from office-bearers of Bholanath's Union who have expressed their disgust with the way Bholanath has acted. I cannot give their names in this letter but I am sure those who are in touch with the Union affairs will tell you all about them.

I hope your meeting will result in a vigorous programme of work.

Affectionately yours,
Jayaprakash Narayan

174. To Jawaharlal Nehru, 2 July 1949[1]

Dear Bhai,

Bishweshwar Prasad Koirala had written to you some time ago seeking an interview. He has now received a letter from Keskar's[2] Private Secretary that he could see the Deputy Minister any time between the 2nd and 7th August. This probably means that you will not see him. Bishweshwar is obliged to the Deputy Minister for agreeing to give him an interview and he will be happy to meet him. But he is anxious to meet you. I personally feel that you should spare some time for him. In fact, I was rather hurt when I learnt that his letter to you was sent to Keskar for action. Probably you are hard pressed for time. But I cannot imagine a more important person in Nepal's public life than Bishveshwar; besides, he has been a comrade-at-arms, having fought by our side for India's freedom. I shall be happy if you see Bishweshwar. I need hardly say that I am not writing this at Bishweshwar's instance; indeed, he might be embarrassed to know that I have done so.

If your reply is likely to reach me after the 1st of August, please address it to me care of Shri Phulan Prasad Varma, 7 Alipore Park Place, Calcutta.

Affectionately yours,
Jayaprakash

[1]*Brahmanand Papers* (NMML).
[2]For biographical note on B.V. Keskar, see *JPSW*, Vol. IV, p. 89.

175. To Achyut Patwardhan, 5 July 1949[1]

Dear Achyut,

Your letter of 27th June. I am camping here [Haveli Kharagpur] with the Provincial Executive since the 28th June and expect to stay on till the 12th morning. This camp is on the lines of the Mahabaleshwar Camp. A good deal of useful work is being done and the statements that you require on the abolition of zamindari etc. are being prepared. They will be sent to you when we return to Patna. As for the Hindi *Janata* I am sure that it is being regularly sent to you. But the post office is probably responsible for irregular deliveries at your end.

Regarding the communists, I do not like to send you anything yet but shall do so from Calcutta where I am going for a week's stay as soon as I am well enough to leave Patna. The plaster on my arm will be finally removed on the 13th or 14th of this month and I expect I will be able to reach Calcutta on the 1st of August. I am going to Calcutta particularly to study the communist situation and to decide our course of action there.

I am happy to hear that Yusuf[2] is better now. I hope he gets better day by day.

Affectionately yours,
Jayaprakash Narayan

[1] *J.P. Papers* (NMML).
[2] Yusuf Meherally.

176. Message to the Railwaymen, 6 July 1949[1]

I am sure railwaymen will warmly welcome the publication of a monthly organ of the All India Railwaymen's Federation. The need for such a journal has been keenly felt and I am happy that the Federation has now found it possible to fulfil this need. For the affiliated unions of the Federation and their far-flung membership, there has been so far no medium for inter-communication. Railwaymen in different parts of the country had no means of mutual contact and those of one part were unaware of what others were doing elsewhere. The unions too had no regular means of contact with one another. On the other hand, the Federation had no means of getting directly at the railwaymen; and the only medium through which it kept in touch with its unions were occasional circulars and letters. This was obviously a very poor medium, and the result was that the men were left almost entirely in the dark about the activities and the policies of the Federation and of the

[1] *J.P. Papers* (NMML).

results and course of its negotiations with the Government. There was thus a hiatus between the Federation and the mass of railway workers.

The *Railwayman* will remove this hiatus and bring the two together. The *Railwayman* will air the grievances of the men. It will serve as a medium of education and information for them. It will also be their organiser, bringing the men and the unions together, discussing organisational problems and showing how to remove weaknesses of organisation. It will place the workers' case before the public and create public opinion in their favour. It will fight for the railwaymen and guard their interests; and it will work for their unity and solidarity.

I hope the affiliated unions and their members and all railwaymen will lend their full support to the *Railwayman*.

177. To Rajendra Prasad, 13 July 1949[1]

Dear Babuji,

Saprem Pranam.

I am giving you trouble regarding Dalmianagar. Phulan Babu would have told you everything regarding arbitration. Until now nothing has happened in that respect. I am very worried because Basawanji had broken his fast at my suggestion. In this regard I am sending copies of correspondence which I had with the ministers of Bihar. Along with it, I am also sending the copy of the letter which I have written just now to Jawaharlalji.[2] Please take the trouble of once reading all those letters. As I have already written to Panditji, the matter has reached such a level that I consider it my duty to undertake a fast. In my letter to Jawaharlalji I have made my position clear. We had chosen you our arbitrator. Therefore I had no intention to give you trouble in this respect. But I thought it necessary to inform you before doing anything. In a few days I shall write a definite letter to the Government of Bihar.

Hope your health is good.

Yours,
Jayaprakash

[1]*J.P. Papers* (NMML). Original in Hindi.
[2]See J.P.'s letter to Nehru dated 30 June 1949.

178. To Sugata Dasgupta, 20 July 1949[1]

Dear Sugata,

Your letter of 5th July. I am glad that after long last the National Preparatory Committee has held its session and taken some definite decisions.[2] But I am sorry that in your letter you do not say anything more about them than that it has been decided to hold the convention of the National Union latest by December next. Obviously, a great deal must be done before the convention can meet. What decisions did your Committee take with regard to all this preparatory work? For instance, take my province Bihar. Here there are ten different student organisations, the names of some of which are:

1. Bihar Provincial Students Congress (Controlled by the Congress Party)
2. Bihar Provincial Students Congress (owing allegiance to the erstwhile All India Students Congress of Narendra Goyal and controlled by the R.S.P.I.)
3. Vidyarthi Parishad (with R.S.S. leanings)
4. Muslim Students Federation
5. Scheduled Castes Students Federation, etc.

There are no unions in the colleges here but there is a University Union which is more or less defunct. Now, if your National Preparatory Committee wants a provincial union to be organised in Bihar, what is the procedure? I had hoped that since Ravindra Varma's[3] group had agreed to the formation of the National Union, the provincial Congress organisations will not encourage the creation of separate students' organisations to be controlled by the Congress Party. Was this question raised at your Simla meeting? Further, I do not understand how a provincial unit of Narendra Goyal's[4] organisation can function when that body has been dissolved throughout the country. I shall be glad if you send me a copy of the resolutions adopted at the Simla session of your Committee and also of the plan of organisation which, I am sure, must have been prepared there.

I do not understand what exactly you mean by your being enabled to

[1]*J.P. Papers* (NMML).

[2]The National Preparatory Committee of the 'National Union of Students', held its first session at Simla on 18-19 June 1949 under the Chairmanship of Prof. Zakir Hussain. The main objective of the Committee was the formation of an organization of students which would not be under the control of any political party.

[3]Ravindra Varma, a student leader of the Congress and Convenor of the National Preparatory Committee.

[4]Narendra Goyal, leader of the All India Students' Organization under Revolutionary Socialist Party of India.

contact Party members in "some official capacity". If you write more explicitly I might be able to do something in the matter. As it is, the Party has already arranged for you to function as a Joint Convenor of the Preparatory Committee. That and your membership of the Party give you enough authority to contact Party members. It strikes me that it is not the lack of official capacity that is hindering the work but complete absence of all knowledge regarding the plans and activities of the National Preparatory Committee. I have a letter from Com. Ramchandra Shukla from Lucknow to say that he is completely in the dark as to what transpired at Simla and that Narendra Goyal has kept everything to himself. Shukla is in charge of the students' section of the Party in the U.P.

I hope you will reply soon and write more definitely and concretely.

Sincerely yours,
Jayaprakash Narayan

179. Inaugural Address at the 22nd Annual Conference of the Railway Mail Service, Patna, 24 July 1949[1]

The hopes with which the Railwaymen's and Postal Employees' strikes had been postponed, have been belied so far. We do not know if these will be fulfilled in future. The strikes had not been postponed because of any weakness of railwaymen or postal employees but out of the consideration and appreciation of the difficulties of the Government. It had been expected that the Government would show a similar consideration for the difficulties of their employees. As a matter of fact Government should have by now done something to show that they constitute the ideal employer. Such expectations, however, to say the least, have not at all been fulfilled.

The leniency showed by the Congress Government to dishonest capitalists is proving diastrous for the wage-earners. While the Government asks the people to produce or perish, the number of shifts in the factories are being reduced in the name of accumulation of stocks and in the case of jute mills, even work is being suspended for some days in a month. This only shows the trend of events which will lead to large-scale unemployment and consequent reduction of wages of both agricultural and industrial labour, and unrest throughout the country.

If Government are sincere in their slogan of produce or perish they must not allow themselves to be dictated to by the industrialists. Why should the number of shifts in factories be curtailed and workers thrown out of employment? Are we having over-production?

[1]Adapted from *Hindu*, 26 July 1949.

The fact is that the capitalists have become too greedy and are not satisfied now with even double or treble the profits they used to earn during the pre-war days. They want to make profits at the same rate as they did during the war. This has brought about the economic crisis. They are causing immense harm not only to labour but also to the country and unless Government deals with them effectively the crisis will deepen and cause widespread unrest and misery.

180. To Zakir Hussain, 24 July 1949[1]

My dear Doctor Saheb[2]

I am writing in connection with the National Union of Students. I understand from Sugata Dasgupta and also Ramkrishna Bajaj[3] that the National Preparatory Committee of the Union held a meeting at Simla on the 18th and 19th of June under your presidentship, at which it was decided to convene the inaugural session of the Union by next December. As I have been interested deeply in this movement I should like to have your advice and guidance in this matter.

In my province there is utter confusion on the student front. There are at present ten students' organisations in this province. There is a Bihar Provincial Students Congress run by the Bihar Provincial Congress. There is another Bihar Provincial Students Congress controlled by the Revolutionary Socialist Party of India. There are eight other organisations, the names of which are:

1. Students Federation (Communist),
2. Independent Students Congress,
3. Backward Classed Students Federation,
4. Hindu Students Federation,
5. Muslim Students Federation,
6. Vidyarthi Parishad (R.S.S.),

[1]*J.P. Papers* (NMML).

[2]Zakir Hussain (1897-1969), Vice-Chancellor, Jamia Millia, 1926-48; Vice-Chancellor, Aligarh Muslim University, 1948-56; Governor of Bihar, 1957-62; Vice-President of India, 1962-7; President of India, 1967-9.

[3]Ramkrishna Bajaj (1923-94), left studies to take part in Freedom Movement; courted imprisonment thrice between 1940 and 1945; Chairman of World Assembly of Youth, India; member Central Advisory Board of Youth Congress until 1962; led youth delegation to Russia and U.S.A. 1958, 1959; member Indian Industrialists' delegation to Africa, 1964; President, Maharashtra Chamber of Commerce, 1964-7; Chairman, Bajaj Tempo Ltd.; Chairman, Matchwell Electricals India Ltd.; Director Bajaj Electricals.

7. Zamindar Vidyarthi Sabha,
8. Momin Students Federation.

While there is such a multiplicity of students' organisations there is no college union in any of the colleges in the province. The Bihar Provincial Congress does not seem to be aware of the joint all-India move to form a National Union of Students of a non-partisan character. The Provincial Congress only recently took active steps to form its Provincial Students Congress. The Bihar Government and the Patna University too seem to have no policy in this regard.

The provincial organisation of the National Union of Students cannot be launched in this province unless the University, the Education Department and the Provincial Congress endorse this move and cooperate in setting up the new organisation. This, however, they will not do unless they receive advice from above. It seems to me that unless you took the initiative in this matter, this will not be done. Steps must be taken to dissolve the existing organisations and to form primary unions in the colleges. Of the ten [or eight?] organisations listed above, one is directly controlled by the Congress whilst several others may be amenable to its persuasion. The R.S.S. and the Hindu Sabha organisations might also agree to fall in line if the Provincial Government, the University and the Provincial Congress were to make a combined effort. In any case, the least that must be done is to advise the college principals to help in the setting up of unions in their colleges. This no principal in Bihar will do unless the Education Department defines its policy in this regard.

I shall be obliged if you could take the necessary steps in this matter and also advise me as to how to proceed in this province.

With kindest regards,

Very sincerely yours,
Jayaprakash Narayan

181. To Rajendra Prasad, 24 July 1949[1]

Dear Babuji,
Saprem Pranam.

Received your following telegram on 18th instant:

"Received letter[2] ascertaining facts. Please do not precipitate matters".

Thanking you for the telegram, I want to say a few words.

[1]Refers to J.P.'s letter to Rajendra Prasad, dated 7 July 1949.
[2] See also Rajendra Prasad to J.P., Appendix 15.

On 5 or 6 April, Anugraha Babu came to me with the proposal of your arbitration. Three and a half months have elapsed since then. Where does the question of precipitating matters arise? The workers are hungry since February when the strike ended. The different kinds of Company's excesses are continuing. Even then we maintained patience for more than three and a half months, frequented ministers' bungalows, and wrote them letters. Then how can I give up patience now after submiting the matters to your and Panditji's hands? Yes, poor workers' difficulties are becoming unbearable.

So far as the question of "facts" is concerned, I do not understand what are such "facts" that have to be ascertained or over which there is any controversy. Phulan Babu's talks that took place with Shanti Prasad are being brought into the centre and it is being said that Shanti Prasad was prepared to make you an arbitrator only to decide whether Basawan Babu's fast was proper or improper. I am as much surprised as pained at this deception. You may ask Anugraha Babu, whether when he came to me with a proposal that we should accept your arbitration, he meant that you would only decide whether or not Basawan Babu's fast was proper. Again, when Krishna Ballabh Babu came and told me that Shanti Prasad had told him on telephone that he accepted your arbitration did he mean that you would decide only on the propriety of Basawan Babu's fast? The "facts" regarding this case are quite clear. The ministers of Bihar, with a view to breaking Basawan Babu's fast, proposed to me in the hospital that the matter should be referred to your arbitration, and they told me that the other party, i.e., Shanti Prasad, had accepted this proposal. We accepted the proposal willingly, Basawan Babu broke the fast; and we wrote a letter to you and to the Bihar Government that we accepted your arbitration.

The fraud began later. Shanti Prasad wrote you a letter, and Pandit Hargovind Misra was also brought into the picture. We do not have any new demand. We only want that the agreements that have been concluded with us should be implemented. What fact remains in it that needs to be ascertained—I did not understand this. Even then you must find out every aspect of the matter. But my only request is that there should not be undue delay in it. The circumstances of Dalmianagar are deteriorating day by day and the fear of some disorder taking place there again is increasing. The old workers whom the company has discharged and those who are looking forward towards you with hope are being evicted from their quarters. Whatever the law may say, we cannot tolerate this injustice and we have sent word to the workers that they should not leave their quarters until arbitrator's decision is arrived at. At this the owner or the police may resort to force. The poor workers depend only on satyagraha. Even then the allegation of violence will be levelled against them by the unjust administration and the owner. The destiny of these poor people is in your hands.

Hope you are in good health and in fine spirits.

Yours affectionately,
Jayaprakash

182. To Jawaharlal Nehru, 28 July 1949[1]

Dear Bhai,

Bishweshwar Prasad Koirala had written to you some time ago seeking an interview. He has now received a letter from Keskar's Private Secretary that he could see the Deputy Minister any time between the 2nd and 7th August. This probably means that you will not see him

Bishweshwar is obliged to the Deputy Minister for agreeing to give him an interview and he will be happy to meet him. But he is anxious to meet you. I personally feel that you should spare some time for him. In fact, I was rather hurt when I learnt that his letter to you was sent to Keskar[2] for action. Probably you are hard pressed for time. But I cannot imagine a more important person in Nepal's public life than Bishweshwar; besides, he has been a comrade-at-arms, having fought by our side for India's freedom. I shall be happy if you see Bishweshwar. I need hardly say that I am not writing this at Bishweshwar's instance; indeed, he might be embarrassed to know that I have done so.

If your reply is likely to reach me after the 1st of August, please address it to me care of Shri Phulan Prasad Varma,[3] 7 Alipore Park Place, Calcutta.

Affectionately yours,
J.P.

[1] *Nehru Papers*—Files at home (NMML).
[2] For biographical note on B.V. Keskar, see *JPSW*, Vol. I, p. 62.
[3] For biographical note on Phulan Prasad Varma, see *JPSW*, Vol. I, p. 62.

183. To V.G. Dalvi, 30 July 1949[1]

Dear Shri Dalvi,

I am very sorry for not replying to your letters till now. I replied to your wire regarding the Agra conference a few days back. I hope to reach Bombay at the beginning of the fourth week of August and expect to stay there till

[1] *J.P. Papers* (NMML).

the middle of October. Could we not fix up the the dates of the Agra Conference after I have reached Bombay. My arm is not well yet and I do not wish to start touring and attending conferences till it is normal. The arm is out of the cast but it will take another couple of months at least to begin to function properly. At present I can hardly straighten it, the joints having become stiff.

I have written a letter today to Shri Kidwai of which I am enclosing a copy.[2] I will be writing to him about the points which are still awaiting settlement and about which he had promised to do something.

I feel more and more that the employees in the Government departments will not be able to fight for their cause till they are united. There is hopeless disunion among the P. & T. employees. Nothing has come so far out of the realignment talks or our own talks about our organisation. You will remember that some time ago I had intended to convene a conference of representatives of the P. & T. unions at Patna. That conference however had to be abandoned due to various causes, among them your inability to attend. I want now that during my stay in Bombay, sometime in September, a conference of this nature be called and we come to some final decision regarding realignment and reorganization. I think the employees are now in a mood to sink their differences and come together. It seems to me that our Union too must show a greater spirit of compromise than hitherto.

I have gone through all the papers you have sent me regarding the dispute in the U.P. Branch and also the proceedings of the Executive Council. I am in agreement with your findings in the U.P. dispute as also with the decisions of the Executive Council.

I shall be glad to hear from you soon.

Sincerely yours,
Jayaprakash Narayan

[2] See the next item.

184. To Rafi Ahmed Kidwai, 30 July 1949[1]

My dear Rafi Saheb,

I am sorry that when you were in Patna a few weeks ago I was not here to meet you.

Shri Dalvi [V.G.] writes that the Secretary, Ministry of Communications, has directed the Director General, Posts & Telegraphs, not to attend to any communications received from the All India Postmen & Lower Grade (Incl.

[1] *J.P. Papers* (NMML).

R.M.S.) Union. The D.G., in his turn, seems to have issued instructions to the P.M.G.s not to attend to correspondence from the provincial branches of the Union. Shri Dalvi has also sent me a copy of a letter which he has addressed to Shri V.K.R. Menon, Secretary to your Ministry.

I find it difficult to express in words my utter amazement at these orders issued by your Ministry. You are probably aware that I am President of the All India Postmen & Lower Grade Staff Union, and I take these orders of your Ministry as a personal insult. If you took the trouble of going through Shri Dalvi's letter to Shri Menon, you would see that there is absolutely no question of the bona fides of the All India Union. There was certainly a dispute as regards the U.P. Branch and I could have understood if instructions had been issued by your Ministry with regard to that branch. I should like to point out that even that dispute was settled in accordance with the constitution of the Union by the General Secretary, Shri Dalvi.

You probably are aware that the All India Postmen & Lower Grade Staff Union has a long history and Shri Dalvi has been its leader for years. A conference of this Union was held last year in Bombay at which the present office-bearers were elected. The next annual conference will be held in October at which the new office-bearers will be elected. This conference would have met earlier but for my illness.

Upon going through the papers concerning the dispute in the U.P. Branch, two conclusions have been thrust upon me: (1) that Shri Shibbanlal Saxena[2] was anxious to capture the U.P. Branch; (2) that he was anxious to become the President of the All India Union. The haste with which your Ministry, without the least reference to me, has acted in virtually withdrawing recognition from the All India Union leads me to believe that your Ministry has been in sympathy with Shri Saxena's ambitions. I have my own views about Shri Saxena both as a trade unionist and as a human being. However, irrespective of my views, if I were assured that my continuing as President of the Union was distasteful to you or to your Ministry I would immediately step down. But in that case it would be for the members of the Union to elect their President and I doubt very much if even with all the pressure that might be brought to bear the members would elect Shri Shibbanlal saxena. I hope you are aware that not a single provincial branch of the All India Postmen & Lower Grade Staff Union has gone with Shri Saxena. Only a section of the U.P. Branch and a few members of the East Punjab Branch seem to be with him.

[2] Shibban Lal Saxena (1907-); one of the prominent political figures of U.P., participated in the Non-Cooperation Movement, 1920-2, Civil Disobedience Movement, 1930-1 and the Quit India Movement, 1942; a trade union leader, member, Constituent Assembly, 1946-50, Lok Sabha, 1954-7 and 1957-62; President of the KMPP, 1952-8; member of the PSP, 1959-60 and of the Socialist Party (Lohia Group), 1961-3.

I take a very serious view of this manner of treating a labour organisation and I least expected that your Ministry will mete out such treatment. As I have said, there is no dispute as far as the All India Union is concerned, and I hope you will appreciate that I cannot associate with any bogus organisation for the sake of either politics or position. I have been deeply hurt by this action of your Ministry and I hope you will be good enough to have the wrong rectified. The least that should be done is, to my mind, to withdraw the orders issued not to deal with the Postmen Union and its branches and to institute an impartial inquiry into whatever dispute might exist as to the bona fides of the Union. Action should be taken only after the enquiry has been completed. You will appreciate that if such summary decisions are taken any group of individuals might at any moment take it into their heads to dispute the bona fides of any established union, thus making trade unionism impossible. I should like to say at the end that I have not written you this letter as President of the Union but just as Jayaprakash Narayan.

I hope you are well.

With regards,

Very sincerely yours,
Jayaprakash Narayan

185. To Three Members of the National Executive of the Socialist Party, 1 August 1949[1]

Dear Comrades,

Your wire to the following effect:

"Request postpone general council meeting. Prolonged session national executive necessary major policy questions demand detailed discussions
Achyut Asoka Suresh"[2]

I was not a little surprised to receive this wire. I do not know what is the latest brainwave that you comrades have got. Doubtless, there are many serious problems which we must consider but I am sure we can consider them at Calcutta and, if necessary, the members can prolong their stay there or the Committee could meet a day or two earlier. After a good deal of deliberation the dates of the General Council were fixed at Patna. Circulars have been issued to the provinces. If these dates are changed now everything will be upset and I do not know when again suitable dates will be found. Moreover, I do not see why the General Council should be postponed if a

[1] *J.P. Papers* (NMML).

[2] Achyut Patwardhan, Asoka Mehta and Suresh Desai.

long session of the Executive is necessary. The two things can go together. Further, when you ask me to agree to postponing the General Council, don't you think you should have written to me explaining what was in your mind. A telegraphic message says so little and I at least fail to understand what urgency there was that prompted you to send the telegram. You could have written more fully and I would have been in a better position to decide.

However, what I have said in my reply telegram and also in this letter is entirely my personal opinion and it is for you people and the Acting General Secretary to decide. You may do exactly as you please.

Sincerely yours,
Jayaprakash Narayan

186. Interview to the Press Trust of India, Calcutta, 4 August 1949[1]

I think the time has come when friends like Mr. Abid Ali,[2] instead of asking us to join the Congress, should consider the question of leaving the Congress themselves and joining the Socialist Party. Personally, I think even Pandit Nehru should leave the Congress and join the Party, because, I am sure, that in spite of his great position, he will not be able to translate his ideals into practice through the instrumentality of the Congress.

Those friends in the Congress who keep on appealing to us (the Socialists) to go back to the Congress, seem to be living in a fool's paradise. They do not seem to understand the development of Indian politics. The Congress is fast fading out and the people of India are realizing more and more that, if they have to solve their urgent problems and create a new society, they must create a new political organisation.

The Railway Ministry has denied recently that the Government have not responded to the gesture shown by the Federation in postponing the railwaymen's strike. The Railway Ministry has misunderstood the position. I fervently hope that the Ministry, presided over by a very able and fair-minded person,[3] will show greater appreciation of the plight of the employees and give better proof of their desire to do them justice. I do not want to create difficulties. But I must warn the Railway Ministry that the discontent of the men is growing rapidly again and they are getting extremely impatient for which I do not blame them.

[1]Adapted from *Hindu*, 5 August 1949.

[2]Mr. Abid Ali, President of the Bombay Provincial National Trade Union Congress had appealed to the Socialists to rejoin Congress. For biographical note see *JPSW*, Vol. III, p. 266.

[3]Gopalaswamy Ayyangar.

Before the strike was postponed, the Federation had discussed about twenty points with the Ministry about which some sort of agreement was arrived. Some of these points had subsequently been implemented and others are probably in the course of implementation, though I must say that in regard to these also, the delay has been unpardonable. But these twenty-odd points are not all that the Federation had placed before the Ministry.

All the points raised by the affiliated unions and the Federation probably have come to over a thousand, and very little has been done with regard to these. I am afraid that the Railway Ministry has not shown appreciation of the tremendous labour problem which it is faced with.

187. Message on Sri Aurobindo's Seventy-eighth Birthday, Calcutta, 5 August 1949[1]

It is in the fitness of things that Sri Aurobindo's birthday is being celebrated for the first time in free India. To those of us who were privileged to be soldiers of Indian Freedom, Sri Aurobindo is not only one of our greatest spiritual leaders but also one of the pioneers of the struggle for freedom. Let us on this auspicious day, which is also the birthday of free India, express our devout wish that Sri Aurobindo be spared to us for another 78 years to lead India to her cultural and spiritual glory.

[1]*National Herald*, 6 August 1949.

188. State of the Country, 6 August 1949[1]

The economic and political situation in the country must cause grave anxiety to every thoughtful citizen. After two years of "Produce or Perish" slogan, the country is faced today with falling industrial production. Mills are closing down and working days are being reduced. The scarcity of goods becomes more serious and the problem of unemployment is further aggravated. There is a danger of fresh attacks on the standard of living of the industrial worker and the white-collared employee. The housing shortage remains as obstinate a problem as before. There is no appreciable fall in the cost of living. The lower middle class, more than any other, is being ground between the stones of inflation and the black-market. The black-market itself flourishes as before. The food situation, after years of Grow More Food campaign,

[1]*Janata*, 15 August 1949; based on a speech delivered by J.P. at a public gathering in Calcutta on 6 August and published in a summary form in all important daily newspapers on 8 August 1949.

and crores of public money having been thrown away, remains where it was.

Inefficiency and corruption in the administration are on the increase. The ruling party seems to be more concerned with maintaining its own power than with serving the people. The liberties of the citizen are in grave danger. With every passing day the Constituent Assembly fashions more and more anti-democratic articles for the country's constitution.

All popular initiative and enthusiasm have been destroyed and there is lifelessness and frustration among the people. Not only Socialists and hot-heads but even such gentle persons as J.C. Kumarappa[2] are talking of the portents of revolution.

While such is the situation in the country the situation in Bengal is even worse. For, added to these national problems, there are problems peculiar to this province which make the situation there far graver. The Prime Minister of India recently visited Calcutta to study the situation at first hand. The only result of his visit and study so far known to us is the decision to hold a general election in this province within six months. While I welcome this decision it is clear to me that it is intended merely to divert the minds of the people from their present problems and give an outlet to the pent-up feeling of discontent. Much more than merely [holding] a General Election has to be done. The pressing problems of the province must be examined and their solution found. It is not enough for the Prime Minister to suggest an outlet for popular feelings, he must also take concrete steps to tackle the problems of the province.

The Central Government should have appointed a commission to go into the problem of refugees, of unemployment, of the surplus population of Calcutta, of falling industrial production, of stagnation of trade and agriculture. The commission would have recommended concrete measures to deal with these problems. When it is realised that the problem of Bengal or of any other provincial unit is a national problem it is not enough to bypass it by the ruse of an election.

Even in this matter of elections the decision of the Prime Minister and the Congress Working Committee is extremely inadequate and even unfair. For some months past, the Provincial Government have been engaged in the preparation of electoral rolls on the basis of adult franchise. This work is fairly well advanced in most of the provinces and I understand, in Bengal, the draft electoral rolls are almost complete. I see no reason, therefore, why within the next few months, these draft rolls should not be finalised and the forthcoming election held on the basis of adult franchise. There seems to be little sense in holding an election six months from now on the basis of

[2]For biographical note on J.C. Kumarappa, see *JPSW*, Vol. I, p. 126.

the old franchise and then another General Election a year later on the basis of adult franchise.

Even if we take the basis of the old franchise, the electoral rolls of 1945 when the last provincial elections were held must be hopelessly out of date. In the last four or five years hundreds of thousands of people must have been qualified under the old franchise to be voters. If we take matriculates alone, their number since 1945 must be a hundred thousand. If the old electoral rolls are not revised, even an election on the old franchise would thus be unrepresentative of the voters.

Further, I am not quite sure whether an election held on the basis of the electoral rolls of 1945 would be ultra vires of the Act 1935. I think even that Act requires that before every general election the voters' lists be revised and brought up-to-date. If this were not so, periodical general elections would lose much of their meaning. In view of all this, I would urge very strongly that the forthcoming elections in Bengal be held on the basis of adult franchise for which, as I said above, the draft rolls have already been prepared.

The main problem seems to me to be that of finding gainful employment for the large number of unemployed in the province. This is not possible unless there is an immediate plan for industrial and agricultural development—a short range plan based on small and medium industries and cooperative effort. A state sponsored and popularly supported plan for industrial and agricultural cooperatives, developed on a war footing, such as the industrial cooperatives in wartime China, would go a long way to solve the problem of unemployment and production. I am sure there is enough talent in the province and enough resources to assure the success of such a plan.

Unfortunately, instead of planning an industrial development of this nature, what we find today, in Calcutta, is the steady decline of small-scale industries which are unable to stand the competition of imported goods. I am told that thousands of artisans have been thrown out of employment in the city due to such competition. It is obvious that there is no economic or industrial plan according to which the Government of Bengal are working. Chaos and discontent are inevitable.

Referring to chaos it is necessary to dwell upon the much spoken of communist danger. This danger has been exaggerated out of all proportion and a fear psychosis created by misconceived publicity about this so-called danger. I have no doubt that communist methods are extremely foolish but they are a danger more to communism than to the country. Pandit Nehru, at his meeting in Calcutta, was right in reminding people that it was their passivity only which encouraged hooliganism and that it was their duty to put down and isolate the handful of mischief-makers. It is gratifying to find that the citizens of Calcutta have taken his words to their hearts and the city today is showing signs of better health. It is heartening to find the people realising that no matter how deep their discontent or sense of frustration, conditions of chaos and anarchy would not help but only worsen their lot. If ordered life were to come to a standstill in Calcutta, the six millions of its population would have no alternative but to starve. Commerce and industry and all other activities would come to a standstill and the chaotic conditions would only lead to greater misery of the people.

From the standpoint of communism, it is a great pity that the Communist Party in India has launched upon this programme of chaos and disorder. Anyone with even a rudimentary knowledge of Marxism and Leninism should be able to see that acid bulbs and kerosene rags cannot bring about a communist revolution. The communists in Bengal have thrown away the greatest opportunity of their lives. If they were interested in communism and not in furthering the policies of the Cominform, namely the policy of weakening those nations which do not fall within the Russian orbit, and had they aimed at establishing a communist society in Bengal, it should have been clear to the smallest among them that the path of acid bulbs would only isolate them from the people and hopelessly destroy their chance of coming to power in this province. Had the Communist Party, on the other hand, followed the path of Marxism, and worked in the open as a freely functioning political party following democratic principles, who can doubt that they, together with the other socialist forces in this province, could have swept away completely, by the consent of the people and upon a direct democratic appeal to them, the present decaying regime and established a socialist government in this province. The communists had political power in their grasp in this province and they have deliberately thrown it away, weakning, for years to come, the forces of communism and socialism. Thus they have once again made themselves the fools of destiny. In 1942 they threw away a golden opportunity that history offered them and again today when destiny stood at their doors they have turned their back upon it. It is important for us to remember that they have behaved in this suicidal fashion at both these times because of their subservience not to the interest of the Indian people but to that of a foreign power. Because of this subservience we must write off the communist movement in this country as a constructive force leading the nation towards socialism.

There is even today in leftist circles a meaningless controversy about the efficiency of democratic means in achieving socialism. I am amazed at this head-in-the-sand attitude of these doctrinaire leftists. In Bengal, we hear on every side that the Congress is completely played out and that the people of the province are fed up with it and further that they are looking hopefully towards socialism. If all the socialist forces in this province

J.P. addressing a public meeting

Portrait of J.P. in thinking mood

J.P. and Prabhavati with the former's host in a Bihar village where he had stayed after his escape from Hazaribagh prison in 1943

J.P. and Prabhavati with Asoka Mehta and other socialist workers of Bombay

J.P. and Prabhavati with prominent socialist workers of Gujarat

J.P. and Prabhavati with socialist workers of Tamil Nadu

Phone : 472

NEW KADAM KUAN
PATNA

En Train
1.5.50

Dear Rohit,

I am enclosing herewith an article on the East Bengal question and ourselves. The article was written primarily for West Bengal, and on this side I am releasing it only to the Statesman. I am also sending to Sadanand. In that case, the article need not appear in the Janata, but that is for you to decide. I should however like the article to be published as a pamphlet by the Central Office. In the pamphlet should also be published Lohia's and Asoka's articles (not press statements) on the question. There should also be the following annexures:

1. The Rewa Resolution
2. My talk at the Nagpur Institute of Journalists as published in the Hitavada. (I am enclosing the relevant cutting)
3. The Lucknow Resolution.

I am sending herewith a small foreword for the pamphlet – see overleaf.

Hoping to meet you at Hyderabad,

Yours affly
J.P.

Facsimile of J.P.'s letter to Rohit Dave

Foreword

One of the most vital questions that faced young India was that raised by the situation in East Bengal. The National Executive of the Socialist Party after carefully considering the matter placed before the people its solution of this vital question. The views of the Party found great favour with the people. Certain misunderstandings were however created, particularly in West Bengal. To remove these and to re-state the Party's policy in this regard, the following article was written which has been reproduced in this pamphlet. Two articles of Rammanohar Lohia and Asoka Mehta, which further elucidate the issues involved, have also been reproduced here. And in the annexures are reproduced the two resolutions of the National Executive and a report of a talk I delivered at the Nagpur Institute of Journalists.

I hope this little pamphlet will help in the understanding and solution of a difficult & dangerous problem.

Jayaprakash Narayan

combine, could anyone doubt that victory would be theirs? It is true that a socialist government in a single province will not be able to establish socialism in India. But even a provincial socialist government would be the beginning of the end of Congress rule and must lead in the near future to the establishment of a socialist government at Delhi itself. To fail to take an objective view of the conditions in the country and in the world and to talk parrot-like of the inevitability of a violent revolution is to deny the dialectics of Marxism.

The issue of left unity has again been raised in the context of the forthcoming elections in Bengal. As I have already said in my public statements, I have not the least doubt that the leftist groups in the province must come together to fight the elections. It is in the national interest to defeat the Congress in Bengal at these elections.

Congress leaders are fond of facing the country with the alternative of Congress or chaos. But I have honestly come to believe that if the Congress continues to be in power for a few years more and carries on in the manner in which it is doing, the Congress itself would be responsible for plunging the country into chaos just as the Kuomintang did in China. Therefore, the defeat of the Congress is essential in the national interest.

I should like, however, to clarify this issue of left unity. People have proverbially short memories. It has been forgotten that the Socialist Party, for years before the war, tried patiently for leftist unity and made considerable sacrifices in that behalf. But the lessons that the Party then learnt at a great cost cannot be easily forgotten. Those experiences convinced us that Left unity, merely by bringing together all manner of left parties into a kind of loose co-ordination and maintaining, at the same time, their separate identities, would not work. Subsequent experiences too, in this country as well as abroad, have shown that such left unity is transient. Sooner or later, conflicts arise and the parties fall out and left unity is wrecked. The Socialist Party, therefore, came to the conclusion that it must set its face against such attempts at unity which are deceptive and ultimately disruptive and try to build up a single party of the forces of the left. In following this policy we are sometimes misunderstood and people think that we are taking a high and mighty attitude in refusing to join Left Consolidation.

In all humility I should like to tell the Left parties that if they really wish to unite they must merge together completely, dissolve their separate identities, and form a single party. If any such venture is undertaken the Socialist Party would be happy to dissolve itself and merge in a larger entity of the Indian Left. But if this is not done, the Socialist Party will try to cooperate with other parties but will refuse to join any make-shift unity arrangements.

I should like here to point out a strange feature of the present left movement. While, on the one hand, the left parties talk of unity, on the other, every one of them, or at least most of them, seem to be disintegrating and giving birth to new left parties whose number is daily increasing. For instance, the Forward Bloc has split into at least two parties, groups have severed from the RSPI, forming different parties, and the RCPI has at least two factions. Similarly the Communist Party too, which has been known for its solidarity and discipline seems to be disintegrating and some groups are breaking away and forming separate parties. An example is the Red Communist Party in the East Punjab. In Bengal too, there have been large defections from the Communist Party and likewise in the other provinces. Thus we have the strange spectacle of unity efforts on the one hand and ever growing splits on the other. Obviously there must be a stop to this disease of splintering. I am afraid left Consolidation Committees which try to bring together all manner of little groups merely encourage these fissiparous tendencies, because even a group with half a dozen members is dignified with the name of a left party and given a right to be represented on such a committee. I believe that the only way to stop this rot is for someone to say "no" to this false process of unity.

Subject to these remarks, the Socialist Party, either in Bengal or in other provinces, is always prepared to go along with other left parties and to co-operate with them on specific issues. As I have said before, on the question of elections in Bengal, the Socialist Party offers its fullest co-operation to all other left parties. The manner of the *modus operandi* of this co-operation is being worked out and I am hopeful about its outcome.[3]

I have spoken above on the state of civil liberties in this country. The Prime Minister in his policy statement published last week says that if a choice has to be made between the security of the State and the liberty of the citizen, the first must take precedence. That sounds like a reasonable proposition and unwary citizens might find themselves in complete agreement with the Prime Minister. But I find his proposition to be an extremely dangerous one. That is the way how all dictators talk. The security of the State is no doubt more important than the liberty of the citizen but who is to be the judge about the security of the State?

Every repressive legislation can be and has been justified on the ground of the security of the State. Does Pandit Nehru, for instance, honestly believe that if Dr. Lohia had been allowed to take out his procession in New Delhi, the security of the State would have been dangered? If not, why was

[3]Jayaprakash Narayan, Sarat Chandra Bose, President of Socialist Republican Party and Sibnath Banerjee, General Secretary of the West Bengal Socialist Party met twice between 2 to 7 August in Calcutta to discuss the possibility of left unity, especially in the context of fighting elections jointly against Congress in the forthcoming polls in West Bengal. It was decided to pursue the unity issue further.

Dr. Lohia denied the fundamental right of assembly? Again, when trade unionists are externed at the instance of bosses of the INTUC, would Pandit Nehru argue that it was necessary in the interest of the security of the State? Today in every province the executive has been empowered to arrest and put under detention any individual without trial. Does Pandit Nehru honestly believe that all these powers are essential in the interests of the security of the State?

There are provinces in this country where there is absolutely no danger of disorder and no need of emergency, yet these sweeping security acts are enforeced there. In no civilised State can a citizen be put under lock and key during normal state of affairs, without having been convicted by an ordinary court of law. Here in our country, even the High Courts have been deprived of the power to interfere in such matters and in Bengal an ordinance has to be promulgated when the High Court holds that there is not sufficient ground for the detention of a particular detenu.

As I have said earliler, every day new clauses of the Indian constitution are fashioned to restrict democracy and install authoritarianism in the country. Does Pandit Nehru honestly believe that all these special and extraordinary powers that the Constitution is giving to the executive and to the majority party, are in the interest of the security of the State? I am afraid Pandit Nehru has been carried away by an attractive phrase and has not been able to go deep into the meaning. All dictatorships have been built upon the theory of primacy of the State and therefore every democrat must beware of it.

189. To Aruna Asaf Ali, 6 August 1949[1]

Dear Aruna,

I received your letter through Arun.[2] I am very sorry to say that it would not be possible for me to go to Delhi at this time. My arm is not normal yet and I am avoiding touring as much as possible. I have come to Calcutta because it was necessary and from here I will go to Bombay, after the meeting of the National Executive, to attend to Central Office work. I shall not go out of Bombay till probably the second week of October by when I hope my arm will be, if not quite normal, sufficiently well to allow me to move about freely.

I am afraid I have no inside knowledge of how the Government or the Congress is working today, though I naturally ponder over national problems

[1] *J.P. Papers* (NMML).

[2] A Socialsit worker.

as I see them. However, it strikes me that if Shri Shiva Rao[3] or anyone else considers it very urgent to meet me he could as well travel to wherever I may be, particularly in view of my present health. Had I any essential work in Delhi I might have considered going there but just at present Calcutta and Bombay are the only items on my programme.

I had your letter in Patna regarding the "Thought" article. You know I am one of those backward people who do not read newspapers or periodicals, but when my attention is particularly drawn to something I cannot overlook it. I had no idea that "Thought" was such a journal as you have described it to be. Had I known it before I would not have taken the trouble to reply to that editorial note.

I am afraid I do not agree with you on the question of civil liberties. The Socialist Party is a political party and in its own interest and in the interest of the growth of democracy and socialism in this country the Party must fight every inch for the preservation of civil liberties. I find a rather strange attitude in the minds of some people. On the one hand they take it for granted that India will soon go fascist and, on the other, they dismiss the fight for civil liberties as bourgeois politics. Civil liberties are important not only in the context of the class struggle, but in the context of all political, social and cultural work. The liberty of the individual is the basis of democracy and whenever that is in danger it is the duty of the citizen to fight. What Pandit Nehru has said in his policy statement, published in this morning's papers, regarding the choice between the security of the State and the liberty of the citizen, is fraught with the greatest danger to democracy in this country. That is exactly how dictators endeavour to justify suppression of liberties and their own dictatorship. Who is to judge when the security of the State is in danger? Did Panditji really believe that if Lohia was allowed to lead a procession in New Delhi the security of the State would have been in danger?

However, I hope you are coming to the National Executive meeting and we shall then be able to discuss this question.

Affectionately yours,
Jayaprakash Narayan

[3]B. Shiva Rao (1891-1969); delegate, I.L.O. Conference to Geneva, 1929-30; Round Table Conference, London, 1930-1; member, Constituent Assembly, 1946-50; Lok Sabha, 1952-7; Rajya Sabha, 1957-60; University Grants Commission, 1962-8.

190. To Jawaharlal Nehru, 7 August 1949[1]

Dear Bhai,

I received your letter about Koirala just before I left Patna and I thank you for it. Koirala must be in Delhi now and might have met you already.

Asoka Mehta asked me sometime ago to write to you in connection with the payment of part of bonus in savings certificates to the Bombay Textile labour. He has already written to you on July 18 and I have not much to add to what he has written. The original proposal of Government, it appears, has subsequently been revised. The savings certificates in which payment is proposed to be made are now cashable at will. In this case this method of payment merely means trouble and delay to the workers, who doubtless will take the first opportunity to cash the certificates. This will not help to check inflation, and, at the same time, it will cause unnecessary irritation to the workers. When the Government has permitted the cashing of certificates at will, payment might as well be made in cash and the trouble and irritation avoided. A section of the workers, it is true, has agreed to accept savings certificates, but as far as my information goes the overwhelming majority of them still remain opposed. Asoka writes that on this issue there might even be a breach of industrial peace and though Asoka assures me that he is anxious to strain every nerve to avoid such an eventuality, he would be helpless if Government merely stands on its prestige and does not amend its order.[2]

After Asoka's letter to you there was no need for me to write, but as he has asked me particularly to do it I am also adding my voice to his and I hope some heed will be paid to it.

With kindest regards,

Affectionately yours,
Jayaprakash Narayan

[1]*Brahmanand Papers* (NMML).
[2]For Nehru's reply see Nehru to J.P., 17 August 1949 in Appendix 16.

191. Socialist Party's Stand on Linguistic Provinces, Calcutta, 8 August 1949[1]

At one time, the Socialist Party felt that this question of linguistic demarcation of provinces should wait till the problems of food and cloth are solved. But the way in which feelings are rising everyday, I personally

[1]Statement at a Press Conference in Calcutta, *The Tribune*, 10 August 1949.

feel that the question should no longer be shelved but should be solved now.

If there is any dispute on the question between provinces, it should be discussed and solved by representatives of the provinces concerned sitting round a table. If they can not come to any decision they should go to the people themselves and hold a plebiscite or they can refer the matter to an impartial tribunal or commission. This is the democratic method of solving such problems.

The dispute cannot be solved by shouting at each other or quarrelling and breaking each other's head. The cult of hatred led to the division of the country and, therefore, a solution of this linguistic demarcation of provinces should be found without any further delay.

192. Message for *Spark*, Patna, 9 August 1949[1]

A fire burnt in the hearts of the people when they fought for freedom. That fire is dead now, and the cold ash of frustration and despondency is suffocating the struggling sparks of new life. That deadening ash must be blown away and the sparks kindled into a flame. So it is good to know that the burning pen of Shri Murli Manohar Prasad is to be active again, and let us hope that through the columns of his "Spark" will blow a blast that will revive this province and help to bring new life to it.

[1] *J.P. Papers* (NMML). This message was published in the Journal 'Spark', on 9 August, edited by Murli Manohar Prasad and published from Patna.

193. To Rajendra Prasad, 9 August 1949[1]

Dear Babuji,
Saprem Pranam.

I received your letter dated 4 August in time. Before that I had received Kala Venkata Rao's[2] letter. He had also sent a copy of the resolution[3] of the

[1] *J.P. Papers* (NMML). Original in Hindi.

[2] Kalavenkata Rao (1900-59); elected to Madras Legislative Assembly in 1937 and 1946; member Constituent Assembly, 1946-9; Revenue Minister, Madras Government, 1947-9; General Secretary, Indian National Congress, 1949-51; Minister for Planning, 1955 and for Finance 1956-9, Andhra Pradesh Government.

[3] The resolution passed by the Congress Working Committee on 18 July 1949 stated that the strike in the Rohtas Industries (Dalmianagar) was illegal and followed by deplorable consequences. But due to some unavoidable circumstances arbitration seemed desirable and the Government of Bihar should make necessary arrangements for it.

Congress Executive Committee. After the passage of the resolution of the Working Committee, I hoped that the matter would soon be settled. But nothing has happened as yet. I had written a letter to Shri Kala Venkata Rao to which he had replied to me on 1 August, in which he said that he was writing to the Bihar Government. But the matter is still in cold storage. After all, there was no intricacy in the matter. After the adoption of the resolution by the Working Committee, all that the Bihar Government had to do was to write to each party that the matter should be referred to your arbitration. We had already accepted the arbitration, we would have gladly given acceptance and I am confident that Shri Shanti Prasad also would have given his acceptance. In that condition perhaps your award also would have been pronounced by now. I have also written to the Bihar Government just now, but they would hardly listen to what I say.

Meanwhile the condition in Dalmianagar is deteriorating. More than five months have elapsed since it was agreed to refer the matter to the arbitration, when the ministers of Bihar had met me in the hospital. And the patience of the workers has almost broken down. Please settle the issue speedily, otherwise further calamity would take place. The bearer of the letter, Shri Narayan Moorthy, had come here from Dalmianagar. I am sending him to you and to Kala Venkata Rao. He has brought a message from Dalmianagar that the elected comrades there would undertake a fast unto death. I am forbidding them from doing so. But, if the Bihar Government continues its indifference, they cannot be forbidden for long. I hope that you would direct Shri Babu to speedily implement the resolution of the Working Committee.

I hope your health is good. I am recovering gradually but I may take at least one month more. Prabhavati is well.

Yours,
Jayaprakash

194. Speech Against India Remaining in the Commonwealth, Patna, 9 August 1949[1]

By agreeing to remain within the Commonwealth, the Congress Government has proved untrue to the Indian slogan, 'Quit India', through which Mahatma Gandhi unleashed the revolution of August 1942. The Congress Government has also proved untrue to the Congress ideal for the achievement of full independence. Apart from that by continuing to stay in the Commonwealth India has also antagonised a great and powerful neighbour[2] with common frontiers with our country.

[1]*Tribune*, 11 August 1949. The speech was delivered at a meeting at Patna in commemoration of the anniversary of the 1942 movement.

[2]This refers to the Soviet Union.

England is seven thousand miles off and America fourteen thousand. ,We have little in common with these countries, whereas more than two-thirds of the Soviet Union is in Aisa. The only way to prevent a worldwide conflict between the American and the Soviet blocs is the creation of a third force in world politics which will not accept the domination of either camp, and which will function in such a way as to limit the destructive potentialities of both. Such a third force in Asia will emerge through the creation of an Asian federation, which would include China, Burma, Malaya, Indonesia and the Middle Eastern countries.

195. Message for Palanpur Comrades, Patna, 10 August 1949[1]

I was happy to meet Sathi Morarji Jeevan[2] who has come from far away Palanpur. He has asked me to send a message to the comrades in Palanpur for the 15th of August. The only message that I can send on this occasion is to remind my comrades that the Freedom Day that we celebrate can have real meaning only when freedom from foreign slavery shall also mean freedom from exploitation, want and poverty. It is for the socialists of India to bring these freedoms to the people of the country. I wish the Socialist Party in Palanpur all success in this great task.

[1]*J.P. Papers* (NMML). The message was sent on the occasion the 15th August celebration by the Socialist Party, Palanpur.

[2]Secretary of the Socialist Party, Palanpur (Gujarat).

196. Message for the *Indian Nation*, Patna, 11 August 1949[1]

I am happy to send on this second anniversary day of our country's freedom my good wishes to the *Indian Nation*. In free India, many high ideals that we had cherished before seem to be in danger—one of them the liberty of the press. Though I have more often than not differed with the policy of the *Indian Nation*, there is no doubt that the paper, as an independent critic of Government has been fulfilling a valuable and unrgent need. There are many reasons why the Congress administrations have proved such utter failures, but one of the more important reasons is the absence of an opposition in the Assemblies and the absence of an opposition press. Absolute power is said to corrupt absolutely and the last two years of our national history have amply demonstrated the truth of the saying. It is good

[1]*J.P. Papers* (NMML).

that in this province at least a paper like the *Indian Nation* is acting as a limitation to this absolutism.

197. To Kalavenkata Rao, 14 August 1949[1]

Dear Friend,

I thank you for your letter of the 29th July.

The resolution of the Working Committee is rather oddly worded but I am happy that the Committee took this decision. It is over two weeks since I received your letter, but I have not heard anything yet from the Bihar Government. I should like to point out that since I agreed to the arbitration proposal and Shri Basawan Sinha gave up his fast nearly three months and a half have gone by. It is cruelty to the discharged workers to delay the arbitration any longer. I am afraid the Bihar Government would unnecessarily delay the matter. I hope therefore that you will be kind enough to see to it that the resolution of the Working Committee is implemented.

Thanking you,

Sincerely yours,
J.P.

[1]*J.P. Papers* (NMML).

198. To Rafi Ahmed Kidwai, 19 August 1949[1]

My dear Rafi Saheb,

Some days ago I wrote to you a letter regarding your orders to your Department not to pay any attention to the letters and representations received from the All India Postmen & Lower Grade (Incl. R.M.S.) Staff Union and its branches, I am surprised to find that you have completely ignored that letter and have not even acknowledged it, much less replied to it. I may inform you that since I wrote to you Shri Kishenchand of Amritsar, who had joined Shri Shibbanlal Saxena and had claimed to be the General Secretary of Shibbanlal's bogus all-India union, has written to your Departmental Secretary, withdrawing his claim to the General Secre taryship. This further strengthens the case of our organisation.

I shall be obliged to hear from you in this matter. Please reply, if you wish.

Sincerely yours,
Jayaprakash Narayan

[1]*J.P. Papers* (NMML).

199. To Mahadev Singh, 31 August 1949[1]

My dear Mahadev Singh,[2]

The National Executive at its last meeting in Calcutta considered the policy of the Party with regard to the distribution of land effected by the Communists, Razakars and others and formulated the policy given below:

> In view of the difficult situation that has been created in Hyderabad due to the method and/or quality of forcible land transfers, the Socialist Party propose as a solution:
>
> 1. The principle of redivision of land be recognised and that no one be allowed to re-acquire his land beyond the maximum allowable to each family under this principle.
> 2. After proper inquiry has been made, confiscation of land of a party-political character be set aside and all such lands be restored to their original tillers.
> 3. In the redistribution of lands above the maximum limit, preference should be given to the previous tillers of these lands, whether tenants-at-will, crop-sharers or landless labourers.
> 4. In all this redistribution, the basic principle of our agrarian policy be recognised that there is only one category of cultivators and the old distinction between share-croppers, tenants, agricultural labourers and others be abolished.

The Hyderabad branch of the Party should henceforth be guided by the above formulation.

Hoping you are well,

Sincerely yours,
Jayaprakash Narayan

[1] *J.P. Papers* (NMML).
[2] Mahadev Singh (1912-); participated in the Quit India Movement, 1942; founder-member of Socialist group within the Hyderabad State Congress, 1946.

200. Corruption: Country's Enemy Number One, Bombay, 5 September 1949[1]

All right-thinking people in this country who are anxious to see the tone of public administration raised, would regret the award that the Prime Minister, Pandit Jawaharlal Nehru, has given in the case of the complaints lodged

[1] Press interview on Nehru's verdict on Corruption Charges against West Bengal Ministers, Bombay, 5 September 1949; adapted from *Tribune*, 5 September 1949.

against certain Bengal Ministers. Some of the complaints might have been vague, but Pandit Nehru's award itself rather suffers from the same fault.[2]

According to my own findings, at least five of the charges were grave and definite; and I am afraid that by brushing aside grave charges against ministers in the manner in which Pandit Nehru has done, it would only further lower the tone of administration in this country.

It appears to me that, if it was found that there was any substance in the charges preferred, the Prime Minister should have ordered a judicial inquiry.

I believe it is not too late yet to institute such an inquiry and I hope that the Prime Minister will reconsider this matter and take the necessary steps to ensure that not even the slightest suspicion might attach to people in high places.

Corruption is today, enemy number one of the country and whenever an opportunity offers itself for something definite to be done to check this malady, it is wrong to let it go.

[2] In a note to the Congress Working Committee on 21 August 1949, Nehru gave his verdict on the allegations made by some Bengal M.L.A.s against certain Ministers of West Bengal Government. The allegations, numbering seventeen, included nepotism, favouritism, corruption, financial irregularities, harassment, illegal confinement, police firing and so on. These allegations Nehru believed, had "no prima facie justification", they were vague and usually made against people in authority.

201. To All the Unions of Post and Telegraph Workers, 5 September 1949[1]

Dear Friends,

You will recall that I have been trying for the past several months to call a meeting of the representatives of all the P. & T. Unions with a view to find out how all these Unions could be brought together. I regret however that this meeting could not be held yet. As I was expecting to be in Bombay during the month of September I had asked Shri Dalvi to write to all Unions to find out whether such a meeting could be held in Bombay during my stay here. In the meanwhile I had gone to Calcutta and met there some of the P. & T. friends. They suggested that a meeting in Delhi would be more suitable. But, on coming to Bombay and discussing the matter with Shri N.M. Joshi and other friends here I have come to the conclusion that it would be better to hold the meeting as soon as possible in Bombay. I am therefore writing to request you to accept the joint invitation to this meeting which I am extending to you along with Shri N.M. Joshi. The meeting will

[1] *J.P. Papers* (NMML).

be held on the 16th and 17th September 1949, at the Servants of India Society's Hall, Sandhurst Road, Bombay 4.

Sincerely yours,
Jayaprakash Narayan

202. To the Chief Secretary, Government of Bihar, 8 September 1949[1]

Dear Sir,

I enclose herewith copies of correspondence that passed between me and Shri Kala Venkata Rao and Dr. Rajendra Prasad regarding the Dalmianagar affair.

It is more than a month and a half now since the resolution of the Congress Working Committee was passed, and the Bihar Government have not taken any steps yet to arrange for the arbitration as directed by the Working Committee. Shri Basawan Sinha had already communicated to the Bihar Government his consent to refer the question of reinstatement of the discharged hands at Dalmianagar to the arbitration of Dr. Rajendra Prasad. If a reaffirmation of his consent is necessary, I have the authority on his behalf to do so, and I am doing so now. I request the Bihar Government earnestly to take immediate steps to arrange for the arbitration and I have no doubt that Shri Shanti Prasad Jain would be happy to give to the Government his fullest co-operation in this matter. The situation in Dalmianagar is as bad as it can be and further delay in carrying out the wishes of the Working Committee would only lead to exasperation and some such desperate step as some of the Trade Union leaders at Dalmianagar are contemplating, namely, that of undertaking a collective fast unto death. I am writing to these friends not to precipitate matters but I am afraid, in the absence of any evidence that the Government are taking steps to arrange for the arbitration, that I may not succeed in persuading them to withhold action indefinitely. It is over five months since arbitration was agreed upon between me and certain Ministers of the Bihar Government at the Patna Medical College Hospital. The workers and the Trade Union leaders showed exemplary patience and I hope Government will take an impartial view of things and act accordingly and urgently.

Sincerely yours,
J.P.

[1] *J.P. Papers* (NMML).

203. To Kalavenkata Rao, 8 September 1949[1]

Dear Friend,

I thank you for your letter of the 18th August.

I regret to find that up-till now the Bihar Government have made no move in the Dalmianagar affair. The resolution of the Working Committee, a copy of which you were good enough to send to me, clearly advises them to arrange for arbitration. After that, all that they had to do was to write to the parties concerned to refer the matter in dispute, namely the reinstatement of the discharged hands, to the arbitration of Dr. Rajendra Prasad. We, on our part, have already agreed to the arbitration, and I am sure Shri Shanti Prasad Jain too would have willingly agreed. However, even though more than a month and a half have passed since the resolution of the Working Committee, the Bihar Government have not done anything yet. In the meanwhile, the situation is getting from bad to worse in Dalmianagar and the workers are becoming desperate. The bearer of this letter, Shri Narayana Moorthy, who is a discharged employee and also one of the leaders of our Union at Dalmianagar, came to me here with a message from his colleagues that seven of them had decided in desperation to undertake a fast unto death. They are awaiting my advice. I am writing to them not to take such a desperate step and, in the meanwhile, I am sending Shri Narayana Moorthy to you so that you might learn at firsthand from him how matters stand and how urgent it is that the decision of the Working Committee is put into effect immediately. I am also writing to the Bihar Government, Dr. Rajendra Prasad and Pandit Nehru.

With kind regards,

Sincerely yours,
Jayaprakash Narayan

[1] *J.P. Papers* (NMML).

204. To Jawaharlal Nehru, 8 September 1949[1]

Dear Bhai,

I thank you for your letter of August 17.[2] I shall be writing to you again regarding the cash savings certificates. In the meanwhile, I should like again to draw your attention to the Dalmianagar affair.

Nearly a month and a half ago I received a letter from Shri Kala Venkata

[1] *Brahmanand Papers* (NMML).

[2] See Appendix 16.

Rao, forwarding to me a copy of the resolution of the Working Committee on the Dalmianagar question. I wrote to you a few weeks later expressing my fear that even though the Working Committee's directive was clear the Bihar Government might adopt a simple method of circumventing it, namely, that of taking no notice of it. I wrote to Shri Kala Venkata Rao also expressing this fear. He replied immediately to say that he was writing to the Bihar Government and trying to find out what they had done. But up-till now nothing whatever has been done in the matter. After all, there was nothing much to do. The Bihar Government had only to write to the parties concerned to agree to refer the question of the reinstatement of the discharged hands to Dr. Rajendra Prasad for arbitration. Basawan Sinha had already agreed to this and he would have been very happy to give his consent again, and I have no doubt that had the Bihar Government written to Shri Shanti Prasad Jain, he too would not have found it possible to refuse the proposal. By this time we would perhaps have had the award of the arbitrator and the matter would have been settled.

A friend has come from Dalmianagar to Bombay to inform me how desperate the situation there is, and he tells me further that seven chosen leaders of our Union there have decided, in utter desperation, to undertake a fast unto death. I am, of course, writing to them advising against that course and I am sending this friend, Narayana Moorthy, to New Delhi, so that he might see Shri Kala Venkata Rao and, if possible, Dr. Rajendra Prasad.

You will appreciate that it is more than five months since arbitration was agreed upon between me and the Ministers of the Bihar Government in the Patna Medical College Hospital. The workers have held their patience till now, but do you think it is fair to them to ask them to do so indefinitely. In one of my previous letters I have rather frankly and even brutally expressed my views about the Bihar Government. I shall not repeat them here but I shall remind you that in view of their attitude I do not expect them to do the right thing unless they are compelled to do so. I hope I will not have to trouble you in this matter again and that it will be settled without further delay.

I did not try to meet you in Bombay because I knew you would be awfully busy. I will be in Delhi from October 11 to 14, and, if you are there then, I shall be happy to come and pay my respects.

Affectionately yours,
Jayaprakash Narayan

205. To Awadhesh Nandan Sahay, 9 September 1949[1]

My dear Awadhesh Babu,[2]

I had a letter from Jamalpur friends who were much annoyed and deeply hurt at your not being able to take up the case of the Labour Union's house in Jamalpur when it came up before the High Court. I wonder how this happened. They write that they were not informed as to when the case was to come up, and in the absence of any lawyer to plead our case the High Court rejected the reference from the District Judge.

When I left Patna we had several activities started in the city, and I have been very anxious to know what progress has been made with regard to them. I should like particularly to hear from you about the Nagarik Samiti movement, the Nagarik Conference and the Civil Liberties Union.[3] Will you please let me know? I have written a letter today to Shri P.R. Das, of which I am enclosing a copy. Will you kindly see him and fix up about the monthly donation. Reyasat has written to me that the finances of the Party are in a desperate state. Kindly do all you can.

My arm is better now though it will be still another month before it is normal. The bandage has been removed. I expect to return to Patna by the 20th October. I hope Savitribehn is fully recovered now.

With the best wishes,

Affectionately yours,
Jayaprakash Narayan

[1]*J.P. Papers* (NMML).

[2]Awadhesh Nandan Sahay, a prominent lawyer at Patna; actively associated with the Socialist Party; treasurer of the Patna Nagrik Samiti.

[3]The Nagarik Conference and Civil Liberties Union's Conference were held at Patna in August 1949 and were followed by other activities to make people aware of their civic rights. The movements wanted citizens to be knowledgeable about the social, economic and cultural needs of the city and to work for all-round development in its civic life, including family and city planning, and municipal functioning.

206. To S.H. Razi, 9 September 1949[1]

My dear Razi Saheb,[2]

I have heard nothing from any of you since I left Patna. I was and am very anxious to know how the Nagarik movement has developed in the city. Will

[1]*J.P. Papers* (NMML).

[2]S.H. Razi, Socialist leader from Bihar; associated with Civil Liberties and Nagarik Movement; became General Secretary of Patna Nagarik Sabha, 1949.

you please write to me at length about it. If you want me to do anything in the matter, do not fail to write to me.

I know how worried you must be about finance. I hope I will be able to send you something within a few days. Please write as soon as you can.

Sincerely yours,
Jayaprakash Narayan

207. To K. Gopal, 9 September 1949[1]

My dear Gopalji,[2]

I have just written to Razi Saheb to complain that since I left Patna I have heard nothing from any of you friends there. You know how interested I was in some of the activities which we had started and since I left I have been very anxious to know what progress has been made. I am particularly anxious to know how the Nagarik movement has fared. Will you please write to me in detail about it. I am also anxious to know what progress our building programme has made, I mean our plan to remodel and repair the Party's house. I hope the hall is well on its way to completion and that the other sheds and verandahs have already been completed. You will remember that the entire drainage system of the house had to be overhauled. Has anything been done in that connection? How is your membership drive going on in the city? The Nagarik Movement should have helped you in the enrolment work.

I shall be happy to hear from you as often and as soon as possible.

Sincerely yours,
Jayaprakash Narayan

P.S. I dictated the above letter yesterday and just now today I have received your letter of the 7th September.Your previous letter to which you have referred has not however yet arrived. I am rather sorry to hear of Baldev Babu's[3] change of opinion. He was, as you say, from the very beginning in favour of preventive detention, but with very strict and precise limitations. He was however, I thought, willing to affiliate the provincial organisation to the Indian Civil Liberties Union, or rather to form a branch of it in Bihar. It seems to me to be very undemocratic on his part to refuse to work with

[1] *Brahmanand Papers* (NMML).

[2] K. Gopal, one of the secretaries of Bihar Socialist Party; connected with the Nagarik Movement.

[3] Baldev Sahay, eminent Advocate, High Court; Advocate General, Patna, Government of Bihar, 1937-42.

Mr. Das,[4] just because he disagrees with him on certain matters. Moreover, the Indian Civil Liberties Union is a national organization and can hardly be considered to be any body's personal affair. It is open to Baldev Babu to try to convert the organization to his point of view. I think in Mr. Das' own presidential address there is a compromise formula in what is described as the Sankey declaration. I am sure, if Baldev Babu is serious about the civil liberties of the people and about building up a democratic society in India, he would not create the difficulties that he is trying to do. I hope, however, that you would be able to persuade the other invitees and will succeed in forming a provincial branch on sound foundations. If Baldev Babu finds himself to be in disagreement, he may be allowed to keep out. It is fantastic for anyone to suggest that there is any kind of an emergency in the province of Bihar. Our definition of "emergency" will have to be modified vastly if one is to accept Baldev Babu's opinion. Now, after what you have written about him, I have begun to suspect whether he will co-operate with us impartially in the Nagarik Movement. However, I hope you will be able to manage and guide both the movements and save them from the difficulties that are threatening.

[4] P.R. Das.

208. To Secretary, Rohtas Industries Mazdoor Sangh, 9 September 1949[1]

Dear Comrade,

Shri Narayana Moorthy came here two days ago and conveyed your message and also told me about your difficulties. I have sent him to Delhi to see Shri Kala Venkata Rao, General Secretary of the AICC, and Dr. Rajendra Prasad. I have also written a letter to the Chief Secretary, Bihar Government, and to Pandit Nehru. I am enclosing herewith copies of these letters as well as a copy of the resolution of the Congress Working Committee. I would advise you and other friends there who are contemplating a fast unto death not to undertake it as long as there is some chance of settlement. I quite appreciate your difficulties but I would still advise patience. When Narayana Moorthy returns from Delhi you will be in a better position to decide what to do, but even then you should not take any drastic step till you have consulted me.

I am also writing to Basawan Babu about this matter.

Sincerely yours,
Jayaprakash Narayan

[1] *J.P. Papers* (NMML).

209. To Basawan Sinha, 9 September 1949[1]

Dear Basawan Babu,

You suddenly left Calcutta and I learned of your going when it was too late. I wanted to discuss with you the organization of the Labour Department of the Bihar Party. I am afraid, even though you are active now, the office of your Department is completely disorganised and therefore there is no steady and organised guidance to the Unions and to our labour workers, or much co-ordination. However, now that the Provincial H.M.S. is soon to be inaugurated, the office of the Sabha might be able to fulfil this need. Before I had left Patna I had talked to Sisir[2] and he had agreed to take up the Joint Secretaryship and the charge of the Labour office. But he seems to have received no encouragement from you and was consequently not in a position to do anything. Regarding his stay in Patna I had told him that he could live in my house and take his meals there. However, when you come to Bangalore, we shall discuss this matter.

Regarding the inauguration of the Provincial H.M.S., I discussed the matter with Asoka. He is going to Jamshedpur on the 25th October to inaugurate the All India Conference of the Union of Post and Telegraph Workers, of which Shri N.M. Joshi is the President. Asoka will be in Jamshedpur till the 26th, after which he has given two days, i.e., the 27th and 28th October, for tour in Bihar. We might utilize these days for the inauguration of the Provincial H.M.S. and also to enable Asoka to have a look around our Unions. I think he should be able to do it.

The inaugural conference of the H.M.S. could be held somewhere in Hazaribagh, i.e., Asoka might be in Jharia on the 27th and in Hazaribagh on the 28th. He is to reach Calcutta on the 29th morning. I also expect to be there with Asoka during his Bihar tour. I will probably be reaching Patna on the 19th or 20th of October and will be in the province for ten days, reaching Calcutta with Asoka on the 29th October.

Narayana Moorthy had come here to see me regarding the situation in Dalmianagar. I have sent him to New Delhi to see Kala Venkata Rao and Dr. Rajendra Prasad. I am enclosing herewith copies of the letters I have written to these friends and to the Chief Secretary, Bihar Government, and Pandit Nehru. I am also enclosing a copy of the Congress Working

[1] *Brahmanand Papers* (NMML).

[2] Sisir Kumar, a young promising worker of the Socialist Party in Bihar; functioned as one of the Secretaries of the Socialist Party and Praja Socialist Party, Bihar; later joined Congress and became a member of Rajya Sabha, 1970-5.

Committee's resolution. I am wiring to the friends in Dalmianagar advising them against undertaking any fast at this time.

I hope you are well.

Sincerely yours,
Jayaprakash

210. To Purnananda Dasgupta, 9 September 1949[1]

My dear Purnananda Babu,[2]

I thank you for your letter of 6th September. You are perfectly at liberty to publish your article and your being the Joint Sectretary of the Party need not come in the way. I will not advise you to resign from the secretaryship on account of your difference with the Party's policy on left unity. As far as the attitude of Shakti and his friends is concerned, I would once again advise you, as I have advised them, to try to remove misunderstandings and work together. In any case, a person of your standing should always take a non-partisan view of things, and I am sure in that way you will be able to remove doubts and suspicions. I would like you to play the role of a cementing factor between the two groups in the Bengal Party.

Hoping you are well.

Sincerely yours,
Jayaprakash Narayan

[1] *J.P. Papers* (NMML).

[2] Purnananda Das Gupta (b. 1900); actively participated in the struggle for freedom, jailed for political activities in 1924, 1931, 1935 and 1942; after release from prison in 1946, joined Socialist Party and became Joint Secretary of the Party in West Bengal, 1947-9; retired from politics in 1950.

211. To P.R. Das, 9 September 1949[1]

Dear Shri Das,

I am sorry I was not able to write to you earlier. I should have written to you soon after my second visit to Calcutta. But I have been rather busy and I hope you will excuse me for the delay.

At Calcutta I had very fine response from the legal profession as well as from other sections of the intelligentsia. I met both Shri Atul Gupta[2] and

[1] *J.P. Papers* (NMML).

[2] Atul Chandra Gupta (1884-1961). Bar-at-Law; joined Calcutta High Court, 1914; joined Calcutta University as Professor in Law Department, 1918; back to legal practise 1928 and continued till end; associated with political and benevolent activities.

Shri Radhabinod Pal.[3] I was surprised to find both of them extremely sympathetic and responsive. Though they said that they never had been directly in politics and did not wish to take direct part in it now, they would do everything to help us. They are both great friends of Sarat Babu but they told me that they did not agree with his move to collect together all manner of hotch-potch parties.[4] Atul Babu very clearly said that though he had been a life-long supporter of the Congress he had lost all hopes in it now and that he did not see any other party except the Socialist Party which could take the place of the Congress. He, however, said that the Party was rather weak in Bengal. I admitted that and asked his help and guidance in strengthening the organisation, which he readily offered.

I shall be returning to Patna by the 20th Ocotber and I hope to meet you then. I shall be going to Calcutta again from Patna on the 28th October.

Our Party has suffered a serious reverse in the District Board elections in Tamilnadu, but I have been told that this was due not so much to lack of popular support as to lack of resources and organisation and to the restricted franchise. When I come to Patna I shall give you the details.

You will remember that when I had met you in Patna I had spoken to you about your giving us some financial help. I wonder if you could give us a thousand rupees a month. We could spend the whole of it in Bihar if you like or share it between Bihar and Calcutta. When I was in Calcutta last I was able to collect some money for the Bengal Party. If you agree with my suggestion I shall be much obliged if you could send for Awadesh Nandan Sahay and give him whatever you wish.

I hope you are well.

With kind regards,

Sincerely yours,
Jayaprakash Narayan

[3] Radhabinod Pal (1896-1967). Bar-at-Law; Judge, Calcutta High Court, 1944-6; Vice-Chancellor, Calcutta University, 1947-8; one of the Judges in the International Military Court, Tokyo, 1946-8, set up to try war criminals; author of many books and articles on law.

[4] Sarat Chandra Bose, a prominent Congress leader of Bengal had been then trying to bring all the leftist parties on one platform.

212. To Shakti Bose, 10 September 1949[1]

My dear Shakti,

I have not heard from any of you since I left Calcutta. This won't do. People should write oftener and keep me informed of the developments. Suresh

[1] *J.P. Papers* (NMML).

must have reached there already and I hope he will be able to give you valuable help and advice. I am anxious to know whether all the numerous contacts that I made in Calcutta during my last two visits are being kept up by your friends. I should like you, Ajit Roy, Sibnath or any other responsible member of the Party to cultivate Shri Atul Gupta and Radhabinod Pal. I am sure if you keep in touch with them they would be of great help. I had also understood from some of you that from the contacts among the Calcutta lawyers you are expecting to get a monthly donation of Rs. 600/-. I wonder if you have succeeded in this.

After I came to Bombay I wrote to Sibnath regarding the differences in the Bengal Party. I hope some via-media has been found now and that you are working as a team. When Suresh left, I explained to him the whole position and told him to follow the line along which a settlement could be arrived at. When we had met last month at Mr. Basu's place I had expressed my opinion that if the editorship of the "Socialist" and the conveners of the Election and Finance Committees were changed in accordance with your wishes there might be smooth working. I do hope earnestly that some such agreement has been arrived at, or at least will be arrived at, before you people come to Bangalore. You also have been invited to the Bangalore Camp. Do come even though for a few days and please write to me as often as you can.

With best wishes,

Sincerely yours,
Jayaprakash Narayan

213. To Nalini Ranjan Sarkar, 10 September 1949[1]

My dear Nalini Babu,[2]

When I was in Calcutta last I had hoped to meet you, but you were unfortunately unable to come for tea at Mr. Basu's place on account of your ill health. Just before I left Calcutta I was rather sad to find an attack from you

[1] *J.P. Papers* (NMML).

[2] Nalini Ranjan Sarkar (1882-1953); participated in the movement against Partition of Bengal (1905-6) as also the Non-Cooperation Movement (1920-1); joined Swarajya Party, founded by C.R. Das and Motilal Nehru, and became Chief whip and Secretary later on; elected to Bengal Legislative Council 1923-8; Calcutta Municipal Corporation, 1932 and Mayor, 1935; President, Bengal Chamber of Commerce; Finance Minister in Bengal, 1935; joined Viceroy's Executive Council as Member-in-Charge of Education, Health and Lands and later on Commerce, Industry and Food, 1941-3; returned to Congress, 1947 and joined B.C. Roy's Cabinet as Finance Minister, 1947; acted as Chief Minister of Bengal shortly in 1949; one of the "Big Five" in Bengal politics.

on the Socialist Party published in the local press. In your statement you had blamed us for following a negative policy. That was, I am sure, due to your lack of knowledge of our programme. You will appreciatc that, however positive an opposition party's programme might be, it is bound to appear as negative till the party has a chance to put it into practice. However, since you want us, and rightly, to follow a positive policy, I am writing to ask you whether your Government will co-operate with us in implementing such a policy.

During my last visit to Calcutta I found that the worst sufferers in the City were people of the middle class. One way to lighten their suffering, to my mind, is to organise them into co-operative societies. I am thinking of asking my Bengal friends to take up this work in right earnest and organise it on as large a scale as possible. But their success will depend entirely on the amount of co-operation they get from the Government. Will you assure us of your full co-operation in this matter? I should be obliged to hear from you in this regard as soon as possible.

I hope you are in better health now.

With greetings,

Sincerely yours,
Jayaprakash Narayan

214. To H.N. Sanyal, 10 September 1949[1]

Dear Mr. Sanyal,[2]

I am writing to say how happy I was to have made your acquaintance in Calcutta and to find your keen interest in our movement. I hope the friends whom I met through you are continuing to take interest in the Socialist Party. I hope to be in Calcutta again towards the end of October and I am looking forward to meeting you then. In the meanwhile I hope you would give all possible help and guidance to the youngmen who are trying to build up the Socialist Party in Bengal. I hope the time will soon come when men like you will come forward and associate themselves more intimately with the Party.

I have sent Mr. Suresh Desai, who is a Joint Secretary of the all India Party, to Calcutta to help and guide the Bengal Party in its work. I hope he will receive your co-operation.

With greetings,

Sincerely yours,
Jayaprakash Narayan

[1] *J.P. Papers* (NMML).

[2] H.N. Sanyal, Bar-at-Law, a senior lawyer in Calcutta and a sympathiser of the Socialist Party.

215. Open Letter to All Railwaymen, 14 September 1949[1]

Dear Friends,

Since my health has improved and I began to move about I have met many railwaymen. I have found that discontent and dissatisfaction are again raising their heads. When the General Council of the Railwaymen's Federation postponed the general strike there was hope created that something definite would soon be done. These hopes, in a large number of cases, remain unfulfilled, with the resulting restiveness among you. But I should like to sound a warning against an unreasonable frame of mind which I have sometimes encountered, namely, that of belittling all that has been achieved so far. Not infrequently have I come across railwaymen who have asserted that nothing had been done for them and that not a single one of their demands had been secured. Among railwaymen there are innumerable categories of employees and men of one category are naturally not interested in what those of other categories have got. Nay, each of you is interested in himself alone. The result is that whereas very substantial victories have been achieved by the Federation in the past three years, victories whose economic value would probably reach the figure of 35 crores, the feeling that nothing has been done still persists. This is unfair to your Unions and to your Federation; and persons who indulge in such loose talk unwittingly injure their own cause and weaken their organisation. The Railwaymen's Federation has been the only labour organisation in this country which, without asking the workers to make any large sacrifices, has succeeded in securing for them large gains.

Let me speak to you more concretely. When I advised you at Danapore on February 16 of this year to postpone the general strike I had placed before you the results of my negotiations with the Railway Ministry.[2] You will find in my address sixteen demands regarding which some agreement was arrived at. These were demands, numbered one to sixteen of our Lillooah resolutions.[3] In addition to these sixteen demands, which you will find in my printed address, I had spoken of two other demands that had been conceded, namely, the grade of switchmen had been raised to Rs. 60-85 and the railway school teachers had been allowed the same dearness allowance as that received by other railway employees. Some of the decisions that had been reached regarding the sixteen demands have already been implemented. The first demand, for instance, was with regard to pay

[1]*J.P. Papers* (NMML).

[2]See ante, item dated 16 February 1949.

[3]Lillooah resolution was adopted by the Railwaymen's Federation in August 1948. It was reproduced in J.P.'s speech at Danapore on 16 February 1949.

fixation formula for pre-1931 staff. This had two parts, the second of which related to the scales of pay of those pre-1931 staff whose scales were inferior to post-1931 scales. With regard to this the Railway Board has already issued orders in its circular E 47 CPC/10 of 31-3-49. As a result of this order employees on the E.I., O.T., M.S.M. and S.I. Railways have received substantial benefits. The case of other pre-1931 staff is being considered by the Joint Advisory Committee. I hope that there will be some improvement in their scales too.

Likewise, demand No. 2 has been conceded in the Railway Board's circular No. E 48 CPC/162 of 3-12-48.

Demand No. 3 has been conceded by the formation of the Joint Advisory Committee.

The question of scales of pay of running staff dealt with in demand No. 5 is being considered by the Joint Advisory Committee and I hope that in this respect too some advancement will be effected.

Demand Nos. 6 and 7 are before the Advisory Committee.

Demand No. 8 was conceded and Bangalore, Lucknow and Nagpur were added to the cities entitled for compensatory allowance.

Regarding demand No. 9, the Railway Board's decision is contained in circular No. E (F) 48 GR 24 of 11-8-49.

Regarding demand No.10, orders have been issued in Railway Board's circular No. E 48 CPC/150 of 12-1-49. With respect to casual labour and temporary staff, though the decision is not wholly satisfactory, the principle involved in our demands has been accepted and it is hoped that the difficulties that are being faced in the matter of implementation will soon be removed. Regarding school teachers I have already said above that the Railway Ministry had accepted our demands.

With regard to demand No.11 orders have been issued in Railway Board's circulars E (R) 48/UN/3 of 3-5-49 and E 48 CPC/27 of 14-2-49.

Regarding demand No.13, new pass rules passed before the Danapore meeting had already met some of the objections raised by the Federation against the previous rules. The question of retirement pass for class IV staff is under consideration.

Regarding demand No.14, the view among railwaymen seems to be that the existing system of payment should be retained, though collective option is conceded to them to change over to 48 hours a week with no variation in emoluments from month to month.

Regarding demands Nos. 15 and 16, the agreement reached is being implemented. With regard to conversion of temporary into permanent saff (demand No. 16), the procedure is somewhat long-drawn-out, but the Federation has been persistently pressing for a quicker decision.

You will thus see that some of the demands made by us have already been conceded and implemented, and the others are before the Advisory Committee. The Advisory Committee, no doubt, is functioning very slowly and its working has to improve considerably before it can fulfil the urgent tasks before it and give satisfaction to labour. It is a matter of regret that the representatives of the Railway Board have not been vested with adequate authority, due to which they are unable to take decisions without consulting the Railway Board on every issue. This not only takes time but also gives the discussions within the Advisory Committee a character of unreality and converts the Committee into more or less a debating society. I am writing to the Railway Minister either to replace the representatives of the Railway Board with men of higher authority or give the present representatives plenipotentiary powers so that they may take decisions without running to the Railway Board every time.

This is the present state of our negotiations. Negotiations concerning such a vast number of employees as railwaymen, who are spread over the whole country, are a complicated affair and naturally much time is taken. But I do not know of any other quicker method to achieve results. The Federation will naturally exert the fullest possible pressure to see that decisions are expedited. I am writing to Shri Ayyangar for a meeting of our Negotiating Committee with him in the second week of October, when I hope to be in Delhi. At this meeting we shall take up the thread of negotiations where we left it before Danapore and, among other things, shall raise this question of delay in arriving at decisions. There were several issues which have not, nor will be, referred to the Advisory Committee. These also we hope to take up at the forthcoming meeting. I shall press for definite decisions on the major issues before our jubilee conference in November next.

In the meanwhile, I want everyone of you to realise that the only manner in which you can succeed in defending your interests and bettering your conditions is by strengthening the Federation and your Union. I am afraid there is a considerable amount of slackness prevalent in our organisational work today. This must go and you must see that your Union is a living vigorous body. Our organisation needs drastic structural changes too, so as to function more effectively and serve your cause better. A draft proposal indicating the main outline of these changes was published in the last issue of the *Railwayman* by Com. Peter Alvares. I draw your earnest attention to the draft proposals, because I feel that unless we adjust our organisational structure to the needs of the times, we shall not succeed in our efforts.

I should also like to draw your attention to an aspect of Union activity which does not receive adequate attention from you. The Union is not merely to formulate your demands and to fight for them but also to serve you in a constructive manner. In these days of high prices one of the most beneficent activities is the formation of co-operative societies through which you can secure some relief from the high cost of living. I should urge you to take up and to also induce your Union to take up this form of activity on as large a scale as possible. The Administrations are bound to give you full co-operation in this work. Where difficulties are created you should write to the office of the Federation, which will do all to help you.

Finally, let me warn you that the economic situation of the country is grave. Where, a balance of forty-five lakhs in the Central Governments budget was expected, a deficit of as many crores, if not more, is threatened. Production and employment are falling. The food situation continues to be full of anxiety. No doubt, a large part of this crisis is due to the bungling of the Government itself. But, whatever be the reasons, we cannot shut our eyes to facts. In view of the present economic position, and further deterioration that is feared, we cannot hope to make any large advances at the present. Nor can threats of strike or strike itself help us. Indeed, it may only hurt our cause. I therefore appeal to everyone of you to realise the gravity of the situation and its risks, dangers and limited possibilities and formulate your hopes and aspiration accordingly.

Jayaprakash Narayan

216. To S. Nagabhushanam, 16 September 1949[1]

Dear Nagabhushanam,[2]

Your letter of September 12.

It is perfectly all right if you do not approve of my staying at the Residency. I only made the suggestion because Mr. Mallayya[3] had spoken to me about it. I hope you will make some other arrangement to suit my needs. The Central Office staff will be reaching there on the 23rd morning. With them will also arrive my Secretary, Shri Parasuram. Please take him to the place where you are putting me up so that he may look into the arrangements made and have everything ready when we arrive the next day by plane. Com. Meherally has written to me from Poona about opening the National Exhibition on the 24th. I shall be happy to do this but I should like to tell you that you should not fix up any public engagements for members of the Executive or those invited for the period of the Camp. We must have ten absolutely undisturbed days for ourselves with no visitors and no public engagements. During the General Council days you may

[1] *J.P. Papers* (NMML).

[2] S. Nagabhushanam, a socialist leader in Karnataka, who was organizing a ten day Socialist Camp and a National Exhibition in Bangalore.

[3] A Socialist leader in Karnataka.

have public meeting and other engagements. I hope you will keep this in mind. I regret to inform you that Acharya Narendra Deva will not be attending the Camp on account of his ill health.

Sincerely yours,
Jayaprakash Narayan

217. To Yusuf Meherally, 16 September 1949[1]

My dear Yusuf,

I thank you for both your letters.

Excepting for rare occasions, Assemblies are always dull. But they give you time for study. I hope you are making use of your time in Poona to do some writing. I am happy to know that the Poona climate is agreeing with you and I hope you will come back much improved in health.

I have written to Nagabhushanam today that I would be happy to open the National Exhibition. At the same time I have also asked him not to fix up any public engagements whatever for any member of the Executive or those invited for the duration of the Camp. We must have ten undisturbed quiet days there. The agenda, I am afraid, is a heavy one. I hope you will come to Bangalore at the very beginning and stay for the whole of the ten days and also the General Council. Purshottam[2] said he was going there towards the end of the month. I am afraid Purshottam will be unable to return to Poona before next Tuesday or Wednesday.

I was very happy to know of Peter's success during the Assembly debate on Jadhav's adjournment motion. I am sure Peter would be an acquisition to the Party in the Assembly.

I am going away to Juhu on the 20th and will stay there till the 23rd night. I have not been able to do any writing work in Bombay and I have to complete it all in Juhu in the four days that I have there.

I am rather disappointed to know that you won't be able to come to inaugurate the Gumasta Conference, but I am sure you are quite right in not coming. Bangalore is much more important and I agree that you must preserve your strength to undertake the arduous journey and to be able to participate in the discussions there.

My arm is improving though very slowly.

Affectionately yours,
Jayaprakash Narayan

[1] *J.P. Papers* (NMML).
[2] Purshottam Trikamdas.

218. To Rafi Ahmed Kidwai, 24 September 1949[1]

My dear Rafi Saheb,

I thank you for your letter of the 22nd August. The orders of the Government of India cancelling their original letter dated the 9th July, 1949, virtually withdrawing recognition of the All India Postmen & Lower Grade Staff Union, did not reach Shri Dalvi[2] till the 29th August, even though the order appears to have been issued on the 6th of August. That is why I wrote to you a second time. I am very thankful to you for the prompt action you were good enough to take in this matter.

You remember that I had met you along with my colleagues of the Postmen Union in February last and, as a result of our talks and the assurances you had given us, the General Council of the Union had postponed the general strike. Soon after that I met with my accident and was unable to take up the thread of negotiations with you again. Nearly seven months have passed since our talks and the postponement of the strike. During this period, certain decisions have been taken by your Department which have met some of the demands put up by the Union. However, there appear to be many questions about which no decision has been taken yet, or which have been decided unfavourably and in contradiction to the assurances that were given to us. The Executive Council of the Union recently met at Bombay and took a rather serious view of that inaction on your part.

I should like to go back to our discussions in Delhi. I am enclosing herewith a copy of the Union's demands, as also a copy of your Department's reply to them, point by point. I shall first deal with the major questions. One of the most important demands of the men was that they should be paid the wages for the strike period of 1946. If you remember you had told me that you might be able to do something in that regard after three months or so. You had said that in a similar situation, as when the employees of the Irrigation Department in the U.P. had gone on a strike, you had arranged for payment for the strike period in the shape of payment against extra-ordinary leave. I had reported your assurance to the General Council, and naturally the men were all expecting that after three months were over something in that direction would be done. Nothing, however, has been done yet, and I am afraid the present economy drive of the Finance Ministry might place in your way insurmountable difficulties. But you will appreciate that when you did give me a definite assurance I expect that everything would be done to have it carried out. Not only my position but yours too is

[1] *J.P. Papers* (NMML).
[2] B.M. Dalvi.

compromised if nothing is done. I had told the men that Rafi Saheb was an honourable man and that if he found he was not able to implement the assurances he had given he would rather resign than carry on in the Ministry. I hope you will attach to this question the seriousness that it deserves.

The other important question which we had discussed and which is threatening to lead to considerable trouble at least in such places as Bombay was with regard to the extra dearness allowance of Rs. 10/-. It was pointed out in the course of our discussion that there was fear that deductions would be made from this allowance in cases where an interim allowance had been previously given. The interim allowance had nothing to do with this extra allowance of Rs. 10/- which was granted by the Government of India after a great deal of agitation and when the P. & T. and Railway workers had completed a highly successful strike ballot. In terms of the Pay Commission the minimum extra allowance that these employees should have been given to compensate for the rise of 120 points in the cost of living was Rs. 30/-, but the Government's financial position did not allow a payment of more than Rs. 10/-. In these circumstances it is very unfair to make deductions even from this meagre allowance of Rs. 10/-. Whatever interim allowance had been granted before, irrespective of what conditions had been laid down at that time, should have had nothing to do with this further increment of Rs. 10/-, which hardly compensated for more than one-third of the rise in the cost of living. Some months ago I had written to you from Patna about this matter but I received no direct reply from you, though the Union was informed that the Finance Department had ruled that the deductions made in the *A* class cities against the interim allowance were just and that there was nothing further that could be done in the matter. I am quite clear in my mind that the Finance Department is taking a very wooden and narrow view of the matter. It seems to me that you cannot allow the Finance Department in this manner to force you to disown your own assurance to labour. I am not trying to give you any threat, for any such thing is as far from my mind as possible, but I should like to tell you that if the deductions that are being made are not stopped forthwith there may be trouble in the cities concerned and I for one would certainly fully back up the workers.

The third important matter is regarding the fixation of pay of pre-1931 staff. During our negotiations we were told that this question would be decided on the lines which the Railway Ministry might follow with regard to its own pre-1931 staff. The Railway Ministry has not as yet taken any decision on this matter and on further study I find that the problem in the Railways is not the same as in the P. & T. The demand made with regard to pre-1931 staff in the P. & T. is that this staff should be continued to be paid what is known as the good conduct pay. When the good conduct pay was abolished,we were told with regard to the post-1931 staff that the good conduct pay had been assimilated in the new scales of pay. For the pre-1931 staff however no new scales have been fixed, and the old scales do not include the good conduct pay. The result is that while, according to the Department's own explanation, the post-1931 staff are getting the good conduct pay as part of their new scales of pay, the pre-1931 staff have been denied that pay completely. This is clearly an injustice to the pre-1931 employees whose number cannot be very large and most of whom are near to retirement. It seems to me that this injustice ought to be removed and the pre-1931 scales should also be revised so as to assimilate, in the case of pre-1931 staff, the amount paid as good conduct pay. I cannot imagine a more reasonable demand and I hope you will see your way to accept it. I might point out that you need not wait for the Railways decision on this point, for the problem there is a different one.

Another question which is vexing the staff is regarding the Departmental examinations for promotion of postmen. If you refer to the reply given by your Department in this matter you will find that the Union was promised that a syllabus would be prepared and texts prescribed and that six months' period would be allowed to those selected for examination. You had also agreed, it seems, to make provision for training schools and dummy post offices. Nothing has been done so far in regard to any of these matters. The result is that the rule that 50% of the clerical posts should be filled up with promoted postmen remains a pious wish. At an examination held in Bombay City, out of 120 examinees only 3 seem to have been successful. This has caused great dissatisfaction among the staff.

Yet another important question was that relating to confirmation of temporary staff. The Department's reply in February was that allied questions were being considered by the Railway Ministry and decisions taken there would be applied to the P. & T. staff also. Quite some months ago the Railway Ministry decided that pending confirmation, temporary staff would receive the same benefits as permanent staff in terms of recommendations of the Central Pay Commission. The Railway Ministry further decided to expedite confirmation and a fair progress has been made in regard to confirmation against permanent posts as and when vacancies were created. With regard to conversion of temporary into permanent posts the Ministry is examining the position and decisions are expected shortly. I am not aware of any steps taken by your Department regarding this whole question of temporary staff.

Many other questions raised by the Union had formed the subject of a report by the Expert Committee and we were asked to await the recommendations of the Committee. Now that the report has been published the staff is expecting speedy implementation of it. Demands Nos. 11, 13 and 17, for instance, concerned matters which are covered by the Expert Committee Report, but hitherto no action has been taken with regard to them. I should like to emphasise here that any unreasonable delay in the implementation of the recommendations of the Expert Committee would only lead to further discontentment and lowering of efficiency. The Report of the Expert Committee was submitted to the Department a very long time ago, even though it is only a few months back that it was published. So it is fair to presume that the Department had enough time by now to examine every recommendation in detail; and therefore any further delay in taking decisions would be unreasonable.

With regard to medical examination we were told that the examination was meant only for communicable diseases, but this assurance has not been implemented.

Regarding leave rules, the distinction made between Class III and Class IV staff has caused a great deal of resentment among postmen, packers and other lower grade employees.

Of the more important demands I shall refer now only to one more, viz: the revision of scales of pay of postmen. This was one of the most important demands that the Union had put forward. You had told us that you were anxious to raise the basic salary of the lowest paid staff as soon as possible and that if and when the economic situation of the Government and the country improved you would do your best to have the scales revised. The postmen were demanding the scales recommended by Shri N.M. Joshi and Sardar Mangal Singh. I do not know if the economic situation of the Government is better than it was last February, but if it is not I am sure it is Government itself which is responsible. However, in view of the high cost of living in which there has hardly been any appreciable difference since February last, I cannot but repeat that the demand of the postmen and lower grade staff is a just one and deserves the consideration of a sympathetic Minister such as yourself.

I shall not go into the details of the other demands, but I would urge very earnestly that you look into each of them yourself and find out what exactly has been done so far and what needs to be done in view of the assurances given to us in February last. It was my duty to have raised these questions months ago, but due to my accident I was more or less put out of action for nearly five months. Since I resumed work again, I have met a large number of P. & T. employees, and I find again a feeling of discontentment and even of desperation arising among them. You are aware, I hope, of the recent fast undertaken by a Bombay postman, Shri Kadam, who is also a member of the Executive Council of our All India Union. His fast had aroused great sympathy among all the P. & T. employees in Bombay. It was only when a mass meeting of postmen requested Kadam that he should break his fast and leave it to them and to the Union to fight for their cause—to which I had added my own personal request and assurance that I would do all in my power—that Kadam was persuaded to give up his fast on the sixth day. I should like to warn that the fast was not a stunt but the symptom of the temper and mind of the men. I hope therefore that there will be no complacency in high quarters and an earnest effort will be made to meet the men at least halfway. I have no doubt that you will make every effort to do so.

I am expecting to reach Delhi on the 12th afternoon. I should like to meet you along with my colleagues of the Union to discuss these matters, so that when we go from Delhi to Agra for the All India Conference of the Union we should be in a position to place definite decisions before them. Some time on the 14th morning or afternoon would suit us. I shall be obliged to hear from you as soon as possible. Please write to me at 40, Ridge Road, Malabar Hill, Bombay.

With kind regards,

Sincerely yours,
Jayaprakash Narayan

219. Appeal for Volunteers to Work for the Relief of the Middle Class People in Calcutta, 26 September 1949[1]

When I was in Calcutta last I had found that the people who were suffering most were those who came from the lower middle class. Among this class there are people of education and talent and it is from this class that the leadership in the province in all walks of life comes. It is also from this class that for half a century men of genius came, who dominated the national life. There is no reason why this class should suffer helplessly and find itself unable to do anything unless the Government came to its rescue. I have no doubt that to a very considerable extent the suffering and misery of this class can be removed by self-help. It is not helpful, however, merely to abuse those who are in power and it is suicidal to be misled into destructive activities such as the Communists are indulging in. If public discontent is not to result in chaos and self-injury we must find a more constructive approach to our problems.

As it appears to me, there are two courses open to the people who are suffering and who are dissatisfied with the ruling powers—one obviously is to organise an alternative political party which will be able to displace the unpopular party in power at the coming elections. The other course is to make concerted efforts to provide relief to immediate suffering as far as possible. One form of such endeavour is co-operative organisation. If in

[1]Press statement issued from Bangalore on 26 September 1949. Adapted from *Bombay Chronicle*, and *Statesman*, 28 September 1949.

Calcutta there are a network of co-operative stores, co-operative canteens, co-operative health societies, co-operative producers' societies, a large part of the middle class problem in the city would have been eased. Are there not enough men of talent and public spirit and enterprise in the city of Calcutta to take up this work? I am sure there are, but someone has to find them and bring them together and get them started on the job according to a plan. I take this opportunity to invite all such individuals, men and women, who may be interested in this programme and are prepared to offer their services, to write to me giving their names and address, their experience and qualifications. This work, to be done properly, will have to be on a locality basis; and in every locality or ward of the city, enough persons should be forthcoming to staff some kind of co-operative activity. After the name have reached me, I plan to go to Calcutta and call a meeting of all these friends and determine collectively our future course of action. I am seeking the help of the Bengal Government in this, as well as of all public institutions and political organisations. This is a non-political work and requires the co-operation of all public-spirited men and women of the state. I am sure that there are large numbers of friends in Calcutta who will come forward and take up this work which, I have no doubt, would yield positive results within a matter of months rather than years. The main requirements of the middle class are cheaper medicine and medical aid and employment. The co-operative stores and canteens and the health societies and the producers' co-operatives would be able to meet this requirement to a large extent. I request those who are prepared to take up this work to write to me at 40, Ridge Road, Malabar Hill, Bombay, up to the 3rd October, and after that at Kadam Kuan, Patna.

220. To Kalavenkata Rao, 29 September 1949[1]

Dear Friend,

I thank you for your letter of September 18. I am grateful to you and Shri Shankarrao Deo for the steps that you are taking to settle this matter.[2] However, some words in your letter have made me rather anxious. You write that the Bihar Ministers have decided to settle the details of the enquiry at Patna on the 20th inst. I fail to understand what this enquiry is to which you refer. We had agreed to Dr. Rajendra Prasad's arbitration and the resolution of the Working Committee also had directed the Bihar

[1] *J.P. Papers* (NMML).

[2] Kalavenkata Rao had written to J.P. that Sri Shankarrao Deo had a series of discussions about Dalmianagar affairs with the Bihar ministers who had decided to settle the details of the enquiry at Patna.

Government to make arrangements for the arbitration. What is this enquiry then of which the details are being fixed on the 20th instant? I do earnestly hope that this matter will not be unnecessarily complicated further. I should like to make it absolutely clear that we shall not accept anything else except Dr. Rajendra Prasad's arbitration.

Thanking you,

Sincerely yours,
Jayaprakash Narayan

221. To All Unions of Post and Telegraph Workers, 3 October 1949[1]

Dear Friend,

It has long been felt by us as also by others working in the P. & T. Unions that a conference of representatives of the different Unions should be called for the realignment of the Unions on a scientific basis and, if possible, to form one central P. & T. organisation for the whole of India. Some efforts were made to call a conference of this kind at Patna in April, but unfortunately it could not be held. Recently an invitation was sent to you over the signatures of Shri N.M. Joshi and myself for a conference of this kind at Bombay on the 16th and 17th of September, but as only a few representatives came we could not do more than have informal discussions. I am therefore calling a conference again at Delhi on the 13th and 14th October for taking a decision on the realignment question. I earnestly hope you would attend this conference and that you would come armed with plenipotentiary powers to arrive at a decision on behalf of your Union.

Sincerely yours,
Jayaprakash Narayan

[1] *J.P. Papers* (NMML).

222. Address at the Meeting of the General Council of the Socialist Party, Bangalore, 7 October 1949[1]

There are three approaches to the problems of the country; the first is to support the present Government at all costs and at all events. Those who believe in this approach feel that the present Congress leaders are irreplaceable. This approach is sterile. Another approach is represented by

[1] Adapted from *National Herald*, 8 October 1949.

the Communist method which means exploitation of the dissatisfaction of the people, leading to disintegration of the State completely. The third approach is the constructive approach of the Socialist Party. It seeks to find out why things are bad and to suggest remedies for them. On the basis of this approach the Party had to go ahead with its propaganda. It should utilise the present situation to convince people that there must be a new political force and that the present Government must go, because it is incapable of solving the problems before the country. The Government can not be made to go by throwing bombs at the leaders. It can go only if the people decide to get rid of it. The will of the people must be crystallised into a new political party and people must be told that the Socialist Party is the new political party.

The appeal for co-operation offered by Pandit Nehru has no value in a situation which is nothing but a "vacuum". From my experience I have come to the conclusion that the Congress and the Congress Government do not want any co-operation. They have developed a kind of totalitarian attitude which precludes the possibility of such co-operation. Pandit Nehru has not made clear how co-operation can be given. The Socialist Party, nevertheless, is prepared to give fullest cooperation to whatever Government is in power in order to remove the difficulties before the country or in an emergency.

223. The Economic Programme of the Socialist Party, 10 October 1949[1]

A detailed analysis of the working of our economy has convinced us that Capitalism in this Country has reached a crisis of its own. For this there is no solution consistent with its stability and permanent working. We have, therefore, to think out steps necessary to transform our capitalist economy into a socialist economy.

The most important problem facing us in the industrial field is the failure of capital formation. This is due to a) lack of savings, b) their inefficient conversion into real capital and c) low productivity which does not leave sufficient margin for savings. The first task is to tackle this problem of capital formation from all these angles.

To promote the growth of savings it is necessary to impose an all-round restriction on consumption. People must realise that placed as we are economically, it is not possible for us to increase our future income and

[1] *J.P. Papers* (NMML). Text of the statement made by J.P. at a Press Conference in Bombay on 10 October 1949. It was published in a summary form in several newspapers on 11 and 12 October 1949.

improve our standard of life without agreeing to restrict present consumption. A scheme of consumption restriction will, however, succeed only to the extent it imposes proportionately greater burdens on the higher incomes than what are put on the lower incomes.

To convert savings into Capital tax concessions and remissions may be given to undistributed profits ploughed back into the industry.

If the consumption of our people is not to be depressed savings can be obtained only by increasing production. This can come only through harder work and better co-ordinated production. It will be necessary to carry out rationalisation of organised and unorganised industries and to insist on harder work on the part of both workers and management.

Physical and psychological bottlenecks hampering the transformation of savings into Capital have to be removed. The depressing effects of uncertainties can be removed by an assurance, from the Government and Monetary Authorities, of maintenance of stable prices and Capital values.

The Indian investor must revise his profit expectations fostered during the years of shortage and inflation. These high profits were made out of the miseries and hardships of the people. That level of profit cannot and must not last. The physical obstacles to be removed are inadequacy of transport, raw materials and Capital goods.

While these preliminary steps will be necessary for the immediate improvement of the situation it must be emphasised that in the set-up of the Indian economy as at present these mesures will not lead to the creation of savings and investments sufficient to meet the needs of our growing population and of improved standard of life. Socialisation of the economy alone will provide conditions wherein men will be induced to make sacrifices in terms of harder efforts and lower consumption.

The analysis of the conditions in agriculture brings out this fact even more vividly. Unless our agricultural economy is completely reorganised on a cooperative basis, there is no hope for solving our agricultural problems satisfactorily. Mere eradication of minor defects through consolidation, reclamation of land, debt relief, agricultural subsidies, land tenure reforms and irrigational facilities will not be of much avail.

As a first step towards socialisation we would suggest the establishment of a National Planning Commission whose function would be to carry out the overall survey of the economy, to ascertain the needs for Capital and resources of the different sectors, to co-ordinate the rates of development of these different sectors and thus bring about an absolute economy in the amount of total Capital required for given quantum of economic development. The Commission will be in a position to prevent the exercise or emergence of monopoly powers.

The Commission should have under it a series of National as well as Regional Supervisory Directorates in charge of different industries. These

Directorates would be made up of representatives of the public, the workers and the management and would be entrusted with the function of carrying out a scrutiny through cost accounting and other methods into the working of the industrial establishments under them.

There should be a Department of the Planning Commission dealing with the small scale and cottage industries. This Department should study the problems facing this sector of our economy and prepare a blueprint to provide technical training, cheap electric power and finance and marketing facilities to those engaged in this sector.

Similarly, there will be an Agricultural Department looking after our agricultural problems, a separate note on which is under preparation.

Another Department of the National Planning Commission should be established to control, develop and direct all foreign trade. In the absence of any overall Planning a mere establishment of foreign trade advisory committee or taking over by the Government of a part of foreign trade will not suffice. This Department should enquire into the question of costs and prices of the articles entering our foreign trade and suggest proper remedies. The Control of the quality of goods exported should also be under its charge.

The Government should evolve a sound Public Finance Policy formulated in the context of general economic policy. It should be used as a weapon for bringing about a new social order based on equality and justice.

Any scheme of Planning of our economy is likely to be frustrated by the alarming rate of increase in our population. It should be viewed as a part of the general programme for the betterment of social life. Moral restraint should be encouraged. But it will not be enough. It will have to be aided by other preventive measures like birth control etc.

This then is our conclusion: Private enterprise has failed miserably to undertake the economic development of the country. An even more far reaching conclusion is that in the conditions of the present-day India private enterprise is incapable of carrying out this task. The inevitability of socialism seems to be unquestioned. The transitional steps to this goal, to be reached through a democratic process, have been indicated in the economic policy enunciated by the Socialist Party at Bangalore, a brief summary of which I have tried to give above.

224. The Congress Overture to RSS, 10 October 1949[1]

The news and the Congress President's statement about the political integration of the RSS with the Congress would fill every Indian who

[1] *J.P. Papers* (NMML). Statement at a Press Conference, Bombay, 10 October, published in the *Tribune*, 12 October 1949.

believes in a secular and progressive democracy with grave forebodings.[2] The drift in this country towards fascism has been visible in many fields of national life; but I doubt whether any single step in that direction was more potent with mischief than the decision of the Congress Working Committee to assimilate the RSS politically into the Congress. How far the Congress has travelled from the high ideals of its creator is perhaps more evident from this single decision than by all that the Congress has been doing so far. Till a few weeks ago, the RSS was an illegal organisation,[3] and today the doors of the ruling party have been opened to it. This no doubt is a historic instance of change of heart; but is it doubtful on which side has the change occurred? It is a tragedy for India that the Congress should have degenerated so rapidly and become such an opportunist and unprincipled body. The Congress has only one concern—to remain in power at all costs. And so it is making use of all such forces as may help it to remain in power. Having set its face against radical social change, it is obliged to make use of racialism, communalism, war-talk to keep itself in power. By this latest alliance with communal and social reaction the Congress stands finally utterly exposed.

This alliance of the Congress with the RSS increases the danger of violence being introduced into the settlement of political and economic issues. Let me therefore warn those who, in their hunger for power, are preparing to thwart democracy and progress, that fascist violence cannot but be met with revolutionary violence and that fascism must ultimately go down in India as it did elsewhere, but the responsibility of plunging the country into chaos and suffering will be on the shoulders of those who are preparing to establish their fascist regime. Let not this warning be in vain.

Jayaprakash Narayan

[2]Addressing a public meeting at Kanpur on 9 October, Congress President Dr. Pattabhi Sitaramaya had justified the Congress Working Committee's decision to give RSS a chance to join the Congress, if it desired, and to work for the national cause. He found no reason to keep the organization away from the Congress fold when the RSS chief after a negotiation with Sardar Patel had agreed to stay away from politics and also to remain loyal to the Government.

[3]The Government of India had imposed a ban on the Rashtriya Swayamsevak Sangh in early 1948, following Gandhi's assassination, but removed it in July 1949 when the latter agreed to work as a socio-religious organization and framed a constitution providing for this.

225. To N.R. Sarkar, 14 October 1949[1]

Dear Shri Sarkar,[2]

I thank you for your very kind letter. I am happy to find such a co-operative an responsive attitude in you which, I hope, is shared by other members of the Government.

My ideas about doing something for the middle class in Calcutta through the development of co-operation are rather nebulous yet and we are still working on our scheme. You may have seen a statement which I have published in the Calcutta papers regarding this question. The response to that statement has been extremely encouraging and I am convening a general meeting at Calcutta on the 31st October of such friends as are interested in my proposal. I am hoping that out of this meeting will emerge a definite plan of action.

I shall meet you in Calcutta this time and discuss the whole matter with you. I shall also have to meet Bidhan Babu[3] and the Minister in charge of co-operation. I hope all this will be possible. I shall write to you later after our plans have taken further shape.

With kind regards,

Sincerely yours,
Jayaprakash Narayan

[1]*J.P. Papers* (NMML).
[2]J.P.'s statement on Calcutta middle-class see item dated 26 September 1949.
[3]Bidhan Chandra Roy, Chief Minister of Bengal.

226. To Shakti Bose and Sibnath Banerjee, 16 October 1949[1]

Dear Shakti, Sibnath

As it was arranged at Bangalore I will be reaching Calcutta on the 29th morning. On the 30th I have the meeting of the Working Committee of the Railwaymen's Federation. On the 31st afternoon I should like to have a meeting of those who have responded to my statement regarding the co-operative movement in Calcutta. I have received a large number of letters in response to my statement and I am writing to each one individually. I shall also issue a public statement later on. I have requested Kamaladevi to be in Calcutta at that time and to preside at the meeting and stay for a few days afterwards to set up the organisation. I am also intending to invite to

[1]*J.P. Papers* (NMML).

this meeting men like Shri Atul Gupta and Radha Binod Pal and other friends from the intelligentsia. I should like you to send me a list of our friends in this class so that I may write to them personally from Patna. I shall send you after I reach Patna a list of the persons who have responded to my appeal, and I would like you to get in touch personally or through other comrades with everyone of them and prepare a note for me on each, giving a characterisation of the person and other information about him.

I found at Jaipur where I met some friends from Calcutta that very little had been done with regard to funds. This means that I will have to stay in Calcutta longer than I had originally intended and the mofussil programme will have to be cut short. These friends told me that unless the money is collected during my presence in Calcutta it would be very difficult to collect anymore than has already been done. I would therefore suggest that my Calcutta Programme should be at least for seven days, i.e., till the 4th I must be in Calcutta. The districts programme might begin from the 5th.

I had met Mr. Dalimchand Sethia[2] at Jaipur and he asked me to stay with him this time. It seems he has taken a new house near Mr. Asim Dutt's, and if you think this is all right please make arrangements accordingly. Or, you may put me up with Mr. A.K. Basu as before, or with Subrata Roy Chowdhury,[3] because he had also invited me to stay with him when I was in Calcutta last. Please don't keep this matter in a confused state and compel me to make a decision at the railway station after I arrive. That is very embarrassing.

Sincerely yours,
Jayaprakash Narayan

[2] A businessman based in Calcutta, sympathetic to Socialists.

[3] Subrata Roy Chowdhury (1923-94), Bar-at-Law; Lecturer, Calcutta University, 1961; nominated Judge, International Court of Justice; Chairman, International Law Association; publications include: *Military Alliances and Neutrality in War and Peace*; *The Genesis of Bangladesh: A Study in International Legal Norms and Permissive Conscience*, and *Rule of Law in a State of Emergency.*

227. Presidential Address at the 23rd Annual Conference of the Postmen and Lower Grade Staff Union, Agra, 16 October 1949[1]

The time has come to bring all rival organisations of posts and telegraph employees under a central body so that they may fight together for a common end. In the deteriorating economic situation of the country, labour is threatened with renewed and concerted attacks on its standard of living and

[1] Adapted from *National Herald*, 17 October 1949

its conditions of work. Labour cannot withstand these attacks unless it is united. Therefore, it is high time that our sectional loyalties are suppressed and unity forged of all post and telegraph employees.

The past was a difficult year for labour and the difficulties seem to be growing with time, and the year before us might well prove more trying yet. After the establishment of the national Government a new hope had arisen in the hearts of labour generally, and particularly in the employees of the State. The erstwhile darling of labour, Pandit Nehru, being the head of the Government had reinforced that hope. Disillusionment, however, was swift and deep. You are all acquainted with that sad story, for it is a story of your own personal experiences, and there is no need, therefore, to dwell on it long. I shall only point out its highlights.

The last conference of our union had formulated the main demands of the postmen and the lower grades staff.[2] At the top of these was the demand for an adequate dearness allowance to compensate for the rise in the cost of living. The demand worked out to a minimum additional dearness allowance of Rs. 30 per month. This was in terms of the Pay Commission's own formula. Among other major demands were pay for the period of strike in 1946, publication of the report of the expert committee, revision of the scales of pay in accordance with the recommendations of Mr. N.M. Joshi and Sardar Mangal Singh,[3] confirmation of temporary staff and fixation of pay of pre-1931 staff. There were many other minor demands, though each was important in its own way. The total number of our demands was thirty-four. These demands were duly communicated to the Government but there was no response.

The story of subsequent developments is one of sad disillusionment. Some of the minor demands have been conceded, and though decision has been taken on the other minor demands they have not been communicated to us. The report of the expert committee has been published, but its implementation has been delayed.

I am happy, however, to be able to say that at my meeting with the Minister for Communications on October 14 last it was agreed that the final dicisions on implementation would be taken within six weeks or so and that the union would be consulted before final orders were passed.

Regarding the major demands, the Government refuse to consider any improvement in the scales of pay. The deteriorating financial position of the Government is pointed out as the reason why this cannot be done. The

[2] The Executive Council of the All India Postmen and Lower Grade (including R.M.S.) Staff Union met at Bombay on 25 and 26 June 1949 and formulated thirty-four major demands and communicated them to the Government.

[3] Sardar Mangal Singh (b.1982), resigned from Punjab Provincial Service and joined the Non-Cooperation Movement, 1920; one of the leaders of the Akali Movement.

position regarding dearness allowance is also the same. The demand for payment for the strike period has been one of the most persistent demands of our union. At the February negotiations, the Minister had given a clear assurance that within three months he would arrange for payment to be made in some form of compensation such as payment against leave due. I am sorry that this assurance too has been given the go-bye.

I hoped that the attitude of Pandit Nehru's Government towards labour, particularly State employees, would be brotherly and that the employees' unions would be treated with respect and every chance would be given to them to work for the betterment of the staff. I have discovered, however, that the unions are regarded merely as a nuisance, and, if their power is not broken by inducing internal disruption, efforts are made to by-pass and disregard them and to wish them out of the way. I am afraid, this attitude, which is no different from that of the average private employer, will sooner rather than later, lead to a terrific show-down between the Government and the State employees.

Let me turn now to the future. There is little doubt that the future is going to be a period of suffering and struggle. The hardy postmen of this country and their brethren in the lower grade are seasoned fighters. But I cannot help sounding a warning. There are divisions in our ranks today. We must close up our ranks and face the Government but the post and telegraph employees as a whole are splitting up into many rival organisations. The time has come to bring all of these into a central body, so that we may all fight together for our common ends.

In the deteriorating economic situation of the country labour is threatened with renewed and concerted attacks on its standard of living and its conditions of work. Labour cannot withstand these attacks unless it is united. Therefore, it is high time that our sectional loyalties are suppressed and unity forged of all post and telegraph employees.

The question of the relationship between politics and the trade unions is often raised. Let me say a few words on this question. Usually this relationship is a matter of one-way traffic, that is to say, political parties standing outside the unions usually attempt to inflict their politics over them. I reject this process, and though I am intimately connected with a political party, I have never attempted to bring the politics of my party into the unions with which I am connected. This does not mean that I want the unions to keep away from politics. Organised labour would commit suicide if it did not also act politically.

I do not want the trade unions to be merely passive receivers of political policies; I want them to participate actively in their evolution and formulation. It is for this reason that I have been advocating collective affiliation of unions to a political party so that the relationship between politics and organised labour may become a two-way traffic and the political exploitation of labour ceases and it emerges as a political force in its own right.

No one can say that the Labour Party in Great Britain exploits the trade unions. Rather, the truth is that the unions control the Labour Party. In this country too, unless a similar relationship grows between labour and its political party, the problem would remain unsolved and labour would forever be at the mercy of political parties, standing outside and above itself.

228. Replies to Questions Asked by Members of the Executive of the East Indian Railway Employees Union, Lucknow, 21 October 1949[1]

Question: Don't you think that the Government of India are taking an unfair advantage of the truce called by the Federation with the Railway Board in order to wreck the award of the Central Pay Commission?

Answer: No, it will be unfair on our part to level such a charge against the Central Government.

Question: Isn't it a fact that the Central Advisory Committee has proved a failure, and isn't it time that the Federation withdrew from this body?

Answer: No. The Committee may be going slow about its task, but it can't be helped. For example, the Committee is examining at the moment the question of anomalies which run to a hundred. I feel that we should give it a fair trial.

Question: Don't you think that the Government of India are using the bogey of financial crisis as an excuse for axing a large number of railway workers?

Answer: The financial crisis is not a bogey but a fact. Bureaucratic squandermania is one factor which brought about the crisis. Another was the unforeseen developments in the Kashmir situation. When the Finance Minister, Dr. John Matthai, budgeted for a small surplus of Rs. 45 lakhs early this year, he was counting on a big cut in our armed forces in Kashmir as a result of the cease-fire. But this could not be achieved because of the continued aggressive preparations by Pakistan. The result has been that the anticipated surplus has turned into a deficit running into crores of rupees.

Of course, it may be argued that since the railways are making huge profits, the railway workers shouldn't be affected by the mounting defence

[1]Adapted from *Pioneer*, 22 October 1949. The question-answer session took place when J.P. met the members of the Executive at tea in the office of the union on 21 October.

budget; but this sort of argument doesn't help. This does not mean that we will submit to any retrenchment move. The Working Committee of the Federation is meeting at Calcutta on October 30 to consider this question.

Question: What is your answer to the growing corruption in the railways and other branches of the administration?

Answer: This is a national problem—a problem which only Government with a revolutionary policy and a pledge to carry out a radical overhaul of the entire governmental machinery can solve. It is now up to the electorate to return such a Government to power, which may successfully carry out a drive against corruption.

Question: Can the Federation do nothing to check the mounting corruption in the railways?

Answer: It can do a lot. For instance, it can clean up its own house. As you know, corruption is not confined to highly paid officials alone. But, are the three lakh odd members of the Federation prepared to pledge themselves to place the nation above self?

Question: Should the workers keep off politics?

Answer: Certainly not, for if they do so, they will be committing suicide. It is true that theirs is a battle for bread; but they cannot hope to win it unless they gain political power. I would advise them to follow the example of the British labour. In Great Britain trade unions are collectively affiliated with the political party of their choice, namely, the Labour Party. The result is that they are not exploited by, but actually control this party.

Question: Which political party should the workers of this country join?

Answer: This is a matter which the workers should decide for themselves. But I should like to mention here that it is only the Socialist Party which has thrown its doors open to the trade unions in this country.

Question: When the policies of the Socialist-sponsored and Congress controlled trade unions are poles apart how could Mr. Ashok Mehta arrive at an agreement with the INTUC. How is unity possible between the two sets of unions?

Answer: Of course, there cannot be any unity between the two, neither did Mr. Mehta seek to achieve it. But surely there can and should be an agreement between them on the presentation of the workers' case before different governmental committees so that labour may speak with a united voice in such committees.

Question: What will be the reaction of the Socialist Party if Netaji Subhas Chandra Bose appears in India again?

Answer: We will offer him our fullest cooperation.

229. To Rohit Dave, 22 October 1949[1]

Dear Rohit,

Kamaladevi may have spoken to you already about this matter. I had asked her to preside over a meeting at which our co-operative work in Calcutta is to have a start. I had issued a statement from Bangalore which was published in the Calcutta papers, a copy of which I am enclosing herewith. The response to that statement has been exceedingly encouraging and the plan is that a meeting of all those who have responded to my appeal should be held at Calcutta and the foundations of our co-operative work in the city laid. Kamaladevi informed me at Delhi that she would not to able to go to Calcutta due to her mother's illness and suggested that you might go there to help us. In her absence I probably will have to take the chair, but I would like you to come to help us in discussing and laying down the lines of our activity.

I am reaching Calcutta on the 29th October and the meeting might be held on the 2nd November. In that case I should like you to reach Calcutta latest on the 31st October. You may return to Bombay on the 5th. Please reply at the *Khoj Parishad* address (24 Chowringhee Road).

Hoping you are well,

Sincerely yours,
Jayaprakash Narayan

[1] *J.P. Papers* (NMML).

230. To Shakti Bose and Sibnath Banerjee, 22 October 1949[1]

My dear Shakti, Sibnath,

I wrote to you from Agra about the initiation of our co-operative work in Calcutta. I am sorry to inform you that Kamaladevi would not be able to be present in Calcutta at that time due to her mother's illness. In that case I am afraid I will have to take the chair, but I am asking Rohit Dave to come

[1] *J.P. Papers* (NMML).

over to Calcutta to help us in our organisational work. In my last letter I had suggested that the meeting be held on the 31st October, but in the absence of Kamaladevi I would require a little more time for study and to meet people. In that case I suggest that you call the conference on the 2nd November. I will of course reach Calcutta as arranged on the 29th morning. I am enclosing a list of names of those who have responded to my appeal. As I wrote in my last letter you will have to arrange for all these persons to be contacted before I reach Calcutta so that I may have a report about them before me.

About my Bengal programme I am afraid a further adjustment will have to be made. Apart from the talks of raising the funds for the Bengal elections I have to try to raise some share capital for the *Janata* Publications. There is a possibility of our being able to take over the *News Chronicle* at Delhi and I want to sell shares to the value of at least two lakhs in Calcutta during my next visit. I therefore suggest that my stay in Calcutta be further prolonged and the mofussil programme be fixed to begin from the 8th November, that is, it should be possible for me to stay in Calcutta from the 29th October to the 7th November. That would give me ten days which ought to be enough.

I hope Suresh has returned to the city by now. If he has please show him this letter as well as the previous one.

Sincerely yours,
Jayaprakash Narayan

231. To Makhanlal Mukherjee, 26 October 1949[1]

My dear Makhan Lal,[2]

I have your letter of 4th October explaining why the Party's work in Jamshedpur has not progressed as well, as expected.

I must tell you that I take very strong objection to your letter. The sum total of what you have to say is that if things have gone wrong at Jamshedpur the responsibility is entirely upon Munshi Ahmed Din. I wonder what all the rest of you are or have been doing. As a matter of fact, I was told by you people that it was better for the work at Jamshedpur that Munshiji was absent from there most of the time. Now you say that everything has gone wrong because he did not give more time to Jamshedpur. Further, at the end of the letter you have raised doubts about Munshiji's bona fides and

[1] *J.P. Papers* (NMML).

[2] Makhanlal Mukherjee; a socialist worker in Jamshedpur Steel Workers' Union.

have even stated that he has "betrayed us". Munshiji, as you probably know, was the undisputed leader of the Socialist Party in the undivided Punjab, and he ran the Party there with ability and distinction. The Punjab Party was then, as now, one of the best parties in the country. Munshiji has also a long record of sacrifice and suffering and loyalty to the cause of nationalism and socialism. When people like you decide to make such wild allegations against him I hope you knew what you were doing. I am afraid such irresponsible conduct cannot go unheeded. There is nothing more that I have to say just now. Appropriate action will be taken in due course.

Sincerely yours,
Jayaprakash Narayan

232. A Plea for Ramanand Tewari, Patna, 27 October 1949[1]

I received the news of the conviction of Pandit Ramananda Tewari[2] when I was on tour in the South. I had learnt earlier that the assessors had returned a unanimous verdict of not guilty on every one of the serious charges framed and I had hoped therefore that he would be acquitted by the Sessions Judge. But, instead, a savage sentence of transportation for ten years was passed on him. After the brave and forthright statement that Tewariji had made before the court and the assessors to convict such a distinguished soldier of freedom was incredible. However, I am glad that arrangements are being made to appeal to the High Court. In the meanwhile it is a pity that Tewariji must languish in prison. Is it necessary that he should be treated as a 'C' class criminal? The least that should be done considering Tewariji's services to the struggle for national freedom is to place him in a higher division and treat him as a political prisoner. I hope the Provincial Government would grant him this status.

[1]Adapted from *Amrit Bazar Patrika*, 30 October 1949.

[2]Ramanand Tewari was arrested for organizing and leading the 'Police mutiny' in Bihar in 1946-7 and put to face trial. He was convicted of waging war against the State and causing disaffection among the police force of Bihar against the lawfully established Government and also inducing them to 'withhold their services' and commit acts of violence. He was sentenced to ten years transportation on 17 October1949.

233. To Kalavenkata Rao, 27 October 1949[1]

Dear Friend,

By the time I reached Patna the Provincial Ministers had gone away to the Congress Camp at Ranchi. So I was not able to contact them. Nor have I been able to find out from other sources here if any final decision has been taken by the Ministry regarding the Dalmianagar affair. I shall be obliged if you will be kind enough to pursue the matter and let me know at my Calcutta address:

> C/o Khoj Parishad,
> 24, Chowringhee Road,
> Calcutta,

if the parties concerned have given their consent to Rajendra Babu's arbitration.

I had met Rajendra Babu at Delhi and he had told me that he would like the arbitration work to be finished before the Constituent Assembly met again. As you know, we on our part are also anxious that the job is finished as soon as possible. I shall anxiously await your letter at Calcutta.

With kind regards,

Sincerely yours,
Jayaprakash Narayan

[1] *J.P. Papers* (NMML).

234. To Rameshwar Rao, 8 November 1949[1]

My dear Rameshwar Rao,[2]

You know that we have been wanting for a long time to start an English daily from Delhi or Bombay. We have finally got a company registered at Delhi, the *Janata* Publications Ltd. An English daily during these times cannot be successfully run unless we have at least fifteen to twenty lakhs. To ensure success and start the paper on a sound footing, we are trying to raise twenty lakhs. I would be obliged if you could help us in this. I have allotted three lakhs to Hyderabad largely on the strength of the help I expect from friends such as you. I am sending you copies of our prospectus. The shares are ten rupees each.

[1] *J.P. Papers* (NMML).

[2] Rameshwar Rao, resigned from the post of Honorary Magistrate (Hyderabad) in response to Non-Cooperation Movement, 1921; participated in the Join Indian Union Movement, Hyderabad, 1947; associated with Socialist Movement in Hyderabad.

I hope you will consider this a first priority job, which it undoubtedly is. With best wishes,

Sincerely yours,
Jayaprakash Narayan

235. Need for a Strong Cooperative Movement, 11 November 1949[1]

There is too great a tendency amongst the people of the country to lean on the Government. There is also a general lack of popular initiative which results in a feeling of frustration and disillusionment among the people, particularly among the lower middle class. Whatever problems the country may be facing and however serious these may be, they can only be solved by popular efforts and initiative.

The people think that the national Government of today would do everything possible to create mass enthusiasm to develop a spirit of initiative among them. But unfortunately the present Governments, both in the Provinces and at the Centre, rely almost wholly on the machinery of administration and have isolated themselves from the people.

One of the most important things the people can do to solve their problems is to launch a co-operative movement. There may be differences of opinion regarding this movement, but it must be admitted that this movement is a fragment of the new social order that they all want to build up. By its very nature the co-operative movement is a non-political one and all the people, belonging to different political organisations, should participate in it. Those who sympathise with the capitalist system of society may probably be hostile to it, because it will cut at the root of the system of a society which is based on private profit. Leaving those, who are the upholders of such a society, all political parties can join together. The Socialist Party and other parties sharing the objective of socialism would wholeheartedly support this movement.

In West Bengal the co-operative movement is not so well developed as it should have been in this premier province of India. It lags behind Madras in this respect.

In Bengal there are 160 co-operative societies in Calcutta and 3,000 in the whole of West Bengal. Some of the societies are functioning properly, but the majority of them exist in name only. The striking fact is that there is no central organisation to co-ordinate the different societies, to guide them and to deal with the Government on their behalf. The first requirement of building up a proper co-operative movement is to have a promoting and

[1]Speech at public meeting in Calcutta; adapted from *Tribune*, 13 November 1949.

affiliating body, which should be in a position to co-ordinate the existing societies and also to take initiative in building new ones.[2] At the beginning we should start our work with four kinds of co-operative societies, namely, consumer societies, refugee societies, canteens and health societies.

The Government of West Bengal has assured me that they will render all possible support and encouragement to this movement.

[2]After the meeting, an eight member committee was formed with J.P. as Chairman to carry on the work of forming cooperatives in West Bengal.

236. To Rafi Ahmed Kidwai, 13 November 1949[1]

My dear Rafi Saheb,

I will be reaching Delhi on the 21st November by the evening plane from Calcutta and shall stay there till the 23rd night. Could we meet Jawaharlalji some time during this period? I won't be able to go to Delhi again for a couple of months and the men are also impatient. I suggest that you fix an appointment with Panditji on the 23rd.

Sincerely yours,
Jayaprakash Narayan

[1]*J.P. Papers* (NMML).

237. Appeal to the Railwaymen to Make Compulsory Savings Scheme a Success, New Delhi, 25 November 1949[1]

You are aware that although there are some long-standing questions pending settlement with the Ministry of Railways, the Working Committee of the Federation, at its recent meeting in New Delhi,[2] decided to make a gesture to the Government and demonstrate that railwaymen are second to none in their anxiety to contribute to the solution of the present economic difficulties facing the country. It was decided that a compulsory savings scheme should be recommended for all wage-earners without exception and that those in the lower pay ranges should be enabled to contribute at least one rupee a head per month towards the compulsory savings scheme in addition to the normal contributions to the Provident Fund.

The Ministry of Railways have decided to make membership of the

[1]*Hindu*, 28 November 1949.

[2]The Working Committee of the All Indian Railwaymen's Federation had met at Delhi on 16 and 17 October 1949.

Provident Fund institution compulsory in cases where it was optional hitherto. This would mean that the workers would be benefited by equal savings provided as retirement benefits. In addition, a voluntary savings contribution of one rupee a month for which there will be no contribution from the employer except interest earned on such excess deposits would show the readiness of railwaymen to play their part in the present crisis. Those who can contribute more will be allowed to do so and I may suggest that those drawing more than Rs. 150 a month may make an individual contribution of two rupees a month towards the savings scheme. This would not mean a wage cut at all. The Federation has already made it clear that this scheme should be tentatively tried for the period ending February 1952, and it should not prejudice any wage claims for proper fixation of pay at any time and in any stage. I appeal to every railwayman to make the compulsory savings scheme a success.

238. Speech at a Kisan Rally at Patna, 25 November 1949[1]

The Congress can never deliver goods to the people nor will it ever establish Kisan-Mazdoor Raj. The policy that was being pursued by the Congress Government had shown clearly that it is totally incapable of ushering in a new era in which social, economic and political iniquities will be a thing of the past.

The partisan policy of the Congress Government of putting obstacles in the way of democratic functioning of the opposition parties has made even a cool-headed man like me to wonder, if it will ever be possible to oust it from power by peaceful means. I wish that the Government should not pursue a policy which may make me take a decision in favour of overthrowing the Government by force.

I do not want anarchy and confusion to prevail in the country. The people should unite and consolidate their strength so as to vote down the Government in the next elections. Organisation and unity are needed for any change, without which only a goonda raj or a communalist raj may emerge.

The reason why I have lost confidence in the Congress Government is the policy it has pursued so long with regard to the exploiting classes, the princes, the zamindars, the capitalists and the bureaucracy. The princes have been left with their vast wealth, accumulated through sucking the blood of the poor subjects and, in addition, have been assured of large sums of pensions to be paid from the pockets of the downtrodden masses.

[1] Adapted from *Tribune*, 26 November 1949.

Some of them have even been made Rajpramukhs with larger powers than provincial Governors. Even the Britishers who gave them a long rope to exploit their subjects did not allow them to dabble in politics. But the benign Congress Government has allowed the Rajpramukhs even to play a political role in the national life of the country.

Similarly the Congress Government has allowed the big zamindars to keep all their wealth, accumulated by exploiting kisans, though apparently it proposed, in name only, to abolish the zamindaris. Then it also proposed to pay compensation to them for ending an evil like the zamindari system. So long as the Kisans do not benefit under the Congress scheme of abolition of the zamindari system, the only change that is to be wrought is that the state will collect the rent now in place of the zamindars. There is nothing to prevent the Government from distributing lands equitably, as has been done in China by Mao Tse Tung. There is, however, no political will to make any such change in India.

To the capitalists the Government has given the assurance that they will not be touched for the next ten years. Public memory is short. They have forgotten now that the Congress has been declaring off and on since its Karachi session in 1931 that it would nationalise key industries immediately it achieved freedom and came to power.

Those who had read Pandit Jawaharlal Nehru's earlier writings on nationalisation of industries have been sadly disillusioned. Even now, if Pandit Nehru threatens to resign on the issue of nationalisation of industry, there is a chance that he will succeed in bringing it about. The capitalists, of course, will be far stronger and in more effective control if the Congress dispenses with Pandit Nehru's services so easily. In any case, there will be no chance of the toilers coming up, on their own, if the Government persists in its present policy of placating the capitalists and appealing to them to help in the industrialisation of the country by giving baits of reduction in income-tax and traffic rates.

239. Statement on the Strike at Indian Steel and Wire Products Company, Jamshedpur, 27 November 1949[1]

It is nearly a month and a half now that the workers of the Indian Steel and Wire Products of Jamshedpur have been on strike.[2] The company belongs

[1]Adapted from *Searchlight*, 28 November 1949.

[2]Workers of Indian Steel and Wire Products Ltd. had gone on strike from 12 October, following the failure of negotiation with the management mainly on the demand of basic pay scale revision (minimum 10 *annas* per day), regularization of services and some other benefits. See also J.P.'s letter to Shri Krishna Sinha, 12 December 1949, reproduced in this volume.

to Sir Inder Singh[3] and has been declared a public utility concern by the Government.

The strike, to the surprise of the Bihar Government and its adviser from Jamshedpur, is a complete success. The strike, further, is a strictly legal one and is also completely peaceful.

There are many issues involved in the strike, but the main issue is the revision of the minimum basic scale of annas ten per day, which for Jamshedpur is an atrociously low scale.

The Government of Bihar is not yet ready to refer this case of labour dispute to adjudication. But the Bengal Government had earlier referred a dispute of the employees of the Calcutta Corporation to adjudication, even though their strike had been declared illegal by the Government. That was done no doubt because the leaders of the strike happened to be Congressmen.

When the Prime Minister keeps on emphsising the urgent need of raising production, it is regrettable that a Provincial Government, out of sheer partisanship, permits stoppage of work for such a long period in an important factory like that of steel and wire products.

The Bihar Government's partisanship does not stop only at refusing to intervene in the dispute, but also in using its repressive arm in the same spirit of party politics. The strike as I have said, has been completely peaceful. Yet on the pretext that some stray individual was assaulted, at least a mile away from the factory, thirty-two workers of the Socialist Party have been arrested from different parts of the city.

[3]Sardar Bahadur Sir Inder Singh, Chairman, Indian Steel and Wire Products.

240. To Purshottam Trikamdas, 27 November 1949[1]

My dear Purshottam,

Goray[2] has written to me for a loan of 2000 rupees to fight the Colaba District bye-election in which the Maharashtra Party has decided to put up Gaekwad.[3] It is important that we win this election. I do not know if there is any money with you, but I would request you to advance a loan of 2000 rupees to the Maharashtra Party from anywhere or any fund. If there is no money I would even ask you to take a loan yourself and give them the money now. I take the responsibility to pay it back.

Achyut writes to me that you have refused even part payment of the

[1]*J.P. Papers* (NMML).

[2]N.G. Goray.

[3]Madhav Rao Gaekwad.

8000 which I had asked you to give him. I do not know what the trouble is. Will you kindly let me know? After all, I do not see how I alone can finance all the activities of the Party. You people also have some responsibility. If there is no money you may ask Achyut to close down the *Janata*. That is all that I can say. I seem to be doing little more than exercising my lungs and passing the begging bowl around. I find it very difficult to bear the strain. However, I would appreciate if you could write to me and let me know what the position is.

Sincerely yours,
Jayaprakash Narayan

241. To Achyut Patwardhan, 27 November 1949[1]

Dear Achyut,

I am enclosing herewith a copy of my letter to Purshottam. I do not know what to do. If you cannot find the money, you may close down the *Janata*.

I hope you are well.

Affectionately yours,
Jayaprakash Narayan.

[1] *J.P. Papers* (NMML).

242. To Madhu Limaye, 7 December 1949[1]

Dear Madhu,

I should have written to you earlier about the meeting of the Executive. At Patna I had a talk with Ramnandan regarding the All India Kisan Conference. You probably know that the C.P. Party was not in a position to hold the conference in December. So Ramanandan postponed the conference and told me that he was fixing the dates sometime in the third or fourth week of January, and he suggested that the Party Executive should also meet at about the same time and same place. Ramnandan told me later that the dates of the Kisan Conference have been fixed immediately after the National Executive dates, which should also meet at Raigarh. I do not think it would be possible for members of the Executive to travel to two different places at the same time, once for the Kisan Conference and then again for the Executive. Therefore, if the Kisan Conference is going to be held at about that time the Executive should meet a few days earlier and at the

[1] *J.P. Papers* (NMML).

same place. You may send a wire to Ramnandan at Patna and find out from him where and when the Kisan Conference is meeting and you may fix the dates of the Executive accordingly.

Affectionately yours,
Jayaprakash

P.S. I had telephoned to Rammanohar from Patna to enquire about his accident. He suggested to me then to call the National Executive to consider the international situation. I told him that it would be better if he called the Foreign Policy Committee. He agreed. I suggested the end of December and Bombay for the time and venue. To that also he agreed. I do not know if he has written to you. If not, please call a meeting of the Foreign Policy Committee on the 28th December at Bombay. Please write to Rammanohar also.

J.P.

243. To Purshottam Trikamdas, 7 December 1949[1]

My dear Purshottam,

I hope you have received my previous letters and I hope I have a reply from you waiting at Calcutta when I return there. I am writing to you now about Madhyabharat. I have received a number of letters from there complaining that the Party is practically defunct there not only in Indore but throughout the province. You are in charge of Madhyabharat. Will you kindly look into the situation there and do the needful? There also seems to be no purpose in giving 500 rupees a month to the Indore Party if things are really as bad as some are trying to make out.

I am enclosing herewith a recent letter that I have received from a Party comrade in Gwalior.

Affectionately yours,
Jayaprakash Narayan

[1] *J.P. Papers* (NMML).

244. To M.S. Rajan, 7 December 1949[1]

Dear Mr. Rajan,[2]

I have your letter of 10th November and regret the delay in replying. I

[1] *J.P. Papers* (NMML).

[2] M.S. Rajan was then Administrative Secretary, Indian Council of World Affairs, New Delhi.

should have been very happy to meet and have a talk with Mr. Straus,[3] but as it happens I am touring during the whole of December and I am not expected at Patna before the end of January. I will be in Bombay from the 24th December to the middle of January and if Mr. Straus is likely to be there during that period I would be very happy to meet him there.

Thanking you for writing,

Sincerely yours,
Jayaprakash Narayan

[3]Ralf Straus (1882-1950); Novelist and biographer; published many books including, *The Man Apart, The Prison without a Wall, Our Wiser Sons, Dickens: a Portrait in Pencil, Five Men go to Prison, Lloyd's: a Historical Sketch.*

245. To P. Tofahrn, 7 December 1949[1]

Dear Friend,[2]

I was very happy to receive your letter of 9th November and to know that you have appreciated the work that we are doing in the Railwaymen's Federation here. I am thankful to you for the kind words you have said about me.

I am rather surprised to know from your letter that you have not officially heard anything from the office of the Federation about its desire to affiliate with the I.T.F.[3] I shall see that a letter goes to you as soon as possible.

We are going to celebrate the silver jubilee of our Federation in March or April next year. I wonder if it would be possible for the I.T.F. to send a fraternal delegate or a guest to our jubilee conference. I shall be happy to hear from you as soon as possible.

Sincerely yours,
Jayaprakash Narayan

[1] *J.P. Papers* (NMML).

[2] P. Tofahrn, Secretary, Railwaymen's Section, International Transport Worker's Federation, London.

[3]International Transport Workers' Federation.

246. To Jawaharlal Nehru, 12 December 1949[1]

My dear Bhai,

I do not know if you would remember that I had spoken to you when I had met you last about the strike in Sir Inder Singh's factory at Jamshedpur.

[1]*Brahmanand Papers* (NMML).

This is the 61st day of the strike. The strike was called by the workers' union of which Munshi Ahmed Din is the President. There is only one union in the factory. Mr. John of the Congress was the President of this union sometimes before but the workers deposed him and elected Munshiji as their President. The strike was called after all the prescribed processes had been gone through. Conciliation proceedings had also been held without any results. The strike is a legal one. This factory is a declared public utility. Under the law the Government has powers to refer a labour dispute in a public utility to adjudication. The Bihar Government has so far refused to do this. The strike would be called off as soon as the dispute is referred to adjudication. But on account of politics the Bihar Government is refusing to do the obvious in the matter and a vital industry has been at a standstill for over two months and nearly 3000 workers have been suffering. The Congress Government of the province wants to wreak vengeance upon the poor workers because they had dared to disown the leadership of the Congress and accept the leadership of the Socialist Party. Not only is the Congress fighting a war of attrition against us but it is taking advantage of its power and has removed our most important workers from the field by putting them in prison under one charge or another. I had sent from Bombay one of our first grade workers, Shri Bagaram Tulpule, to Jamshedpur. He is the Secretary of the Tata Mazdoor Sabha. Before he came to Jamshedpur he was a Joint Sectretary of the Bombay Socialist Party. In 1942 he graduated from the Engineering College of the Bombay University and topped the list in the whole presidency, and jumped into the August movement forthwith. Even such a man is in prison on a charge under Sec. 307. Ultimately of course nothing would be proved against him, but the object would have been gained, namely, of removing him from the field of action and preventing him from being released on bail.

You will again get angry that we are trying to waste the time of the Prime Minister over such petty matters, but firstly the matter is not petty and secondly one just does not know what one is to do in a situation such as this. There seems to be no one in the Congress today from whom we could hope for justice except you. I hope therefore that you will be patient with Munshiji and listen to him and do the needful. After all we are not asking for much. All that has to be done is to refer the demands of the strikers to adjudication and to assure them that there will be no victimisation. If I may inform you, in a recent strike which took place, when you were in the United States, of the employees of the Calcutta Corporation, the dispute was referred by the Bengal Government to adjudication even though the strike had been declared *illegal* by the same Government. This was done because the leaders of the strike were Congressmen and the union concerned was the INTUC.

Our strike being legal, cannot we expect the same treatment at least?

With kindest regard.

Affectionately,
J.P.

247. To Shri Krishna Sinha, 12 December 1949[1]

My dear Shri Babu,[2]

You know Munshi Ahmed Din well enough and I need not introduce him to you. He is going to discuss with you the strike in the Wire Products factory at Jamshedpur.[3] This is the 61st day of the strike. The Wire Products factory is, I believe, a declared public utility. A strike in such a unit of industry should not have been allowed to continue so long. The Government has powers under the law to refer a dispute in a public utility to adjudication. If this were done at any time the workers would have gone back to work. I should like to inform you, if you do not know it already, that the strike was launched only after all the prescribed processes had been gone through. Conciliation proceedings had also been held, but the management was not prepared to accept even the minimum demands of the workers. The strike was therefore called as a last resort and it is a legal strike. Sardar Ajaib Singh, the Director, has no doubt in a leaflet declared the strike illegal. He has of course no right to do so because the Provincial Government alone can take such action. Having declared the strike illegal without any authority or power to do so, the Director has further proceeded to withdraw from the workers all privileges and benefits including medical aid in the company's hospital.

The Wire Products Labour Union, which is the only union in this factory, is a registered trade union and is recognised by the management. Mr. John was the President of the Union till a few months ago when a vote of no confidence was passed against him and Munshi Ahmed Din was unanimously elected President. There is a fear in our minds that the attitude of the authorities is on this account partisan and that every attempt is being made to starve the workers and force them to fall at the feet of Mr. John again. I can find no other explanation than this for the Government's failure to get the wheels of such an important industry running again and to save the poor workers from starvation. If you remember, in a recent strike of the employees of the Calcutta Corporation, even though the strike was illegal the dispute was referred to adjudication by the Bengal Government, only because the leaders of the strike were Congressmen. In our instance, on the

[1] *J.P. Papers* (NMML).

[2] Shri Krishna Sinha, for biographical note, see *JPSW*, Vol. II, pp. 221-2.

[3] See item no. 239 and fn. 2 (item dated 27 November 1949).

other hand, even though the strike is a legal one,.the Government has so far refused to take action. Not only that, but in one way or another the most important of out workers have been put out of action by arrest or detention. Even a colleague of the standing of Shri Bagaram Tulpule[4] has been hauled up on a charge under Sec. 307, which is fantastic.

I am sure that you will take an impartial view of this matter and see that the workers are not victimised for their political views and that justice is done to them. If the demands of the workers are referred to adjudication and we are assured that there would be no victimisation, the Union would withdraw the strike. Munshiji will explain to you the situation more fully.

I hope you are well.

With kind regards,

Sincerely yours,
Jayaprakash Narayan

[4] Bagaram Tulpute, graduated from Bombay Engineering College, 1942; joined Quit India Movement, 1942; Joint Secretary, Bombay Socialist Party, 1947; Secretary, Tata Mazdoor Sabha, 1949.

248. Speech at a Public Meeting, Hyderabad, 14 December 1949[1]

I remember my earlier visit to the State in 1947, when I was arrested and deported to Bombay. If the people of India had been allowed to help the people of Hyderabad, there would have been no need for a police action. I have come to know that after the police action, the people of Hyderabad had been badly disillusioned. As in the past, it depends upon the people of Hyderabad to shape their own future. The burning problems today are how to provide food to the people, how to stop profiteering and black-marketing, how to remove poverty and establish a *Janata Raj*, where all will live comfortable lives.

The Socialist Party does not think in terms of Hindu Raj or capitalist Raj. It wants that only those should govern who earn their living by sweat and labour. They should not think in terms of Hindu or Muslim, or else the whole country would be enveloped by the communal disease. The partition was the result of mutual differences among various sections and communities.

In the map of India, which is before the Ministry of States under Sardar Patel, only the rajas and capitalists are there, and the poor have no place in it. After going through the state of affairs in the States I can say that if there

[1] Adapted from *Janata*, 25 December 1949.

is no change in the Indian map, Hyderabad will also have a reactionary government. When the Indian people fought the war of independence they thought that after the Britishers' exit the poor would get their bread but at present 999 out of 1,000 go without bread. When the Congress Government came into power, they said that poverty would be removed, but two years have passed and nothing has been done. Nor has any scheme been chalked out to help the common people. Only handful of people have the monopoly of all the wealth which India produces. There are crores of people, who through their sweat and labour are producing the national wealth, but getting nothing in return of their toil. When this fact is brought before Pandit Nehru and other Congress leaders, they ask for time. Under the rule of the Congress Government corruption has become manifest and there is no honesty left.

The ruling class is being encouraged by the Government of India so the people's progress is checked. Wherever the States had been merged the rulers were intact, and they were being paid very large amounts in the shape of allowances. Under such circumstances, how can Pandit Nehru say that there is a people's raj in India. Lakhs of rupees which were given to these rajas were looted from the poor. Recently, Pandit Nehru went to America and asked for a loan. How ridiculous it was for a big leader like him to beg for a loan. He ought to have used the wealth, which these 500 to 600 rajas are keeping idle with them; he could have confiscated the 500 crores black money hidden by the capitalists. Why not the people of Hyderabad go to the Nizam's Palace and ask him to vacate it as they have no place to take shelter. I appeal to the people to bestir themselves and fight for their rights, or else they will be engulfed by the capitalist flood. In every such struggle of the people, the Socialist Party will always side with the toilers against the exploiters.

249. Address to Students, Nagpur, 16 December 1949[1]

Both small and great problems are there before the country. Among the great problems one is the growing discontent among the working people. The feeling of frustration is spreading and it will ruin the country. If it continues, India will go the China way. The Kuomintang had to meet with its doom because of corruption and nepotism in its ranks. Fortunately that stage has not yet been reached in India, but considering the present set-up of the administration, the future looks gloomy.

When freedom came to India the people thought they would be happy and content. But gradually that feeling has undergone a change. There is

[1]Adapted from *Janata*, 25 December 1949.

frustration and discontent all-round. The same old machinery of the British raj continues. There are a handful in India, who are working honestly for the country, but the highly paid officers of the Government are lazy and incompetent. With great difficulty the working class get their wants and needs fulfilled. What is the use of freedom if the basic salary of a person is Rs. 30 and that of the head of the State is so enormous? But still the Government expects the people drawing that paltry basic salary to produce more. How can the people produce more when they are starved and discontented.

Production alone would not solve all our problems. If India is to be industrialised, it cannot be done by the capitalists in whose hands the wealth of the people is at present concentrated. For more production, the industries of the country must be run by the people. With a long-range and short term production policy and with proper redistribution of wealth, the country's outlook can be changed.

If the industry of the country is in the hands of the capitalists, there will be unemployment. Even in the United States there is unemployment because there is inequality in the distribution of wealth.

If this state of affairs continues, the working class will one day rise and seize power and wealth from the hands of the capitalists.

250. Statement at a Press Conference, Hyderabad, 23 December 1949[1]

After the great struggle of the people of this State against the Nizam's tyranny and Razakar atrocities, and after the intervention of the Government of India, the least that the people expected was that the Nizam would be deposed, and that steps would be taken to destroy the feudal system root and branch and then to carry through a quick and drastic agrarian reform.

The Government of India's administration has resulted in deep and widespread disillusionment. I am afraid that the policies the Government seem to be contemplating for this State have added further to the people's disillusionment and discontent.

It is a denial of democracy to impose a government over the people of Hyderabad. Nobody can be sure when the first general election will be held in the country. In view of this uncertainty, it is unjust to prevent the people of the State from forming a popular government of their own by continuing a nominated Ministry.

If elections to the State Constituent Assembly are going to be held in March as announced, that Assembly should not be dissolved after deciding

[1]Adapted from *Hindustan Times*, 25 December 1949.

the issue of accession, but should be turned into a Legislative Assembly of the State and power should be handed over to those who command a majority therein.

251. To Rafi Ahmed Kidwai, 4 January 1950[1]

My dear Rafi Saheb,

I am informed by my General Secretary and other colleagues in the All India Postal Union that you have finally expressed your inability to do anything regarding your promise about the strike period pay. It also appears that the Prime Minister has not accepted the demand which was supported by you regarding the deductions made from the additional ten rupees dearness allowance. I also understand that the recommendations of the Expert Committee have all been thrown overboard wherever they involve any additional expenditure. All this has created a very difficult situation and I am sure that the workers would be for a general strike. I should however like to save the workers and the public from trouble and suffering if possible. For me there is not only a matter of industrial dispute involved but also a moral issue. It would be impossible for representatives of labour to deal with Government if the latter showed such scant respect for the pledges given by its own Ministers. I have no complaint to make about you in this regard because I do freely admit that you have been considerate and fair all along, and I am sure you are even now anxious to carry out the promises you had made to me. And, if I may say so, I wonder how you find it possible to continue in office when you are not allowed to carry out your own pledges. Be that as it may, I have decided to go on a fast from the 5th of February to compel Government to kept its word. In this connection I have written a letter to Panditji, of which I am enclosing a copy.[2] My fast, of course, will be only on the issue of carrying out the promises made and I cannot tell what my Union would decide regarding the enforcement of the other demands.

I hope you are well.

With kind regards,

Sincerely yours,
Jayaprakash Narayan

[1] *J.P. Papers* (NMML).
[2] Could not be found.

252. To Gopalaswami Ayyangar, 8 January 1950[1]

Dear Shri Ayyangar,

You are probably aware that the Co-ordinating Committee of the Rajasthan Railway Workers' Union met in Jaipur recently and authorized the Bikaner State Railway Employees' Union and the Jaipur State Railwaymen's Union to serve strike notices on their Administrations. The strike is to begin from the midnight of January 24, 1950. If this strike comes about, I am afraid it will not be confined only to the Bikaner and the Jaipur Railways but will involve the other railways in Rajasthan also.

The demands of the Bikaner and Jaipur Railway workers are simple and reasonable and should have been conceded without delay. The workers are asking for nothing more than the application of the C.P.C. scales to their railways, particularly in regard to basic scales of pay, dearness allowance and house rent allowance. It is difficult to understand why these demands have not been conceded up-till now. As far as my information goes the employees of the Hyderabad and Jodhpur Railways have already been granted these scales. Moreover, to allow the employees on a section of the Rajasthan Railway Administration, namely the Jodhpur Railway, a distinct advantage and to deny the same to the employees on other sections appears to be unjust and cannot but be detrimental to the smooth working of the Rajasthan Railways.

The refusal to grant the demands of the Bikaner and Jaipur Railway employees for the C.P.C. scales appears further to be unreasonable in the light of the Krishnamachari Report, according to which all the "State" railways will be integrated with the Government Railways from 1st April 1950. If from the 1st of April 1950 the employees concerned would automatically be entitled to the C.P.C. scales, why should not justice be meted out to them now? I understand that the Rajasthan Government's refusal to accept these demands is due to instructions from the States Ministry to freeze all expenditure until integration has taken place. If this is so, it is unfortunate that the question of expense should arise in connection with the wages of poor employees.

There is another important aspect of this matter. When integration takes place, the Railway Ministry would find itself faced with complex problems arising out of multiplicity of scales in the same administration. The employees too would be at a serious disadvantage with respect to pay and seniority, both amongst themselves and in relation to the employees of the Government of India Railways. This disadvantage would seriously affect their seniority and promotion, crippling their prospects for the entire period

[1] *J.P. Papers* (NMML).

of their service. This important aspect of the matter should also receive earnest consideration.

I request you to intervene in this matter so that a serious crisis my be avoided. I need not add that these demands and any action taken to secure them have the entire support of the Federation.

Please reply at the above address.

With kind regards,

Sincerely yours,
Jayaprakash Narayan

253. To Pattom Thanu Pillai, 9 January 1950[1]

9 January 1950

Dear Shri Pillai,

I should have written to you earlier but I hope the telegram that I have sent you today would be adequate. The telegram reads as under:

> Herewith confirming our Bombay talks. Welcome you and your friends in the Party. Please apply individually for admission to membership immediately, When state assembly opens please announce decision to join party.

I am also sending a telegram to Wilson[2] as follows:

> Sorry you could not come. Discussed Pattom Thanu Pillai's entry into Party with friends and the objection raised by some Travancore comrades. Having considered all aspects have decided welcome these friends who will all apply individually for membership. On opening day State Assembly Thanu Pillai will announce his decision to join party with his friends. Letter follows.

You know that when you left I had sent out wires to friends in Travancore to come up to Bombay to discuss this matter. But except for Prabhakaran[3] no one else turned up. So I am afraid there might be some local opposition at the initial stage but I have no doubt that Dr. Menon[4] would be able to explain the position and remove the objections that might be raised.

I hope that soon after my wire all of you would have applied for membership and that on the opening of the State Assembly you would have announced that you have joined the Socialist Party.

I shall be happy to hear from you as soon as possible.

Sincerely yours,

Shri Pattom Thanu Pillai,
Trivandurm.

[1] *J.P. Papers* (NMML).
[2] P.P. Wilson, Secretary of the Socialist Party in Kerala.
[3] Prabhakaran, one of the leaders of the Socialist Party in Kerala.
[4] K.B. Menon.

254. To P.P. Wilson, 9 January 1950[1]

9 January 1950

Dear Com. Wilson,

I have sent you today the following telegram:

Sorry you could not come. Discussed Pattom Thanupillai's entry into party with friends and the objection raised by some Travancore comrades. Having considered all aspects have decided welcome these friends who will all apply individually for membership. On opening day state assembly Thanu Pillai will announce his decision to join party with his friends. Letter follows.

I was really sorry that you could not come to the Secretaries' meeting and later even in response to my telegram. I wish you had come. It is good to meet comrades from other provinces and to take part in discussions. I am afraid comrades from the South are inclined to keep themselves away from what is happening in the Party elsewhere.

The most important question that we wanted to discuss with you here was the admission of Shri Thanu Pillai and his group into the Party. Technically, according to the Party constitution, no one can prevent anyone from coming into the Party except on the ground that the person belongs to a communal organisation or to a political party whose aims and objects are opposed to those of our Party. As such if Shri Thanu Pillai and his friends had applied for membership in the normal course they would have had to be admitted. But it is natural that when persons of position wish to join the Party they should discuss their acceptability and utility to the Party in all their bearings. We went into the whole question here in Bombay at two sittings at which com. Asoka Mehta and Prem Bhasin were present and at the last of which Dr. Menon was also present. At these talks we also went into all the various objections that have been made against Shri Pillai and his group by various comrades from Travancore. We considered carefully the explanation offered by Shri Pillai and felt satisfied that in the circumstances his joining the Party along with his friends would be an accession of strength to us. Already in certain parts of the country there are too many leftist groups and it would have added to the confusion if in Kerala a new party had been allowed to be formed. That would surely have been the result if we had not welcomed Pillai and his friends.

As to what these new friends may do and how they may function within the Party depends not only on them but also on how you and the other comrades in the Travancore-Cochin Party react towards them. If there is any vitality in the Party in your province these new friends could easily be assimilated and made to serve the best interests of the Party and the socialist

[1] P.P. Wilson, Secretary of the Socialist Party in Kerala.

movement. If there be anyone among them whose activities might harm the Party, you would always be free to take action against him as against any other member of the Party and I am sure shri Thanu Pillai would wholeheartedly support such action. I hope therefore that this decision to welcome these new friends to the Party will be worked out by you and the Travancore-Cochin Party in the right spirit.

Shri Thanu Pillai and his friends will apply for membership individually and on the day on which the State Assembly opens, i.e., on the 12th of this month, he will announce in the Assembly his decision to join the Socialist Party with his friends. The question whether these friends will be asked to resign from the Provincial Assembly can only be decided by the National Executive, but I am sure that the decision would be against their resignation. In that case these friends would function in the Assembly as the parliamentary wing of the Travancore-Cochin Party.

I would like to hear from you regarding the steps taken in this matter as soon as possible.

Sincerely yours,
J.P.

255. To Ramnandan Mishra, 9 January 1950[1]

My dear Ramnandan Babu,[2]

I have both your letters. I would be very happy to help you to the best of my ability in running the Hind Kisan Panchayat[3] but you know the incessant demands that are made upon me and I am afraid I shall find it very difficult to take on extra burdens. Just now the finances of the Central Party are rather low and I am not in a position to hold out much hope. I shall, however, do my best to try to find out as large a part of the [Rs.] 5000 that you want as possible.

Regarding the Kisan Committee expenses of the last year it is not enough to say that 400 rupees per month was sanctioned and nothing was paid and so 4800 are due and should be sent to you. Against expenses already incurred we can make payments only on receiving the actual accounts of the expenditure. If nothing was actually spent, nothing can and should be paid. In any case, if I succeed in raising the amount I wanted during this visit to Bombay, I shall send you Rs. 1000 before I leave. In the course of the next one or two months I shall try to send you the rest of the amount from time to time. But it would not be possible to send all the 5000 at once.

[1] *J.P. Papers* (NMML).

[2] For biographical note on Ramnandan Mishra see *JPSW*, Vol. II, p. 186.

[3] Hind Kisan Panchayat (All India Kisan Sabha). For note see *JPSW*, Vol. IV, p. 231.

You will have noticed that the dates and venue of the Executive have been changed according to your suggestion. I hope you will ask the Vindhya Pradesh comrades to make all the necessary arrangements. I wonder by the way if the present disturbances will affect the conference arrangements. News has been received today of Rammanohar's arrest.

I hope you are well.

Affectionately yours,
Jayaprakash

256. Statement on the Arrest of Rammanohar Lohia, Bombay, 10 January 1950[1]

The curtain over Vindhya Pradesh has not yet been lifted. How grave the situation must be and how stark mad the administration must have gone are evident from the arrest of Dr. Lohia.

The Congress Government without consulting the people of Vindhya Pradesh decided to split the Union and merge the parts in the provinces of U.P. and C.P. The people disapproved of this decision and agitated and demonstrated against it.

They have every right to do so in a democracy. But the officers of the Central Government administering the Union met the people with bullets and lathis and a reign of terror reminiscent of the days of imperialism.

It has been alleged that the repression was occasioned by the violence indulged in by the people. This too, like the firing, lathi charge and curfew, has a familiar ring. In any case, Dr. Lohia left Bombay for Rewa for the very purpose of enquiring into the reported incidents. He was promptly put under arrest and taken to an unknown destination.

Dr. Lohia's arrest fills one with anger and bitterness and there is no doubt that millions of people if and when they hear of it will share these feelings. Outside India, too, this arrest will be taken as an eloquent commentary on our much vaunted democracy.

The arrest of Dr. Lohia and the events of Vindhya Pradesh are a serious warning to the people of this country. It is time that the power-drunk and power-hungry rulers of this country are made to realise that they derive their power from the people and that the freedom and the rights of the people cannot be trampled upon.

It is instances such as the Vindhya terror that bring to the surface the evil forces that are at work at the very base of our national life. The inclination to brush aside such instances as partisan propaganda or stunt-making will

[1] Adapted from *Janata*, 15 January 1950. Published also in *Tribune* dated 10 January 1950.

cost us heavily. So let us take the warning while there is time.

The precipitate action against Dr. Lohia who went to Rewa for the very purpose of inquiring into the reported incidents there, fills one with anger and bitterness. The release of Dr. Lohia outside Vindhya Pradesh does not necessarily mean that he is free to enter Rewa.

It clearly shows that the administrators in Vindhya Pradesh have been guilty of heinous act, which they are trying to hide from the world.

The least that must be done is to order an impartial non-official or high-level judicial inquiry into the recent happenings in Vindhya Pradesh and to remove the officers concerned from the scene of terror. I hope that there is enough vitality in the people of this country to force the Government to carry out these urgent measures.

257. Reasons for the Proposed Fast from 5 February 1950, Bombay, 13 January 1950[1]

Mr. Rafi Ahmed Kidwai, Union Minister of Communications, had given me an assurance in March 1949 that after three months he would do what was possible to settle the demand for payment for the period of the strike of 1946. He had further told me that he would have a formula worked out to make this payment not in the shape of payment for a strike period but as payment against leave due or special leave.

The Government of India announced in January last a flat increment of Rs.10 per month as the minimum dearness allowance. As it happened, certain categories of postmen and lower grade staff in the P. and T. Department had been given an extra interim dearness allowance sometime earlier. In these cases, the sum already sanctioned as interim allowance was deducted from the additional ten rupees that the Government granted in January. My union protested vigorously against this cut and Mr. Rafi Ahmed Kidwai was good enough to assure us that there would be no deduction made from the additional dearness allowance of Rs. 10, granted by the January announcement.

It is ten months now that these assurances were given, but they yet remain to be implemented. At no time during the last ten months did Mr. Rafi Ahmed Kidwai disown his word, as of course as an honourable man he could not do. It seems, however, that the Ministry of Finance and the Cabinet have over-ruled him. This puts labour and its representatives in an awkward position, and it seems to me that the Government, too, can't be in an enviable position when its assurances and pledges carry no weight. When I met

[1]Adapted from *Hindu*, 13 January 1950.

Mr. Nehru last with Mr. Rafi Ahmed Kidwai, I tried to impress upon him that whatever the financial difficulties, the Government was honour bound to carry out the assurances given by one of its Ministers to labour.

After a Minister of Cabinet rank has made definite promises to labour, on the basis of which labour makes a responsive gesture, it is meaningless for the Government or any other Ministry to go into the right or wrong of the question concerned. Internally, the Cabinet may say what it likes to the Minister concerned but this promise must be carried out. As a matter of fact, I cannot see how Mr. Rafi Ahmed Kidwai can permit himself to continue in his present position when he is unable to carry out his word himself.

The other demands which were the subject matter of negotiations between us and the Ministry of Communications have also not been satisfactorily disposed of. With reference to the Expert Committee's report on the working of the P. and T. Department in relation to the staff, when the representatives of the Union met the honourable Minister and his colleagues they were told that there was no purpose in discussing the matter because no recommendation of the Expert Committee which involved the expenditure even of a single additional pie could be implemented. This had given to the employees a very rude shock indeed.

I am not in favour of using the method of fasting to solve industrial disputes. We are dealing here not with an industrial dispute but a moral issue.

No less a person than a Cabinet Minister gave me certain assurances and I find that these assurances are not being carried out. It is wrong of any Government to act in this manner, but it is much more so for a Congress Government because the Congress had in the past years laid so much stress on Truth. I, therefore, find that the only course open to me is to undertake a fast till the Government agrees to carry out the promises made by a member of the Cabinet.

I express my opposition to a general strike which was the other course open before us, as I do not desire to put the public to serious inconvenience or to make them suffer the privations and difficulties of a strike.

258. To Reyasat Karim, 21 January 1950[1]

My dear Reyasat Saheb,[2]

I have your letter,[3] It is perfectly alright about the house that you have bought. When I come to Patna I shall do the needful about it.

[1] *Brahmanand Papers* (NMML).

[2] For biographical note on Reyasat Karim see *JPSW*, Vol. IV, p. 222.

[3] Not available.

News from Jumhri Talaiya has been very disquieting, but I wish there were fuller reports. I have received a report from Hitnarayanji, but it does not go beyond what the Special Number of *Janata* contained. I was informed quite some days ago that Basawan Babu had gone to enquire into the matter, but there has been no report from him. I am writing to Shri Babu and Panditji also. If there is time when I am in Delhi on the 27th, I shall talk over the matter with the people there.

The news from Jharia is still more disquieting, but in a different sense. It appears that a meeting of workers arranged by Alakh Narayan Jha,[4] Tripathi[5] and others backed by B.P. Sinha,[6] passed a motion of no-confidence in Munshiji[7] and Pinakin[8] and Indu Patel.[9] I have received a report from Pinakin regarding this matter and also a letter from Munshiji which I have not been able to read yet because it is in Urdu. You will remember that at Kodarma I discussed with you the Jharia situation and you too agreed that Munshiji should be given overall powers to deal with it as he thought fit. But the vested interests there seem to have proved too strong for him. The vote of no-confidence becomes much more serious when one takes into account the fact that the arrangement concerning Munshiji was made by me in consultation with you. It is therefore a vote against me and the Bihar Party too. Secondly, this practice of motions of no-confidence should never be encouraged within the Party. If any member or group of members has any complaints to make against any other member of the Party, who may be holding office, the complaint should be made to the higher committee of the Party. You will have to deal strongly with this matter. Will you write to B.P. Sinha, and Alakh Narayan Jha to explain? I believe you are calling a meeting of the Provincial Executive on the 30th or 31st of Jan. and I should like you to put this matter also on the agenda. I am also writing to B.P. Sinha.

I will be reaching Patna on the 28th of this month.

Yours Sincerely,
Jayaprakash Narayan

[4] Alakh Narayan Jha, Secretary, Workers Union, Lodna (Jharia).

[5] For biographical note on V.D. Tripathi see *JPSW*, Vol. IV, p. 222.

[6] For biographical note on B.P. Sinha see *JPSW*, Vol. I, p. 161.

[7] Munshi Ahmaddin, President, Koyala Mazdoor Panchayat, Jharia.

[8] Pinakin Patel, General Secretary, Koyala Mazdoor Panchayat (Jharia) and member Executive, Socialist Party, Bombay.

[9] Indu Patel, prominent Socialist worker and Trade Union leader.

259. Message to the *Indian Opinion* for the Independence Day [before 26 January 1950][1]

I am thankful to the Editor of the *INDIAN OPINION* for giving me this opportunity of sending a message of greetings to our long suffering brethren in South Africa on such an auspicious occasion as Independence Day on which our country is to be declared a Republic. This, no doubt, is a day of rejoicing for Indians all the world over. But for me the rejoicing is more than coloured with sorrow and pain. On this day we are trying to give birth to a monstrosity, i.e., a republic which is a member of a family of nations over which presides a King—a King withal under whose rule and the rule of whose forebears we struggled and suffered for our freedom. Having won our freedom we are going on this freedom day to accept that very King, or Crown, as the symbol of the unity of this family. And look at this family itself. There are members of this "united" family who are not prepared to treat other members even as fellow human beings.

To you members of the Indian community in South Africa this Republic Day must bring mixed feelings. Among so many uncertainties that lie in the womb of the future, one thing is an absolute certainty. The Republic of India must march far ahead before it can give dignity and security to its nationals in every land, and lay low the monster of racial arrogance and tyranny which stalks half the world today. I have faith that soon a new India will arise which will be a hope for all the downtrodden and disowned of the earth. On this Republic Day I hail that India of the future and offer her my homage and salutation.

[1] *J.P. Papers* (NMML).

260. To Nalini Ranjan Sarkar, 30 January 1950[1]

Dear Nalinibabu,[2]

You will recall the talk and the correspondence I had with you in connection with the cooperative movement in Calcutta. We have formed a central cooperative society and some two months ago I wrote to you in connection with the registration of the society. I understand from my friends in Calcutta that the society has not yet been registered. I am sure the usual red-tape is the cause of delay. It is a pity, however, that such essential constructive work should be held up in this manner. You had promised your full support

[1] *J.P. Papers* (NMML).

[2] Nalini Ranjan Sarkar, then Finance Minister in the Government of West Bengal.

in this kind of activity. Therefore I am giving you this trouble again. I hope you will be good enough to look into this matter and issue the necessary instructions.

I hope you are well and with kind regards,

Sincerely yours,
J.P.

261. To Satyabrata Sen, 30 January 1950[1]

Dear Satu,[2]

I had your letter in Bombay. I quite realise your difficulties. You certainly have done your test and the failure is not yours but ours. I too feel completely helpless in the absence of cooperation from anywhere and agree with you that the institution should be closed down. I will be in Lucknow on the 1st of February and if Acharyaji is there I will talk to him about it. Lohia also, I hope, will be there.

I am sorry that an institution[3] of such importance has to be wound up, but there seems to be no other alternative. In any case before we take the final decision, a meeting of the Council of Governors must be convened. Indeed it is only the Council that can take the final decision. I should like to discuss with you the whole matter. Could you see me here on the 4th of February?

I hope you are well,

Sincerely yours,
J.P.

[1]*J.P. Papers* (NMML).
[2]Satyabrata Sen, Secretary, Khoj Parishad, Calcutta.
[3]Khoj Parishad.

262. To Jawaharlal Nehru, 31 January 1950[1]

Dear Bhai,

I am sorry to encroach upon your busy and valuable time, but I could not reject the request of a person who has been languishing in prison for ten long years. This lady is the wife of Pandit Tunk Prasad Acharya[2] of Nepal, who is in the Khatmandu prison for the last ten years for a political offence.

[1]*J.P. Papers* (NMML).
[2]Tunk Prasad Acharya, eminent fighter against Rana rule in Nepal.

Tunk Prasad has written a letter for you which his wife is going to deliver to you personally.

I had heard of Tunk Prasad before and I know that he is an honest and brave fighter. In a long letter that he has written to me, he has expressed his views regarding the struggle for freedom in Nepal and the role of the Indian people and Government in it. I was particularly impressed by the fact that he has said not a word about himself or asked me to persuade you to intercede in his behalf and secure his release. His courage, detachment and devotion to the cause of the Nepalese people are beyond question.

I understand that the Prime Minister of Nepal is shortly visiting Delhi and that the Government of India is to settle with him the question of Indo-Nepalese relations. I thought that at this moment it would be useful if you heard a genuine voice from Nepal so that your decisions could be tempered by it.

In addition to Tunk Prasad there are four other political prisoners in Nepal who are serving life terms which, in Nepal, means literally imprisonment for life. One of them, Khadag Prasad,[3] has been in prison already for twenty years. It appears that it will only be his dead body that will be able to leave prison. There are of course about a hundred other political prisoners in that kingdom.

I do not know if the Indian Ambassador in Nepal has kept you informed of the situation there. If he has and if he himself is at all in touch with what is happening there, you must be aware by now that among the conscious public of Nepal, particularly of Khatmandu, which holds the key to the entire politics of the State, a large number has turned communist. Communism or socialism in the context of Nepal has little relation with the body of principles that these terms represent. To say that the people of Nepal have turned or are turning communist merely means that (a) they have become anti-Indian and (b) they are turning their eyes towards China and Tibet for their deliverance. After the 15th of August 1947, great hopes had arisen in the bosom of the Nepalese people that the Government of free India would come to their rescue. But all that the Indian Government has done so far has not only succeeded in destroying these hopes, but even in persuading the people that the Government of India is really behind the Ranas. Whenever the leaders of the Nepalese have met the Indian ministers, Central or Provincial, they have been given sweet assurances, but except in the matter of Koirala's release, there was very little done to give effect to these promises. In the small matter of the imprisonment of some Nepalese workers by the Bihar Government, even though both the Provincial and Central Governments were moved, nothing so far has been done. Some of the people in jail are prominent nationalist workers and their continued

[3] Khadag Prasad, a colleague of Tunk Prasad.

detention is causing grave injury not only to the cause of Nepalese freedom, but also to that of Indo-Nepalese relations.

The essence of the situation in Nepal today unquestionably is that the people there have lost faith in the Government of India, have largely turned against it and are eagerly looking to China for help. I have not the least doubt that the Chinese Communist Government is not moved by the same scruples as your Government and in the Communist Party of Nepal they have a ready-made fifth column; and undoubtedly they will supply it with the necessary tools. I have no objection to Nepal becoming Communist, but I would have preferred it to go that way as a result of help and cooperation from India and the Indian Government. Communism and socialism in Nepalese conditions have hardly any distinction; the only distinction being in the field of international loyalty. I have no doubt that even the socialist movement in Nepal cannot but follow the same pattern of revolution as the communist, but whereas Communist Nepal would be violently anti-Indian and pro-China, a Socialist Nepal might be friendly both to India and China.

I believe there is still time for your Government to save the situation. This to my mind can be done in two ways: (a) by exerting political and economic pressure on the Rana Government by the Government of India (in both these matters we undoubtedly have a whip hand); and (b) by rendering all possible help to those of Nepal who are fighting for their freedom. I am sure, the Chinese Communist Government would be willing even to supply arms to their friends in Nepal. I wonder if the Government of India has equal courage to do so. I am sure there are all sorts of difficulties, as in everything else; but we will hardly achieve anything if we were merely to tackle problems which offered no difficulty.

If the visit of Mrs. Tunk Prasad and the letter of her husband could induce you to think afresh on your Nepalese policy, this poor lady's journey from Khatmandu to Delhi would have produced a considerable result indeed. The lady herself would not be able to speak to you much because she hardly talks our language or hardly understand much of politics.

I am sending Mrs. Tunk Prasad with a young socialist worker of Bihar who is going merely to escort her and put her in touch with you. He has nothing to do with the Nepalese question.

With regards,

Affectionately yours,
J.P.

263. To M.O. Mathai, 31 January 1950[1]

Dear Mr. Mathai,[2]

I am sorry to give you a little trouble again. This lady who is going with my letter is the wife of Shri. Tunk Prasad, Nepalee Nationalist leader who has been in prison at Kathmandu for the last ten years. Shri Tunk Prasad has written a letter for Panditji which Mrs. Tunk Prasad is going to deliver to him personally. I too have written a letter for Panditji in this connection which the lady is taking with her. I shall be obliged if you kindly arrange for Panditji to give her a little time. The lady herself has not much to say to Panditji, but I do consider it useful for Panditji to see her.

I hope you are well. When I went to see Panditji last, you were unfortunately laid up in bed. I hope you have fully recovered by now.

Yours sincerely,
J.P.

[1]*J.P. Papers* (NMML).

[2]M.O. Mathai, Nehru's Special Assistant, resigned in 1959 on account of certain allegations by Communists. Publications include *Reminiscences of the Nehru Age,* Vikas, 1978 and *My Days with Nehru*, Vikas, 1979.

264. Speech at a Public Meeting, Lucknow, 2 February 1950[1]

The Congress has utterly failed to fulfil the hopes and expectations of the people and the only alternative before the country is Socialism. The Socialist programme alone can liquidate the abject poverty of the people and solve the urgent problems of increased agricultural and industrial production and equitable distribution of wealth.

I demand a categorical assurance and convincing proof from the Congress Government that they are really serious about establishing kisan-mazdoor raj in the country as they have promised time and again.

I urge the people to rally round the banner of the Socialist Party which does not hanker after office but aims only at the good of the country. The deplorable conditions under which people are living in this country, calls for a strong opposition to the Congress which is provided by the Socialist Party in the interest of peace, progress and economic prosperity of the country.

The outcome of the next general elections would finally determine the

[1]Adapted from *National Herald*, 2 February 1950.

shape of things to come and decide the fate of the country for all times.

There are four enemies of the country: maharajas, zamindars, capitalists and the high-salaried bureaucracy—who have bled the people white. The Congress leadership has been giving them every encouragement, preserving and even enhancing their status in some cases and giving them a long lease of life at the expense of the poor. Even the Prime Minister, Pandit Jawaharlal Nehru, has accepted the Congress position in regard to these four classes of people. The rajpramukhs of the various unions of states would retain their status and receive unduly large privy purses for years to come. Sardar Patel was given the sole credit for the unification of the country but the truth is that it was the states people's agitation which made it possible.

As for zamindari abolition and the establishment of a Kisan raj I challenge the Government to confer on the kisan proprietary rights over his holding after realising from him ten times his annual rent. More than 40 per cent of the peasantry is landless and would continue to be so under the scheme of zamindari abolition. The entire scheme, as envisaged in the bill, is doomed to failure and would never succeed in bringing happiness and contentment to the kisans. When even the law had not been enacted in the past three years how is one to believe that zamindari would be abolished before long as claimed by the Congress Government.

Our new Constitution has become a serious obstacle to the nationalisation of industry and the liquidation of landlordism. Nationalisation of industry is indispensable for the setting up of mazdoor raj because all profits accruing from industry must go into the state exchequer in order to help implement development schemes and projects. The Constitution lays down that for the next ten years there shall be no nationalisation of industries, except the state-managed atomic industry. Even the distant future looks obscure and dim as it is hitherto undefined.

The bureaucratic machinery of the Government i.e. the I.C.S. cadre, has been responsible for the mal-administration of the country, but it continues to be maintained at a huge cost. I deplore the disparity in the salaries of high officials and those of other Government employees and demand fixation of a minimum salary of Rs.100 for the humblest employee and a maximum of Rs. 1,000 for the highest paid official.

The Congress has been giving a call for increased production. I ask what success has been achieved in the much boasted drive for it during the past three years. The Congress is merely playing for time, being unable to satisfy the aspriations, needs and expectations of the people. The problems of poverty and unemployment exist in the United States also in a stark form in spite of the highest agricultural and industrial production and wealth in that country. The only way to remove poverty is to make the worker owner of the goods he produces by his toil. Likewise, the tiller of the soil must also be the owner of his land.

Black-marketing, profiteering, and rising prices can be checked if the Government encourages the setting up of consumers' cooperative stores by subsiding them and affording them all possible facilities. The problem of poverty can not be solved with the disappearance of the black-marketeer or the profiteer alone, but would require recourse to several hard measures. Mere paper plans and airy talks and promises would not do the trick.

Regarding the causes of the poverty of the masses, I would like to point out that India's social structure is mainly responsible for it, since it allows the capitalist to grab and swallow the fruits of production. Production of wealth and profit-making are entirely different things and cannot be put together in one category. Without labour and toil there can be no wealth. I advocate a radical change in the present defective social structure so that the worker may be enabled to enjoy the fruits of his labour.

265. Presidential Address at the General Council of the All India Railwaymen's Federation, Lucknow, 2 February 1950[1]

Friends,

We are meeting after a year. We met last February at Dinapore where we decided to postpone the general strike in view of the assurance given by the Railway Minister, Shri Iyengar. The whole atmosphere has been one of hopes and expectations and prolonged negotiations. The result of these negotiations will be placed before you by our Secretary and it will be for you to decide whether you find it satisfactory and what your next step should be. The main part of our negotiations has been carried through the machinery of Joint Advisory Committee which was constituted in last May in fulfilment of the assurances given before we met last year. The work of the Joint Advisory Committee has not yet concluded and a great deal remains yet to be done. If you examine carefully the Secretary's review of what has been achieved since last February, you will agree with me that the results are not inconsiderable. We have gained on many points and many categories of staff, including the ministerial staff, have made considerable progress. Some of the decisions, however, of the past year have fallen far short of our demands and expectations. It is a matter of deep regret that the Railway Ministry rejected the unanimous recommendation of the Labour Representatives on the Joint Advisory Committee with regard to pre-1931 staff. I should like to make it clear that we stand by the unanimous recommendations of our representatives and reject the decision of the Ministry.

[1]*Tribune*, 29 August 1949.

We had hoped that when we meet in the General Council today we would have before us the decision of the Government at least on all the important outstanding issues. But in the first place we have noted that the Joint Advisory Committee functions inexcusably slowly and, secondly, even the recommendations of the Committee are not quickly enough acted upon by the Government. When we had met Mr. Iyengar and his colleagues last November, they had assured us that every effort would be made to pass final orders on the Committee's recommendations as expeditiously as possible. But the progress made in this respect since last November has been unsatisfactory in the extreme and I cannot but express my deep resentment at this unconscionable delay. Scores of issues have been discussed and decided upon by the Joint Advisory Committee and it is unfair for the Railway Ministry to hold up final decision so long. I fear you may have to do something drastic to impress upon the Railway Board and the Ministry the urgency of the situation and the need to act with despatch and expedition.

I would also like to say a word about the functioning of the Joint Advisory Committee. While I do appreciate the good work done by the Committee, I cannot but express my dissatisfaction with the pace at which the Committee functions. I think that the practice of working intermitently should be given up and henceforth the Committee should sit from day to day without any break till its work is completed. It would further be advisable for the Committee to fix a date before which it should conclude its sittings and I think it would be unfair to prolong its work beyond March 31, 1950.

You may have seen a report in the papers that another all India organization of railwaymen has been recognized by the Government. I found it difficult to believe the report when I read it, but subsequent enquiry shows that it was not unfounded.

At our last meeting with the Railway Minister we had raised the question of the recognition of rival labour organizations and we were told that the whole question was under consideration in connection with the comprehensive labour legislation that was being drafted by the Labour Department. We had hoped therefore that till the new act was passed the *status quo* would continue. I was therefore surprised that recognition was given to this new organization which has been set up with no other purpose than to disrupt the unity of railwaymen and to make them tools in the hands of the ruling party. The All India Railwaymen's Federation has for the last 25 years been the sole representative of railwaymen in this country and it is the greatest disservice to them to try to weaken it.

It is always possible for a few interested people to set up a labour union and if recognition were given by Government or the employer to every such splinter organization, it would spell the end of the labour movement.

It is necessary therefore to lay down definite conditions for the recognition of the unions and to deal with only the most representative one. There could be no doubt that in the field of railway labour, the All India Railwaymen's Federation has been and is the most representative organization and it was to my mind the clear duty of the Government which in this case is the sole employer to countenance no other rival body till it was proved through some democratic process that the new body was more representative than the old one. I therefore cannot but condemn this act of the Railway Ministry of giving recognition to the new organization. The Ministry should have at least waited till the new Labour Relations Act had come into existence. However, I hope that the railwaymen throughout the country will take up this challenge and prove decisively that it is the All India Railwaymen's Federation that is their sole representative organization. This act of the Government has put you all under a test and I am confident that you will come out of it with flying colours.

I should like to remind you that on the 7th of June next, the Federation will be completing 25 years of its life and I hope all our affiliated unions and railwaymen throughout the country will celebrate the Silver Jubilee of the Federation in a fitting manner and will utilize the occasion to raise higher the status and strength of their great organization.

266. To Rafi Ahmed Kidwai, 3 February 1950[1]

My dear Rafi Saheb,

I thank you for both your letters. I should like to have some further clarification, so I am writing to you again. But I am afraid there will not be enough time for your reply to reach me before the 5th. I shall therefore try to telephone to you from Patna on the 4th night.

First of all let me make it clear once again that I never complained that it was you who was breaking his word. In my letter to Panditji I had said that you had all along stood by whatever promise you had given me. In my public statements also it was not you whom I had blamed, but the Finance Department or the Government as a whole. I hope that this misunderstanding would be cleared up now.

Coming to the points at issue, I am thankful to you and to the Government for agreeing finally to restore the cut that was being made from the extra dearness allowance. In this connection too there is one point which I should like to have cleared up further. When I met you in Delhi on the 27th of January you told me that this restoration of the cut would have retrospective

[1] *J.P. Papers* (NMML).

effect, from the time that the extra dearness allowance was granted. In your letter you have not made this clear. Will you please confirm this point?

Regarding the strike period pay, it was clear to us from the very beginning whatever payment was made, that would not be treated by Government as payment for strike period and we had accepted that position. In my letter to Panditji also I had said that the payment was promised to be made against leave. You told me at Delhi when I met you last year that it was found subsequently that in most cases either the leave had been availed of or had lapsed, and therefore that formula could not be applied. But you told me that you will evolve some other formula to make the payment in the form of bonus or some such things; and you authorized me to assure the postmen and also to announce to the press that a satisfactory formula would be worked out. I found from both your letters that you have not made a definite commitment to that effect. That makes my position difficult and it would help me to reach a decision regarding my fast if you wrote to me repeating the assurance that you gave me at Delhi. In one of your letters you have asked me to suggest a formula, but I am afraid it is not possible for me to do so because I am not acquainted with your rules and regulations. I thought the bonus formula, or for that matter, any other, would be satisfactory, provided the men who were on strike received payment for the days on which they were on strike. I hope I shall be able to talk to you tomorrow night and clear up this matter and that I shall have your letter too at the earliest possible moment.

With kind regards,

Sincerely yours,
Jayaprakash

267. Announcement Postponing Fast, Patna, 5 February 1950[1]

I had announced in Bombay last month that I would go on a fast for an indefinite period from February 5 unless the Government of India redressed the grievances of the postal employees.

Since I wrote to the Government of India a month ago that I would be compelled to undertake an indefinite fast, I met the Communications Minister, Mr. Rafi Ahmed Kidwai, twice and there has been correspondence. There were two points on which the Minister had given an assurance in February last. As it has been already announced in an official communique, one of the points regarding the deduction that was being made from the

[1] *Tribune*, 7 February 1950.

dearness allowances has finally been conceded now. Government have ordered that no deductions would be made and that this decision would take effect retrospectively.

On the question of payment for the period of the 1946 strike, the Minister had not yet reached any decision, but had assured me that he was trying his best to find a solution. Some method might be evolved to make the payment, treating the strike period as leave with pay. Otherwise, payment might be made in the form of bonds.

While I do not find this position entirely satisfactory, I am convinced that a genuine attempt is being made to carry out the assurances that were given. Indeed half the assurances have already been carried out. I, therefore, feel it would be wrong on my part to launch upon the contemplated fast to-day and it seems but fair to give Mr. Kidwai time to work out his solution. I am, therefore, postponing my fast for the time being.

268. To S. Vaidyanath Aiyar, 6 February 1950[1]

Dear Mr. Aiyer,[2]

I am sorry that I have to admit failure in the English daily undertaking. All the friends who had promised to help have failed to carry out their promise. In this circumstance, I am afraid, we must give up the entire scheme. When I had discussed this matter with you in Bombay last, you had suggested that we might have another company registered so that if we failed to get the first one going, we might start the other one. But I think it is unnecessary now for you to go through all that trouble. Please carry out all the necessary legal processes to wind up the Janata Publications limited. Please also let me know the total expense that you have incurred from the beginning up to the winding up of this company.

You had very kindly undertaken to meet the monthly requirements of the East Punjab Party for November and December. Will you please continue to bear this burden for another two months, i.e. January and February? If you are agreeable, kindly send a thousand rupees immediately to Tilakraj Chaddha for the month of January.

I shall be here [Sonepur, Bihar] at the Bihar Party's Camp till the 18th and I shall be obliged if you reply to me at this address.

With kind regards to Mrs. Aiyer and you.

Sincerely yours,
Jayaprakash

[1] *J.P. Papers* (NMML).

[2] S. Vaidyanath Aiyer, Chartered Accountant.

269. To Rameshwar Rao, 6 February 1950[1]

My dear Rameshwar Raoji,[2]

I should have written to you earlier, but I regret I could not do so.

As regards the Janata Publications Limited, I am sorry I have to give up the entire scheme. You wanted me to give you more time, but the law requires that by the middle of this month, we should collect at least three lakhs share money and deposit it with the bank. So far not even 3,000 has been deposited. You of course have been doing your best, but several other friends who had promised to collect large sums have completely let me down. I have therefore advised Mr. Aiyer to wind up the company. The job was too big for me to tackle single-handed and it would be folly to persist in it any longer. So will you please return all the moneys that you may have collected to the parties concerned? I am very sorry for having given you all this trouble.

I hope you are well. I shall be at this place [Sonepur, Bihar] till the 18th of this month.

Sincerely yours,
J.P.

[1] *J.P. Papers* (NMML).
[2] Rameshwar Rao, a sympathiser of the Socialist Party based in Hyderabad.

270. To Suresh Desai, 6 February 1950[1]

Dear Suresh,

Your letter regarding your visit to Burma. I think under the circumstances you should not go there.

I should like to discuss with you your future programme. Will you kindly come to this Camp [Sonepur, Bihar] as soon as you find it convenient? I am here till the 18th. I had written to both Sakti and Satu Sen to see me at Patna on the 4th of this month. They neither came nor wrote me any letter. Will you please ask them both to come here and see me as soon as they can? Sonepore is just across the Ganges. The climate is lovely here and the Camp is very nice. Do come as soon as you can and bring them with you. Sibnath also has promised to come. Please remind him and ask him to let us know when he is coming.

By the way when you come here, you will have to deliver some lectures to the students on elementary economics. Please send a wire when you are arriving.

[1] *J.P. Papers* (NMML).

I hope your wife is well now and has fully recovered.
With best wishes,

Yours Sincerely,
J.P.

271. To Purshottam Trikamdas, 11 February 1950[1]

Dear P.T.,

I should have written to you earlier about the Jharia affairs. Things have not improved yet, but we have decided to deal firmly with the matter. The Provincial Executive has asked both Munshiji and Pinakin to continue as President and General Secretary of the Koyala Mazdoor Panchayat. We are again calling the workers from Jharia to Sonepore on the 18th when final decisions will be taken. In the meanwhile both the Panchayat and Pinakin are in serious financial difficulties. I shall try to do something for Pinakin, but I shall be obliged if you too can help in the matter. For the Panchayat, I am afraid, it would be necessary for some one of us to go to Jharia again to raise a little money. Can you go to Jharia some time within a month or so? It is necessary once again to have a talk with the colliery owners on the lines you had once before, so that the relation between the Panchayat and the owners might be regularized. Do write to me in the matter and also to the Provincial Secretary, and to Munshiji and Pinakin direct.

Regarding the finance of the Party, I know that when I left Bombay there was not much in the bank, perhaps not more than fifteen or sixteen thousand. I may be able to send you something from C.P. again where I am going early in March. Till then you will have to carry on with what you have.

When I had left I had asked Madame[2] to tell you to contact Jain. I hope you did this and that it was fruitful. I had also told her to ask you to pay my bills from the Sahakari Prakashan and the Bookland. Shanker[3] had told Parasuram[4] the amount that had to be paid. This money is a loan and I shall pay it back to you.

Regarding the *Janata* you know that it was agreed that till the end of June, Rs.9,000/- will have to be paid by the Party to cover the deficit which was estimated to be Rs. 2,000/- per month for the first three months and

[1] *J.P. Papers* (NMML).

[2] Madame: wife of Purshottam Trikamdas.

[3] Shanker: Socialist worker in Bombay at that time; later Secretary to J.P. for several years.

[4] Parsuram, at that time working in the central office of the Socialist Party in Bombay; worked earlier with Gandhiji.

Rs.1,000/- a month after that. [M.V.R.] Iyer who is the Manager of the *Janata* had asked me to arrange a deposit of Rs.12,000/- including this Rs.9,000/- plus Rs.3,000/- as reserve with the *Janata*. This of course I could not do, but I think you should pay the monthly demands from the Manager in accordance with what we had agreed upon. Otherwise the re-organization plans would be upset. As I said above, I shall try to send you some more money by March.

You are a worse correspondent than me. But I hope you will at least reply to this letter.

Prabha and I send our greetings to both of you. I hope Madame's health is steadily improving.

Affectionately yours,
J.P.

272. To Jawaharlal Nehru, 12 February 1950[1]

Dear Bhai,

I hope you are aware of the recent happenings in Rewa. During the British days whenever the executive authority perpetrated an atrocity, the Congress demanded and rightly, an un-official, impartial or, at the least, high level judicial enquiry. Now under Congress rule every time the executive commits an atrocity no heed is paid to the public demand for a similar enquiry. At the most, the Congress organization sometimes appoints a committee of "reliable" Congressmen to report on such incidents.

Ghastly things were done in Rewa and such eminent publicmen as Lohia and Seth Damodar Swarup[2] visited the affected area and demanded a proper non-official or judicial enquiry; but nothing has so far been done. The attitude of Congressmen seems to be that the Congress Governments can do no wrong. This is a very dangerous mentality which will not only spell the ruin of the country but also destroy the Congress itself.

It had been decided sometime ago before the Rewa incidents occurred that the inaugural conference of the Hind Kisan Panchayat would be held at Rewa on the 26th and 27th of February. In the meanwhile terror was let loose in Rewa and elsewhere in Vindhya Pradesh. Nevertheless the committee of the Hind Kisan Panchayat decided not to make any change in the venue of the conference. It was a commendable decision and every sensible person would support it.

It appears now that the authorities are determined to make it impossible

[1] *J.P. Papers* (NMML).
[2] For biographical note on Seth Damodar Swarup see *JPSW*, Vol. I, p. 85.

for the conference to be held at Rewa. I have just received a wire from Ramnandan Mishra, who is the General Secretary of Hind Kisan Panchayat, and who has gone to Rewa to make preparations for the conference in view of the fact that most of the local socialist and Kisan Panchayat workers are in prison, to the effect that all the petrol, hotel and tent facilities have been denied. Giving of petrol coupons is, of course, directly in the hands of the authorities, and in the Republic of India it is still possible for the latter to frighten people to such an extent that they will shut their doors to the opponents of the Congress and deny them the use of their goods.

The conference of course is at all events going to be held at Rewa even if all of us have to sleep under the naked sky.

My purpose in writing this letter is not to beg you to intervene and see that the facilities denied are given, but merely to inform you so that if you thought a wrong was being done you could rectify it. There is no use my writing to Sardar Patel, to whom everything that we do appears to be creating disturbance. I am referring to his speech during the debate on the President's address. I cannot imagine even a Maxwell[3] outdoing the Sardar's performance.

You may recall that I had spoken to you when I met you last about affairs in Bihar. You told me that if I placed before you any specific matter, you would be prepared to look into it. I am collecting material regarding the firing in Jhumri Talaiya in the district of Hazaribagh and I shall write to you in a few days about it.

With kind regards,

Affectionately yours,
J.P.

[3] For biographical note on R. Maxwell see *JPSW*, Vol. III, p. 150.

273. Statement on the Denial of Facilities to the Socialist Party for Holding the Inaugural Conference of Hind Kisan Panchayat at Rewa, Patna, 12 February 1950[1]

I condemn the action of the Government of Vindhya Pradesh in denying facilities to the Socialist Party to hold the inaugural conference of the Hind Kisan Panchayat at Rewa. I have just received a telegram from Pandit Ramanandan Mishra, who is the General Secretary of the Hind Kisan Panchayat and has gone to Rewa to make arrangements for the conference, as most of the local Socialist and Kisan Panchayat workers are in prison. In his telegram, Pandit Mishra says that all petrol, hotel and tent facilities had

[1] Adapted from *Tribune*, 15 February 1950.

been denied and every other obstruction is being put in the way of the preparations for the conference. Giving of petrol coupons is, of course, directly in the hands of the authorities and in the Republic of India it is still possible for the latter to frigthen people to such an extent that they will shut their doors to the opponents of the Congress and deny them use of their goods.

The conference, of course, is going to be held at Rewa, as decided, even if all the delegates have to spend their days and nights under the open sky. However, it is of vital importance for the future of our country that the people are made aware of the lengths to which a Congress administration is prepared to go to suppress its critics and crush any independent movement. If the people of India are silent, they would find sooner than later that they have forfeited their liberties and that they have been enchained to a new autocracy.

It was hoped that after the inauguration of the Republic and of the democratic sovereign constitution, things would take a new turn. But the words and deeds of the Congress seem to be as different from each other as white from black.

274. Statement regarding Firing in Salem Prison, 13 February 1950[1]

I cannot imagine a more shocking news than that of the recent firing in the Salem Prison in the State of Madras. According to official reports 19 persons were killed and 40 injured. Apparently the prisoners were communists. I am one of those who consider communist methods and the communists themselves as one of the serious dangers to this country; and the communists too have never hesitated to return the compliment and to treat me as their enemy number one. But I cannot allow my views to influence my attitude towards such fundamental issues as human values and civil liberties.

Prisoners, no matter how dangerous they were as free individuals, are the most helpless of creatures and to treat them as wild animals of the jungle and to shoot them down by the dozen is a kind of savagery which cannot but be condemned in the strongest language by all right-minded citizens. It has been reported that the prisoners had armed themselves with glass panes and iron rods, but no matter how armed they were they surely had no guns with them and it should have been the care of the authorities who were armed with superior weapons to use them with the utmost restraint. I cannot imagine any situation in a prison in which it would ever be necessary

[1]*Brahmanand Papers* (NMML).

to kill outright as many as were killed at Salem to control only a group of prisoners.

If the Congress Government at all desire to vindicate their claim to be a civilized government, the least that they must do is to suspend forthwith the officers concerned and to institute a high level judicial enquiry.

275. Statement Condemning America's Decision to Support Chiang Kai-Shek, Patna, 14 February 1950[1]

The peoples of Asia desire and need the friendship of such world powers as America and Russia, but they are awakened enough now to spurn any gesture of domination. America by its obstinacy in supporting Chiang not only at Formosa but also at Lake Success is laying a spark into the staggering powder dump that is the world today.

America's decision to defend Formosa to the last in the interest of Generalissimo Chiang Kai Shek cannot but producc a violcnt reaction against America among the peoples of Asia. There was a civil war raging in China for a number of years and the Communists have at last come out as victorious as any victory can ever be. Chiang not only met with a military defeat at the hands of Mao Tse-Tung[2] but there is no doubt that he was completely disowned by the Chinese people. Whatever may be the view of America about the Chinese Communists, there can be no doubt that the Kuomintang has hardly any friends left among the common people of China.

In these circumstances, the decision of America to bolster up Chiang Kai-Shek and his discredited and corrupt party can have no other meaning to the peoples of Asia except that America is seeking to suppress the democratic voice of the peoples of Asia in order to create its own spheres of influence.

If America followed its professions of democracy and freedom, the only course open to it was to recognize the Government of Mao Tse-Tung and to accept the new shape of things in Asia and as its corollary to replace the representatives of a non-existent Nationalist China on the United Nations with the representatives of the new China. It is a pity that the successors to the great tradition of Roosevelt are acting as the swaggering imperialists of an age that has ended for ever.

[1]Adapted from *Searchlight*, 15 February 1950.

[2] Mao Tse-Tung (1893-1976); Chinese revolutionary and statesman; founder of Chinese Communist State; acted as Librarian of Peking University in 1918, founded Chinese Communist Party in 1921, Mao became Chairman (Chief of State) in 1949. After Stalin's death his influence grew throughout the Communist world.

276. Presidential Address at the Uttar Pradesh Provincial Kisan Conference, Ballia, 20 February 1950[1]

During the struggle for national freedom it was a common place of politics to talk about the urgent need of an agrarian revolution. Now that freedom has been achieved, that talk has been forgotten and the urgency seems to have receded. Perhaps the circumstances in which freedom was achieved, earlier than expected, left the Congress unprepared to effect the social changes, the urge towards which had pitchforked it into power. A further development of the freedom struggle would perhaps have further revolutionized the Congress. But this development was suddenly arrested, with the result that the Congress has been found to be utterly incapable to fulfil the social urges of the masses. The most tragic instance of this incapacity is the failure of the Congress to effect the agrarian revolution which its leaders had championed before. In the place of basic and vital changes, we have pale agrarian reforms which do not touch even the fringe of the problem. In this part of the country half-hearted abolition of zamindari is being boasted of as red revolution. The Socialist Party in Uttar Pradesh and the Provincial Kisan Panchayat have so utterly exposed the hollowness of this attempt that it is waste of time to criticize the Zamindari abolition legislation. I would content myself with pointing out that in those parts of the country where the zamindari system did not obtain, the agrarian problem was hardly less acute. There are few places in the country where for instance the agrarian situation is more explosive than in Tamil Nadu. The time therefore has arrived even in the zamindari areas to turn public attention from the issue of abolition of the system to more basic agrarian issues. Zamindari was destined to die, but we have to see that the manner of its death does not create more problems than it solves. The apologists of the present agrarian policy of the Congress governments assert that it is wise to hasten slowly and that all changes can not be made overnight. Planned, slow change is better than a chaotic upheaval. But present changes, no matter what their speed, must fit in with the picture of an ultimate plan. Contrary to this, the present agrarian reforms are not part of any plan and do not subserve any ultimate policy. Indeed, they are creating powerful obstacles in the way of future revolutionary changes.

I would like to define the basic principles that should govern the revolutionary reorganization of our agrarian economy. The first principle is that the land, in the ultimate analysis, belonges to the community as a whole and must subserve the interests of all and not of a few. The other principle is that only they have a right to the possession of land and enjoyment of its produce who cultivate it themselves. The third principle is

[1] *J.P. Papers* (NMML).

that there should be no class differentiation in the rights and privileges pertaining to the use of the land. The fourth basic principle is that the land should not be used as a means of exploitation.

To put these principles into practice, it is necessary not only to abolish zamindari, but also other intermediaries between the State and the tiller. It is further necessary to redistribute land, to fix the upper and lower limits of the size of holdings, to consolidate the latter, to prevent alienation of land except to the village as a whole, to replace the present wasteful, individual and fragmented agriculture with cooperative and collective farming, to resuscitate village industry and to rehabilitate the landless labourer. Such a far-reaching revolution can not be accomplished only through legislative and administrative measures. To carry through such a basic transformation of society it would be necessary to secure the active and enthusiastic cooperation of the agricultural masses themselves. It is the Kisan Panchayats that would be the spearhead of this revolution.

If the problem of landless labour is not properly handled every village would face, with the awakening of the backward and depressed sections of the people, a virtual civil war. Even the poor peasantry and the landless labourers might be divided into two hostile camps. Nothing can be more disastrous to both. There is no final solution of this problem on the present basis of individualistic agriculture. It is only in cooperative and collective farming that the conflict is fully resolved. The peasant brings into the cooperative his labour and his land as his share and the share of the landless labourer is his labour, and both become shareholders in a joint undertaking, the success of which depends on their mutual cooperation. As cooperation developes and begins to serve every economic need of the people concerned, the community of interests of the peasant and the labourer would be complete.

The development of collective farms on newly reclaimed land, where the landless labourer receives the first choice, is another important solution of the same vexed problem on the same lines.

While the industrial labourer finds it easy to discover that capitalism is his enemy and must be destroyed before he achieves his economic freedom, the peasant in the village does not see his relationship with capitalism so easily, and therefore the development of the socialist movement in the village takes mostly an anti-feudal form. But it is necessary for the peasants to realize that it is not enough that the land system is reformed, no matter how drastically, and that capitalism is as much their enemy as that of the industrial workers. Capitalism means a two-fold exploitation of the peasantry. First, the capitalists always try to reduce the prices of agricultural commodities to the lowest levels. Secondly, it is always their desire to sell to the agriculturists the produce of their mills and factories at as high rates as possible. In that manner under capitalism, the helpless individual farmer is cheated at both ends, and as long as capitalism lasts, exploitation of the peasants in this manner, not to speak of the exploitation by usury and interest, would continue. Therefore it is necessary for the peasants to join hands with the industrial workers in overthrowing capitalism at the earliest possible opportunity.

I am convinced that as long as agriculture is organized on the present basis of individual farming, India can not achieve self-sufficiency in food. The root of the problem is the yield from the land. The yield is dependent upon improvements on the land and better implements and seeds. But ninety per cent of our peasants are so poor and their holdings so small that it is beyond their means to make the necessary improvements. It is only by banding together and pooling their resources that the peasants can ever hope to be able to do this. Such banding together is possible only in cooperative and collective farming. Thus reorganization of our agriculture on a cooperative or collective basis is the only real solution of our food problem. I would also like to refer to the frightful rate of growth of population and warn that unless steps are taken to limit families, starvation would become the country's chronic disease.

There is urgent need of extending agriculture and reclaiming new land. I regret the official neglect of the suggestion to organize a 'land army' for the purpose. Despite official pusillanimity, I stress the need for voluntary effort on the part of the peasants to reclaim land, to build up irrigation works and to make the necessary land improvements. The peasants should learn to rely upon their voluntary efforts, then they would be nearer to their salvation. I commend the Kisan Panchayat's slogan of "an hour a day for the Nation" and advise the peasants among other things to establish "grain banks" in their villages. The goal of economic emancipation of the workers and peasants can be achieved only through the conquest of political power. Effective economic and political power is today in the hands of the vested interests. In order to seize political power, it is not necessary to create chaos and anarchy, to loot and murder, but to develop the class consciousness of the masses and to build up their class organization and their political party. The Hind Kisan Panchayat is trying to organize the peasants for the struggle against economic exploitation, and by electing its representatives to the Socialist Party, it would enable the peasants to carry on their fight for political power in cooperation with the representatives of the industrial workers and other groups of working men. The enforcement of adult franchise makes it possible for a peaceful capture of power by the people. There is growing fear that if the fundamental liberties continue to be limited and tampered with, an explosive situation might be created leading to violence, anarchy and civil war. Those in power being concerned exclusively with the task of maintaining themselves in power at all costs, seem to be unaware of the dangers of the situation. The inauguration of the new Constitution is expected to usher in a new era of freedom and democracy, but the dividing line between the old period of Dominion and the new age of the Republic is so thin as to be hardly noticeable. The Government's policy with regard to the princes, to capitalist ownership of industry, to the vast divergence between incomes, to agrarian exploitation, its handling of rationing and controls, profiteering and blackmarketing, all lead to this conclusion.

I hope that the peasants and workers would be organized soon enough to be able to establish their rule at the very first opportunity in the coming year when a new government is to be elected.

277. To Asoka Mehta, 27 February 1950[1]

Dear Asoka,

It was a shock to learn that you could not come to the Executive for reasons of health. You will remember the dates were changed to suit your convenience. However, no one can help illness.

Your letter about the Bihar Conference[2] gave me another shock. I thought at least the Bihar Party Conference would have some importance in your eyes. It is too late to say now that you have no stomach for conferences. I do realize your heavy responsibilities, but you must make some time and preside over the conference. This should be easier for you to do since you have been unable to come to Rewa.

I was happy to hear of Sadanand's[3] public announcement regarding the Party. I shall be writing to him in a day or two.

With best wishes,

Yours affectionately,
J.P.

[1] *J.P. Papers* (NMML).
[2] See Appendix 17 for Asoka Mehta's letter to J.P.
[3] Sadanand, Managing Editor, *Free Press Journal*, *Bharat Jyoti* and *Janashakti*.

278. To Rafi Ahmed Kidwai, 4 March 1950[1]

My dear Rafi Saheb,

It is exactly a month since I postponed my decision to fast. On the 5th February last, I had issued a press statement explaining my position after which a communique was published by your Ministry which I had failed to

[1] *J.P. Papers* (NMML).

understand. However, I did not write to you then, because after our talk in Delhi and the subsequent correspondence between us, I had no reason to have any anxiety in this matter.

Out of the two items which I had taken up, one has already been conceded. The only question to be settled now is regarding the payment for the strike period.[2] In this connection the position, as I understood it, was that while no payment could be made for the strike period, some formula would be evolved to meet the demand. When I discussed the matter with you at Sodhani's place, you had told me that as there was no leave due, payment might be made in the form of some kind of bonus. I had asked you then what statement should I make to the Executive Council of the Postmen's Union, which was meeting that afternoon and also to the press. You had told me to tell both that some form of payment was being considered which would be found to be satisfactory. Subsequently in your letter of January 30, you wrote to me that "I had admitted that while I had not agreed to pay for the strike period, I had promised to consider some formula by which the strike period could be converted into absence on leave or to make some other adjustment which will ensure that the strike days were not wasted".

Again in your letter of February 3, you wrote to me that it was discovered that the rules of leave at the time of the strike were different from what they are today, and possibly a very large majority of the strikers had their leave due. You said further that the whole position was being reviewed and that after the information was collected a suitable formula would be evolved. It is a month now since you wrote and I hope all the necessary information has been collected. The last part of you letter of February 3, made me somewhat anxious, but I hope that after you asked me to make a definite statement to the postmen in Delhi that a satisfactory formula would be evolved, you will not let the position be altered at this late hour. I expect to be in Delhi by the 12th of this month when I hope to see you. I also hope that by then your Department will have reached a final solution of this problem.

I hope you are well and with Holi's greetings,

Sincerely yours,
Jayaprakash Narayan

279. To K.B. Menon, 4 March 1950[1]

Dear K.B.,[2]

Your various letters. It was a pity that you could not come to Rewa. I hope, however, that you will come and meet us some time before the Party

[1] *J.P. Papers* (NMML).

[2] For biographical note on K.B. Menon see *JPSW*, Vol. IV, p. 52.

Conference. I hope to be in Bombay in the second week of April and I wish you would come there for a couple of days, to discuss the details of the Conference. I am writing to Kamaladevi about what you have said regarding collections. I hope you will be able to secure the college building for the delegates. That would surely reduce your burden and anxiety by at least fifty per cent. Did you write to the Bihar Party for the relevant information and did they send you what you wanted?

I am enclosing a copy of a letter that I have written to Wilson.[3] I hope you will see that the Pattom affair is settled soon.

Now that the Hind Kisan Panchayat has been formed, it is necessary that its work should be taken up in all seriousness by the Party in every province. In the South its work has made very little progress and there has been a great deal of confusion regarding it. There should be no more confusion now as the Hind Kisan Panchayat has a constitution and its relations with the Party are clearly laid down. The Kisan Panchayat is an independent organization, the primary committees of which are to be affiliated to the Party (with at least 60% vote of the members concerned) and members of the Party working in the Kisan Panchayat are under the same disciplinary jurisdiction as other members working in other fields.

Dr. Lohia, as you might know, is going to Trichinopoly on the 26th or 27th March to preside over the Provincial Kisan Conference. You should make it a point to meet him there and take his help to set the situation right. S.R. Subramaniam should also be present. I am writing to him too in this connection.

Please write to me at my Patna address.

With greetings,

Yours sincerely,
Jayaprakash

[3] P.P. Wilson, an active member of the Socialist Party from Kerala.

280. To Achyut Patwardhan, 4 March 1950[1]

Dear Achyut,

I hope you have received my letter from Rewa. Every one there felt disconsolate at your decision[2] but what could any one do in view of the fact that you have inexorably made up your mind? Every one hoped, however, that you would soon come back after your creative pause and give your best to the movement and render it even greater service than hitherto.

[1] *J.P. Papers* (NMML).

[2] This has reference to Achyut Patwardhan's decision to give up political work.

The Executive considered the question of *Janata's* editorship and decided that Rohit Dave[3] should take your place. I hope this will meet with your approval.

I am spending my Holi in the quietude of Sanchi and tomorrow shall resume my infernal tour. Have you ever been to Sanchi? The Stupa and other monuments around it are marvellous indeed. Archaeologists and art lovers have written a great deal about it, but what impressed me most was the social significance of such a hallowed place for the times when it was created. The monasteries and the noble temples could not but have exercised the deepest influence on the life of the people of those days. One contrasts the significance of such institutions with the Hindu temples of the present day which are lifeless centres of a dead society. The only impression I have of our present day temples is of the filth in and around them, and of the priests plaguing the worshippers at every step for coined offerings. There is no inspiration in them and no life, not even the life of dead stones that one finds in a place like Sanchi, nor are they centre of piety, devotion, education or service. One wonders whether there will be a renaissance in Hinduism or its decay will soon end in its ultimate death. But I have strayed into domains which are not my own, so I better stop.

I would like you to be in Bombay in the middle of April or where will you be about that time? I hope to be in Bombay then. Do write to me at my Patna address.

With Holi's greetings,

Affectionately yours,
J.P.

[3]Rohit Dave (1908-87): M.A., L.L.B, member P.S.P Gujarat, M.P. Rajya Sabha 1958-64; Joint Secretary P.S.P. 1948-9.

281. To P.P. Wilson, 4 March 1950[1]

Dear Com. Wilson,

I had your letters regarding Mr. Thanu Pillai and his group. I had hopes that some one would come from the South to the Rewa meetings, but no one except Com. Rahim turned up. In your letters you had said that we had not taken into account all the aspects of the case, but you have not taken the trouble of pointing out what those aspects were . Prior to the Bombay meeting, certain letters had been received from friends in Kerala making certain accusations against Mr. Pillai and some members of his group. We had discussed all these specific points with Mr. Pillai and found his

[1]*J.P. Papers* (NMML).

explanation completely satisfactory. Under the circumstance, I find the refusal of Travancore comrades to admit Mr. Pillai and his friends rather unreasonable. When Dr. Menon wrote to me some time ago, after your Ernakulam meeting, all he said was that you people wanted some time to prepare the mind. After that I have no clear idea as to what happened. You all probably realize that there is no provision in the Constitution by which any one can prevent any one from entering into the Party, provided he fulfils the conditions of admission. Mr. Pillai and his friends surely fulfil these conditions inasmuch as they accept the policy, programme and discipline of the Party and do not belong to any other political or communal organization. I therefore advise you not to delay the matter any further and admit these friends and let them work for the Party.

You had written some time ago that I had over estimated the strength of Mr. Pillai's group. But there was no question of over estimation. Even a group of half a dozen people which begins to call itself as a socialist party creates confusion in the public mind. The formation of the Kerala Socialist Party caused no end of confusion, not only in Kerala but also in other parts of the country. There are already dozens of socialist or leftist parties in the country and it does not do any good to the socialist movement to let other groups to form.

It is possible that someone on behalf of the National Executive might go down to Travancore to have this matter fixed up. But if that were not possible, you should settle this matter yourself.

I am glad to know that the Party is making steady progress in Travancore. Wishing you success.

Yours sincerely,
J.P.

282. To Jawaharlal Nehru, 4 March 1950[1]

Dear Bhai,

I am enclosing herewith copy of a statement on Indo-Pakistan relations issued by the National Executive of the Socialist Party and wish to draw your earnest attention to it. The situation is grave and effective action cannot long be delayed. The enclosed statement clearly sets forth our policy. Your policy appears to be satisfactory as far as it goes, but it is obvious that it must go much further to reach even a relatively lasting solution.

You will see from our statement that we desire a united national policy to be evolved on this question. I wonder if you would agree with this

[1] *J.P. Papers* (NMML).

viewpoint and also if you would at all consider it worthwhile if some of us meet you in this connection.

With regards,

Affectionately yours,
J.P.

283. To Gopalaswami Ayyangar, 5 March 1950[1]

Dear Mr. Ayyangar,

I trust Mr. Guruswami has sent to you a copy of the resolutions adopted at the General Council of the Federation at Lucknow. Now that the Budget business is over, I hope you will have some time to look personally into the issues raised. I am afraid, the resolutions of the Federation did not receive the attention they deserve at the hands of the Railway Board.

As you will see from resolution no. 2, the General Council has fixed May 31, as the last date by when the work of the Joint Advisory Committee should be completed as far as the issues pending before it are concerned. If this is not done, you will note, that the Federation would withdraw its representatives on the Committee. The same resolution has also expressed resentment at the delay in implementing the recommendations of the JAC When we had met you last, you had assured us that decisions on the report of the JAC would be expedited. I am afraid, however, that this has not been the case.

In your Budget speech, on which I congratulate you, you had painted a fairly satisfactory picture of the Railways and you had made an appreciative reference to labour. I should, however, like to sound a warning that under the surface there are grave rumblings. The Lucknow meeting of the General Council showed an ugly mood. The financial position of the Railways being as indicated in your Budget, labour is entitled to a better deal. I, therefore, hope that the main outstanding issues would be settled before the 31st of May to the satisfaction of labour. What these issues are, is apparent from the resolutions of the General Council. Among other things, you will have seen, that there was universal dissatisfaction with your Ministry's decision regarding the vexed question of weightage for length of service. If the other issues are also settled in a like manner, you will have a serious labour trouble on your hands.

I had wanted to write to you earlier about the recognition of the rival railwaymen's federation. I had thought that when we agreed to have Mr. Hariharnath Shastri[2] on the JAC, the question of giving recognition to

[1] *J.P. Papers* (NMML).

[2] For biographical note on Hariharnath Shastri see *JPSW*, Vol. I, p. 62.

a rival body would not arise. I had also thought that it was Government's desire not to have a multimplicity of labour organizations in the same industry. Mr. Hariharnath Shastri and Khandubhai Desai make a great deal of the fact that the B.B. and C.I. Railway Employees' Association was not admitted into the Federation, but later on when the Federation opened its doors to all the unions on the Railways and particularly invited the Congress unions to come into its fold, I do not see what stood in the way of Messrs. Shastri and Desai. They make also a good deal of the argument that the Federation is a Socialist body. This kind of propaganda is sickening in the extreme and I for one have made up my mind to leave the Federation so that this socialist obsession may go. The organization which Messrs. Shastri and Desai have set up is far more under the control of a political party than the Federation ever was or could be. However, I hope that the new Industrial Relations Bill, will, in its final form, have some provision by which the evil of rival trade unionism might be stopped.

I hope you are well and with kind regards,

Sincerely yours,
J.P.

284. To P.C. Dasgupta, 5 March 1950[1]

Dear P.C.,

I duly received your letters regarding Danapore and Allahabad and also copy of Rambabu's letter regarding Allahabad. I was sorry to learn that there was such irregularity and hooliganism at Allahabad. I am sure that in the interest of the Union such practices must be put down with a firm hand. You should, however, make a careful enquiry into what actually happened. Disciplinary action should be confirmed only after you have satisfied yourself of the breach of discipline in every case. If you wish you may appoint a committee of Dubeji[2] and Shri D.P. Joshi[3] to enquire into the whole affair. As for the election of the Allahabad branch, I am afraid, I would have no time for a couple of months. Moreover, I think you should not drag me into such affairs. If you agree, I may write to D.P. Joshi to accompany you to Allahabad to supervise the election. I shall be in Patna on the 14th of this month and I expect to hear from you on this matter there.

We should also fix up the dates for the annual conference of the Union at

[1] *J.P. Papers* (NMML).

[2] Dubeji, a Socialist leader from U.P.

[3] D.P. Joshi, Socialist leader from Lucknow.

Jamalpore some time towards the end of the second week of April, say, about the 11th or 12th.

With season's greetings,

Yours sincerely,
J.P.

285. To Asoka Mehta, 5 March 1950[1]

Dear Asoka,

Now the *alibi* is complete, the accused must be acquitted. I have no option now but to relieve you from the Bihar Provincial Conference. But if in any case the dates of your Delhi conference are changed, I hope you will still favour us with your visit to the conference.

I received your letter[2] at Rewa about Lohia's 13-point programme. As the matter will be discussed at the next meeting of the Executive on the 3rd, 4th and 5th of April at Lucknow, it was not taken up at Rewa. I hope you will find it possible to attend the Lucknow meeting. You have a long notice in any case. Some days ago Achyut had written to me that he had finally made up his mind to leave. I naturally had to write to him that he was free to do as he liked. I am enclosing a copy of my reply to him. The National Executive appointed Rohit in the place of Achyut as editor of the *Janata*. I hope this will meet with your approval.

I hope you have recovered from your last attack and with season's best wishes.

Affectionately yours,
J.P.

[1] *J.P. Papers* (NMML).
[2] See Appendix 18 for Asoka Mehta's reply to J.P.

286. To Kamaladevi Chattopadhyaya, 5 March 1950[1]

My dear Kamaladevi,

I had your letter regarding your inability to attend the Rewa meeting. I hope your mother is better now.

K.B. [Menon] wrote to me that all that he wanted you to do was to help him collect some funds for the Conference in Madras and of course you will have to write your address as Chairman of the Reception Committee. I

[1] *J.P. Papers* (NMML).

hope you will find at least two weeks to go to the South for collection work. I think at this stage it is not advisable to make any change in the Chairmanship of the Reception Committee.

What is this Nekhroll refugee township of which the Prime Minister has spoken so highly. It seems to be a co-operative community built under the inspiration of some American engineer. I should like to know something more about it. Are you in touch with it?

I hope you are well and with season's greetings.

Yours sincerely,
J.P.

287. Address at the Nagpur Institute of Journalists, Nagpur, 7 March 1950[1]

If all peaceful methods by India fail and Pakistan can not guarantee justice and security for the minorities, the only alternative left is to send out our own forces into East Bengal to protect the minorities there.

This may sound odd for international behaviour, but under the conditions existing this is the sanest, the least harmful of solutions. And if Pakistan takes that as a declaration of war, which it is not meant to be, it cannot be helped.

I am, however, in favour of international intervention for the protection of minorities, provided it is not of the type which we have seen in Indonesia and elsewhere. If that kind of intervention is allowed probably the situation would save itself before this intervention reaches its conclulsion.

It is a conflict of principles between nationalism, secularism and democracy represented by India on the one hand and theocracy and denial of equality and democracy represented by Pakistan on the other. India is making a serious attempt to build up a secular State and, as a consequence, whatever might happen in Pakistan, the minorities in India must live without fear. I stress the duty of the majority community in India to assure the Muslims absolute equality and hope that they would assist the Government, whatever their differences with them may be, in maintaining peace and communal harmony.

This, obviously, is only the beginning of the solution of the problem facing us at present. Whatever we do here there is no guarantee that in Pakistan, which is built on communal foundations, events would not take place which would disturb the minds of the people here. Nevertheless, we should set our house in order and demand of Pakistan to mete out to the minorities there, the same treatment as Muslims here are being given.

[1]Adapted from *Bombay Chronicle*, 8 March 1950.

I regret the Pakistan's Prime Minister, Mr. Liaquat Ali Khan's rejection of Pandit Nehru's proposal for joint tour of affected areas. Such a joint tour would have reassured the minorities on both sides and produced a psychological change among the people as well as those officers of the two Governments who have not been free from communalism.

I suggest that India should make the same proposal again to Pakistan. Further, we should place the facts of the case and methods proposed by India to solve the conflict before the world, particularly our neighbours. If India fails in all these methods, then it would be better for us to tell Pakistan that if it is not able to protect the minorities, it should take India's or international help for the purpose. We in India have been able to give freedom and justice and sense of security to the minorities, but if Pakistan does not agree, then, there does not seem to be any other solution possible except to send our own forces into East Bengal to protect the minorities there. We do not want to fight against Pakistan. Our forces will only be sent to protect minorities there.

The Socialist Party has always taken an uncompromising stand against Hindu communalism. To preserve the basic principles on which our state is founded and to preserve peace in Asia, this armed intervention in East Bengal by India, if it becomes necessary, would be justified in my eyes.

288. To Purshottam Trikamdas, 15 March 1950[1]

Dear Purshottam,

I wrote to you about clearing the bills of the *Janata*. Now that the *Janata* is moving to Free Press, it is essential that we pay up all arrears to the NIP. Madhu has written to me that you paid only Rs. 2000/-. The C.P. tour unfortunately was not very profitable from the monetary point of view. I got only a thousand rupees out of which I have sent to you Rs. 800/- keeping Rs. 200/- for my camp office expenses. The Gondia programme was cancelled, otherwise I would have probably got a few thousands more. Now I will be touring Bihar and I may be able to send you something at the end of the tour. In the meanwhile you must make some arrangement for the *Janata* bills.

Yours sincerely,
J.P.

[1] *J.P. Papers* (NMML).

289. Remarks at a Press Conference on Socialists' Cooperation with the Government, Calcutta, 23 March 1950[1]

In case of a national crisis and formation of an emergency Government on the East Bengal issue my partymen or I may not join the Cabinet. We are, however, always ready to support the Government on any firm action they take.

I suggest that Pandit Nehru should immediately call a conference of representative Indians for evolving a national policy to deal with the situation. At this hour when the nation is in great peril, people should cease talking in different voices and should evolve a common policy of action. If there is any time for dispassionate thinking and united action, it is now.

Let those who are talking loosely of ministerial resignations and change of Government realize that if India has to face the present menace with success there must be national unity and joint effort of all patriotic citizens and parties.

Whatever national policy might eventually be formulated it is the duty of men of all parties to preserve peace in this country and guarantee to our Muslim citizens not only freedom from fear but also an equal and honourable status with other citizens of the country. Some recent incidents in India, and particularly in West Bengal, have weakened the hands of those who want firm action to be taken with regard to Pakistan.

My earlier statement has been misunderstood in certain quarters. If for certain events Socialists have suggested armed intervention to protect human rights and decencies in East Bengal, that does not mean that they should conquer or annex East Pakistan.

But before any armed intervention we must maintain peace and guarantee full security to the Muslim minority in India. Then only we can demand of Pakistan to create similar conditions there, and if they fail to do so, India would be justified to send her troops to create that condition in East Bengal. I have placed before the Prime Minister, and have also sent a telegram to him, our views on the present problem and how to solve it. It is for the Government to decide the future course of action. If they fail to do it, people have a right to have another Government. But before they talk of changing the Government they must realize that the situation calls for united national effort.

[1]Adapted from *Bombay Chronicle*, 24 March 1950.

290. Speech at a Public Meeting, Patna, 29 March 1950[1]

People in India as well as the Government should strive to assure the minorities living in the Union of all safeguards and convince them that their lives and properties are safe in this country. Then alone would the Union Government be justified in taking action or demanding that Pakistan should afford similar protection to the minorities living in that country. Sending of troops to Pakistan to protect the minorities there would be necessitated only in the event of Pakistan failing to provide that protection.

Sending of troops, presumably with a view to capturing Pakistan, as advocated by the R.S.S. and the Hindu Mahasabha these days, is no solution of the problem. Such moves are likely to bring India down in the eyes of the world. All talk of exchange of population as a solution of this issue is bound to fail, as it is both impracticable and unwise, likely to affect the economy of the country adversely.

I am for an all-party conference to exchange opinion and explore ways and means of solving the problem. I had referred to such a conference in my telegram to the Prime Minister of India. Pandit Nehru has expressed his difficulty in calling such a conference. I am going to write to the Prime Minister again suggesting a way out. The question of the safety of the minorities of Pakistan is an issue over which all parties should join hands. A common solution should be evolved for the protection of the minorities of East Bengal and maintenance of peace in India. The issue should not be exploited for gaining political ends.

After the meeting of the national executive of the Socialist Party, which passed the resolution on Pakistan, I had an opportunity to come to Patna for a day and I learnt from friends that there had been some misunderstanding among a section of Muslims with regard to the policy of the Socialist Party. I am also told that some of the erstwhile Leaguers, in reaction to my Nagpur speech, are of the opinion that whether it be a Golwalkar[2] or a Jayaprakash Narayan, every Hindu is ultimately a rank communalist and as such an enemy of the Muslims.

Such reactions are painful to me. They remind me of the days of the last Bihar riots (1946) when the same section of the Muslim population in this state held me responsible for the riots and openly said that after my release from jail, while taking classes in Anjuman Islamia Hall I had really prepared plans for the mass killing of Muslims in Bihar. Similarly, during the days following the murder of Mahatama Gandhi the Hindu communalists openly said that after Gandhiji it was going to be the turn of Pandit Nehru

[1]Adapted from *Searchlight*, 30 March 1950 and *Amrit Bazar Patrika*, 31 March 1950.

[2]Madhav Sadashiv Golwalkar (1906-73); Chief (*Sarsanghchalak*) of Rashtriya Swayamsevak Sangh (RSS) 1940-73.

and Jayaprakash Narayan to be killed. Thus it was curious that both the Hindu and the Muslim communalists have dubbed me as an enemy of their community.

Socialists have been working for the uprooting of communalism among both Hindus and Muslims and have contributed significantly to the maintenance of peace and harmony in the country. It is, therefore, a matter of deep regret that they are being branded as communalists by a section of Muslims and as enemies of the Hindu community by a section of Hindus.

We do not want that India should wage war against Pakistan. We must create confidence among the Muslims in India that their lives and properties are safe and secure and that they have equal rights and opportunities for self-expression and self-development along with the Hindus. We believe that one day India and Pakistan will become reunited. We hate communalism. We reject all notions of Hindu Raj. We reject the theory of a theocratic State in India. We firmly believe in nationalism. We maintain that we are all Indians and we observe no distinction between Hindus and Muslims. We reject the theory of exchange of population between India and Pakistan. Indians constitute one, single united nation. We think in terms of politics and economics and not in terms of religion. We shall protect the lives and properties of Muslims at the risk of our lives and ensure that they enjoy full religious freedom. Implementation of the above is the only way of dealing with Pakistan and putting it to shame. In this way only can all Hindus in East Bengal and other parts of Pakistan remain safe.

India would progress and develop if it maintains unity and peace on all its fronts. War with Pakistan would create a lot of complications. If any country wages war in disregard of world opinion, it would be branded as aggressor. Exchange of population would be no solution for India's problems with Pakistan. Exchange of population would take decades to materialize and during the period of exchange of population there would be dislocation of political, economic and social order of the country.

A section of the people is trying to bring pressure on Pandit Nehru for armed intervention in Eastern Pakistan for the protection of minorities there. But with what face can they make such a demand if they can not guarantee the same protection to their own minorities. India must pledge to give full protection to Muslims in India. Here everybody must be treated as an Indian. The State must be secular. In that way alone lies the solution of India-Pakistan problems.

291. To the Provincial Secretaries, Socialist Party, 30 March 1950[1]

Dear Comrade,

May I remind you of the decision of the National Executive taken at Bangalore that the General Secretary may suspend from Party membership those Provincial Secretaries who fail to submit monthly reports to the Central Office for two consecutive months. The last report received from you was for the month of. . . . If you do not send immediately to the Central Office the reports which are in arrears and are not regular henceforth in your reports, I shall have regretfully to take action in terms of the Executive's decision. You should treat this as a final warning.

Sincerely yours,
General Secretary

Province	*Last report*
Assam	November
Bombay	October
Madhya Bharat	November
Delhi	November
Hyderabad	November
Mysore	No reports
M.S.T.C	October
Tamilnadu	November.

[1] *J.P. Papers* (NMML).

292. To S.K. Saxena, 11 April 1950[1]

Dear Saxena[2]

I have already written to you about the case of Com. Brijnandan Sharma. Some months ago he was served with an Order of Extermment from the district of Manbhum. (Com. Sharma is running the Tata Colliery Union at Jamadoba near Jharia.) After the promulgation of the new Constitution a petition was filed in the Patna High Court against the Government's Order. The High Court ruled that the Order was invalid. The Bihar Government have moved the Supreme Court. We shall be obliged if you can arrange a

[1] *J.P. Papers* (NMML).

[2] S.K. Saxena, an active member of the Socialist Party in Delhi.

good lawyer to take up this case. When I meet you in Delhi I shall talk to you further about it.

I hope you are well and with best wishes,

Yours sincerely,
J.P.

293. To U.S. Malliah, 11 April 1950[1]

Dear Mr. Malliah,[2]

You remember I had spoken to you once about Achyut's sister, Vijaya.[3] After that I spoke to Mehra Masani and on her suggestion Vijaya had gone to Delhi recently to take a voice test. I do not know what her prospects are after that test. I should, however, like you to help me in this matter. You had told when I had spoken to you first about this matter that you would wait till the Secretary of the Department arrived whom you know. I hope this officer is in Delhi now. I am reaching Delhi on the 17th and shall stay there till the 18th evening. I hope you will be in Delhi on these dates. I shall get in touch with you as soon as I reach there.

Hope you are well and with regards,

Sincerely yours,
J.P.

[1] *J.P. Papers* (NMML).

[2] U.S. Malliah (1903-65), belonged to South Kanara district (Karnataka) imprisoned in 1925 for two years for his underground activities, member AICC from 1936 onwards, General Secretary of K.P.C.C. 1939-40 and its acting President 1941-6; member of Constituent Assembly of India; whip of Congress party in Central Legislature 1947-52 and chief whip in Lok Sabha from 1952 onwards; member of Provisional Parliament 1950-2 and later got elected as an M.P. from Udipi constituency for two consecutive terms.

[3] Vijaya Patwardhan (1924-), younger sister of Achyut Patwardhan; had accompanied J.P. to Nepal in 1943 and spent a few weeks there when he was engaged in training a group of young men in guerilla warfare.

294. To S. Vaidyanath Aiyar, 11 April 1950[1]

Dear Mr. Aiyar,

I expect to be in Delhi on the 17th and 18th of this month. I hope you will be there. I want you this time to help me collect some money for the Central Party from Delhi. I am writing to you in advance so that you might talk to

[1] *J.P. Papers* (NMML).

your friends in the meanwhile. I want to collect at least Rs. 10,000/-. I will get in touch with you on the 17th evening.

I hope you are both well and with kind regards,

Sincerely yours,
J.P.

295. Inaugural Address at the Civil Liberties Conference, Patna, 15 April 1950[1]

Pandit Jawaharlal Nehru, Prime Minister of India, talks in the language of a dictator when he maintains that if we have to choose between security of the State and the freedom of the individual, we must choose the former.

In the name of emergency-(which I describe as 'sankatvad')- and security, there have been numerous cases of arrest and detention in the past year, which had no relation to the security of the State. Dr. Ram Manohar Lohia, for instance, had been arrested for taking out a procession in Delhi in order to register the Socialist Party's protest against repression in Nepal. This had nothing to do with the security of the State. If Dr. Lohia had been allowed to take out the procession, the State would not have crumbled down.

There are two views about the relation between the society and the individual. One holds that the individual lives for the glory of the society, while the other holds that the society lives for the utmost good of the individual. The culture and civilization of India ordains that the society must be organized in such a manner as to afford every individual ample opportunity for self-development. Such a society is possible only where fullest freedom exists. I believe that the Indian people as a whole subscribe to this ideal and I have reason to think that the constitution makers of India also had this ideal in view.

It appears that an attempt is being made to escape from the implications of this ideal. While lip service is being paid to the ideal of democracy, freedom and civil liberties, those in power do not mean what they say.

A serious danger to civil liberties is growing with a tendency to identify the Government with the Congress Party and the Congress Party with the Government. I have found officers of Government doing party work. If officers take sides, they would no longer remain servants of the people. If the bureaucracy behaves as a limb of a party, what would happen?

The Constitution confers on all adult citizens the right of franchise, but I can not see how people can exercise this right, if different parties are not allowed to approach the people. In Bihar there are standing orders that no meetings can be held without the previous sanction of the authorities. Such

[1]Adapted from *Tribune*, 17 April 1950.

standing orders mean that the Congress Party would be free to hold meetings without hindrance, while opposition parties would be put in a position of disadvantage.

In the labour field also, this is being used as a favourite weapon to put down all independent trade unions and workers' organizations. The creation of an official labour front is nothing but open fascism.

A favourite argument of the Government is that the new-born State must stabilise itself first, before it can put inio practice theoretical concepts of civil liberties. Such an argument from the disciples of Mahatma Gandhi is surprising. After all, on what basis are we going to build a new India? It is not merely by maintaining law and order. Britishers also maintained law and order.

It seems to me that the greatest danger to civil liberties is from the people themselves as they are apathetic or indifferent to such a fundamental question. For many years they have lived in slavery and by freedom they understand only national freedom. National freedom and civil liberties are two different things. A country might have national freedom, but might live under a dictatorship. People take the question of civil liberties as something abstract and not as a vital question of life and death for them. They do not realize that if the Government blunders, they must have the liberty to change the Government.

No Government can be changed in a peaceful manner, if the people have not the right to organize peacefully. I do not know what shape the national life is going to take, but everybody seems to adhere to the objective of promoting a democratic way of life. It is necessary, therefore, to clearly define the place of the individual in a democratic set-up. The question of civil liberties is at the root of the problem of a democratic way of life. I want the Civil Liberties Conference, therefore, to make people aware of the importance of this question. The responsibilities of the people regarding defence of civil liberties also should be impressed.

There are some persons in the country, who believe in non-violence but actually practise violence. Such persons cut at the root of civil liberties and democratic way of life. Under certain conditions violence may be used as a weapon of social change, but in such an event all talk of civil liberties would become meaningless. No individual can demand liberty for murdering and looting others. Those who believe in violence as a means of social revolution need not bother about civil liberties. The path of peaceful social revolution is for those who cherish civil liberties.

Fascism can be established by the ruling authority only if the people acquiesce or remain indifferent. Its rising tide can be checked only by making the people conscious of their rights. I believe that the people of the country, who could effectively fight against their alien rulers, would also be able to fight fascist tendencies that are growing in the country.

I believe that the Civil Liberties Conference would become a public movement of such dimension that the civil liberties of the people would become safe.

The question of civil liberties is not a partisan question. It is an all-party question. It should be made a national issue by different political parties, who should put up a united front, so that this priceless element of a democratic life is not lost.

296. To Shakti Bose, 16 April 1950[1]

Dear Shakti,

Your letter. I have to go to Delhi on the 17th to meet the Defence Ministry on behalf of the Civilian Employees of the Defence Dept. I shall start from Delhi for Calcutta on the 18th night by the Delhi Express, reaching Calcutta on the 20th morning. I shall stay this time with Pachisiaji[2] at Regent Park and have to leave Calcutta on the 25th night for Patna. When I again return to Calcutta will be decided when I am there.

I shall like this time to lay down a daily routine during my stay at Calcutta. I shall give the Bengal Party five to six hours every day from 3 p.m. to 8 or 9 p.m. The rest of the time will be my own. Will you kindly follow this regime strictly? Also in fixing up my engagements, please see that my time is not wasted in all kinds of petty interviews or avoidable visits. You should discuss with Sibnath and other senior comrades there as to what use should exactly be made of my time there. This time I do definitely wish to address at least one large mass meeting at Calcutta, preferably towards the end of my stay there. I should also like to address a labour rally in the Howrah-Hooghly area. Please fix one dinner or lunch engagement with Dr. P.C. Ghosh[3] and also an appointment with Dr. B.C. Roy.[4] I should also like to meet the more sensible of the leftist leaders. The rest of the engagements you must fix up yourselves. Don't forget I shall have to make fresh contacts to collect more money for the Bengal Party. I should like to meet Dr. Hemant Sanyal.[5]

More when we meet,

Yours affectionately,
J.P.

[1] *J.P. Papers* (NMML).
[2] Pachisiaji, a Calcutta based socialist sympathizer.
[3] For biographical note on P.C. Ghosh see *JPSW*, Vol. III, p. 187.
[4] For biographical note on B.C. Roy see *JPSW*, Vol. IV, p. 228.
[5] Hemant Sanyal, a socialist sympathizer in Calcutta.

297. Speech at a Public Meeting regarding India-Pakistan Minorities Problem, Delhi, 17 April 1950[1]

After examining various solutions put forward by different political organizations for the India-Pakistan minorities problem the only practicable solution is for us to create an atmosphere in which all Muslims can remain here as honoured citizens of India.

My party is strongly opposed to communalism, because that would make the establishment of a Socialist State in India impossible. If we follow the communal policy to its logical conclusion, the country would be divided into several parts and its economic structure would be shattered.

Exchange of population is no solution of the minorities problem in the two countries. Even if a peaceful exchange is agreed upon by both the Governments it would take them years before it can be completed and all normal nation-building activities would stop during this period.

I have recently visited Calcutta and was told that if one million Muslims migrate from there, nearly half the industry would come to a standstill.

If over forty million Indian Muslims migrate to Pakistan and over ten million Hindus from East Pakistan come to India, Pakistan may demand more territory to accommodate the additional Muslim population.

Similarly, if after this exchange of population, India becomes a Hindu State, the Sikhs, the Christians and the Adibasis would be justified in demanding separate States for themselves. If a country can be divided on the basis of religion, what can prevent its further division on the basis of castes and sects.

If the secular character of the country vanishes, it is bound to give a philip to the growth of fissiparous tendencies which might express themselves in the shape of demands by various smaller communities for independent States of their own. It is, therefore, imperative that India maintains here secularity at all costs. A strong and well-knit nation should to be built up and the country's economy placed on a sound footing.

The most effective way of protecting the life and property of the minorities in Pakistan is to afford protection and safeguard the honour of minorities in India. If Indians indulge in retaliation against innocent people to avenge a wrong done hundreds of miles away, they would be playing the imperialist game of divide and rule.

Pakistan is the outcome of our old rulers' policy to keep different communities apart by encouraging religious differences. If we continue to pursue that policy, wittingly or unwittingly, we would be sowing the seeds of many more Pakistans in the country, which happens to be a mixture of many creeds, communities and languages.

[1]Adapted from *Statesman* and *Searchlight*, 18 April 1950.

Communal disturbances in the past led to the vivesection of our motherland. If they are repeated or an atmosphere conducive to violence or communal hatred grows unchecked, India will have to shelve perhaps for ever all her nation-building plans. She will have to let her workers continue to be ground in poverty and her visions of a glorious India remain only a dream.

The only way, therefore, by which we can strengthen our country would be to make it possible for every member of the minority community to live here as a free citizen of India. If the Muslims are safe and happy here, India can demand that the Hindus in Pakistan also lead an honourable life. If Pakistan does not treat the non-Muslims properly, India can compel her by all possible means to realize her duty.

This is the way Mahatma Gandhi had suggested over two years ago, and it still remains the sanest course possible.

298. To P.R. Das, 17 April 1950[1]

Dear Mr. Das,

I hope you will excuse me for giving you this trouble. I did not wish to speak to you about this matter in the midst of the Conference work, and I am leaving this morning for Delhi.

It is about your kind and generous help to the Provincial Socialist Party. Your monthly aid was a great standby for us, and the fact that for the past couple of months your donation has not been received. It has put us in some difficulty. May I therefore request you to give us something before you leave Patna? The last two months' plus the current month's donation would enable us to tide over our present difficulties.

Wishing you a pleasant holiday,

Yours sincerely,
J.P.

[1] *J.P. Papers* (NMML).

299. To the Workers of West Bengal, 22 April 1950[1]

Dear Brother Worker,

A great danger faces the workers and the poor of our country. This danger is of communal riots and violence. You very well know that these riots

[1]Adapted from *Janata*, 1 May 1950.

caused the partition of country and gave birth to Pakistan. If the Hindu and Muslim workers and the poor did not kill each other, then Pakistan could never have been formed. Today, again, this mutual slaughter is going to damage the interests of you, poor people.

What does the worker want? He wants the abolition of poverty. He wants the liquidation of capitalism and the establishment of the rule of the poor. This mutual slaughter is never going to result in this. To establish a workers' government, workers must be united. The working class contains Hindus, Muslims, Sikhs, Christians and others, from all castes and all provinces and States of India. But if the workers, forgetting the differences of religion, caste, province and language, do not get together as one, then they can never attain their destiny and end their oppression and exploitation.

In the recent riots (in West Bengal), some Hindu workers took part, and they killed their Muslim fellow-workers and also looted their homes. It is a matter of great shame and sorrow. It has harmed the interests of all the workers including those who have perpetrated these crimes. These incidents have destroyed the unity of the working class, and as a result the days of workers' regime have become distant.

Now the riot is over. But I have heard that many Hindu workers have decided that they won't work if the Muslim workers were taken back in the factories. I was not only amazed but shocked to hear it. It hurt me to the heart. This decision of the Hindu workers is against the ideology and principles of the whole working class movement. The slogan of the workers is 'workers of the world unite' and we are dividing the workers' fraternity in our country. This will result in only one thing, that the fratricidal quarrels and riots will continue and the strength of the workers will become insignificant and the owners of capital will go on merrily ruling the country.

Therefore, I request and appeal to you, Hindu workers, that if you want your own welfare, then by ending these religious differences and riots, establish the workers' real class unity. Ask your Muslim brother workers back to work, stand all united together like before and begin the joint fight for the daily bread and the ultimate establishment of a workers' State.

Yours fraternally,
Jayaprakash Narayan
General Secretary, Socialist Party

300. To Rohit Dave, 24 April 1950[1]

Dear Rohit,

I was very much surprised to read in the *Janata* of 16th April 1950, a write-up by the Political Correspondent about the Nehru-Liaquat Ali Pact. The correspondent writes about Sardar Patel wanting to arrest Liaquat Ali. I am pained that such irresponsible statements should find a place in the *Janata*. Firstly, there is absolutely no foundation for it and secondly, even if there were, it was not for a journal like the *Janata* to give publicity to it. Sardar Patel was not at all keen about the Nehru-Liaquat Ali talks at the beginning, but when the talks were concluded in which he too participated at the later stages, he gave the Agreement his unstinted and whole-hearted support. While we all desire that the *Janata* be made a popular journal, the editors of the *Janata* must take care to keep away from sensationalism, vulgarism, cheapness and falsehood. I am afraid, some of the headlines in the *Janata* remind one of the "Blitz", which I dislike more and more every day. I want you to make amends in some suitable manner for this false and vulgar story about Sardar Patel which was published last week and the publication of which I considered a piece of national disservice.

I hope you are well,

Yours sincerely,
sd/- Jayaprakash Narayan

[1]*Nehru Papers*—Files at home (NMML).

301. To H.M. Jagtiani, 25 April 1950[1]

Dear Mr. Jagtiani,[2]

Mr. Pratul Chatterjee,[3] Treasurer of the All India Railwaymen's Federation and a representative of the latter on the Joint Advisory Committee brought to me yesterday a case of great hardship and suffering. The case is that of Shri Sachindra Chandra Bhowmick[4] who was a Station Master in the ex-B.A. Railway. Shri Bhowmick had provisionally opted for Pakistan, but after the Radcliff Award[5] when he discovered that his place of residence

[1]*J.P. Papers* (NMML).

[2]H.M. Jagtiani, a High Official in the Eastern Railway headquarters at Calcutta.

[3]Pratul Chatterjee, Treasure of the All India Railwaymen's Federation and later member on the Joint Advisory Committee.

[4]Sachindra Chandra Bhowmick, Station Master in the ex-B.A. Railway.

[5]Radcliff Award—After the acceptance of the Mountbatten Plan (3 June 1947) providing for India's partition, it was deemed necessary to have a body to settle boundaries of the new dominions of India and Pakistan. Two commissions were constituted—first to deal with partition of Bengal and separation of Sylhet from Assam; the second with the partition of Punjab. Radcliffe was the common chairman of the two bodies.

fell in India, he made his final option for India on the 7th of September 1947. It is more than two and a half year since then, but this employee has not yet been absorbed anywhere on the Indian Railways. I was rather pained to learn that a person who once was a station master has to earn his livelihood by working as a cook in Calcutta. I do not know what technical difficulties have stood in the way of his being absorbed on the E.I.R. But it seems to me that the human tragedy involved should have been enough to obviate technical or other difficulties. In writing to you in this matter I am hoping that you will take a human view of this case and do the needful.

I am enclosing herewith a petition of Shri Sachindra Chandra Bhowmick.

With kind regards,

Yours sincerely,
J.P.

302. To Jawaharlal Nehru, 30 April 1950[1]

Dear Bhai,

I have just read your statement about the report published in the *Janata* of 16th April regarding Sardar Patel's wanting to arrest Liaqut Ali Khan. I have nothing to say about your statement, but should like to tell you that I was very deeply distressed to read that report in the *Janata* and that I wrote a letter soon after to Rohit Dave who is now editing *Janata* in the place of Achut, you might know, has retired from politics, having been impressed with their inadequacy. I am enclosing herewith a copy of my letter to Rohit and also of that of his reply. Even before my letter had reached Bombay, the *Janata* had expressed regret on the front page in its very next issue.

I am sorry that this unfortunate thing has happened, but I hope you will understand that the fault was that of the assistant editorial staff. Madhu Limaye, a joint secretary of the Party, has explained to me how the mistake was made by the assistant editors, Bhargava and Indra Sen. I am also enclosing an excerpt from Limaye's letter regarding this matter.

With kind regards,

Affectionately yours,
J.P.

[1] *J.P. Papers* (NMML). See Appendix 20 for Nehru's reply to J.P.

303. To Provincial Secretaries of the Socialist Party, 1 May 1950[1]

Dear Comrade,

As you know, the Hind Kisan Panchayat has opened a Training School at Patna to train Kisan workers. The School started from the 15th April. But the response from the States has been very poor and a very small number of students have come for the first term. The second term would begin from July 1, 1950. You should arrange, in cooperation with the State Kisan Panchayat, to send an adequate batch of selected trainees to the School from your State for the next term.

Each term is of three months and the fees per term per trainee are Rs. 100/- out of which Rs. 90/- are for hoarding at the rate of Rs. 30/- per month, and Rs. 10/- are the tuition and entrance fees to the School. Some provision should be made in your budget to help poor students.

For other particulars you should write to the Director, Kisan Training College, c/o Hind Kisan Panchayat, Kadam Kuan, Patna 3.

At Party workers' meeting, I have always found a demand for training centres. But it is rather regrettable that when facilities for training are actually provided for, our workers are reluctant to avail of them. I hope, therefore, that this matter will receive your particular attention.

If you wish to send any trainees for the current term, you may do so.

[1] *J.P. Papers* (NMML).

304. May Day Message to Workers, Patna, 1 May 1950[1]

The May Day has brought the message of bondage for the workers in India. The Government is attempting to enact laws that will bind you hand and foot and will crush your sole strength, the strength of your organization.

The Trade Union Bill, 1950, and the Labour Relations Bill, 1950, have been introduced in Indian Parliament. These bills will deprive you of your priceless right to strike and will inflict compulsory arbitration. Cancellation of registration of your unions will become an easy affair. The Labour unions in the railways and post and telegraph departments will be reduced to mere tools in the hands of the Government. The labour movement will be segregated from politics which will means that labour will be denied the opportunity of establishing its own Government.

[1] Adapted from *Searchlight*, 3 May 1950.

Comrades, are you going to take this challenge lying down or will you take the vow to fight to the bitter end for your birthright? This is the question which this historic day poses before you this year. This is a question of life and death for you. If you express your disapproval of these black bills, with one voice, there is no doubt that the Government will be compelled to take them back. But if you are not vigilant you will be crushed.

305. Remarks at a Public Meeting regarding Implementation of the Indo-Pak Agreement on Minorities, Hyderabad, 4 May 1950[1]

I hope that the implementation of the Indo-Pak agreement on minorities in both Bengals would pave the way for the conclusion of a treaty for a united foreign policy between the two countries, ultimately leading to their re-union.

Irrespective of what Pakistan did, India should not only implement the latest agreement but ensure security of life and property to every Muslim so that not a single member of that community should be made to leave for Pakistan. Having made India a secular State in a real sense where everyone has equal opportunities, the Government should conduct negotiations with the Pakistan Government if the minorities in that country contunue to live under fear for life and property. If a direct approach for ensuring the peaceful living of Hindus in Pakistan fails India should, if possible, seek the help of an international body like the united Nations with a view to making Pakistan realize the need to protect the Hindu population there. If even this method proves fruitless, then there is no alternative for India but to send her army to Pakistan not to annex her but to protect the life and property of the minorities. I emphasise that this should be our last resort and is possible if the hands of India are clean and not a single Muslim feels insecure in this country.

The creation of Pakistan did not in any way solve the question of minorities in both the countries. Ever since the attainment of freedom, communal clashes have occurred in India and Pakistan almost by rotation. The energies of the Government are directed mainly to the rehabilitation of thousands of refugees and we can hardly think of solving the economic problems. The recent disturbances in the Bengals have brought to the fore the minority problem in all its grimness. One of the solutions suggested is exchange of populations which, if accepted, would negate the principle of a secular State which we have cherished from the days of Mr. Dadabhai

[1]Adapted from *Hindu*, 6 May 1950.

Naoroji[2] to the present day. Besides it would lead to interminable conflicts which might ultimately ruin both the States politically and economically. The division of the country on a religious basis holds dangerous possibilities which might result in the Balkanisation of the country.

Some of my Bengali friends suggest the re-union of Bengals to form an independent State. The suggestion is not only impracticable, but its acceptance is also likely to result in the creation of a number of independent States on a linguistic basis which is detrimental to national interests. Therefore, the only way to the establishing peace between India and Pakistan is that India should become a secular State in the real sense of the term. It is gratifying that this principle is accepted by the Government of India and an earnest effort is being made to build the State on a secular, democratic basis.

I hope that if there is a Government of the poor in the saddle in Delhi as well as in Karachi, India and Pakistan would come together and a re-union would be effected not by force but by love and friendship.

[2]Dadabhai Naoroji (1825-1917); generally known as the grand old man of India; one of the stalwarts of the Congress in its early phase.

306. Rermarks at a Workers' Rally on Trade Union Unity, Secunderabad, 6 May 1950[1]

The greatest danger facing the Indian working class today is contained in the two contemplated Bills, The Trade Unions Bill and The Labour Relations Bill. They would not only restrict the workers' fundamental rights, but reduce the workers to the position of serfs.

Mr. R.S. Ruikar has suggested that the Hind Mazdoor Sabha should form an united front with the All-India Trade Union Congress and the United Trade Union Congress to oppose the new Bills. We stand for unity among workers for securing the workers' demands, but can not overlook the peculiar atmosphere in which the trade union movement has grown in this country. The A.I.T.U.C. is no doubt the oldest trade union organization, but even a person of the stature of Mr. N.M. Joshi was forced to resign from it after being a member for 20 years. The reasons that made him and several other labour leaders like him leave that organization still exist. No useful purpose would be served by trying to come to an agreement with it. It is an open secret that the A.I.T.U.C. follows a policy which advocates sabotage, creation of anarchic conditions and use of violent methods. The Communists who dominate this organization want to take advantage of any opportunity to further their own political ends even at the cost of the interests of workers.

The Hind Mazdoor Sabha, on the other hand, believes in peaceful methods

[1]Adapted from *Hindu*, 7 May 1950.

to defend the workers' rights. The difference in means is a fundamental one and there can be no meeting ground between the A.I.T.U.C. and the Hind Mazdoor Sabha. In my opinion the only way to create unity among the entire working class is to bring all the workers under the banner of the Sabha.

At the other end is the Indian National Trade Union Congress. Its General Secretary has already extended his support to the two bills affecting the Indian workers so adversely. I characterise the approach of the I.N.T.U.C. to labour problems as detrimental to the well-being of workers.

Thus the Hind Mazdoor Sabha can come to an agreement neither with the A.I.T.U.C. nor with the I.N.T.U.C. I am, however, prepared to arrive at an agreement with the U.T.U.C

I refute the criticism of some persons that the International Confederation of Free Trade Unions is dominated by the agents of Anglo-American capitalists. While the World Federation of Trade Unions is a Communist organization, the I.C.F.T.U. is a federation of free trade unions in spite of some of its defects.

307. To K.K. Menon, 12 May 1950[1]

Dear K.K.,[2]

I have a copy of your circular on the People's Representation Bill. I am glad to find the election office function so well.

In this connection I should have written you earlier. I was in Delhi just when the Bill was in Parliament and I talked to Panditji as well as Dr. Ambedkar about certain points which you have raised in the circular.

Ambedkar told me that he had deliberately left out matters such as system of voting and that would be taken up in another bill which he would introduce in October. He made a statement to this effect in Parliament too, as you will remember.

I am considering a joint conference of representatives of the opposition parties some time in the 4th week of June in Bombay to consider the entire election business. I shall soon be writing to the parties concerned. I intend to write to the Hindu Mahasabha, the Scheduled Caste Federation, and the United Socialist Organization. Would you suggest some other names?

How about issuing a pamphlet for Party workers on the election procedure and election work.

You should also prepare a memorandum on the procedure of election to

[1] *J.P. Papers* (NMML).

[2] K.K. Menon was at that time one of the secretaries of the Socialist Party.

be placed before the President and the Election Commissioner—that is, concrete suggestions so as to make the election really democratic. If you send me a draft, I shall send you my suggestions,

I hope you are well.

With affectionate greetings,

Yours sincerely,
J.P.

308. Why the Socialist Party Supports the Delhi Pact,[1] 14 May 1950[2]

For a brief space of recentmost history I rose to dizzy heights of popularity in West Bengal. I must confess it was a rather pleasant experience; for who does not relish the acclaim of the crowd? Now again I have dropped down to the usual pedestrian level that has always been mine in the Province.

Incidentally this personal history has shown how cheap is the price of popularity. A mere statement can make one the darling of the people and a mere statement again can make the same people jeer and boo. Unfortunately it is not popularity that I have ever sought in politics, but the right path to serve my country and my people. History shows that popular clamour has not always coincided with national interest, and that nation-builders had often to discipline mass frenzy and sometimes even face martyrdom in the process. Mahatma Gandhi is the most illustrious example in all history. Let me not be misunderstood. I am not placing myself in the ranks of nation-builders. I am but a humble servant of the nation. My purpose in drawing attention to history is merely to correct perspective.

I have been accused of turning a somersault. Nehru again has been discovered to be the villain of the piece, for it was he who is alleged to have persuaded me to change my mind. Nehru-phobia seems to be a disease no less epidemic today in some parts of the country than cholera.

Let me, in view of this psychopathic climate, state at the outset my position with regard to Nehru. It was twenty years ago, early in 1930, soon after my return from the United States that I started my political career under Nehru in the office of the AICC as secretary of the Labour Department.

[1]Delhi Agreement on Minorities; signed by Jawaharlal Nehru and Liaquat Ali Khan in Delhi on 18 April 1950; popularly known as Nehru-Liaquat Pact. Under it, the Government of India and Pakistan solemnly agreed that each shall ensure to the minorities throughout its territory complete equality of citizenship, irrespective of religion, a full sense of security in respect of life, culture, property and personal honour, freedom of movement within each country and freedom of occupation, speech and worship subject to law and morality.

[2]*Janata*, 14 May 1950.

Nehru was President of the Indian National Congress. Since that time I have held Nehru in high regard and affection and I have learnt a great deal from him. It has always been a source of happiness to me that, as in the case of Gandhiji, whether in agreement or opposition I have always had Nehru's confidence and affection. Unfortunately for the past some years it has been my misfortune to find myself more often than not in disagreement with him on major issues. Soon after the August Revolution, it may be recalled, when the AICC assembled at Bombay [in 1946] it was Nehru who moved that the Committee accept the Pethick Lawrence Plan of independence for India.[3] I, on behalf of the Socialist group, opposed him and urged for a total rejection of the Plan. It was because of that policy of total rejection that, and spite of pressure, we kept out of the Constituent Assembly, which was but a part of that Plan.

When the Nehru Government was formed, our divergence with his Government's policy ultimately compelled us to leave the Congress and form an independent Socialist Party. Our main difference with him today is that whereas we would like here and now to lay the foundations of a socialist India, Nehru has put socialism on the shelf and his Government is proceeding to reconstruct the economic and political structure of this country on the existing basis of private enterprise.

Had I been inclined, as I am painted to be, to suspend my independent judgment in favour of Nehru's persuasion, I would have been today not in the ranks of the Opposition but elsewhere. Opposition, however, has never meant to me abuse and ranting or exploitation of a national calamity to party advantage. Nevertheless, those who are accustomed to ranting and who raise amoralism to a basic theorem of politics will not appreciate the decencies of public life.

Almost every time I have met Nehru in the last years, the papers, or at any rate some papers, have been thick with rumours about a Congress-Socialist coalition. Every time, in turn, these wishful thinkers and equally wishful detractors, have been proved false. But undaunted they merrily carry on the game.

II

Let me—now that the heat of controversy has abated somewhat—state the position of the Socialist Party in regard to this difficult problem in the hope that cooler minds will find reason more acceptable. Incidentally, I shall also examine the alleged shifts in our policy.

[3]This refers to the Plan issued on behalf of the British Government by the Cabinet Mission on 16 May 1946 and usually known as the Cabinet Mission Plan. Pethick Lawrence, Secretary of State for India, was the leader of the Mission. Its other members were A.V. Alexander and Stafford Cripps.

Pakistan owed its birth to a fallacious principle and a vicious practice. The principle was that religion alone constituted the basis of nationality. According to this principle it was contended, for instance, that the Bengali Muslim, and frontier Pathans were members of one nation, while the Bengali Hindu and Bengali Muslim belonging to the same ethnic group, speaking the same language, sharing the same culture and living in the same village belonged to two separate nations!

The principle was so fantastic that even imperialist machination would have failed to establish it, had not ugly and vicious facts been produced to support it. These facts were the riots. Whether Hindu killed Muslim or Muslim killed Hindu, whether it was the great Calcutta killing, or Noakhali, Bihar or Garhmukteshwar, the result was the same: demonstration of the fact that Hindus and Muslims could not live together because they were two separate nations.

The principle and the practice combined to partition the country. But the partition solved nothing. While the two nation theory brought into being two separate States, the two separate "nations" still faced each other on both sides of the border. The prime question then was: would these *separate* "nations' live together in amity and be welded into a common nationality? The question was the same that had faced undivided India; and if the answer was found to be affirmative, partition and all the attendant bitterness and hostility had been unnecessary: the two nations might as well have lived together in undivided India.

The two countries started to answer the historic question in two different settings. When the Congress accepted partition, it did not accept the two nation theory. It still believed in a common Indian nationality and explained the acceptance of partition as a choice of the lesser of the two evils, the greater being continuous communal strife. Thus with the exception of a small section of Hindu communal opinion, India started with a firm faith in a common nationhood. The party that came to power was a non-communal body. The organic law of the nation laid down clearly that the Indian State would be secular and democratic. The task of welding Mr. Jinnah's two nations was thus not too difficult in India. The Indian Muslims, fed on Mr. Jinnah's theory might have found it rather difficult at the beginning to adjust themselves to the prospect of common nationhood. But the theory being artificial their adjustment could not have ultimately been difficult.

The situation was different on the other side. Pakistan was born out of the two-nation theory. The advocates of that theory were themselves in power, and the ruling party, the Muslim League, was a frankly communal party. The objectives resolution of the Pakistan Constituent Assembly prescribed an Islamic basis for the State that was to be built up there. It may be remarked parenthetically that Mr. Liaquat Ali Khan's recent reference to Ramrajya in this connection was irrelevant, because while there is a considerable loose talk in this country about Ramrajya, it finds no mention in the Constitution or in any documents connected with it.

In view of this setting in Pakistan, the emergence there of a common nation of Muslims, Hindus, and Sikhs was, to say the least, problematical.

Then followed the Punjab and the Sind tragedies. It appeared that the two nation theory was still at work and Pakistan was determined to squeese out the minorities. Whatever might have been the real intentions of Pakistan, the facts seemed to fit that assumption.

Then came Bengal. It appeared again that the squeesing out process was still at work.

What is the solution of this awful problem? This was the anguished question that millions asked. In the opinion of the Socialist Party there are only two solutions of this problem and no third.

One solution is to accept the full implications of the two nation theory. That would mean the expulsion of all Hindus from Pakistan and of all Muslims from India. I understand that exchange of the Hindu and Muslim populations of East and West Bengal was the solution suggested by Dr. Syama Prasad Mookerjee. Some others too have made that suggestion. But it is not realized that such an exchange of population can never stop with East and West Bengal. The logic of the situation would drive us to its inexorable end.

This solution is wholly repugnant to me, as it must be to all who believe in the principles of human civilization. To be forced to accept the principle that two human beings could not live together just because their religions were different was to go back to the dark ages and to deny everything that one has stood for.

The practical aspects of this solution are no less repugnant. People cannot be forced out of their homes except by force. Application of force on such a mass scale cannot but brutalise the whole people and reduce life in this country to the brutest level. Further, such gigantic migrations must disorganize the country's economy and put a strain on the State that must prove unbearable. Again, exchange of a crore of Hindus for four crores of Muslims must start the train of a new conflict, because Pakistan would feel justified to demand new territory to settle the excess population. The remedy would thus have created a new disease.

The acceptance of this solution would also mean the victory of the Hindu communalism and the ascendancy of the *Hindu-Rashtra* mentality. That would inevitably stimulate separatism further; and then the separatist mentality might not be restricted to religious communities, but might spread to racial, linguistic and even caste groups. That would be the end of India.

Thus considered from every point of view, the idea of exchange of populations must be given up.

That leaves only one possible solution; namely that both India and

Pakistan be secular States and the minorities in both do have full security and equal citizenship.

It was in the light of this basic analysis that the Socialist Party Executive had enunciated at Rewa its policy in regard to the East Bengal situation. Since it still remains our policy, let us bring out the main points. The main points are three. First, India must hold fast to its secular character. Whatever might have happened in Pakistan, India must give full protection and security to its Muslim citizens and guarantee them equal rights of citizenship.

Second, India should, by friendly approaches to Pakistan, try to persuade that country to join hands to guarantee in words and deeds full protection and opportunity for development to all minorities. The Executive went on further to say that in this connection the Prime Minister's suggestion for a joint enquiry commission and a joint tour with Mr. Liaquat Ali Khan was a commendable beginning. The suggestion bore no fruit. But further attempts should be made and the idea of a joint tour and enquiry should be expanded to wider joint action.

The last point provides for a way out in case of a possible failure of these efforts. To quote the Executive again: "If the earnest attempts of our Government do not succeed and the people and Government of Pakistan persist in their present policy, India must finally, and sooner rather than later, *act on her own and take every measure to protect the minorities and human rights in Pakistan*".

I still stand four square by this policy and hold that there is no alternative. Where then is my famous somersault? In the imagination, I must say, of my critics who do not take the trouble to understand but are ever ready to misjudge.

A few days after the Socialist Party Executive had issued its statement I addressed the Nagpur Institute of Journalists and elucidated the Party view-point. Asked to explain the words 'take every measure to protect the minorities and human rights in Pakistan', I told the Nagpur Institute that every measure included as the last resort the sending of our forces into Pakistan to protect the minorities. The next morning the papers flashed my statement: 'Jayaprakash demands armed intervention'. And my stocks soared high in West Bengal. And Mr. M.N. Roy[4] denounced my war-mongering and Mr. Khwaja Ahmad Abbas[5] my sabre-rattling. Attempt was even made to show that there was a rift in the Socialist Party on this issue and

[4]For biographical note on M.N. Roy see *JPSW*, Vol. II, p.124.

[5]Khwaja Ahmad Abbas (1914-88); Novelist, Filmmaker and Journalist. Worked in Bombay Chronicle as journalist 1935-47; shifted his weekly column entitled "Last Page" from Bombay Chronicle to Blitz; awarded President's gold medal for his film "Shehar aur Sapna", 1963; got Padma Shri 1968, Mirza Ghalib Award for Urdu Prose 1983-4, Soviet Land Nehru Award for Indo-Soviet Friendship and World Peace 1985.

Mr. Asoka Mehta's fine efforts to contact the Pakistan Trade Union leader were represented as being in contradiction to my views. I wish both critics and friends tried to understand.

While it is true that I had suggested what is known in International Law as "measure short of war", it was not right to overlook the qualifying conditions and fasten attention only on the final step. Let me remind the reader of the conditions I had set forth. First, I had emphasised that there must be peace and order in India and our Muslim citizens must live without fear and in enjoyment of equal rights with Hindus. As I had said in a later statement, we cannot rush to protect minorities and human rights elsewhere when we fail to do so at home. Second, I had insisted at Nagpur that though Nehru's friendly approaches had proved infructuous, fresh attempts should be made to reach a peaceful solution. This is how my "war-mongering" statement was summed up by the *Nagpur Hitavada*, in whose office incidentally the Institute of Journalists had met: "A plea for exploring all possible avenues of peaceful settlement of Indo-Pakistani relations arising out of the situation in East Bengal was made by Mr. Jayaprakash Narayan at the Nagpur Institute of Journalists this evening". It will thus be seen that it was only in the event of all peaceful efforts failing and when we had succeeded in keeping peace at home and doing justice to our own minorities, that I had suggested what was described as armed intervention.

After that it was not I who changed but the objective situation. The communal position rapidly deteriorated in West Bengal and incidents took place on a large scale, the dimensions of which have not yet been made known to the people of this country. Pandit Nehru had spoken of an iron curtain in Pakistan but I found a steel curtain in Calcutta itself, where practically nothing of what was happening next door in Howrah or Hooghly found the light of publicity. To say, as it has been said *ad nauseum*, that the people acted when the Government failed to act, does not unfortunately alter the terrible facts. In view of these facts, to have persisted in the demand for police action would have been perverse and without any moral justification whatever. I shall concede that there was perhaps a full week in which the Government of India would have been justified to act. But perhaps the hope of a peaceful settlement prevented Nehru from taking a step which was not only fraught with grave danger but was sure to cause greater suffering and hardship to the whole people.

As it turned out, Nehru's hope was justified, and a peaceful settlement was arrived at. To oppose that settlement or to sabotage it is to play with fire, for as Nehru has said the alternative is war. War is a frightful affair and no sane person would rush into it when other avenues of settlement are open. Nor would war necessarily save the Hindus of East Bengal nor help in the rehabilitation of the refugees.

There is a great deal of talk about the honesty of purpose of Pakistan. Will they implement the Agreement? We are asked on all sides. It occures to no one to ask if we will implement it. Judging from the temper of the people of West Bengal and the attitude of its press, one may well ask that question. Let us remember that if we implemented the Agreement and Pakistan did not, a solution—though a tragic solution—would yet be available. But if we both failed to do the job, no solution could ever be found. A war fought in a communal climate on both sides could only result in mutual destruction. It would be quite a different affair, however, if an India which had upheld the principles of civilization and respected human rights used force for the enforcement of these very rights and principles. The result of such force cannot but be the defeat of the forces of evil and reaction.

III

Let me say a word to those who accused me of sabre-rattling. As a socialist, I have ever been an enemy of communalism. I was a bitter opponent of the League and its two-nation theory and of partition. I was also, and am, an opponent of Hindu, Sikh and all other communalism. When Gandhiji was assassinated, it was common talk in certain circles in Delhi that Nehru was second on the list and my turn came next. I have not changed since then.

Let me remind my critics of what Gandhiji had said at the time of the Punjab riots. When the gigantic forced migrations began, Gandhiji firmly set his face against them. He declared solemnly that he would never accept the migrations as final and would never bow his head before the principle that human beings could not live together just because they professed different faiths.

Congenial conditions must be created in India so that every Muslim who has fled to save his life may return to his home and live here in peace and with honour. In Pakistan too similar conditions must be created so that every Hindu and Sikh may go back to live with honour and happiness.

If we succeed in creating such conditions in India and Pakistan fails, I would be prepared to fight with Pakistan on that issue. Let it be remembered that it was in trying to create these conditions in India that the nation's father was martyred.

My proposal is no different in principle from what Gandhiji has said. There is no doubt, of course, that the Mahatma was sure that if he succeeded in creating the conditions for which he was working, the moral force of this success would have conquered Pakistan and the fight of which he talked would have been unnecessary. Lesser men like me might nurse the same hope. At any event, let it be remembered that there is no room for *force majeure* in my proposal if we fail to create the conditions for the Muslims of India that we are demanding for the Hindus of Pakistan.

But if we do that, and Pakistan does not and rejects all peaceful methods of settlement, then I do expect all Muslims in India, including Mr. Khwaja Ahmad Abbas, to join honds with other Indians in compelling Pakistan by force to do its duty to its citizens. If that is sabre-rattling then words have ceased to have any meaning.

Let me, before I conclude examine certain other solutions that have been suggested. One suggestion, fashionable in Leftist circles in West Bengal, is about the creation of an independent, united Bengal. If finding a solution of a serious practical problem merely means wishful thing, the above may be considered a solution. But there is absolutely no chance, to my mind, of either India or Pakistan agreeing to a second dismemberment. And without the agreement of both, independent united Bengal must remain on paper.

Further, it is not clear to me how, when a communal division of the country has failed to bring peace, a linguistic division would succeed. Let it not be forgotten that the East and West Bengal question in not the only source of conflict between India and Pakistan.

Another solution, also emanating from Left circles, is that of two autonomous provinces of East and West Bengal—one Hindu and the other Muslim, and both under the Indian Republic. As in the previous case, it is not clear how East Bengal would be detached from Pakistan, nor, why when it was detached must it remain separate from the rest of Bengal. One has thought that the linguistic, cultural and economic pulls are so great that the two Bengals would inevitably come together once the artificial partition is undone.

Lastly, a few words about *Akhand Bharat*. There is a great deal of talk about the re-union of India and Pakistan in Hindu communal circles. It is tragic, however, that these circles do not realize that by their actions they do everything possible to defeat their purpose. It was communalism, both Muslim and Hindu, that was responsible for the division of the country. Communalism now can only further divide and alienate. If the Hindu communalist is dreaming, as he well might, of reuniting the broken pieces by a war of conquest, he is living in a fool's paradise.

Ten crores of Muslims of Pakistan and India can never be forced to be citizens of India by the sword. Even if the world allows the battle to be fought and India is victorious, its victory would become its defeat, for it would have a hundred million rebels on its lands, backed by millions outside.

It would be a task beyond the power of any nation to keep a hundred million people under subjugation. And why should India want to subjugate any one? Did we win our freedom from subjugation only to subjugate others? If I understand my countrymen, their overwhelming answer surely would be no.

Strange as it may appear I too dream of a re-united India. I dream of it because I am a Socialist. I dream of it because I have faith in the toiling peoples of the earth. I dream of it because I dream of an Asian Federation and ultimately of a World Government. But a World Government is a far cry from Hindu Imperialism.

309. Statement regarding Scandals in the Bihar Ministry, Patna, 19 May 1950[1]

Almost since the formation of the present Bihar Ministry all manner of scandals about corruption and nepotism have been afoot. Public opinion in this State has unfortunately been unassertive and the Opposition has suffered from lack of proper means of publicity.

Molasses, iron and Bettiah lands on the one hand and certain Ministers, public servants and Congress Party leaders on the other have been the main actors in this sordid drama.

At one stage the matter was referred to the Congress Working Committee which appointed Sardar Patel to investigate and report. After many months of comings and goings between Delhi and Patna and hesitations and negotiations, the Sardar's final verdict was given and published. In furtherance of that verdict the Provincial Government has introduced a Bill in the Legislature to force Shri R.P.N. Sahi to return the raj lands settled with him.

As this entire episode reeks with shady politics and the methods and measures used are likely to lower public life and administration further in this State, I feel compelled to say a few words in this connection.

First of all, it seems to me that the Congress High Command is attempting to make an escape-goat of a public servant to save Congress Ministers and party chiefs. If the Sardar and the Congress High Command do really desire to build traditions of clean and honest administration, the findings of Sardar Patel are enough to warrant a dismissal of the Bihar Ministry or, at the least, of certain notorious ministers who have figured in these scandals. An inadvertent slip sent a British Chancellor crashing down. But in this country, alss, in spite of so much chanting of hymns to the Apostle of Truth, even the most palpable misbehaviours in high circles go unpunished. It happened in Bengal, it happened in Madras and it is happening in Bihar. By making escape-goats of smaller fry the Congress is only encouraging misconduct in high quarters and strengthening the belief that Congress Ministers and leaders can do no wrong. If Shri Sahi is found to be at fault for accepting the Sathi lands, those who are custodians of the raj property are still more guilty. But instead of being punished they are being made to play the role

[1] *J.P. Papers* (NMML).

of the people's tribune enforcing justice with a strong arm! Can political chicanery go any further?

Again, it is not clear why only Shri Sahi is being forced to return the lands settled with him. It appears that thousands of bighas have been settled with outsiders. Why does the present Bill exclude them? Is it because, as it has been suggested, most of them are Congress Party stalwarts? By restricting the Bill to the Sathi lands alone, the Bihar Ministry is attempting to perpetrate another fraud upon the people of this State.

Finally, I must draw attention to the habit of the Congress Party of identifying itself with the Government. Sardar Patel was appointed by the Congress Party executive to investigate certain matters. In that capacity, while he had full authority to examine the conduct of Congress Ministers, he had no authority to ask for official files or summon public servants or decree action against them. Wherever the conduct of officials is concerned or even where the conduct of Ministers in their official capacity is concerned, it is dangerous for party bosses and party committees to hold enquiries. The proper course, which alone can inspire public confidence, is to appoint judicial committees of enquiry or other properly constituted official or non-official committees of enquiry. In any case a party boss, acting in that capacity, can never be permitted to order action to be taken against public servants. One of the greatest injuries Congressmen are causing the nation is by reducing the Public Service to more limbs of the Congress Party.

I reiterate that if the findings of Sardar Patel are well-founded, the ends of public morality demand not the Sathi Lands Restoration Bill alone but resignation of the Bihar Ministry and of the Provincial Congress Chief.

310. To Jawaharlal Nehru, 19 May 1950[1]

Dear Bhai,

You are perhaps aware of the doubts raised in opposition circles as to whether the coming general elections would be free and fair. I had brought to your notice what had happened in the U.P. Legislative bye-elections some two years ago. Events that have followed in many parts of the country have not in the least put our doubts at rest. I have heard that it is common talk in Congress high circles that no means would be spared to ensure a Congress victory. The complete and precipitous fall from Gandhian ideals of the Congress rather confirm one's doubts and all these gossips. I wish to bring to your notice certain incidents that took place in connection with a recent bye-election in Bihar. As a result of Dr. Sachchidananda Sinha's death a

[1]Prime Minister's Office, File No. 16(49)/50-PMS, Sr. No. 1-A.

seat had fallen vacant in the Bihar Assembly. Dr. Sinha represented the University Constituency in which there are only 325 voters of whom 145 are Govern-ment or semi-Government servants. One of my friends, Shri Awadhesh Nandan Sahay, who is a member of our Party was contesting the seat as an independent candidate. The Congress had put up its own candidate, Shri Awadh Bihari Jha. Awadhesh Nandan Sahay lost the election by 95 votes. The defeat did not matter in the least, but the methods used by the Congress Ministry filled me with the utmost fear that every kind of foul means would be used in the forthcoming general elections.

In this by-election the Ministry sought to bring all manner of pressure on the voters and officers of the Government including District Magistrates, Deputy Commissioners and Education and Police officers were used to canvass and to collect ballot papers from the voters. Ministers, including the Chief Minister, personally telephoned to Government servants advising them to vote for the Congress candidate. It is true that the Ministers did make it clear that they were speaking not in their official, but merely in their individual, capacity. You will appreciate that for employees of the Government, the distinction is hardly of any significance. Even so in some cases it happened that after the Minister had spoken to a voter in his "individual" capacity, a magistrate immediately turned up to collect the ballot paper from the person concerned. How could a Minister in his individual capacity instruct a magistrate to go about collecting ballot papers for a party candidate?

Further, Muslim voters were intimidated by high Government officers to vote for the Congress candidate under the threat that it was only the Congress which could protect the Muslims and not Shri Awadhesh Nandan Sahay.

The questions that I should like to frame for your consideration are:

1. Should the party in power use Government servants for party purposes, such as influencing voters?
2. Should Ministers canvass the voters of Government servants?
3. Should the minorities be intimidated into voting for the party in power, on the plea that the latter alone could offer them protection?
4. Keeping in mind the morale of the general public in this country, do you think that elections could ever be free if the party in power were to utilise Government officers and officials machinery for party purposes?

You might be told that some Government servants canvassed for Awadhesh Babu also. While it may be true that some of them—a very few—showed enough character and resisted all pressure and voted for Awadhesh Babu, I do not think any one did any actual canvassing for him. Even so, in the very midst of the election, three officers were asked, without any previous enquiry, to explain why they acted against the Service Rules in canvassing votes in an election. The same Government, or rather Ministers of the Government, as I pointed out above, actually directed their officers to work for the Congress candidate and collect ballot papers for him. This kind of double standard cannot but compel one to give up all faith in the honesty of the Congress ministry and to raise grave doubts about the fairness of the coming elections.

Let me warn that in the very nature of things the allegations I have made above cannot be proved in an official enquiry. But I have not the least doubt that were you to enquire from trustworthy private sources, they would all be amply substantiated.

To ensure free and fair elections is a big task. I have brought only one incident to your notice to show that the task cannot be handled with complacency.

With regards,

Affectionately yours,
Jayaprakash

311. To Mahadeo Singh, 20 May 1950[1]

My dear Mahadeo Singhji,[2]

You remember the promise you made to collect some money for the Central Office. Badri Vishal[3] wrote to me a few days ago that he was going to raise something with your help and the help of other friends in the next few days. I should like to impress upon you the urgency of the situation and to urge you to do what you can as soon as possible. I have written to Badri Vishal and also to Rameshwar Rao separately.

I am touring Bihar till the 4th June after which I will go to C.P. I will be at the Balaghat Camp from 10th to 15th June.

I hope you are all well.

Sincerely yours,
J.P.

[1] *J.P. Papers* (NMML).

[2] Mahadeo Singh, Hyderabad based Socialist Leader.

[3] Badri Vishal Pitti (1928-2003), Socialist Leader, member Legislative Assembly, Andhra Pradesh, 1967; Trustee Dr. Rammanohar Lohia Samta Trust, Hyderabad.

312. Reply to Bihar Revenue Minister's Charges, Patna, 29 May 1950[1]

I find that my statement about the Sathi land scandal has stung my friend, Babu Krishna Ballabh Sahay.[2] Among other things he has complained in the Bihar Assembly that I had not named the notorious ministers. True, but I had not done so because there was no need for it. No one in Bihar is in the least doubt about the identity of these ministers. But if Babu Krishna Ballabh Sahay finds it difficult to recognize these worthy characters let me help him out.

Shri Sahay might remember that it was one of these notorious ministers who was to have been turned out of the Government years ago but was saved by two leading Socialists of Bihar who interceded on his behalf with Gandhiji.

So much about that identity of the notorious ministers. Shri Sahay went further in the Assembly and threw out a challenge that if these ministers were named, he too would have to name the two Socialist leaders who had received settlement of some lands in the Saharsa district. Such exercise of restraint by a person of Shri Sahay's scruples would have indeed been surprising had it not been false restraint; because Shri Sahay on other occasions and to other audiences had already named at least one of these Socialist leaders.

His statement in the Bihar Assembly was also so worded that the insinuation was clear that one of these persons was my humble self. As the Congress party thrives on lies, and as this particular lie about me has been sedulously propagated for some time past, let me state the truth. I had taken no notice of these lies before because I was sure that the people concerned will not find it difficult to discover the truth.

It was many years ago that in the course of a talk with the late Babu Shiva Prasad Gupta[3] of Banaras about the economic difficulties of whole-time Congress workers, Shiva Prasadji, generous as he was, offered me some virgin land for cultivation in the Bhagalpur district. It was arranged later that three others would join me in taking settlement of these lands. These three friends were a second cousin of mine Panna Babu, and Babu Devakinandan Singh and Babu Kamala Prasad Singh of the village of

[1]Adapted from *Searchlight*, 30 May 1950.

[2]For biographical note on Krishna Ballabh Sahay see *JPSW*, Vol. II, p. 254.

[3]Shiv Prasad Gupta (1883-1944), a big landlord of Eastern U.P. and Bihar; a noted philanthropist; contributed one million rupees to help in founding Kashi Vidyapeeth and gave large sums to Banares Hindu University; imprisoned in Singapore for 3 months for his association with Indian revolutionaries in South America, Japan, China etc; associated with Congress since 1916; opposed the Congress adopting the parliamentary programme in 1937; believed in complete independence.

Khaspur in the district of Patna. In due course about 250 bighas were taken and these three friends started reclaiming and cultivating parts of the land. No legal settlement had yet been made. Most of this time, those being the war years, I was in prison. When I came out of prison, it did not seem right, on reconsidering the matter, that I should take any share of those lands. So I wrote to Babu Satyendra Prasad Gupta, Shivaprasadji's grandson, who with his brother had become the proprietor of the estate after Shiva Prasadji's death, that I was no longer interested in the land. Later on, the land was settled with the gentlemen who were to be my partners because they had in the meantime invested money in it and reclaimed it for cultivation.

As far as I know they paid some salami too, but that is their concern. These are the facts. Originally, the intention was that I should take a share of those lands, but as it turned out, the partnership never became effective and at no stage did I have anything to do with it. I neither invested a pie in it nor received a pie in return, nor a grain or corn.

Let me also make it clear—for a suggestion of that character has been made—that I have made no surreptitious deal either in regard to this or any other piece of land or of other property—a deal such as receiving settlement in the name of my wife or any other relation or friend. I shall be obliged to Shri Sahay if he will discover for me properties that I or my wife might possess—other than the little ancestral property at Sitabdiara.

As for the other Socialist leader of the country who has taken lands in Saharsa according to Shri Sahay, I should like him to name him, even though I have not named the notorious ministers. But let him make sure of his facts before he does so.

As for the Lohia commission surely the commission is welcome to begin its labours from Saharsa and I personally and the Socialist Party would give it all cooperation. And I hope Shri Sahay and his Government will in their turn give full cooperation to the commission in its labours in Champaran.

Before I conclude, let me warn Shri Sahay not to mix up issues and try to cover up his lapses by accusing others. While a private proprietor is free to give his property away to whomsoever he desires, ministers of Government in charge of public or private properties cannot misuse or throw them away. Nor does the present issue involve the principle of the maximum of the size of holdings. That issue is important, and I wish Shri Sahay had raised it in his land reform legislation. At any rate Shri Sahay would receive the full support of the Socialist Party if he ever shows courage enough really to reform the land system in this state and not merely did window dressing.

Finally, I cannot help referring to the cynical and unprincipled manner in which the Revenue Minister has handled the Sathi legislation in the Assembly. In the same breath he has defended his Government's action in settling the Sathi farms with the Sahi brothers and also asked the legislature to annul the settlement. Can cynicism and lack of principle go further?

The Revenue Minister's sole defence of this extraordinary behaviour was that the Sardar's will had to be carried out. That was a great insult to the Sardar, but that alone would not have mattered, for it was no concern of mine how Congressmen quarrelled among themselves. But issues of grave public importance are involved.

Can a state Legislature be made to enact a law merely because a person outside it, no matter how eminent, wills it?

Further, should our political life be allowed to fall so low that a Minister should openly declare that what he was doing was wrong but yet he had to do it because such was party discipline.

Would it not have been better for the morale of public life if the minister concerned resigned rather than publicly carry out what he considered wrong.

Lastly, by arguing that there was nothing wrong in the settlement of the Sathi farm or of the other Bettiah raj lands, and by refusing to extend the principles of the Sathi lands restoration bill to the other settlements, the Bihar Ministry has utterly exposed itself and proved its complicity in what the Sardar himself considered wrong.

That such a self-condemned ministry should last another day is a national tragedy.

313. To Leaders of Opposition Parties regarding a Proposed Conference on Free and Fair Elections, 30 May 1950[1]

Dear Friend,

We have in our country today an almost single-party State. Under this single-party State we are going to have general elections next year. Most of us in the Opposition feel that the party in power would not run the elections in an honest and fair manner. Therefore, it is the responsibility of the opposition parties to come together to consider what appropriate steps must be taken to ensure free and fair elections. Obviously education of the masses and creation of an independent public opinion is the most important guarantee of a free election. That of course is the task which I presume the opposition parties are trying to fulfil each in its own way. But there are also other necessary steps that must be taken to this end, particularly by the Government. For instance, there is the vital question of the system of voting and the character of constituencies. Then there are such questions as that of

[1] *J.P. Papers* (NMML). Similar letters were issued to leaders of opposition parties, and some eminent persons in public life on 14 June 1950.

number and location of polling booths, regulation of transport facilities, check on election expenditure etc.

I am therefore suggesting that we should meet together to discuss these matters so that a united front might be presented to Government and the maximum pressure might be exerted on them to take the necessary steps to guarantee honest elections. I, therefore, invite your organization to join the conference which I am convening of representatives of the opposition parties in Bombay on 1st and 2nd July. I hope earnestly that you will accept this invitation and intimate to Shri K.K. Menon, Socialist Party, National House, 6 Tulloch Road, Apollo Bunder, Fort, Bombay, the time of your arrival and that of your other comrades in Bombay so that arrangements might be made for accommodation etc. I suggest that *not more than five* representatives should attend on behalf of any single organization that is being invited.

In addition to representatives of opposition parties, I am also inviting some distinguished public men who are interested in the future of democracy in this country. My address till June 13, is:

Socialist Workers' Camp,
Balaghat C.P.

and thereafter till early July: Socialist party, National House, 6 Tulloch Road, Apollo Bunder, Fort, Bombay.

Yours sincerely,
Jayaprakash Narayan

314. To Jawaharlal Nehru, 30 May 1950[1]

Dear Bhai,

I thank you for your letter of May 23.[2] I am afraid, you have treated a very grave problem in a rather light manner. There was hardly any need for you to answer the questions which I had formulated. Your answers were of course never in doubt as far as I was concerned. The real problem is as to what should be done to ensure fair elections. Considering the moral tone of the Congress organization and the Congress Ministries, I too have no doubt that unless very special efforts were made and strict measures adopted, the elections would never be fair. Not only would there be intimidation, violence and dishonesty of every kind, but, I am afraid, even ballot boxes would be tampered with. In one para of your letter you have mentioned circumstances which accentuate irregularities and unfairness. And all that you say that will be done is to "draw" the attention of all provincial Governments and

[1] *J.P. Papers* (NMML).
[2] For Nehru's letter to J.P. see Appendix 21

others to this question of governmental interference in elections. I am afraid, this ,is, as I have said above, a very light treatment of a serious question. Mere drawing attention of the provincial Governments, etc., would hardly do. One assumes that the provincial Governments too are aware of the danger of governmental interference in elections. The question is how such interference can be stopped or reduced to the minimum and fair elections can be held. When the decision was announced to appoint an Election Commissioner, I thought the first step had been taken to ensure that the elections would be free from the control of the executive and the normal administrative machinery. But as things are developing, it appears that the Election Commissioner would function merely as the secretary of a new department of Government, that is the Election Department. Theoretically, the Election Commissioner's office may not be of such a nature, but I am referring to the actual practice.

I am not very clear as to the details of the independent election machinery that must be set up and of the election rules that must be drafted to ensure as free and fair elections as possible at this stage of our political development.

I am convening a conference of representatives of the important opposition parties where, I hope, it would be possible to settle these details which in due course would be communicated to you and the President and which I hope would receive due consideration. I have no doubt that you appreciate that were the people to lose faith in the honesty of elections and therefore in democracy itself, there would be nothing to prevent a civil war in this country, whatever your views or mine may be regarding such a civil war. Already there is a growing lack of faith in political parties and in parliament and assemblies and if this mood were to be reinforced by dishonest and unfair elections, even a match would be enough to start a general conflagration.

I do not expect you to reply elaborately to every letter that I write. I would be content to know that the matters which I bring to your notice receive your earnest consideration.

I hope a previous letter that I wrote to you about the two labour bills is under your consideration.

Yours affectionately,
Jayaprakash Narayan

P.S. After writing the above I read a letter from K.K. Menon, who is the head of our election office at Bombay. I am quoting from his letter:

"As the Election Commissioner had Orissa first on his itinerary I asked Surendra[3] to interview him and represent our view-point. I wanted Mr. Sen[4]

[3]Surendra Nath Dwivedi, socialist leader of Orissa.

[4]Sukumar Sen, Chief Election Commissioner.

to know wherever he went that the Socialist Party was serious about its job. An appointment with Mr. Sen was fixed by the Orissa Government (through which intermediary it had to be done). As Surendra fell ill he contacted the Government who agreed to the Joint Secretary meeting Mr. Sen. But for some reason the Government did not allow the interview. Surendra is quite sore about it and has sent in a protest." (Surendra Nath Dwivedi is Provincial Secretary, Orissa Socialist Party.)

I fail to understand why a representative of an opposition party must see the Election Commissioner through the provincial Government. The Government in such a matter and in the present circumstances can hardly be considered as different from the Congress Party. The Election Commissioner should have his own secretariat and appointment with him should be made through his own office. It should be entirely his job to decide whom he should and whom he should not interview. This is just one instance which goes to prove what I have said above that the office of the Election Commissioner is also being made subservient to that of the Government.

315. Address at Silver Jubilee Convention of the All-India Railwaymen's Federation, Nagpur, 7 June 1950[1]

Sometimes it is rather humiliating to hear railwaymen say that they got absolutely nothing from the Federation. I do not know whether this kind of irresponsible talk does any good, either to the railwaymen or to the Federation. However, every railwayman who has worked for the Federation knows that the Federation has rendered very valuable services to the railwaymen's cause. I hope that this record of progress would continue and the Federation would grow from strength to strength.

I call upon the Railwaymen's Federation to elect a new president for the ensuing year. I have decided not to stand for election this year. For over two years I occupied the office of President of the Federation. But I feel that, owing to other preoccupations, I can not devote as much time as I would have liked to. The plan of developing the Federation which I had in mind when I took office, has remained unrealised and I think that you should elect as your president one who can devote more time to the Federation and give you a better lead.

I warn the railwaymen of the dangers they are facing, external as well as internal. External dangers are the activities of rival unions, the two labour bills that are before the Parliament, and the attitude of Government towards its employees. I am, however, confident that you can meet these dangers if you are able to remove your internal weaknesses.

[1]Adapted from *Tribune*, 9 June 1950.

The Federation did not receive during the past year the co-operation it was entitled to from the affiliated unions and railwaymen. I find great lethargy in the affiliated unions. I ask the unions to shake off this lethargy, and put in hard work to enable the Federation to consolidate its strength.

As for the two labour bills now before the Select Committee of the Parliament, except the I.N.T.U.C. all trade unions are unanimous in calling them black bills. I assure the Federation of my full support in its fight against these two bills and suggest that the Federation at this present session should formulate a definite plan of action for this fight. The Federation should enlist the co-operation of other labour bodies in the country in fighting these two bills.

316. To Sisir Kumar, 15 June 1950[1]

My dear Sisir,

As you know Gangababu[2] has gone to Madras on my behalf to look after the arrangements for the Annual Conference. He is not likely to return before the 3rd week of July. Your election office, however, should not be inactive in the meanwhile. I should therefore like you to collect all the necessary information including population statistics, maps, relevant Government publication and so on. I should also like you to advise the Provincial Party to take up the work of scrutiny of electoral rolls as soon as they are published. The first examination of the rolls should be to ascertain whether all eligible members of the Party are enlisted, particularly all possible candidates. Then it should be seen whether in every locality all the qualified voters are enlisted and whether there are bogus entries, etc. You should also give effect through the Provincial office to all circulars that you receive from Com. K.K. Menon and you should reply to all the correspondence you receive from him. I had asked you to write an article on your experiences at Jamalpur and elsewhere. If you have not done this, will you do so immediately? You should also keep me in touch with your activities.

I believe my house in Patna is not entirely closed down and whenever you are in Patna you should stay there and have your meals. If there is any difficulty please let me know. I shall be in Bombay from now till the beginning of the Annual Conference.

I hope your brother is better now.

Yours affectionately,
J.P.

[1] *J.P. Papers* (NMML).

[2] For biographical note on Ganga Sharan Sinha see *JPSW*, Vol. III, p. 81.

317. Reply to K.B. Sahay's Statement in the Bihar Legislative Assembly, Balaghat, 15 June 1950[1]

Immediately after replying to Shri Krishna Ballabh Sahay's statement which he had made in the Bihar Legislative Assembly, I had to leave the State for Madhya Pradesh. Therefore I was not able to see Shri Sahay's rejoinder when it appeared in the press. I have now a copy of the rejoinder sent to me here from Patna.

Shri Sahay has argued like a lawyer with a bad case and instead of arguments has relied on abuse and untruths. Also instead of confining himself to the issues raised by the Sathi Land Restoration Bill, he has produced a long dissertation on the achievements of the Bihar Government and the failures of the Socialist Party in the agrarian and labour fields. By indulging in all this irrelevance, Shri Sahay has confirmed the conclusion that he has no case whatever and that he has found public criticism unanswerable.

This is no place for me to go into the success or failures of the Socialist Party and the achievements of the Congress Party, but I should like to take this opportunity to state that I find myself in complete agreement with Shri Sahay when he says that it will take the Socialist Party, if it ever comes into power, four generations to achieve what the Bihar Congress Ministry has done in the course of four years. I confess I cannot imagine even the worst possible socialist government perpetrating even in forty generations such scandals as the molasses scandal, the iron scandal and the Bettiah land settlement scandal, to mention only a few of the achievements of the Bihar Government.

As regards Shri Sahay's gloating reference to the imagined debacle of the Socialist Party at Dalmianagar, Jhumri Telaiya and Agartala, let me make him a sporting offer. Let a plebiscite of the workers be taken at these centres under impartial and honest auspices, and if the majority of the workers are found to vote for the INTUC unions, the Socialist Party would close down its shop there.

Regarding the personal attack he had made on me, Shri Sahay returns to the charge by merely asserting that I never divested myself of the lands in Saharsa. I am not accustomed to have my facts contradicted. Shri Sahay had challenged the Lohia Commission to investigate into the two land deals in Saharsa which he had mentioned in his first statement in the Assembly. As far as my information goes, the Lohia Commission took up the challenge and offered to investigate the matter and wrote to Shri Sahay, but his co-operation was not forthcoming. However, as I am anxious that this matter be investigated and as the charge was made by a responsible Minister on the floor of the Assembly, may I make a request to the Hon'ble Speaker of the Bihar Legislative Assembly? Will he be good enough to enquire

[1] *J.P. Papers* (NMML).

personally into the said charges of Shri Krishna Ballabh Sahay or ask someone else, of whose honesty and integraity he is assured, to conduct the enquiry on his behalf? I shall unfortunately be away from Bihar till the fourth of week of July, after which I shall be in a position to offer to the Hon'ble Speaker my fullest cooperation.

Regarding the real issues involved, there has been a remarkable unanimity in Bihar in non-Congress circles and the non-official press. What I had said in my two statements was an echo of the voice of the people of Bihar. But the Bihar Ministry and Shri Sahay, secure in the unshakable majority they possess in the Legislature, can afford to flout public opinion with impunity. Let us hope the public will teach them the lesson that sooner or later all disloyal governments have to learn.

318. To Karpoori Thakur, 15 June 1950[1]

My dear Karpoori Thakur,

I am enclosing herewith a copy of my statement in reply to Krishna Ballabh Sahay's latest rejoinder. I am sending copies of this statement direct to the local press. So there is nothing that I want you to do about the publicity of this statement. I am writing to you about another aspect of the matter. As you will find from Krishna Ballabh Sahay's rejoinder, instead of replying to the issues raised he has gone into all kinds of irrelevant matters such as the achievements of the Bihar Ministry in the agrarian and labour fields. What I want you to do as Secretary of the Bihar Kisan Panchayat is to answer Krishna Ballabh Sahay's statement as far as it relates to agrarian matters. I hope you will soon issue an effective reply to him. I am writing to you in English because of the facility of dictation.

I hope you are well and with best wishes,

Yours sincerely,
J.P.

[1] *J.P. Papers* (NMML).

319. To Reyasat Karim, 15 June 1950[1]

My dear Reyasat Saheb,

I am enclosing herewith a copy of my statement in reply to Krishna Ballabh Sahay's rejoinder. I have had copies of it sent to the local press directly from here. All I want you to do is to ring up and find out from the editors

[1] *J.P. Papers* (NMML).

concerned whether they have received the statement already. I have also written to Bindababu[2] and I am enclosing a copy of the letter herewith. Please keep me informed of developments in the Province and all the progress that you friends are able to make.

I hope you are well and wish best wishes.

Yours sincerely,
J.P.

[2] Bindeshwari Prasad Verma, speaker of the Bihar Assembly.

320. To Bindeshwari Prasad Verma, 15 June 1950[1]

My dear Bindababu,

I am enclosing herewith a copy of my statement in reply to the rejoinder issued by Shri Krishna Ballabh Sahay to my previous statement. As you know, Krishna Ballabh Sahay has made a statement on the floor of the Assembly making certain pointed insinuations against me. Previously in his speeches in the Palamu district he had openly attacked me on the score that I have taken settlement of hundred of bighas of land in the district of Saharsa. In my last statement I gave the facts concerning this matter. Krishna Ballabh Sahay, however, has virtually made me out to be a liar and without giving any proofs has denied my facts. In his statement made in the Assembly he had challenged the Lohia Commission to investigate his charges against two prominent socialist leaders who had taken more than five hundred bighas of land in the district of Saharsa. As far as I am aware, the Lohia Commission wired and wrote to Krishna Ballabh Sahay offering to investigate into his charges, but the latter did not come forward to cooperate with the Commission. At the same time he goes on persisting in his lies. I am, therefore, seeking your protection and help. Krishna Ballabh Sahay made his first statement on the floor of the Assembly and therefore, as an aggrieved party, I have a claim upon you as the Speaker of the Assembly. I therefore request you to enquire into the charges made by Shri Krishna Ballabh Sahay in the Assembly or to ask someone else in whose honesty and integrity you have faith, to do the same. Krishna Ballabh Sahay's charges were very definite and it should be easy to find out the truth about them. I shall offer you or your delegate my fullest co-operation. My only difficulty is that I shall be out of Bihar till the fourth week of July after which I shall give you all the time that you need for investigating this matter.

I hope you are well and with kind regards,

Yours sincerely,
Jayaprakash

[1] *J.P. Papers* (NMML).

321. To K.T. Shah, 19 June 1950[1]

Dear Prof. Shah,[2]

I thank you for your letter of June 12. I am happy to know that you have accepted my invitation to the forthcoming Conference of Opposition parties. I have invited only political parties and such political organizations as the U.S.O. and the Scheduled Castes Federation. I have not invited trade unions or peasant organizations. At the same time I have invited certain eminent publicmen as yourself, Mr. Kunzru,[3] Mr. P.R. Das and others.

If you refer to the circular letter a copy of which I had enclosed with my letter of invitation to you, you will find that my object in calling this Conference is not to consider the formation of leftist front, but to consider what the Opposition parties must do to ensure that the forthcoming elections are honest, free and fair. For this reason I have invited even those political parties with whom my Party at least has fundamental ideological differences such as the Hindu Mahasabha. This does not mean that I do not appreciate the need of a leftist front, but that is a separate question and we might discuss it separately.

I am now in Bombay and shall be here till the Conference. I shall, therefore, like to meet you some time and discuss the problems involved. I shall be happy if you could have tea with me on Friday the 23rd June between 4 and 5 p.m. at the residence of Shri Purshottam Trikamdas at 40, Ridge Road (Tel. 43379). If this time does not suit you, you may suggest any other suitable time for you or if you want me to come over to your place I shall be happy to do so.

In a day or two I shall be sending you a short note on the agenda for the Conference.

Sincerely yours,
J.P.

[1] *J.P. Papers* (NMML).

[2] K.T. Shah (1888-1953); taught at Bombay, Mysore, Patna and Delhi Universities, 1914-31. Economic & Financial Advisor to Indian Princes at Round Table Conference, 1930, and Princes' Chamber in 1931; Hony. General Secretary National Planning Committee 1938-49; member Constituent Assembly, 1946-50 and Provisional Parliament, 1950-2.

[3] For biographical note on Hirday Nath Kunzru see *JPSW*, Vol. I, p. 49.

322. Statement to the Press regarding the Purpose of the Conference on Free and Fair Elections, Bombay, 20 June 1950[1]

The purpose of the opposition parties conference to be held in Bombay on July 1 and 2 is to take steps to ensure complete freedom to vote, fair chances of competition and impartial conduct during the coming elections. The purpose of the conference is not to form an opposition bloc to the Congress or to build a united leftist organization. Obviously education of the masses and creation of an independent public opinion is the most important guarantee of a free election. That, of course, is the task which, I presume, the opposition parties are trying to fulfil, each in its own way. But there are also other necessary steps that must be taken to this end, particularly by the Government. There is the vital question of the system of voting and the character of constituencies. Then there are such questions as that of the number and location of polling booths, regulation of transport facilities and check on election expenditure.

I am, therefore, suggesting that we should meet together to discuss these matters so that a united front might be presented to the Government and the maximum pressure might be exerted on them to take the necessary steps to guarantee honest elections.

One of the recommendations that the conference might make would be that the Congress ministries should resign a few months before the elections and the Governors should take over.

It is the job of the Election Commission to see that the rolls are complete and accurate. I am afraid that this is not being ensured and the official machinery is not carrying on adequate propaganda or offering adequate facilities to enable every voter to register himself.

It has also been announced that the work of delimitation of constituencies has already started. It has been made to appear that it is merely the mechanical part of the work that is being done. This, however, is untrue and behind the backs of the people and their Parliament, questions of principle are being decided. It is clear that before the territorial delimitation of constituencies can be made, the character of the constituencies must be decided upon.

Parliament has not yet decided whether in this country there will be single or plural constituencies or if plural, whether the system of voting would be cumulative or distributive. These are vital principles which the Constitution itself should have defined. But not even Parliament has defined them, and if I am not mistaken, Dr. B.R. Ambedkar gave an assurance in

[1] Adapted from *Hindustan Times*, 21 June 1950.

the course of the debate on the People's Representation Bill that he would place another Bill before the House in the next session to cover these and other issues. It is difficult then to understand how the Election Commission, even if advised by committees of Parliament, can proceed with the work of delimitation.

According to Article 327 of the Constitution, only Parliament is competent to make provision for delimitation of constituencies, and that power cannot be delegated to the Election Commission or even the President. I am afraid that in the name of provisional arrangements, the people and Parliament are going to be faced next autumn, with a fait accompli.

It is for the proposed conference to make the people conscious of this danger and to compel the Government to drop their underhand policy and consult Parliament and public opinion before proceeding with the work of delimitation. I also remember that the Prime Minister had given an assurance on the floor of the House that in the work of delimitation, opposition parties would be consulted. I am not aware that this assurance is being carried out.

Besides there is at present in the country an atmosphere of fear and intimidation and the people, especially in the rural areas, are afraid to stand up to the local bureaucracy and the local Congress chiefs. The minority community also lives in fear.

It is feared that the Congress would utilize the civil servants in the elections. Only the other day, a civil servant of the standing of Mr. V.P. Menon,[2] made open propaganda for the Congress at his Press conference in Travancore.

Further, Government have certain monopolistic sources of propaganda today, such as the radio, which are used exclusively in the interest of the Congress Party. All parties must be allowed access to these vital instruments of propaganda.

[2] V.P. Menon (1894-1966); joined government service as a clerk (1914) and rose through hard work to one of the top positions in the bureaucracy and became Constitutional Advisor to the Government of India (1945-6). As Secretary of the States Ministry (1946-9), he ably assisted Sardar Patel in negotiating the accession of princely states to the Indian union. Later, he was appointed Governor of Orissa. He wrote *Story of the Integration of Indian States* (1955) and *The Transfer of Power in India* (1957).

323. To J.R.D. Tata, 20 June 1950[1]

Dear Mr. Tata,[2]

I am writing in connection with the Khoj Parishad. You have been good enough to donate Rs. 5,000/- per year for the last two years. We are expecting your third year's donation every day. Meanwhile certain changes are taking place in the organization of the Khoj Parishad. You will be glad to know that we have decided to shift the Head Office of the Parishad to Bombay and for the time being to place it under the direction of Mr. M.L. Dantwala. After Prof. B. Ghosh left for the United States there was no competent person in Calcutta interested enough to look after the Parishad and we did not have the finance to employ a first-class economist. These decisions were taken by the Council of Governors at Lucknow some time ago under the presidentship of Acharya Narendra Deva. They have to be ratified by the meeting of the General Body which I expect will be done at the end of July. I, therefore, write to advise you to send this year's contribution to me at Bombay instead of to Acharya Narendra Deva.

Thanking you for you kindness and hoping you are well,

Yours sincerely,
J.P.

[1] *J.P. Papers* (NMML).

[2] J.R.D. Tata (1904-93); a leading industrialist; pioneer of civil aviation in India; started Tata Aviation Service in 1932, later known as Tata Airlines. After partition of India in 1947 he was made Chairman of Air India, formed after the nationalization of Tata Airlines in 1948. Tata was awarded Tony Jannus Award in 1985, Edward Warmer Award in 1988 and Bharat Ratna in 1992.

324. To K.B. Menon, 20 June 1950[1]

My dear K.B.,

I have received a letter from Gangababu since he arrived in Madras. I am glad that you are all making progress. I sent a wire to Gangababu yesterday to enquire when should Com. Keshav Gore reach Madras. Will you please inform us telegraphically?

I spoke to Kamaladevi about her going down to Madras for collection work. Due to her mother's illness, she will not be able to go for some time yet. But she is expecting a cousin of her's to come to stay with her mother by the end of this month. So she has told me that she would be reaching

[1] *J.P. Papers* (NMML).

Madras on the 1st of July. Even during the last days it is always possible to raise money. I am hoping therefore that by the time she reaches you will have the ground prepared so that you will be in a position to make the fullest use of her presence there.

I shall appreciate it if you keep me informed regularly on progress made in the conference arrangements.

With greetings,

Sincerely yours,
J.P.

325. To the General Secretary, Servants of India Society, 21 June 1950[1]

Dear friend,

As you probably know, I have invited Mr. Kunzru and Mr. Vaze[2] to the Conference that I have called on July 1 and 2, to consider the question of free and fair elections. I understand that my not having invited the Servants of India Society has been misunderstood. I hasten to remove the misunderstanding. It was my intention to invite only political parties, that is those that are expected to participate in parliamentary work. I thought the Servants of India Society was not a political party in that sense. So I invited Pandit Kunzru and Mr. Vaze in their individual capacity. I assure you that I would always consider it an honour to participate in any deliberations jointly with the Servants of India Society and I do hereby extend a most cordial invitation to the Society also to send its representatives to the Conference which has been convened.

Sincerely yours,
J.P.

[1] *J.P. Papers* (NMML).

[2] S.G. Vaze, Vice-President of Servants of India Society in 1952. Secretary of the All India Civil Liberties Council in 1951-2, edited *Indian Civil Liberties Bulletin.*

326. Statement to the Press regarding the Activities of the Election Commission, Bombay, 22 June 1950[1]

Mr. Sen[2] has said that at present there are only two activities in which the Election Commission is engaged—registration of voters and delimitation

[1] Adapted from *Bombay Chronicle*, 23 June 1950.

[2] Sukumar Sen (1898-1963); educated at Presidency College Calcutta and University College London; competed for I.C.S. 1921; Chief Secretary, West Bengal, August 1947-March 1950; Chief Election Commissioner of India, 1950-3, awarded Padmashri in 1954.

of constituencies. I hope to discuss these matters with him.

Adult franchise is being introduced for the first time and the people being so backward, there is need for the Government to do active propaganda to make the adult citizens conscious of their right of franchise and to induce them to take interest in registering themselves. I find that only the Madras Government has done some propaganda in this behalf . The example of the Madras Government should be followed by the other States also. In this work the State Governments and the State Election Commissions, if and when they come into being, should take the help of political parties and other public institutions.

I should also like to draw Mr. Sen's attention to the inadequacy of the arrangements made for the scrutiny of the electoral rolls when they are published. It has been announced that the rolls will be hung up at the taluka headquarters. It would not be possible for the people of the whole taluka to go to the headquarters to scrutinize the list. Therefore, it is necessary that the lists are hung up in a larger number of places such as selected post offices, libraries, schools etc.

Regarding the problem of delimitation, the issue of single or plural constituency, as of the system of voting, is a very vital one and I am anxious that the issue is not prejudged by the Chief Election Commissioner or the President before public opinion is consulted and Parliament decides the matter.

The decisions of the coming conference will be communicated to the Chief Election Commissioner and I am happy to find that he has expressed his readiness to give them due consideration.

327. To S.G. Vaze, 24 June 1950[1]

Dear Mr. Vaze,

I had a talk with Pandit Kunzru last night. I am very happy that he is attending the Conference and that you and other friends from the Servants of India Society are also attending. By the way, I have invited Servants of India Society, too.

Last night I told Pandit Kunzru that we desire that he should preside over the Conference. His difficulty was that he was to be touring till almost the beginning of the Conference and was not in a position to prepare an address. He proposed Mr. P.R. Das's name or Dr. Paranjpye[2] for the

[1] *J.P. Papers* (NMML).

[2] Sir Raghunath Purushotam Paranjpye (1876-1966); Minister of Education, Bombay (1921-32); member of the India Council (1927-32); Vice-Chancellor, Lucknow University (1932-3); Indian High Commissioner in Australia (1944-7); Vice-Chancellor, Poona University (1956-9).

address. He proposed Mr. P.R. Das's name or Dr. Paranjape[2] for the presidentship, but I still am anxious to have Pandit Kunzru as the President. The difficulty about the presidential address can be removed if you come to the rescue. If you are able to prepare a note on the questions involved, in other words a rough draft of the presidential address, and come to Bombay on the 30th morning when Pandit Kunzru is due, he may be in a position to prepare his address in the time available. We could then get it printed also before the 1st afternoon. We shall also send you a note on the subject. I hope you will do this and oblige us.

I am sorry, I had not thought of Dr. Paranjape before and had not sent him the invitation. I am sending him a wire today and also writing a letter of invitation. Will you be good enough to meet him and persuade him to accept the invitation? Pandit Kunzru thought that his participation would be very valuable. I also agree.

Looking forward to meeting you here.

Yours sincerely,
Jayaprakash Narayan

328. Interview to the Press on the Korean Question, Bombay, 29 June 1950[1]

There is no justification for North Korea to invade South Korea and try to annex it. I do not think that India is in a position to do anything effective in the matter, although I am sure her sympathies would be on the side of South Korea.

I do not feel that the present trouble in Korea would lead to a third world war. However, if such a thing is not checked in time, the world would be reduced to a jungle where there will be no rule of law.

I cannot see any justification for North Korea to invade the South and try to annex it. If North Korea had cooperated with the United Nations Korean Commission, there might have been to-day a properly constituted representative government for the whole of Korea. But the Commission was not even allowed to enter the Northern territory.

It is also a bad augury for the future of the world that the North Korean Government refused to comply with the directions of the United Nations Security Council to withdraw to its side of the 38th Parallel. In the face of such defiance, there were only two courses for the United Nations—either to accept failure or to take steps to enforce its decision.

I observe that some effective action is called for if the world is not to be presented with the accomplished fact of a strong nation having gobbled up

[1]Adapted from *Tribune*, 30 June 1950.

To whitewash a full-scale invasion as a civil war, does not make any sense. If the North Koreans had co-operated with the U.N. Commission for Korea, we might have helped United Korea today and the world would not have been torn with fear of another world war as a result of any flare-up in that region.

I think it is possible to localize the conflict in Korea because the issues are so clear and so narrow.

I regret the defiance of the United Nations direction for an immediate ceasefire. I do not find fault with the decision directing member nations to render such assistance to South Korea as they deem necessary for the restoration of peace, and I do not see how Russia looks upon that decision as illegal. Surely, the invasion by North Korea is not a legal act. Yet Russia seems to have kept silent on this point.

The only effective guarantee for peace in the world today is the United Nations, even though the latter's actions in the past have not always appeared to us to have been free from partisanship. Yet the fact remains that as a result of its timely action on several occasions, local conflicts have been prevented.

329. Welcome Address at the Conference on Free and Fair Elections, Bombay, 1 July 1950[1]

Friends,

I am very thankful to you for accepting my invitation to attend this Conference.[2] I am sorry that one of the organizations which I had invited kept away on the ground that there was no prior consultation about this matter. In the very nature of things it was not possible to consult all those who were invited about dates, venue, etc., because that would have delayed the Conference too long and even then it is doubtful whether unanimity could have been reached about the dates and the venue and other matters involved. I hope however that we shall have the co-operation in the future of those who have kept away in furthering the objects of this Conference, objects which are common to all who have faith in democracy.

I am also sorry that some friends have not been able to attend for unavoidable reasons. We have, however, their best wishes and suggestions.

You know the object for which we have gathered here. In one sense it is a limited object; in another a very fundamental one. Our country has but

[1] *J.P. Papers* (NMML), summary published in almost all newspaper in India on 2 July 1950.

[2] See Appendix 23 for the Resolutions adapted by the Conference on Free and Fair Elections, Bombay, on 1 and 2 July 1950.

recently embarked upon the democratic way of life. The first general elections in Free India have been announced to be held in the next year.[3] How these elections are going to be conducted, what laws and rules are going to govern them, how is the ruling party going to behave, to what extent are the voters helped or hindered in exercising their franchise freely, whether violence is used or otherwise, are questions which are going to determine vitally the future of democracy in this country. In this sense it is a fundamental problem that we are gathered here to consider.

It has been pointed out in some quarters that the real problem is to consider how an effective opposition can be created. Representing one of the major opposition parties in this country I cannot but heartily agree with this view. But that is a problem which may be considered elsewhere, and it does not in any way lessen the importance of the problem that we have come here to discuss. Some of the parties represented here, might find themselves opposing one another at the next elections. But that does not mean that they are not interested in the common problem of free and fair elections. As I have said before, who wins the next elections is of vital importance. But even more important than that is how the elections are conducted. I have talked to a great number of persons about this matter, persons belonging to different parties or to no party at all, and I have found that there is a widespread fear that the ruling party would so conduct the elections that they would be no more than a farce. I do not say that it will be necessarily so. If there is a strong opposition it would not be so. Yet, I am pointing out that there is this climate of suspicion. Now, democracy has already suffered heavily since the rise of fascism and totalitarianism, and if it is found that elections are a farce, the field would be clear for the forces of violence and chaos in this country. People in Bombay City, where there is a high degree of political consciousness and a fairly ordered civic life, may not appreciate the danger, but the danger is real.

Since this Conference was mooted, I have watched the reactions to it. I have been amazed to find how oblivious people are to the issues involved and how the whole matter has been attempted to be brushed aside as being a stunt. It has been assumed in some quarters that the only issue involved was that of the honesty of the ruling party. So it was argued that when such upright men as Pandit Nehru and others were the leaders of the Congress, how could there be any doubt raised about the honesty of that organization. I shall come to this question later but I should like to emphasise that, while the question of the honesty of the ruling party is important, there are many other basic questions—questions of political principles and of procedure—involved. Whatever may actually happen, Government has announced that

[3] The first general elections were actually held in 1952.

the elections would be held next summer. To that end the Representation of the People Act, 1950, was hurried through Parliament. Another Representation of the People Act will be introduced in the next session. A Chief Election Commissioner has been appointed and other important principles and procedures are being settled. And yet it is remarkable that in a country that aspires to become a democracy there is so little understanding of and concern with the issues and problems involved. If the whole matter was to be settled by pointing to the honesty of Pandit Nehru and Sardar Patel, surely there was no need for Representation of the People Act, for a Chief Election Commissioner and all other steps that have been or will be taken. In other democratic countries, there had been long and serious controversies regarding such questions as the system of voting, but here when that question is raised we are simply reminded of the honesty and integrity of the Congress leaders or are told that Parliament was in any case going to settle that matter; as if the people have no concern with the question at all.

Let me now turn to a few issues that have to be considered.

The very first question connected with the coming elections is that of registration of the voters. I am afraid very little has been done by Government to enable the people to understand the implications of adult franchise and to ensure that the voters were made conscious of their right to vote and were made interested enough to see that their names were listed on the rolls. However, the preparation of rolls is nearly complete, and now it is only after the rolls are published that it would be the duty of political parties and other interested bodies to see that enough interest is roused among the voters to take the trouble of finding out whether they have been enrolled and to see that the rolls are corrected where necessary. It is desirable that political parties, no matter what their mutual differences may be, should co-operate in this work. I hope after this Conference we shall address ourselves to this task. I may add in this connection that originally it had been announced that the electoral rolls would be published only at district and taluka headquarters. I am glad to say that after our representation to the Chief Election Commissioner he agreed that as far as possible each village might be posted with its own roll.

The very next question, and perhaps the most important to be considered, is the delimitation of constituencies. This task is being tackled at present by the Chief Election Commissioner. Delimitation of constituencies, as you know, involves a question of principle as well as that of honest and fair demarcation of territory. The question of principle involved is whether there should be single-member or plural constituencies. This question is yet to be decided by Parliament, and till it is decided actual delimitation is not possible. The Government, however, seems to have come to its own private decision and delimitation work is proceeding on the basis of single-member constituencies. This is prejudging the issue and our strong voice of protest must be raised against it. The issue of single or plural constituency is not a minor issue but one of vital importance, and till public opinion is consulted it is not right that this issue should be treated as settled.

As far as the physical demarcation of constituencies is concerned that is just the field where gerrymandering is possible and has been practised in many countries. It has often happened that the party in power has attempted so to draw the line that concentration of opposition opinion is dispersed, and the areas are broken up and added to one another in such a manner that in no constituency the opposition might have a chance. During the British days, whenever a new constitutional reform was made, a commission was appointed to delimit constituencies, which toured from province to province and district to district, took evidence and consulted all sections of public opinion and then made its recommendations regarding delimitation. After the 1935 Act, the Hammond Committee was appointed. But under Congress rule, when for the first time constituencies are to be delimited on the basis of adult franchise, the task has practically been left in the hands of a single party, the Congress. The procedure laid down in the Representation of the People Act has empowered the Chief Election Commissioner to make recommendations regarding delimitation to the President. The Chief Election Commissioner is to be advised by Committees of the Parliament appointed by the Speaker for each State. In the very nature of things these Committees are practically entirely made up of Congressmen. The Committee appointed for the Bombay State, for instance, has no non-Congress member, because there is no non-Congress member of Parliament from the Bombay State. Further, the Chief Election Commissioner has asked the State Governments to prepare proposals for delimitation. These Governments are all Congress Party Governments and their recommendations are likely to serve the interests of the Congress Party alone. Only in the U.P., as a result of much pressure from the opposition groups in the State Assembly, was a committee appointed by the Assembly to advise the State Government on delimitation work. On that Committee some representatives of opposition parties were taken. It is necessary that this procedure be at least followed in other States. It is true that Shri Sukumar Sen assured us when we met him that whatever proposals would be made by the State Governments would not be finalised before consulting different political parties. Such consultation at least might be of some value, but it cannot be an effective check on gerrymandering.

I shall not take your time with discussing every issue we have to consider here but I shall briefly refer to a few. A fuller note on the subject has been prepared by Shri K.K. Menon, who is functioning as Secretary to this Conference. That note is in your hands already.

The system of voting, to my mind, is of the utmost importance. If there are single-member constituencies, the question does not arise. But we have to consider whether we want single-member constituencies or not. Speaking for myself, and after considering all aspects of the matter, I am not opposed to the system because I am anxious to see developed in this country a two-party system of government under which democracy has the best chance. However, if there are plural constituencies, and I have an open mind on the question, the system of voting assumes a very great importance. I understand that it is the intention of Government to have plural constituencies where reservation is to be made for scheduled castes and tribal peoples, and I understand further that in these constituencies they are going to introduce the system of distributive voting. Whatever system of voting we ourselves may desire we must see that in no case is the distributive system adopted because that would make it possible for a 51 per cent majority to capture 100 per cent of the seats in every such plural constituency. These constituencies are likely to become pocket boroughs of the Congress. Speaking for myself I should like, wherever there are plural constituencies, the cumulative system of voting to be adopted.

The location and number of polling booths are also of great importance. If the voters have to be made to walk long distances the poll would be poor and the party which is in a position to supply private transport would have an advantage. Therefore, polling booths should be so constituted that no voter would have to walk more than two miles.

The question of private transport for bringing voters to the polling booth is also important. If private transport is allowed, parties whose purses have long strings will have an advantage over the poor man's parties. Therefore, it is my opinion that we should all combine and demand that the use of private transport for bringing voters to the polling booths be completely banned.

I shall not take you into other questions of detail. I shall now say a few words about the holy indignation in which the Congress supporters have spoken about the possibility of the ruling party using unfair means at the next elections. I have nothing to say against the honesty and integrity of Pandit Nehru or Sardar Patel. But they are not the entire Congress. We have all had a taste of four years of Congress rule in States. I wonder if it is the verdict of the people that these administrations have been honest and fair. As a matter of fact, the most common charge levelled against them is that of corruption. Recently, Congress Panchayat elections were held and Congressmen openly charged one another with malpractices.

In this connection I shall read to you an excerpt from a letter of a constructive worker published in the *Harijan* of June 24, 1950. The writer asks the editor, Shri Kishorelal Mashruwala:

Looking at the rowdy scenes at Congress election booths,—free fights, hurling of shoes, abusive language, rudeness towards women and many more ugly features—, and the foul and ultra-constitutional means which candidates and even polling and returning officers resort to, one wonders what the Congress is coming to. What lesson may the people take from an organization, in which there is no discipline, no consideration of complaints, and the elections are reduced to a farce giving rise to rampant hooliganism?

That requires no comment.

Recently, there was an election for municipal chairmanship at Raipur, Madhya Pradesh. There was no official Congress candidate set up, and Congressmen were contesting each other. The candidate belonging to the Chief Minister's group won. Thakur Pyarelal Singh, a well-known Congress leader, was one of the other contestants. In a statement published after the election, Thakur Saheb made serious allegations against election and polling officers. He said that before polling started the ballot boxes were not shown to be empty, nor were the locks on the boxes sealed. Inside the booth the polling officer actually took ballot papers from the voters and dropped them into the box of the officially favoured candidate. He gave a specific instance of the wife of Principal Yoganandam, who resisted the officer's attempt to take her ballot paper away.

I take it that you have all seen the letter in *The Times of India* written by Shri Shankarrao. More alleging that in two specific instances at least there was clear official interference in the elections in the Bombay State. Instances can be multiplied indefinitely, but that is not necessary.

I therefore submit to those Congressmen, who have regard for honesty in public life, not to dismiss the possibility of widespread corruption in the elections as malicious propaganda against the Congress, but to be realistic and take steps to stop it.

The problem of the use of government resources and government funds in the elections is also not an imaginary one. In many elections held, the Congress Party has been allowed to use Government Publicity Vans and Congress Ministers have used Government cars and Government petrol to do Congress Party propaganda. In many cases officials have been found to exert pressure to vote for the Congress.

To stop all this, what is needed is not so much as assurance from the Congress Party or the Government, but vigilant and strong public opinion. I hope this Conference will go some little way in creating this opinion as also an awareness among the people of the issues and tasks involved. I hope further that at the end of your deliberations definite proposals will emerge to be placed before the Government and we will have arrived at some *modus operandi* to create public support for these proposals.

With these words, I once again thank you for your kindness in accepting my invitation to this Conference.

330. On the Demise of Yusuf Meherally, Bombay, 3 July 1950[1]

After Mahatma Gandhi's death Yusuf Meherally's death has given me the greatest shock.

The country would not see another Meherally—a pillar to the Socialist Party, friend of all, lovable and faithful to his ideals.

His was a death to be envied by all—a sacrifice in the cause of the motherland.

[1] *National Herald*, 5 July 1950.

331. Statement on Problems of the Depressed Classes, Madras, 6 July 1950[1]

Shri P.N. Rajbhoj, General Secretary of the All India Scheduled Castes Federation, and Shri J.H. Subbiah, Hyderabad leader of the Federation, discussed with me recently at Bombay the problem of the scheduled castes and the promise that socialism held for them. I explained to them that as socialism stood for all the exploited and downtrodden, the Harijans could not but acquire equal social and economic status with other sections of the people in a socialist society. While the scheduled caste leaders appreciated that view, they were particularly anxious about certain specific guarantees. The scheduled castes form the bulk of our landless labour population. They therefore have the first claim on our waste lands. The Socialist Party has already been advocating this policy, and I had no difficulty in endorsing the plea of the Scheduled Castes Federation leaders.

They also demanded guarantee for proportionate place for the Harijans in the Services. I have no doubt that those who had been suppressed and kept backward should receive special attention and the lag in their case should be made up. Accordingly, I endorsed that demand too. I also see no reason why if proper provision is made for education and training, the Harijans should prove less competent than others.

The third specific guarantee they desired was proportional reservation of seats in the legislatures and ministries. The Constitution has already guaranteed such reservation in the Legislatures for ten years. We endorse that provision. Whether reservation would be necessary after ten years would depend upon the efforts made to raise the depressed castes to the level of others. As for proportionate reservation of seats in the Cabinets, I see no reason why this guarantee should not be given.

[1] *J.P. Papers* (NMML); also published in *Bombay Chronicle*, and other newspapers, 7 July 1950.

I might add that merely guarantee would not solve the Harijan problem. A great drive would be necessary to raise these depressed peoples. The Socialist Party would like to spend, say, a hundred crores in the first ten years of its government on the education and technical and vocational training of the scheduled castes.

All this may appear to be an opportunistic concession made to communalism. I have, however, never looked upon the organized efforts of the depressed and backward castes to regain their proper place in society as an expression of communalism. The attempt of the higher castes to preserve their privileges through caste organizations is certainly communalism. But the attempt of the depressed castes to band themselves in order to raise their status is a sign of revolt and a progressive social force. There is danger, of course, of this force remaining confined within caste boundaries. But I have no doubt that the socialist movement will gradually absorb the communal revolt and give it a larger expression in the socio-economic programme of socialism.

332. A Note on Steps to ensure Free and Fair Elections (some time after the Conference on Free and Fair Elections)[1]

It will be recalled that a conference was held recently on "Free and Fair Elections" at Bombay under the presidentship of the famous liberal leader, Dr. R.P. Paranjpye, for some time our High Commissioner in the Commonwealth of Australia.

That Conference did a good deal to focus and crystallise public opinion on the important issues involved; and its Memorandum seems to have found general acceptance and served as a guide to opposition parties in formulating their proposals for the Chief Election Commissioner. If the press reports are to be relied upon, the Chief Election Commissioner himself has expressed opinion very identical on several points with the Bombay Memorandum.

However, one single conference cannot be enough to create adequate public opinion, particularly in a country where the public is so unaccustomed to democracy and its problems. The work begun at Bombay must therefore be continued and enlarged.

With this end in view, the Bombay Conference set up a Standing Committee on Free and Fair Elections, with Dr. Paranjpye as chairman and Shri Naushir Bharucha, Bombay Municipal Corporator and secretary of the Bombay Provincial Association; Shri S.G. Vaze, general secretary of the All India Civil Liberties Union and Shri K.K. Menon, secretary of the

[1] *J.P. Papers* (NMML).

Parliamentary Board, Socialist Party, as the secretaries. The office of the Standing Committee is at National House, 6, Tulloch Road, Fort, Bombay.

This All India Standing Committee, while it would be able to continue the good work of the Conference, will not be enough by itself. Therefore, it is proposed to set up State Standing Committees on Free and Fair Elections, consisting of representatives of opposition parties and other leading public men. These committees will watch, guide and coordinate all activities in furtherance of the objective of ensuring free and fair elections.

The Bombay Memorandum laid down a six-point programme about which there is constant need to educate public opinion. There are two issues however on which there is urgent need to concentrate immediately. These issues are: (a) delimitation of constituencies and (b) the system of voting.

In every State the Government concerned is in the process of preparing a concrete picture of delimitation of constituencies. In some of the States, at conferences called by the Election Commissioner, it was revealed that the official proposals for delimitation were utterly devoid of any guiding principle and were drafted merely to suit party ends or intra-party conveniences. Constituency delimitation is just the sphere where gerrymandering at its worst can be practised, and there is evidence already that as in other spheres here too the Congress has no desire to act with fairness. It has been found that according to the official proposals even small areas, such as thanas in Bihar, have been split up and joined together artificially to other areas in order merely to suit the interests of the likely Congress candidates who may belong to this or that caste or power-group. Unless therefore a concerted effort is made in every State so that delimitation is carried out in accordance with well-defined principles and not to suit party conveniences, the ruling party will succeed in perpetrating a fraud upon the electorate and vitiate the elections by gerrymandering. The principles to be universally accepted to govern delimitation should be (a) that as far as possible existing administrative units should not be split (b) where, from population considerations, an excess area has to be split from an administrative unit, it must be added on to another contiguous and most convenient administrative unit. I shall advise opposition parties not to wait quietly till the official schemes of delimitation are published but to prepare their own schemes and after coordinating their proposals send as far as possible agreed schemes to the proper quarters. When the Governments have finally cooked up their schemes, it might be too late to have them amended.

The question of the system of voting is even more important. It appears from public comments that the importance of this question is not adequately realised nor are the issues properly understood. The Bombay Conference advocated single-member constituencies for the House of the People and three-member constituencies for the State Assemblies. The system of voting advocated was the cumulative vote in order that the assemblies might be properly representative of the electorate. The object of elections under a democracy is not merely to return the majority to power, but also to enable the minority—at any rate the substantial political minorities—to be represented. Nothing is so destructive of democracy as one-party rule. It is true that if proportional representation is carried to its end, it leads to instability of representative institutions and to weakness of government. But the proposal of the Bombay Conference was mindful of this danger. Three-member constituencies with cumulative voting would still ensure stability and strong government and allow at the same time substantial minorities polling more than 25% of the votes to be represented.

It appears, however, that Delhi has made up its mind on this issue and we are going to have single-member constituencies. Speaking for myself, I am prepared to accept that as a second choice. But, it is also known that, in view of the reservation of seats for the scheduled and tribal castes, some constituencies must of necessity be multi-membered. It is here that the Congress is trying sleekly to carve out a number of pocket boroughs for itself and defeat democracy. This is being done by attempting to introduce the distributive system of voting in these plural constituencies. First the Congress waxes eloquent on the evils of the multi-member system and decides in favour of single-member constituencies; then it brings in multi-member constituencies as necessary evils and further multiplies the evil by introducing the distributive vote.

The difficulty is that the public at large, including even its educated section, firstly, does not understand the different systems of voting and their comparative merits, and secondly, is not sufficiently interested in these technical issues to be able to influence official policy. The Congress is trying to take the utmost advantage of this lack of public understanding and interest. In doing so, the Congress might be serving its party interest, but not the interest of the nation.

If we honestly intend to build up a democracy in India, proper representation of the people must be one of our particular cares. The single-member system is not a very sound system of representation, but as it has other advantages, it might be accepted as a second choice. But to combine multi-member constituencies with the distributive vote is to combine the disadvantages of both the single and plural system and at the same time eliminate the advantages of both.

In the case of single-member constituencies, the system of voting has no difficulties, except where the second poll is in vogue. But due to the expense and trouble involved in the second poll, the simple majority vote is the usual practice; i.e. of several contestants the one securing the largest vote is elected, irrespective of whether or not the number of votes secured by him forms a majority of the total votes cast. Because of the smallness of single-member constituencies and the comparative small expenditure involved, minority parties are able to nurse some of these constituencies and poll majority votes in them and thus secure representation for themselves in the legislatures.

In plural constituencies, however, these advantages do not exist for the minority parties. Therefore, any proper system of voting for these constituencies must be such that at least substantial minority opinions are represented in the legislature. Under the distributive system, no matter how many seats there are in a plural constituency the majority party—even though it has a bare majority—will capture all the seats.

It seems to be the intention of the Congress that the plural constituencies should be two-membered. Now suppose there are a hundred voters in such a constituency and 51 out of them are supporters of the Congress and 49 of the Party A, these hundred voters have to elect two representatives using the distributive vote. According to that system each voter has as many votes as there are seats in the constituency, but he cannot give more than one vote to a candidate. In our imaginary constituency there are two seats; so each of the hundred voters has two votes. Suppose the Congress party has two candidates and party A has also two candidates, the 51 Congress supporters will give one vote each to the Congress candidates, who will thus have 51 votes each, while the 49 other voters will give one vote each to their candidates who will have 49 votes each. Both the Congress candidates will be declared elected.

This would mean that while 51 adult citizens would have *two* representatives in the legislature, or 25.5 would have one representative each, 49 adult citizens would go completely unrepresented! Can any thing be more unfair?

By introducing distributive voting in two-member constituencies, the Congress is attempting by a sleight-of-hand as it were to just double its strength. This fraud upon democracy must be resisted. Whatever other system of voting is adopted, the distributive system must never be allowed.

The Bombay Conference advocated three-member constituencies with the cumulative vote. The restrictive vote may do equally well.

Let these systems be properly understood so that the public might induce Parliament to legislate wisely and justly on this important question. The cumulative and restrictive vote are crude forms of proportional representation. They are opposed on the ground that they lead to multiplicity of parties and weakness and instability of government. Firstly, these objections have little application in the case of three-member constituencies with cumulative or restrictive voting; and secondly, these pleas should not be made the justification for giving the Congress, which is the majority party today such terrific weightage.

Under the cumulative system every voter has as many votes as there are seats in a plural constituency, but he is permitted to distribute his votes as he likes among candidates of his choice. He might cumulate and give all his votes to one candidate or distribute them in the proportion he likes. In a three-member constituency, he might give all his three votes to one candidate, or two to one and one to another, or one vote each to three candidates of his choice.

Under the restrictive system each voter has only one vote, no matter what the number of seats, and he can vote for only one candidate of his choice.

Under either of these systems in three or even two member constituencies, a substantial minority, more than 25% in one case and 33% in the other, have a chance of being represented. Nor are these systems so complicated that even the illiterate voters cannot be trained to use them. Certainly, they do not require any higher understanding than the distributive vote. It is true that parties entering the contest must estimate their strength properly so as to determine how many candidates they must set up. But this has no relation to the backwardness of the electorate itself.

There is thus no case against the cumulative or restrictive system of voting and every thing in their favour, if proper representation of the people is the object. On the other hand, the only merit of the distributive vote is that it enables the Congress artificially to multiply its strength. That cannot be the desideratum of any one who believes in democracy. If plural constituencies were not being introduced at all, these questions would not have arisen. But when plural constituencies have become a constitutional necessity, as it were, fair play requires that they are not used to eliminate the opposition and bolster up the Congress. The distributive vote is being introduced to achieve just these ends. Will lovers of democracy raise their voice against this fraudulent move?

333. General Secretary's Political Report Circulated at the Eighth National Conference of the Socialist Party, Madras, 8 July 1950[1]

The Patna Conference, last year, met in an atmosphere of hope and enthusiasm. The Conference was a striking success, both as a political demonstration and from the point of view of the quality of the debates and the importance of the decisions.

[1] *Socialist Party Eighth National Conference, Madras, 8-12 July 1950*, pp. 129-48.

A year earlier, at Nasik, when we took the daring step to cut the integuments that bound us to the Congress and emerged as an independent political party, many had predicted our rapid demise and disappearance from the political scene.

Those prophecies were belied, and the Party stood its ground.

On the other hand, there were also facile hopes raised at that time that the disillusionment with the Congress being so great we had merely to come forward to oppose and the people would rally at once round our banner. Those hopes too were belied.

That the people showed a natural reluctance to be hustled and wanted time to test and discern was a sign of health rather than the contrary. A party that seeks the allegiance of the people must have patience and must give proof of its worth by hard and loyal work.

If the people were to be moved merely by slogans and political circuses, that would be an indication of mental sickness, and that moment would be appropriate for any unscrupulous demagogue, with adequate command over funds, to establish his dictatorship. That the people, once bitten, have not merely been twice shy, but have also shown discernment and native caution and shrewdness, augurs well for the growth of the political life of the nation.

I should like, therefore, to warn the Party that there is no quick road to victory, and that while history may come to our aid, nothing can take the place of hard, honest and quiet work.

II
OUR FAILINGS

There is a tendency in some sections of the Party to want to live from excitement to excitement. This tendency to my mind is one form of expression of the tendency to shirk steady work. As our work develops and the situation matures, moments of intense excitement, of masses moving and struggling, would come. But to seek synthetic excitement at inappropriate moments is to invite reaction and demoralisation. The workers of the Party, at least, should need no artificial tonic to invigorate them. Their faith in their ideal, their Party and its methods should be enough to drive them onwards.

At Patna two important decisions were taken. One, as you all know, was the adoption of the new Party Constitution, and the other, the formulation of a programme to mobilise the masses for a move forward in the political, economic and cultural fields. Our achievements in these two respects have been partial and below our expectations.

If I may be permitted to offer a personal explanation in this connection, I should like to recall how only three weeks after the Patna Conference I met with a motor accident which put me out of action for four long months. Thus the momentum that had been gathered was, as far as I was concerned, lost. When I returned to active duty, I did not find the situation as I had left it on April 1, the day of my accident, and I could never re-create the post-Conference momentum.

The new Constitution was adopted after a long and able debate by a large majority. But its enforcement has been tardy and difficult.

The two pillars of the new Constitution were mass individual membership and the collective affiliation of such organizations as trade unions and kisan panchayats. For this country it was a unique constitution for a political party to have, and it naturally was not so simple as the conventional patterns of political organization.

The uniqueness and the complicated forms stood in the way of speedy enforcement. But after making all concessions on those scores, it has to be admitted that the Party structure is grievously incomplete today, and of the two pillars, only one has so far been raised to any height at all. Up-till 15th June our individual membership totalled up to 1,29,694. But as far as collective affiliation, which was conceived as the stronger of the two pillars, is concerned, hardly any thing has been achieved so far. One reason, no doubt, is that the kisan panchayats started to be properly constituted only after the recent Rewa Conference[2] of the Hind Kisan Panchayat. But even in the trade union field, the progress made towards collective affiliation has been negligible.

In the coming year all of us, particularly the organisers and active workers of the Party, must give more attention to building up the structure of the Party. Without organization effective work is impossible, just as without work, organization ceases to grow and atrophies.

In the course of the last year certain defects have been discovered in the Constitution and the National Executive is going to place before you certain amendments to streamline the Constitution and to remove the internal frictions and maladjustments.

As regards the "On The Move" resolution, the achievements have been equally unsatisfactory. Our efforts made in that direction were not sustained, nor co-ordinated. No doubt the unequal development of the Party in different parts of the country was one of the factors responsible for this, but that alone cannot explain everything. The leadership of the Party and the Central Secretariat and the Party Journal failed to give the necessary sustained guidance, direction and education to the Party workers on whom devolved the responsibility of putting that important decision into practice. At the top, further, there was lack of that effortless cooperation and team work which inspire the rank and file and create confidence among the public.

[2]Rewa Conference, Hind Kisan Panchayat, held at Rewa (then in Vindhya Pradesh).

Local Party units too were in many cases constituted of small groups of inexperienced youngmen without any real contact with the people and intimate understanding of local problems.

It is a universal shortcoming of socialists to be busy more with generalities and first principles than with the specific day-to-day problems of the people in different sectors and localities.

During my tours I have found entire State branches blissfully ignorant even of major pieces of legislation in their State and of its peculiar economic and political problems. This is another aspect of the negativism to which Rammanohar Lohia referred in a recent article in *Janata*. Positivism requires study of objective problems and situations.

On account of these and other shortcomings the mass mobilisation which was envisaged for a move forward in the Resolution moved by Lohia at the Patna Conference could only be partially implemented. I may briefly refer, however, to what was actually done in this regard. There were the two famous kisan marches and rallies in the U.P. and Bihar; there were large workers' demonstrations in Bombay and Jharia; there was some constructive effort made in the form of raising voluntary land brigades for road and bund building, tank repairing and excavation and other forms of village reconstruction in the States of U.P., Bihar and Orissa. There was a brave struggle against the proposed merger of the State without ascertaining the will of the people of Vindhya Pradesh, which, for the time being at any rate, put a stop to the merger scheme. There was agitation among the people of the merged states in Bombay against nomination of their representatives to the Bombay legislature. There was a successful peasant satyagraha in the district of Hissar [Punjab] against ejectment and there is at present a mass satyagraha going on again in the Indian Punjab. There was satyagraha by the Adivasis in Madhya Bharat and Rajasthan for the enforcement of prohibition.

Indian political life was slowly taking shape and the people's attention was being more and more concentrated on the solution of their real problems, when there was again an eruption of communal violence in the two Bengals. People's attention was suddenly drawn from the issues of political and economic reconstruction to that of Indo-Pakistan conflict; and a wave of communalism again swept over the country, practically submerging West Bengal and affecting large parts of North India. A good part of the energies of the Party was absorbed in dealing with this situation and into the plans for developing political action a tremendous spanner was thrown. In large part of the country all Party work came to a standstill and anti-riot and refugee work absorbed all the energies of our comrades. In an atmosphere vitiated by communal strife Socialism could hardly make any headway. Indeed the anti-communal stand of the Party often resulted in considerable setbacks.

But it gives me pleasure to state that the Party came out with flying colours through the communal fire, and where many were swept away by the communal tide our comrades held fast to their socialist faith and upheld the Brotherhood of Man which is a basic article of that faith.

III
DEMOCRATIC SOCIALISM: OUR GOAL

At this Conference while we must take stock of what we did in the past year, we must also plan for the future. The coming year would be a crucial year, far more important than the two years that have gone by. The future of the Party will depend to a large extent on what we are able to do in the next twelve months. I am sure, at this Conference, you will prepare a plan for this year and give an inspiring lead to the country.

But if we were to succeed in what we undertake to do, we must have faith in ourselves and in the ideals that we hold and the methods that we follow. It is in this sphere that I have to point to a serious weakness within ourselves.

It seems to me that there are some at least in our Party, however small their number may be, who have no faith in the very fundamentals on which the Party stands. The existence of such individuals irrespective of their numbers makes for confusion and hinders effective team work.

Now the Socialist Party is not patterned after maxims mechanically lifted out of Marxian textbooks, nor is the Party a puppet show, the leading strings of which are in the hands of powerful agents outside.

Since its birth, as the Congress Socialist Party sixteen years ago, the Party has slowly and painfully been working out its basic ideals and its methodology. This process is not complete yet, but a fairly clear-cut body of thought has already been created which distinguishes the Socialist Party from other Left parties in the country.

The roots of the Socialist Party are in the Indian soil. Indian history and background and experiences of the past sixteen years have moulded and shaped it; as also international socialist thought and the experiences of socialist re-construction in Europe and elsewhere. It was as a result of this process of ideological evolution that when the Party was reorganized at the end of the August Revolution and was meeting in its first post-war conference at Kanpur, Democratic Socialism came to be inscribed so indelibly on its banner.

Those, however, who have not gone through the same experiences and shared the same background, will not easily understand either the need for laying stress on Democratic Socialism or the real significance of that term. For the new enthusiast, with a smattering of the obvious writings of Marx-Engels-Lenin, the issue of Democratic Socialism is likely to appear to be a fruitless repetition of the issue settled long ago at Zimmerwald. Mentally he still lives in the age when one contrasted the failures of European social democracy with the brilliant success of Lenin.

But years have rolled by since then, years of poignant and tragic history of lost dreams and of the very God that failed. Of all this he is blissfully ignorant and is hardly aware of the basic problems of present-day Socialism and of the brave efforts still being made to rescue the heart of Socialism from its shell.

He still bandies the words 'reformist' and 'revolutionary' and has not yet realised that the revolutionary has turned a reactionary.

One reason why the new enthusiast is in this state of mental development is that in the enthusiasm of his conversion, the new words he has learned, the new phrases and formulae, become all important and their substance is taken for granted. Socialist theories are more real to him than socialist values, to achieve which those theories were evolved. He assumes that the theories will inevitably lead to the values; so, when the theories become a State religion he assumes that the values have been realised and Socialism established on earth. The phenomenon is common in the history of religions.

Socialism is not merely anti-capitalism, nor statism. Nationalization of industry and collectivization of agriculture are important aspects of socialist economy; but in themselves they are not socialism.

Under socialism there is no exploitation of man by man, no injustice and oppression, no insecurity and an equitable distribution of wealth and services and opportunities.

Now, even in a nationalised and collectivised economy there may be exploitation, injustice, oppression, insecurity and glaring inequalities. If under such an economy, all political and economic power is concentrated in the hands of a party oligarchy, irreplaceable and self-perpetuating, there can be no Socialism but its suppression, no revolution but reaction. The communist inasmuch as he believes in and works for just such an oligarchical society is a reactionary rather than a revolutionary.

The Party, therefore, felt that unless the goals of socialism were clearly defined and steadfastly adhered to, there was danger again of the revolution being betrayed. The aims of the socialist movement which needed to be emphasised were not mere overthrow of the capitalist order and establishment of a party dictatorship, but the creation of a society of free and equal peoples, a society based on certain values of human and social life; values which could never be sacrificed in the name of theory or the Party line or expediences of any sort. In the noble words of Ignazio Silone: "On a group of theories one can found a school; but on a group of values one can found a culture, a civilization, a new way of living together among men."

Socialism is not just a school of thought, but a new culture, a new civilization.

Since the Party declared its faith in Democratic Socialism two attitudes seem to have developed among the membership. A common and rather widespread attitude has been that of acceptance of the objective but without any living faith in it. Democratic Socialism did not become for these comrades a burning inspiration or an article of faith. Where arguments convinced the mind, the heart remained cold. Democratic Socialism was intellectually satisfying perhaps, but it failed to evoke that emotional response which makes men die for their ideas. This was due to the pre-occupation with theories and neglect of values. These comrades have not fully understood the objectives they are fighting for. If we are not fighting merely for power or the "dictatorship of the proletariat", but for certain values, if we are fighting against exploitation, injustice and tyranny of every kind, Democratic Socialism alone can be our goal; and it cannot but evoke in us that loyalty, zeal and devotion with which even a handful of men can move a mountain. That intensity of feeling is lacking in many of us. That is why though there are thousands of workers in the Party, the total output of work is comparatively so little, and that is also why there is such lack of teamwork and co-operation.

I am confident, however that as convictions deepen and as the understanding of the values of Democratic Socialism grows, faith and devotion too will grow.

There are other comrades as I have said above—their number though is small—who accepted Democratic Socialism with the tongue in the cheek, and who fancy themselves as real revolutionaries.

They have never ceased to sneer at the very fundamentals of the Party to which they belong. To such I have a very clear advice to give: "For heaven's sake, go". I do not wish to argue with them as to who is the real revolutionary among us. That issue is being decided by history.

Therefore, I say to those who have no faith in Democratic Socialism: "go". Their going will not mean disintegration of the Party, rather, it would mean integration and the acquisition of greater strength by greater internal unity and harmony. There are many parties in this country selling revolution on easy terms. I say to our pseudo-revolutionaries: "Go and choose from them and make your revolution even though it may be in a tea cup". And I say further to them: "For heaven's sake, don't go and practise a fraud upon yourself and the socialist movement by glibly professing verbal allegiance to Democratic Socialism and doing everything by word and deed to deny it". If there are agents of other parties trying to infiltrate, let me say to them: "You are wasting your time; not even the Communist Party was able to disrupt or swallow up the Socialist Party".

The methods of the Democratic Socialist Movement are different from the methods of Communism. We eschew the unclean and unscrupulous methods that the Communists follow. Even in intra-party struggles between power groups, they practise lying and deceit, character assassination, kidnapping and shooting. There is evidence that there are some in our Party who too are not averse to these unclean methods. Let me warn that these methods will be given no quarter and where reasonable proof is available, drastic action will be taken.

Recently attempts have been made to form groups within the Party and though these groups are mainly based on personal ambitions, some times an ideological cloak is thrown over them.

But whether the groups are ideological or personal, groupism or factionalism will never be allowed. The Party is democratic in its constitution and working and every member of the Party has full freedom to express his view.

Even office-bearers of the Party have been given the opportunity to express disagreement with the official Party line through the Party Letter. But permanent groupings and factions will never be permitted. If ever they are, the Party will cease to be a party and will become a loose conglomeration of groups fighting among themselves for power and position. Such a party can achieve nothing.

IV
DEMOCRATIC METHOD

For the last three years we have debated the correctness of the method to be used to achieve Socialism. While the Party as a whole has accepted the democratic method, here too as in the case of the final goals, there has been an undercurrent of stubborn scepticism and lack of faith. As a result, all of us have not worked as a team, and our actions have often had the stamp of tentativeness.

The Party's Policy Statement clearly says that there are two roads to the social revolution: (1) the road of armed mass rising or the insurrectionary method; (2) the peaceful or democratic method. The Policy Statement elucidates these terms further and distinguishes the insurrectionary method from mere violence or terrorism or putschism, and the democratic method from mere constitutionalism. The Statement goes further and declares categorically that in the present conditions of India, and future anticipated conditions, the democratic mehtod is the "only" right method to work for Socialism.

There is thus no ambiguity in Party policy on this score. Yet, there are complaints that our policy is not clearly defined in this regard. The confusion, no doubt, is in the minds of the critics, for they do not fully understand the implications of the democratic method.

There are other critics whose complaint is not that our policy is ambiguous, but that it is wrong. According to them, to say that it is possible to establish Socialism without bloodshed is to dupe the workers. For them there is only one road to Socialism: that of a blood-soaked revolution. They quote Marx's authority for this dogmatic assertion. Let me therefore quote Marx.

This is what Marx said in the course of a notable speech on tactics at The Hague Convention of International Working-men's Association (the "First International") in 1872:

> The worker must one day capture political power in order to found the new organization of labour. He must reverse the old policy, which the old institutions maintain, if he will not, like the Christians of old who despised and neglected such things, renounce the things of this world. But we do not assert that the way to reach this goal is the same everywhere. We know that the institutions, the manners, and the customs of the various countries must be considered, and we do not deny that there are countries like England and America, and, if I understand your arrangements better, I might even add Holland, where the worker may attain his object by peaceful means. But not in all countries is this the case.

If the critics do not hold that Marx was temporarily demented when he delivered his famous inaugural address, they will see that they had completely misunderstood him.

Let it, therefore, be clearly understood that it is as un-Marxian to hold that *only* an armed revolution can lead to Socialism as to assert that only a peaceful method can do so. The correct Marxian position is that either method can be used, but that which of the two is suitable to a particular situation can be determined only by the relevant historical and objective conditions.

In a given situation only one method is the right method, but only the facts of the situation, and no 'a priori' dogmatising, can decide which method is right.

To this the critics reply that the situation today is not what it was in Marx's days, and that in the existing world conditions Socialism can never be achieved by peaceful methods ! It is a healthy sign to try to correct Marx, but if the process of re-thinking does not follow the scientific method of Marx, it is likely to degenerate into mere rationalisation of pre-conceived notions. When Marx spoke at The Hague Convention, reaction was reigning supreme in Continental Europe and even in England and Holland political democracy had not fully developed. Today, one-sixth of the world is under Soviet communism and China and the whole of Eastern Europe and part of Central Europe are communist. In Scandinavia and Great Britain there are socialist governments and strong co-operative movements. In other countries of Western Europe there is at least full political democracy and, as a result of the last war, European capitalism lies shattered. Imperialism is also on the decline and India, Pakistan, Burma and Ceylon are already independent countries. Elsewhere also the chains of imperialism are loosened. In America the New Deal initiated a progress towards the welfare state which has not yet been checked and there has been since the war years a tremendous resurgence of Labour. Elsewhere in the world too the forces of democracy are to the fore more than even before. Therefore, while it is true that the situation today is different from what it was in the days of Marx, the difference is all in the favour of a peaceful evolution of socialism.

The forces of socialism are incomparably stronger today than in the last quarter of the nineteenth century. In India, in spite of the limitations on civil liberties and the Preventive Detention Act, the fact remains that there is a large scope for the democratic forms of political activity.

Even the present restrictions on civil liberties might go if the democratic forces in the country grow stronger. There can be no manner of doubt that if Marxian methodology were to be applied to India it would be the democratic method that would have to be selected. In any case, what is the alternative that the critics suggest? To this question there has been no positive answer.

One alternative is that offered by the Communist Party. In a democratic climate they deliberately embraced violence and committed murder, loot and arson. They, of course, believed that they were working for an insurrection and following a revolutionary method.

But in reality they were merely practising terrorism. What fruits the Communist Party of India has gathered from the use of violence, the past two years have clearly shown. Not only communism stands discredited today in this country but even the much-vaunted unity and solidarity of the Communist Party have proved to be a myth and there is utter disruption and ideological confusion in their ranks.

I have not come across a single member of the Party who actually advocates communist methods, and yet there has been criticism and scepticism about our own methods of work. I have vainly tried to find a middle course between our own democratic methods and the violent methods of the Indian Communist Party. There are more than half-a-dozen small socialist groups in the country, most of them in Bengal, who are loud in their denunciation of the Socialist Party. I have, however, not discovered that any one of them is following any new technique. Whatever lip service they may be rendering to brave revolutionary slogans, in actual practice they seem to be following exactly the same method as ours. Those that are not, are following the only alternative: the communist method.

I should like to digress here a little. There has been a considerable talk about recent changes in communist strategy. It is necessary that we fully appreciate these developments. The policy that Ranadive[3] seemed to be following was to bring about a social revolution on the classical lines of Russia, i.e., a revolution in which there was a general and armed mass upheaval which smashed established authority and gave birth to a new revolutionary state.

That method was bound to fail and has failed. An armed mass insurrection cannot be engineered at will. Failure of the method was bound to force a change in policy. The changed strategy seems to mean substitution of the Chinese pattern in place of the classical Russian. Terroristic and violent activities will on the whole stop, and in the urban areas the communists are likely to follow a more respectable policy and strive once again to win over the middle class.

At the same time, in certain selected rural areas they are likely to concentrate and their violent activities are likely to be intensified with a view to establish in some part of the country a communist pocket—a 'red' India.

This method too is bound to fail, because Republican India is not only different from Czarist Russia but also from war-torn China of a quarter of a century ago.

At the time when the communists succeeded in establishing their little state in a red pocket of China, the Nationalist Government was fighting a life and death struggle with powerful war lords, some of whom had even the support of certain foreign powers. Chiang Kai-shek[4] considered Chang Tso-lin[5] and the other war lords a greater danger to the Chinese Republic than Mao's[6] small Red China; so while, one by one, he crushed the war lords and integrated China, Mao's red pocket grew in strength and area. When at a certain stage Chiang turned to the reds in South China, the entire communist State migrated hundreds of miles away to the north-west. Meanwhile, Chiang's attention was drawn elsewhere, and in that remote corner of China, more or less contiguous with Soviet Asia, Mao's State developed and grew.

[3]B.T. Ranadive, then General Secretary of the Communist Party of India.

[4]Chiang-Kai-Shek, for biographical note see *JPSW*, Vol. III, p. 143.

[5]Chang-Tso-Lin (1873-1928), Chinese war lord who dominated Manchuria and north China during 1913-28; he rose to power as the protégé of Japanese and in return granted them vast concessions in Manchuria. Chang was thwarted by the armies of Kuomintang which invaded north China in 1927 under the leadership of Chiang-Kai-Shek.

[6]Mao-Tse-Tung (1893-1976), Chinese revolutionary and Statesman, founder of Chinese Communist State, became chief of the State in 1949; visited Russia in winter 1949-50 and secured all possible aid for China's economic development; after Stalin's death in 1953 his influence grew throughout the Communist world.

While Nationalist China was slowly integrated, the State remained a military dictatorship. There were no democratic forms and no constitution and no elections were held.

Now, none of these conditions exists in this country. Here we have a central government whose writ runs from the Himalayas to the Cape. We have a central army and no war lords. We had a Constituent Assembly which has given us a democratic constitution however inadequate it may be. There is adult franchise in the country, and Opposition parties that do not openly embrace violence are allowed to function. General elections have been announced for the next year. Under these conditions it would never be possible for a 'red' India pocket to be created or for that pocket slowly to envelope the whole country. Even in China it is doubtful if Mao could ever have achieved a victory over Nationalist China had not the Japanese war intervened and had not Japan surrendered in Manchuria to a Russian army.

Therefore, I repeat that the Cominform's[7] latest directive to Indian communists to follow Mao Tse-tung is bound to be as total a failure as the previous directive which was the basis of the Calcutta Thesis of the Communist Party, passed two and half years ago.

Coming back to the question I was examining, it seems to me that the only difference between the Socialist Party and the other Socialist groups that criticise us for our insistence on the democratic method is, that, while in actual practice all of them follow the same method, they keep on repeating to themselves, in order to fortify as it were their faith in their revolutionary character, that Socialism can never come through peaceful means.

To follow peaceful means today and to hold dogmatically that at the last stage violence would somehow be essential seems to be the position of these groups. On the other hand, the position that the Socialist Party takes is a perfectly Marxian one, namely, that in the present conditions democratic means alone are the right means, and further that, if the democratic way of life develops and abides in India, the same means would be right even at the final stage of the struggle for Socialism.

If, however, conditions change, and all of us, including the bravely talking revolutionaries, fail to stop the growth of fascism in this country, it is elementary Marxism that democratic methods would become ineffective. But in the first place, there is no need to be faint-hearted and accept defeat before the battle has been joined. I am confident that, if the democratic forces in this country functioned properly and effectively, it would be

[7]Cominform—a name given in the West to the information office of the Communist Parties. This was an agency of international revolutionary Communism from 1947 to 1956. It was formed in September 1947 at Wilcza Gora by representatives of the Communist Parties of the USSR, Eastern Europe, France and Italy.

possible to prevent fascism and to build up and preserve democracy. In the second place, even if the situation were to change later, what is it that has to be done today in anticipation except what is being done now to prepare and organize the masses through the present methods.

If by following democratic methods the Socialist Party succeeds in winning the allegiance of the masses and in making them politically conscious and organizationally strong, even an appeal to mass insurrection would be likely to receive an effective response.

That the masses may have to resort to such a course and seize power by mass action, if the ruling powers make democracy ineffective is and should always be a part of the political education that we endeavour to give to them.

In the course of my talks with Party members I have sometimes come across an undercurrent of feeling that while violent methods yield speedy results the democratic methods might mean a long drawn out slogging game at the wickets. Nothing can be farther from the truth than this. Russia itself is an example of how long it took for violent methods to succeed. And, without the first World War, who can tell if the Bolshevik revolution could ever have come in 1917? At present China has become a common illustration of the effectiveness of violence.

It is forgotten, however, that the struggle in China has taken at least two decades and but for the intervention of World War II, Mao's victories could never have been assured or come at the time they did.

We come back to the conclusion, therefore, that in our given conditions there is no alternative to the democratic method. What then is this method?

Before I proceed to answer this question, let me remove a possible misunderstanding. Just as there are those for whom there is no alternative in any circumstances to the insurrectionary method, there are also those who would under no conditions take recourse to insurrection. The attitude of the later would be equally incompatible with the Party's fundamental faith, and there can be no place in the Party for them.

Returning to answer the question posed above, it will be remembered that the Policy Statement has distinguished the democratic method from constitutionalism. The Socialist Party is not a mere parliamentary party. As a matter of fact, the Socialist Party hardly exists in the Parliament. The Party is a revolutionary party and while it may use the parliamentary method it relies for its success mainly on its work outside parliament and among the people.

While it is a part of the democratic method to capture parliament through elections and to form a government, the Socialist Party believes that a social revolution, even after the capture of power, would have to be carried out by the people themselves, aided and guided as they may be by the socialist State.

A mere parliamentary party is little more than an election machine and relies on propaganda alone. But the Socialist Party is not an election machine and it does not rely on propaganda alone. The Party organizes at the same time trade unions, kisan panchayats, youth leagues. It carries on agitation and fights for the people. It conducts local struggles, strikes and 'satyagrahas'. It may have to launch even a national struggle if and when the situation demands and advises. It also carries on constructive work. It builds co-operatives, roads, tanks, bunds. It conducts workers' education and it does many other things.

V
MILITANCY AND STRIKES

Organization, propaganda, agitation, struggle and constructive work may be summed up as the five different kinds of activities which we carry on today and which are all comprised within the term "democratic method".

The object of all our activities is not merely to win elections, but to serve the people, to organize them to fight for and protect their rights and interests and ultimately to enable them through collective mass effort to establish a socialist state and create a socialist society.

There is one type of criticism which I shall admit is valid. In applying the democratic method mistakes may be committed. Where action was needed, inaction might have been ordered, and 'vice versa'.

The railway strike is an instance in point. It might have been wise to postpone the general strike or it might have been a mistake. But the kind of criticism that sometimes has been made even in our Party ranks is neither helpful nor well-informed nor *bona fide*. I should like to say a word about this matter for it has been a source of some confusion in the Party. I have heard that in some quarters it has been said that I betrayed the railway workers. Now, betrayal is a serious matter, and it is not the same thing as a mistake. A mistake is always *bona fide*, but betrayal implies a moral wrong.

Anyone in the Party who has betrayed the workers has no place in it, and whoever thinks that I have betrayed the railwaymen should arraign me before the Party, and, if I am proved guilty, I should be expelled.

If I may point out, the railway worker does not think that he was betrayed. This will have been clear to any one who was present at the last Jubilee Conference of the All-India-Railwaymen's Federation. As you know I had made up my mind to leave the Federation because I wanted more time for political work.

But at the Conference I witnessed a demonstration of affection and confidence that I shall cherish all through life and that compelled me to change my mind. For forty minutes the entire proceedings of the Conference were brought to a standstill while delegates demonstrated with one voice as it were that they wanted no one else but the one who is alleged to have betrayed their cause.

The leaders of the Federation, most of them railwaymen themselves, came in groups and singly to remonstrate and to say that the very future of the Federation was in danger if I did not carry on for at least another year. I am saying all this not in self-praise but merely to show that the railwaymen do not seem to agree with my traducers.

I concede, however, that it is possible to hold that a mistake was committed, though nothing that has happened since the decision was taken has persuaded me to change my opinion. Let it first be understood that the Railwaymen's Federation is not a political party but a trade union formed to fight the cause of railwaymen.

As President of the Federation, my primary task was to safeguard the interests of railwaymen and not to further any political policy or theory.

When the decision was taken to hold a strike ballot the situation roughly was that the Railway Board had said: so far and no further. In other words, the door to further negotiations was closed or, at any rate, it was made plain that nothing further was to be gained by negotiations. During the course of the strike ballot the Hon'ble Shri Ayyangar, the Railway Minister, offered to talk it over with the Federation and indicated that no item was beyond the pale of negotiations. Negotiations naturally followed, and their result was placed before the General Council of the Federation at Danapore, along with my personal advice that the strike was no longer necessary and that it should be postponed till full results of the negotiations were known.

The General Council, with only ten dissentient votes, decided to postpone the general strike. The Communists, notwithstanding the Federation's decision, gave a call for a general strike, but railwaymen paid no heed to that call. This indicated, if anything, that the postponement of the strike was generally approved of.

The communists and the others who wanted the strike in any circumstances were prompted not by trade union considerations but had political motives. The Federation is not a political party and I, as its President, would have betrayed the railwaymen if I had used it to further a political policy. Considered merely from the trade union point of view, i.e., from the point of view of the interest of the railwaymen, the decision taken at Danapore was a right decision, and it has never been regretted by those who took it or by those on whose behalf it was taken.

I am convinced that had a strike been actually called, the Federation would have been seriously weakened and the rival federation formed by the INTUC would have been pushed to the fore.

There would have been discharges and victimisation on a large-scale, and, while a few militants might have been born out of the catastrophe, there would have been general demoralisation in the ranks of railway labour. Nor was it ever possible to achieve more through a strike than what was done by a grand demonstration of strength through the strike ballot and by the negotiations that followed.

An important by-product of the tactics then used was that the Federation was cleared of the communist disruptors who virtually were manoeuvred into committing a suicide.

In any case, I admit that in the application of a method, however correct, mistakes can be made and may have been made. However, in examining any specific application of a method, we should not be guided by preconceived notions. For instance, there is a tendency in some quarters to say that it matters little whether a strike succeeds or fails. The real object is not to achieve specific advantages for labour through collective bargaining but to create a spirit of militancy and hostility to the established order.

I cannot conceive of a more foolish and shortsighted principle than this. This is exactly the policy which the communists had been following for the last twenty-five years in this country. But where are their militants among the working classes today and what have these militants achieved? The communists have brought more demoralisation by their ill-conceived methods and militancy.

Militancy is not inculcated by a mood of defeat and bitterness but by understanding and conviction. That worker is militant who has deep convictions and a clear understanding of what he is fighting for. We can help the workers to acquire convictions and understanding by political education and hard, patient work. Struggle mellows and hardens the worker, but this does not mean that we must rush into every foolhardy strike or get up a synthetic struggle every day. An ill-conceived, ill-timed and ill-organized struggle will do more harm than good. As far as creation of feeling against the established order of things is concerned, it is not necessary to manufacture struggles to do that.

The feeling exists today, engendered by the misdeeds of the ruling classes. The task is to convert all this dissatisfaction into organized political consciousness and vital political action. I have tried in this report to sum up the controversy that has been going on in the ranks of the party for the last three years, and I should like this Conference finally to put a stop to it. We cannot go on arguing about our fundamentals indefinitely. If the foundations were to be pulled out every time they are laid, no structure can be ever built.

I am aware that in achieving this ideological clarification in the Party we too have failed to discharge our duties. The literature that was necessary for this was not produced. But it will not be denied that slowly a body of writing has been growing on this matter. It has, however, been my unfortunate experience that our comrades do not even try to read the literature that is available. The Party journals are obviously the best instrument for Party Education, but it is not unoften that I have found that while Party members would read cheap, sensational and vulgar journals with avidity, they would not even look at the organs published by the Party. I have also come across Party comrades who have not even studied the Policy Statement, much less the the resolutions of the Party. It is not unnatural, therefore, that there should be so much ideological confusion.

Clarification of fundamentals has become essential from another point of view too. With the recent shift in communist policy there is likely to be a drive at infiltration and the familiar slogans of united front and left unity are again likely to be raised.

If our workers are not very clear as to what they stand for, the Party is likely to be weakened by unnecessary internal controversies engineered by stooges of others.

In this connection, I should like to draw your attention to the Bangalore statement of the National Executive on left unity, which is a part of the Policy Statement and which clearly defines the Party's policy in regard to that question.

A sign of infiltration is already visible. There is already a talk in certain quarters in the Party about the "reactionary leadership". It is a familiar Communist tactic to try to destroy a party by creating a gulf of distrust between the rank and file and the leadership. In the Socialist Party there never has been a division between the leadership and the Party membership, nor any struggle for power within the Party. The difficulty has rather been to persuade the "leaders" to accept positions in the Party. The will to keep behind rather than to fight for offices has been the characteristic of the party leadership.

I, therefore, wish to warn you against these disruptive tactics of dividing the rank and file from the leadership. If the leadership is reactionary, the Party too is reactionary, because the leadership is one with the rank and file and vice versa.

VI
DISINTEGRATION OF THE PARTY?

There has also been some talk about the disintegration of the Party. Nothing has amazed me more than this talk because, while other parties, including the Communist Party, are showing signs of disintegration, our Party alone has preserved its integrity. Sometimes, the so-called differences between the leaders have been exaggerated. I see no reason why on every issue Party leaders must speak with one voice. It is desirable that we do, but where differences exist they should be expressed and there should be mutual criticism. It is another matter that after the Party has taken a decision the minority should submit to that decision and carry it out. But even then there should be freedom for the minority to propagate its views in an effort to convert the majority to its side.

Sometimes ago news items appeared in some papers to the effect that certain important members of the Party were resigning. These reports were without any foundation. It was laughable to say that our able Chairman, Asoka Mehta, was thinking to resign. He never even dreamed of it. Regarding Achyut Patwardhan, I shall read out his letter which will show you that it is not because of any differences with the Party that he is not in the front line today. Rammanohar Lohia, always original and bold in his thinking and sharp and hard-hitting in his phraseology, was never more active and close to the Party than now. The only member of the National Executive about whose future line of action I have any misgivings is Aruna Asaf Ali. It has been known for some time that she is not in agreement with the objective of democratic socialism nor with the democratic method. But what she will actually do on her return to India is more than I can say. I have no doubt that in these critical moments her post of duty was here. But I am sorry to report to you that since the Patna Conference she never took the trouble of attending even a single meeting of the National Executive nor of doing much Party work. If Aruna Asaf Ali does not agree with the fundamentals of the Party her resignation, I am sure, will not mean disintegration but, as I have said above, a closer integration of the Party.

VII
THE TASKS AHEAD

From the report placed before you by my colleague Madhu Limaye, you will see that in the last year we have failed to progress as we had expected to do. The next year you know is going to be a testing year for us. Let us hope that in the past year we have got over all the hesitations and doubts that were natural when we took a new turn at Patna. In the spirit of the "On the Move" resolution of the Patna Conference and in furtherance of it the Executive has placed before you this year an inspiring Programme for National Revival.

As Rammanohar Lohia pointed out in his recent article, we failed in the last year to set the people on the move. Let us hope that we have by now sufficiently understood our task and reorganized ourselves to be able to carry through his programme of national reconstruction.

Before I conclude, I should like to say that while our aims and hopes are high we should work with the detachment that the *Geeta* teaches and neither success nor failure should enthuse or dishearten us. Our joy should be in our work and in the conviction that victory ultimately is bound to be ours. We must carry on no matter how long the struggle. I am afraid there is a mentality growing in the Party which is only interested in quick results. Many have been heard to say that the results of the forthcoming general elections would decide the future of the Party.

I have no doubt that the Party will make a great showing at the elections, but it will not make the least difference to me if the Party were completely swept off the board. Indeed, for me, such a result would be a further challenge and a spur to greater efforts.

I hope all of you will work in that same spirit and the only return that you will seek will be the satisfaction that you have done your duty.

Madhu Limaye, in his report, has dealt with many grave organizational problems which should receive your serious consideration. I endorse wholly the views that he has expressed and the suggestions that he has made.

I have refrained in this report from summing up the political and economic position in the country. That has been done in the resolutions and the National Revival Programme.

334. Some Remarks on the Political Report, Madras, 8 July 1950[1]

My report[2] and the report of my fellow secretary are in your hands. I do not want to add to these printed reports. I shall only draw your attention to the character of these reports and the purpose for which they have been prepared. In my report I have tried to sum up the controversies and doubts that have been raised in the last three years, that is, ever since we reorganized our Party at Kanpur. I have also tried to re-state the fundamental principles and policies of the Party. I believe that now we have arrived at a stage of maturity where we should be able to say without any doubt or hesitation as to what the fundamental principles for which we stand are. If we do not clearly define our fundamentals, I am afraid we would suffer from continued paralysis and we shall not be able to make progress, at any rate rapid progress, in the direction in which we want to move. We cannot go on changing our goals and casting doubts on our goals.

When we discussed our Policy Statement at Kanpur and finally adopted it at Nagpur, it was felt that now at last the Socialist Party knows what its goals are. You will excuse me for saying so, but I have found during my tours that there exist doubts in the minds of our co-workers about the fundamentals of our Party. I have found that they don't even try to understand

[1] *Socialist Party Eighth National Conference, Madras, 8-12 July 1950*, pp. 2-9.

[2] See Appendix 24 for debate on the General Secretary's Report at the Madras Conference of the Socialist Party, 9 July 1950.

what democratic socialism means. I have also observed with regret that many Party workers have not read the Policy Statement. Only the other day on my way to Madras, I was addressing nearly 150 workers of the Maharashtra branch, a branch which is known for its systematic and efficient working, a branch which has produced some fine men, a branch which has a number of young and earnest men who are constantly trying to study and understand and yet I have found that less than half of the number present there had read our Policy Statement. In a mass party like ours I don't expect all our members to read our Policy Statement. Illiterate Party comrades cannot do so, but I do expect active workers and office-bearers, working in the various fields of activities, to study the Policy Statement. The Policy Statement has been translated in most of the Provincial languages so that nobody can excuse himself on the ground that he does not understand English.

Secondly, in the ranks of the Party, there is a tendency to disregard what the Party has defined as its fundamental goal and to follow individual predilections and preferences. It would be impossible for us to build up a cohesive Socialist Party if we continue like this. No member of the Party is entitled to say that he does not believe in Democratic Socialism. We cannot build up the structure of the Socialist movement and Party, if we go on laying the fundamentals and pulling them out day by day. Therefore I have tried in my report to impress upon you the need to put a stop to these doubts, to these controversies that are still going on in the ranks of the Party.

In the second part of my report, I have dealt with the methods that we have to follow. About that also, the Policy Statement has left no room for doubt. The Policy Statement has categorically stated that under the present conditions in India, democratic methods are the *only* correct methods to follow. The Statement does not say that in *all* circumstances these are the only methods to follow. It states that if conditions change our methods will also change. It is not denied that democratic rights and civil liberties are encroached upon today. Yet there is room for democratic work. I have therefore tried to sum up the discussions on that question also. I have not said in my report that whatever we did was wholly right. There might have been situations where some felt that a more militant policy should have been followed. What that militant policy should have been, I fail to understand. All that I can say is that in the present state of organization we have followed the methods that should have been followed. Wherever our Party branches have been in a position to follow a policy of struggle, nothing has been done to stop them from going ahead. Today over 800 workers and members of the Punjab Party are in prison. Their Provincial Joint Secretary, Meherchand Ahuja,[3] himself is in prison. The Punjab Party has not been in

[3] Meherchand Ahuja: for biographical note see *JPSW*, Vol. IV, p. 226.

a position to hold elections for this conference and therefore I request you to allow two comrades who have come from Punjab to function here as delegates. The National Executive has no power to do so; only the conference can do it.

I should be happy if it were possible for our Party to follow a more militant policy. I have absolutely no quarrel on that issue. I should, however, like to tell you that it is not possible to enter or launch upon struggle without preparation, that is to say, without fulfilling certain conditions. But wherever we thought we had a fairly good organization, we did not avoid struggle. However, that does not relate to the fundamental issues that I have placed before you in my report. I shall therefore like this conference to endorse that report. For it merely re-states the fundamental policy of the Party. We have always distinguished democratic methods from mere constitutionalism. I have only reiterated this in my report. I have further tried to draw your attention to certain growing diseases in the Party. For instance, the rise of groupism in the Party to which a very pointed reference was made by Rammanohar Lohia in his recent article in the *Janata*. He has dealt with that problem more fully. All I expect you to do is to endorse our fundamentals and put an end to the controversy on this point. Those of us who do not subscribe to Democratic Socialism have no place in this Party. I want you to categorically and clearly endorse that statement. What the full picture of Democratic Socialism would be is a different matter. I do concede that we have not yet been able to place before you that full picture. However, our people have written articles and pamphlets which give an outline of the principles of Democratic Socialism. We have also evolved ideas which we can claim to be our own. Nevertheless, it is true that a coherent philosophy of Democratic Socialism has still to emerge, and I hope that in the course of the next year, something positive and concrete will be done in that direction.

I would, however, like a major part of the discussion on the report to be centred round the organizational problems which have been raised in the Joint Secretary's Report. We were prone in the past to discuss ideology more and leave organizational matters alone, with the result that serious defects have crept into our organization. Madhu Limaye[4] has in his report made some suggestions as to how these organizational defects could be remedied. I should like this conference to endorse these suggestions and make in them such modifications and alterations as it deems fit. You will, perhaps, remember that I have referred in my report to the loose talk that has been going on in certain circles regarding the disintegration of the Party. There I have referred to a letter which Achyut Patwardhan[5] wrote to me.

[4] Madhu Limaye: for biographical note see *JPSW*, Vol. IV, p. 186.

[5] Achyut Patwardhan: for biographical note see *JPSW*, Vol. II, p.162.

He has also sent his statement which he desires me to read out to the conference. This statement was received by me yesterday night. In his letter written to me on 16th February 1950, Achyut says:

I shall not attend the Rewa meeting of National Executive and I hope you will take care to see that no fresh responsibilities are put on me during this year. Knowing how my mind is moving, I hope you would be kind enough to give me a little time to myself. This request is not made in a huff. You know that I have come much closer to you during recent months. I do not think it would be an exaggeration if I said that you and some other co-workers mean more to me than some of my brothers—emotionally as well as in work. Still I need a little time to myself and I hope you will let me have it.

In another letter written on the 24th February 1950, he further says:

I do not think, I shall be able to continue to do political work hereafter. What precisely I propose to do I cannot say today. I would most likely fade out quietly and completely for the time being. You know, people like you and me cannot do anything half-hearted. It is only fair that I should end all the uncertainty and vacillation and take a final decision on this matter. For my part I have taken that decision and I hope you will believe me when I say that I would feel terribly double-faced if I continued as though I was carrying on.

You can retain my name on the *Janata* up-till the Annual Conference. Then you could make new arrangements in the general shuffling of work.

I am keenly aware of the difficulties I am causing you by this step. If they were not absolutely unavoidable, I would have cut my hand rather than put you to so much trouble. You have probably hardly realised that you mean more to me than my brothers and sister. But I must be true to myself if I am to be true to anyone else. Please forgive me for the pain I am causing.

The views expressed by him in these two letters are further elucidated in his statement which I will now read out:

Close association with the Socialist Party since its inception and ties of deep friendship with some of my colleagues in the movement make it desirable that I should say a few words to explain my decision to withdraw from all party political activities and organizations.

From early youth, most of the thinking men of my generation recognised that individualism and the liberal philosophy could not explain or remedy the deeper social evils around us. Neither was personal salvation a meaningful response to the challenge of social inequalities and injustice in the midst of which we live.The core of the prevailing misery and cruelty was directly traceable to the institutional basis of our lives. Particularly in India, British domination was the keystone of the arch of inequity. From Vivekanand[6] and Tilak,[7] Annie Besant[8] and Gandhiji we had been advised to seek personal enlightenment through closer identification with social struggles.

Thus the struggle for political freedom, the emancipation of the working people on land, and, in the factories, from an outmoded system of ownership of social resources, and ending of the tyranny of caste and outcaste—these three-fold ends seemed to define the task-sheet of our generation.

In the course of the past twenty years we have pursued these ends with all our humble capacity jointly through organized efforts, for these ends demanded effective organization and collective resistance. The success of the Russian Revolution, the rise of fascism and the fall of the Spanish Republic led most of us to seek political power as the major instrument of social change. Thus political power became the sole immediate objective of our organized efforts. This deviation of social philosophy into power-philosophy has led towards an outlook of seeking power at any price.

The effectiveness of ideology and the strength of an organization are at present judged by the single test of attaining power as soon as possible. The inevitable result of this quest for political power is the growing vogue of ruthlessness in our public life. It has also led to the glorification of toughness and the rise of new theories of "MINORITY REVOLUTION". Practice between parties and even within each party has reflected the decay of social standards and this tendency has debased our public life. On the one hand, it has led to the glorification of the State as the new Church Militant; it has, on the other hand, led to a total lack of brotherliness and tolerance between persons with marked differences in outlook or loyalties. These are not isolated developments. They are the prevailing political tendency all the world over. In this perspective, social changes are treated as a function of the compulsive authority of the State. The movement of men's minds and the quickening of human sentiment are ignored and even come to be viewed as the results rather than the prime cause and source of all political authority. Thus political parties degenerate into hand-picked cliques of professional revolutionaries or Tammany-hall bosses, and men and women are led towards new and frightful wars in the name of social philosophy. This tendency is not more particularly at work in the Socialist Party. It is the prevailing mode of political action all the world over. This drift towards STATISM is less obvious in a party in opposition,

[6] Vivekananda (1863-1902); a sage and social reformer, his original name was Narendra Dutta, came under the influence of Ramakrishna Parmahansa; attended Parliament of Religions at Chicago in 1893; visited England in 1896 and lectured on Vedanta; visited England and U.S.A. in 1899; again founded a Vendanta Society in San Francisco. His writings and speeches influenced several national leaders who fought for Indian's freedom.

[7] B.G. Tilak: for biographical note see *JPSW*, Vol. IV, p. 247.

[8] Annie Besant: for biographical not see *JPSW*, Vol. I, p.187.

none the less, the direction is the same in all political organizations and it is the price of immediate effectiveness.

This tendency has led to a growing indifference towards politics among millions of people who are disillusioned by the debacle of political cults. However, this is but a negative response and it cannot provide an alternative movement by earnest men of good will who are anxious to end the framework of social injustice and inequality. There must be another approach to social regeneration which does not negate itself in the vicious circle of power politics. There must be a path of social redemption which can forge for itself an instrument as worthy and sane as the end it seeks to attain.

I must confess, that there is no ready-made alternative of this type to which one could subscribe *en masse*. It is an exploration in a region of human behaviour which is still shrouded in uncertainty. Yet any new movement must begin in the first instance as the adventure of a single perplexed mind, which is prepared to move away from the shore of certainty which is recognised as inadequate. In this sense it must begin as a lone trail in a pathless wilderness. It is however by no means a personal quest. This social import alone gives it a meaning.

You will see from this statement that it is not because of any difference on fundamentals or policies of the Party that Achyut had decided at least for the time being to go out of active politics or active party politics. He has raised in this statement some of the issues which have the deepest significance. All that I shall say with all humility is that Achyut's place is still in the Socialist Party. We are aware of the limitations to which he has drawn attention. It is not possible for a political organization to convert itself into a spiritual organization, but as I have stated earlier the Socialist Party by subscribing to the principles of Democratic Socialism is endeavouring to safeguard those very human values which he wants to preserve by other means. For, if capture of power and the establishment of a Party dictatorship were to be the only goals of the Socialist Party, there was no need for us to declare that we stand for Democratic Socialism. It is precisely because we are interested in preserving and creating certain values of social life, it is precisely because we are interested in building up a *socialist society* and not merely in the establishment of a *socialist State* that we have raised the banner of Democratic Socialism. I hope that Achyut will realise that after all human beings have their own limitations. But we have at least the satisfaction that we are endeavouring to establish a society which also is his dream. I therefore hope that it will be possible for Achyut to return soon to the Party to which he rightly belongs.

You have probably been reading in the papers that there is going to be a change in the policy of the Communist Party. I believe they are again coming forward with a facade of united front behind which they would continue to carry on their disruptive activities. I do not exactly know what the nature of that facade will be—whether it will be known as Workers' and Peasants' Party or a consolidation of the so-called left parties. But, it is obvious that they have now realised that the methods which they were following so far have resulted in their complete isolation from the people, and therefore there is going to be a change of front. They will now try to woo not only the lower and upper middle classes but also a section of the Indian bourgeois which they consider 'democratic'. The word 'democratic' in communist parlance means one who is prepared to follow blindly the Soviet Union. The Communist Party is going to set up a 'democratic front' not for the creation of a democratic society nor for the preservation of democratic values but in order to canvass and organize support for Russia. They are doing this not because the objective conditions in India demand such a policy, but simply because they have been ordered to do so by the Cominform. Today they are concerned with only one thing and it is: in the tense international situation today on which side are the people of India and on which side are the people of the world. They will, therefore, do everything to drag India into the Russian camp. If you, comrades, do not know your minds and do not hold fast to your ground, you will be swept off by these new communist manoeuvres. I trust our ranks would achieve greater clarity and no matter what happens, what slogans they put forward, would march forward with firm determination under the banner of Democratic Socialism.

With these words I present my report and the organizational report of the Joint Secretary.

335. Reply to the Debate on the Political Report, Madras, 9 July 1950[1]

I have been somewhat disappointed to find that the discussion again centred round the ideological part of the report. I had thought that most of us have now reached a stage where we should act rather than talk about our fundamentals. Very few delegates have given attention to the organizational problems and the programme of work placed by Madhu Limaye. I hope, however, that in the coming years, we will be able to devote more time to discuss the organizational problems—the basic task before us.

I shall reply in two parts to the debate. First, I shall make some general remarks about the ideological discussion. Most of the speeches have been helpful, but I have a very serious complaint against Com. Basu Krishnamurthi's[2] speech. He spoke of the Democratic Socialism of the

[1] *Socialist Party Eighth National Conference, Madras, 8-12 July, 1950*, pp. 52-9. See Appendix 24 for debate on General Secretary's Report.

[2] Basu Krishnamurthi, an active Socialist worker.

National Executive and me. I submit in all humility that there is no such thing as the Democratic Socialism of the National Executive; the Democratic Socialism of which I have spoken, is the Democratic Socialism which forms the basis of our Party. He talked of "true" Democratic Socialism and scientific Socialism. I do not know what he means by these phrases. The Policy Statement has clearly defined what Democratic Socialism means. I have only re-affirmed it in my report. Comrade Krishnamurthi said that there is nothing wrong in discussing the fundamentals of the Party. I hope that there is none among you who would support his contention. There is everything wrong in discussing fundamentals time and again. As I said yesterday and as I have stated in my report, we cannot go on laying the foundation today and pulling it out tomorrow. Either we stand for some definite ideals or we do not. The Socialist Party is not a joint front, nor a loose conglomeration of all kinds of ideologies, but it has a certain distinct body of ideals which shall always inspire and guide us. There is no room in the Party for the kind of attitude which Comrade Krishnamurthi has shown.

Those who believe in the fundamentals are welcome in the Party.

There can, of course, be different points of view. Even the leaders can differ among themselves. These are healthy signs and the discussion, if carried on proper lines, can help our comrades in their education. But, some of our comrades feel that they have a right to differ among themselves while the leaders have not. May I remind our friends that during Lenin's time, members of the Bolshevik Party openly discussed party policies in party papers? Lenin used to criticise others and was in turn criticised by them, sometimes even in strong language. There was democracy inside the Bolshevik Party. All this is common knowledge. In our Party also, there is room for discussion. It, however, does not mean that we should go on discussing the very fundamentals. Because such interminable discussions would undermine the very foundation on which the superstructure of the Party rests. We will fight for those fundamentals till our death. We will die fighting, but under no circumstances will we barter away those ideals for something which is Socialism only in name—a Socialism in which there is complete denial of political and economic freedom.

I was rather surprised to hear Comrade Genda Singh.[3] He seems to believe that I have a brand of Democratic Socialism of my own, because I described the Constitution of India as fairly democratic. He also seems to think that the messages we have received from different parts of the world tend to add to the confusion. I am sorry to say that this is a superficial observation. If Genda Singh had only gone through the Policy Statement, there would have been no confusion about Democratic Socialism in his mind. We have contrasted Democratic Socialism with Totalitarian Communism. We have

[3] Genda Singh, one of the prominent leaders of the Socialist Party in U.P.

also described the basic elements of Democratic Socialism in our Policy Statement. He seems to believe, however, that Democratic Socialism is the private property of Jayaprakash Narayan. I have only tried to sum up the discussion that has been going on for the last three years. I hope that during the course of the next year we will be able to put forward a fuller picture of Democratic Socialism, in which task I shall also do my bit. While referring to my inaugural address at the Civil Liberties Union Conference held at Patna, he reminded me that I had characterized the Nehru Government as fascist. And therefore he says that to describe the Indian Constitution as fairly democratic is a contradiction. I would like Genda Singh to know that the Constitution is different from the Government. Pandit Nehru and Sardar Patel may be in the Government and they may be and are at times showing fascist tendencies. But in my report I have discussed only the Constitution. When I say that it is a fairly democratic constitution, it does not mean that it is satisfactory. Under this constitution we have adult franchise. It guarantees elections. The political parties can function in an open manner and the opposition parties can take part in the elections. But I am not characterising it as fully or wholly democratic.

There are many aspects of Democratic Socialism which have to be examined and defined as a result of collective discussions in the Party. But its fundamental character has been adequately defined in the Policy Statement.

There are complaints that I have tolerated too much of looseness in the Party. Perhaps this is my weakness and I own it. But I hope that my successor will enforce stricter discipline. I say this in connection with the talk of witch-hunting which is going on in the Party. If the Party has been guilty of anything it is of looseness. And therefore, there need be no fear of witch-hunting.

Every member of the Party has full freedom to criticise Party policy, in the columns of the *Janata* and the Party letter.

Tulsi Boda complained that the publication of the resolutions just ten days before the conference does not leave enough time to think over them. May I inform him that the Central Office has been repeatedly reminding the provincial offices and through them the Party members to send their resolutions and suggestions either directly or through provincial offices? But unfortunately neither the provincial parties nor the members have responded.

Some questions have been raised about certain aspects of the ideological discussion I have summed up in my report. At least two speeches were made on the question of values. I am afraid, both of them did not understand what I said. The values of which I have spoken are not traditional moral values, as Abhyankar seems to believe. I have not talked of ethics in this report, but of the abiding values of socialist society. Are not these values, after all, the driving force behind the socialist movement? The socialist theories, I submit, are instruments for the achievement of these ultimate values. The socialist theory, for instance, talks of nationalization of industries. But you will agree that by itself, it does not lead to socialism. Nationalization is meant to serve some purpose. It is a means to industrial democracy. It would, therefore, not be enough to take away these industries from private enterprize and put them in the hands of a few bureaucrats. Nationalization will have no meaning if the industries are to be run by a few people appointed by the Government. It will not be Socialism. Socialism requires active participation of workers in running the industry. There can be wage slavery under state management. That is why I have insisted on these values. Hence you will see that I have not talked of changing moral values nor of the Christian and liberal values as some friends suggest, but of absolute social values alone.

A lot was said about Marxism and Gandhism. An Andhra friend came here and talked about Marx and condemned the Stalinists. Capitalists and Stalinists were branded together. Does he not know that the only prophet the Stalinists claim is Marx himself? Every one of the Stalinists feels that he is the direct descendant of the Prophet. Does this comrade not know what Ranadive says of Joshi and Joshi of Ranadive, all in the name of Marx? Ranadive has charged Joshi with Titoist and Trotskyist deviation and Joshi in his turn hurls back these very epithets at Ranadive, again in the name of Marx.

There are so many kinds of Socialism that Socialism seems to have lost all definite meaning. Different schools of thought, often contradictory and thirsting for each other's blood, are found swearing by Marx. I am also a Marxist. But that means nothing. It, therefore, becomes necessary to define what we mean by Marxism. I believe that Socialism which Marx pictured was the Socialism which we are trying to describe by the term Democratic Socialism. Only that Socialism can bring about the emancipation of toilers and no other. We are following in the footsteps of Marx, but we must avoid dogmatism because dogmatism is foreign to Marxism. Marxism is a scientific attempt to understand and change society. Every dispute cannot be settled by bringing in the name of Marx. We must apply the method that Marx gave us to the objective conditions obtaining in our country.

People have also talked of a choice between Democratic Socialism and dictatorship of the proletariat. I am sorry to note that these friends have not understood either. Dictatorship of the proletariat is not socialist society. All that Marx and Lenin have said is that the dictatorship of the proletariat is a transitional stage, under certain conditions, between Capitalism and Socialism. Therefore the talk of a choice between Democratic Socialism and dictatorship of the proletariat is a gross mistake. Under certain circumstances dictatorship of the proletariat may become necessary. But, let me make it abundantly clear to you that the dictatorship of the proletariat is different from the dictatorship of the party. The two are fundamentally opposed to each other. The proletariat is not a party. It is far bigger than a party and no party has any right to say that it alone represents the will of the entire proletariat. Please try to understand that when Marx spoke of the dictatorship of the proletariat in connection with the civil war in France and the Paris Commune, he was not thinking in terms of a party dictatorship. He was thinking of a new kind of democracy, in the sense that a vast majority of the people, the toiling masses would establish a dictatorship over a small class of feudal lords, capitalists and exploiters. It is a dictatorship of a vast majority over a very tiny minority. It is a dictatorship which must disappear in the course of time. If, however, that dictatorship degenerates into a party dictatorship, as it has degenerated in Soviet Russia, it will be a denial of Marxism.

In India, we are trying to build up a socialist movement keeping in view the prevailing objective conditions and the country's historical background. Mahatma Gandhi was a great social force. His life and teachings have a significance not only for India but the entire world. He gave us a weapon—the weapon of Satyagraha, which has been effectively used by thousands of our countrymen in the Punjab, Champaran, Maharashtra, Tinnevelly and other places. Gandhi is the one tremendous fount in India from which Socialism will continue to derive inspiration. If Marx were to be alive today, I am sure that he would certainly not have withdrawn himself into a shell and closed his eyes to Gandhiji's precepts and practice.

There has been some discussion about democratic methods. Some delegates have said that our Policy Statement states that if all other methods fail, we will have to take to insurrectionary methods. These comrades seem to have completely misunderstood the Policy Statement. The Policy Statement says that democratic methods will be followed under certain conditions and in others insurrectionary or violent methods will be adopted. It further says that under the *present conditions* democratic methods are the *only* right methods. If the conditions change, then, of course, the methods also will change. I may, however, refer the members to what I said at the Patna conference. Whether there is to be full democracy or Fascism in this country will not be decided by the Congress alone, but it will also to a great extent depend upon what we do and how actively we shape events in this country. The Socialist Party cannot be a passive spectator of the events. We will fight to prevent Fascism from coming. But, some of our comrades have a tendency to accept defeat and say that democracy has failed. To all those who talk of Fascism in India, I appeal not to waste their time in such loose talk but devote themselves to constructive work, to the organization of the peasants, the workers and other toilers. They seem to think that if we are swept off the board in the coming general elections, it will mean the failure of democratic methods. All this seems to me only a cover for our weakness.

B.P. Sinha raised a very subtle point. It is a matter of definition. It is true that when we use a word we have to make clear what we mean by it. After all we live in a world of double standards. In this strange world, words have a tendency to lose their meaning. Therefore, if B.P. Sinha wishes to say that if the majority of the people rise up in arms, it would also be a democratic act I have nothing to say. But I should prefer to call it a popular rising. We are not working today for an insurrection. By following the democratic methods we shall be able to mobilize the people in vast numbers and thus obviate the necessity for an armed insurrection.

A reference has also been made to the conference on free and fair elections which I had recently called in Bombay. Basu Krishnamurthi sought to show that I was more keen on elections than on people's liberties, rise in the workers' living standards, food problem, etc. I am very sorry that he does not seem to follow what appears in his own papers. In Bombay we had called a conference sometime ago to discuss inflation, falling wages and other allied problems. The Hind Mazdoor Sabha was born out of it. I may say with all humility that this anti-inflation conference was called on my initiative. Another conference, though not initiated by me, was called at Calcutta under the auspices of Khoj Parishad to consider the problem of inflation. The All India Civil Liberties Union Conference which met at Patna was inaugurated by me. The Bombay Conference was called merely to ensure that the elections if and when they are held, shall be free and fair. It is a part of our fight for democracy and not election-mongering.

Some members have talked about the opportunists getting into the party. I should like to include in my report what B.D. Joshi has suggested. Self-seekers, job hunters and electionists have no place in the Party and my advice to them also is to quit. But the only guarantee against the infiltration of opportunists in the Party is to bring in workers and peasants in large numbers so that the opportunists might get crushed under the weight of the toiling people.

Some complaints have been made about some opportunist alliances with the communal elements. I want to make it clear from this platform that our Party shall have nothing to do with the RSS or the Hindu Sabha in elections. And all those who are guilty of such alliances will be severely dealt with.

During the debate some members tried to bring in local matters. This was unfortunate. This is hardly the place for voicing such petty complaints. Whatever complaints they have should be referred to the National Executive and the Executive would appoint an impartial committee to go into these.

May I point out that on the one hand, you complain that there is looseness and lax discipline in the Party, and on the other wherever an effort is made to tighten the discipline, all kinds of false issues are raised and an attempt is made to show that the disciplinary action was not taken in good faith? With the tightening of discipline this year, such complaints are bound to increase and I would like to caution you against them.

Verghese was very unfair to the National Executive and to me when he referred to the incident in which an ex-Chief Minister was involved. There is a long history behind it. The National Executive and I myself have shown the utmost consideration to the Executive of the Cochin-Travancore Party. Here I say only this that this question will be finally decided before we leave Madras.

Tulsi Boda complained about the working of the Bombay Party. He said that some of the members of the Corporation have voted against the mandate of the Party. The incident, he refers to, related to members' attitude to birth control. The same comrade earlier said that not only discussion but even differences on methods should be permitted. But he is intolerant of those who differ on minor questions. Does he mean to say that those who have differences on vital issues should be allowed to continue in the Party and those who have differences on such issues as birth control should be expelled from it?

It must have come to you as a surprise, when I made certain remarks in my report about Aruna Asaf Ali. But I thought it necessary to do so in the interest of the Party. She has no faith in Democratic Socialism. In private talk she is wont to deride those who talk of Democratic Socialism. Just before she left for Europe, I met her in Bombay and asked her why did she not attend three successive meetings of the National Executive. She told me that she did not understand what Democratic Socialism means and further said that she would send her resignation to the Party after reaching Delhi. The resignation never came. Apparently she still continues to be a member. Her activities in Europe have not brought strength to the Party. I cannot anticipate what she will do on her return to India. One thing is certain that the report that she has joined the Communist Party is entirely false. I put this in my report because I feared that one fine morning you might be shocked to read in the newspapers that she has resigned from the Party. If she comes back to India and says that she has faith in the ideal of Democratic Socialism, I shall make amends and apologise.

336. Remarks in Course of the Debate on the Resolution[1] on the Indian Constitution at the Madras Conference, 10 July 1950[2]

Tushar Pawar has called for an explanation from me.[3] I wish to inform him that I stand by every word I have said with regard to the Indian constitution and the slogan of a new Constituent Assembly.

But, it is also necessary that we should look at the problem from the point of view of tactics and strategy. In the event of the Socialist Party being returned to power with only a bare majority, any move by them to convene a Constituent Assembly to frame a new constitution would evoke little enthusiasm among the people. Such a move might not be very meaningful for many. The Party should, therefore, stay its hand and instead introduce legislation nationalising industries and banks, abolishing all forms of landlordism, etc. These enactments would certainly be challenged in High Courts and the Supreme Court, and I have no doubt that they could be declared *ultra vires* under the provisions of the present constitution. Under those circumstances we could go to the people with a call for a "new Constituent Assembly—a new constitution". We can then appeal to the people to help us remove the impediments in the path of realisation of Socialism. The people would then easily grasp the need for a new Constituent Assembly and would extend their overwhelming support to the move.

I still firmly hold that the present constitution cannot be an instrument of full and complete democracy. It will have to be changed radically through amendments if possible. Should this be impossible, we will call a new Constituent Assembly for this purpose.

[1]See Appendix 25 for the Resolution on the Indian Constitution adopted by the Madras Conference of the Socialist Party, 8-12 July 1950.

[2]*Socialist Party Eighth National Conference, Madras, 8-12 July 1950*, p. 70.

[3]This has reference to the speech of Tushar Pawar in course of the debate on the resolution on the Indian Constitution in which he had reminded J.P. that when the Socialist Party came to power, it would get another Constituent Assembly elected on the basis of adult franchise for framing a new constitution, ibid, p. 68.

337. Speech while moving the Draft Programme for National Revival at the Madras Conference, 12 July 1950[1]

I have suggested a few corrections and additions to the National Revival Programme, which have been circulated. We have already discussed this

[1]*Socialist Party Eighth National Conference, Madras, 8-12 July 1950*, pp. 118-19.

draft in the group meeting. I do not wish to make a long speech. I would however like to point out the main features of the Programme.

I wish to make it clear that this Programme is not our election manifesto. It is our answer to the most urgent and grave problems which our country is facing, as also a programme of work for Party members. A mood of negativism prevails among the people and it is our supreme duty to find a way out.

It has been our practice to criticise the Congress Party and the Congress administration. The people want to know, and naturally so, as to what alternative the Socialist Party has to offer. I am confident that this programme offers an excellent opportunity to our workers to approach the people.

I agree that there is much in this programme which can only be implemented if the Party comes into power. But there are also many items which can be implemented by us here and now. If we succeed in creating the necessary enthusiasm among the people, if we are able to mobilise them, then we can surely compel the Government to accept this Programme.

It contains both combative and constructive items; the two are integrated into a whole. As a party in opposition we will have to agitate for certain aspects of the Programme and fight for certain others. But while doing all this we will also have to carry on our constructive activities to help the people.

In this Programme we appeal to the nation as a whole and not merely a section of the populace and that is why I prefer to call it National Revival Programme. It stresses the importance of creating mass enthusiasm. People can be enthused only if they find that what they are called upon to build up will be theirs and that they will get a fair deal. Small schemes of development must be initiated in which the people can directly participate and in which there will be scope for voluntary effort. The Programme is for the whole nation. We therefore appeal to all to co-operate with us in putting through this programme. I am confident that you will endorse it unanimously.

338. Reply to the Debate on the Resolution[1] on National Revival at the Madras Conference, 12 July 1950[2]

Apart from the amendments moved so far I have received numerous others. I am afraid it will not be possible for me to accept all of them.

I accept the amendments of Raja Kulkarni, Pinto, Sukumar Pagare and

[1] For Resolution on National Revival see Appendix 26.

[2] *Socialist Party Eighth National Conference, Madras, 8-12 July 1950*, pp. 122-3.

Mir Mushtaq Ahmad. I will however redraft them. I also accept Baburao Jagtap's amendment with regard to rural indebtedness. Vinayak Purohit has suggested that paras 8 and 9 of column 1, page 1, be deleted. I am sorry it cannot be done. I however promise that the language will be changed. I accept his amendment in regard to Foreign Trade. Commodities such as mica, manganese, jute, etc., suggested by him will be included. Tushar Pawar has suggested that no land revenue should be collected from those whose holdings are uneconomic. I accept this suggestion.

The other amendments are not acceptable to me. With regard to the various suggestions made, I promise that I will consider them when I retouch the Programme.

A number of speakers have suggested that nationalisation should be without compensation. I would like to remind these friends that even if compensation were to be paid, there would not be any great difficulty, since under our plan, the range between the maximum and minimum incomes is to be fixed.

Prabhakar More is needlessly apprehensive regarding our suggestions of hard work and austere living. I submit that if we tell the peasants and workers that the National Revival Programme aims at bringing about a great social revolution and the first step in that direction will be nationalisation of industries, banking, insurance, etc., and abolition of landlordism, all for their benefit and therefore they should work harder, I am sure they will respond to our call.

APPENDICES

APPENDIX 1

From N.G. Goray, 6 April 1948[1]

Dear J.P.,

We are making every effort to put the office into shape. But for the last few days Parshuram is laid up with chicken pox and both our typewriters have broken down. Lot of work is therefore held up.

I am forwarding for your information copies of the circulars we have so far issued. Much of our success will depend on the co-operation we get from the provincial units. Without their prompt co-operation the organizational & publicity work that is to be carried on from the centre must necessarily suffer. I request you therefore that whenever you go, please insist on the provincial secretaries to reorganize their offices, and to put a special man incharge of information Department, who would always keep contact with us.

The Bombay Government have banned the Motor workers rally, which was going to be held at Kolhapur on the 11th instant with Asoka Mehta as the chairman. They have also banned the activities of Rashtra Seva Dal though they have not banned the Dal itself. The Public Safety Act has been amended and the Government have assumed the most autocratic powers. We are in for a spell of stormy weather, I am afraid.

In the meeting of the Foreign affairs Sub-Committee it was decided that the Milan Conference is a conference of a section of the socialist movement in Europe and our party should not identify itself with it. The situation has also changed materially in the last two months. So we should not send any delegation. But before taking the final decision the secretary should write to Jayaprakash, as he has agreed to be one of the conveners of the conference.

Suresh is proceeding to Calcutta for a fortnight stay and he will be meeting you in Calcutta on the 1st of May.

Hope your Tamil Nad Tour was a success.

Convey my greetings to Prabhavati Devi & Dr. Menon.

Yours sincerely,
N.G. Goray

[1] *Brahmanand Papers* (NMML).

APPENDIX 2

From Rajendra Prasad, 13 June 1948[1]

Sj. Jayaprakash Narayan,
General Secretary, Socialist Party,
Bombay.

Dear Sir,

I have received your letter dated the 30th May, 1948 forwarding to me resolutions passed by the National Executive of the Socialist Party at its meetings held at Belgaon on May, 24 to 26, 1948.

As regards the first resolution regarding the Constituent Assembly, the question about its competence and character has never been raised before this and the assembly has so far acted as a duly constituted assembly having the right and the power to frame a constitution. Even persons belonging to the Socialist Party like Seth Damodar Swarup never raised any question about this competence and character. It is also not for the Government of India, which did not create the Constituent Assembly, to dissolve it and to convene another in its place. The Constituent Assembly would have appreciated and given due consideration to any comments and criticisms on the Draft Constitution as prepared by its Drafting Committee. The Draft has been published for public criticism and suggestions received from various individuals and associations are being considered by the Drafting Committee and will be in due course placed before the Constituent Assembly. I trust it is not yet too late for the Socialist Party to offer any constructive criticism on the Draft.

As regards the 2nd resolution regarding India's relation to Britain, I am not aware of secret talks now going on between the Governments of India and United Kingdom. Whatever decision the Government of India may take will be made public. If you have any information about any secret negotiation, I shall be obliged if you let me have it so that I might take up the matter with the Government of India.

As regards Linguistic provinces, the matter has been referred to a Commission which I have appointed on behalf of the Constituent Assembly. The Commission will go into the question and make a report in due course, taking into consideration all aspects of creation of new provinces. After creation of new provinces is recommended and accepted by the Constituent Assembly, the question of delimitation of boundaries will be referred to a Boundary Commission. The points raised in the resolution will undoubtedly

[1] *J.P. Papers* (NMML).

be considered by the Commission. I am passing on the resolution to them and if the Socialist Party would like to amplify the points raised in the resolution in a memorandum, it may do so and I have no doubt the Commission will consider the points.

Yours sincerely,
Sd. Rajendra Prasad

APPENDIX 3

From U.S. Bajpai, 28 July 1948[1]

Government of India
Ministry of External Affairs &
Commonwealth Relations

Dear Shri Jayaprakash Narayan,

I am directed to refer to Mr. Nair's Demi-Official letter to you No. D.2023-CA/48 dated the 16th June 1948, and to say that this Ministry may kindly be informed at an early date the address where your articles seized in 1944 are to be despatched.

Yours faithfully,
U.S. Bajpai

[1] *J.P. Papers* (NMML).

APPENDIX 4

From Jawaharlal Nehru to Achyut Patwardhan, 12 September 1948[1]

Personal & Confidential

My dear Achyut,

You will remember that some ago I suggested to you to accept a diplomatic post abroad. You told me then that you could not do so and you said that

[1] *Nehru Papers*—Files at home (NMML).

you would send me some names of suitable persons for our consideration. I do not remember having received any such list from you.

Later we invited you to join our U.N. delegation this year. Again you refused. I was sorry for this but I did know what I could do about the matter. Jayaprakash met me long afterwards and he told me that he had advised you to accept, and so had Narendra Dev. I did not know this and in any event I could hardly do anything about it after your refusal and at that late stage.

I had a general talk with Jayaprakash when I met him last and I expressed the wish that we should try to lessen the gap which had unfortunately come into existence between the Congress and the Socialist Party. It was not easy to bridge this suddenly but it was certainly possible to improve the situation and to find out some avenues of cooperation. Each step might well lead to another.

This becomes even more important in the present crisis. I hope every one realises that we are up against something which will strain our resources to the utmost. We cannot waste our energy in mutual squabbles and conflicts when we have to face these dangers.

Because of these larger considerations I would very much like you to reconsider the previous decision that you had made. I should like you to accept an Ambassadorship. I know the objections that you can raise to this. Nevertheless, I feel that the time has come when all of us should take some steps forward in a new direction. In the balance the good will outweight the objections.

To be precise, I would like you to be our Ambassador in Italy. This is an important place and as you know many forces are in conflict there. It is important to us from the political and economic points of view. World affairs, whatever some people may think here, press upon us more and more and we just can't ignore them.

Italy as you know is just a day's journey from here, indeed less. I am sure that if you accept this offer it will be good for all concerned, including you. The Socialist Party tends to become very sectarian and rather isolated. That is not good for it or for the country. I shall not write much more to you about this but I do feel strongly that your going there is a right thing.

I am sending a copy of this letter to Jayaprakash. I should like to have an early reply.

Yours sincerely,
Jawaharlal

APPENDIX 5

From Jawaharlal Nehru, 22 December 1948[1]

My dear Jayaprakash,

I have only today received your letter of December 13th from Meerut. As also a copy of your letter to Shri Gopalaswami Ayyangar.

So far as the railways are concerned, I am naturally greatly interested in their future, in the well-being of the railway workers, and in the avoidance of any conflict. I am afraid it is difficult for me to consider the various points you have mentioned in your letter. They require a more detailed knowledge than I possess. But in the past I have often discussed this matter with Dr. Matthai and I felt confident that he would view every such matter with the greatest inclination to meet the wishes of railwaymen. You yourself say in your letter to me that had Dr. Matthai been in the Transport Ministry, there would have been no break between the Ministry and the Federation. You seem to think that Santhanam's coming into the Transport Ministry has led to this break. I am very much surprised to find that you think so. Santhanam, to my knowledge, is eager and anxious to benefit the railwaymen and Gopalaswami Ayyangar is certainly at least as favourable to their cause as Dr. Matthai. I believe that there has been a feeling that the Railwaymen's Federation is exceedingly difficult to deal with and even when agreements are arrived at, they are not treated as final and something new is always cropping up. Dr. Matthai told me some time back, and he has repeated it since, that he has made every effort to meet the wishes of the All-India Raiwaymen's Federation and spent a tremendous deal of time and energy in this effort. But he had been grievously disappointed at the response he had received and at the way agreements and promises made were not kept. I am not myself fully acquainted with all these negotiations, but it is worthy of note that a man like Dr. Matthai should come to feel this way. Anyway I am quite convinced that you could have no fairer and more friendly person to deal with in such a matter than Shri Gopalaswami Ayyangar. I am equally convinced that whatever Santhanam's other views might be, with which you may differ, in this matter he is equally eager to find an honourable settlement.

It so happened that Gopalaswami Ayyangar wrote to me today on this subject and sent me a copy of your letter to him. He also sent me a copy of the telegram he had sent you. You will notice from this how friendly his

[1] *Brahmanand Papers* (NMML).

approach is and how eager he is to give you every opportunity to discuss every matter with him fully. I hope you will take advantage of his offer. He told me that he had made several efforts to meet you previously, but they had not succeeded.

It is rather difficult for me to discuss in a letter the various other points that you raise. It may be that you are right in some matters, but I feel sure that you have taken an exaggerated view of many other matters, just as no doubt others have taken an exaggerated view about your activities. It is unfortunate that in the strees and strain of our public activities nearly all of us tend to lose our balance of mind.

So far as I know, there is no politics in the Transport Ministry, though there may be politics elsewhere.

It is possible that I may be wrong or that my judgement of a situation may not be correct. Naturally I have to balance various factors. There is no such thing in life as an isolated decision in vacua. It may be that many of the factors that are before me are not present to your mind. You know well that we have had to steer a very difficult course in stormy waters. Few people fully realize how stormy the waters have been and how many dangers continually threatened us. Again I repeat that we may have erred, but surely I may lay claim to one thing and that is that I would not deliberately do anything to injure the cause of the workers which I thought just. If I am convinced of this in any particular matter, I would do my utmost to advocate it. Unfortunately even a just cause sometimes has to be seen in relation to other factors and we have to choose the lesser evil or lesser injustice.

Whenever I have had the chance of speaking to you, I have frankly told you of some of the problems and difficulties that we were facing. I want you to realize and appreciate them, because only then can you really give useful advice. It is immaterial whether you agree or disagree. Your advice would be of value, but only if the facts are before you. The international situation at present is a critical one. The Kashmir situation is also very delicate. It is impossible to talk about all this in detail before the public, and our people and our newspapers have yet to develop a balanced way of looking at things. At this stage any grave upset in our economic life might have disastrous consequences. If the railwaymen struck, it is obvious that any government would try its utmost to run the railway services for essential supplies etc. That might be called strike breaking. But the only alternative is for the Government to resign, if it cannot fulfil its primary function. I feel sure that a railway strike at this juncture would be deeply injurious to the country as well as to the railwaymen. The latter would inevitably lose the sympathy of the great majority of the people in the country and that is never a good risk to face.

For the communists I can understand this policy because their aim in

India is and can only be a destructive one at present. They want some kind of chaos to weaken the country as a whole politically and economically. But for any one who does not want to weaken the country, I cannot understand the adoption of any policy which must inevitably lead to such weakening and chaos.

Have you thought that the result of any such weakening need not necessarily be the success or even the strengthening of more progressive or socialistic elements in the country? It may well result in pushing forward far more reactionary groups. You will remember the recent history of Nazism in Germany. While the progressive groups quarrelled with each other, Hitler and his Nazis took charge of the situation and entrenched themselves, crushing socialists, trade unionists and the like. This is not an impossible development in India, for the reactionary forces in this country are strong. If these reactionary forces get the sympathy of the middle elements which are not politically advanced, but which are normally sympathetic with progressive and socialist elements, then the strength of the reactionaries becomes great. That is how Fascism has come on the scene in other countries. It may be said that fascism cannot last long and it destroys itself in the end. That is probably true, but meanwhile it might well ruin the country.

Therefore no responsible person can take the risk of upsetting the applecart in the vague hope that something better will emerge. Nor can any of us be led away by the emotion of the moment to a course which may lead to evil consequences.

I am frightfully busy and I shall be out of Delhi for most of the time during the next two weaks. But however busy I am, I shall gladly find time to help in the solution of the railwaymen's problems. Personally I think that you could not have a better man to deal with than Gopalaswami Ayyangar. But if I am wanted, I shall be there.

Yours affectionately,
Jawaharlal Nehru

This letter has been hastily dictated and deals with some of your points in a scrappy manner.

APPENDIX 6

From Asoka Mehta, 22 January 1949[1]

Dear J.P.,

Your letter of the 19th inst.

2. The enclosed letters will show that I have informed Peter and the Secretaries of Bombay and Maharastra Parties about your definite view that Peter should be set up for the railway seat. As far as that matter is concerned, the question is closed.
3. Certain observations in your letter leave me, to put it mildly, surprised.
4. As I wrote to you in my earlier letter, no less a person than Nanasaheb Gore himself told me that one of the two seats must go to the Maharashtra Party. And he had suggested Gaikwad's name for the Railway seat. Yesterday, Bandu Gore requested Yusuf to recommend Nanasaheb's name for the Railway seat. This evening, I received a telephone message from Suresh informing me that the Maharashtra Party executive has recommended Gaikwad's name for the railway seat. These facts deceively disprove any statement that S.M. and Madhu might have made to you. Your following observation in your letter: "they were completely surprised and told me definitely that the matter was never discussed in the Executive and the idea that one of the two seats should go to Maharashtra had never crossed their minds"—needs to be carefully enquired into in the light of the facts I have cited above. All that I can say is, I am completely surprised at the surprise of theirs and at their suggestion, especially Madhu's, that the idea had never crossed his mind.
5. The next sentence in your letter is even more disturbing: "It appeared", you write, "that Gaikwad's telegram was in reply to a specific suggestion that the Maharashtra Party should recommend the political (as different from labour) name." Here again facts have got distorted. The Bombay Party wrote to other parties—Maharashtra, Gujarat and Karnatak—inviting them to suggest nomination to the Parliamentary Board and sent them certain rules, which in the opinion of the Bombay Party, should govern such nominations. There was no occasion to make similar suggestions earlier because this is the first inter-provincial seat that is being contested. It is necessary to realize that these rules were not specially pieced together for the railway seat. They are the generalizations of

[1] *J.P. Papers* (NMML).

the considerations that led the Bombay Party to recommend its two outstanding leaders—Maherally and Purshottam—for the first available openings in the legislature. To believe that ulterior motives were behind the drawing up of the Rules and their circulation is to do less than justice to the Bombay Party.

6. If the Executive Committee of the Bombay Party rejected Peter's name with virtual unanimity, it was not because it was biased against Peter Alvares but because it does not believe that a seat in the Assembly should be a reward for a particular type of work. If Peter's work in Railways entitled him to the railway seat, the seat in the E & F Wards should go to men like Bapurao or Prof. Bhatt who have built up the Party in the two wards and the Muslim seat to Adam or Harris. The logic that led the Bombay Party to select Yusuf and Purushottam, led them to oppose Peter's candidature. The Bombay Party is unable to have one standard for the territorial constituencies and another for the functional.
7. It deeply hurts me to find you believing that the Bombay party would do anything out of a spirit of antipathy while I am actively associated with it. The words "conspiring to keep Peter out" suggest a lack of objectivity. It is possible that "insufferably petty" things happen in the Bombay Party, but may I beg of you to enquire carefully as to where is the focus of the pettiness before you arraign a party and condemn its devoted workers?
8. Your advice and guidance, believe us, will never be received as interference by the Bombay Party. While we shall not hesitate to place our views before you, we shall loyally carry out the directives of the General Secretary. You are not only entitled to have your say in the railway seat but in the selection of all candidates. Speaking for myself however, I would like to point out that it is unwise to treat railways as an *imperium in imperio*.
9. There is one more thing that I would like to add: from the point of view of the development of the Party in Maharashtra, Gaikwad's election to the Legislature would have been not without meaning. Our comrades in Maharashtra are working against heavy odds and if an opportunity presents itself to help them, we may miss it only at our peril.
10. I had a useful visit to Hyderabad. I shall send a report of it before long. You will be glad to know that notwithstanding the hard work that I put in at Hyderabad, I had no attacks of Asthma. Does it mean that Hyderabad climate is more congenial to me than Bombay's ?

Yours sincerely,
Asoka

APPENDIX 7

From Madhu Limaye, 30 January 1949[1]

My dear J.P.,

Your letters dated the 22nd and 23rd Jan. 1949. I was away from Bombay busy with the Maharashtra Provincial conference in Poona and returned only two days back.

Before leaving for Poona I had sent a reply to Gunawardhan's telegram stating that the Conference will be held in the 4th week of February and discuss the question of Indonesia and Asian Socialist co-operation. I also requested him to invite other socialist groups and individuals.

A file containing the addresses of Asian Socialist Parties and prominent political leaders was sent to Phulan Babu on the 17th. A copy of Gunawardhan's telegram and my reply to it was also sent. After my arrival I wrote to Phulan Babu saying that I shall be going to Patna in the first week of Feb. and shall be glad to go to Calcutta from there and discuss with him this question.

Invitations to Socialist Parties and friends abroad have already gone out. Yusuf has gone through the list and suggested a few additions.

The Central Office has no information about Dr. Lohia's future programme. Nevertheless, I am writing to him care of his Lucknow address.

If the letters I have received from the various Provincial Parties since our sub-committee meeting in Bombay and proceedings of the Maharashtra Provincial Conference which met from the 21st of Jan. to 25th, are any indication, I think we should be prepared to face a great deal of opposition to the clause of individual mass membership and the ratio of representation as between the various classes of members.

As for the railway seat, I think that it won't be useful to write to you about it in this letter. I hope to clear up many things when I meet you in Patna.

Yours sincerely,
Madhu

[1] *J.P. Papers* (NMML).

APPENDIX 8

From Achyut Patwardhan, 17 February 1949[1]

My dear Jayaprakash,

I am hearing high praises for your performance at Danapur among the first impressions I have collected so far. I have tried to put through the gist of our talk on the Editorial Page. I hope it will help the more belligerent section of our co-workers to use the decision usefully.

I am writing to remind you that we need some money rather urgently. Can you not ask PT to send me something this week.

Asoka has come here for the Fair Wages committee. It is so useful to talk things over so that we give something fresher. The Banking Bill and the Hindu Code Bill are both on the anvil. I wish we could give a really well informed commentary on the measures. The Railway Federation ought to issue a critique of the RLY Budget to project its own views. They ought to be extremely relevent on an issue of this nature.

I am sending you some questions. Will you kindly give some time and send me your replies?

With loving regard to Prabhawati and yourself.

Asoka tells me Yusuf is better psychologically and in health.

Your affectionately,
Achyut Patwardhan

[1] *J.P. Papers* (NMML).

APPENDIX 9

Debate on the Draft Constitution of the Socialist Party at the Seventh Annual Conference, Patna, 6-10 March 1949[1]

Chairman: 36 delegates have intimated their wish to speak. This is too large a number. I would, therefore, call upon only a limited number of delegates to speak.

Ramnandan Mishra: I oppose the new Constitution. The present Constitution meets our needs and I submit that it is a proof of the revolutionary character of our Party.

[1] *Report of the Seventh Annual Conference of the Socialist Party, Patna, 6-10 March 1949.*

Jayaprakash has said that the Socialist Party should become a mass party. Who does not agree with him? But when he recommends the new Constitution and says "here is something which will make the Party a mass party", I fail to understand his logic. It has pained me to note that he has misunderstood the objective conditions. The proposals for mass membership are astounding. Jayaprakash wants Kisans and Mazdoors to come into the Party in millions. Is it possible? Is it advisable?

What is the level of consciousness of Kisans and Mazdoors? We organize the mazdoors and kisans. We lead them in their struggle for bread and butter. Once they get what they want they give up the fight. Kisans and Mazdoors to-day are not conscious; they are after economic gains. Have they understood socialism? Have they reached a level where they can understand the full implications of socialism, freedom and liberty? We talk to them about the creation of a new society—a society of fearless and freemen. Do they understand this talk? When they themselves will feel the urge within themselves and will actively work for the establishment of a new order; when they will prepare themsevles for utmost sacrifice in the cause of democratic Socialist Society, only then can they be admitted in the Socialist Party. And, therefore, there is still need for a Party of active members. The Party must for a long time to come remain a party of select revolutionaries. It is our responsibility to teach the Kisans and Mazdoors that socialism means much more than mere bread and butter, something fine—a higher culture. We must first help the masses to come into their own. This can only be achieved by a Party of the select. If you accept the proposed constitution you will be asking the masses to do things which they are incapable of doing. You will put difficulties in their way. You will check the pace of their coming of age. If you agree to mass membership it will mean that different classes will enter the Party. Their interests may clash.

It is not enough to proclaim our faith in socialism. It must express itself in action. Do you want the Socialist consciousness to express itself through more and more work? Nothing can be achieved by pious intentions. Therefore, we should not accept the proposals regarding individual membership. Democratic Socialism has a definite meaning. It does not mean constitutional socialism. If you want reformist socialism then the proposed constitution is good for the purpose.

This proposed constitution will not strengthen us. The Government is systematically opposing us everywhere. Our Conferences are banned. Our workers are arrested. The Government is creating all sorts of difficulties in our path. We need strength to fight the Government. The present constitution makes for greater mobility and concentration of our forces in this struggle.

We must continue to remain a Party of select workers, fired by revolutionary zeal. A party of revolutionaries cannot afford the luxury of a constitution which can lead them only to constitutional socialism. I, therefore, request you to oppose the new proposals.

D.P. Joshi: Mishraji has been rather severe in his criticism of the proposed Constitution. He is not prepared to touch it with a pair of tongs. He has developed an utter dislike for collective affiliation. But he does not realize that collective affiliation will give us an opportunity to grow. I have no apprehensions regarding the proposed individual membership. It seems that Mishraji is suffering from a peculiar complex. Why should we oppose the entry of the masses into the Party? This is a middleclass complex. I say it with Jayaprakash that the present constitution has outlived its utility. Let us replace it by adopting the new one.

Vasu Krishnamurthy (Bangalore): I strongly oppose the Draft Constitution. We will head towards a disaster if we accept it. It is an irony of fate that the hero of August Revolution is leading us to disaster. The new constitution will dilute our revolutionary character. The exploiters will enter through the wide door of individual mass membership. And the soul of the Party will be lost. We must have a well equipped, strong and disciplined organization. It is tragic that when the Congress is excluding revolutionaries we propose to admit opportunists! Let us stick to the present constitution\.

Shri. Purshottam Trikamdas: Mr. Chairman, I feel we are digressing too much. Why not consider the draft constitution clause by clause?

Chairman: I am unable to accept the suggestion. Let us proceed.

Acharyajee has suggested that out of the list of 36 delegates 17 be given a chance to speak. He has selected the speakers as follows:

Eleven who wish to oppose and 6 who wish to speak in support of the draft Constitution. The speakers have to be so selected that every province will have a say.

S.D. Shastri (U.P.): I am in complete agreement with Ramnandanji. I oppose the entire Constitution.

Shri. Annapurnia (Andhra): It seems that the rank and file of the Party is opposed to the proposed Constitution. I belong to the rank and file. But I wish to support the proposed Constitution. It is unfortunate that some delegates have made harsh speeches against it. I do not think we are abandoning the revolutionary path.

Let us understand the spirit of the proposed constitution. It seeks to increase our revolutionary strength. Can a handful of persons achieve this glorious revolutionary task? Revolution cannot be the work of a few individuals.

I admit that conversion of a party into a mass party does carry with it some dangers. Indiscriminate admission of individual members must be avoided. We have learnt a bitter lesson in Andhra. Due to the Communist infiltration the Party in Andhra was wiped out.

How to overcome these dangers? The remedy is implicit in the proposed constitution. Collective affiliation is its principal plank. It is a guarantee against infiltration. Let us accept the proposed constitution.

Ajit Roy: I oppose the proposed constitution. I am not very happy about the development of the Party. I do not know much about the state of Party organization in other provinces but I can say from my experience of Bengal that there is a great deal of truth in what Jayaprakash has said about it. I agree with Jayaprakash when he says that our Party should become a mass Party but I differ from the solution, he has offered us. The problem is how to become a mass Party. The objective of the Party is to bring about socialist revolution. The Party must become a fit instrument of this revolution. While broadening the basis of the Party, we must preserve its revolutionary character and its theoretical foundations. The German Social Democratic Party was a mass Party. Yet we know how it collapsed in the face of the fascist advance. The Socialist Party must admit in its fold only revolutionaries, i.e., people who are conscious about their task and their responsibility. If we succeed in spreading revolutionary consciousness among a large mass of people we will be able eventually to increase our membership.

S.P. Mishra (C.P.): I oppose the proposed Constitution. Its acceptance will lead to a dangerous situation in spite of the attractive way in which it has been drafted.

Adhir Bannerji (Bengal): A revision of the present party constitution is necessary. I am in complete agreement with the central idea of the new constitution. Its approach is healthy and sound.

Those who have opposed it also want that our Party should become a mass party. Some of them also recognize the need to effect some structural changes. But none of them has suggested how.

Nargolker (Bombay): I oppose the proposed constitution. It seems that we are trying to create a machinery for elections. Civil liberties have been severely curtailed. The Congress does not want any opposition. They are trying to liquidate all opposition. Then why do you need an election machinery when democratic climate necessary for elections is being denied?

There is a falacy in the proposal regarding collective membership. Class character of the Party does not depend upon who comes into the party or by its class composition. It is entirely determined by our principles, programme and policy.

If constitutional democracy is going to be your creed then the proposed constitution adequately meets the need. But if you do not wish to abandon your revolutionary tasks then let us stick to the present constitution.

Vijayanand Kabra (Hyderabad): Who can deny that the pattern of Indian life is communal. People have not yet developed the necessary democratic sense. Under these circumstances it will be unwise to admit people in large numbers to the membership of the Party.

The Government has scant regard for Democracy. Fascism is knocking at our doors. Can we give up our revolutionary character at this juncture? The proposed constitution will open the doors to parliamentarianism. We have two tasks before us. The first is to represent the masses and the second is to make them revolution-conscious. The proposed constitution only offers us an opportunity to represent the masses.

Purshottam Trikamdas: The salient features of the new constitution are that firstly it drops the restrictions on individual membership and secondly it provides for collective affiliation.

According to the present constitution we have restricted individual membership. Every member undergoes a probationary period of six months and must work for fourteen hours a week. How many actually put in that amount of work? Hardly 25%. Are the remaining useless? Then remove them from Membership Register. No that is not the way. Though they do not put in the prescribed work, they are useful. They are advocates of the Socialist Party. If we have larger membership it will not harm us in any way.

There is yet another aspect. You cannot ask a mazdoor or a kisan to obey the work clause. They do hard manual labour for eight hours. And after this hard labour to ask him to do a specific job for the Party for another two hours is to be cruel to him.

We have failed to create organizational loyalty amongst those who came to us momentarily. If you want that they should be permanently loyal to the Party, I see no reason at all why such people should not be admitted to the Party membership straightaway.

You are also unnecessarily apprehensive regarding collective affiliation. A mazdoor panchayat for example cannot be affiliated as member unless 60% members of the panchayat vote in favour of affiliation. It means we will have to educate them. Does this not offer us new opportunities?

It gives us a picture of how and what we are going to build up. The proposed constitution is not meant to create an efficient machinery. It is ridiculous to say that it will. Why are you afraid of middle-class infiltration? Why do you look at it from this angle? Why not say that it will lead to a large influx of workers. Let us not raise the bogy of middle-class infiltration, this infiltration and that inflitration.

The present constitution was meant for the effective functioning of a ginger group within the Congress. Today we are a party in opposition. Don't you want to become an alternative to the Congress? If you want to, then a revision of the constitution is necessary. Why should you call yourselves revolutionaries if you dread change? The sole test is, do you or do you not want a few thousand to enter the Party?

What is happening elsewhere is immaterial. Do we want to become a Party for the Masses and of the Masses? The constitution gives a convincing yes to this question.

Keshar Gupta (U.P.): I feel that when the new constitution was drafted objective conditions were wrongly interpreted and understood. I feel that revision of the present constitution is out of the question.

Sadashiv Bagayatkar (Maharashtra): I agree that the present Constitution should be changed. But such drastic revision as proposed by the draft is not wanted. The Party is as yet weak. Let us consolidate what we are. I accept collective membership. But I oppose individual mass membership.

Manorama Sinha: I have listened to your speeches. You are unnecessarily quarrelling like the proverbial daughters-in-law. The proposed constitution is good. Let us adopt it.

Jagannath Sinha: Also spoke against the constitution.

M.R. Dandawate (Bombay): I am going to speak in support of the draft moved by Jayaprakash. This question of structural change is related to our strategy and tactics. In the political resolution we have rejected the insurrectionary approach. We have said that in the conditions prevailing to-day adventures in insurrection would prove suicidal and lead to the victory of Reaction. What is our method of social change? We have to advance towards the goal by democratic means. The Communist approach of encouraging sporadic and violent outbursts is not at all revolutionary. Therefore, we have pledged ourselves to developing people's organization and people's initiative. We have declared that we will lead their peaceful struggles against all forms of exploitation. Thus alone can we make progress in the direction of socialist society. Only a mass Socialist Party will be able to achieve democratic socialism. I, therefore, urge upon the delegates to accept the present draft which gives us an opportunity to expand the basis of the Party.

Chairman: The Conference will now adjourn till 8-30 A.M. tomorrow.

Fourth sitting (Wednesday 9th March 1949)

The Conference reassembled at 8-30 A.M. with Acharya Narendra Dev in Chair.

Bapurao Jagtap (Bombay): When people like me oppose this proposal we do so because we honestly feel that its acceptance will result in slackening of our revolutionary effort. I talk the language which our experience has taught us. I do not talk about bookish things. Yet just because we oppose the Constitution we are branded as Communists. This sort of intolerant attitude pains me. We are fighting for socialism. We have to build up class-organizations to lead class-struggles. The Party will not grow if these struggles are not developed. And only a Party of tried and selected workers can do this. During struggles our workers receive training. But if we open Party membership to all and sundry, by removing the work clause, it will only weaken the Party.

Chairman: I think we have had enough of speeches. I now call upon Madhu Limaye, Secretary of the Committee to clarify some points. Jayaprakash will reply thereafter.

Madhu Limaye: When the draft constitution was circulated, Clause 5 of Article XIII was not there. That has led to some misunderstanding. That Clause says that only those who have been members of the Party for at least a year, will be entitled to stand for any elective post.

Please do not excite sentiments by saying that something is being imposed upon you and that there is a conspiracy to lead the Party in the direction of Parliamentarianism. The only test which we should apply to the proposals under consideration is whether it will lead us forward or not. No one has suggested that the adoption of the draft proposals in itself will make for a mass party. We will have to work hard to transform it into a mass organization. The new constitution is not being offered as a substitute for hard and patient work.

The present constitution was evolved during a particular stage of the development of the Party. That is to say when we were an ideological group within a big mass movement. Socialism was not an immediate issue then. A mass movement could be built up then, only on the basis of an anti-imperialist programme. To-day we are free. 'Socialism here and now' is our battle-cry. We are an Opposition Party to-day.

It is wrong to say that the proposed constitution is meant to build up an efficient election machine. The New Constitution cannot make miracles. Some of the speeches betrayed unscientific and confused thinking about constitutionalism and revolution. People seem to fight shy of elections and constitutional activity. But let us not forget that even Engels stressed the importance of elections and he and Marx even visualised democratic transformation. Achievement of socialism cannot be the work of selected individuals. Marx described the socialist movement as "self-conscious movement of an immense majority". We want to build up precisely such a Party. This does not mean that we will surrender to any Party. We are not giving up our revolutionary tradition. We will continue to fight repression.

Today our Party workers organize the peasants and workers, work for the redress of their grievances and lead their struggles and yet no one can deny that the feeling of belonging to the Party, of being a part of it is absent among the people. The new proposals seek to remove this hiatus by bringing the masses into the Party. There is only one valid objection. Have we got to-day the resources and organizational capacity to lead a mass Party? But this is really a challenge and not an objection. Let us accept the challenge.

APPENDIX 10

Text of the Constitution of the Socialist Party adopted by the Seventh Annual Conference, Patna, 6-10 March 1949[1]

I. *Name:*

The name of the Party shall be: The Socialist Party.

II. *Objects:*

1. *National:* To establish a democratic socialist society in India.
2. *International:* To work with Socialist forces in other countries with a view to eradicate imperialism, racialism, colonialism, all other forms of national oppression and economic inequalities among nations and to create a democratic socialist world.

III. *Membership:*

1. There shall be two classes of members:
   (a) Individual members;
   (b) affiliated members.

2. *Individual Members*: Any person who is of the age of 18 or above and who accepts the Objects, Policy, Programme and Discipline of the Party shall be eligible for membership provided that:
   (a) he does not believe in or observe caste and communal distinction;
   (b) he is not a member of any other political party or organization whose membership is inconsistent with that of the Party;

(*Note:* The National Executive shall decide whether a particular party or organization comes within the purview of this clause.)

   (c) in case he is eligible to be a member of a trade union or kisan panchayat or any other *bona fide* association recognized by the Party, he is a member of such organization.

3. *Affiliated Members:* Affiliated members shall consist of:
   (a) trade unions, including unions of agricultural labourers;
   (b) kisan organizations;
   (c) organizations of professionals, artisans and technicians, etc.
   (d) socialist youth organizations;
   (e) cultural organizations;

provided that:

[1]*Report of the Seventh Annual Conference of the Socialist Party, Patna, 6-10 March 1949.*

(i) they accept the Objects, Policy and Programme of the Party;

(ii) they decide to affiliate with the Party by a majority of 60 per cent of those voting, in such manner as may be prescribed in the Rules; and

(iii) they are, in the opinion of the National Executive, *bona fide* bodies.

4. REPRESENTATION OF AFFILIATED MEMBERS:

(a) Members enumerated in III 3, shall be affiliated to the Socialist Party and not to the branches or units of the Party. The National Executive alone shall have the right to accept affiliation to the Party.

(b) Affiliated members shall be entitled to be represented on constituency and city branches and upwards and not on the primary units.

(c) Affiliating bodies shall be the lowest unit of the organizations concerned, e.g.:

(i) primary trade unions;

(ii) village (or group of villages) Kisan panchayats.

IV. *Affiliation and Membership Fees:*

1. Each individual member shall pay a minimum membership fee of Re. 1 per annum.
2. Each affiliated trade union shall pay a minimum affiliation fee of Rs. 5 *plus* an additional fee of As. 4 per member per annum.
3. Each affiliated kisan panchayat shall pay a minimum affiliation fee of Rs. 5 *plus* an additional fee of As. 2 per member per annum.
4. Each affiliated organization of professionals, artisans and technicians, etc., shall pay a minimum affiliation fee of Rs. 5 *plus* an additional fee of As. 4 per member per annum.
5. Each affiliated socialist youth and cultural organization shall pay an affiliation fee as fixed by the National Executive.

V. *Organization:*

1. the organization of the Party shall consist of the following:

(a) NATIONAL:

(i) National Conference;

(ii) National General Council;

(iii) National Executive.

(b) PROVINCIAL:

(i) Provincial Conference;
(ii) Provincial General Council;
(iii) Provincial Executive Committee.

(c) DISTRICT AND CITY BRANCHES:

(i) District or City Council;
(ii) Executive Committee.

Provided that cities having a population of 3 lakhs or more shall have city councils and executive committees with a staus equal to district branches.

(d) CONSTITUENCY BRANCH:

(i) Constituency Council;
(ii) Executive Committee.

(e) PRIMARY UNITS:

(i) Ward Units;
(ii) Local Units.

2. The provincial organization of the Party shall be known as the Provincial Branch (e.g. Socialist Party, West Bengal Branch. For the purpose of provincial organization the constituent units of the Indian Union shall be the basis.

Provided that non-viable states or unions of states may be included in the adjoining constituent units if the National Executive so decides.

3. (a) The primary unit shall be the smallest territorial organization of the Party. The territorial area, for this purpose, shall be a ward or a group of wards in urban areas and a village or a group of villages in rural areas.
(b) The primary unit shall comprise of all the individual members residing in its area.

VI. *National Conference:*

1. The National Conference of the Party shall be convened annually at such time and place as may be fixed by the National Executive. A Special Conference may be convened by the National Executive or by the decision of the General Council.

2. The National Conference shall consist of delegates elected by:

(a) individual members; and
(b) affiliated members.

3. (a) The number of delegates to the Conference which shall not exceed 1,500 shall be fixed by the National Executive for each conference.

(b) The number of delegates to be elected by:

(i) individual members;

(ii) members of the affiliated trade unions;

(iii) members of the affiliated kisan panchayats;

(iv) members of the affiliated organizations of professionals, artisans, technicians, etc.

shall be in the proportion of 3: 2: 1: 2 for an equal number of members such number to be determined by the National Executive from time to time.

(c) The number of delegates to be elected by the affiliated socialist youth and cultural organizations shall be fixed by the National Executive, irrespective of their membership. The total number of delegates to be elected by these organizations shall not, however, exceed 30.

(d) At least 10% of delegates elected by individual members from each Provincial Branch shall be women.

(e) The members of the National Executive shall be exofficio delegates without right to vote, unless they are duly elected as delegates.

4. THE NATIONAL CONFERENCE SHALL HAVE THE POWER:

(a) to lay down the policy and programme of the Party for the ensuing year. The decisions of the Conference shall be binding on the members of the Party, its branches and its affiliated organizations;

(b) to consider the Report and Audited Accounts presented by the General Secretary on behalf of the National Executive;

(c) to elect at the annual conference, the General council, the Chairman, the General Secretary and 23 members of the National Executive from amongst the delegates for the ensuing year. The Chairman, the General Secretary and the members of the National Executive shall continue in office till a fresh election is held at the next annual National Conference;

(d) to amend the constitution.

VII. *General Council:*

1. The number of members of the General Council shall be one-fifth of the number of delegates to the National Conference. Members of the National Executive shall be ex-officio members of the General Council.
2. The General Council shall meet at least once between two Annual

Conferences and shall have the power to take decisions regarding policy, programme and organization of the Party, provided that they are not inconsistent with those of the Annual Conference. Extra-ordinary meetings of the General Council shall be convened on a requisition made by not less than one-fourth of its members.

VIII. *National Executive:*

1. (a) The National Executive shall consist of the Chairman, the General Secretary and 23 members elected at the Annual Conference.

   (b) The Chairman shall preside over the meetings of the National Executive, General Council and the next Annual Conference and Special Conferences and act as the spokesman of the Party throughout his period of office.

   (c) The National Executive shall, on the recommendation of the General Secretary, appoint not more than three Joint Secretaries from among its members, to assist the General Secretary in his work.

   (d) The National Executive shall appoint one of its members as Treasurer.

   (e) Any vacancy during the course of the year in the National Executive shall be filled up by the National Executive.

2. THE DUTIES OF THE NATIONAL EXECUTIVE SHALL BE:

   (a) To carry out the policy and programme as laid down by the Annual Conference and the General Council;

   (b) To organize provincial branches and supervise their working;

   (c) to enforce the Constitution and Rules of the Party and to take any action it deems necessary for such purpose whether by way of disaffiliation of an affiliated organization, dissolution or suspension of a branch of the Party, suspension or expulsion of an individual member of the Party. Any such action shall be reported to the next Annual Conference of the Party, to which appeals shall also lie from the organizations, branches and members concerned;

   (d) to appoint an Election Committee which shall deal with the complaints arising out of all Party elections;

   (e) to appoint a Parliamentary Committee with power to select. Party candidates for Parliamentary elections, settle all disputes arising out of them and co-ordinate and guide the parliamentary work of the Party.

   (f) to maintain accounts and submit a Report and Statement of accounts to the Annual Conference;

(g) to undertake all such activities as may further the aims and objects of the Party;

IX. *Quorum:*

The quorum of the General Council and the Annual Conference shall be one-fifth of members and delegates respectively and the quorum of the National Executive shall be nine.

X. *Provincial Branch:*

1. PROVINCIAL CONFERENCE:

(a) The Provincial Conference shall be convened annually by the Provincial Executive. A special Provincial Conference may be convened either by the Provincial Executive or on the request of at least one-third of the District Branches of the Party in the Province.

(b) The Provincial Conference shall consist of all the members of the district and city councils in the province, acting as delegates for the purpose.

(*Note*: The members of the National Executive from the province concerned shall be ex-officio delegates to the Provincial Conference with full rights.)

2. THE PROVINCIAL CONFERENCE SHALL HAVE THE POWER:

(a) to lay down provincial policy and programme for the ensuing year not inconsistent with the basic policy and programme of the Party;

(b) to consider the political and organizational reports and statement of accounts presented by the Provincial Secretary on behalf of the Provincial Executive;

(c) to elect at the Annual Session the Provincial Council, the Provincial Chairman and Secretary and not more than 19 members of the Provincial Executive for the ensuing year. The Chairman shall preside at the next session of the Provincial Conference as well as special conferences held during the year. The Chairman, Secretary and members of the Executive shall continue in office till a fresh election is held at the next annual Provincial Conference.

3. PROVINCIAL COUNCIL:

(a) The number of members of the Provincial Council shall be one-fifth of the number of delegates of the Conference;

(b) The Provincial Council shall meet at least once between two Annual Provincial Conferences. Extraordinary meetings of the

Provincial Council shall be convened on a requisition of not less than one-fourth of its members.

4. PROVINCIAL EXECUTIVE:

(a) The Provincial Executive shall consist of the Chairman, the Secretary and not more than 19 members. The Executive shall on the recommendation of the Provincial Secretary appoint from among its members not more than three Joint Secretaries, to assist him in his work. It shall also appoint one of its members as Treasurer. Any vacancy in the Provincial Executive during the course of the year shall be filled up by the Provincial Executive.

(b) Members of the National Executive from the Province concerned shall be ex-officio members of the Provincial Executive.

(c) Duties of the Provincial Executive shall be:

(i) to organize district, city and other branches and units; to supervise, co-ordinate and guide their activities and work;

(ii) to carry out the Policy and Programme of the Party and instructions and directives received from the National Executive, enforce its constitution and to take such action as it deems necessary for the purpose, by way of suspension of an affiliated organization or individual member attached to the Provincial Branch. Any such action shall be reported to the National Executive. The Provincial Executive shall be entitled to make recommendations to the National Executive in the matter of affiliating and disaffiliating or dissolving or expelling affiliated organizations, branches and members of the Party respectively;

(iii) to manage, control and guide the work of the Party in the Provincial Legislature and elections thereto as well as the work in local bodies and municipalties under the general supervision of the National Executive;

(iv) to undertake all such activities as may further the work of the Party in the province.

XI. *District or City Branch:*

1. The District Council shall consist of all the members of the executive committees of the Constituency Branches in the District.
2. The city Council shall consist of one representative for every 90 or such number as may from time to time be determined by the National Executive of the individual members and representatives of the affiliated members in the proportion mentioned in VI 3(b).
3. There shall be a District or City Executive Committee consisting of

note more than 15 members including one Secretary, elected by District and City Council as the case may be.

4. The District or City Council shall meet at least three times in a year.

XII. *Constituency Branch:*

1. The Constituency Council shall consist of representatives of individual members and representatives of affiliated members in the proportion mentioned in VI 3 (b). Till otherwise determined by the National Executive there shall be I representative for every 18 individual members.
2. The Provincial Executive shall determine the quota of representatives of the affiliated socialist youth and cultural organizations.
3. The Constituency Council-shall meet at least three times in a year.
4. The Executive Committee shall consist of one-fifth of the number of the Constituency Council. The Executive shall elect from its members one Secretary.

(*Note*: For the purposes of this Constitution a Constituency stands for a Provincial Legislative Assembly constituency under the new Indian Constitution. Till such time as these constituencies are delimited such areas as may be determined by the Provincial Executive shall be treated as constituencies.)

XIII. *Party Elections:*

1. Every delegate and reprentative must be an individual member of the Party.
2. Delegates and representative representing the affiliated organizations must also be members or office-bearers of those organizations.
3. No person shall act as a delegate or representative for more than one organization.
4. No person shall act as a delegate or representative who does not pay the political levy of his trade union, kisan panchayat, etc.
5. No person shall be eligible for any elective post in the Party unless he has been a member of the Party for a period of not less than one year. This does not however apply to members who were on rolls on March 6, 1949.
6. No person shall be eligible for membership of any executive committee in the Party unless he puts in atleast 14 hours of work per week for the Party in accordance with the directives of the National Executive.

XIV. *Ward and Local Units:*

1. All the individually enrolled members of the Party in a particular

locality shall constitute the General Body of the Ward (in urban areas) or Local (in rural areas) unit of the Party for that locality.

2. The General Body shall meet at least four times in a year.
3. The General Body shall elect a Ward or Local Committee consisting of not more than 7 members, including one Secreetary.

XV. *Method of Election:*

Voting at all Party elections shall be by *multiple distributive* vote and by ballot, provided that in case of ward or local committees the voting may be by show of hands.

XVI. *Full-time Secretaries:*

The National, Provincial, District and City Secretaries of the Party shall be full-time workers.

XVII. *Rules:*

The National Executive shall have powers to frame rules not inconsistent with the constitution of the Party, subject to the approval of the National Conference; provided that the Rules framed by the National Executive after this Constitution comes into force shall be valid till the session of the National Conference under this Constitution meets.

XVIII. *Constitutional Amedments:*

Amedment to the Constitution of the Party can only be made at the Party Conference by two-thirds majority of those present and voting.

APPENDIX 11

From Basawan Sinha to Works Manager, Rohtas Industries Ltd., 8 March 1949[1]

Dear Sir,

I met you on 28 February 1949 and understood the position regarding all those workers whom you have refused to take back to work following the end of the strike. I had made it clear to you on that day that unless the company changed its decision, I would undertake a fast in protest and would continue it till all striking workers are taken back to work. After that a number of days passed, but your decision is as firm as it was before. Two and a half thousand workers and their several thousand dependants are

[1] *J.P. Papers* (NMML).

starving as usual. Therefore I am informing you with regret that I am going on fast with effect from today morning. This fast will continue till your decision is changed and all those workers whose name was on your register prior to the strike are taken back to work without any conditions. If I die as a consequence of this fast, the responsibility for it will lie entirely on the intransigence of the company.

I am not taking the decision to fast in haste or impelled by emotion. I am doing so after considerable deliberation. If there had been some other way open for ending the injustice inflicted upon the workers securing them justice I would have had recourse to that, and saved myself from the torments of fast and probable death.

You have not formally mentioned any reason for removing the workers from their jobs. My guess is that you have removed them only for their participation in the strike. I would like to submit that the full responsibility for the strike and for the circumstances in which the strike has taken place is on the Company. All old agreements with the labour union have been put on the shelf. After having set up a rival union, the recognition was given to it despite our opposition with a view to depriving the workers of their just dues and breaking the organized strength of the labour union. The merciless pressure of hunger was exerted by illegally withholding earned salaries so that the strike could be broken. The different repressive forces of the Government were used. Even those who are working in the factories are being oppressed in various ways by snatching and breaking their economic and trade union rights secured as a result of years of organization and struggle.

I think that the desire for daily increasing profit after accelerating the growth in production in an atmosphere of industrial peace through this unwise, greedy and cruel policy is a day dream. The workers are also human beings. They are not lifeless parts of a machine; their desires and legitimate aspiration for living as civilised human beings cannot be repressed permanently. If my comrades and I, who work and want to work in the labour movement in a peaceful and democratic manner, will be looking helplessly, as the Company's repressive and selfish policy gives rise to the feelings of vengeance, violence and anarchy among the workers, this will create a fertile ground for the Communist expansion, as a result of which the Rohtas Industries, the workers and the national interests will all be destroyed. I am not wasting your time by preaching to you; I am writing all this only with a view to performing my duty so that you may eschew obstinacy and be guided by a desire to do justice.

Yours,
Basawan Sinha
President
Rohtas Industries Workers Union

APPENDIX 12

From Jawaharlal Nehru, 14 April 1949[1]

Personal

My dear Jayaprakash,

Thank you for your letter of the 10th April.

I am greatly worried about Bishweshwar Prasad Koirala and we are trying to do what we can diplomatically. The position in regard to Nepal is very delicate and we cannot do very much more at present.

About India and the Commonwealth issue, it is a little difficult to write fully in a letter. But I think your argument is not a sound one. If our foreign policy continues to be one of complete neutrality, even when we are supposed to be a Dominion of the Commonwealth, surely a lesser association will not affect that neutrality. Neutrality ultimately depends upon the strength of a country and not on any vague association. Most of the independent countries today are not neutral and cannot be so, because of their weakness and they depend upon others.

India today, as you mentioned to me when you saw me, is about the only stable country in Asia, barring the Soviet Union. I have no doubt in my mind that our association with the Commonwealth during the past year and a half has helped greatly in our maintaining our stability and in largely settling the States problem. For a variety of reasons, into which I need not to go now, I have equally no doubt that some such association will be of great practical help to us during the next two or three years at least. We cannot purchase that help by giving up any principle. But if no principle is given up, then there is no payment for an advantage received, or the payment is very slight. India has learnt to stand on her own legs or is learning to do so fairly rapidly and I am not aware of any matter in which we have changed our policy, internal or external, because of our association with the Commonwealth. In regard to some policies, we have opposed British policy openly and directly.

It may interest you to know that the two Commonwealth countries that are opposed to our being in the Commonwealth are South Africa and Pakistan.

As for the British trying to exploit India and Pakistan, that may or may not be so, so far as the British Government is concerned. I rather think that this is so to a slight extent still. But the British Government is realising more and more that it is India that counts and not Pakistan. Britishers in Pakistan are certainly very anti-Indian. But presuming British desire to create

[1] *Nehru Papers*—Files at home (NMML).

trouble between India and Pakistan, will that be any less if we are out of the Commonwealth? Indeed it will be much more.

As for your saying that to consult with one group means not consulting with another group, that is only partly correct. We are at present in close consultation with almost all Asian nations and this method of consultation is growing rapidly. The Commonwealth does not come in the way. If we were not associated with the Commonwealth, curiously enough, it would have been more difficult to develop closer relations with Asian countries, as many of these are very timid and dare not take a risk. With the Russian Bloc it is anyhow rather difficult to consult. Nevertheless we deal with them in the United Nations and elsewhere probably more than many other countries.

I think we are apt to think too much of India in past terms. We imagine that she is weak enough to be made the camp-follower of any other group, with which she may be associated. India's position is completely different and grows more different daily because of her actual and potential power. Where she is, she plays a prominent and independent role, influencing others more than she is influenced herself.

Practically speaking, there is no doubt that a sudden break with this association would be injurious to us in many ways and our progress would be hampered. One aspect is that the $9^1/_2$ millions of our countrymen abroad in Moratious, Fiji, Guiana, etc., would be put in a most invidious position.

I hope you and Prabha will soon be quite well again.

Yours affectionately,
Jawaharlal Nehru

APPENDIX 13

From Jawaharlal Nehru, 14 May 1949[1]

Personal & Confidential

My dear Jayaprakash,

Your letter of May 12th. I have already told you that we are intensely interested in what is happening in Nepal and we are bringing continous pressure on the Government, more especially in regard to political prisoners there. We shall continue to do this. You will appreciate that it is not possible for a Government to deal publicly in such a matter. The case of Indonesia is very different.

[1]*Nehru Papers*—Files at home (NMML).

You refer briefly to my press conference. I can assure you that I was neither impatient nor did I lose my temper and I do not in the least feel that I have a weak case. That of course does not mean that I am necessarily right. What I said at the press conference was that the Socialists could not get out of their past complexes and this came in the way of their judging a situation in terms of actuality. I think I pointed out this to you and to others on several occasions during the past four years or so, ever since I came out of Ahmednagar prison. I think if you look back in this period, you might even agree with me somewhat that the Socialist Party's judgement of the situation and of what was likely to take place turned out to be wrong. I may be right or wrong about any particular matter. But I do feel that the Socialist Party is extraordinarily static in its approach to many problems, notably the foreign policy one. Lohia whom as you know I like very much, normally represents the Socialist Party's outlook on foreign affairs. I think he has been consistently wrong in this matter.

It is, as you know, the easiest thing in the world to break the Commonwealth link. There is no difficulty about it whatever and it can be done at any moment by any party. But any responsible government or party has necessarily to think of the advantages and disadvantages of doing so. The least than can be said is that it is unwise to proclaim a future policy in this regard without balancing all these factors and without knowing more or less what that future is going to be. We are apt to be too sure of our stability and security, internal as well as external. Taking that for granted, we proceed to endeavour to remodel the world. Yet the most powerful nations have to admit limitations to the accomplishment of their wishes and desires. The principal thing for India to aim at today is to ensure that stability and security so as to make as rapid progress internally as possible, and at the same time, of course, ensure that we have the fullest freedom to do what we like.

I hope you have nearly recovered.

Yours affectionately,
Jawahar

APPENDIX 14

From Sushila Koirala to, 30 May 1949[1]

Kadamkuan, Patna

Yesterday B.P. was released and he broke fast on 28th May, sends you and Prabhaji his regards—Sushila.

[1] *J.P. Papers* (NMML). The telegram was sent by Smt. Sushila Koirala, wife of B.P. Koirala on 30 May 1949.

APPENDIX 15

From Rajendra Prasad, 13 September 1949[1]

Dear Jayaprakash Babu,

I received your letter through Shri Narayan Murti of Dalmianagar. I came to know about matters regarding Dalmianagar. I am not keeping good health. It is the usual complaint of asthma and cough. I have been able to participate in the meetings of the (Constituent) Assembly somehow on the strength of medicine and injection. Previously it had been assumed that the meeting of the Assembly would be over in the month of August, but the pressure of work was such that the meeting could not be over as yet, and now whenever the work is completed in this month, the meeting will have to be called once again in the month of October. I wanted that after the closure of the meeting I should go to some other places from here so that my health could improve, but this could not happen. Apart from attending the meetings of the Assembly and attending to its work, I have neither any strength to do nor am I doing any other work.

I talked to Anugraha Babu and Krishna Ballabh Babu regarding your letter. Anugraha Babu and Krishna Ballabh Babu have said that after consulting Shri Babu they would tell me in a week what they are going to do. So far as I know, they have written to Shri Shanti Prasad regarding this, but nothing has been settled as of now. I have talked today with Shri Shankar Rao Deo in the Legislative Council regarding your letter. He is also thinking regarding it. So far as I am concerned what can I do unless all persons concerned write to me that they will accept my arbitration? However, I shall endeavour to do on my part whatever can be done. I shall write to you again after I get a definite reply from the Bihar Government.

Meanwhile, my request to you is that you should advise the workers of Dalmianagar that they should not undertake a fast.

Yours,

Rajendra Prasad

[1] *J.P. Papers* (NMML).

APPENDIX 16

From Jawaharlal Nehru, 17 August 1949[1]

My dear Jayaprakash,

Thank you for your letter of August 7th. You have referred in this to the issue of savings certificates to the Bombay Textile labour. I must confess that I do not understand why any person should object to accepting certificates which are cashable at will. Even supposing it means a slight additional trouble to the individual, surely this cannot justify strikes etc. As a matter of fact, it should be our policy, not only Government's but of Trade Union leaders, to encourage investment in this way. In most countries this is being encouraged. The Communists here, who are out for trouble at every possible opportunity, oppose issue of cash certificates in any forms. Others, who look to the interests of labour as well as the country's interests, cannot take up that attitude.

There is no question of prestige. But it is obviously the right thing to do which meets even the point of view of those who do not want cash certificates. Obviously there are or there may be workers who are prepared to keep the certificates. Why should they not be allowed to do so when it is open to others to cash them at any moment?

When you come to Delhi, please let me know as I should like to meet you and have a talk with you.

Yours affectionately,
Jawaharlal Nehru

[1] *J.P. Papers* (NMML).

APPENDIX 17

From Asoka Mehta, 1 March 1950[1]

Dear J.P.,

I sent you this morning the following Express Telegram:
"Yours telegram. Government calling Labour Conference Delhi 20th & 21st. Request relieve me Bihar engagement—Asoka".

[1] *J.P. Papers* (NMML).

As I wrote to you earlier, it is very necessary that I give my uninterrupted time to work here for the next few weeks. I can go to Delhi or a central place like that, which can be reached easily by air, but not into the interior. I am sure, Bihar Party can always find somebody else to preside over the Conference. I hope you will appreciate my difficulties and relieve me of the responsibility of presiding over the Bihar Party Conference.

As you are aware, the Govt. of India have introduced two highly controversial bills in the Parliament: one deals with industrial relations and the other with trade unions. Government is convening a tripartite conference on 20th & 21st and if the Working Committee of the HMS wants me to go there, I must keep myself available for it. This is another reason why it will not be possible for me to come to Bihar.

Yours sincerely,
Asoka Mehta

Copy to:
J.P., Patna

APPENDIX 18

From Asoka Mehta, 4 March 1950[1]

Dear J.P.,

I have called a meeting of the Working Committee of the Hind Mazdoor Sabha to meet in Bombay on the 13th & 14th of March to consider the Labour Relations Bill and the Trade Unions Bill now before the Parliament. I need not tell you how important these Bills are and how serious the restrictions of these Bills will be on their enactment on the labour movement in the country. It is necessary that we meet and discuss not only our attitude towards the Bills but also decide upon a campaign we are going to organize to get the Bills amended or at least to make the workers conscious of the menace the bills constitute to free trade union movement. Under these circumstances, I think it is very necessary that you should find time for the meeting of this Working Committee. It is being called in Bombay because there are 10 members and we shall also have the benefit of the mature advice and guidance of N.M. Joshi. The dates have been fixed to suit the convenience of Com. Joshi. Even if it causes you some inconvenience to come here for the meeting, I think, in the interest of the labour movement which is facing a major crisis today, you should spare some time and make it possible to attend the meeting of the Working Committee.

Yours sincerely,
Asoka Mehta

[1] *J.P. Papers* (NMML).

APPENDIX 19

From Jawaharlal Nehru, 23 March 1950[1]

My dear Jayaprakash,

I have just received your telegram suggesting representative Indians should be invited to forge a national policy with regard to Pakistan and unite to preserve peace and decency in India. I like the idea, but I do not quite know whom you consider representative. Can you make some further suggestions?

The more I think of it, the more I feel that we should avoid war if we possibly can. The consequences are terrible to contemplate. Some people are trying to push and bully us into war. The Hindu Mahasabha's attitude is clearly to exploit the situation in order somehow to bring about what they call Akhand Hindustan. They will never do so of course, but their statements to this effect are revealing. They are not out to settle this question, but just to have war in the hope of conquering Pakistan. Because of public feeling, many people fall into this trap.

While we must accept those refugees who come to us and look after them, I feel that the only way to solve this problem is to produce condition of security for minorities where they are. As things are at present, declarations by Government to this effect do not go very far. We have made declarations. We might make a comprehensive approach to the problem. But ultimately, it seems to me that possibly some international agency might be asked to see that these declarations are carried out in practice. This agency may be the Red Cross or some other

Yours affectionately,
Jawaharlal

[1] *Nehru Papers* (NMML).

APPENDIX 20

From Jawaharlal Nehru, 2 May 1950[1]

My dear Jayaprakash,

Thank you for your letter of April 30th with its enclosures regarding the statement in *Janata*. The contradiction in *Janata* related only to one particular matter. There were as a matter of fact several other wrong statements in that article.

Yours affectionately,
Jawaharlal Nehru

[1] *J.P. Papers* (NMML).

APPENDIX 21

From Jawaharlal Nehru, 23 May 1950[1]

My dear Jayaprakash,

I have your letter of May 19th.

To the questions that you have put to me the answers are clear. Government servants should bot be used for party purposes. Ministers should bring no pressure on Government servants. Minorities should on no account be intimidated be the party–in power for voting for them. Indeed no one should be intimidated.

While this is quite clear, obviously some difficulties might well arise. ministers are no doubt interested in elections and are members of a party. They are bound to participate in the elections and to some extent, it may be difficult to distinguish between their individual and ministrial capacities. We are in the early stages of large scale elections. We have not yet developed the conventions and the habits of mind which, say, a country like England has achieved through long course of years. We should try to do so of course and I hope that we shall largely succeed.

So far as I am concerned, I shall certainly draw the attention of all provincial Governments and others to this question of Governmental interference in elections.

Yours affly,
Jawaharlal Nehru

[1] *Shri Jayaprakash Narayan's Sixty-first Birthday Celebration – Commemoration – 1962-1963*, p. 158 (Madras).

APPENDIX 22

From Jawaharlal Nehru, 26 May 1950[1]

My dear Jayaprakash,

Please refer to your letter of May 12th in regard to the two Labour Bills before Parliament. I sent your letter to the Labour Minister, who has taken the trouble to write at length about them to me. I shall not burden you with all that he has written, but he has specially asked me to request you to let us know what specific provisions in the Bills you take exception to and how you would like them to be modified. We shall gladly examine each one of these points and if need be, invite you for a discussion about them.

We do not consider the draft Bills as final and we are always willing to consider any suggestions for alteration. Indeed the representatives of the Hind Mazdoor Sabha have participated in some of the conferences and no doubt will participate in others.

In these circumstances, do you think it is right to carry on a vehement propaganda against these Bills, calling them black Bills, and raise the plea of trade unionism in danger? Surely, it would be more helpful to all concerned, if specific points were raised and discussed instead of a blanket condemnation.

Yours affectionately,
Jawaharlal

[1]*Nehru Papers* (NMML).

APPENDIX 23

Resolutions adopted by the Conference on Free and Fair Elections, Bombay, 1 and 2 July 1950[1]

I

This Conference appoints a Standing Committee consisting of the following members, with power to co-opt one-third of its strength, to take all steps as may be necessary to ensure free and fair elections:

1. Dr. R.P. Paranjpye (Chairman)
2. Pandit H.N. Kunzru
3. Shri Jayaprakash Narayan

[1] *J.P. Papers* (NMML).

4. Shri N.C. Chatterji
5. Shri P.N. Rajbhoj
6. Shri P.R. Lele
7. Shri Moinuddin Harris
8. Shri Naushir Bharucha
9. Shri Purshottam Trikamdas
10. Shri N.M. Joshi
11. Dr. N.B. Khare
12. Dr. V.K. John
13. Shri S.G. Vaze
14. Shri B.K. Gaikwad
15. Shri K.K. Menon
16. Shri N.M. Joshi.

II

This Conference authorises the President to forward the memorandum adopted by this Conference to authorities and bodies concerned.

MEMORANDUM ON FREE AND FAIR ELECTIONS

Whereas general elections on adult franchise basis will be held next year and apprehensions have been expressed in various quarters that they may not be conducted in a manner so as to ensure proper representation of various political parties in the country, and whereas all shades of political thought are unanimous about the need of having purity and freedom of elections held under the Constitution of Free India, the Free and Fair Elections Conference held on 1st and 2nd July at the Blavatsky Lodge, Bombay, after careful consideration, places the following concrete suggestions before the authorities concerned for their acceptance:

I. *Elections and Civil Liberties:*

The Conference feels that for assuring the freedom of propaganda by candidates it is necessary that the various Provincial Public Security Measures Acts, the Preventive Detention Act, 1950, and promulgation of prohibitory orders under Section 144 C.P.C. and under similar restrictive measures should at least be suspended and that action taken against members of political parties that have not been banned should be withdrawn. The Conference regards this as basic and vital to free and fair elections.

II. *Electoral Rolls:*

The Conference feels that electoral rolls are far from perfect and that the following measures should be taken to make them such as to inspire confidence in the masses:

(1) Test checks should be carried out to eliminate fictitious names.

(2) Efforts should be made by sending out enumerators to bring on record names left out. Care should be taken to enroll scheduled caste voters who may be denied facilities in villages by appointment of scheduled caste enumerators.

(3) Representative non-official bodies should be associated with election offices for the above purpose.

(4) Preliminary or first publication rolls should be made available to the public in sufficient numbers for inspection at convenient places.

(5) Necessary legislation should be undertaken for enfranchising refugees from Pakistan, who, by reason of immigration into India at a later stage, are not regarded as citizens under Articles 5 and 6 of the Constitution.

III. *Delimitation of Constituencies:*

(1) The Conference is of the view that having regard to the peculiar conditions prevailing in India there should be for Legislative Assemblies multi-member constituencies, preferably three-member constituencies, with cumulative voting. In no case whatever distributive system of voting should be adopted. The Conference realizes that in case of elections to the House of the People, multi-member constituencies may perhaps present difficulties, excepting in the case of Delhi and similar areas, having regard to the bigger sizes of the constituencies. Care should be taken not to prejudice the interests of scheduled castes in delimitation of constituencies.

(2) It is necessary that delimitation committees for States, as well as the Union, with representative non-official bodies should be immediately appointed to assist the Election Commission to deal with the problem of delimitation.

(3) Early publication of proposals for delimitation of constituencies is highly desirable as sufficient time should be left to the public to express its views thereon before they are finalised.

IV. *Election Propaganda*:

(1) The Conference feels that since broadcasting in this country is a State monopoly, and as broadcasting is a powerful propaganda weapon these days, broadcasting facilities for election purposes

should be made available to all parties in a fair manner and that an all-party non-official board should be created to see that broadcasting facilities are made so available.

(2) It is also desirable as in the case of England that the facility of free postal transmission of his election manifesto should be made available to every candidate.

(3) Schools, halls, maidans, under control of Government, and other places of access to the public should be made equally available to all political parties for holding election meetings and rallies.

V. *Election Legislation and Election Commissioners:*

(1) The Conference feels that Election Commissioner and Regional Commissioners required to be appointed under Article 324 (2) and 324 (4) should be forthwith appointed.

(2) In view of the fact that Election Advisory Committees appointed by the Speaker from the members of the Parliament consist mainly, if not exclusively, of the Congress Party members, it is highly desirable with a view of inspiring confidence in the masses that representative non-official committees in States should be created, and associated with the Chief Election Commissioner, Election Commissioners and Regional Commissioners.

(3) Early enactment of legislation should be undertaken to supplement the Representation of the People Act, 1950, to *include inter* alia the following provisions.

(a) Prescribing a maximum limit of expenditure by a candidate for the State Legislative Assemblies and for the House of the People;

(b) Provision of State aid to candidates for election expenses, based on the number of votes polled by the candidate;

(c) Provision of a certain number of free copies of electoral rolls to all candidates.

(d) Prohibition of use of private or hired conveyance for election purposes on the polling day;

(e) Tightening of the law so as to prescribe minimum imprisonment for impersonation and other election offences which are not merely technical in character;

(f) Marking a voter's thumb with indelible ink, in big cities and big towns, to prevent same voter voting more than once.

VI. *Conduct of Elections:*

(1) In order to ensure that a large number of voters have facilities of polling, the Conference is of the opinion that sufficient number of

polling stations should be established so that voters do not have to walk more than two miles for recording their vote.

(2) As is done in England, every voter should be informed by the election agency in advance, by issue of cards, indicating his roll number, page of the electoral roll and the address of his polling station.

(3) Demonstration of political parties or by their agents or canvassers on the polling day should be prohibited.

(4) The first general elections should be simultaneous both for State Legislative Assemblies and the House of the People on one day. In case this is not possible, at least there should simultaneous counting of votes and simultaneous declaration of results.

(5) Ballot cards should be printed with candidates' names in alphabetical order for each constituency together with his symbol and with instructions to mark a cross.

APPENDIX 24

Debate on the General Secretary's Report at the Madras Conference of the Socialist Party, 9 July 1950[1]

Kulomani Mohapatra (*Orissa*):

The General Secretary in his report has referred to the so-called revolutionaries and has served a 'quit' notice on them. Is that the only remedy? The report does not suggest any remedies to clear up the ideological confusion that exists in the ranks of the Party.

I feel that the General Secretary has tried to look at every problem in pedantic Gandhian manner. Our ideal cannot be achieved merely by reforming on Gandhian ideas and dressing them up with Marxism.

Another point which I want to make is that we have not been able to make our democratic socialism an international force. The General Secretary should amend his report in the light of the suggestions I have made.

Gobind Das (*Orissa*):

I am persuaded to say that the General Secretary's report is singularly remarkable for its vagueness. The report is not a complete exposition of democratic socialism.

[1]*Report of the Eighth National Conference of the Socialist Party, Madras, 1950.* pp. 40-52.

The report is a ethico-political utopia. He asks us to fulfil certain tasks to achieve this utopia. Was it not on account of these utopian conceptions that social democracy failed in Europe?

He also talks of human values. What type of values should we follow? Should we follow liberal values of the European type? Or should we follow Indian cultural values? Or else should we rather follow the Gandhian values? I am afraid that if the Socialist Party does not stand with its feet on the ground but soar high in the sky, the common man will remain puzzled and will run away from the Party.

Amolesh Muzumdar (*Bengal*):

I have some grave doubts regarding the methods suggested by the Policy Statement for the achievement of our objective. Mention is made of democratic or peaceful methods as opposed to insurrectionary or violent methods. I submit that insurrectionary methods are democratic, if and when they have the backing of the demos, the people. Moreover democratic methods and insurrectionary methods are complementary.

The organizational picture of the Party is not at all encouraging. Why? I do not agree with Madhu Limaye's diagnosis. At Patna and after, much stress was laid on affiliated membership; and yet some party leaders kept on insisting that the labour movement should be above party politics. Labour could not be persuaded to affiliate because of this confusion.

The enrolment of individual members was undertaken in isolation. It should, on the contrary, have been the culmination of a process. I submit that this has been due to lack of discipline in the Party leadership. If we wish to remedy this, we must strictly enforce the active membership clause. Then only the Party will be lifted from the morass of stagnation.

Raja Kulkarni (*Bombay*):

I draw your attention to organizational report and commend it to the house.

Old ideas about trade union work are a hindrance. Undesirable tendencies have developed in the labour movement. For, some people economism seems to be the basis of the movement, and therefore, economic struggle is considered to be the only method. This approach has failed to bring the masses in the political struggle. While it fails to create proper class consciousness, it, at the same time, offers no opportunity to the workers to develop socialist consciousness.

If these unhealthy tendencies are to be checked, it will be necessary to evolve a new theory and practice of trade unionism compatible with our goal of democratic socialism.

D.S. Mahajani (*Bombay*):

At Patna some people had expressed the fear that if the mass Party constitution is adopted, it will lead to calamities. Bogus membership is one such calamity. As the report says 'Men of means' are trying to enroll bogus members. What steps are being taken to stop this?

The idea of affiliated membership has failed. It is not possible to persuade unions to affiliate because we cannot explain to the workers what democratic socialism means. This is again due to the fact that we ourselves are not clear about it. There is an utter lack of literature also.

There is no ideological revolt in the Party. Confusion and doubts do exist and are growing. The reason is that the party is not clear about the methods we should follow. To say that there are quite a few who have no faith in democratic socialism is to challenge their *bona fides*. This is not proper.

There is bound to be difference of opinion as long as there is confusion regarding methods. But this does not mean that there are fundamental differences.

Vishwanath Pande (*Orissa*):

I commend the reports to the house. Every one must accept the fundamentals of the Party. Those who do not, must be asked to quit. Formation of groups either personal or ideological must be strictly prohibited.

There is lot of indiscipline and organizational looseness. I have to make a complaint against our leaders. The members of the National Executive must observe greater discipline. Our leaders issue conflicting statements. This creates confusion in the minds of the ranks of the Party. It is true that there should be democracy in the Party. But then, groupism, indiscipline and contradictions is not democracy.

Sen Gupta (*Bengal*):

There is one point which I should like to emphasise. In trade union field we are not following proper methods. Mere partisan policies must not be followed. We must follow a clear political policy to meet political ends.

Regarding bogus membership, I would only say this that this tendency must be checked.

Mohan Kali Biswas (*Bengal*):

We must go into the reasons why our Young Socialist League failed. Youth organizations are necessary for the growth of our Party. It was through such organizations that other countries succeeded in their efforts to bring about a social revolution.

The Young Socialist League failed because of lack of organization. It is to such organizations that groups of intellectuals of the middle classes can be drawn. But unfortunately, our leaders pay little attention to youths.

Madhu Limaye has referred to the National Union of Students. We should not co-operate with the Congress in this matter. We should form healthy homogeneous party organizations of the youth.

Gulabrao Ganacharya (*Bombay*):

Madhu Limaye seems to be very much displeased with the organizational state of the Party. If that is how he feels, then why should we expect the ranks to be satisfied with it? But he has failed to point out how to rectify these mistakes.

I submit that there is inefficiency, confusion and want of clarity at the top. This is bound to percolate down. And when the ranks of the Party 0discuss the very things which Madhu Limaye has said, the bogey of groupism is raised.

We all accept democratic socialism. If we did not, we should not be in the Party. In a mass party, ideological differences, if they exist, should be welcome.

Bapurao Jagtap (*Bombay*):

I joined the Party in 1942 because I believed that the Socialist Party is the Party of kisans and mazdoors. But since last year some disquieting happenings in Bombay have shaken our belief. If we do anything we are branded as disruptionists. When we say that only revolutionary methods will bring socialism, we are ridiculed by the office-bearers.

But when office-bearers do anything nothing happens. Take for example the arbitrary selection of candidates for the Bombay Corporation elections.

The report has referred to bogus affiliated membership. Why does the Secretariat not take courage in both hands and announce the names of the culprits?

Madhu Limaye:

Comrade Chairman, I am sorry, I have to intervene. I should like to inform the house that action has been taken against those involved in cases of bogus membership. Please do not emphasise the point again and again.

Verghese (*Malabar*):

The General Secretary's report is, no doubt, a brilliant and final answer to the controversy going on in the Party. Nevertheless, the tone of the report is that of a defence counsel and not of a General Secretary giving a comprehensive analysis of political situation and outlining the future course of action. During the last sixteen months, many things have happened. He should have dealt with the ideological and structural changes which have occurred in the Congress.

Why is it that the people are not enthusiastic? It is because there is ideological confusion, and there is a lack of effort on the part of the Party leadership to create clarity which can soak down to the people.

The National Executive has failed on some occasions to show common courtesy to subordinate organizations. For example, recently the ex-Chief Minister of Travancore and his group were invited to join the Party without consulting the Provincial Executive.

P.V. Khandekar (*Bombay*):

The General Secretary, in the first part of his report, has said that those who have no faith in the fundamentals of the Party should quit. There is one difficulty in this. While some workers publicly declare their faith in the fundamentals during private discussions they say that the Party leadership has become reformist. This is, of course, difficult to prove. But let it not be forgotten that difficulties arise in day-to-day work if differences with regard to approach and methods persist. This is the cause of confusion such as exists in the Party.

This can only be tackled by accepting Raja Kulkarni's suggestion.

Madhu Mahuakar (*Bombay*):

What should we do to remove our shortcomings? Can it be achieved by making rules of conduct for the Party members and members of the National Executive? Many have said that we should follow a more militant and co-ordinated policy. I agree. But then do not forget that it puts great responsibility on the ranks of the Party. I object to certain remarks made by some delegates. The discussion is generating.

Madhu Limaye has admitted that confusion exists regarding the function of the Central Office. I feel that the Central Office should be both a co-ordinating and directing organization.

B.D. Joshi (*Delhi*):

As far as I am concerned, no confusion exists in my mind regarding the questions discussed in the General Secretary's report. But then I must emphasise one point. The General Secretary has asked those who do not believe in Party fundamentals to quit. I am afraid that the General Secretary will be open to the charge of being partial if he does not show the same strictness to other types of people, communalists and corrupt people, who have entered the Party. Such and others profess faith in democratic socialism, but declare that they have no faith in struggles and militancy.

Both these undesirable types exist in the Party today. The General Secretary has asked one type to quit. How about the other type? They must also be asked to quit the Party.

I will give you one unfortunate example. In the Alwar Municipal elections the Hindu Mahasabha and the local Socialist Party were to be seen on the same platform. Our workers heard the shouts of "Veer Savarkar Zindabad", and "Jayaprakash Narayan Zindabad" from the same platform.

Why are such unholy, ridiculous pacts tolerated?

Then there is another thing I must refer to. I feel that the General Secretary should have written to Aruna Asaf Ali before making a mention of her name in the report. He should have given her an opportunity to explain.

B.P. Sinha (*Bihar*):

I am not satisfied with the definition of democratic methods given by the General Secretary. I want to ask him if by democratic methods, he means peaceful methods only. I believe that democratic methods include armed insurrection also. Majority insurrection is certainly democratic, while minority insurrection is not.

He has said that under Fascist conditions, democratic methods will not work. Instead, he should say that peaceful democratic methods will become ineffective under Fascist conditions.

It seems that the General Secretary considers 'peaceful' and 'democratic' synonymous. I am afraid he is wrong. He should also include armed insurrection in democratic methods.

Sadashiv Bagayatkar (*Maharashtra*):

The General Secretary has said that those who do not believe in our goal of democratic socialism have no place in the Party. I submit that this is not enough. Some people say that they believe in democratic socialism but have no faith in democratic methods. If we are convinced that under the existing conditions democratic methods are the only right methods, then the General Secretary must make it clear that those who do not believe in both democratic socialism and democratic mehods have no place in the Party.

Ishwari Singh (*Rajasthan*):

I have to observe that while the National Executive is moving in one direction some of the rank and file members are trying to pull in another direction. This has created confusion.

The General Secretary must clearly define democratic methods. We should make it absolutely clear that we shall adhere to peaceful revolutionary methods. We must clearly define how we are going to effect peaceful social revolution.

Regarding the organizational report I have sent some written suggestions to Madhu Limaye. We must give specific work to every active workers. They should be made to send regular reports.

Madhavrao (*Andhra*):

The General Secretary submits that the new philosophy of democratic socialism is not yet evolved fully. He says that it will be done during the course of the next year.

But I believe that there is no need to evolve a new philosophy nor can it ever be done. Such a philosophy already exists. I refer to the Communist Manifesto. If struggle of toiling millions is not democratic socialism, then what is it?

Our hatred of Stalinism is no excuse. We must study Marx. We will have to adopt such policies and formulations as are in conformity with Marxism.

Ramkrishna (*Tamil Nad*):

The General Secretary's report is a good thesis on democratic socialism.

I submit that many of you are making a mistake about democratic socialism. You are probably equating democratic means with constitutionalism.

Madhu Limaye has rightly complained that our Party members going abroad do not submit reports. We must know where we stand in the international field.

Shankar Kurtakoti (*Bombay-Karnatak*):

We must see how far the Party has made progress not only organizationally but also as a political party. Instead of seeing the bright side, Madhu Limaye has thought it fit to play up the gloomy side.

We may have defects. But I feel that within a short time we have built up a healthy Party. Bihar and U.P. have made good progress. We are also doing our best.

N.R. Abhyankar (*Madhya Pradesh*):

Socialism is concerned with the material needs of man. Therefore we must talk of material values only. Why bring in moral and spiritual values which rightly belong to the field of religion? Religion is concerned with things after death.

We are a political party. We do not exist for the uplift of an individual. Socialism is a force which seeks to fulfil the material needs of human beings.

The General Secretary has mixed up issues and this mixing up has created confusion.

Genda Singh (*Uttar Pradesh*):

Quite a large majority of our comrades have not understood the fundamentals of the Party. Misconceptions exist regarding democratic socialism. These must be removed.

One reason why this is so is that we have connections with such Socialist Parties abroad as are betraying socialism. The Labour Government of Britain claims be a socialist government. But then look at what they are doing in Malaya. Look at France and its Indo-China policy. We should sever our connections with such Socialist Parties.

I have grave doubts regarding our Party's attitude to the Indian Constitution. Excepting adult franchise, there is nothing else in it which is democratic. At Patna the General Secretary recently said that the government is showing Fascist tendencies, that the constitution was bad, and now he says it is fairly democratic.

I submit that confusion becomes worse confounded because there is tendency to equate revolutionary methods with insurrectionary methods. This confusion must be removed.

S. Krishnamurti (*Mysore*):

The General Secretary has threatened us, and in the same breath has asked us to endorse his report.

At Patna, I had said that we will head towards a disaster if we accept the new Party constitution. We do face a disaster today. Can the fundamentals of a party be static? Have we no right to analyse them? Have we no right to argue and discuss them? If all this is denied, what becomes of scientific socialism and Marxism?

We have been told either to accept the democratic socialism of the National Executive or to quit. If this is conceived as a challenge, then indeed it is a great tragedy.

Recent happenings have shown that the Party is definitely drifting towards parliamentarianism. This is evident from the fact that the General Secretary does not care to call a conference of progressive people to discuss such burning issues as inflation, food problem, industrial and other unemployment, refugee problem, etc., but calls a conference to discuss elections and invites reactionaries to it. It is evident that the Party is drifting more and more towards constitutionalism and if this process is not combated we will be lost. We must therefore change the leadership and the personnel of the National Executive.

Ajit Roy (*Bengal*):

There is today a deep and fundamental crisis of thought throughout the socialist movement all over the world. A century ago when Karl Marx in his writings, was laying down the basic ideas of socialism, there was no doubt in the peoples' mind about the essentially democratic character of the socialist state. The socialist state, according to him, was one which would guarantee to the individual greater and not less democracy than even the most liberal of the capitalist states.

Notwithstanding a century of democratic traditions of the socialist movement, we find in one country after another the growth and worship of a new theory of "statism". This new theory assails the working class movement from within and totally denies to the toiling masses the role of controllers and inspirers of the state and its policies. In Soviet Russia as well as under the Labour Government in England the significance of the toiling man and of his freedom and initiative is completely lost under the weight of the gigantic bureaucratic machinery of the state.

It is therefore necessary for the international socialist movement to rediscover its ancient democratic foundation, and to assert its faith in a society where the state will not rise above the masses but be controlled and shaped by them. The Socialist Party, by raising the banner of democratic socialism, is therefore performing a great service to international socialism in its search for its ancient, democratic values.

We have declared ourselves in favour of democratic or peaceful means. But we cannot say beforehand whether socialism will come about peacefully or through an armed insurrection. That does not rest entirely with us. We will do our utmost to adhere to our declared methods. But our enemies, the landlords and the capitalists, have also something to say about it. If they are ready and willing to accept a verdict of the people in favour of socialism and against capitalism and landlordism, and are prepared to hand over power peacefully, then there can be no doubt that socialism will come to power without any civil war. But if the capitalists like their brothers in other parts of the world are unwilling to accept the democratic verdict of the people and seek to crush our movement through violence and illegality then the Socialist Party will know, I am sure, how to fight for socialism under the new conditions.

There is yet another thing to which I wish to draw your attention. We are not a constitutionalist party. But we must not underestimate the importance of elections in our struggle for socialism. Parliamentary work without activity among the masses is sheer reformism and useless but to deny the importance of election and parliamentary struggle is to fall into dangerous sectarianism. If we go to the masses, penetrate every village and factory with our message of democratic socialism, we need have no fear of our Party degenerating into meaningless parliamentarianism.

With these words I commend the General Secretary's report to you.

M. Harris (*Bombay*):

The reference made by Madhu Limaye in his organizational report to the Bombay Party and the Coporation elections is too sweeping. He has referred to the two elections which we lost in recent months. But he has failed to mention the number of votes we secured, the number of votes by which we lost and the conditions under which we had to fight the two elections.

A few comrades from Bombay have complained against the selection of candidates for the Corporation elections. May I ask these friends to mention a single instance when the Party was not consulted? Comrade Jagtap was consulted on every occasion. Has he forgotten that he had approved of every selection except one?

Mr. Mustaq Ahmed (*Delhi*):

B.D. Joshi has raised a fundamental issue. This conference must give a general direction with regard to elections. We must decide once for all as to where elections should be contested and where not. I suggest that we should not contest elections which are not held on the basis of adult franchise.

This conference must also view with concern the tendency among some of our Party units to join hands with all sorts of groups, individuals and parties at the time of elections. This conference should direct the National Executive to take drastic action in such cases.

Tilak Raj Chadha (*Punjab*):

Those comrades who perpetually talk of armed insurrection and revolution should come to Punjab and see things for themselves. If the struggle conducted there really had shown anything, it is this that peaceful methods are the only practicable methods under the existing circumstances and that the toiling masses are not yet ready for armed insurrection. There is no doubt that we have yet to achieve a great deal. But, come what may, we will not waver from our principles and our path.

Let us all endeavour to imbibe the spirit which underlies the General Secretary's report.

Karpoori Thakur (*Bihar*):

There are no differences in Bihar.

The General Secretary has presented a brilliant exposition of democratic socialism and democratic methods. Are you angry with him because he has condemned groupism and asked non-conformists to quit? What do you want to do with the Socialist Party? Is the Socialist Party a loose united front? Do you want to convert it into a debating society?

I have to observe that a majority of those who oppose democratic socialism and democratic methods are pseudo-revolutionaries. They are book-worms and not field workers.

I have a suggestion to make. We urgently need a volunteer organization. We have failed so far to organize the students. We must concentrate on the students and youths front.

Kabra (*Hyderabad*):

There exists an atmosphere of distrust in the Party today. Let us not distrust any of our comrades. Let us try to appreciate those who have failed so far to understand democratic socialism. It is not possible that they are only keen on preventing its metamorphosis into something similar to European social democracy?

Hareshwar Goswami (*Assam*):

I have observed a tendency in the house to equate democratic methods with parliamentary methods. A fraction is being taken for the whole. I submit that when the Socialist Party thinks of elections, it considers them as one of the ways to reach the masses. Elections held on a wide basis offer an excellent opportunity. Where the franchise is limited, we can ask the voters to boycott the elections. We did that in Assam and we have had a good response.

Tulsi Boda (*Bombay*):

I oppose the way in which the organizational report has posed the issue of grouping. Both the diagnosis and prescription are wrong and will lead us nowhere. There are groups and personal cliques because of the new Party constitution.

I admit that there is considerable democracy in the Party today. But it is not enough.

The draft resolutions reach us too late. There should be enough time to discuss them in Party journals and Party meetings.

Sisir Dhar (*Bengal*):

There is a significant omission in the General Secretary's report. In Bengal today there is a floating population numbering nearly 50 lakhs. A rational solution should be found for their problems.

The Central Office does not supply literature which is so very necessary for the education of the members.

I have to request the General Secretary not to start a witchhunt in the Party.

Chairman:

Madhu Limaye will now reply.

Madhu Limaye:

I am aware that there are some serious omissions in the organizational report. For instance, no mention was made of the cultural activities of our comrades in Bengal. They are conducting a music centre and have also organized a Contemporary Writers' Association. The membership figure for the Mysore State was also left-out by oversight. These and such other omissions will be corrected.

I am sorry to observe that the delegates did not properly respond to the self-critical report which I had submitted. I had expected them to criticise their own mistakes and suggest positive remedies and not use my criticism against the leadership and the Central Office.

I should like to tell Tulsi Boda that my diagnosis of groupism is correct. A distorted version of Party policy is presented to the members, and our revolutionary democratic methods are equated with reformism. Formation of groups is then characterised as a reaction to parliamentarianism. This is wrong. There may be deviations from the Party line, but this does not mean that the line itself is wrong. Groupism cannot be tolerated in the Socialist Party.

APPENDIX 25

Resolution on the Indian Constitution adopted by the Madras Conference of the Socialist Party, 8-12 July 1950[1]

This Conference strongly feels that the Constitution of India falls considerably short of the democratic principles enunciated in its preamble. It, no doubt, recognizes the principle of adult franchise, bases representation on common and equal citizenship and assures the system of responsible government. But the legislative authority is vitiated by bicameralism which has invariably proved to be a clog in the working of democracy and a hindrance in the implementation of people's wishes. It is also adversely affected by the ordinance-making powers of the executive. The Constitution, though federal in form, is unitary in spirit. It is highly centralised in character and leaves only limited autonomy to the constituent units. Parliament can grant to the Union Government concurrent administrative powers over subjects which are assigned by the Constitution to the exclusive charge of the States. The question of finance has been dealt with in a most perfunctory manner, and the resources left at the disposal of the States are of a meagre character. Emergency powers are so wide in character that the Federal Executive may at its sweet will suppress liberties of the people and the autonomy of the States and with the consent of the Parliament establish its dictatorship over the States. Princes are guaranteed privy purses and titles, Rajpramukhs are allowed to act as heads of States Unions and Civil Services are guaranteed high Salaries. Even representative institutions are not provided for Chief Commissioner's provinces.

Provisions with regard to fundamental rights have to an extent enabled the judiciary to protect people's liberties against laws and orders of despotic character.

These rights and liberties could however be made more absolute. Limitations, conditions and provisos, to which they are subjected in the name of the interests of the general public and safeguarding of public order, morality, etc., have deprived these rights of much of their guarantees. Persons can be deprived of their life and personal liberty in accordance with the procedure laid down by the executive through ordinances, and political opponents can be detained under preventive detention order.

Provisions with regard to economic rights and property are very clumsily drafted and are definitely pro-capitalist in character. While no guarantee is given against the exploitation of property-less workers, the interests of property-holders, specially capitalists are safeguarded through specific guarantee with regard to compensation for the acquisition of property for

[1]*Report of the Eighth National Conference of the Socialist Party, Madras, 8-12 July 1950*, pp.72-3.

public purposes. Powers of legislative authorities of the States with regard to the acquisition for public purposes are restricted by the provision that all laws on the matter shall require the consent of the President.

Directive principles of the State policy are kept purposely vague. They include no directive to the State with regard to the liquidation of landlordism and capitalism or the protection of economic interests of peasants who constitute the bulk of the Indian nation. The State is no doubt required to regulate national economy with a view to promoting the welfare of workers and to preventing concentration of economic resources in the hands of a few persons. The implementation of these directives may guarantee regulated capitalism but cannot create a real and effective social democracy.

Thus, the constitution not only lacks brevity, clarity and precision, but also contains many undemocratic principles and cannot claim to provide a proper mechanism of full democracy. The people will have to be ever vigilant about their rights and liberties, to strive to institute healthy democratic conventions and to march ahead towards democratic socialist order regardless of the directive principles of the State policy. Provisions with regard to property rights will have to be repealed so that economic reconstruction on socialist lines may not be hindered by the requirements of compensation and the veto of the President. Other democratic principles of the constitution will also have to be excluded to make it a fit instrument of full democracy. The Socialist Party pledges itself to work for the establishment of healthy democratic conventions and traditions and for a radical change in the constitution to ensure full democracy, through amendments in Parliament or by a new Constituent Assembly.

APPENDIX 26

Programme for National Revival, adopted by the Madras Conference of the Socialist Party, 8-12 July 1950.[1]

PROGRAMME FOR NATIONAL REVIVAL

Introduction

Freedom Day, August 15, 1947, was a historic day that filled every heart in the country with pride and hope. The people had celebrated that day as no other day had been celebrated in recent history.

It is barely three years since that historic day, and the hope is dead, and disillusionment and despair have gripped the people. There is stagnation in

[1]*Report of the Eighth National Conference of Socialist Party, Madras, 8-12 July 1950*, pp. 189-202.

national life. Stagnation, if not removed, will lead to decline and death.

Therefore the Nation's Life Must Be Revived.

Gandhiji who had the power to breathe life into the nation is no more.

The Congress relied upon the Government machinery to reconstruct the nation. That was bound to fail, and has failed. It is only the people who can create. Government can guide, co-ordinate, help, inspire. Since the Government has no plan of reconstruction, nor the will, nor the drive, there is stagnation.

But if the Government has failed, should the people fail too? Every citizen has a stake in the country, no less than the Government. It is in their very self-interest that the people must act. But how should they act? There must be a programme, co-ordination, initiative.

In all humility the Socialist Party makes bold to place before the people this Programme for National Revival and pledges to put forth every ounce of energy for its fulfilment. The Party seeks the co-operation of the people in this task. It seeks particularly the co-operation of the YOUTH, the Trade Unions, the Kisan Panchayats, the intelligentsia, and the depressed, backward and tribal peoples.

This Programme cannot be implemented by popular effort alone. The Government must also join in and enact and enforce the appropriate legislative and administrative measures.

Therefore, a vital part of the National Revival Programme is for the people to compel the Government to adopt the necessary measures. Mere condemnation of the Government or discontented sullenness is fruitless. The people must either force the Government to act or dismiss it and choose another that will carry out their will.

One Nation: National Integration

Under the challenge of the foreign ruler, a certain amount of national unity had been achieved. With the disappearance of that challenge, disintegrating tendencies are raising their head: communalism, provincialism casteism, linguism, racialism, tribalism. We cannot survive as a nation, indeed we cannot become a nation, unless this separatism is checked and there is a National Integration. All patriotic citizens must therefore declare war on the forces of disintegration. Cultural peculiarities, including those of the tribal peoples, will be preserved and nourished, but we must forge, not in theory but in living reality, that all-governing unity that shall transcend all diversities and make us One Nation.

One Caste: Social Integration

India cannot grow unless the distinctions and oppressions of caste are destroyed. The system of caste is like an iron shell which, while it protects a dried-up social order, denies release of social energies; isolates India and prevents her from participating in that process of give and take which is the law of historical progress. Further, and no less important, by checking social mobility and perpetuating vocational rigidity, it also stands in the way of economic development. Freedom must mean to the socially oppressed millions a release from the humiliation and pain of social inferiority and the fullest possible social mobility. Like one nation we are all of One Caste: the Human Caste. National integration must be accompanied with social integration.

The YOUTH of the nation must take in both their hands these two torches of National and Social Integration and light up the path through the surrounding darkness to National Revival. We can conceive of no higher ideals for the Youth to work for and die for if need be.

Our writers, artists, thinkers must become the instruments of this all-sweeping cultural revolution.

"Meherally Youth Homes" and "Janata Centres of Culture" must spring up in town and village and become the catalytic agent in this change.

Poverty: Problem Number One

There is intense poverty in the country. At least 90 per cent of the people are its victims. To remove poverty or to reduce its rigours is our first task. This admits of no controversy.

Poverty depends on two factors: (a) how much we produce, and (b) how we share the produce.

We do not produce enough. Production per man-hour is too low: we must work harder. Not all who should work find employment, and even those who do are under-employed. There must be full employment and the incentives to work harder must be created. All this will take a little time and require great social changes. This Programme suggests below some immediate measures to increase production.

The question of *distribution*, however, can be tackled without delay.

All wealth is produced by labour: mental or physical. That each should receive a proportionate return for his labour no one can deny. That those who labour more, or whose labour is more valuable to the nation, should get more than the others, too, cannot be denied.

But at present the distribution of wealth is not governed by these unexceptionable principles. Many who do not labour at all own large amounts of wealth. On the other hand, many of those who labour hard have not enough to live on. Many others who perform certain specific forms of labour such as running trade or industry derive incomes that are fantastically disproportionate when compared with the incomes of those who perhaps perform even more valuable labour, such as engineers or scientists.

Clearly in a *people's raj* such a state of affairs cannot exist. If there is not enough for everybody, that is the more reason why, what there is, should be equitably distributed. Austerity must be shared. Sacrifice must be equal.

Therefore, the first step towards ending poverty is equitable distribution of wealth.

Money incomes that range today from a few rupees to several lakhs of rupees a month must be brought within a narrower range, and the difference between the highest and the lowest should not be more than between 1 and 10. The minimum income should as soon as possible be raised to the living standard.

The allowances of the Princes must be stopped and their huge treasures must be taken over and applied to productive use.

Land, the chief form of wealth in this country, must also be equitably distributed. In an agricultural country, land reform was the first essential. But even after four years of Congress administration in the States, no vital reform in the land system has been made.

Subject to the ultimate right of the community land must belong to the tillers and all intermediaries should go. Just as a worker must have a living wage, every peasant family must have a 'living holding.' The minimum holding for every peasant family should not be less than 12.50 acres of land of average productivity. The maximum holding should not be more than 30 acres of average quality land. Ejectments from land and homesteads should stop and pasture and other common lands should not be settled.

Land revenue should be charged on a basis similar to that of income-tax, and peasant families with incomes below a prescribed minimum should be exempt.

Provision should be made for cheap rural credit, and the agricultural debts of the poor peasants should be cancelled.

Except for rehabilitation compensation to small landlords, no compensation should be paid for the abolition of landlordism.

Agricultural labourers should be assured of a minimum living wage and dispossession of their homesteads should be made illegal. In the settlement of newly reclaimed lands, agricultural workers should have priority.

All this requires legislation. But if vested interests delay the law too long, the peasants will have to carry through these reforms by their own motion. That would not be anarchy but the smashing of the dams of stagnation.

We Must Produce More

Above all, we must produce more from our land: more FOOD and other crops. For this certain basic measures must be adopted.

Our agriculture must be *reorganized.* If the present basis of individual, uneconomic, fragmented farms continues, agricultural production cannot rise. Co-operative farming operations and pooling of holdings, without interfering with proprietary rights (except to the extent necessary to effect the above reforms) is the first essential. This is admitted on all hands, but here as elsewhere governmental intertia stands in the way. Development of co-operative farming on a planned mass scale must become the first priority job of the State.

Irrigation, manuring, better seeds, better ploughs and better bullocks are the other primary needs that must be fulfilled before agricultural production can rise. But if these needs are to be fulfilled in accordance with the streamlined plans prepared by the sahebs in the Government Secretariats, involving unimaginable amounts of steel and cement, we are afraid the plans will ever remain on paper, as they have hitherto. The old sources of irrigation that have fallen into disuse must be revived, and new irrigation projects, based on the use of home-made and locally available materials, should be undertaken on as widespread a scale as possible. Composting, fuel, tree planting, fodder-growing, establishment of grain banks, etc., should take the form of a mass movement. For all this the people's initiative and voluntary effort must be harnessed.

There is a vast acreage of arable land that is lying waste today. To bring this national wealth into productive use, a land army, as far as possible locally recruited, should be raised by the Government. The equipment should be provided by the Government, though the people should be encouraged to pool in their own lighter equipment such as shovels, etc. New lands, thus brought under cultivation, should be settled with co-operative colonies of landless labourers or the poor peasantry. A considerable part of these settlers may be drawn from the land army itself.

Village Reconstruction

The reconstruction of India is largely a question of the reconstruction of her five and half lakhs of villages. A new life, a wave of new activity, must surge through these villages so that, with them India too might rise and move forward.

It would be impossible through State effort to reconstruct the five and half lakhs of villages. That task must be fulfilled by the village folk themselves. If every able-bodied villager gave not more than one hour of his time every day, there would be crores of hours available, and even a year of this voluntary constructive effort would transform the countryside completely. We appeal therefore to the people in every village to band themselves together and give one hour's collective labour each day to the work of reconstruction, such as making of village roads, planting trees, repairing or excavating tanks, making bunds and channels, clearing swamps, compost making, opening grain banks, education, sanitation, etc. The State should come forward with such assistance as may be necessary. We pledge to make this gigantic mass reconstruction the corner-stone of our rural programme.

For village reconstruction other conditions too must be fulfilled. At present the villages are being drained for the benefit of the towns, economically and culturally. This should stop and there must be a movement "back to the village". Let the educated who have their homes in the village, go back to it to teach, to look after its health, to revive its industries, to establish co-operatives, and, not the least, to plough.

Further, the land revenue that the villages pay today, directly or indirectly, is used to support a costly urban administration. At least 25 per cent of the State revenue should be spent by the village panchayats and self-governing bodies in the district.

An adequate proportion of the capital resources available for development purposes should be used for rural reconstruction.

Industrial Production

In the industrial field production is stagnant mainly because (1) there is very little capital available for industrial investment; (2) those who have the capital lack the spirit of pioneering and enterprise and are not prepared to work at the necessarily low margins of profit that the poverty of the country and the needs of austerity economy demand; (3) there is lack of technical know-how; (4) there is uncertainty in the economic policies of the Government; and finally (5) because the existing Managing Agency system is a drag on industry and exercises a deterrent effect on the small investors.

At the same time, while private enterprise is unable to expand production, the State remains inactive, and the dam of stagnation remains unbreached.

Further, the implications of a backward economy such as that of India are not fully realized. Capital, machinery and technical personnel for large-scale industrialisation are not available in an adequate measure in a backward economy. But there is one factor of production that is plentifully available: manpower. The harnessing of the immense manpower of this country requires not only the climate of egalitarianism and social justice, but also industrial activity *suited* for its absorption. Therefore, to expand India's industrial production, it is necessary that medium and cottage industries, based on equipment that can be made at home and organized on co-operative lines, are developed. Research, invention, technique and training suited to such industries must be stimulated and organized. In all this it is the State that must take the initiative.

The lack of adequate capital, which is at the root of present industrial stagnation, can be removed only in two ways: (1) by stimulating saving at home, and (2) by import of foreign capital and technical know-how.

To stimulate saving, we have to tighten our belt. The poor have already their belts tightened to the limit. It is conspicuous consumption that has to be controlled and austerity living enforced.

Economic uncertainty should be removed by clearly demarcating the domain of private enterprise; and defining the terms on which the private sector is to operate. These terms once fixed must be strictly enforced, and a new economic morality and behaviour pattern, in consonance with the ethics of austerity and equitable sharing in the wealth and poverty of the nation, should be developed.

Every effort should be made by the State to obtain foreign capital, as also technical know-how, on terms suitable to our national development and in consonance with our national sovereignty.

Foreign technical personnel would be costly and inadequate. Therefore, a vital part of industrial planning must be a provision for planned technical and vocational planning.

Abolition or a drastic reform of the Managing Agency system in the private sector of industry has become necessary.

We firmly hope that the economic and social measures advocated in this Programme will create a climate in which all of us will work harder. Productivity of labour will thus grow. To stimulate that productivity further we suggest that provision be made for the education and technical training of the workers, so that the chances of promotion might become an added incentive to work.

All the available and created factors of production must be applied in accordance with a plan. Investment, private, public and foreign, should therefore be directed and planned. For this Banking and Insurance must be nationalised.

Ownership of the basic industries places private enterprise in a position of such vantage that it might stand as an impassable barrier on the road to a new social order. Questions of political power, planning, equitable distribution are all likely to be deeply affected by the interests owning the basic industries of a country. Therefore an essential part of a programme of industrial reconstruction that aims to create a just and equitable social order must be the Nationalisation of the Basic Industries.

The entire programme of development of cottage, medium and large-scale industries and of agriculture should be integrated together in an overall Plan.

A new Economic Civil Service should be raised and trained to carry out this planned economic development.

Trade: Internal

There must be trade, like production, in every society: goods produced must be exchanged or distributed. Those engaged in exchanging goods today are performing a useful function. But there is intense profiteering and black-marketing; and there are unnecessary layers of middle men. In these days of licences and permits, the normal traders are being pushed out and nepotism and political jobbery are pushing forward new agents who are untrained and incompetent, with the result that the consumer and the normal trader both suffer. Another result of the present system is that the small trader is being ground down and a few big fish are prospering.

The small trader who performs the real service of distribution should receive encouragement in preference to the big trader. The middle men should be eliminated. Nepotism should go. Consumers' co-operatives in the urban and mutli-purpose co-operatives in the rural areas must receive top priority, and an attempt should be made within a prescribed period so as to develop the co-operative movement that at least half of the internal trade of the country comes to be handled by the co-operative societies. That would constitute the most effective check on profiteering and black-marketing.

Trade: Foreign

In the sphere of foreign trade, there should be State monopoly in such commodities as mica, manganese, jute, tea, cotton textiles, etc., in which India has peculiar advantages. All other foreign trade should be under State control. The import-export policy of the country should be a part of the larger National Economic Plan and should be used as an instrument of economic development.

Lower Prices

High prices continue to cause great suffering, particularly to the working and middle classes. The measures suggested above to raise industrial and agricultural production, coupled with compulsory saving on a wide scale, deferred payments to the high salaried groups, freezing of bank balances and control of consumption would go a long way to solve the problem of prices.

As long as high prices continue there should be fair price shops for essential commodities for families of incomes lower than 250 rupees a month in urban areas.

Black Money

Black money which, among other things, causes inflationary pressure and retards industrial development should be ferreted out. Businessmen have not co-operated with Government and the Income-Tax Investigation Commission has been a failure. More stringent measures should be adopted.

Unemployment

The working out of the above economic programme can alone solve the problem of unemployment, which is growing apace.

Corruption

The one greatest single enemy of the nation today is the evil of corruption. Slowly this evil is becoming all pervading.

The first job is to purify the Services. No serious attempt has hitherto been made to do this. On the other hand, the complacency with which corruption or alleged corruption at even higher levels has been treated is only aggravating the disease. In at least five States of this country, namely, Madras, Bengal, Bihar, U.P., and Punjab, serious charges were made by Congressmen themselves against Congress Ministers. In one case, Bengal, the Prime Minister himself investigated and found five of the charges "grave". In another, Bihar, the Deputy Prime Minister investigated and found irregularities in land settlements and the issue of licences. But while there was a great deal of intra-party controversy and Congressmen gave an unedifying exhibition of mutual mudslinging, and some Congressmen rebelled, nothing was done about the charges themselves. The Ministers in the State may all be Congressmen but the State Governments are not the concern of the Congress alone but of the people as a whole. Therefore, where a doubt about a Minister or a high State Officer is raised, the people and the needs of honest administration must be satisfied by a judicial enquiry and not merely a party investigation. In the five cases named above, such judicial enquiries must immediately be ordered.

The Anti-Corruption Departments have been a total failure. They should be replaced with independent Anti-Corruption Commissions like the Election Commissions defined in the Constitution. These Commissions should be made statutory and they should be appointed by the President and should enjoy the status of the highest judiciary of the land and should have independent staff and machinery for investigation. They may act on their own motion or on the motion of private citizens or of Government. These Commissions should also have power to deal with charges of nepotism. Official records and documents should be freely available to the

Commissions, who will maintain the secrecy of the documents where necessary. The decisions of the Commission should not be subject to revision by the Government but must be acted upon without delay.

Further, every Government employee, high or low, should be asked to declare his property every year. Many Government servants are found living today in a style completely beyond their means, and many have acquired properties, which their salaries could never permit. As a first step, they all must be made to account for these.

Black-marketing, tax evasion and other corrupt practices should be more vigorously fought. Purification of the Services should go a long way in rooting out corruption from this sphere. Traders' organizations, merchants' association and similar bodies should be charged, on the pain of punishment, with the task of checking corruption in their spheres. Punishment should be made deterrent. Co-operative trade, particularly in the controlled articles, should be developed on a large scale to fight the black market. Even if 25 per cent of the total trade in any controlled commodity is carried by co-operatives, that would be an effective check to black-marketing.

Administration

The Congress took over and has preserved intact the system of administration created by the British. That system was efficient for the purpose of collection of revenue and maintenance of law and order and the *status quo*. It is obvious that the same system can never answer the needs of nation-building or of a welfare State. This is admitted on all hands, but, as in other fields, no step has been taken to reform the system of administration. New recruitment and training are also on the same lines as before.

The British system was based on distrust and on a process of shifting responsibility to others, higher up or lower down. Among other things, this led to red-tape and mountainous rise of files. The spirit of mutual distrust should now go and responsibility should be fixed and goods should be asked to be delivered. Red-tape should be cut out and delay should be punished. Officers in high places should be made clearly and concretely responsible for achieving specified results within a specified time limit and those who fail to deliver the goods must be dealt with severely and no attempt at passing the bucket should be encouraged. With the progressive disuse of English, public servants should be recruited from newer sections of the people and training should be suited to the jobs required to be performed.

In the present system there is no or little co-ordination between different departments. There should be better co-ordination, not through circuitous files and notings, but through human contacts.

Democracy and Decentralisation

Experience has shown that only that democracy is real where the people are most able directly to manage their affairs. In India the State is decentralised into two tiers: the central and provincial. Further decentralisation is necessary to make democracy living and real by enabling the people to manage their affairs more directly. So the district state and the village state, with distinct economic and political (including administrative) powers, should be brought into being, thus giving the entire Indian State a sort of four-pillar structure.

Among other instruments through which democracy can function are the co-operatives, which in a large sector of the national economy enable the people to manage their affairs.

In the nationalised industrial undertakings, democracy will be expressed through workers' participation in management on equal terms with the State, that is, through industrial democracy.

Education

There should be free and compulsory primary education. At the secondary stage every effort should be made to impart vocational and technical training. University education should be restricted to those who intend to pursue higher studies in the Arts, Sciences, and Technology and Research. Except for religious academies, all education should be secularised and communal and denominational institutions should be prohibited.

Youth, women and children centres should be organized for cultural activities.

Harijans, backward communities, tribal peoples should receive special attention in our educational programme.

Health

Trained, scientific doctors and modern medicines are beyond the means of the overwhelming millions of the people in town or country. Therefore, a judicious and scientific use of such ancient systems of medicine as Ayurved or Hikmat and of native drugs and herbs must be made. Mobile hospitals or mobile medical vans based on field hospitals should be organized. Manufacture, import and prices of drugs must be severely controlled and profits in this sphere must be reduced to the very minimum. Co-operative health societies should be encouraged. Sanitation, clearing of swamps and supply of pure drinking water should receive urgent attention. The medical profession should be persuaded to change its mentality from that of looking upon the profession as a career to that of considering it a social service. A beginning towards socialization of the medical and health services should be made in the larger cities.

Scheduled Castes and Tribal Peoples

The scheduled castes and tribal peoples are the most backward sections of our community. Special efforts must therefore be made to raise their economic and social level. For their education and technical training special provision must be made so as to bring them abreast of the advanced communities within a prescribed period. In the settlement of reclaimed lands and the redistribution of large holdings these communities should have the first priority. In the Services, Legislatures, Central and State Executives they should be represented in proportion to their population. Free access to wood and timber should be allowed for domestic purposes to the tribal peoples living in hills and forests; and in any economic development of these regions they should be given a favoured place.

Women

Women in this country suffer from a variety of social and economic injustices. They should enjoy equal rights with men and their disabilities in the matter of inheritance and property must be removed. Special effort should be made for girls' education and vocational training. In the Services and Professions, there should be no discrimination against women. Organizations of women to fight for their rights and for their constructive uplift must be encouraged and fostered.

Refugees

There is perhaps no other sphere where the Government have bungled more than in that of the rehabilitation of refugees. This problem must be treated as an integral part of the national problem, and Refugee Rehabilitation must be dealt with as a part of the general plan of national development. The question of evacuee property and compensation should not be mixed up with rehabilitation benefits. The object of rehabilitation should not be to re-instate the uprooted individuals in the same social and economic niches that they occupied in Pakistan, but to fit them into the economic reconstruction of the country. A semi-autonomous Board of Rehabilitation and Development should be set up with wide powers of planning, supervision and execution. The Board should co-ordinate and guide the work of rehabilitation in the States as well as at the Centre.

Housing

Housing is one of the most crying needs of the country in town and village. First of all, there must be equitable rationing of existing living space, particularly in the urban areas. Owners of vacant plots should be compelled to build within a prescribed period, or else the plots should be acquired and handed over to co-operative housing societies. Full and planned encouragement should be given to co-operative and self-labour building activities. In the industrial areas the employers should be compelled to build tenements. State housing schemes, in which the workers may also be persuaded to participate, should be prepared and completed within specified periods of time.

Control of Population

We are multiplying at a very rapid rate, so that the growth of population, unless checked, is likely to nullify economic development. There is little awareness of this danger today. The first task, therefore, is to make the people understand this problem and its seriousness, so that they may be compelled to think of its solution.

As a preliminary step towards the solution of this grave problem we suggest: (1) raising the age of marriage and enforcing the law in that regard; (2) provision for proper birth-control clinics in urban areas by municipalities.

Those who may have conscientious objection to practise artificial birth-control methods shall have freedom to use such moral means as may be prescribed by their faiths.

People's Freedom

The fundamental freedoms of the people guaranteed by the Constitution must be made real and all the restrictions placed upon it by the Constitution itself or legislation must be removed. Arrests and imprisonment without trial must be outlawed except in times of war or other national emergency.

This is the Programme for National Revival that the Socialist Party places before the country. We seek the co-operation of the people in working out this Programme. This Programme will not take us to the achievement of the ultimate objectives of a classless and casteless society, but it will be a big jump towards that final goal. We believe that only such a Programme can dissipate the present mood of despair and frustration and create that psychological revolution without which India cannot move forward.

INDEX